CORRECTIONS

BY THE REV. CANON RUPERT H. MORRIS, D.D.

Page 36, l. 2 from foot; p. 46, l. 12; p. 48, l. 24; p. 49, l. 11 from foot, *for* Examinato *read* Examinatus

p. 47, l. 6; p. 73, l. 25; p. 94, l. 10 from foot, *for* interrogato *read* interrogatus

p. 50, l. 28; p. 51, l. 4; p. 71, l. 30, *for* reddenda *read* reddendo

p. 145, l. 15 from foot; p. 146, l. 6, *for* comite *read* comitatu

p. 146, l. 10 from foot; p. 160, l. 6 from foot, Gamull *is right.*

p. 146, l. 3 from foot; p. 155, l. 16; p. 157, l. 12 from foot; p. 158, l. 10 from foot; p. 162, l. 8, 32, *for* Interiori *read* Interiore

p. 149, l. 11 from foot, Mr. Paull Chauntrell *is a well-known name in Chester Records: omit* of

p. 152, l. 14, Richard Birkhenes: *read* Birkenhed *which is well known.*

p. 153, l. 13 from foot, *for* Carnificesium Ciuitate Cestrie, *read* Carnific[es]ium Ciuitatis Cestrie

p. 154, l. 11, *for* your god *read* yow god

p. 157, l. 3, eidem: note about masculine Elizabeth: 'eidem' is of common gender, and has no feminine.

p. 159, l. 9 from foot, *for* maiorum *read* maiorem (*by the Mayor's order*).

p. 162, l. 4, 8, *for* Justicia *read* Justiciario

p. 166, bottom line, *for* Richardi *read* Ricardi

p. 169, per maiorem: (*by the Mayor's order*).

p. 171, l. 13, porkigell = Portuguese; l. 24, *for* beand *read* beard; l. 25, *for* norpold *read* Norfolk

p. 175. In Bond of Patrick Ford the names should be in the accusative, in apposition with *nos*, after *nouerint*. *Read* Nouerint vniuersi nos, Patricium Foord . . . mercatorem, et Alexandrum Cappock . . . mercatorem, teneri, &c.

p. 176, l. 2, Ad quamquid: ? quam quidem.

For 'moram' instead of 'morans,' see p. 253.

F. J. Furnivall
64 ½
Oct. 12 1889

Heliogr. J. Blechinger, Wien.

Child-Marriages, Divorces, and Ratifications, &c.

In the Diocese of Chester, A.D. 1561-6.

DEPOSITIONS IN TRIALS IN THE BISHOP'S COURT, CHESTER,

CONCERNING

1. Child-Marriages, Divorces, and Ratifications.
2. Trothplights. 3. Adulteries. 4. Affiliations. 5. Libels.
6. Wills. 7. Miscellaneous Matters.
8. Clandestine Marriages.

ALSO

Entries from the Mayors' Books, Chester,

A.D. 1558-1600.

EDITED FROM THE MS. WRITTEN IN COURT WHILE THE WITNESSES MADE THEIR DEPOSITIONS, AND FROM THE MAYORS' BOOKS,

BY

FREDERICK J. FURNIVALL, M.A.,

TRINITY HALL, CAMBRIDGE; HON. DR. PHIL. BERLIN.

LONDON:

PUBLISHT FOR THE EARLY ENGLISH TEXT SOCIETY

BY KEGAN PAUL, TRENCH, TRÜBNER & CO.,

PATERNOSTER HOUSE, CHARING-CROSS ROAD.

1897.

KRAUS REPRINT
Millwood, N.Y.
1988

Unaltered reprint 2002

ISBN 0 85991 720 7

Distributed for the Early English Text Society by
Boydell & Brewer Ltd, PO Box 9, Woodbridge, Suffolk IP12 3DF
and Boydell & Brewer Inc, PO Box 41026, Rochester, NY 14604-4126
Website www.boydell.co.uk

Printed and bound by
Antony Rowe Limited, Eastbourne

DEDICATED TO

THE ANTIQUARIES OF CHESHIRE,

IN THE HOPE

THAT THEY WILL AT ONCE HANG ONE OF THEIR NUMBER,

TO ENCOURAGE THE REST

FORTHWITH TO PRINT ALL THE DEPOSITIONS AND OTHER VALUABLE MATERIAL

IN THE DIOCESAN REGISTRY AT CHESTER

WHICH THEY HAVE SO LONG AND SO CULPABLY LEFT IN MS. ONLY.

F. J. F.

CONTENTS.

PAGE

Forewords: See the Contents of the 14 Sections xiii

Afterwords: Depositions in other Dioceses (*Notes*, p. lxx) ... lxviii

Contents of the Manuscript Volume of Depositions whence the extracts below are taken lxxi

DEPOSITIONS.

I. **Child-Marriages.** (See other cases, p. xxi—xxxiv.)

§ 1. Child-Marriage Divorces 1

1. Elizabeth Pole (born Tilston) *v.* Wm. Pole (she 8 (?) at marriage, he 11) 1
2. Humfrey Winstanley *v.* Alice Worsley (he under 12 at marriage, she over 17) 2
3. Elizabeth Hulse *v.* George Hulse (she 4 at marriage, he 7) 4
4. John Bridge *v.* Elizabeth Bridge (born Ramsbotham). (He 11 or 12 at the marriage, she ? 13-14) 6
5. Andrew Haworth *v.* Constance Entwisell (boy 9 at marriage, girl 11) 9
6. Peter Haworth *v.* Margery Haworth, born Heydocke: girl 8 at marriage, boy less 11
7. Joan Whittall (born Leyland) *v.* Rafe Whittall ... 12
8. Ellen Dampart *v.* John Andrewe. (Her 2 Sisters put between them in bed on the wedding-night.) Girl under 8 at marriage, boy 10 12
9. Grace Boyes *v.* Robert Talbot 16
10. Margery Vernon *v.* Randle More (she 9-10 at marriage, he 7-8) 16
11. Peter Hope *v.* Alice Ellis (? both of Hawarden. He nearly 13 at marriage, she 9) 18
12. Elizabeth Dampart (born Page) *v.* Thos. Dampart. (Boy under 10 at marriage. Wife leaves Husband) ... 22
13. Thomas Fletchar *v.* Anne Whitfield (he between 10 and 11 at marriage, she about 9) 22
14. Jane Sommer *v.* Roger Massy 25
15. John Somerford *v.* Jane Somerford (born Brerton): (boy 3 at marriage, girl 2; carried in friends' arms, who spoke the words of Marriage for them) 25
16. Jenet Parker *v.* Laurence Parker 28
17. Margaret Hawke or Whittacres *v.* Henry Whittacres (girl 11, boy 10, at marriage) 29

PAGE

18. Robert Mason *v.* Margaret Mason or Dugdale (he 9, she 10, at marriage) 30
19. Thos. Bentam *v.* Ellen Bentam (born Bolton): (he 12, she 10, at marriage) 31
20. Rafe Fishe *v.* Katherine Fishe (born Bolton). (He under 14 at marriage)... 33
21. Alexander Osboston (Osbaldiston) *v.* Margaret Osboston (born Hothersall): (he nearly 11 at marriage, she 6 or 7, partly borne in arms, and partly led to Church. See p. 183) 34
22. Wm. Westby *v.* Anne Sothworth (boy under 10 at marriage, girl under 11) 35
23. Brigitte Dutton *v.* George Spurstowe (she 4-5 at marriage, he 6) 38
24. Roland Dutton *v.* Margaret Dutton (born Stanley): (he 9 at marriage, she 5) 41
25. Wm. Spakeman *v.* Leticia Unsworth (he about 10 at marriage, she about 11) 43
26. James Ballard *v.* Anne Ballard. (She gives him, when 10-11, two apples to marry her. The curate acting, is punisht) 45
27. William Stanley *v.* Anne Stanley (born Dutton): (he 12 at marriage, she 10) 47

I. § 2. Child-Marriage Ratifications 49
1. John Starkie and Alice Dutton. (Depositions as to the parties' ages: both now 14; married at 10) 49
2. Elizabeth Culcheth and Rafe Culcheth, A.D. 1562. (She had 4 children by him) 51
3. Thos. Wicksted (16-17, married at 9-10), and Ellen Wicksted (15-16, born Ball, married at 8-9) 51

I. § 3. Suit for Restitution of Conjugal Rights 52
1. Margaret Stanley *v.* Thomas Stanley. (She 16 at marriage; he 14-15. She starvd by his Parents) 52

II. **Trothplights.** (See the *Supplement*, p. 184—201, 210) ... 56
1. Jane Walkden *v.* Richard Lowe. (A girl born) ... 56
2. Christian Grimsdiche *v.* John Smith. (He gives her money) 57
3. Anne Yate (Victualler) *v.* George Johnson (married another) 57
4. Ellen Ricroft *v.* Thomas Snelson. (Banns askt. A Child born. He marries Joan Wily. See p. 196) 59
5. Hugh Pollett *v.* Elizabeth Eccles (spinster), alias Burton (widow. Her water sent to a Physician, 63.) ... 62
6. Katherine Man *v.* Richard Pickforth. (She had a child by him) 63
7. Thos. Sothworth *v.* Marg. Sothworth. (Runaway Match) 65
8. Eleanor Manwaring *v.* Roger Bybbye. (Going to Sea) 67
9. Alice Ince *v.* John Brotherton. (Two forms. Child born) 68
10. Sybil Blakhurst *v.* Randle Ramshae. (See p. 210) ... 69

PAGE

III. **Adulteries** 72

1. Mr. Rafe Holden. (Adultery and Bigamy) 72
2. Margaret Alatt *v.* Richard Pierson (alledgd incompetent) 73
3. Henry Price *v.* Mawde Price or Gregorie (she precontracted) 76
4. Elizabeth Shuttleworth's Confession (her girl is P. Hartley's) 80
5. Jane Downes *v.* Reginald Downes. (See p. 202) ... 81
6. William Eiton *v.* Mary Eiton. (Chaplain-Doctor. Woman's water) 82

IV. **Affiliations** 85

1. Anne Wadesworthe *v.* John Whitwham. 19 Feb. 1561-2 85
2. Randle Fradsam *v.* Marg. Wilkinson. (Church-Affiliation) 85
3. Oliver Leghe *v.* Rose Sworton. (Wrongful Affiliation) 89
4. John Cotgreve *v.* Margaret Monelay. (Suit for Cancellation of Affiliation. Couple behind the Mill-door) ... 91
5. Wm. Clare *v.* Ellen Gardiner. (Suit for Cancellation of Affiliation. 'Clare hath a house, & Holt hath non') 97
6. Jn. Thirlewind and Elizabeth Crosse. 3 Nov. 1563 ... 99
7. Robert Walton *v.* Anne Doxie. (Affiliation-Cancelling) 100
8. Thos. Underwood *v.* Ellen Key. (To cancel Affiliation) 101

V. **Libels.** (See the *Supplement*, p. 204—210; Durham cases, lvii) 102

1. Jane David *v.* Robert ap David, and *v.* John ap John (for calling her "a strong hoore"). And John ap John *v.* Jane David (for calling him Cuckold) 102
2. Wade *v.* Rile. (Alledgd Adultery of Custance Wade, wife of Randle Wade, with young Robert Rile) ... 111
3. Margaret Wirrall *v.* Henry Fazakerley. (See p. 204) ... 117
4. Mrs. Katherine Claiton *v.* Margaret Tauliour (for abusing her. Drink at an Inn. Letter written in a Loft) ... 117
5. Margery Morgan *v.* Philip Jenkin (said she lay with W. Bathoe) 120
6. Matilda Holme *v.* Elizabeth Tilston, widow, (for calling her 'Roberte Soundes hoore') 121
7. Constance Frost *v.* Wm. Ball and others. (She a 'whore Jade') 122
8. Joan Ashley *v.* Margaret Stele and others (for saying she was with Child by John Jackson) 123
9. Ellen Gillam *v.* Agnes (or Anne) Gillam (for calling her a 'hoore') 126
10. Isabell Pattele *v.* Rafe Hare (for calling her 'a hoore and a thief') 128
11. Thos. Grenehalgh *v.* Fras. Grenehalgh (for saying he committed Adultery) 129

VI. **Wills** 130

1. Jn. Crompton *v.* Isabella Crompton, testator's widow, and Jn. Crompton. (Hinge-nails of Will-chest drawn) ... 130
2. A Deposition as to Richard Pendleton's Will 131

PAGE

3. Nuncupative Will of Roger Hodson 132
4. Thomas Pole *v.* Randle Rope, executor of Laurence Rope 133
5. As to the Sanity and unexecuted Will of Alice Brodhurst 134
6. Robert Olton *v.* R. Dod and the other Executors of John Olton's Will 135

VII. **Miscellaneous Matters** 137

1. Henry Blagburne's Answer to his Wife's Exceptions to his suit about an Impediment in her body 137
2. The Tithing of Pigs and Geese in Whalley, Lancashire 138
3. Depositions under Commission. (Clergyman and Plague) 139

VIII. **Clandestine Marriages** 140

1. Phillipe Mainwaringe and Jane Serjant 1588 140
2. Thomas Walker and Isabella Walker, *alias* Bamford. 1609 140
3. Richard and Anne Stockley. 1622. (Notes, p. 142) ... 141

English Entries from the Mayors' Books, Chester. (Notes, p. 144) 143

Bond by Jn. Church of the City of Chester, and John Rodorye, fisher, to bring their grain into the City, and not carry any out of it. Penalty £40. A.D. 1558 ... 145

Bond of Thomas Mercer, barber, not to play at unlawful Games, or let them be playd in his house. 1558 ... 145

Bond to secure Hy. Gibbons his Sword, on payment of 3*s.* borowd on it, and 3*d.* interest. 1590 146

Surrender by a Mason of his Patent to keep the City Walls in repair. 1591 146

John Barker's Bond to secure the due Nursing and keeping of his Bastard Baby till Michaelmas. 1591 146

Award of the Mayor, William Massie, in a Dispute about a Lease of a house in Northgate St., and a Bond for due keeping of its Covenants. 1591 147

Richard Porter's Bond to secure the due Nursing and Keeping of his Bastard Baby for a year. 1591 ... 149

Agreement as to the payment and re-payment of a Rent-charge on a house. 1591 149

Commitment to Gaol, of a County Bailiff who arrested a man in the City Market-Place 150

Agreement as to the Ownership of the Hautboys, Recorders, Cornets and Violins, of the City Waits. 1591 ... 150

Bond of a Slater, to buy Slates only for his own use and Buildings. 1591 151

Acknowledgment of a Debt, to be paid at Michaelmas. 1591 151

Acknowledgment of a Debt. On default of payment, Debtor to be sent to Prison. 1591 151

Certificate of a Statute Merchant of £800. 1591 152

Censure of an Alderman for sueing a Fellow-Citizen and late Sheriff for damages. Friendly arrangement as to the Debts. 1591. (See p. 159) 152

Acknowledgment of Debt for Rent. 1591 153

PAGE
Oath of the Butchers in Chester. 1591 153
Oath of the Bakers in Chester. 1591 154
A Chandler's Bond to sell Candles at 4*d*. a Pound. 1591 ... 154
Bond by Sellers of Meat, to bring the animals' Skins and Tallow for sale too, and charge only 3*s*. 4*d*. for the Tallow 154
Bond by a City Merchant to keep and produce 6 Butts of Sack—belonging to Outsiders, which are enterd in his name in the City Customs' Book—or pay £50. 1591 ... 155
Bond by George Title, the Father of a Bastard Child, to provide for the Child, and marry its Mother. 1591 ... 156
Bond by a Sadler to pay his Fine for putting red and white Harness in his Shop before taking it to the Common Hall 156
Bond by a young Goldsmith to provide for his Bastard Child when born, and for its Mother till a month after its birth 157
Bond to secure a debt of 50*s*. to a City Servant. 1592 ... 158
Censure of two men for entering an Innholder's, a Freeman's house, and arresting him. 1592... 159
Order on the late Sheriffs to pay 28*s*. 10*d*. for an Execution Debt and costs. 1592. (See p. 152) 159
Certificate by the Mayor of the due payment of £400 secured by a Statute Merchant. 1592 160
The names of those who haue the keies of the Thresure howse, and Chestes therin. 1597 161
Bond by a Merchant not to sell 70 Bushels of Rye without leave of the Mayor. 1597 162
Bond by a Searcher of Tand Leather and Leather-ware, for his due Fulfilling of his Office. 1597 162
Agreement by a Hatmaker, that, on his failing to pay £12, by 3 instalments, his Creditor may take possession of his Shop, Tools, and Goods. 1598 163
The Stewards of the Fishmongers' Company sent to Gaol, for buying Ling and Cod for their Company, instead of letting the Mayor buy it for the Citizens. 1598 165
Award of the Mayor as to the possession and use of a Table and Frame. 1598 165
Letter from Lord Burleigh to the Officers of the Port of Chester, authorising them to enter, without tax, the Gascony wines of a City Merchant's Widow. 1598 166
Fine for not bringing Brass for Sale in the Common Hall. 1598 167
Receipt and Forwarding of Letters by Post. 1597 167
Gifts of Money by the Mayor and Common Council. 1597-8 168
Description of men for the "Hue and Cry." 1598 171
Distribution of Lady Savage's and Robert Offlee's Gifts to the Poor. 1597 172
Order by Justices of the Peace, at Sessions, that a well-off Son shall pay his poor old Father 20*s*. a Quarter, and give him a Gown. 1598 173
Order against a Plaintiff for not being ready for his Trial ... 174

PAGE

Bonds to produce, on warning, Patrick Ford, a Dublin Merchant come to Chester, and not let him leave without the Mayor's license. 1600 174
Entries of Writs of Error. 1600 175
Bond to secure the appearance of Patrick Ford, on his return to Dublin, before the Lord Deputy of Ireland. 1600 ... 175
Order for Stay of a Trial till Counsel are appointed on each side 177
Order that the Keeper of the Conduit shall let the Stalls near it and take their rents, he cleaning the Street thro it, and paying 8*s*. a year. 1600 177
Promise that a Mariner and his Bark and Crew shall be ready by 25 July 1600, for the Queen's service. 1600 ... 178
Receipt of 9*s*. 8*d*. for the Highway-rate. 1600 178
Receipt and Forwarding of Letters by Posts. 1599-1600 ... 178
The names of those that have landes within the Countie of Chester, and do not dwell within the same. 1578? ... 180
The Queen's Cheshire Wards in 1578 180
Petition of the Men of Staines, Middlesex, that their Bridge over the Thames may not be wholly broken down. 1549 181

SUPPLEMENT.

I. i. 21 *b*. Alexander Osboston *v*. Margaret Osboston or Hothersall. (See p. 34) 183
II. 11. Katherine Strete *v*. Nicolas Jepson. (Trothplight, 1562) 184
II. 12 *a*. Morgan Edmund *v*. Elizabeth Bird. (Trothplight. She married another) 187
II. 12 *b*. Cross-suit. Henry Dilon, Elizabeth Bird's Husband, *v*. Morgan Edmund. (She, trothplighted to Edmund, married Dilon, 1562) 194
II. 4 *b*. Ellen Ricroft *v*. Thomas Snelson. (Trothplight Evasion. See p. 59) 196
II. 13. Alice Wodfall *v*. Thomas Torbock. (Trothplight. Referees) 196
II. 14. Alexander Winstanley *v*. Ellen Sonkie. (She marries R. Gidlowe) 198
II. 15. Ellen Carter *v*. Thomas Middlehurst (an inconstant man) 200
III. 5 *a*. Jane Downes *v*. Reginald Downes. (A Child-Marriage. See p. 81) 202
V. 3 *b*. Henry Fazakerley *v*. Margery Wirrall. (Libel. See p. 117) 204
V. 7 *a*. Constance Frost *v*. William Ball and others. (Libel. See p. 122) 208
V. 12. Elizabeth Basnett *v*. Anne Venables. (Libel. Referees) 209
II. 10 *b*. Sybil Blakhurst *v*. Randle Ramshae. (Trothplight. See p. 69) 210
Index of Names of Persons 211
Index of Names of Places 229
Glossary 235
Index of Subjects 241

FOREWORDS.

§ 1. *How I came across these Child-Marriage Depositions*, p. xiii.
§ 2. *The value of all the Depositions for the Social Life of their time* (p. xv). *Child-Marriages: Details of the Children's Ages, Parents' Motives, Hours of Marriage, Bride-ales, Bedding at Night* (p. xvii), *Causes of Divorce* (p. xviii), *Meetings at Christmas Merriments* (p. xix), *Ratifications or Dissolutions of the Marriages* (p. xix).
§ 3. *Other cases of Child-Marriage, in Cheshire* (p. xxi), *Durham* (p. xxiv), *the Berkeley family* (p. xxvii), *the Bible* (p. xxvii), *the Fathers* (p. xxviii), *Sir Simonds D'Ewes's* Autobiography (p. xxix), *Lord Anglesey's* Diary, 1673 (p. xxxi), Notes and Queries (p. xxxii), *Philip Stubbes's* Anatomy, 1593 (p. xxxiv), *Indian Child-Marriages* (p. xxxiv).
§ 4. *The Law on the point, from Judge Swinburne, who died in* 1624, p. xxxv.
§ 5. *The reason for these Child-Marriages: abuse of the Sovereign's right of Guardianship*, p. xxxix.
§ 6. *Social Life as shown by the Trothplight cases*, p. xliii.
§ 7. *Social Life as shown by the Adultery cases*, p. liii.
§ 8. *Social Life as shown by the Affiliation cases*, p. lv.
§ 9. *Social Life as shown by the Libel cases*, p. lvi.
§ 10. *Social Life as shown by the Wills cases*, p. lx.
§ 11. *Social Life as shown by the Miscellaneous cases*, p. lxi.
§ 12. *Clandestine Marriages, and the state of the Clergy*, p. lxii.
§ 13. *Social Life as shown by the Mayors'-Books entries*, p. lxiii.
§ 14. *Conclusion*, p. lxiv. *Ought a Cheshire antiquary to be hangd?*

§ 1. Having to work for one Society or another, in August holidays as well as ordinary months, I went to Lichfield in 1889, to collate a Hampole MS. and try the Probate Office Wills (which proved too late); to Lincoln in 1890 (whence, with Mr. T. Austin's help, I got copies which will make a good volume of Wills and Documents when the E. E. T. Soc. has funds to print it); to Norwich in 1891 (which yielded half a volume of Wills, the other half being stopt by the death of our copier); to Salisbury in 1892 (where little was to be had for us); and to Chester in 1893, drawn thither by Mr. Cordy Jeafferson's Report on the City Documents in the Appendix, Pt. I., to the Fourth Report of the Historical MSS. Commission, 1881, p. 355—403. But on asking for the likeliest MS. book, I was told it was lent to Canon Morris, for his nearly-ready work on the Chester City-Records, &c. So I turnd to the Mayors' Books, which Canon Morris was said not to have used, and copied from them the few English documents and entries that seemd suited to us.

Then I went across to the Diocesan Registry, and askt for their earliest English books. A grand folio of Wills was shown me; but as the Lancashire and Cheshire Chetham Society had printed several volumes from it, I left it to them to go on with, and I turnd to the second tatterd MS., the 'Depositions in Trials in the Bishop's Court from Nov. 1561 to March 1565-6.' I started at the first moderately solid leaf, 9, p. 4 below, and, to my astonishment, read, that Elizabeth Hulse said she was married to George Hulse in the Chapel of Knutsford, when she was but three or four years old, while the boy himself deposed that he was about seven. I had heard of the betrothal of royal children by proxy, but never before of the actual marriage in church of the little boys and girls of middle-class folk. However, there proved to be 27 instances of this latter custom in this one volume; and a report of Mr. J. P. Earwaker's Paper on the subject from the *Manchester Guardian* of March 9, 1885, was handed to me,[1] with a Leader on it, which showd that he and his North-Western folk were in this matter 8 or 10 years ahead of us poor know-nothing Southerners. Still, if we don't know much, we don't wait eight years before printing the important fresh matter we find, on the social state of Elizabethan or earlier England. I at once set to work, copied hard for six or eight hours a day[2]—as long as the office rules allowd,—till my eyes were tired, and then went up again for three weeks in October, to get out of the MS. all its non-tithe and non-church or merely local matter.[3] Within three months of my starting at the MS., all the text of this volume was in type,—thanks to Messrs. Clay and Sons,—and within 4 months I began writing these Forewords. Some hours had to be given to patching up the rotting leaves, and some more to completing the partial Index to the volume which the Rev. Mr. Piccope, a former Vicar of Farndon (11¼ miles up the Dee, where a lock is wanted), had made, and out of which he had left all the Adultery, Affiliation, and Libel cases, which contain so much material for the social historian. But I hope the present Text holds most of the MS. that will interest the general student; and

[1] Mr. Earwaker tells me that he read this Paper before the Lancashire and Cheshire Antiquarian Society on March 6, 1885—see their *Transactions*, vol. iii (1885), p. 167—and before the Liverpool Historic Society on March 19, 1889. He afterwards enlarged the Paper, and read it, as one on "Marriages between Children," before the Archæological Institute at their Meeting in Chester in 1886. But he has never printed this Paper, altho often askt to do so, because he was constantly adding to it, and was anxious to make it as complete as possible before it was publisht. He has some thoughts of writing a little monograph on the subject. The sooner the better, we all say.

[2] At night I had to edit Shakspere for three or four hours.

[3] On going thro the Contents of the MS. at more leisure in London, I found that I'd unluckily left out a few bits of my cases, and also some other good ones. These, I askt Mr. Price for; and he has kindly sent me copies of some, for the *Supplement*, p. 183, &c., and extracts from others, for Notes to the *Contents of the MS.*, p. lxxi below.

I ask all its readers to join with me in thanking Mr. W. H. Price, the Chief-Clerk of the Registry, who, with the kind consent of Mr. J. Gamon, the Registrar, has read all the proofs or revises of my copy, and corrected very many mistakes that my tired eyes and want of familiarity with late Record writing had left-in. Mr. Phil Davies of the Town-Clerk's Office has joind Mr. Price in reading the proofs and revises of the Mayors'-Books extracts; and to him too our thanks are due,—to say nothing of my own, for the two delightful Sundays on the Dee in which we sculd above Farndon, he cheering us with his fine bass songs.

§ 2. Now for the Contents of the MS. (see p. lxxi below) and this volume.

Having given myself specially to the social side of our forefathers' lives—witness my editions of *Handlyng Synne* (1303), *Fifty Earliest English Wills*, the *Babees Book*, *Queene Elizabethes Achademy*, *Harrison's England*, *Stubbes's Abuses*, *Tell-Troth*, *Ballads from MSS.*, *Fraternity of Vacabonds*, *Andrew Boorde*, *Stafford's Examination*, *Laneham's Letter*, &c.,—I can safely say that no MS. or print that I had previously handled seemd to so let me into the life of its time as this volume of Chester Depositions. The 'Child-Marriages' start us with birth, the 'Wills' take us to death, while between the two lies many a scene of Life in olden days which needs but little fancy to call up before one's mind's eye now. In the 'Child-Marriages' we see the servant hurrying for the midwives (p. 49-50), the baby born, and suckled by the wet nurse (pp. 40, 50), then christend (p. 9), and sent to its foster-mother's for a year (p. 27). Soon, a consultation of parents and friends of boy and girl is held, and a marriage of the children arranged. The girl, between 2 and 3, the boy between 3 and 4, are carried into the parish church in the arms of friends, who speak some of the words of matrimony for them, because their baby-tongues cannot say them all for themselves (p. 26).[1]

If the girl is about 6 or 7, she is "partlie borne in armes,[2] and partlie led to" the church where she is married to her boy-husband (p. 34). If the parent of either child is mercenary, a money-bargain is made for it: the father of a boy of two, gets from an older girl's father, "monie to bie a pece of land," and executes a Bond to repay the money if his boy doesn't marry the girl, (p. 6—9). In another case, the boy's father is in debt, "and, to get somme money of William Whitfield, to the discharge of his debtes, maried and bargained his sonne to the said Whitfeildes doughter" (p. 23, 24). Again, a girl of 3 or 4 is married to a boy of 7 "biecause her frendes thought she shuld have had a lyvinge bie

[1] See also p. 39 below. [2] See too p. 183, and p. 25, below.

hym" (p. 4), and her father-in-law is under Bond to marry them (p. 5). So again, a girl's father says that she married a boy of her own age, 11-12, "biecause she shold have had bie hym a prety bargane, yf they cold have lovid, on the other" (p. 12). Another girl of 11 is married to a boy of 9, because, on her father's death, the boy's father gets the landlord's leave to take-on the girl's house (p. 10). Another girl of 8 is married to a boy of 10, because the boy's father feard "lest he shuld lose his parte of his lyvinge" in a tenement which he held in common with the girl's protector (p. 14). In another instance, the girl's grandfather "was a very welthie man; and it was supposed that he wold have bene good vnto" her & her boy-husband, "and bestowid somme good ferme apon her" (p. 32), so a boy of 12 married her when she was 10. Other children are married "bie the compulsion of their frendes" (p. 11, 13, 23, &c.); another "by a wile" (p. 16), the girl being invited by a relation of the boy's to come and make merry, and then married to the boy against her consent. But in one case, a girl arranged her own marriage. She was "a bigge damsell, & mariageable" (p. 47), that is, past 12, and evidently fancying a nice boy of 10-11, "intised hym with two Apples, to go with her to Colne, and to marry her" (p. 45). No wonder that this boy 'repentid' next morning, and that others say "at the tyme of their mariage they knewe not what they did" (p. 15), "they were both so ignoraunt, they knewe not what the matter meanid[1]" (p. 1), &c.

These Child-Marriages took place in parish churches (p. 6, 9, 11, 25, 33, 44-5, &c.), or chapels[2] (p. 4, 17, 52, &c.), or the private chapels of rich parents or friends at their country-seats (p. 39, 41; 2, 3, &c.), or at private houses or rectories (p. 13, 15, 50, 51, &c.), on a workday (p. 53), on Sunday (p. 30), at Christmas (p. 48), Twelfth-Night (p. 46), or other feast-days (p. 7, 36, 41, 45); and at all times of the day, from "a morninge about Cockes crowinge, with Torche-light and Candell-light, in the

[1] 1893, *Westminster Gazette*, 25 October, p. 7, col. 2. "A little Indian boy and girl have just been tried at the criminal sessions at Berhampur on a charge of bigamy. The girl and boy, aged respectively six and nine, were indicted for marrying, the former being at the time, to the knowledge of the bridegroom, already, under the barbarous Indian custom of child-betrothal, the wife of another. As the Act only allows presumption of death after seven years' continuous absence of one of the parties, it was justly observed that a bride of six could not possibly plead that excuse. For three days little Lilith stood beside her fellow bigamist in the dock, while their respective parents were charged with abetting their offence. Ultimately the jury returned a verdict of 'Not guilty,' and 'the youngsters went cheerily home again with the smallest possible conception of what all the bother was about.'"

[2] By chapels is to be understood the smaller churches, "Chapels of Ease" to the mother churches, not Nonconformist Chapels, as some present-day readers might hastily imagine.—J. P Earwaker.

parishe churche[1]" (p. 2), to 10 or 11 a.m.[2] (p. 2), and to the night-season (p. 16), "inconvenient tymes" like 10 p.m. (p. 45), for which the Curate acting gets punisht by the Archbishop of York.

The marriage ended, the bride-ale or feast at the girl's-father's follows (p. 31), or, in 1673, the grandfather gives the wedding dinner, dance, and supper (p. xxxi); [3]and at night the child-bride and -bridegroom are,—sometimes, at least,—put to bed.[3]

In one case, p. 15 below, the boy says, "the first night they were maried, they lay both in one bed; but two of her sisters lay betwene hym & her." In another case of an unwilling boy of 11-12, the girl of 13-14 says he wept to go home with his father, but "bie his fathers intreating, and bie the perswasion of the priest, the said John did comme to bed to this Respondent far in the night; and there lay still, till in the morninge, in suche sort as this deponent might take unkindnes with hym; for he lay with his back toward her all night": as the boy says, p. 8, "he never touchid her bare skin." In the rest of our 27 cases, no bedding of the children is mentiond; and Alice Worsley of 17, who married Humfrey Winstanley of 12, says that "he neuer came in bed with her" (p. 4). The Downes case also, in the Supplement, p. 203, seems to imply that the parties were not bedded till 'they did comme to the yeres of Consent.' This was a case of Child-Marriage ending in the husband's adultery, leading to a separation by friends' counsel and the parties' consent, p. 192, 203, and then a suit for divorce.

After the wedding-night, the boy either stopt with the girl's father or went home to his own folk (p. 24), and was sent to school or service, while she stayd with her relations or went to service too.[4] It depended partly on the wealth of the families. Crack ones, like the Stanleys of

[1] Compare, in the 'Clandestine Marriages,' p. 140, the marriage 'in a meadowe, in the night season, by the lighte of the moone.'

[2] For a later marriage of runaway folk, see the striking case, p. 65-7 below: Thomas and Margaret Sothworth.

[3—3] For this line, Mr. J. P. Earwaker would substitute: "and after that, the children were taken home to their parents, or to the house of one of them, to wait till they reached their 'years of discretion.'" He says: "I don't think you find this putting to bed anywhere else; and it is a *most* important point. The two cases cited are clearly exceptions to the rule; and, as you see, no carnal copulation took place. These 'child-marriages' were never consummated till the children reached their 'years of discretion.' If they came together then, all well and good, but it was *before* this consummation of the marriage that these divorce proceedings had to be taken. A marriage once consummated could only be set aside for adultery, &c." See Notes at end.

Of course the 'putting to bed' of very young children involvd no fleshly act. But here are our two cases of bedding. I took them at first as samples of the general custom; Mr. Earwaker says they are exceptions; and as his experience is so much greater than mine, no doubt he is right. See Notes at end.

[4] But sometimes she stayd with the boy's father, p. 10.

Hooton, sent their boy to Dr. Standish's school[1] at Lathom, and then to learn manners and arms, in service with the head of the Stanleys, the Earl of Derby (p. 48). A poorer boy, who'd lost his expected living or inheritance, would straggle off to a town near, like Congleton, apprentice himself to a shoemaker (p. 5), and be thrown over by his bride accordingly, for "she neuer did fansie or love the said George, for biecause the said George had lost his lyvinge, . . and was not able to maintaine her." But if the boy stayd in the girl's house, differences with her father or her might arise. In the case on p. 12, the boy stays with his father-in-law[2] for less than a month, then goes to his own mother's till he is 15 or 16, and then comes back to his bride's father for two years, but is 'ordred' or treated 'worse than any servant in her father's house'; and this bride "dealid so unkindly with him, he will never have her; for whie, she ever lovid other boies (to his knowledge) as well as hym"; and so he goes to service elsewhere: as another girl says, "dislove fell betwene them" (p. 11).—I never saw the word *dislove* before: it is used a second time in this volume at p. 55.

When the boy married "biecause it was his mothers mynde, [&] he durst not displease her" (p. 20), he would still refuse his little wife, tho she dwelt for three years in his mother's house (p. 19), and tho 'the said Alis wold comme and bring the said Peter his sheetes to bed; and this deponentes sonne [his bedfellow] wold say to hym, "Peter, whie do not you take your wief to you?" and he wold answere, "Peace! she is non of my wief"' (p. 20).[3] So, where a boy married a girl for his father's property's sake, "the said Ellin went to London,[4] and the said John went to the warres, & abrode to service." In another property case, the boy says, "Father! gyve me your blessinge, and I will go into an other Cuntry [county] to seke my Livinge; for I will never take her as my wief." One boy Robert gives as his reason, "he cold never fansy her [his child-bride], nor her father; biecause he [her father] kept the mother of the said Roberte to paramour, afore he maried her, & consumed the said Robertes goodes," p. 30.

Another boy John says, that even before his marriage—to save his father from the penalty of a Bond—his girl "beynge a bigge woman, and

[1] A poorer boy is also sent to school away from home, p. 19. On 'Education in Early England,' see my Forewords to the *Babees Book* (or *Manners and Meals*), E. E. T. Soc., also to *Queene Elizabethes Achademy*, and p. 182-6 of Starkey's *Dialogue between Pole and Lupset*, E. E. T. S., 1870.

[2] See p. 28 for another instance of disagreement with a father-in-law.

[3] See also p. 21, where Peter won't take drink from Alice.

[4] As to London, compare Katherine Strete's case in the Supplement, p. 185, deposition of Wm. Sidall.

the said John but a child, she delt shrewdlie with hym: and that made hym to cast his love so from her, that yf hit had not bene for savinge of the band [Bond], he wold never have maried her," p. 9. A boy at school writes to his mother-in-law and aunt to his bride, "that if his father wold have hym to take her as his wief, he wold rather be banished out of the Cuntrey," p. 38.

When the children of gentlefolk dwelt apart after their early marriages, they yet dined and supt together occasionally, and foregatherd at Christmas merriments and other guestnings (p. 17, 18, 43, 48). I *should* like to have seen how the little married folk treated one another, and how they were made much of by parents and friends, at table, in dances, games, &c.[1]: and whether they were demure, and fild with the consciousness of their wedded state, or rompt and flirted with other children, turnd jealous, and got into pets, &c. When chicks act a Marriage now, how do the bride and her groom behave for the rest of the evening? If only the Lord Mayor would marry a hundred couples for the one evening, at his next children's Christmas party, it would be a pretty sight, and an interesting character-study.

Well; when the girl became 12, and the boy 14, either of them could, by suit in the Bishop's Court, avoid their child-marriage, if it had not been completed by dwelling-together, kissing, giving of tokens, treating one another as man and wife, or copulation. To the 27 cases in which marriage was a failure in the diocese of Chester in 1561-6, we owe the records printed below. No doubt scores of others ended happily; the child-husband and -wife just livd on together, and—when they had reacht their years of discretion, (girls 12, boy 14) or attaind puberty—ratified their marriage by sleeping in one bed and having children (p. 203). But if either objected, he or she was free to marry before the Bishop's Court pronounst their Divorce,[2]—see Lord Eurye's case below, p. xxiv-vii,—tho the new spouse could hardly feel sure that the rejected one hadn't proof of the ratification of the first marriage, which would have invalidated the second. The proceedings in the Bishop's

[1] Mr. Earwaker says he could give me several instances of this if it were not that they'd make these Forewords too long. No fear of that, so long as the matter is fresh and good.

[2] Mr. Earwaker writes, "This is not so. Neither could marry till the Divorce had been granted." I hold to Lord Eurye's case, and reject Mr. Earwaker's dictum. Swinburne says only, *Spousals*, p. 31, "nor is [either] to be licensed to marry elsewhere in the mean time"; but this implies only adviseability, not illegality. Mr. Earwaker, however, maintains his point, and adds: "If this were so, there was no occasion to go to the expense and trouble of procuring these divorces in the Spiritual Courts. I am sure that no marriage could possibly be valid until the Divorce had been granted and enrolled." (How obstinate some folk are!) See note, p. xxv.

Court ought to have been taken soon after either child attaind the age of consent (girl 12, boy 14); but if the party seeking relief was poor, the suit could be brought later. On p. 12 below, one girl's father "beynge askid whi the said Joane did not begin her sute afore, he sais that she was poor, and had no money; and nowe she hath gotten somwhat in Service, and nowe spendes hit in triall of the Lawe." If the parties are to be rich, and family property is concernd, the Ratification of the marriage is sometimes recorded in the Bishop's Court, after Depositions made by witnesses as to the children's ages, p. 49—52 below; and the Dissent is also a formal matter. In one case (p. 44), "ther was diverse daie-holdinges to get them [the wedded children] to abide together; which they [the relatives and friends] never cold bringe to passe"; in another (p. 41-2), the boy disclaims before the Bishop of Chester: "the said Roland, within a smale while after he was xiiij yeares of age, did, before his ordenarie, declare, that he would refuse to take the said Margaret to his wief; and that he would not consent to the said mariage which was solempnized in his minoritie /." In the case of Sir John Southworth's daughter Anne, p. 36-7, the boy's father comes to Sir John's house, and asks little Anne "what she could finde in heart to doe concerninge the said mariage." Her father repeats the question, and she answers, 'she could not phansie the said William; and that she wold not consent to take him, the said William, to her husband' (p. 36). A twelvemonth after, Sir John asks the boy William 'what liking he had of her [Sir John's girl Anne], and whether he could so well phansie her as to have her to wief'; who made answere in the presence of diverse worshipfull, 'that he would not haue her to wief, nor ratifie mariage with her in any wise (p. 36).' Another witness says, p. 37 :—

about S^t^. James day last past, at my Lord Bushops beinge at Sampsbury,[1] the said William, in the presence of diverse Worshipfull, was demaundid by sir John Sothworth and others, 'whether he cold be content to fansy the said Anne, and take her as his wief': who answerid, that 'he wold not take her as his wief, biecause she had afore refusid him.'

So the boy, Wm. Westby, brought a suit for Divorce against the girl in the Bishop's Court, and would get it as a matter of course, after proof given that their child-marriage had never been ratified.

Now, before I go on to quote some of the illustrations of social life from the Trothplights and other Divisions of this volume, I think I had better deal with the few other cases of child-marriage that have turnd-up in my small search for em, and quote Judge Swinburne (15 . . . 1624) on

[1] Samlesbury, a well-known old Lancashire Hall of the Southworths.—J. P. E.

the law of the subject. But I first notice the case (p. 22) of Elizabeth Dampart *v.* Thomas Dampart,—in which the Child-marriage was ratified by carnal intercourse, the wife afterwards leaving her husband, and which I suppose to be a suit for Divorce;—and the more curious and interesting case of Margaret Stanley *v.* Thomas Stanley (both members of county families), in which the loving young couple livd with the bridegroom's father and mother; then the mother, 'a straite woman' (p. 53, at foot), or the father and mother "beynge a heady folk, toke a folish opinion against" the young bride, "and almost clemmid her for defaulte of meate," p. 54. Then the girl's father gave her a chest, and

"meate, as bred, cheese, & other victualles, which she for a tyme kept lockt in the chest, till they [the mother- & father-in-law] beyng ware of it, convaid the kay away from her, & so toke away her victualles, and fell worse out with her, that her father was faine to fetch her home, for feare she shold be clemmid [starvd]."—p. 54, at top.

There seems to have been an attempt at a separation or divorce between the young couple before the parson (rector) of Bury in Lancashire; but as he couldn't divorce them, I suppose the young wife brought her suit for Restitution of Conjugal Rights, and not for Divorce. The boy Tom Stanley, of 16 or so, couldn't stand up to his "heady" father and mother, I suppose; and England not being then a 'free' country, the neighbours didn't shoot the old ruffians.

§ 3. Now for the other cases of Child-Marriage. I do not propose to give these in order of time, because that plan would break up John Smith's and Judge Swinburne's quaint statements, and mix the Chester cases with those from other parts. I shall quote, i. such additional instances in the diocese of Chester as I know of; ii. that of young Lord Eurye (10-11) and Lord Darcy's daughter (4), from the Durham Depositions; iii. give John Smith's Berkeley and Bible cases; iv. Judge Swinburne's from the Fathers; v. that cited by Sir Simonds d'Ewes, and his own case; vi. that of Lord Anglesey's grandson in 1673; vii. others from *Notes and Queries* and *The Academy*, and viii. from my edition of Stubbes's *Anatomy of Abuses*, 1593.

i. In the Diocese of Chester. Our pioneer leads the van, with 4 fresh cases.

In his Paper on this subject, before the Lancashire and Cheshire Antiquarian Society on Friday, 6 March 1885, Mr. J. P. Earwaker cited the additional cases[1] of (1) ISABEL ORRELL, who deposed that she could

[1] These, Mr. Earwaker says, were only selected instances out of a large number of divorce cases which he had met with in his searches amongst the Consistory-Court Records.

not perfectly remember her marriage, but knew by credible report that it was celebrated in Turton Chapel when she was 7 years old, and when her bridegroom was of the age of 5 or 6. (2) When GILBERT GERRARD and EMMA TALBOT were married at Leigh Church, the boy's uncle held up the bridegroom, who was 5 years old, and "spake the words of matrimony for the child's part; and the woman"—who was not 6 years of age—"spake for herself, as she was taught." (3) JOHN RIGMARDEN, at the age of 3, was married to a bride of 5. He was carried in the arms of a clergyman, who coaxt him to repeat the words of matrimony. Before he had got through his lesson, the child declared he would learn no more that day. The priest answerd: "You must speak a little more, and then go play you." (4) In 1582, JOAN CHADERTON (a Bishop's daughter) was, at the age of 9, married to RICHARD BROOKE, who had nearly completed his 11th year; and the marriage was ratified by the consent of the young folk in 1586, as shown by documents still preservd in the Bishop's Registry at Chester. Joan's father was Wm. Chaderton, successively Bishop of Chester and Lincoln, and a well-known scholar and distinguisht ecclesiastic in Q. Elizabeth's reign. During his residence in Manchester,—where he and the Earl of Derby were virtual rulers of the district,—he was notable for the encouragement he gave to ministers, and for his zeal in establishing lectureships and daily morning prayer. His child was married in his own Bishop's palace. Twenty years later, Sir Jn. Harington tells us that the Bishop had "no great comfort of that matrimony" of his only daughter, "who was then living apart from her husband." "A harvest of domestic unhappiness and disaster must frequently have resulted from these ill-assorted unions."—*Manchester Guardian*, March 9, 1885.

Next comes the volume of earlier Depositions—July 1548 to March 1550-1—uneartht in the Diocesan Registry at Chester, by Mr. W. H. Price and Mr. W. F. Irvine last September. An infant-marriage from this, Mr. Irvine has just printed in the *Birkenhead News* of Dec. 9, 1893, page 6, column 7. In 1538 or '9, Robert Parre, of Backford, was married at the age of three, to Elizabeth Rogerson. "He was hired for an apple bie his uncle to goe to the Church," and was borne thither "in the armes of Edward Bunburie his uncle . . . . wich helde hym in hys armes the tyme *that* he was maried to the said Elisabethe, att which tyme the saide Robert colde scarce speke." The Depositions will be printed in full by Mr. Irvine and Mr. W. H. Price in the volume they will edit for the Early English Text Society in a year or two.

In turning hastily over the leaves of the volume backwards, I notist three other cases, *a.* (Piccope's No. 67) lf. 127-8, Harie Accars, at the time of his marriage with his child-wife Jane, was "abowt the age off viij yeres, and the said Jane about iiij' or v' yeres old." She deposes "*that* both she and hyr husbonde dwellid at hyr father aft*er* the said matrimonie, the space off xij yeris / but she was neuer myndit to haue hym, nor he hyr, off all that space." *b.* (Piccope's No. 37) Just before Corpus Christi day in 33 Hen. VIII. (the Thursday week after Whit-Sunday, 1541), Alexander Woodward, when married to his wife Cicelie, in the parish church of Wigan, was "vnder the age off eghte yeris," "and Cicelie abowt the age off x yeris and vnder a xj." *c.* (Piccope's No. 23) In about 1539, John and Ellen Aynscoe, at their marriage, were both "vnder the age off xij yeris."

Mr. Earwaker tells me that "a great many instances of Child-Marriages might be given from the *Inquisitiones post mortem*, taken after the deaths of persons holding lands under the Crown, or, in the case of Cheshire, under the Palatine Earls. It is by no means unfrequent to read that so and so was heir to his father, and then aged, say, ten years, and was already married." [1] Mr. Ponsonby Lyons says the real things to search are the Inquisitions in the Court of Wards and Liveries: this must be true. Let the next Editor of a Child-Marriage volume work them. Time fails me. (For the Duke of York's case, see Notes, p. lxxxvii.)

ii. A.D. 1541. Child-Marriage at Eynsham, Oxfordshire: girl 4, boy 10-11. Divorce of the parties, 3 Nov. 1554. The boy married another girl in or about 1548. Mary Darcye, daughter of Lord Darcye, *v.* William, Lord Eure. (From "*Depositions and other Ecclesiastical Proceedings from the Courts of Durham, extending from* 1311 *to the Reign of Elizabeth.*" Surtees Society, 1845, p. 54-8).

[1] The following cases I've seen in a hasty run thro vol. i. of the Lanc. and Cheshire Record Soc. *Lancashire Inquisitions:*

Pt. i, p. 149. *Richard Walmisley*, died 23 Oct. last [1609]; and *Richard*, his son and heir, who was married to *Elline Gerrard* in the lifetime of his father, is now [4 Jan. 1609-10] aged 11 years, 4 months and 19 days . . .

Pt. i, p. 168. *Edward Stanley* died at Aighton, 30 March last [1610]. Bridget, his wife, yet survives at Aighton; and *Peter Stanley*, his son and heir, who was married in his father's lifetime to *Elizabeth*, daughter of *Thomas Woodfall*, is now [9 Oct. 1610] aged 11 years, 2 months, and 13 days.

In Part ii. is one case: *Christopher Anderson* died 2 Dec. last past [1619], and *Christopher*, his son and next heir, is 'aged, at the time of taking this Inquisition [21 March, 1619-20], 12 years, 1 month, and 11 days, and not more. The said *Christopher* (the son) married at Lostocke, in his father's lifetime, *Agnes*, daughter of *John Preston*, Esq., which Agnes is now aged 12 years and more.'—p. 164. (The Inquisition of Henry Southworth, who died at Samlesbury on 24 Jan. 1615-16, is at p. 292-3). I cannot see any instance of a Child-Marriage in Part III.

In the *Yorkshire Inquisitions*, i. 102, is one case in 1265. Roger de Merlay, or Merley, had 3 daughters and heirs: the third, 8 years old, and she was married before his death to the son and heir of Marmaduke de Tuenge (Thweng).

LV. Extracts from "Processus Divortii inter Mariam Darcye, filiam domini Georgii Darcye, Domini Darcye, et Willielmum Dominum Eure."[1] [Reg. Pilkington, f. 61, b. &c.]

Willielmus Farefaxe de Alne in com. Ebor. armiger, ætatis circiter xxviij annorum, testis super libellum per partem Mariæ Darcye, alias Euers, unius filiarum domini Georgii Darcye, Domini Darcye,[2] contra Willielmum Euers, Dominum Euers, judicialiter oblatus, productus, admissus, juratus—dicit, quod dictam Mariam Darcye, alias Eurye, a nativitate sua, et dictum Willielmum Dominum Eurye per duodecim annos, vel circiter, bene novit.

Super primo articulo examinatus, dicit, quod articulus continet in se veritatem. Interrogatus de causa scientiæ suæ, he saithe that he was presente at the solemnizacion had beytween the parties articulate, in the said parishe churche of Eynsham, and see all rites and cerymonies used and doon betwixt them, as is commonlye doon bytwixt man and wife at the solemnizacion of matrimonye; savinge that one Marye, beinge nursse to the said Marye Darcye, articulate, at that tyme, did first speke the wordes of matrimonye, and the said Marye Darcye did repete them after her; presentibus tunc ibidem, Thoma Matham armigero, Petro Hoothorne generoso, Ricardo Allerton yoman, et multis aliis.

[1] He was the second Baron: see Cokayne's admirable *Peerage*, iii. 293: Eure [or Evers]. II. 1548. 2 WILLIAM (EURE), LORD EURE, grandson and heir, being son and heir of Sir Ralph Eure, Warden of the East Marches, by Margery, da. of Sir William Bowes, of Streatham; which Ralph was s. and h. ap. of the first Lord, but was slain v. p. by the Scots, 6 March 1544-5, at the battle of Ancrum moor. He was *b.* 27 Feb. 1530-1,* was Warden of the Middle Marches, *temp.* Ed. VI., Mary and Eliz., and was Capt. of Berwick Castle; was one of the Commissioners to negotiate with Scotland in 1587. He was contracted in marriage (at his age of 11, the lady being but 4), at Eynsham, Oxon, in 1541, to Mary, da. of George (Darcy), LORD DARCY, by Dorothy, da. and h. of Sir John MELTON, of Aston, co. York. This contract was, however, set aside by decree at Durham, 3 Nov. 1554. He then *m.* before 1558 [? had previously married, by or before 1548: he could legally repudiate his Child-marriage when he was 14, that is, in 1544], Margaret, da. of Sir Edward DYMOKE, of Scrivelsby, co. Lincoln, Knight Banneret [Champion of England], by Anne, da. of Sir George TALBOYS. She was *bur.* 15 Sept. 1591, at Ingleby, co. Lincoln. He *d.* 12, and was *bur.* there 13 Feb. 1593/4. Will dat. 22 Dec. 1592. *Inq. post mortem*, 24 Sept. 1594, at Stokelsey, co. York.

[2] See Cokayne, *Peerage*, iii. 20:—

DARCY, DARCY DE DARCY, or DARCY AND MEINILL.

Sometimes (*erroneously*) called Darcy of Aston.

Barony in tail male I. 1548.

1. SIR GEORGE DARCY, s. and h. of Thomas, LORD DARCY, next above named, by his 1st wife, Dowsabel, da. and h. of Sir Richard Tempest, of Ridlesdale, co. Northumberland, was Knighted at the battle of Flodden, 9 Sept. 1513, and was, ten years after his father's death, restored in blood by Act of Parl. (1548) 2 Edw. VI. to the dignity of BARON DARCY, "to him and the heirs male of his body." He *m.*, before 1537, Dorothy, da. and h. of Sir John MELTON of Aston (hence the designation of the Barony as "DARCY of *Aston*"), co. York, by Catharine, da. of Sir Hugh HASTINGS of Fenwick. She, who was aged 38 at the death of her father, 26 Feb. 1544/5, died before her husband, and was *bur.* at Brayton (*not* Bempston), co. York. He *d.* 28 Aug. 1557, desiring, in his will, to be *bur.* there.

* Later information from Mr. Cokayne. The printed text says 1530.

Super secundo articulo examinatus, dicit, quod continet in se veritatem. Interrogatus de causa scientiæ suæ, he saithe, that the said Marye Darcye, alias Eurye, articulate, was, at the solemnisacion of the matrimonye, caryed in hir nurse armes, and could scarse well speke the wordes of matrymonye at the said solemnizacion after the teachinge of hir nursse, as he hathe byfore deposed. And he saithe that he herd at that tyme Sr Raff Eurye, father to the said Lord Eurye, saye that the said William Lord Eurye was ten yeres old, and no more.

Super tertio articulo examinatus, dicit, quod articulus continet in se veritatem. Interrogatus de causa scientiæ suæ, he saithe, that the said William Lord Eurye and she never sawe togither, nor came in companye togither at any tyme save ons, synce the said Marye came to thaige of xij yers; and at that tyme he is well assured she woold scarse looke or speke to the said *Lord* Eurye, but at his desyer and request. And further saithe, that byfor that tyme, by the space of a yere at the leaste, the said William Lorde Eurye was maryed to an other woman,[1] so that she had the lesse occasion to cast hir favor unto hym.

Super quarto articulo examinatus, dicit, quod articulus continet in se veritatem, so longe as he contynuithe in Eyton, in Pikeringe Lyth, wher he now remaynethe.

Petrus Hothorne, serviens domini Georgii Darcye, Domini Darcye de Aston, ætatis circiter xxviij annorum.—He saithe, that he was presente in the said parishe churche of Eynsham, and see when the solemnizacion of matrymonye was had betwen the parties articulate, and did also here and see all other ryts and ceremonies doon and ministred at that tyme, as is commonlye used and doon in all mariages, savinge that the said Marye Darcye, alias Eurye, spake the wordes of matrymonye as hir nurse, who had hir then in hir armes, taught hir.—

Dicit, that the said Marye was, at the said solempnizacion, not above foure yeres of age; for she was not able well to go nor speke, but as she was caryed and taught by hir nurse, who caryed hir in hir armes to the churche, and there taught hir what she shuld saye, as he haithe byfore

[1] "See my note on p. 5," writes Mr. Earwaker. "If this second marriage had taken place or not, it was invalid until the divorce had been pronounced. Else why trouble to get a divorce?" Why, to stop questions arising thereafter. I do not admit that the validity of the 2nd marriage depended on the Divorce from the first, because the 1st was only a void marriage, turnable into a valid one by the doing of certain acts. If these acts were never done,—if there was no dwelling together, token-giving, kissing, or copulation,—the void first marriage remaind void, and didn't and couldn't stand in the way of a valid 2nd marriage, as a prior Trothplight between older folk would have done. But tho the first marriage was void, it was of course sensible of persons of position and property, to prevent any future question arising, and to have this void wedding declared null by the Bishop's Court. I think Mr. Earwaker plainly wrong on this point. But he won't give in. He writes: "I differ from you on this point entirely. These 'child marriages' were absolutely binding marriages, and no further ceremony was required to make the parties 'man and wife' for their lives. They had simply to come together when they reached their 'years of discretion.' But if they wished to contract another marriage, or to be free from one another, they were *obliged* to get a separation or divorce from the Spiritual Court, and so annul the first and binding marriage. Many of the people in the cases you print were poor, and held no 'position' or rank whatever."

deposed. And he saithe, that he hathe herd Mr William Hotham esquier,—who was the doer in all things for the makinge of the said marriage,—and others at that tyme that the said mariage was solempnized, saye, that the said William Lord Eurye was then aboute ten yeres of age.—

Dicit, that he haithe dwelt in house with the said Lord Darcye, father to the said Marye, ever sence the said Marye Darcye cam to thage of xij yeres, and long byfore, where she, the said Marye, haithe ben contynuallye ever-sence his comminge. And he saithe, that the said Lord Eurye was neuer with her at any tyme, save twyse, sence she came to xij yeres of age; and at the one tyme she wold not speke with hym nor see hym; and at thoder tyme, when they met togither, the said Lord Eurye wold have kissed hir, and she refused so to do, and went frome hym. Further he saithe, that he could never see nor perceyve any token of favor that she bare towardes the said Lord Eurye, sence she came to xij yeres of age, but haithe herd her at dyvers tymes say that she wold never have hym.—

Ricardus Allerton, de Swyne in Holdernes, ætatis circiter lx annorum.—He saithe that he was presente in the parishe church of Eynsham, articulate, about xij or xiij yeres ago, and see [the] said Marye Darcye, alias Eurye, and the said William Lord Eurye solempnyse matrymonye togither; and did then and there see all other rytes and ceremonyes doon and used as is commonlye doon at all mariages; savinge that the said Marye Darcye was so yonge that she could not speke the wordes of matrymonye, but as hir nursse, who had hir in hir armes, taught hyr.—He saithe he haithe knowen the said Marye Darcye ever sence she was born; and he is well assured that she was not past foure yeres of age at the said mariage. As for the said Lord Eurye, he saithe that he haith herd Sir Raff Eurye his father, and one Davyson his servaunte, saye, that the said Lord Darcye was, at the said solempnizacion, but x yeres olde, or a xj at the most.—

He saithe he could never perceve, or here tell of, any favor that the said Marye Darcye shuld bere towardes the said William Lord Eurye, sence she came to xij yeres of age.—He lyvethe at Eyton, in Pickeringe Lyth, whiche is notoriouslye knowen to be of the dioces and jurisdiction of York.

[*Letter of George Lord Darcye, with his and his Daughter's consent to the Divorce, and authorizing a Proctor to act for her.*]

Tenor vero literarum domini Georgii Darcye, Domini Darcye, judicialiter, ut præfertur, exhibitarum, sequitur in hæc verba:—

To my very lovinge frende, M*aste*r John Shillito, at Yorke, deliver this. After hertie commendacions. Where, by the opynyon of counsell learned, is thought requisite that a divorce be sewed between the Lord Euers and Marye Darcye, one of my doughters, for the more clere extinguishmente of a mariage solempnized betwixt them in their infancies, thes shalbe therfor to signifie you, that bothe I and my said doughter ar contented and wollinge that the said divorcement be had and doon, with convenyente spede; and doo require you to be proctour for my said doughter in that byhalf.

Ye have here, enclosed, an answer to certayn instructions. And what instrumente or proxye you shall devise for your further procedinge in the premisses, I and my said doughter shall signe and seale, and shall ratefie, approve, and confirme your lawfull doings therein accordinglie; and the ordinarye charges herof, and also your paynes, shalbe thanckfullye considered, by Gods grace, who kepe you! Frome Aston, this xxvijth of August, Anno 1554.

Your lovinge frende, G. Darcye,
Marye Darcye.

[Sentence of Divorce pronounced 3 Nov. 1554, by Dr. John Dakyn, Canon Residentiary of York, in the absence of the Dean, on behalf of the Dean and Chapter of York, the Guardians of the Spiritual Jurisdiction, the See of York being vacant.]

Canon Raine tells me there are more Depositions about Child-Marriages, &c., in the Diocesan Registry at York, and he hopes that the Surtees Society will soon issue a volume or two of them.

A.D. 1289. *Boy and Girl married at* 8, *are Father and Mother before they are* 14.

iii. In his *Lives of the Berkeleys*,[1] 1618 (ed. 1883), i. 224-5, John Smith, of Nibley, says of Maurice, the third Lord :—

"Then was this lord Maurice born in the year 1281, being the ninth of King Edward the first, and near the month of Aprill wherein his grandfather the lord Maurice dyed; And was, by his father the last lord Thomas, marryed at *eight yeares old*, in the 17th. of that King, to Eve, daughter of Ewdo lord Zouch and of the Lady Millicent de monte alto his wife; and was by her made *father of Thomas, his eldest son, before hee was fourteen years old himself: Neither was his wife above that age*" . . . . .

The worthy Smith then cites parallel instances from the Bible stories :—

Boy (*King Josiah*) 13.

"2 Kings. 23. 26. Sutable is that of King Josiah, whom ye holy scripture doth assure us to be but thirty nine years old when hee dyed: That at eight years old he began to reigne, and raigned one and thirty years. And sith, (as the text sayth,) his son Eliakim was twenty five years old when he began to raigne after his fathers death, *Then could not Josiah exceed fourteen yeares when his sonne was born.*

Boy (*King Ahaz*) 11.

"2 Kings: 16: 2. chap. 18. 2. In like sort we are assured by the same holy Authority, That King Ahaz lived but thirty six yeares in the whole; That hee was twenty years old when hee began to raigne, and raigned

[1] Mr. Graham Wallas kindly referd me to the book.

Sixteen years, And that his son Ezechias was 25 years old at his fathers death: Then it must needs follow that *Ahaz was marryed and begat Ezechias at Eleven years old or before.*

King Solomon 11.

"1 Kings. 11: 42; et ch: 14 vers. 21. In like sort it is generally taken by Jewe and Christian, (and but fewe think otherwise,) That Solomon came to his crowne at twelve years old; and the Text saith hee raigned but fourty, and soe dyed at fifty two: And when Rehoboam his son, who imediately succeeded his Father, began to raigne, hee was one and fourty years old; *then could Salomon bee but Eleven years old at most, when he begat Rehoboam.*

"I approve not of this match of this lord Maurice, by the examples of the former matches, with any desire that the nuptiall bed should soe soone be known; but by instanceing those of authenticall verity, to lett in esier beleafe to what I find of this lord: With whom my small reading could paralel more then a dozen other parents which have been fathers and mothers at fowerteen years: And the Fathers of the Church do tell us that the blessed Virgin Mary brought forth our Saviour at fifteen years old, or under."

Smith also gives two other instances of Child-Marriage in the Berkeley family:

1338: *boy and girl* 8.

In the 'Life of Maurice the Fourth, Lord Berkeley,' Smith says, i. 364:—

"In the 12th year of that king [Edw. III. 1338-9], and *the 8th of his age* . . . . hee was marryed to Elizabeth, daughter of Hugh lord Spenser, *then about eight years old* . . . . But, though thus maryed at eight, yet had hee no issue by her till about .12. or .13. years after."

1366: *boy* 14½, *girl* 7.

Thomas the Fourth, Lord Berkeley, was married [A.D. 1366], at about fourteen and a half, to Margaret, daughter of Gerrard Warren, Lord de Lisle, at about seven (Smith: *Lives*, ii. 2, 3).

Maurice the Sixth, "Anno 1484, then in the 17th year of his age, hee was, by his fathers means, marryd to a gentlewoman of his own age" (*Lives*, ii. 641).

St. Jerome tells of a boy-father at 10-11.

iv. On this point, Judge Swinburne writes, *Spousals*, p. 52-4:—

"An ancient Father of the Church, of no less Learning than Credit, Jerome by name, writeth thus . . . . 'The Lord is my Witness, I do not lye, a certain Woman, when she had nourished an abject Child (*expositum infantem*), and fed him with Meat, and performed the duty of a Nurse, with whom also the Child did lye till he was Ten years old; it fell out that (more than modesty will suffer) the Woman gorged her self with sweet Wine, and being inflamed with Lust, provoked the Child by her unchast Motions to commit the Act: the first Drunkenness being iterated the second Night, caused a Custom of the other Nights following. But ere two Months were past, behold her Belly began to swell. What will ye have more? by the Providence of God it came to pass, that she that did abuse the simplicity of the Infant, to the Contempt of God, was discovered by the Lord of Nature.'"

St. Gregory of a boy-father at 9-10. *Boece, of a Girl ravisht at* 8.

Gregory likewise, in a certain Dialogue, doth witness of a Boy in his time, which being of the Age of Nine years, begot his Nurse with Child, whose Testimony is without exception received for true. Albericus maketh mention of a young Damosel in his time, who being of the Age of Nine years, brought forth a Child. Hostiensis reporteth, That in the Castle of S. Michael, within the Diocess where he dwelt, a Boy of Ten or Eleven years begot a Child. Henry Boich our Countryman, and of all Canonists the most methodical, telleth us of a Child, which was defloured in his time when she was but Eight years of Age.

Girl a Mother at 9.

Boy a father at 11.

How many years old was Solomon when he begot Rehoboam of the Daughter of Pharaoh? or Ahab when he begot Ezechiah of Abiah, the Daughter of Zechariah? By the testimony of sundry, both Divines, Canonists and Civilians, the Fathers were not past Ten or Eleven when they begot these children. The Histories are rich and plentifully furnished with such Examples.—*Spousals*, p. 52-4.

About 10-11.

1606. v. *Child-Marriage under* 14: *Husband incompetent.*

In Sir Simonds D'Ewes's *Autobiography*, i. 87-9 (1845), he says: "in the year 1606, when the Earl of Essex was scarce fourteen years old, he [the Earl of Suffolk] caused the espousals to be solemnized between him and the Lady Frances, his second daughter, about thirteen years old, and then a most sweet and delicate lady. It seems the Earl of Essex made choice of her, for else her younger sister named Katherine, after married to William Earl of Salisbury, had been much the fitter spouse for him. Certainly this first bred the coals of discontent between them, that the Earl of Essex was unfit to pay the rites of marriage for many years after she was ready to receive them. They lived about four years after they were man and wife, separated from the very converse of each other; by which, doubtless a great estrangement and alienation of affections was wrought between them. Afterwards, in the year 1610, when they were first suffered to be together, the Earl was a mere boy, and little past eighteen, and so unable to consummate his forepast matrimony. This was a real and true affliction to the lady; for remedying whereof, had she first sought that divorce which was afterwards [in 1613] procured, and not satisfied her inordinate lust by that unlawful means, she had never been plunged into that deluge of sin with which she was afterwards overwhelmed. For, as the Earl's deficiency caused her distaste of him, so her known and common advowtries with Viscount Rochester caused him at last to abhor her. And therefore, she, fearing that her lord would seek some public or private revenge against her . . . consulted and practised with Doctor Forman and Doctor Savory, two conjurers, about the poisoning of him. Her letters to the said Forman were very passionate, that her lord did yet thrive, and would survive, she feared, all her good fortunes, and that therefore she desired the hastening of his end . . . . this made the Commissioners, in the year 1613, hasten the divorce between the said Earl and the Lady Frances . . . . he did freely confess that he could never know his said wife."

She procured the poisoning of Sir Thomas Overbury for threatening to make known her adultery with Rochester, who was afterwards made Earl of Somerset, and whom she married in 1614. They were both condemnd to death for Overbury's murder, but, by the influence of her father, the Earl of Suffolk, with Queen Anne and Villiers, were pardond. Their daughter, Anne, was born before their trials, on 24 May, 1616.

1626. *Child-Marriage of a Girl* 13½-14 : *Husband* 23-4.

On 24 Oct. 1626, Anne Clopton, nearly 14, married Sir Simonds D'Ewes, who was nearly 24 : he was born 18 Dec. 1602. D'Ewes gives a long and interesting account (*Autobiography*,[1] i. 306-326, ed. 1845) of the negotiations for his marriage and its fulfilment, from which I take two extracts, 1. on his gift of a 'token' after the engagement; 2. on his forbearance to his child-bride :—

1. "August the 31st [1626]. I sent my servant over to Clare [Priory, where the girl's uncle lived] with a diamond carcanet, to be presented to Mistress Clopton, and a letter with it; which, being the only lines I sent her during my wooing-time, and but short, I have thought good to insert in this place:

'Fairest,

(A.D. 1626) Blest is the heart and hand that sincerely sends these meaner lines, if another heart and eye graciously deign to pity the wound of the first, and the numbness of the latter: and thus may this other poor inclosed carcanet, if not adorn the purer neck, yet lie hidden in the private cabinet of her whose humble sweetness and sweet humility deserves the justest honour, the greatest thankfulness. Nature made stones, but opinion jewels; this, without your milder acceptance and opinion, will prove neither stone nor jewel. Do but enhappy him that sent it, in the ordinary use of it, who though unworthy in himself, resolves to continue your humblest servant,

Simonds D'Ewes.'

2. (p. 328) "The day following [on Sept. 20] I had some serious discourse with the old lady touching the speedy consummation of my future marriage . . . . (p. 319) The only objection arose from her grand-

[1] The Bishop of Bath and Wells, Lord Arthur Hervey, was good enough to refer me to this case and book. Mr. Earwaker tells me he knew of this Dewes case, and that it is one of the most curious instances extant.

child's tender years, which persuaded her to make some long pause before she yielded to the consummation of her marriage: for she did not only doubt what danger might ensue to her very life, from her extreme youth, but she was also in some fear that the very interest I had already gained in her grandchild's good will and affections, was no solid or real love grounded on judgment, and might therefore alter and lessen again after marriage—she being at this time but little above thirteen years and a half old. To these objections I answered fully to her own abundant satisfaction; that I only desired to have the marriage consummated, and would forbear to reap the fruits of it till all danger in that kind should be passed; which, through God's blessing, I afterwards performed, (p. 320) although there were no separation between us, it being perhaps the first example that ever was of that kind; and so impossible it seemed, as others could scarcely be brought to believe it. And for the second objection, I told her I did not doubt but easily to mediate and prevent it; for the same means I had used to gain her affection before I married her, should be continued afterwards to maintain and increase it."

They were accordingly married on Oct. 24, 1626, in Blackfriars Church.

1673. *Child-Marriage: Boy not* 8; *Girl about* 13.

vi. Lord Anglesey's Grandson in 1673. From the Report of the Historical Manuscripts Commission, 1893. Extract from the Diary of the Earl of Anglesey.

1673, May 20. "This morning about ten of the clock at Lambeth, the Archbishop of Canterbury married my grandson John Power, not eight years old, to Mrs. Catherine Fitzgerald, his cousin german, about thirteen years of age. I gave her in the chapel there, and they answered as well as those of greater age. The wedding dinner and supper I gave them, and the rest of the day, and till 12 at night, was spent in dancing &c., and they lay in my house. I did duties, and commended them to God's blessing." (Sent me by Mr. Walter Rye: printed 2 or 3 weeks after, by Mr. W. E. A. Axon, in the *Academy*, Nov. 1893.)

vii. In I. *Notes and Queries*, vii. 526, col. 1, 28 May 1853, is the case of a Child-mother under *eleven years and a half* old. She was the wife of a Brazilian traveller, who applied for leave to pay the reduced passage money for her by the S.S. Severn, as being 'under twelve years of age.' But as the rule said "*children* under twelve," the request was refused.

In Scotland, early marriages were so frequent that—says Calderwood, *Hist.* vi. 24—an Act of Assembly was past in 1600, "to correct divers and great inconveniences arissing by the untimeous marriage of young and tender persons." It orderd "that no minister presume to join in matrimony any persons in time coming, except the man be *fourteen* years of age, and the woman *twelve*, complete."—III. *Notes and Queries*, vi. 129.

In Chambers's *Domestic Annals of Scotland*, vol. ii, "the following instances occur: A.D. 1659, Feb. 9, the Countess of Buccleugh, a child of *eleven* years of age, was married to Walter Scott, a youth of *fourteen;* A.D. 1685, Jonet Pringle, an heiress of about twenty years of age, was carried over the Border, and married to her cousin Andrew Pringle, a boy of *thirteen*, p. 481. See also pp. 319, 390."—*ibid.* See a notice on this subject in *The Derby Household Books*, edited by the Rev. F. R. Raines for the Chetham Society, pp. 210, 211.

"In Nicholas's *Leicestershire*, vol. iv, part ii, p. 156, under the head of 'Dunton Basset,' is a pedigree of the family of Hewett of that place, in which occurs the following marriage of an infant at 3 years old:—

'Mary, born 1666; married Oct. 28, 1669, facultate concessa; dec. 1743, æt 77' . . . . .

In Burn's *Eccl. Law* it is stated that 'Both by the civil and canon law, infants under seven years of age cannot contract any kind of spousals.' In whose power, then, did it lie to grant any faculty?—IV. *Notes and Queries*, v. 489.

In some Chancery proceedings in Ireland in 1676, cited in IV. *Notes and Queries*, vii. 105, the Earl of Tyrone, uncle of the bride, admitted that she was married in the previous March to Edward Villiers,

"*de facto, sed non de jure*, for on the 9th of May, 1670, the plaintiff Catherine was lawfully married, by Gilbert, Archbishop of Canterbury, to John Power, then Esquire, and now Viscount Decies, the eldest son and heir-apparent of this defendant: she being then about *twelve* years old, and John Power being about *seven* or *about eight years old.* That she cohabited with John Power, and subscribed her name and took her place as Viscountess Decies, until she stole away clandestinely out of the house of the Earl of Anglesey, grandfather of Viscount Decies."

In VI. *Notes and Queries*, vi. 347, is an instance of a squire's son of 14, marrying a daughter of Sir Richard Lowther of 16. Vol. vii, p. 91-2, gives the following cases: At *six*, Elizabeth, daughter of Thomas Lord Clifford of Skipton Castle, marries Sir Robert Plumpton of Plumpton Castle, who is not much older. He dies three years later, and his child-widow, at *twelve*, marries his brother William: this in the 15th century. In Hen. VIII.'s time, Margaret, daughter of Richard Smith, Esq., heiress of Shirford (near Nuneaton in Warwickshire), was married to William, third son of Sir John Lyttlelton: the children were both *nine* years old. ("Generally the custom followed with these marriages was, that, after the ceremony, the bride lived with her parents for some years, and the bridegroom continued his education, or was sent abroad with a tutor.")

"On June 8, 1721, Charles Powel, of Carmarthen, Esq., of about *eleven* Years of Age, marry'd to a Daughter of Sir Thomas Powel, of Broadway, Bart., deceasd, aged about 14."

VI. *Notes and Queries*, viii, adds these instances: Bridget Clarke, 25 years old in 1883, the mother of 7 children, and was married at *thirteen* (p. 94). At Deeping St. James's, Lincolnshire, a bride of *fourteen* married a bridegroom of 21. ('It was somewhat of a novelty to observe the interesting bride the following day exhibiting her skill on the skipping-rope on the pavement in the street,' p. 176.) In 1729, a girl of *nine* years and three months was taken from a boarding-school by one of her guardians, and married to his son, 'who had no estate, and was an apprentice to a peruke-maker.' Goodall *v.* Harris in 2 *Peers Williams's Reports*, pp. 560-1.—*ib.* In 1719, Lady Sarah Cadogan, daughter of William, first Earl Cadogan, was married at the age of *thirteen*, to Charles, second Duke of Richmond, aged 18. On Aug. 1, 1672, John Evelyn 'was at the marriage of Lord Arlington's only daughter (a sweet child, if ever there was any) [aged *five*] to the Duke of Grafton, the king's natural son by the Duchess of Cleveland.' And on Oct. 6, 1679, Evelyn was also present at the remarriage of the child-couple, the girl then being *twelve*. In Sir Wm. Cope's book on Bramshill (p. 9), Elizabeth Rogers is shown to have married, at *eleven* (A.D. 1487), a boy Wm. Essex of *ten* (p. 413). In VI. *Notes and Queries*, ix. 236, Mr. Longstaff says he has searcht thro the tables of the Annual Reports of the Registrar-General for the 31 years, 1851-81, and finds that out of 11,058,376 persons married, 154 boys married before *seventeen*, and 862 girls before *sixteen*. Of these, 11 boys of *fifteen* married girls of *fifteen* (four cases), 16, 18 (2 cases), 20 and 21. Three girls of *fourteen* married men of 18, 21, and 25. Five girls of *fifteen* married boys of 16; in 29 marriages, both girl and boy were *sixteen*. In the *Westminster Gazette* some months ago was a statement that four families were in one house, in London, of which the husbands and wives were all under *sixteen*.

The Academy of 3 Feb. 1894 (p. 104, col. 2) contains the following, by the Editor, Mr. Jas. Sutherland Cotton:

A comparatively late example of child marriage in England may be found in Number 1 of *Dorset Records* for January, just published by Mr. Charles J. Clark, of Lincoln's Inn Fields.

Among the abstracts of Inquisitiones post Mortem, *temp.* Charles I., there printed, is one relating to Sir Robert Seymor, of Hampford, *alias* Hanford. The jurors duly find that the said Sir Robert died on July 7, 22 James I. [*i. e.*, 1624], leaving as his son and heir Henry, then aged 14 years, 4 months, and 20 days. And they further find that the said Henry was married to Mary Welstead, on July 22, 1623, at which time he would have been only 13 years and 5 months old.

No doubt in this case, as in others, the object of the early marriage was to evade the liability for feudal dues; for Sir Robert held his manor of Hampford of the king in chief.

viii. Lastly, Philip Stubbes,—in his *Anatomie of Abuses in Ailgna* [Anglia, England], 1593, p. 97 of my edition for the New Shakspere Society, 1877-9,—says on early Marriages:—

Maring of infants in swadling clothes.

"in *Ailgna* there is one great libertye permitted therin; for *little infants in swadling clowts*, are often maried by their ambicious Parents and frends, when they know neither good nor euill; and this is the origene of much wickednesse, & directlie against the word of God, and examples of the primityue age. And besydes this, you shall haue euery sawcy boy of x, xiiij, xvi, or xx yeres of age, to catch vp a woman & marie her, without any feare of God at all, or respect had, either to her religion, wisdom, integritie of lyfe, or any other vertue; or, which is more, without any respecte how they may lyue together with sufficient maintenance for their callings and estat. No, no; it maketh no matter for these things: so he haue *his pretie pussie to huggle* withall, it forceth not, for that is the only thing he desireth. Then build they vp a cotage, though but of elder poals, in euery lane end, almost, wher they lyue as beggers al their life," &c. &c.

Euery Boy snatcheth up a Woman to wyfe.

Cottages in euery Lane end.

The rest of the passage, and the whole book, should be read by every student of Elizabethan England. Against the nuisance of such Cottages as Stubbes speaks of, the Act 31 Eliz., c. 7, was past in 1589, ordering no Cottage to be built by any one 'for habitacion or dwellinge, unlesse the same person doe assigne and laye to the same Cottage or buyldinge, fower acres of Grownde at the least.'—*Stubbes Notes*, p. 281.

Mr. Eccles has cald my attention to the "Papers relating to Infant Marriage and Enforced Widowhood in India.[1] Calcutta, 1886." On p. 4, Mr. Malabari says:—

[1] "From the Five Rivers" (1 vol., Heinemann), also from the pen of Mrs. Steel, is a collection of short stories, treating of the superstitions that hold the Indian mind in thrall, and make the position of the Hindoo woman so pitiful. The author has evidently studied closely the conditions of lives darkened by unnatural creeds. In "Gunesh Chund" she makes us understand the longing of the native for a man child, and the desperate plight in which the wife finds herself, the sorrow of whose travail is not turned to joy by the birth of a son. In "A Girl's School" the tragedy of children's marriages is poignantly brought home. Fatma, the child-mistress of the infant class, motherly of heart, old of face, sweet, strong, grotesque, is saved just in time by death from marriage, the thought of which she loathes. The story enacted in the school held in the various stages of a disused palace is quaint and deeply pathetic. A glimpse of the terror of the fate attending the child-widow is given in *A Citron Garden*, the setting of which is a brilliant example of the author's descriptive powers. Every story in the volume is worth reading; those that treat of the position of women in native social life are especially valuable and interesting.—*Daily News*, Dec. 1893.

"The most obnoxious amongst early marriages (which are often unequal in point of age) are—(1) the marriage of an infant girl with an old man,—the object generally being for the bride's father or relatives to secure money from the bridegroom. This is much the same as selling the child, selling her into slavery, and worse . . . . 2. Another objectionable form of marriage, so-called, is a girl of 12 to 15 married to a boy of 8 or 10. When we know that the marriage is brought about by the father or the elder brother of the boy, who (the father or elder brother) is a widower, we may guess the object. It is a criminal arrangement, leading to sin all round, and to much suffering for the unfortunate girl, who must in name remain the wife of the boy. When the boy-husband realises his position, he may murder the wife, the father, or the brother. In proof positive, the reader may search the records of a Magistrate's Court here and there: of presumptive evidence there is no lack."

On p. 56, Mr. T. R. Venkatesh says:—

"9. As regards girls, the proper age prescribed [by ancient Hindus] for the marriage of Brahman, Tshetria and Vysia classes is between 6 to 8, but never under 6 years of age . . . . 10. If a girl were to attain her puberty, *i. e.* commence her monthly sickness [generally after 10], before being married, her parent and brothers go to Hell, as it was their duty to have got her married before that period."

Mr. Eccles also refers me to the 'Spirit Basis of the Rule in favour of Child-Marriage.' *Bombay Gazetteer*, ed. 18, pt. 1, Appx. A.

§ 4. The Law on the point is stated by Henry Swinburne, Judge of the Prerogative Court of York, in his *Treatise of Spousals or Matrimonial Contracts*, publisht in 1686, sixty-two years after his death in 1624:—

"In the Civil and Ecclesiastical Laws, by Infants (most commonly) are understood those Children which have not as yet accomplished the Age of *Seven* years; and so is the word accepted in this place.—p. 19 . .

"They therefore which are not Seven years old cannot contract Spousals . . . . .

"Spousals contracted during Infancy are utterly *void*, whether the Infants themselves, or their Parents for them, do make the Contract, p. 20, ... as Infants cannot contract Spousals, so they cannot Matrimony, because they which cannot do the lesser, cannot do the greater."

But this statement is subject to certain Limitations.

"14. The Limitations are these: First, when the Infants, after they have accomplished their several Ages of Seven years, do either by express word ratifie and confirm the Contract made during their Infancy, or by other words of like importance, as by calling and naming each other Husband and Wife; for by the reason of this *new consent*, the Contract (otherwise void) is become of no less force than if they had now made a new Contract.

"15. The second Limitation is, when as by Deeds only they do approve and confirm the Contract made during their Infancies, as if they laye together, imbrace, or kiss[1] each other, or give and receive Gifts and Tokens, either of them, to or from the other, after both their Ages of Seven years[2]; for by *Deeds* the former Spousals are confirmed, as well as by *Words*.—p. 21.

"16. The third Limitation (like unto the second) is, when the Infants, after the accomplishment of their said several Ages, do mutually cohabit or dwell together, and are not ignorant of the Contract made betwixt them, during their Infancy; for otherwise they do not ratifie that which they know not.—p. 21-2.

"17. The fourth Limitation is, when two contract Spousals, of whom the one is more than Seven years old, the other near Seven years, suppose six and a half; if these Persons ever, during the Infancy of the younger Party, do either lye together, or cohabit together, by occasion whereof it remaineth doubtful whether they have essayed to know each other; in this Case the Contract hath like effect as if the Parties had both accomplished the Age of Seven years.

"18. The fifth Limitation is, when the Infants which do contract Spousals are of that *Wit* and *Discretion*, that albeit they have not as yet accomplished the full Age of Seven years, yet doth their supraordinary

[1] Another part of the ceremony of Espousals was a kiss: thus, in the "Twelfth Night":

'A contract of eternal Bond of Love,
Attested by the *Holy close of Lips.*'

In this part of the ceremony [if performd in church, or by a priest] the Priest very probably joined: it is quite certain that he did so on the solemnization of *matrimony*, since, in the articles of Visitation in the Diocese of London in 1554, is the following: "Item, whether there be any that refuseth to *kysse the Prieste* at the solempnisation of matrimony, or use any such lyke ceremonies heretofore used & observed in the Churche."—J. S. Burn, 'Sponsalia' in *Coll. Top. and Genealog.* iii. 325 (1836).

[2] The Laws of our Realm say, That the Wife which is of the Age of *Nine* years at her Husbands death, shall be endowed of the third part of his Lands and Tenements, which be held either in Fee-simple or Fee-tail, and which he had either by Purchase or Discent.—Hy. Swinburne. *Spousals*, p. 51, citing Fitzherbert's *Natura Brevium* fol. 149, and Littleton, on Dower, at the beginning.

Swinburne, speaking of a girl of seven being married, adds, "say that the Infant was known Carnally (which thing is no less incredible to be spoken, than horrible to be heard), yet the Infant not having discretion to understand what is the Nature of Matrimony, cannot give her Consent to that whereof she is ignorant, and consequently the Marriage cannot be good: For it is a clear Case, That without Consent there cannot be any Matrimony."—*Spousals*, p. 51.

Michael Dalton—giving his authorities—says, in his *Countrey Justice* (1618), p. 248:

"The taking away of a maide vnder sixteene yeares of age, without the consent of her parents or gouernors, or contracting marriage with her, or deflowring her, is no felony, but yet shall be punished with long imprisonment without baile, or with grievous fine.—4 & 5 Ph. & Mary, Par. Women 7, 8. See Co. 3. 37, &c."

"But vnlawfully and carnally to know and abuse any woman child vnder the age of ten yeares, is felony, although such child consents before.—*Cromp.* 47; 18 Eliz. 6; Par. Fel. 14."

There is a curious doctrine on this page, which I apprehend that modern physiology does not sanction:—

"If the woman at the time of the supposed rape, doe conceiue with child by the rauishor, this is no rape, for a woman cannot conceiue with child, except she do consent.—Britton 45; Stamf. 24."

Understanding fully supply that small defect of Age, which thing is not rare in these days, wherein Children become sooner ripe,[1] and do conceive more quickly than in former Ages."—p. 22.

The void Spousals of Infants could thus be made valid ones by the little ones lying or dwelling together, calling one another 'husband & wife,' or "by Conjectures only, as by Kissings, Embracings, Gifts, &c." (p. 31) after they were seven years old.

At seven, Infants became Children, and so continued, till Girls were twelve, and Boys fourteen; at which times they were respectively 'of ripe age'[2] and marriageable, tho' ability to bear or beget children earlier, pre-dated the period 'of ripe age.' Of Childhood, says Judge Swinburne, p. 25: "During this Age, Children cannot contract Matrimony or Spousals *de præsenti*, but only *de futuro*." But their Spousals could be easily turnd into actual Marriages, by fit words or deeds after girls were 12, and boys 14. Says Swinburne, p. 27:

"By what means, Spousals contracted during *Infancy*, and therefore void at the beginning, are notwithstanding afterwards made strong and confirmed—namely, by mutual Cohabitation,[3] by Kissings, by Embracings, by giving and receiving of Gifts and Tokens, &c., or by Words expressing the continuance and perseverance of the mutual Consent, as by calling each other Husband and Wife;—By the same means practised, after the Parties be of *ripe Age*, fit for Marriage, are those Spousals by them contracted in their Minority by words of present time (being then Spousals *de futuro* by interpretation of Law only) resolved or turned into Matrimony; from that time enjoying the same Properties and Effects belonging to Spousals *de præsenti*, contracted betwixt Persons of full and perfect Age, unless the Parties, after they be come to perfect Age, do first *dissent*, and so dissolve the Contract before they consent."

[1] Compare Ascham's complaint, in his *Schoolmaster* (1563, prob. 1570), p. 131 (ed. Giles), 'of the little child of four, roundly rapping out his ugly oaths.' Also *Babees Book*, p. 350.

[2] But what may be the Reason wherefore Women are sooner ripe than Men?
I will not Answer with the Gloss, *Quia citò crescit herba mala* [Ill weeds grow apace], for this is but a Jest. Macrobius (he saith) it is *propter votorum festinationem*, for the forwardness of their Desire: Some do yield this Reason, *Quia facilius est pati quam agere*; this is something, but it is not all: Others, because the Female Bodies are more tender and moister than the Male: And so, Mens Bodies being harder and drier, they are more slow in ripening; and Womens Bodies, because they are softer and moister, are more quickly ripe; like as it is to be seen in Plants and fruits, whereof that which is more soft and moist is sooner ripe, than that which is hard and dry. And this I take to be the best Reason, and is agreeable to that which followeth, namely, That even that Fruit which is sooner ripe, doth sooner decay: So Women, as they are sooner able, so they sooner become unable to bring forth, than Men to beget. —Hy. Swinburne, *Spousals*, p. 48-9.

[3] Compare "*A Treatise of the Cohabitation of the Faithful with the Unfaithful*, whereunto is added a Sermon made by the confessing of Christ and His Gospel, and of the denyinge of the same." Black Letter, 8vo (Zurich), 1556.

Either party on attaining ripe age may dissent, tho the other is under it, and must not wait 'a good space after,' or the elder will have to "expect until the younger come to ripe Age, nor is to be licensed to marry elsewhere in the mean time."—p. 31. And, p. 43,

"The dissent is to be made and published before the *Bishop* of the Diocess where the disliking Party dwelleth, or before his *Chancellor*, or in their absence, before the *Parochial Pastor* or *Minister*, and other honest Witnesses. The time of manifesting this dissent, is so soon as he or she shall attain to ripe Age, or years of Consent; for to dissent before that time, is to no purpose; and to prolong the same afterwards, is dangerous. p. 44. (p. 47) "a Man so soon as he hath accomplished the Age of *Fourteen* years,[1] and a Woman so soon as she hath accomplished the Age of *Twelve* years, may Contract true and lawful and individual Matrimony, in case there be no other impediment to hinder the same."

Tho the Ratification of a Child-Spousal was made formerly in the Bishop's Court when property was concernd, and a record of the marriage was needed,—see below, p. 49-52, and Bp. Chaderton's daughter's case cited by Mr. Earwaker, *Manchester Guardian*, 9 March, 1885, p. xxii above,—no such proceeding was necessary. Swinburne says, p. 40,

"That if the Parties, after they be come to lawful years, being then free from former Contracts, do by plain and direct words, without fear or fraud, express their mutual Consents; as if they say [*We do ratifie and confirm the Marriage contracted betwixt us*, &c.] the Marriage (which before was no more but Spousals *de futuro*, in construction of Law) is now made true and undoubted Matrimony. This also is without Controversie, That if the Parties willingly, or of their own accord, know each other *carnally*, the Marriage before contracted in their Minority, is from henceforth of no less force in Law, than if the same were now again contracted by words of the *present time*, during their lawful Ages. By voluntary *Cohabitation* likewise (as I have before declared), and by *Subarration*, or giving and receiving of Rings, (as hereafter shall be shewed) is this former Contract, having but the form of Marriage, indued with the virtue and very nature of true substantial Matrimony" . . . . .

The reader will now see why the Child-Marriage Depositions in the present volume are so full of the children not having dwelt together, kist, given tokens, treated each other as man and wife, or copulated carnally.

Swinburne, who died in 1624, says in his "Treatise of Spousals," 1686, that the custom of spousals was then in great measure gone out of use; and the Marriage Act of 1753 enacted that no suit or proceeding should be had in any Ecclesiastical Court in order to compel a celebration

[1] "If a Husband was then incompetent, the Wife had to wait till he was 18 before she could divorce him on that account."—Swinburne, p. 49. (See Lady Somerset's case above, p. xxix-xxx.)

of any marriage 'in facie Ecclesiæ,' by reason of any contract of matrimony, whether 'per verba de præsenti,' or 'per verba de futuro.'—1836. J. S. Burn, 'Sponsalia,' in *Collectanea Top. et Gen.* iii 320.—But it is still the English law that boys and girls of full age (which, for this purpose, is fixt at the age of puberty as defined in the Roman law, namely 14 for males, and 12 for females) can marry with the consent of parents or guardians, and that marriages under age are cured and made good by later consent. And tho, 'if either party is under age, the dissent of the parents or guardians exprest at the time of publication of banns renders such publication null and void, yet it doesn't affect the marriage if it has been solemnized.' [1]

The person to consent is 1. the father or lawful guardian, 2. the Mother, if unmarried, or 3. the guardian appointed by the Court. If any such person is a lunatic, the Lord Chancellor takes his place.

If by fraud or false oath, a valid marriage is made between 2 persons, one of whom is under age, the offending party forfeits all property that otherwise might accrue to him from the marriage. From the *Encyclopædia Britannica.*

§ 5. To nineteenth-century folk these child-marriages seem unnatural and absurd. And tho' we all agree that most Englishmen are fools,[2] by education in prejudices or by birth—else, why does the House of Lords exist?—yet we must seek for the causes that led our forefathers to pledge their children to one another as they did. Property-arrangements were one cause, as the cases show. Another—and perhaps the chief one—was, I suspect, the desire to evade the feudal law of the Sovereign's guardianship of all infants. When a father died, the Crown had the right to hold the person and estate of the propertied orphan[3] until it came

[1] The absence of the necessary consent is not a disability invalidating a marriage actually solemnized.—*Encycl. Britann.*

[2] Cp. Hamlet; and Lydgate's *Order of Fools*, in his *Minor Poems*, Percy Soc. p. 164, and *Q. Eliz. Achad.* p. 79.

[3] On Wards, Michael Dalton says in his *Office and Authoritie of Sherifs* (1623), p. 40-1:—

"by the Statutes made 32 Hen. VIII, c. 46, & 33 Hen. VIII, c. 22, & 34 Hen. VIII, c. 46, All the Kings Wards are to bee within the order, suruey, and gouernance of the Court of Wards; together with their lands, rents, and issues thereof.

"The King (by his Prerogatiue Royall) shall have the wardship of all *their* lands, which hold of him in chiefe by knight seruice, whereof the tenants were seised in their demesne as of fee, the day of their death, of whomsoeuer they hold, &c.—17 Edw. II, c. 1.

"Also the King, by his perogative of the wardship of the heire, shall have rent-charges, commons, estouers, annuities, aduousons, offices, and the like, which descend, &c, to the heire: 12 Hen. VII; Br. Prerog. 63."

The uncle of the first James, Lord Berkeley (1417—1463),—who had four wives seemingly—"sold his mariage twyes for a thousand markes, and another time for one thousand two hundred markes."—Smyth, ii. 80. He also 'pursed' the portion of

of age, and it could be sold in marriage for the benefit of the Crown or its grantee. If the orphan refused such a marriage with a person of its own rank, it had to pay its guardian a heavy fine for refusing his choice, and selecting a spouse of its own.[1] The founder of the Yorkshire branch of the Furnivalls fought in the Holy Land with Richard Cœur de Lion. When they got home, the King pickt him out a Yorkshire heiress (Maud Lovetot), and handed her over to him. In 1375 the Poet Chaucer was granted the guardianship and marriage of a Kentish squire's heir till 1378, and may have owd his later M.-P.-ship for Kent in 1386 to his ward's estate. A reference to the heading 'Wards and Wardship' in any of the Rolls Series of Calendars is almost sure to show several grants of wards. Take the eight cases in June 1552.

Calendar of State-Papers, Domestic Series, 1547-1580 (publ. 1856), p. 41-2.
June 1552.

No. 47 (all Docquets). (1) Grants to the Duke of Northumberland of the wardship & marriage of Wm Flamock and of Margaret Whorwood.

(2) Grant to Tho. Welden of the wardship and marriage of Tho. Welden, son and heir of Edw. Welden.

(3) Grant to Sir Ric. Lister of the wardship and marriage of Richard Lyster.

(4) Grant to John Payne of the wardship and marriage of Henry Chamber.

(5) Grant to Michael Wentworth of the wardship and marriage of Gervays Storthes.

six hundred marks given with the first wife, the daughter of Sir Humphry Stafford of Dorsetshire.

[1] Chas. Roberts says in his Introduction to his *Excerpta, de Rotulis Finium*, temp. Hen. III, A.D. 1216—1272, vol. 1, p. xv (1835): If on the death of a tenant—the custody of whose heir belonged to the crown—the heir were a minor, the King either retained the profits of the estate till his majority, or else we find the enrolment of a fourth description of instrument, wherby the King sold the wardship, or granted it to enrich some favourite. The value of this wardship depended on the extent of the possessions, and the probable duration of the minority, and, when sold, immense sums were paid for it.[1] For, according to Hargrave (Co. Litt. n. 11), "the guardian was not accountable for the profits made of the infant's land during the wardship, but received them for his own private emolument, subject only to the bare maintenance of the infant. And this guardianship, being deemed more an interest for the profit of the guardian, than a trust for the benefit of the ward, was saleable and transferable, like the ordinary subjects of property, to the best bidder; and, if not disposed of, was transmissible to the lord's personal representatives. Thus the custody of the infant's person, as well as the care of his estate, might devolve on the most perfect stranger to the infant; one prompted by every pecuniary motive to abuse the delicate and important trust of education, without any ties of blood or regard, to counteract the temptations of interest, or any sufficient authority to restrain him from yielding to their influence."

[1] Simon de Montford paid King Henry II, 10,000 marks to have the custody of the lands and heir of Gilbert de Umfraville, with the heir's marriage, a sum equivalent to 100,000*l.* at present. See p. 436.

(6) Grant to William Hellard of the wardship and marriage of John Rokeby.

(7) Grant to Robert Carr of the wardship and marriage of Augustyne Smythe.

(8) Grant to John Holte of the wardship and marriage of Richard Seyman.

A later and an earlier case may be quoted:

p. 43. Aug. 4, 1552. No. 57. Earl of Pembroke to Sir Wm Cecill . . . for Mr. Sharington to have the wardship of Mr. Hall's heir . . . . .

Aug. 14. No. 59. Wm Thomas (Clerk of the Council) to Cecill. The Earl of Pembroke is well contented with the wardship (Hall's heir) procured for Cecill's sister.

Acts of the Privy Council, ii. 542 (1890). 1547. xij February. To my Lord Archebishope of Yorke, wher it was reported God had calid to his mercye the Earle of Comberlande, who had nowe lefte behind him a daughter, beinge the Kinges Majestes warde, his Lordshipe was required to take order (upon receipte herof) for the sendinge of her up hether, so as by the conducte of some discreate gentlman of that houshold, two sober gentlweomen and xij servantes of that famelie, shee might come up hether by convenyente and easie jurneyes; and yf ther shoulde not be money allotted by the offyceres of her late father for that purpose, if his Lordshipp disbursed it, he should be repaide it, with thankes. (If the Earl wasn't dead, the Archbp. was to wait, 'to stay therin till he should be soe.')

Now, tho Elizabeth took better care of her well-propertied wards than any sovereign before her[1]—see my *Queene Elizabethes Achademy* in the Early English Text Society—yet in ordinary country cases, the orphans must have been liable to be exploited, and made money out of by any one with influence enough at Court to get a grant of them. A father would naturally desire to stop this; and I suppose—thro a weakening of the early Royal Prerogative—that if he had child-married his offspring, and, when illness threatend him, procured the turning of the void or voidable union into valid matrimony, he would save his child, if not its estate, from a strange guardian's sweating, and the practical sale of the boy or girl to the best bidder of its own rank, the guardian pocketing the purchase-money.[2] That parents of older boys, of 17 or 18, tried to

[1] I assume this, from Sir N. Bacon's and Sir Humphrey Gilbert's proposals for their education, and from the enforcement of the actions for waste against grantees of wards, of which instances occur in the Calendars of State Papers.

[2] Knighthood had the same effect, according to John Smyth, 1618. He says of Maurice the Fourth, Lord Berkeley (*Lives* i, 364, see above, p. xxviii):

"In the eleaventh yeare of the said king [Edw. III], about the seaventh of his age, what tyme his mother dyed, his father placed him at Portbury under the tuition of Will*iam* de Syde, parson of Awre and his fathers Receivour . . . And yet his father the same year took him alonge with himselfe in that martiall voyage which hee made into Scotland; perhaps to mollify the griefe of his wifes death: In which Journey this Maurice was knighted, then about seaven years old."

A younge knight, to prevent wardship.

marry them when young[1]—no doubt to stop them running on the loose—we know from Shakspere's handsome friend, William Herbert, to whom (I doubt not) the Poet wrote his Sonnets. The boy's mother was Sir Philip Sidney's sister, and she and her husband, the Earl of Pembroke, tried to marry the young fellow, when 17, to Cecil's grand-daughter. But the plan fell thro: the gay youngster came to London in 1598, evidently pickt up Shakspere at the Globe or Blackfriars theatre, and took away his 'dark lady.' If she was Mary Fitton—Sir Edward F.'s daughter,—she drest like a man, went across to the young fellow's rooms, bore a child by him; and then he was popt into the Fleet prison by Queen Elizabeth for the dire offence of so misconducting himself with one of her Maids of Honour. Whatever the evils of early marriages may be, they tend (at least) to keep young men straight, and stop the parades of women for hire in the Strand, Piccadilly, Regent St., &c.—as well as in other cities than London—at night. Still, no one with an idea of what Marriage ought to be, can wish now for a return of the Child-Marriages of those "good old times" which men, who don't work at Records and evidence, are so fond of praising.[2]

"Significant also, as illustrating the system of child-marriages in India, are the remarks on p. 74 as to the habit of the Burmese to engage their daughters while young, in real or fictitious marriages, in order to save them from the hands of the king's ministers, custom having established a rule, which is rarely if ever violated, that no married woman can be seized, even for the king himself."—Review of *The Burmese Empire a Hundred Years Ago, as described by Father Sangermano,* with an Introduction and Notes by John Jardine, in *The Athenæum*, 13 Jan. 1894, p. 43.

[1] The only early betrothal in Mr. Reynolds's *Old Ways in Olden Days down West* (1892) is at p. 102-3: William Foot 'was only sixteen years of age, and she [Joane Priste] twelve, when they were thus betrothed in 1536.' But Hugh Prieste, who betrothd them, says he thinks 'that Joane was XIII. from the appearance of her body—or rather *habit.*'

[2] As an illustration of the "good old times" for Women in Tudor days, take the Preamble of 39 Elizab. (1597), chap. 9: "Whereas, of late tymes, divers Weomen, as well Maydens as Widowes and Wyves, havinge Substance, some in Good*es* moveable, and some in Land*es* and Tenement*es*, and some being Heires Apparant to their Auncestors,—for the Lucre of such Substance bene oftentymes taken by Misdoers contrary to their Will, and often maried to such Mysdoers, or to other by their Assent, or defiled, to the great Displeasure of God, and contrary to your Highnesses Lawes, and Disparagement of the said Weomen, and great Heavyness and Discomfort of their Friend*es*, and ill Example of others," &c. The offence was Felony under 3 Hen. VII. c. 2: "Yet forasmuch as Clergye hath bene heretofore allowed to such Offendors, divers *per*sons have attempted and comitted the said Offenc*es* in hope of lyfe by the Benefit of Clergye, that Benefit is abolisht, and every Offender shall suffer Paynes of Death without any Benefit of Clergye." (See Notes, p. lxxxvii.)

Compare the case of Girls in China now: "Pastor Gottschalk, of the Berlin Foundling House in Hong Kong, draws a sombre picture of the effects of the custom of polygamy among the Chinese. Among these is the lack of marriageable girls. At present, girls are sold at a very high price; a girl of fourteen to sixteen can scarcely be purchased for less than one hundred dollars—a price which, as Herr Gottschalk quaintly says, 'poor people can ill afford.' Some buy for their infant son an infant wife, who is occasionally nursed at the same breast as her future husband. If this

On this point of the benefit and purpose of early marriages, the reader will like to hear Judge Swinburne:—

And albeit this Age [boys 14, girls 12] may seem over-tender and over-timely to prevent those Inconveniencies so long ago foreseen by Lycurgus, Plato, and the rest, yet considering the Lord and Maker of all Creatures, in the beginning of the World, hath by Divine Providence, for the propagation of his Church, proclaimed an universal Liberty *Crescite & Multiplicamini.*[1] And therefore that this Liberty is to be denied to none, whom otherwise the Almighty hath naturally disposed and enabled to encrease and multiply; considering also, that like as the little Sparks are to be extinguished at the very first, lest afterwards they mount to an unquenchable Flame: So whosoever have any such Sparks of Natural Provocation, whereby their hearts may be kindled, or set on fire by ungodly Lusts, To these persons, albeit very young, the Remedy against Lust is not to be denied, especially seeing it is *better to marry than to burn.* These things (I say) considered, it is a large and clear case, That we may not so foresee the avoidance of Temporal Discommodities, with Lycurgus or any other Philosophers, that we oversee greater Dangers by abridging the general Liberty of Generation, established without distinction of years by our *eternal Lycurgus*, and heavenly Lawmaker, or by denying or deferring to any that are stinged with Carnal Appetite, the blessed and Sovereign Remedy against this Poison, invented by Divine Philosophy.—*Swinburne*, p. 48.

§ 6. The Trothplights take us to later ages than those of the Child-Marriages; and ten of the seventeen cases show us men trying to sneak out of their contracts[2] when they've had their fill of pleasure with the women.

economical device fails, the matter is regarded as serious, as they may have no offspring to perform the sacrifices at their tombs. Young girls (adds Mr. Gottschalk) dare not leave their homes for fear of being kidnapped, as they not unfrequently are. In a place one day's journey from Hong Kong, three or four years ago, twenty young girls were stolen in a night, taken on board a junk, and carried no one knew whither. Unfortunately the Berlin Foundling House derives no benefit from the brisk demand for marriageable girls, partly because the institution limits its choice of suitors to Chinese Christians, and partly because there is in China a superstitious belief that an evil fate hangs over a Foundling girl."—*Daily News*, 16 Jan., 1894, p. 5, col. 4.

[1] The Harl. MS. 980, lf. 74, says that "A weaver in Scotland had by one woman 62 children, all living till they were baptised, of *which* ther wer but fower daughters onely who lived till they were women, and 46 sonns, all attaining to man's estate." (She regularly bore triplets.) . . . "John Delavall of Northumb*erland*, Esq. . . . ann. 1630, rid about 30 miles beyond Eddenburrough to see this fruitfull couple, who were both then living."

Mr. Ricketts, the father of the present (1837) Lord St. Vincent, was the 23d of 27 children of the same mother. ". . . in the year 1698, Thomas Greenhill, surgeon . . . petitioned the Earl Marshal," stating that he was "the 7th son & 39th child of one father & mother." In the Gentleman's Magazine for Feb. 1743, is recorded the death of Mrs. Agnes Milbourne, who was aged 106, and had 30 children.—*Coll. Top. and Gen.*, iv. 53 *n* (1837).

[2] A case in the Supplement, p. 200, shows us that the woman's friend and landlord, "knowing the inconstancy of the said Thomas Middlehurst, biecause he had been diuerse tymes at intreaties of mariage to be had between them, the said parties, and the said Thomas wold ever shrink from the same," took care to make him regu-

The most picturesque case is the Sothworth run-away match, p. 65-7. The suit is brought by the man against the woman; but whether to cancel or confirm the marriage, I cannot say.[1] One Michaelmas night the man calls for the girl at her father's house; she steals out and goes with him, about midnight, to the house where a sickly old priest lives. They knock at the door, which the householder (who knows them, and tries to dissuade her from the marriage) opens. They all go into the priest's room at the end of the house: he "beinge a very old and a sicklie man," sits up in his bed, upon his pillow, and marries them, saying the "wordes of Matrimony used in the church," and putting a ring on the bride's finger.[2] After the wedding, the house-owner, "being somwhat offendid with the matter, wold not suffer them to be in his house the rest of the night," and so they went to Thomas Ireland's, of the Green; "there had meate and drink"; and so to bed together.

The most sneakish case on the man's part is George Johnson's, p. 57-59. He trothplighted himself, before witnesses, to Anne Yate, a victualler of Chester,[3] one evening near the fireside, a fortnight before Christmas 1566, then drank together, and eat a couple of woodcocks. Then the man used the woman's house as his own,—evidently for a long while,—slept there, and with her, as man and wife, brought his dogs, horse and hawks there, took her money, "by 20s. at once": and then went off and married another woman. But Anne Yate brought suit against him, and would, as a matter of course, get a Decree declaring his pretended marriage void, and her own Trothplight valid,[4] since she wasn't content to be well rid of a rogue. Morgan Edmund was a bad lot too, p. 192-3.

larly trothplight the woman, Ellen Carter: but she had to bring suit against him to make him carry it out.

[1] I have assumed that it was a Trothplight case,—as the courtship was evidently a long one, and the woman was willing,—tho no ceremony except that of the marriage is cited.

[2] Compare other 'Clandestine Marriages' in Section VIII below, p. 140-1. In the Supplement, p. 189, John David says that Henry Dilon and Elizabeth Bird "did steale a marriage without banes askinge."

[3] A hopping or dance on a Sunday about 1570 in a namesake Chester—Chester-le-Street, in Durham—is worth a note:

George Grondye, of Hedley near Lamesley, husbandman, aged 60 years. He saith that, as he remembrith, the Sonday next after Trinitie Sonday last past, which was the day that one John Fletcher of Chester maid a hopping,* this examinate came to Chester Church: at what tyme the said [John] Catchesyd came to this deponent, and thei tow satt in a stall togither ther.—*Durham Depositions*, p. 102. (Surtees Soc. 1845.)

[4] Spousals *de futuro* do become Matrimony by carnal knowledge betwixt the parties betroathed; The Ampliations of which Conclusion are these.

First, albeit either Party betroathed should after-wards marry another Person in the face of the Church, and should also lye with the said new married Person; Yet,

* A 'hopping' is defined by Canon James Raine, the editor, as 'A merry meeting accompanied with dancing.'

Richard Lowe was, at any rate, a better fellow than George Johnson; for, tho he trothplighted Jane Walkden,[1] had a wench by her, and then married an old woman, Helen Stonis,—"he saith he is hartelie sorie that he hath disceyvid them bothe; and will do any thinge for the health of his soulle," p. 56. As soon as the old woman found that her marriage was unlawful, she 'partid from' Lowe, 'and refusethe to take hym as her husband.' Thomas Snelson (p. 59-61), too, shows some signs of conscience; for, tho he tries to shirk his trothplight with a servant, Ellen Ricroft, he still offers her twenty nobles to let him off, and gets her a Citation before the Bishop against himself (p. 59). And when she says "she wold not relese hym for no gold; 'for I am your lawfull wief; and so take me.' 'Well,' quod he, 'sticke to that,[2] and I will never leave thee,'" p. 60. He also tells a witness that he will confess before the Bishop that Ellen is his wife (p. 61). But the further Depositions, p. 196, show that in the previous February or March, Snelson had sneakt

this Marriage solemnized and consummate notwithstanding, the Party so marrying is to be compelled to return to his or her foresaid Spouse, formerly known.—Swinburne, *Spousals*, p. 224. But 'Spousals do not become Matrimony, when as the Parties did lye together before they were contracted, but not after.'—Swinburne, p. 227.

[1] They first had a promise 'secretlie betwene them self, and therapon had carnall dole together. then Jane Walkden desired this respondent [Richard Lowe] to make her a promisse before witnes; and so he did.'—p. 56.

A somewhat like case is given in Mr. Reynolds's *Old Ways in Olden Days down West* (Exeter, 1892), p. 106-7. It occurd at Wotton Phippyn (now Wootton Fitzpaine) in the diocese of Salisbury, and the Depositions were taken in 1540. William Sampson had had four children by Joan Smith. He sent for his neighbour, Richard Barcumbe, to Wm. Sprack's house, and said:

"Goodeman Barcumbe, I have causede you to cum hither, bycause I wolde desyre you to ber wittnes in a cause of matrimonye betwixt this woman, Joane Smyth, and me. and bicause I have myseused here, I intende to make [her] a goode woman; therefore I desyre you to betroght usse."

Mr. Reynolds carelessly gives no date for this; but presumably after it, the same William Sampson, a fortnight before Whitsuntide 1539, betrotht himself to Agnes Beyne, in the presence of witnesses, by the words "I, William, take thee, Agnes, to my wiffe, *before God and man*": 'an expression which we do not often meet with in these narratives.'

As to 'secret promises' or contracts like that between Jane Walkden and Rd. Lowe, above, J. S. Burn in his article on 'Sponsalia' in *Collectanea Topographica et Genealogica*, iii. 325 (1836), says:—The following caution is in "A Werke for Householders" (1537). "It is a great jeopardy to make any such (private and secrete) contractes, specially among themselfe secretely alone, without *recordes*, which must be two at the lest."

One of the interrogatories for the doctrine and manners of mynisters in the reign of Elizabeth, is the following:

"28. Whether they have exhorted yung folke to absteyn from *privy contracts*, & not to marry without the consent of such their parents and fryends as have authority over them, or no."

An ancient Canon forbids private contracting of marriage, and charges the contractors not to use words of the present tense (that they might not be construed into matrimony itself).

[2] I suppose this 1563 use of the phrase to be one of the earliest recorded.

out to Rishton Chapel in Staffordshire, in another diocese, and there married Joan Wily, after Ellen Ricroft had forbidden their banns, perhaps in his own parish. Ellen would of course upset this marriage.

Richard Pickforth's conscience moved him only to take "as his owne, and set it to nurse" (p. 65) the child that he had by the woman he had trothplighted—'not in his house, but in the Towne field of Warburton.'

Morgan Edmund, in a case in the Supplement, p. 187-195, trothplighted and exchanged tokens with Elizabeth Bird. He then left the town, and was reported to her as dead. She, having law-suits, married Henry Dilon—out of several suitors—to carry her causes thro for her. Then Morgan turnd up, and sued or threatend Dilon for marrying Elizabeth: not because he, Morgan, meant to marry her himself—he said she was a priest's whore,[1] and he wouldn't marry her,—but because he wanted to get some of Elizabeth's property out of Dilon. Another rejected suitor, out of spite, applied to the Sheriff of Chester to arrest Elizabeth and Dilon as adulterers; but he got off by declaring, that tho she was in the house with him, she wasn't in his bed.

In another case, the Mayor of Liverpool is a witness to the Trothplight, and performs the ceremony. 'A travailer bie the Seas' (p. 67) says to the Mayor that, "having a voiage beyond the sea, toward Ireland," I "wold have one in the meane season to loke to thinges in myne house; and therefore, I pray you, let her [Eleanor Manwaring] be made my wief; and then I trust you will suffer her to be my housekeper without suspicion." On which, the Mayor "toke the said parties and this deponent with hym on his backside[2]," and there and then trothplighted them. They "kissed together, and callid together man and wief, and dronke a Cuppe of ale together in the Maiores house; and so departid."

The case of Alice Ince (p. 68-9) is interesting, not only for the scenes of her and her lover John 'sittinge together bie the fire in the eveninge tyme ... afore dailight was done,' and then,—because company was in the house,[3] —going out before the street-door, on the green, and there holding a Psalter-book, and trothplighting one another, but also because it shows the

[1] See, on this subject, my *Ballads from MSS.*: the first Introduction to the first Ballad.

[2] and ever, when a mylner came to the towne, [Mrs. Isabell Richardson] folloed hym up and doune, whill she wer droken, and had no delit upon hir husband; and that she left hir left-fott shoe vpon Mr. Andersons *bacsyd* when she clamme over the wall for such intents.—1563. *Durham Depositions*, p. 77. (Surtees Soc. 1845.) she would sett her horse in one of his *backhouses.*—*ib.* p. 83. See the Supplement, p. 187 below, 'in a parlour there, on the *backside.*'

[3] For nearly the same reason, Katherine Strete and Nicolas Jepson go into 'a worke-house, which is an out-house ... an inconvenient place' ...—*Supplement*, p. 185 below.

unfounded common belief that a special form of words was necessary to the trothplight.[1] Alice thinks the words "I take thee, Alice, to be my wief, and non other woman, so God me helpe, and the Contentes of this boke," were not well and sufficient; but when the latter words are changed to "So God me helpe, & holidame,[2] and bie this boke," she is satisfied.

[1] True it is, we are not to stand upon Terms, but upon truth; and any words will suffice to Contract Matrimony, so that the meaning do appear.—Swinburne, *Spousals*, p. 63.

The form of Trothplight given in the *Ripon-Chapter Acts*, 1452—1506 (Surtees Soc. vol. 64, p. 161-2, A.D. 1875), in the case of Margaret Donnyng *v.* John Owlthwayt, A.D. 1471, is: "Here I take the, Margaret, to have to my wyff, to dede [= till Death] us departe; and therto plyght I the my trouthe." et mulier viro: "Here I take yow, John, to have to my husband, to dede us departe, and therto plyght I yhoue my trouthe." The joining hands, kiss, and following cup of Ale accompany these words: "et contraxerunt manus dexteras adinvicem, utraque vice, osculo interveniente. Et post contractum, praefata Margareta afferebat ciphum servisiae, et tradidit [in] manus ejusdem Johannis, et potavit, et reddidit mulieri, et ipsa potavit."

The Editor of the *Ripon-Chapter Acts*, the Rev. J. T. Fowler, adds a Note: "There are some scores of similar cases in the York Registry, from which the following examples are taken.

In 1484, at Easingwold, a man says, 'Here I take the, Margaret, to my handfest wif, to hold and to have, at bed and at burd, for farer for lather [*pro pulchriori pro difformiori*], for better for wars, in sekenes and in heil, to dethe us depart, if holy Kirk it will ordand; and therto plight I the my trowth.'

In 1516, at Thornton in Craven, a man says to a woman, 'Here I take the, Anne, to my wif, to have and to hold, in sekenes and in heele, for richer for porer, til deth us depart; and therto I plight the my troth.' (York Registry, Eccl. Court.)

The words in the *York Manual*, now in course of publication by the Surtees Society, are as follows:—

"'Here I take the, *N*, to my wedded wyfe, to haue and to holde, at bedde and at borde, for fayrer for fouler, for better for warse, in sekeness and hele, tyl dethe us departe †; and thereto I plyght the my trouthe': *manum retrahendo. 'Deinde dicat mulier, sacerdote docente:* 'Here I take the, *N*, to my wedded husbande, to haue and to holde, at bedde and at borde, for fayrer for fouler, for better for wars, in sekenes and in helth, tyll dethe vs departe; and there-to I plyght the my trothe.'"

At "departe, †" says Mr. Fowler, "all the MSS. have in the text, or in margin, 'if holy kirk it will ordayn.' [That is, allow the Marriage to be lawful.] The Sarum and Hereford forms may be seen in the Preface to "Maskell's Ancient Liturgy."

In the second Marriage-Contract case in the Ripon volume, p. 199—203, Jn. Wardell *v.* Margaret Kendale, in 1468, there was no real contract; and no Trothplight words are given.

[2] This asseveration is in *Piers Plowman*, B text, Passus V, l. 376 (Clarn. Press).—P. Z. Round.

The form of Trothplight given by Robert Cleaver in his *Godly Form of Household Government* (1598), p. 36, is:

"*I, N., do willingly promise to marry thee, N., if God will, and I liue: whensoeuer our parents shall thinke good and meet: til which time, I take thee for my onely betrothed wife, and thereto plight thee my troth. In the name of the Father, the Sonne, and the Holy Ghost. So bee it.*"

"The same is to be done by the woman, the name onely chaunged, and all in the presence of the Parents, kinsfolkes, and friends.

"After this, the Parents are to be admonished, to set and appoint the day of marriage, neither too neare nor too farre of, but to appoint a competent space of time, that it may be sufficient for the learning and triall of all lets and impediments,

The case of Sybil Blakhurst *v.* Randle Ramshae, p. 70-1, shows us the parties strolling home from Nantwich market on a Saturday, overtaking one of the overseers of the girl's father's will (which gave her "an honest porcion of gooddes to mary her withall"), and talking over their intended marriage. The form of words used to the girl in the trothplight here was "I will marry thee, if ever I marry any"; and this, being only a contract *de futuro*, would not have been enforceable, had it not been followd, as it was, by copulation and the birth of a child. For "when the Parties, after they have contracted Conditional Spousals *de præsenti*, or *de futuro*,[1] do, before the event of the Condition, knowe each other Carnally, . . . by this Corporal Copulation they are deemed to have *renounced* the *Condition*; and presently to yield their mutual Consents to Contract and consummate pure and perfect Matrimony."[2]—Swinburne, *Spousals*, p. 121. As an Example of Conditional Spousal, he gives, "I will contract Matrimony with thee, if thou wilt give me 100 l."—p. 120. (See below, p. 210.)

The case on p. 57 raises, like[3] other cases do, the question of tokens. How far are gifts from one contracted or copulating person to another, evidence of intended marriage or not? On that p. 57, a poor man who gives a woman 10*s.*, or about a mark, 13*s.* 4*d.*, declares that he gave it only

whereby promised marriage might be hindered, and yet giue no occasion, by reason of the length thereof, to prouoke the parties to incontinencie. In the meane time, the parties affianced are to be admonished, to abstaine from the vse of marriage, and to behaue themselues wisely, chastly, louingly, and soberly, till the day appointed do come. And so with a Psalme and prayer, to conclude the holy action.

"1. Because there might be some preparation for the things pertaining to house-keeping, betweene that time and the celebrating of marriages: but this is not a chiefe cause.

"2. Because the Lord would by this meanes make a difference betwixt bruite beastes and men, and betwixt the Prophane and his children.

"For they, euen as beastes, do, after a beastlike manner, beeing led by a naturall instinct and motion, fall togither: but God will haue this difference, whereby his children should be seuered from that brutish manner, in that they should haue a certaine distance of time, betweene the knitting of affection, and the enioying one of another, and a more neere ioyning of one vnto another.

"3. That they should in that time, thinke on the causes why they are to marrie, and the duties of marriage: For many enter thereinto, not considering at all, of the great duties belonging to them in the same, nor thinke of the troubles and afflictions that followe marriage.

"But the Lord would haue these thinges thought on, and a consideration to bee had, both of the causes of marriage, and the duties to bee performed, and the troubles to be undergone."

'Had Cleaver's opinion of Shakspere been asked, he would evidently have set him down as a "bruite beast," and one "of the prophane."'—F. J. F. in *The Academy*, 14 Oct. 1876, p. 385-6.

[1] See the Supplement, p. 186, and 210, the first of the Blakhurst case.

[2] See also Cranmer's *Miscellaneous Writings* (Parker Soc.), p. 360. Cranmer says in a Letter to Thos. Cromwell (? 1538):—"I and my doctors that are now with me are of this opinion, that this matrimony contracted *per verba de præsenti*, is perfect matrimony before God."—Cited by E. B. Peacock, in *Academy*, 21 Oct. 1876, p. 409, col. 3.

[3] *Like* is a conjunction (*like as*), as well as a prep. (*like to*).

"because he had, and wold have, to do with her . . . & not for that he wold marry her. as for any other *token*, he sais ther was non sent from hym, or receyvid from her," tho he acknowledges that "he hath had of her a sate [sute ? MS.] of silver and a handcheverchefe," which she evidently intended as tokens.

In a Durham Deposition case (Surtees Soc.) in 1575-6, Edmund Hodgson of Cockermouth, husbandman, aged about 40 years, "saith that ther was never any tokens gyvin nor sent to this deponent by or frome the said Margarye [Wormely], no, not so moch as a handkeircher. Marye, this examinate gave the said Margarye an olde grote, upon frenship, *but as no token*[1]." He 'had an ox that torfled,' dislocated a joint, and applied to Margarie's father to give, or borrow for, him, enough to buy another ox. The 'father refuside'; Margarie lent him 20*s.*; and then he didn't either repay her or marry her. Such, alas, is man!

Of course the question of money turns up in marriage. Richard Lowe, mentioned above, p. 56, gives his reason for not carrying out his trothplight with Jane Walkden: he "sais, her frendes promysed hym a pece of good, and wold not performe hit, so that this respondent was lothe to marie, and not well able to kepe her, except he had had that mariage good." In Man *v.* Pickworth too, p. 64-5, the money-point seems to turn up. And Hugh Pollet's case, p. 62-3, appears to be one of a man trying to hook a well-off widow. But the widow won't have it, and declares that Hugh's silver ring[2] was not meant as a token in con-

[1] 1571. "Jn. Simpson . . saith that, about harvest this time 2 yeres now last past, this examinate caried a *bowed grote* and a *bowed 2d.* as tokens, sent by this examinate from the said William, to the forsaid Anne, being then spynning in a little house within hir mother Margaret Smith dwhelling house."—*Durham Depositions* (Surtees Soc. 1845), p. 238.

A.D. 1575-6. "immediately after the said Helinor [Colson] had plight her faith and treweth to the said Thomas, and Thomas Manwell had doon to hir, then the said Manwell took a *rose noble* of gold out of his purse, and *bowed the same*, and, in the presence of this examinate and his said wyf, gave the same noble to the said Helinor for a token. And then she, the said Helinor, imediatly then after opened hir pusse, and gave the said Thomas Manwell a rynge of silver havynge 2 hands, one of them in another, and gilte with golde."—*Durham Depositions*, p. 282. Surtees Soc. 1845.

1587. "Allison Browne . . saith that . . the said Clement and Agnes . . talking of mariag to be had betwixt them, the said Clement did say, by his trouth, that he would never have other woman in middle earth then the said Agnes, and she said she wold never have other man but him; and then he gave hir an old *grote*, and she gave him a napking."—*ib.* p. 327.

Cp. Fletcher (ab. 1613), *Henry VIII*, II. iii. 36, "a Threepence bowd would hire me, Old as I am, to Queene it." (Shakspere didn't write any of *Henry VIII.*)

[2] Compare *Old Ways*, p. 82: "John Cragge did take out of his purse a rynge of sylver, and gave hit to Atwode [the betrother], who did give it even to Alson [Badcocke], and they did drynke together." 'They had kissyd.' See the gold ring in the Supplement, p. 187-192 below, and in the Index.

See an interesting Paper by S. R. Bird in *The Antiquary*, Nov. 1881, vol. iv. 185-8, on four 'Early Breach of Promise Cases,' to recover presents made, and (in one

firmation of a contract, but was merely a loan, which she returnd. The most interesting thing in the case is the bit at the top of p. 63, that the widow, after her husband's burial, was ill from anxiety, and from the birth of two children, and sent her water "to a phisicion at Chelford, to knowe his opinion, what was good for her: which bade her take spice, nutmegges, ginger and old Ale, and drink them, and she wold mend; for it was no sicknes, but that her braine was wastid with taking thoughtes."

In the case of Alice Wodfall *v.* Thomas Torbock (Supplement, p. 197) the parties each appoint a referee or Daiesman, and these two meet, "and eate a pigge, and cold not agree." But on a second meeting, when (as Mr. Price notes) the 'good chere' was put off till they'd finisht, they award that the man and woman shall be formally trothplighted; which they are; and a day is appointed for their marriage.

A case in the Supplement, Winstanley *v.* Ellen Sonkie, p. 198-200, is curious for the man's delay of 20 years in bringing his suit.[1] He heard that Ellen, who had bound herself by oath to him, was going to marry Robert Gidlowe; so he went to her house at night, when her father and mother were in bed, and challenged her as to her pledge to him. She acknowledgd it. They finally trothplighted one another in the presence of witnesses. Three or 4 weeks after, she married Gidlowe; and 20 years after, Winstanley took process to annul the marriage. Her father "was offendid that [Winstanley] came to his house"; and this explains (I suppose) the daughter's throwing over her trothplighter. There's an interesting touch, in this case, of the continuance of the Romish custom of abstaining from meat on Fridays:

> beinge askid 'howe she knoweth it was done apon a Thursdaie'; she saies, 'bie her supper; and biecause they made an end of flesh meat that night for that weke.' p. 200.

The most amusing bit that I've seen in a Trothplight case was given me by Mr. W. H. Price from the 1548-50 Depositions at Chester, which he and Mr. Irvine are to edit for our Society. Hitherto we have always thought that Shakspere was poking fun at us when he made Biondello say, in *The Taming of the Shrew*, IV. i. 95-6, "I knew a wench maried in an afternoone as shee went to the Garden for Parsley to stuffe a Rabit"; but Mr. Price's case shows us that this might easily have happend: the gardener or some man trothplighted her on the spot, then copulated with her, and the "perfect Matrimony before God" (as Cranmer

instance) money expended to keep the lady (and cure her during her illness from neglect) and her servant for the ten years during which the man betrotht to her was abroad.

[1] See the more delayd Price case, p. liii, 76-9.

and his Doctors call it, p. xlviii, n. 2) was accomplisht. The case is one of a clergyman of St. Peter's, Chester, "Johannes Cotgreue, cl*er*icus, p*a*roch*ie* s*an*cti Petri, Civ*itat*is Cestrie," and Alice Gidlowe, who, during his later absence from Cheshire, married Thomas Belen.

On 6 Feb. 1549-50, John Cotgreve deposes, "that upon a mydsom*er* daie comeinge, the tyme shalbe ix' yeris, this deponent w*ith* iiij' other p*er*sons, as he nowe reme*m*bres, and Alis Belen, al*ia*s Gidlowe, articulate, aft*er* theye hade made merie the same day, in the evenenge he, this deponent, accompanied w*ith* Bartime Dood, Rondall Philippe, Hugh Aston, and one [*blank in MS.*] Picton, went to bringe the said Alis homward toward Saltneye,[1] wher*e* then she dwelled, Vt dicit; and beynge in Hanbrige,[2] this depone*n*t spied forth a vacant howse or a berne, wher*e* no ma*n* dide dwelle att that tyme; & beyng att *tha*t tyme in familiar acquentains w*ith* the said Alis before named, desired that theye ij' soole [alone] toge*th*er to goe into the said howse, for the intente *tha*t he, this deponent, (as he sais) wold haue hade his pleasure off hyr; the wich thinge the said Alis wold not grante, excepte he wold att that tyme promesse to marie hyr. wher*e*apon this deponent spake to his companyons before named, desiring them to come into the said vacant howse w*ith* hym and the said Alis, for he intended to make a co*n*tract in ther*e* w*ith* the said Alis. and so ther*e*, and att that p*rese*nt tyme, and before the p*er*sons afore speciefied, he toke the said Alis bie the hande, speyking thes*e* words, "I, John, take the*e*, Alis, to mye wedded wiff; and therto I plight the*e* mye troth": whervnto the said Alis i*m*mediatlie then and ther answaringe, said, "I, Alis, take the*e* John, to mye husbonde; and therto I plight the*e* mye troth"; and so they toe kissed toge*th*er. And this deponent desired the p*er*sons before named to bayre record off this contracte when theye shuld be called thervnto. And forther required them to goe a litill before towarde Saltney, and he, this deponent, w*ith* the said Alis wold shortlie come aft*er*. aft*er* whos dep*ar*ture, this deponent, Vt dicit, in that vacant howse and att that present tyme, did knowe carnallie the said Alis; and so did often and manye tymes afore she was maried to Thomas Belen, Vt dicit. And forther he sais, that he was absent and forth off the contrey when the said Alis was maried w*ith* Thomas Belen; and iff he hade ben*e* present att *tha*t tyme, he wold haue forbiden the same, for his consciens sake, Vt dicit; and that he has told to his secrett frend*es* off the said contracte made w*ith* the said Alis, Vt dicit.

Another curious case of Trothplight under compulsion, of which the present Text contains no instance,[3] occurs in Mr. Price's volume. A grown-up girl is induced to trothplight herself to a man, by the threats of her father and mother (the father thrashing her with his walking-staff);

[1] A village near Chester, up the Dee estuary.

[2] Handbridge, a suburb of Chester, across the Dee.

[3] We have a compulsory Marriage of a grown-up girl, Maude Gregorie, to Henry Price, p. 78 below.

and she then marries the man, from her feeling of politeness to some neighbours, who came three miles to see her wedded. She evidently felt that she must not disappoint them: so she was accordingly married, and went to her husband's house, but would not let him touch her. He set a watch on her; but she one day took her clothes and ran away, and stopt away more than three years. He then took proceedings to annul the marriage. Here are the details, from my letter in *The Academy*, 14 Oct. 1893, p. 321:—

In February 1548-9, William Wittoun, of Frodsham, says that he married his wife Alice five years before, in his parish church, and

"*that* he thinke*s* verelie *that* the said Alice his wiff was compellid bie hyr father and mother to marie *with* hym"; and "*that* after he hade maried the said Alis, as long as she taried *with* hym, he cold neu*er* obteyne hyr luff or fauo*ur*; nor yett, be anye feare meanes or foule, the said Alis wold not suffer hym to have carnall knolege *with* hyr; and often tymes the said Alis has declared to this deponent, *that* she neu*er* agreed nor consentid in hyr harte to marie with hym, but bie the manesyng, beytinge*s*, and compulsion off hyr father / and forther, this deponent sais, *that* for a certen space he desired his frendis to wache the said Alis, *that* she ra*n* not awaie. And as sone as the said Alis p*er*ceyved *that* ther was no such strect wache laid for hyr, she toke hyr clothis and ra*n* awaie, and has ben*e* from this deponent iij' yeris and more."

Richard Massie, of Budworth, deposes, among other things,

"that the daie befoir the said William and Alis were maried together, the said Alis told this deponent *that* she hade rather the devill had hym, than she wold co*n*tract to marie hym; but she most ned*is* do itt, bie the compulsion off hyr father."

Then comes the most important witness, "Margareta Walchwoman, of Budworth," and she

"sais that the daye wich Allis was assured to William Wittoun, she bie no meanes wold haue gone to haue ben*e* assured to the same partie, although the said Alis father and hyr mother did intise and allure hyr bie meanye feare mesurs and promesses, vntill the tyme *that* the said Alis father did beate hyr *with* a walkyng staff, and threten othirwise to handill hyr, iff she wold not go *with* hym to the Northwich, to be co*n*tracted *with* the said William Witto*un*; and for all that, the said Alis wold not goe *with* hyr father vntill the tyme *that* hyr mother did co*m*pelle hyr *with* manesyng word*is* and threatening*is* to go to the Northwich aft*er* hyr said father. And forther now this deponent sais, *that* the said Alis told this deponent, aft*er* she was assured to the said William, *that* she wold ru*n*e owt off the cu*n*trey, rather then she wold marie *with* the said William; in so moch, *that* this deponent has seen the said Alis wepe dyu*er*se tymes, bie cause hyr father wold compelle hyr to marie hym *that* she cold neu*er* luff / And the daye off the mariage off the said p*ar*ties, the said Alis wepped bitterlie, as this deponent sais; and wold not have goen to *the* church to have ben*e* maried, but lie so long*e* in hyr bed, vntill neybo*urs*, *that* dwellid iij' mylis off, came to the mariage to the howse; and then the said Alis was compellid to rise, and goe to the church to be maried /"

The wife Alice herself briefly confirms these statements.

§ 7. Adulteries. One of the cases I have clast under this head, Henry Price *v.* Mawde Price (p. 76-79), might perhaps have been better put under *Trothplights;* but as Mawde actually married Hy. Price, and then had two children—a boye and a wench—by Randle Gregorie (to whom she was previously betrothd), I have placed the case in the present section as one of apparent adultery. Mawde, at 18, trothplighted herself to Randle Gregorie, and was then "compellid bie her parentis, and other hyr frendis, to marie the said Henrie Price," tho "bie hyr owne mynde, she wold rather have drowned hyr, than maried" him, p. 78. Randle Gregorie didn't forbid the banns "biecause he hard men say that the said Mawde and [he] were too nere akinne to marry in those daies, forbiecause [his] father was brother to the said Mawdes grandfather." After her marriage, Mawde refused to let her husband Henry Price have "his pleasure apon her"; whereupon he, "perceyvinge and judging that she lovid an other man better than hym, fell into such sorowe that he was not his owne man; & went out of the Countrey to service." There he stayd while his nominal wife had two children by her trothplighted lover; and he waited 21 or 22 years before bringing his suit for a divorce, or a decree that his marriage was null and void from the beginning. He would of course get it; and she would marry Randle Gregorie.

The most touching case in this volume is that of Elizabeth Shuttleworth (p. 80), who, moved "only to save her othe, and discharge her Conscience, biecause hit is a matter of Truthe," confesses that after she had had six or seven children by her husband, she set him aside in favour of her lover Peter Hartley, and past off Hartley's child as her husband's. She will make no excuses for herself, but confesses her sin; and, "beynge askid how she will lyve hereafter, sins she cannot mary, & her husbande hath refusid her"; she sais 'she knowis not, but as God will provide for her'; and she will do such penance as 'she shalbe assigned to do.'

The first case of Mr. Rafe Holden, p. 72-3, is full of local colour. We have a bit of the Tudor fortification of our coasts (see my *Andrew Boorde*, pages 119, 329[1]), the workmen at Hull, there "to make one bulwarke & two blockhouses for the defence of the Towne"; we have the packman, one of the body who carried on the inland trade of the country, one who "draweth packes of Cloth from Holifaxe to Hull, and ther lodethe hymself home againe with stockfishe, red heringes and such marchaundrie wares"; we have this packman visiting and chatting with an old gentlewoman of his county, not telling her of her husband's marrying another young woman, "biecause he wold not discomforth an old auncient gentlewoman," but accepting her token of a 'bendid grote'[2] for her faithless spouse, and her commendations to him, besides 'a paire of Flemynge knyves [imported into Hull] and a Ribon' for his sisters. We have this nice sample of a country gentleman,—supposed to have 'bene up at London in the Court,'—having shunted his old wife on to her married daughter, marrying a new wife, and being about 'to build a newe house.' But he had the grace to send his old wife some rents.

The second case, Margaret Alatt *v.* Richard Pierson (p. 73-6), is an amusing one. The husband is eager for his marriage, but when it is solemnized, he finds himself incompetent, from a hurt. He goes to physic; his wife waits eight weeks; and then

"perceyvinge that he could not do any more than afore, she commensid a sute, and sekid for a divorce to be had bie the lawe betwixe them; wherof Richard Pierson was so ashamid, that he wold have runne his way; and had gon xxx^{tie} mile on his way, and was fett againe bie his frendes, and bound to abide the award of the lawe."—p. 74.

The husband, on the contrary, alleges that he has had a child by another woman; and that tho, at his marriage, he *was* incompetent, from a hurt, yet a parson-doctor's drink soon cured him, and made him 'lustye'; but he wouldn't use his wife's company in bed, because she had associated with 'one Thomas Pawton' (? adulterized with him) and with 'one Jane Sidebotham, who is knowne to be a naughtie woman.'—p. 75.

The Downes case, p. 202-3, p. 81, is one of a wife stopping on at her mother's house, and not going to her husband's, while he indulges in other women, and has illegitimate children. The Eiton case shows us again (p. 82-85) a woman sending her water—if it was hers—to a parson-

[1] Also Harrison's *England*, p. 265 (my edn.), and Halle's *Chronicle*, p. 827, ed. 1809. The allusions to public affairs are but few in the Depositions. Besides this fortification one, we have that to the battle of St. Quintins, p. 106 at foot, the ship for the Queen's service, July 1600, p. 178, the Earl of Essex's soldiers for Ireland cast away on the Welsh coast, p. 168, and the Letters by Post, p. 178-180.

[2] "The syluer of England is Grotes, halfe grotes, Pens, halfe pens; and there be some Fardynges."—Andrew Boorde, *Introduction* (written 1542, publisht 1547), p. 121 of my edition.

doctor for the disease of the Mother.[1] It gives us also a lady drinking with men at an inn; her servant walking her horse about as she waits; her giving birth to a (? bastard) child as she is riding to London with a male relation or friend; her making a posset 'of a herbe callid Mugge-wede'[2] with her maid, the daughter of one of her husband's tenants, &c. We now come to

§ 8. Affiliations. As I turnd over the leaves of the MS., my eye caught Ellen Gardiner's despairing cry (p. 98), "Alas! I am undone; for he whom I wold father my Child on, will forsake it"; and this made me copy her case, and the rest of its class. They are full of the life of their time, and of course have an illustration or two of Shakspere: 'the little *peltinge* alehouse' (p. 98 at foot)—to compare with the '*pelting* Farme,' *Rich. II.*, II. i. 60, 'Poore *pelting* Villages, Sheeps-Coates and Milles,' *Lear*, II. iii. 18, &c.—and the proof that the dramatist when he said in *Winter's Tale*, III. iii. 72, of the babe Perdita, "this has been some behinde-doore-worke," knew more about what could be done standing 'behind the Milne dore' (p. 97) than John Cotgreve.—There are few things about women (and men too) that Shakspere didn't know; and few Elizabethan records and books that don't illustrate him.

We see what went on at smart[3] houses like Sir Philip Egerton's, p. 87: two servant-girls in bed; a man gets into bed with them;[4] the proper girl goes to another bed; the improper girl and the man keep together half the night. Another time, the same couple are found on a truckle-bed together; but the male finder declares they are not there, for fear of the consequences to them. When, however, the discoverer is a female (p. 91-2), and she finds that her bedfellow secretly steals to the bed of John Barnes, and stays there two hours, she dresses, sees they are 'nought' together, and peaches on the woman,[5] refusing the bribe of a pair of shoes to hold her tongue. This naughty Margaret Monelay was a hard-working woman; for when she says she is not to be brought to bed till Christmas, she is told, "thou art happy; thou may have a pece of harvest to get somwhat in." In another case, p. 101, the girl is riding behind a young man,

[1] A hysterical malady. 'Oh how this *Mother* swels vp toward my heart!' Shakspere, *Lear*, II. iv. 56 (1 Fo. 293/2). 'The *mother* is a pestilent, wilful, troublesome sickness.' Middleton. *Michaelmas Term*, III. i.—*Century Dict.*

[2] *Mug-wort*, an Herb, which being carry'd about a Man, is said to take away Weariness: It is good for Wounds, and Fits of the Mother (womb).—Kersey's Phillips, 1706.

[3] In earlier stages of English, 'smart' meant rough, wild,—'smerte londe,' Dublin MS.; 'will[d]e londe,' Rawlinson MS.,—p. 128, 129, of my edition of *The English Conquest of Ireland*, E. E. T. Soc. 1896. It's a curious change, from 'uncultured' to 'cultured,' at least in Society ways.

[4] See note to Contents of MS., p. lxxxi, note 1.

[5] The misdeed was also reported on Dee bridge, p. 92.

"and when they came to a suspicious place, they light both; and the horse was rayned in the midest of the Lane; and they went both over a stele [stile], and backside a hedge, very suspiciously, & did continue together for the space of a quarter of an howre & more; but what they did there, this deponent cannot certenlie tell; but he supposed it was for no good purpose."—p. 101.

In almost all the cases, we see the childing (p. 95) of the woman, with her friends and midwives round her; we hear the midwife ask her, in her extreme pains, who is the father of the child; and when she declares him, I for one incline to believe her, tho an Ellen Gardiner may have said before, "Clare hath a house, and Holt hath non; and therefore Clare shalbe father of my Child," p. 98. Then we see the woman going with her kinsfolk to the vicar or rector of the parish to declare the child; and he in church proclaims it, p. 86. Afterwards, if the reputed Father will not own it, he brings suit to cancel the Affiliation, and the Depositions follow. I was told in the Town-Hall at Chester, that one Welsh magistrate would never listen now to a plea that a child might belong to one of half-a-dozen fathers who had been with its mother; he said a woman had a perfect right to choose her child's father out of the set of likely ones; and he decided the cases accordingly.

The scene on p. 98 foot, 99 top, is to the life: the woman going for turfs;[1] the keeper of the little ruinous alehouse pulling her in; the neighbour entering for a coal to light his fire, and seeing the couple in bed together, thro the unclosing door and windows [shutters]; then the man trying to get rid of the woman, and his mother reproaching him for it.

The existence of venereal disease is, alas, evident, p. 33, 100, &c.

§ 9. Libels. Our forefathers and foremothers cald a spade 'a spade,' and not 'a horticultural implement.' The raciest instances of this here, are on pages 122, 123, 128-9. But after skimming hastily the Durham Depositions, Cheshire folk 'll have to confess that they are no match for their Northern rivals.

These *Durham Depositions*, publisht by the Surtees Society in 1845, show the following terms of abuse (among others): 1. as to women: 'this plaintiff should [= did] give her daughter such drinkes as did slee the childe that she was with,' p. 50; 'Go thy way, like nowghth as thou art, and cut a purse, as thou haist doon bifore tyme; and thou may be duckt in Tyne, as thou haith beene,' p. 71; "drabe, and rotten drabe, and biche foxe," p. 81; "hoore"; 'she had borne 2 children, and that the fathers of them was hanged,' p. 81; 'his wyf was a lymer,' p. 83; 'for certaine

[1] Cp. 'she went downe to fetche a baskett-full of Turves.'—*Supplement*, p. 207.

things lackinge, she turned a seve upon a pair of sheres' (was an exorcist, or witch); 'she was a drabe, and that she was worthie a tar-barrell, a cart,[1] and a whip,' p. 84; 'she was a barrell drome, and that she was ever kend for nought all the daies of hir lyf'; 'she had stolen one silver spoone'; 'she should teir a cheffe and a neckurcheffe of a dycke [off a hedge],' p. 84; 'Had she stolne a purse? Ye, marye, had she, and was caried to the New Yaite for the same,' p. 88; 'hyte hoore; a whipe, and a cart, and a frame hoode,[2] (waies me[3] for the, my lasse!) wenst[4] have a halpeny halter for the to goo up Gallygait and be hanged?'; 'she was a Spanyell hoore'; 'she was whippet out of Morpeth for a skolde,' p. 89; 'she caul me hoor,' p. 90; 'she was a horse godmother water wych,' p. 91; 'noughtie pak': 'I am neyther goos-steler nor steg [gander]-steiler': 'What, noughty hoore, caull thou me goose-steiler?' p. 104; 'crowket-handyd wytch,' p. 247; 'Skotts hore': "Thou caulde hir 'hoore' to my face," p. 253; 'hange-lipped witche': 'clarted witche,' p. 313; 'Thou haist A witch to thy eldmother,' p. 318. 2. Of men: 'why cannot the young theefe learne at the old?' p. 318; 'he haithe kept hir, and doethe kepe her still, as his leman,' p. 312; 'thou droncken horemonger preist,' p. 292; 'hooremaster preiste,' p. 264; 'cockold, knave, cockold,' p. 248; 'thou art a cookhold, and ye ar a pair of cockholdlye knaves,' p. 249; 'Goo, Bayker, thou art a knave, and thy wyfe a hoore,' p. 244; 'Thou art a vacabound, a wagwallet, and syde-tayled knave'; I called him openly 'beggerly harlot and cutthrote,' sainge that he was 'a covitous snowge, and such as he, by Godds worde, aught to be weded out of the Coomenwelthe,' p. 107; 'theiff, fals knave, busy knave,' p. 101: 'he was a gouse and a hen thefe, and all his,' p. 91; 'he was so fals of his toung, that ther was [not] a worde of his mouth worthie to be trusted': 'he shuld steill his own goodes, hens and duckes, and gyve the same to

[1] See the instance below, p. 128. Shrove-Tuesday was the special day for this carting: see Brand's *Popular Antiquities*, i. 50-52, ed. Hazlitt, 1870. "BAWDRY.—The punishment for this offence was riding in a cart through the parish where it was committed, and sometimes through the adjoining ones also, with a paper attached to the front of the dress, descriptive of the particulars, and a basin ringing before them to draw the attention of the people to their disgrace. Occasionally the culprit went on horseback. The examples given by Stowe and others, of this class of chastisement, are not only very numerous, but we cannot fail to be struck by the great frequency of cases, where parents were guilty of the crime towards their own offspring, and of the respectable position of many of those who were implicated. The publication of the delinquency on a sheet of paper pinned to the person, was common to many other crimes, such as perjury, &c.; but then it seems to have been more usually fixed over the culprit's head." Several instances of carting are cited on p. 51; among them, "In 1559, 'The wife of Henry Glyn, goldsmith, was carted about London, for being bawd to her own daughter.'"

[2] Probably the *branks* or headdress used in Newcastle to punish scolds.—Raine.

[3] Woe is me.—R. [4] Wilt thou?—R.

Lightons wyfe, whome withall he, the said Bartram, shuld lyve ungodlye: she cauled them Scottes Martyn sonnes,' p. 91; 'maynsworn harlots': 'he wittinglye solde one stolne shepe skyn': 'he or his wyf stole a silver whistell': 'he was a skott,'[1] p. 39; 'she wolde nott go to supper with no such vile vyllands as he was, saing, "Falsh vile knave, thou wold have my husband to bryng the pox to me, as thou brought them to thi wyfe" . . . than the said Janet cauld him "falsh pokye theiff"', p. 88; 'he was a thief, and wold be hanged, as all his fore ellers [elders] was,' p. 84; a 'hold eyed lymber thief,' 'and that he shuld recett certain corne of S*i*r Robert Brandlyngs, so moch as wold fyne his house one hole yere': 'he shuld have murdered and put down his two wyfes,' p. 83;[2] 'the said Foster was a perjured person,' p. 82; 'shew not your croweltye upon the boy, as ye use to your wife,' p. 77; 'Skotts mangerell, Skotts browll,' p. 76; 'thou falsse olde carle,' p. 73; 'he murdered his own son,' p. 71; 'the said Dicson did breake the churche of West Awkelande, and toke forthe of the same, a chalice and certayne bookes and money, and for the same the said Dicson did open penaunce,' p. 49.

After these lists, the Cheshire and Flintshire 'cuckold,' 'grinning thief,' user of another man's wife as his own, 'hore & thief, strong hore, provid hore, jade hore,' 'thou liest like an arrant howre, as thou art,' &c., make but a poor show. The long Flintshire case, p. 105—110, arose out of John ap John's mare breaking into Roger David's close. Roger turnd the mare out, and John said, 'Bid that foul Cuckold seek me my mare again.' The ground of the imputation was, that when John's wife Jane was very young, she got into bed between her husband and another man, instead of sleeping with her maid (p. 105, 110), and then John was foolish enough to tell his friends of it.[3] Another case, p. 117, 204-7, rises out of a woman asking a man for 7 groats she'd lent him 3 years before. He said he didn't owe it her; she said he did; and she cald him 'a grinning thief.' He cald her 'a strong whore.' He was working at a paling with an axe, and rusht after the woman,

> "to have smit her with the axe; and she runne into Wolfall(s) house; and Toppinges wief, who stode by when they were at thes wordis, shutt the dore against Fazakerley; & so hit fortuned that he hitt her not. and he confessid in that tene, he carid not yf he had knockid her downe."

In the second long case, Wade *v.* Rile (p. 111—116), a Mother

[1] See Andrew Borde's 'Trust yow no Skott,' p. 59 of my edition.

[2] Wm. Loye of Newcastle, says of Wm. Rand and Janet Wood going 'suspeciouslye' together: 'thoise two wold one day make thre.'

[3] In this case a Welsh witness isn't examind on certain points because he doesn't know English.—p. 108.

accuses a neighbour's wife of adultery with her stepson Robert Rile. The mother is milking: Wade's servant rides by; she asks him how his master and mistress agree; and tells him and others that his mistress came one snowy Saturday morning to young Robert Rile's room; and she, the Mother, lookt thro a 'tote' or spy-hole in the door, and saw them use one another as man and wife. On this, Wade's husband put her away; but a friend of hers took her case up, and got a Citation against Mrs. Rile for libel. Mrs. Rile's answer is interesting, not only for her evident drawing-back from what she'd said to Wade's witnesses against her, but for her having taken charge of a Cross and other ornaments of Mrs. Wade's, and lent the Cross to a young woman to go to a wedding or wake (p. 116). She also complains that when Mrs. Wade was sick, she, Mrs. Rile, "as one neybour wold do to another, did bringe her chickens, spice, and other thinges to comfort her"; whereas, when she, Mrs. Rile, was sick, Mrs. Wade only brought her a little befe[1] 'to release her mouth,' and a little salt eel; and nothing more: p. 116.

In the fourth case, p. 117—120, we have a respectable woman inviting her husband's friends to drink with her at the Bell inn at Nantwich; we have a man going into a high loft there, to write a letter for one Browne; and the indignant lady bringing to him, Browne, one of her friends, to hear what a bad character a wrong-minded Margaret Tailiour had given Browne of her and her husband, the absent Mr. Claiton: "he was a very evill & noughtie man," and as to his wife, "like as the one, like [is] the other," p. 118.

In the amusing Pattele case, p. 128-9, already referd to, we see a curate, offended at a libel on one of his female parishioners, take 'one other honest man in companie,' and exhort the libeller 'to geve over those sclaunderous wordes'; but he stands to them. In the case of John and Elizabeth Seaton, they were wrongfully 'rid in a cart,' for their fornication, inasmuch as they "were trouthplight together afore, & maried imediatlie after," p. 128. (See p. lvii above.)

In the Gillam case, Elizabeth Walley says sensibly, that though Agnes Gillam was cald by another woman 'a liar and arrant whore,' she thinks her good name "is not hurt herebie, biecause the wordes were spoken in anger[2]," p. 127.

[1] I read it 'beste,' beestings, the thick rich milk of a cow after calving; but Mr. Price decided on 'befe.'

[2] Proverb: 'Two pots, a feast presage; two women, mickle rage.'—Cotgrave, *Fr. Engl. Dict.*, 1611, under *Pot.*

Sometimes there is a suggestion that very poor men have been subornd as witnesses, so that their testimony is of no worth. Thus,

"Alexander Liney is a light person; and nowe latelie it was provid before Sir Rafe Leycetour, . . . that he did consent to the Convaieng away ["Convey," the wise it call—Shakspere] of certen butter & cheese from this deponent, delivered to the said Alexander & his wief bie one Ellin Bodley; and for the same, both he & his wief were ponished in the stockes / . . . John Apshawe is a light person, and a fugitive, and hath flitted twise within this half yere," p. 125.

In the Supplement are two interesting cases of the reference of disputes about Libels to Daiesmen or Arbitrators. In the second of these, a widow, Anne Venables, says that Elizabeth Basnett "was a hoore, and had plaid the nought with Raffe Venables, her [Anne's] husband decessid" (p. 209). Daiesmen (or Referees on each side) are appointed to settle the dispute, and they give their award against the widow;

"the daiesmen of Anne Venables did promes vnto the daiesmen of Elizabeth Basnet, that Anne Venables shuld comme before a dosen or xvi persons, in a place and daie appointid, & there aske forgevenes of Elizabeth Basnet for such wordes as she had wrongfullie spoken by" her.

"and at the daie and place appointed, the said Anne Venables did refuse, and would not comme to ask the said Elizabeth Basnet forgevenes, but came not there at all." p. 209-210.

Whereupon Elizabeth rightly went to the Bishop's Court for redress.

In the case of Constance Frost *v.* William Ball (Supplement, p. 208), a Deposition is made that a man heard it said at the Chester Council, that Constance had two husbands.

§ 10. *Wills.* The most striking case here is that of the widow, Isabella Crompton, p. 130-1. During her husband's illness she wanted to get hold of his Will and other documents, and make away with the Will. So she gets a man to draw the hinge-nails of the chest the Will is in, takes out the papers, and then brings the man some fresh nails to fasten the hinges again, as if they had never been toucht. Luckily the nail-drawer was an honest man; and when question and suit were raisd about the Will, he was movd by his Conscience to tell the executor, and then come into Court and depose to the facts.

In the case about Alice Brodhurst's will, p. 134-5, we see the Curate administering the Communion to the deaf old dame at 9 o'clock one morning in her own dwelling, six days before she died, and then, an hour after, taking "a certen note of her Will," which he couldn't read over to her because she was so deaf. This note was no doubt admitted to or offerd for Probate, and objection was made that the old lady was 'lunatique'; but the curate repudiates the notion, and Margerie Piers says she "did never knowe that euer she (A. Brodhurst) was Lunatike or furiouse." In other cases, no Note of a man's Will is made; and it is only nuncupative, or by word of mouth. Roger Hodgson, tho urgd by his parson,—after he "had gevin hym the rites of the church"—to make his Will (p. 132), wont do it till his sick Brother comes, whom he wishes to be his executor. But the Brother doesn't come in time, and no Will is made. In Pendleton's case, the parson is again (as usual) the drawer of the Will (p. 131); and we can see the old testator sickening after his first recovery, telling his neighbour "of thinges done eighty years ago," his friend tarrying "with hym when the breath went out of his mouth."

§ 11. Miscellaneous. The most amusing bit here is on p. 138: the farmer of the tithes of Clitheroe sent one

"Michaelmas to Christofer Hargrevis house, and demaundid a tieth goose of his wief, who had ix geese this yere; and she wold have gevin him none but one that haltid, and tralid the winge. And this deponent wold not take it, biecause the use is, to have the best, savinge two; and that was the worst."

One can fancy the couple in the farm-yard; the woman trying to palm off the lean lame bird on the tithe-renter's man, while he sticks up for his master's rights.

Henry Blagburne's case (p. 137-8) is a curious one: he says he had the use of his wife's body when a spinster, and she persuaded him that she was with child by him; so he married her, and they livd together 12 years, but could have no carnal connection because of an impediment in her body. This she refused to have removed by an operation: so, in the 8th year "they partid; & then the Justices of Peace compellid him to take her againe till the Spirituall Lawe had orderid" a Separation or Divorce. Accordingly, he brings suit in the Bishop's Court; but as he acknowledges having had a child by one other woman, and isn't yet certain about another child by a second woman, he surely couldn't expect the Bishop to be anxious to help him.

In the long Depositions under a Commission (which I couldn't make time to read thro), my eye caught a nice bit about a good clergyman, John Leigh, who was without a curate, but was "continually travaylid in visitinge of his parishioners, when the newe sicknes was hote and extreme within" his parish. So I copied it, and it is printed on p. 139. Mr. J. P. Earwaker has kindly written the notes on the places named on that page, &c., besides looking thro my revises, and calling attention to slips in the text, before its final collation with the MS. by Mr. Price.

§ 12. Clandestine Marriages. Those in our Trothplight cases, both in the Text and Supplement (p. lxxviii, 57, 56, 194, 196), were made by men in order to get out of their trothplights and enjoy fresh wives, except in the Sothworth runaway case. But the three later cases sent by Mr. Price from separate documents, to form Section VIII, p. 140-1, seem not to have anything to do with men's evasion of former trothplights. Two marriages were solemnized by Clerics, the third by a 'Master Kendricke.' The two would, I assume, be valid marriages, while the third would be a good trothplight. The first of the two was performd in the bride's house [p. 140]; the second 'in a meadowe neare the towne of Ashton-under-Lyne, in the night season, by the lighte of the moone' [p. 141]; and the third 'in the heighe waie that leadeth to Mellinge meadowes.'

The question has been askt me, How clergymen came to commit such gross irregularities as the performances of these unlicenst and un-band marriages? Their want of money was the main cause, I take it; and their probable friendship for one or both of the parties, the less cause. Any one who wants to know the impoverisht and ignorant state of the clergy in Q. Elizabeth's time, should read part of Chapter i, Book II. of Harrison's *Description of England*, 1577-87, p. 26-35 of my edition, and the authorities cited in the notes there. He denounces

"the couetousnesse of the patrones, of whom some doo bestow aduousons of benefices vpon their bakers, butlers, cookes, good archers, falconers, and horse-keepers, in sted of other recompense for their long and faithfull seruice, which they imploie afterward vnto their most advantage," p. 26-7.

Harding calls the English ministers, tinkers, tapsters, fiddlers and pipers. Bernher says of the patrons (A.D. 1562):

"these greedy men have spoiled the livings, and gotten them into their hands; and instead of a faithful and painful preacher, they hire a Sir John, which hath better skill in playing at tables [backgammon], or in keeping of a garden, than in God's word."

Edward Dering, in his Sermon before Q. Elizabeth, 25 Feb. 1569-70—in Brydges's *Brit. Bibliogr.*, i. 260-1 (1810)—on the state of the ministry &c., benefices &c., says of patrons

"some are selling theyr benefices, some farming them, some keepe them for theyr children, some giue them to boyes, some to seruingmen; & very fewe seeke after learned pastors . . . Looke vpon your ministery, and there are . . some shake-bucklers, some ruffians, some hawkers and hunters, some dicers and carders, some blinde guides, and cannot see, some dumme dogs, and wil not barke: and yet a thousand more iniquities haue now couered the Priesthode" . . .

Is it likely that clergymen of this kind, thus treated and appointed, would hesitate to marry any couple, any where, if they got a fee for it? Or would a parson of the Chester John-Cotgreve type, p. li above, stick at a trifle of banns or license, when cash was to be had for the job?

§ 13. The Mayors' Books. Only the English bits in the volumes I lookt at, did I copy, for we are an Early English Text Society. The earliest books are rotting, so that it is hardly safe to open them. The Mayor and Corporation ought to pass a self-denying ordinance, that they'll eat no feeds till they've had the leaves of their old volumes properly dried, sized, and lookt-to. It is not creditable to a Municipality like Chester, that its old records should be in the sad state they are.

The English entries speak well for the care of the old citizens for the common good. The Butchers and Bakers are made to take public oath that the food they supply to their fellow-citizens shall be wholesome, and fair in price, p. 153-4. (See too Rafe Haselwall's Bond, p. 154.) A Chandler in like wise executes a Bond that his Candles shall be only 4*d.* a pound. If any trader tries to forestall buyers, he is had up, and bound to bring 1. either the wares into the general market or Common Hall (p. 157, 167), where every one has like chance of buying, or 2. not to interfere with the Mayor's buying fish 'for a common bargaine, to the use of this Citie' (p. 165), or not to sell the goods without the Mayor's license (p. 162). Corn and grain also are not to be taken out of the City without the Mayor's leave (p. 145). Wine-merchants are stopt from cheating the Customs, p. 155, and bound to deliver their Butts of Sack to the City Sheriffs on demand. A slater is allowd to buy slates only for his own use and buildings (p. 151); he mustn't hold a lot, and raise the price to his customers. A Barber has to execute a Bond not to let unlawful games be playd in his house, p. 145. If a woman has a bastard by any man (like, say, George Title) he is made to enter into a Bond to provide for the Child—for a time at least—and prevent the City being charged with them, p. 156. Nay, in one case, before the baby is born, its father, Jn. Lingley, has to execute a Bond to find it suck and other necessaries, p. 157.[1] Men must pay for their own larks, and not saddle fellow-citizens with them. The City is jealous, too, of its own privileges. A Deputy-Bailiff of the County Exchequer dares to arrest a defaulter in the open market-place of the City. Off he is packt to jail (p. 150); and his prisoner would be of course set free. Another time, one citizen—helpt by another man—breaks into a neighbour's house, and hauls him out to the Castle-jail, p. 159. He is set free,

[1] Compare the City Sheriff searching for adulterers, to send them to prison.—*Supplement*, p. 194 below.

and his captor rebuked for his 'such injurious dealing.' A Letter from Lord Burleigh, p. 166, confirms the trading rights of City merchants' widows equally with their dead husbands. Well-off sons are forst to support their poor fathers 'wholy decaied, and in greate yeares,' under the powers of a Statute past two years earlier, p. 173, 182.

Then, private disputes are referd to the Mayor for decision, p. 147, 149, 151-2, 165. One of the City Waits dies: his widow claims a share in their Hautboys, Trumpets and Viols. They go before the Mayor; and all is set straight (p. 150). The City Wall-mender grows old, and resigns his post and his livery, p. 146. The City Conduit-Keeper and another man arrange before the Mayor, that the Keeper shall let the Market-stalls, and take their rent, and clean the street there, paying the other man 8*s*. a year, p. 177. The Searcher of Leather gives a Bond for his due execution of his Office, p. 162-3. Hue and Cry for culprits, lays before us a description of their persons, p. 171-2. Letters of State, &c. arrive, and are sent off by posts, p. 178-80. The shares of the City-parishes in Charity-gifts are stated, p. 172. The Corporation's own small gifts of money (p. 168-171) include doles to two dozen poor soldiers,—of eleven, the ship was 'caste awaie in Wales';—one to a Doctor's wife and her children to go to her native Ipswich, 'upon her promis never to retorne hither to be troublesom to this Citie'; two for burials; four for three lame folk and a cripple; one for 'Cranes wife, her legg broken'; 6*d*. to three people 'dangerus sick'; one 'to a woman, for to cary her to Hardn whom (Hawarden home),' &c.

As we've had to deal with Wards, I have added a list of the Queen's Cheshire Wards in 1578 (p. 180-1), and of the absentee Landlords, which it follows in a State Paper. A notice of the orderd pulling-down of Staines Bridge, Middlesex, on account of the South-Western rebellion, I have also put in, to raise the question, whether the Citizens of Chester were ever bidden to pull down their Dee Bridge for a like cause: p. 181.

And so at last we draw to

§ 14. Conclusion. No reader of these Depositions, who has any brains, will deny their great value as illustrations of the life of their time. What, then, ought to be done to those Cheshire Antiquaries who have known of them for the last ten years and more, and have left them unprinted? Certainly one of these naughty folk ought to be hangd; and the rest dragd thro' the Dee, or stood in sackcloth and ashes at the Cross. Every outsider in the land has a legitimate personal grievance against these Cheshire old-timers. And if the Records are interesting to us, how much more so are they to Cheshire folk! As Mr. St. Chad Boscawen said to me after I'd read bits of the Child-Marriage cases to a

Meeting at Mrs. Haweis's: "Interesting? Why, I know all the names, the families, the places, the old phrases! These things mean ten times more to me than they do to you." And so they do. More shame, then, to the Cheshire Antiquaries for not having publisht them before, and for leaving them to an overworkt old Londoner to put thro in a spurt, when he's had, in the same time, to turn out two books for his Early English Text Society—*The Three Kings' Sons* (ab. 1500), and *The English Conquest of Ireland*, 1165—1186 (2 texts, c. 1425, 1440)—as well as edit Shakspere's *Comedies and Histories* in his evenings, for Mr. Wm. Morris's grand black-and-red edition. I am an ill-used person. And if any reader will curse the Cheshire Antiquaries for me, I shall feel grateful to him. On them, too, he must in fairness lay all blame for the shortcomings of this edition,[1] and the want of the final Decrees in the Suits,[2] &c., of local notes. One of these Cheshire demons ought to have issued a complete print of the 1561-6 Depositions ten years ago. They may depend upon it that Satan has them down in his black book (or is it red?) for their neglect.[3]

[1] "When in doubt," swear at a Cheshire Antiquary.

[2] I hadn't time for the search, and took little interest in the Decrees, tho they should be added for completeness' sake.

[3] Mr. J. P. Earwaker writes:—"About these Chester Depositions:—The entering of them into the folio volumes which you saw, ceased about 1580, or possibly earlier. After that date the depositions of the witnesses in each case which came before the Court there, were written upon sheets of folio paper, which, at the conclusion of the case, were folded up lengthwise, and endorsed on the back with the date and the names of the parties in dispute. These were then packed away year by year; and there are now very many thousands of them in the Chester Registry, tied up in enormous packages without any order or arrangement, and stowed away at the top of the large cupboards in some of the rooms there.

"I have often had one of these bundles down, and have spent many hours going through the Depositions, picking out any which specially interested me, either from the names of the persons or parishes mentioned, to go through at my leisure.

"There is material enough there to enable you to print a volume of the size of the one now finishing for the next 20 years, and I shall only be too glad if you will do so. [This is local men's duty, not ours of the E. E. T. Soc.] I cannot tell you when they cease; but I think I have met with them as late as 1680, and possibly later, but I do not recollect any after 1700. Between 1580 and 1640 they are very numerous, and full of the same quaint information, old English words and expressions, which are to be found in those you have printed.

"I expect there should be many more of the bound volumes found, if a good search were made. Anyhow I hope you will pay Chester a visit next summer, and we will have a hunt together; and you shall see for yourself what an immense mass of material there is to be culled from.

"I hope you have no very thin-skinned members, or they may be voting this volume of yours a most 'improper' one, and full of 'naughty' doings."

Mr. Price showd me some of those folded and bundled Depositions, and I read one or two, but had no time for more. Mr. Price does not believe that there are any more bound volumes in the Registry, and says that it contains material for many more volumes than Mr. Earwaker estimates. So there's plenty for the Cheshire Antiquaries to do. The question is, Will they do it?

The next person who wants talking-to is the Bishop. Why are the old Records of his Court in the dirty, decaying, uncalendard, and unindext state that many of them are? Why isn't the Chief Clerk of the Registry enabled, and properly salaried, to put all the documents in order, tin-boxes, &c., and have a complete list of them, with an Index to their contents? No one can fairly make the present Bishop responsible for the sins of his predecessors; but something he ought to do.[1] As a last resource, 'the Duke' could be appeald to; and if he wont listen to reason and sign a cheque, a Football Club might carry him off, and hide him in a disused mine till he sends for Mr. Parker with the necessary bags of sovereigns as his ransom. Then the Registry could be set straight. It would be a much more useful result than getting goals and points for kicking a football about.

To the present Registrar, Mr. John Gamon, I am much indebted. Not only did he refrain from charging me a guinea a day for copying, which the Salisbury Registrar charged,[2] but he let me off the usual moderate fees that other searchers for private matters have to pay; and, far more, he allowd his chief Registry-clerk, Mr. W. H. Price, to help me in reading and collating the MS. Such correctness as the text of the present book has, is greatly due to Mr. W. H. Price, as I have said before; and I again thank him heartily for his help; as well as Mr. Phil Davies for his work at the Mayors' books.

As this volume may have a few readers not accustomd to our E. E. T. Soc. ways, I note that all contractions in the MS. have been expanded in italics in the print; perhaps mistakingly now and then. The MS. 'in vī' ought probably to have been always expanded 'in vi*m*,' as the word is occasionally written 'vim'; but as it is englisht 'by virtue (of his othe),' I have generally printed 'vī' vi*rtute*. The tꞌ of 'examinatꞌ,'

[1] The Registrar, "Mr. Gamon, and his partner Mr. Farmer, have personally arranged and indexed many documents, at the cost of a great deal of time; and cleaning and arrangement of documents have been going on slowly since Mr. Gamon has been Registrar"; but the work wants years of undivided attention. Had all prior Registrars been John Gamons, and all Chief-Clerks W. H. Prices, everything would now have been right.

[2] The Bishop found this system establisht, and could not alter it, tho he'll not continue it if he has a chance of breaking it. When he came to the Diocese, being an antiquary himself, he exhorted all his clergy to write the histories of their parishes. Two or three tried to begin, but were met by the Registrar's demand of a guinea a day for searches,—a charge of which the Bishop was then, I need not say, wholly ignorant. So he had to give up his idea of Parish Histories in his Diocese.

At Lincoln, no hint of a charge was made. The Bishop put me (and later, my copier) into the hands of his Secretary, Mr. Smith, who set us down his own room in the Tower, and let us copy freely all we wanted: this is the right thing. At Somerset House, literary searchers into Wills, &c., above 100 years old, are free from fees, and get most valuable help from the Superintendent, Mr. Challenor Smith.

the scribe of the MS. expanded as 'to,' the few times he wrote it at full length, for he treated the word as an ablative absolute—'B. being examind';—but, as its far-off noun—the name of the examinee—was in the nominative case (to its verb), the rule of Latin Grammar obliged me reluctantly to abandon the scribe's precedent, and print 'examinat*us*.' To the word 'the,' the scribe has often added a kind of wavy tail, which may have meant 'y,' and may not. When 'the' was wanted by the sense, I've printed 'the,' and when 'they' was wanted, 'they.' In the Mayors' Books, a few of the contractions beat me, and I could only do my best with em.

In some of the Cases, I have printed the whole of the Depositions. In others, I have left out the tedious Latin repetitions of the deponent knowing nothing about a certain Article of Complaint, &c. In others, I have left out the later Depositions, which only repeat former ones; and in still other cases I have abstracted the main statements. Time faild me to copy everything; and as Canon Raine said of his doing, in his Preface to his edition of the Durham Depositions, Surtees Soc. 1845, p. viii: "In some suits, where, perhaps, ten witnesses were examined, he [the Canon] has contented himself with printing the deposition of only one. Neither has he deemed it necessary to detail the result of the litigation, which in most cases might have been obtained from the Contemporaneous Act Books."

For the Glossary, I am indebted to my friend Mr. P. Z. Round, B.A. —who made part of it in the Temperance Hospital while under Dr. Collins's care,—for the Indexes of Places and Names, to Mr. W. H. Price. To them and all our Members, readers, and friends, I wish a Merry Christmas and a Happy New Year. To those Cheshire Antiquaries, deep repentance, frequent flagellations, and the outpouring of large subscriptions to print all their Records before they themselves depart to Purgatory, to be punisht for their sins.

F. J. Furnivall.

British Museum, under the Electric Light,
December 21, 1893.

---

p. lxiv, lxv. Some folk seem to be under the impression that Mr. Earwaker discoverd the Child-Marriages about ten years back. Mr. St. Chad Boscawen told me that the late Dean Howson described them to him more than twenty years ago, and that other people then knew of them as well. Mr. Piccope of course read all in the Registry volumes, and would not keep his knowledge to himself. But doubtless no prior Antiquary made such a thorough study of them as Mr. Earwaker did.

AFTERWORDS.

In the hope that Depositions like the Chester ones might be in all our old dioceses, I sent every Bishop a copy of my Child-Marriage letter in the *Academy* of Sept. 1893, and askt him to request his Registrar to tell me what Documents of the kind he had. The answers of those who replied are briefly as follows :—

Bath and Wells. "There are books or depositions from the year 1500 to the present time; but most of the earlier ones are in a very bad state from damp, the pages most rotten, and stick together; and even where that is not the case, the books are kept in abbreviated Latin, which is often faded, and almost impossible to decipher. Most of the books break to pieces when you try to separate the leaves."—Richard Harris.[1]

Durham. "The Depositions here in Ecclesiastical Suits begin about 1570. It is possible that they contain similar records to the Chester ones; but if so, it is odd if they escaped the keen eye of the late Dr. Raine, who made some use of them in Vol. 21 of the Surtees Society publications. [See p. xxiii-xxvii above.] It is always a pleasure to me to afford literary enquirers facilities; and I shall be happy to do so in Dr. Furnivall's search, of course without charge to himself."—John Booth.

Ely. See A. Gibbons's printed Calendar of the Ely Episcopal Records, Lincoln, 1891. It shows no Depositions in Trials, and only a few on other points.

Gloucester and Bristol. "The documents of this Registry can be inspected whenever you can attend, between 10 and 4, except on Thursdays, when the hours are 10 to 2. I fear there are no documents here, likely to assist you."—B. Bonnor.

Lincoln. "I have not in this Registry any such Depositions as those referred to in the printed slip enclosed with your letter."—John Swan.

Oxford. "I am not aware that there are any Depositions, or any reference to Child-Marriages here; but you or your friends are welcome to search here without fee."—Thomas M. Davenport.

Peterborough. "There are no records of Marriages of Divorced persons in this Registry. The only records of Marriages here are those contained in the Marriage-License Bonds, which commence about 1660." —H. N. Gates.

[1] Mr. Harris suggests that a short Act of Parliament or Order in Council be obtaind, to transfer all the earlier documents to the Public Record Office in London.

Rochester. "I shall be happy to produce the Register-Books for your inspection if you will give me a day's notice when you are coming. You will not find any 'Deposition-Books.' Whatever records (if there are any) of the kind you mention would be found in the general Register-Books of the periods. These books unfortunately are not indexed. The Office-hours are from 10 to 4; Saturdays, 10 to 2."—Geo. Hy. Knight.

St. Asaph. The Bishop writes: "Our Registry was burnt down in the 18th century, and all documents destroyed."

St. David's. "Diocesan Registry, 2, Notts Sq., Carmarthen. As to all public Records in my charge, which may be open to the Public, I am always prepared to let them be inspected free of fees, for literary purposes. I am quite unaware of there being in this Registry any papers that may throw light on the subject with which you are dealing. I have some Books of Records, and also some papers, relating to Consistory Court proceedings; and it would be in such only, I take it, that any reference to such subject would be found."—John H. Barker.

Sodor and Man. "There are not any Depositions of the period named in your letter, in the Bishop's Registry, relating to Child-Marriages."—Claude Connell, Advocate, Douglas, Isle of Man.

Winchester. The Registrar, Mr. Chas. Wooldridge, kindly askt Mr. Baigent, the well-known antiquary, who writes: "There are no entries or depositions as to children's marriages. The few books preservd, mostly relate to Tithe-suits & non-payment of Tithes; to Church-rates, cases of defamation and immorality—mostly as the result of Visitations—and *ex officio* proceedings: bare entries of a few lines, with entries of repeated adjournments of causes. I do not think the books contain sufficient for any one to be sent to examine them for the object Dr. Furnivall is engaged upon. There are also some entries now and then as to Recusancy, and non-attendance at church. Anything in the shape of Depositions of the 16th century rarely occurs; and I have noticed only a very few entries worth copying, except as regards local interest. There are no books of Depositions in Trials till a later date: these processes do not appear to have been preserved, or entered into books."

We know about Chester, Salisbury, and York (p. xxvii above); but still want tidings from Bangor, Canterbury, Carlisle, Chichester, Exeter, Hereford, Lichfield, Llandaff, Norwich, (St. Paul's?), and Worcester. To the Bishops or Registrars of these Dioceses, I shall apply again; but I want volunteers who'll give up their holidays, or some spare days now and then, to search the Registries and copy their likely documents. Mr. Henry Littlehales will kindly do what he can. Who else will help?

p. xxxv, &c. *Girls at* 7, 9, *and* 12. Mr. Round sends the following from 'Iohn Cowell. The Interpreter: or Booke containing the Signification of Words. Cambridge, 1607.'

leaf C 2. *Age* (*ætas*) . . . is in the common lawe particularly vsed for those especiall times, which enable men or women to do that, which before for want of age, and so consequently of iudgement, they might not do. And these times in a man be two, in a woman sixe. The age of 21. yeres is termed the full age in a man, the age of fourteene yeares, the age of discretion, *Litleton li.* 2. *ca.* 4. In a woman there are sixe seuerall ages obserued, that seuerally enable her to do sixe seuerall things. *Broke. Gard.* 7. First, at 7. yeares of age the Lord her father may distraine his tenents for ayde to marry her: for at those yeares she may consent to matrimonie, *Bract. lib.* 2. *cap.* 36. *nu.* 3. Secondly, at the age of nine yeares she is dowable: for then, or within halfe a yeare after, is she able *promereri dotem, et virum sustinere. Fleta. li.* 5. *cap.* 22. *Litleton lib. prim. cap.* 5. which *Bracton, loco citato,* doth notwithstanding limit at 12. yeares. Thirdly, at twelue yeares she is able finally to ratifie and confirme her former consent giuen to matrimonie. Fourthly, at 14. yeares she is enabled to receiue her land into her owne hands, and shall be out of ward, if she be of this age at the death of her ancestor. Fiftly, at sixteene yeares she shal be out of ward, though at the death of her auncestor she was within the age of fourteene yeres: *Instit. iure com. cap.* 24. [ed. 1727]. 'The Reason is, because then she may take a Husband able to perform Knight-Service. Sixthly, at Twenty one Years she is able to alienate her Lands and Tenements.'

As to the effect of Marriage, note that it evidently stopt Guardianship, for the Statute 13 Charles II, ch. 24, gives the Father power to appoint a Guardian to his under-age child, when such child is 'not married at the Time of his [the Father's] Death.'—Cowel: *Gardiene.*

p. xxxvi, note 2, at foot. The doctrine quoted in your note at foot of p. xxxvi was current; cp. Beaumont and Fletcher, *Four Plays in One*, scene viii of *The Triumph of Love,* where one of the "States" says, "Who ever knew a rape produce a child?" [He was a lawyer, I suppose, though.] Darley's edn., vol. ii, p. 514, col. 1. The date of this is put at before 1611.

p. xxxviii. *Child-Marriages.* Girl 8. In 1396, King Richard II (aged 30) married Isabella, the daughter of King Charles VI of France, when she was 8 years old.

p. lxiv-lxv. *The Cheshire Antiquaries.* Mr. Earwaker defends them:

"Although the Cheshire antiquaries may have neglected the printing of these particular Records, they have been by no means idle within the last 10 or 12 years. They have printed no less than 7 volumes of Indices to the old Wills, relating to Lancashire and Cheshire, now preserved at the Probate Court, Chester, thereby opening up an immense amount of most valuable information to all searchers into the past history of those two counties. They have also printed volumes of Inquisitions *post mortem,* and many other valuable Records, and so hardly deserve to be condemned in quite so unsparing a manner. They can give a good account of themselves whenever called upon to do so."—J. P. E.

CONTENTS OF THE MS. VOLUME OF CHESTER DEPOSITIONS.[1]

November 1561 to 14 March 1565-6.

A.D. 1561.

LEAF

1-2 (Piccope's No. 1). **Cowhouse.** Imperfect Depositions concerning a place called the Cowe House near Stanlowe Abbey: whether it had been part of the Demesne Land of that Abbey,[2] and free from Tythe.

3 (P.'s 2). **Child-Marriage.** Imperfect Depositions concerning the marriage of Wm. Pole or Poole (when 11) and Elizabeth Tilston (when 8). *Extracts printed below, p.* 1.

4 bk. (P.'s 3). **Adultery and Bigamy.** Depositions concerning the marriage of Ralph Holden, Esq., with Isabel Houghton during the lifetime of his first wife.* *Extracts printed below, p.* 72.

7 (P.'s 4). **Child-Marriage.** Depositions concerning the marriage of Humphrey Winstanley (12) and Alice Worsley, 17. *Printed below, p.* 2.

9 (P.'s 5). **Child-Marriage.** Further Depositions in the matter of Ralph Holden, Esq.* *Extracts printed below, p.* 72.

11 (P.'s 6). **Child-Marriage.** Depositions concerning the marriage of John Bridge (under 14) and Eliz. Ramsbottom.† *Printed below, p.* 6.

12 bk. (P.'s 7). **Child-Marriage.** Depositions concerning the marriage of George Hulse and Elizabeth Hulse. *Printed below, p.* 4.

14 (P.'s 8). **Trothplight.** Depositions concerning a Contract of Marriage between Rich. Lowe and Jane Walkden. *Printed below, p.* 56.

A.D. 1562.

15-17 (P.'s 9). **Trothplight.** Depositions concerning Contract of Marriage between Nicholas Jepson and Cath. Street. *Printed below, p.* 184.

[1] These 'Contents' are by Mr. Piccope, a former Vicar of Farndon, near Chester, with additions by Mr. Price and me. Mr. Piccope writes in his copy, "All Depositions in cases of Adultery, Fornication, and Defamation are omitted in this Index."

[2] Roger Cowper 'sais that he knewe stanlowe abbey before hit was suppressid, when thre monk*is* dwellid there; and he neu*er* kne[we] other but the Cowe house, whereas John Hine now dwellith, did belonge to Stanlowe, and was [a] house for Cattall and best*is*, and [other] thing*is* that belongid to husbandrie, [and was] of the demaine of Stanlowe' . . . (leaf 2).

LEAF

17-18. **Affiliation.** Hugh Pollet and Ellen Maddocke.[1]

18 bk. (P.'s 10). **Child-Marriage.** Further Depositions concerning the marriage of John Bridge and Eliz. Ramsbottom † (he neuer touchid her bare skin). *Printed below, p.* 7.

20-1. **Libel.** Jane David *v.* Robert Ap David. *Printed below, p.* 102.

21-23 (P.'s 11). **Inventory.** Depositions that Ann, widow and Executrix of Henry Halsall, had given in a false Inventory to the Dean of Warrington. (See no. 18, lf. 45.)

24-5 (P.'s 12). **Child-Marriage.** Ratification of Marriage of boy and girl, each 14 (married younger). Depositions as to the age of John Starkey, who had married Alice Dutton, and as to her age too. *Printed below, p.* 49.

25-27. **Libel.** Custance Wade *v.* Robert Rile. *Printed below, p.* 111.

28-29 (29 bk.: 30 front, blank) (P.'s 13). **Tithe.** Deposition concerning Tythes in Haigh, in Wigan Parish.

30 bk., ⅔rds of a page (P.'s 14). **Divorce.** Deposition (20 Feb. 1561-2) in a matter of Divorce between Ric. Livesay and Ellen Livesay. (Only that Jas. Whitonge had heard that Richard and Ellen Livesay were married in Blagburne parish church 'a yere agoe & more.')

30 bk.-31 bk. **Affiliation.** Anne Wadesworth and Jn. Whitwham. *Part printed below, p.* 85.

31 bk.-40 (P.'s 15). **Cowhouse.** Further Depositions concerning the Cowe House near Stanlow. One of these Deponents was Sir Rowland Stanley, and another "*Dominus* Ric*ardus* Coke," aged 70 years, and formerly Curate of Eastham. He mentions his going with a former Vicar to enquire of the Monks of Stanlowe concerning some Tythes, and that he knew Stanlawe before it was suppressed. The place was called the Cow House from the Monks keeping their "Kye" there. These Depositions extend over 16 pages.

40 (P.'s 16). **Child-Marriage.** Deposition concerning the marriage of Andrew Howarth and Custance Entwisel,§ Minors. *Printed below, p.* 9.

(leaves 41, 42 blank).

43-44 (P.'s 17). **Tithe.** Deposition concerning the right of John Orrel to the Tythe corn of the Hamlet of Turton, in the Parish of Bolton [le Moors].

45-6 (P.'s 18). **Inventory.** Further Depositions concerning the Inventory of Hen. Halsall. (See No. 11, lf. 21-23.)

[1] From the Deposition of Anna Smithe, of the parish of 'Mancester,' aged 22, it is clear that servants of both sexes slept in the same room.

"Ad iiij ar*ticulum*, This deponent sais that she neuer knewe or se any evill bie the said Ellin, whie she shuld be of evill lief ['about seven yere afore, she had a child by an other man,' says Randle Hannet], but only for this matter [of her child by Hugh Pollet]; neuertheles this deponent think*es* this suspic*ion* to arise, biecause ther were [lf. 18 bk.] one [or] two servinge men in Chambre w*ith* the said Ellin, havinge in their Cumpanie a gent*lewoman*, one, m*is*tres Diconson; but she think*es* in her Conscience that is no true suspic*ion*." Compare the Hilton case at Sir P. Egerton's, below, p. 87; and the notes to the MS., lf. 147 bk., 170, p. lxxxi, lxxxii, below.

LEAF
46-48 (P.'s 19). **Adultery** of Wife and Incompetency of Husband. Depositions in the matter of Margaret Alatt, the wife of Richard Pierson, seeking for a Divorce. *Printed below, p.* 73.
In this Deposition, the Parson of Little Budworth is called Vicar.[1]—P.

48-49. **Libel.** Wade *v.* Rile. Alice Rile's Answer. *Printed below, p.* 115.

49 bk.-51. **Affiliation.** Randle Fradsam *v.* Margt. Wilkinson. *Printed below, p.* 85.

51 bk.-53. **Libel.** Margaret Wirrall and Henry Fazakerley: also at lf. 61. *See extract below, p.* 117.

53 bk. (P.'s 20). **Child-Marriage.** Further Depositions concerning Andrew Haworth and Custance Entwisel.§ *Printed below, p.* 10.

54-55. **Libel.** Kath. Claiton *v.* Marg. Tailiour. *Printed below, p.* 117.

55 bk.-57 (57 bk. and 58 front, blank), (P.'s 21). **Adultery** or **Trothplight.** Depositions to prove a Contract of Marriage between Randle Gregorie and Maude Gregorie* previous to the marriage of the latter with Henry Price. *Printed below, p.* 76.

58 bk. **Libel.** Margery Morgan *v.* Philip Jenkin: Wm. Colly, as to the marriage proposed between Margery Morgan and John Gam. (See lf. 68 bk., p. 121 below.) *Printed below, p.* 120.

59 (P.'s 22). **Tithe.** Deposition in a case of refusal of Tythe of Hemp and Flax in the Parish of Warrington.†

59 bk. (P.'s 23). **Child-Marriage.** Deposition concerning the marriage of Peter Haworth and Margerie Heydock, Minors. *Printed below, p.* 11.

60 (P.'s 24). **Tithe.** Another Deposition concerning Tithe of Hemp and Flax in Warrington Parish.†

60 bk. (and at 99 bk.). **Affiliation.** Oliver Leghe *v.* Rose Sworton. *Printed below, p.* 89.

61 (P.'s 25). **Trothplight.** Further Deposition in the Case of Randle Gregorie and Maude * (and 25,* lf. 63 bk.). *Printed below, p.* 78.

61-63 bk. **Libel.** Further Depositions in Margt. Wirrall and Hy. Fazakerley (see lf. 51 bk.-53). *Printed below, p.* 204.

64 (P.'s 26). **Inventory.** Deposition of Isabel Crompton concerning an Inventory.

64 bk. (P.'s 27). **Child-Marriage.** Deposition of Eliz. Culcheth concerning her marriage with Ralph Culcheth, when children: 4 children afterwards born to them. *See extract below, p.* 51.

65-6. **Libel.** Jane David and Jn. ap John. (See lf. 75 and 86 bk.) *Printed below, p.* 103.

[1] 'Why shouldn't he be?' writes Mr. Earwaker. Little Budworth is a Vicarage. It is also a township, village and extensive parish 4 miles from Delamere station on the Cheshire Lines railway, and 4 m. E.N.E. from Torporley. It was formerly a part of the parish of Over, and is described as such in the charter for endowing the bishopric of Chester, 38 Hen. VIII. (1546-7).—Kelly. Over is a small market-town and a parish on the West bank of the river Weaver, 4½ m. W. from Middlewich, and 15 E. from Chester.—*ib.*

LEAF

66 (P.'s 28). **Tithe.** Further Depositions concerning Tythe in Warrington Parish.†

67 bk.-68 (P.'s 28*). **Tithe.** Further Depositions concerning Tythe in Warrington Parish.† (See lf. 59, P.'s No. 22.)

68 (P.'s 29). **Trothplight.** Deposition of John Smith as to Contract of Marriage with Christian Grimsditch. *Printed below, p.* 57.

68 bk.-69. **Libel.** Margery Morgan *v.* Philip Jenkin. (See also p. 120.) *Printed below, p.* 120.

69-70 (P.'s 30). **Will.** Depositions concerning the affairs of Jenkin Crompton, deceased. (Testator's wife had his chest opend, and stole his Will and other Papers.) *Printed below, p.* 130.

70 bk.-72 (P.'s 31). **Will.** Depositions concerning the Will of Rich. Pendleton. *Printed below, p.* 131.

72 bk.-73 bk. (P.'s 32). **Adultery and Separation.** Depositions concerning the separation of Reginald and Jane Downes. (He has children by 2 or 3 other women. See p. 81 below.) *Printed below, p.* 202.

73 bk.-74 (P.'s 33). **Child-Marriage.** Depositions in the Divorce suit to annul the marriage of Ralph Whittle and Jane Leyland, Minors, married when both were above 11, and under 12.
See extracts below, p. 12.

75-77. **Libel.** John ap John *v.* Jane David. *Printed below, p.* 105.

77 bk. **Adultery.** Elizabeth Shotilworth's confession of Adultery.
Printed below, p. 80.

78 front (P.'s 34). **Tithe.** Depositions as to the right of the Vicar of Aldley (Audley, co. Stafford) to Tythe in the Parish of Church Lawton (Chester), and the right of the said Vicar to "Tythe Herbage" in the Parish of Aldley. (See lf. 103 bk.-105, Piccope's No. 50.)

78 bk.-79 (P.'s 35). **Tithe.** Depositions as to personal Tythes payable to the Farmer of the Tythe of Plempstow.

79-80 bk. (P.'s 36). **Child-Marriage.** Depositions concerning the marriage of John Andrew and Ellen Dampart (Davenport), Minors.
Printed below, p. 12.

80 bk.-81. **Affiliation.** John Cotgreve *v.* Margaret Monelay. (See leaves 84 bk., 90, 105, 120 bk., 124 bk.) *Printed below, p.* 91.

81 bk.-82. **Libel.** Lady Anne Houghton *v.* John Hoterhall, for saying she was not the lawful wife of Sir Richard Houghton.[1]

[1] 22nd Oct. 1562. William Skelicorne of the Parish of Kirkh*am*, Gentleman, aged 26, "sais that he neu*er* h*a*rd my Lady Houghton but to be eu*er* of gode name & fame; and so this depone*nt* think*es* her worthie to be"; and "yif such word*es* of sclaunder were spoken, she hath good cause of complaint." Edward Houghton, Gentleman, of the Parish of Standish, aged 55, states that he never "hard John Hotersall, articulate, or any other p*er*son, speake or say that my Lady Houghton was not Lawfull wief to S*ir* Ric*hard* Houghton, afore this sute com*m*ensid; but that he hard one of my Lady Houghtons men say nowe, that the said Hotersall alledgid [it] in a play [in fun] at Lanc*aster*." Sir Richard Bretten appears also in this suit for Lady Houghton.—W. H. P.

LEAF
82-84 (P.'s 37). **Trothplight.** Depositions as to a Contract of Marriage between Morgan Edmund and Elizabeth Bird (see P.'s Nos. 46 and 47). *Printed below, p.* 187.

84 bk.-85. **Libel.** Cotgreve and Moneley. *Printed below, p.* 91.

85 bk.-86 (P.'s 38). **Trothplight.** Another Deposition in the case of Morgan Edmund and Elizabeth Bird (*see p.* 93). *Printed below, p.* 191.

86 bk.-87. **Libel.** Jane David *v.* John ap John. *Printed below, p.* 108.

88 (P.'s 39). **Child-Marriage.** Further Deposition in the case of Andrew and Dampart (Davenport): see lf. 79. *See below, p.* 15.

88 bk.-89 (P.'s 40). **Child-Marriage.** Depositions in the Divorce of the Child-marriage of Robert Talbot and Grace Boys, Minors: she 9-10, he 12-13. *Extract below, p.* 16.

89 (P.'s 41). **Church and Curate maintenance.** Depositions concerning the liability of the occupiers of Tenements in the chapelry of Witton to maintain the Church and Curate at that place, tho' the occupiers should reside out of the Parish. The rate in Hartford was 8*d.* in the pound on the Rental.

90 front. **Affiliation.** John Cotgreve and Margaret Moneley. *Printed below, p.* 94.

90 bk.-93 (P.'s 42). **Tithe.** Depositions as to the right of Sir Thomas Langton to certain Tythes in Walton Demesne. They were claimed by Sir Thos. Gerrard under a Lease from Sir Thos. Talbot, who held by Lease from the Abbot and Convent of Whalley (Lancashire).

93-94. **Affiliation.** Wm. Clare *v.* Ellen Gardiner. *Printed below, p.* 97.

94 bk.-95 bk. (P.'s 43). **Tithe.** Depositions as to the customs of Tithing Hay in the Parish of Rostherne (Cheshire).

95 bk.-96 bk. (P.'s 44). **Restitution of Conjugal Rights.** Depositions concerning the marriage of Thos. Stanley and Margaret Southworth, Minors,§ and their being separated or Divorced before the Parson of Bury, Lancashire. *Printed below, p.* 52.

97 (P.'s 45). **Tithe.** Depositions concerning the manner of Tything in Budworth Parish, and the illegal carrying away of Tythe.

98. **Libel.** Matilda Holme *v.* Elizabeth Tilston. (E. T. cald Maude Holme 'Roberte Soundes hoore.') *See extract below, p.* 121.

98 bk.-99 bk. (P.'s 46). **Trothplight.** Further Depositions in the case of Morgan Edmund and Eliz. Bird. (See No. 37.) *Printed below, p.* 192.

99 bk.-100. **Affiliation.** Oliver Legh *v.* Rose Sworton. *Printed below, p.* 89.

100 bk.-101 (P.'s 47). **Contract of Marriage, Tokens &c. (turquoise Ring).** Further Depositions concerning Harry Dillon and Elizabeth Bird. (See lf. 82-4, No. 37.) *Printed below, p.* 194.

102. **Impediment in Wife.** Henry Blagburne. Deposition as to an impediment in his Wife, and his dealing with 2 other women. *Printed below, p.* 137.

LEAF

102 (P.'s 48). **Tithe.** Deposition as to the Tythe of Hay in Tatton, in Rostherne Parish. (See lf. 107 bk., Piccope's No. 52.)

103 (P.'s 49). **Restitution of Conjugal Rights.** Further Deposition concerning the marriage of Thos. Stanley and Margaret Southworth.§ (See lf. 95 bk.) *Printed below, p.* 55.

103. **Adultery.** Rafe Yate *v.* Joanna Yate: her alledgd Adultery with Rafe Smith.[1] (See also lf. 115 bk., Piccope's No. 54.)

103 bk.-105 (P.'s 50). **Tithe.** Depositions concerning "Tythe Herbage" to the Vicar of Aldley (Audley, co. Staffs.). See lf. 78, Piccope's No. 34.

105-6 (?) **Affiliation.** John Cotgreve *v.* Margaret Monelay. *Printed below, p.* 95.

105 bk.-106.† **Libel.** Matilda Holme *v.* Elizabeth Tilston. *Printed below, p.* 121.

107 (P.'s 51). **Adultery and Separation.** Downes's answer to his wife's charge. (See too p. 202-4, below.) *Printed below, p.* 81.

107 bk. (P.'s 52). **Tithe.** Another Deposition concerning Hay Tithe in Rostherne Parish. (See leaf 102, Piccope's No. 48.)

108. **Tithe.** Two Depositions as to Tithe Geese and Pigs in the parish of Clitheroe, a chapelry of Whalley.[2]—Piccope. *Printed below, p.* 138.

109 (P.'s 53). **Right to attend a Church.** A Commission from William (Chadderton), Bishop of Chester, to John Fernhed, Rector of Limme, Edward Newson, Vicar of Prestbury, and Humphrey Buron, Curate of Chedill, to examine witnesses concerning a claim on the part of the Inhabitants of Baguley, in Bowdon Parish, to attend service and receive the Sacraments at Northenden Church. Dated 24 Oct., 1562.

[1] 3rd Dec. 1562. Thomas Huyton, of the Parish of Wigan, aged 50, [3] "sais that Rafe Yate and Joan Yate were maried together, and vsid either other as man and wief shuld do, for ix or x yeres space, till after the said Rafe Yate had her in suspic*ion* of Rafe Smith, and she went away from her husband. beynge askid 'what is the cause he is brought in as witnes for'; he saies, 'apon a tyme, about xij moneth ago, hard bie Leighe church, he mett the said Joan and Rafe Smithe, like x' road [rods or perches] a-sonder, in a morning, like an howre afore day; and this depone*nt* askid the said Rafe Smith, whether he went; and he said, to Lashawe; and the said Joan followid hym.' but he saies, 'he neither see them together suspiciously otherwise then [he] hath deposid, nor knewe of any evill conversac*ion* betwix them, but as this depone*nt* hath hard that the said Rafe Yate toke the said Rafe Smith & his wief in his own house together, w*ith* the dores closid against them.'"

[4] Robert Cowdale, aged 38, relates that Henry Haliwall told before a gret nomber in Mr. Urmistons house, that about iij or iiij^or yere ago, he found Joanne Yate and Rafe Smith together in a Corne field; but whether they were sett downe or laid downe, this depone*nt* hard hym not declare. and the said Smith said to Haliwall, "I pray the, play the good fellowe," and so dep*ar*tid away; and the said Haliwall and she went home together; and the said Haliwall said to her, he wold declare what he had sene; and she said she wold geve hym a shert to sey nothinge. and the said Haliwall wold have had his pleasure of her; but she grauntid hym not. and this tale he told afore the said company, im*m*ediately the day after; but *per contra*, this depone*nt* knowes nothinge.—W. H. P.

[2] Lancashire. Kelly says, under Clitheroe, that St. Mary Magdalene, now a parish, was formerly a chapelry in the civil parish of Whalley.

[3] leaf 103. [4] leaf 103, bk.

LEAF

110-115. The Depositions which follow this Commission are very interesting and curious.—Piccope. *See an extract printed below, p.* 139.

115 bk. (P.'s 54). **Adultery.** (See lf. 103.) Deposition [14 Dec. 1562] for a Divorce between Rafe Yate and Joan Yate. [She has been seen suspiciously in an Orchard with Rafe Smith, and he has been seen to come suspiciously half a dozen times from her house when her husband was away.]

A.D. 1563.

116 (P.'s 55). **Will?** Deposition concerning a Panne (worth 4*s.*, to which the holders say they have the right; sold by deceast during her life to Elizabeth Dudson for 20*s.*) and a Kirtell.

116 bk.-117 (P.'s 56). **Nuncupative Will.** Deposition concerning the Nuncupative Will of Roger Hodson. *Printed below, p.* 132.

117 bk. (P.'s 57). **Marriage without Banns or License.** Deposition by Hamlet Tailiour, Curate of Northwich, as to his having married George Johnson to Ellen Sudlowe, without proclamation of Banns or the Bishop's Dispensation.[1]

117 bk.-119 (P.'s 58). **Child-Marriage.** Depositions concerning the marriage of Randle More and Margery Vernon, Minors. *Printed below, p.* 16-18.

119-120 (P.'s 59). **Child-Marriage.** Depositions concerning the marriage of Minors, Peter Hope and Alice Ellis. (See No. 61.)* *Printed below, p.* 19.

120 bk.-121. **Affiliation.** John Cotgreve and Margaret Moneley. *Printed below, p.* 95.

121-122 (P.'s 60). **Trothplight.** Depositions concerning a Contract of Marriage between George Johnson and Ann Yate. *Printed below, p.* 57.

123. **Child-Marriage and Separation.** Deposition by Thos. Dampart as to his marriage with his wife Elizabeth Page. *Printed below, p.* 22.

123 bk. **Marriage out of Church.** Answers of John Heighfeld and John Clarke,[2] as to the former's marriage in a private house, with Margaret Edge or Ellis.

123 bk.-124. **Evasion of Trothplight.** Depositions as to the Marriage of Thomas Snelson and Joan Willy out of their Parish. (See p. 59-61 below.) *Printed below, p.* 196.

[1] 21st February, 1562-3. Hamlet Tailio*ur* Clerk, Curate of Witton, says in his defence, that the proceedings against him in this instance "shuld be but a check of my Lord for it; and [promised] amendment not to do the Like again, or els he wold not have done it yf [he had known] the ponishm*ent* had bene so gret."—W. H. P.

[2] **Answer of John Heighfeld,** (March 1563) that he was married to "M*ar*garet Edge, al*ias* Heighfeld, nowe his wief, by v*er*tue of a Licence to hym directed in that behalfe; and . . . they were not maried in the church, but in an honest manes house,—biecause his wief was somwhat sicke,—before honest witnes; and that they receyvid the Co*mmun*ion at Pever the next sonday."

Answer of John Clarke. He "saies, that of simplicity he sufferid John) Heigh feld and M*ar*garet Edge to be maried in his house, biecause the Curate of Rostorne said he had a Licence to discharge hym w*i*th."

LEAF

124 (P.'s 61). **Child-Marriage.** Further Depositions concerning the marriage of Peter Hope and Alice Mathue, Minors.*

Printed below, p. 21.

124 bk. **Affiliation.** John Cotgreve and Margaret Monelay.

Printed below, p. 96.

125 (P.'s 62). **Evasion of Trothplight: Marriage out of own Parish.** Further Deposition concerning the marriage of Thos. Snelson and Joane Wily out of their parish, at Rishton, 'through the p*ro*curemen*t* of Thomas Snelson; and she thought it was not so gret Daung*er* as she thinkes it nowe be. and forther she saies, the banes were aske twise; and the iij[d] tyme, Ellin Ricrofte forbade the same.' (See her Trothplight case, p. 59-61.) *Printed below, p.* 196.

125 (P.'s 63). **Marriage out of own Parish.** Deposition concerning the marriage of Gilbert Wright and Eliz. Whatton out of their own Parish. She "saies that she was married to Gilberte Wright in Formby Chapell, bie the Curate there, w*i*thout banes asking there, or in ther owne p*ar*ish of Ormskirk, and w*i*thout any Licence. beynge askid, 'whie they went out of their owne p*ar*ish to marry in any other place,' she saies 'it was biecause of her frendes, that were against her, that she shuld not marry hym; and not for any title or Claime that, to this re*spo*ndent*es* knoledge, that any woman had against hym: what Gilbert, her husband, did it for, she knowes not; but this re*spo*ndent saies she will obey the Lawe; and yf she be not p*ro*vid to be his Lawfull wief, she wilbe Content to do that w*hi*ch shalbe thought reasonable.'" (No doubt a case of Evasion of Trothplight, like Snelson's. See Wright's Trothplight to Margery Barton, on lf. 136, Piccope's No. 72, note 1, p. lxxix below.)

125 bk. (P.'s 64). **Will.** Deposition of Catherine Eiton, alias Billinge, concerning her husband's Will.[1]

125 bk.-126 (P.'s 65). **Child-Marriage, Ratification.** Depositions concerning the marriage of Thos. Wicksted and Elline Ball, Minors: he 10, she 9. *Printed below, p.* 51.

126 bk.-127 bk. (P.'s 66). **Tithe.** Depositions concerning the subtracting of Tythe of Rye in Neston Parish.

127 bk.-128 (P.'s 67). **Tithe.** Depositions concerning Tythe in Budworth Parish.

128. **Libel.** Arrowsmith *v.* Horton. Depositions that Richard Horton said Alice Arrowsmith was 'naughtie, and had bene nought with ij or

[1] 29th April, 1563. Katherine Eiton, alias Billinge, in her answers, says, 'that the Testam*ent* was provid, and she was sworne well and truly to execute the said Testam*ent* and eu*ery* clause therin, accordinge to the extent of *the* good*es*, when she toke thadministracion of the goodles apon her; that ther was xl m*arkes* bequeathid to Anne, the doughter of John Tailio*ur*, bie the said Testam*ent*, w*hi*ch she [Kath. Eiton] hath not paid, nor yet any p*ar*cell therof; but [she] myndeth to pay it as sone as she can be able. and concerninge the sheet*es*, &[c], she knowith not that they be in her husband*es* will, nor no*n* other will that she knowes of, that she, this depone*nt*, is bound to p*er*forme. That she was not req*ui*red to pay the xl m*arkes*, nor the other thing*es* libellate, at any tyme to her knoledge, before she was callid to this Court.'

LEAF
iij men besides the said Ric*hards* brother' Roger, who wanted to marry her, she being Rafe Goodman's servant.

129 (67*). **Inventory.** Depositions in Henry Whitbe and Robert Tench *v.* Elizabeth Page, widow, as to the inclusion of six silver spoons, cattle, &c., in the Inventory of Rafe Page.§

130. **Tithe.** Depositions as to the non-payment of Tythes by Thos. Masterson. No tithe of Milk payable. Budworth Parish.

130 bk.-131 bk. (P.'s 68). **Child-Marriage.** Depositions concerning the marriage of Thos. Fletcher and Ann Whitfield, Minors. *Printed below, p.* 23.

131 bk. **Will.** Deposition in Tailiour *v.* Eiton, ? as to a Legacy.

131 bk.-132 bk. (P.'s 69). **Trothplight.** Depositions concerning a Contract of marriage between Thos. Snelson and Ellen Ricroft. (See lf. 123 bk., 133, and p. 196 below.) *Printed below, p.* 59.

133. **Trothplight.** Further Deposition in the Trothplight case of Ellen Ricroft and Thomas Snelson. *Printed below, p.* 60.

133 bk.-134 bk. (P.'s 70). **Inventory.** § Further Deposition concerning the Inventory of Rafe Page. Tench and Whitbe *v.* Widow Page.

134 bk.-135 bk. (P.'s 71). **Tithe.** Depositions concerning the subtraction of small Tythe in Bowdon Parish, and the Custom of gathering them.

136 (P.'s 72). ‖ **Trothplight.** Deposition concerning a promise of marriage by Gilbert Wright to Margery Barton.[1] (See his Marriage to Elizabeth Whatton, lf. 125, Piccope's No. 63.)

136-137 (most of 137 front is blank) (P.'s 73). **Trothplight.** Deposition concerning a Contract of Marriage between Thos. Torbock and Alice Wodfall. *Printed below, p.* 196.

137 bk.-138 (P.'s 74). ‖ **Trothplight.** Further Deposition in the case of Wright and Barton, leaf 136.

138. **Affiliation.** John Dutton *v.* Kate Jenkin. Depositions of Joan Fisher ('Peter had rid a pack a pack on the said Kate'), and of Katherine and Elizabeth Sharp, on lf. 138 bk.[2]

[1] Gilberte Wright deposes, on 25 June 1563, that "he had Co*mmuni*cacion w*i*th Margery Barton, as younge folk*es* ar vsid and wont to have; but neu*er* they made co*n*tract or troth-plighting." Also "that the word*es* of mariage that were spoken betwixe them parties libellate, were spoken on the back side of W*illia*m Asmall viij or ix' yeres ago; the w*hi*ch word*es* were: this R*es*pondent said that 'he wold marry the said M*ar*gery, and no*n* other.' & the said M*ar*gery said, 'and I will marry you and no*n* other.'"

[2] 'Joan*na* Fisher' deposes, on 3 July 1563, "that the said Kat*e* is of suspectid name and fame, biecause she hath had a child before; and also she hath hard the wief of W*illia*m Kitchin, who is suster to Peter Rodon, say that her brother Peter had Rid a pack a pack on the said Kat*e*, in the field beneth Pulf[o]r*des* house /"

On leaf 138 back, Katharine Sharpe deposes, on 8 July 1563, that "she knowes not that Edward Collen articulate had carnall dole w*i*th the said Kate Jenkin; but this deponent saies, that about Michaelmas last, she hard the said Collen say, that 'whosoeu*er* did beate the bush, John) Dutton shuld have the bird*es*.'" And Elizabeth Sharpe "saies that a young man callid Ed*ward* Collen did resort into the Company of the said Kate, insomuche that it was susposid that the said Collen had got her

LEAF
139-140 (P.'s 75). **Tithe.** Further Depositions concerning Tythe in Neston Parish.

141 (P.'s 76). **Tithe.** Further Depositions concerning Tythes in Bowdon Parish.

141 bk.-142 (P.'s 77). || **Trothplight.** Further Deposition in the matter of Wright and Barton.[1]

142 (P.'s 78). **Tithe.** Deposition of William Arderne concerning his refusal of Tythe in Bowdon Parish.

143 (P.'s 79). **Trothplight.** Further Depositions concerning contract of marriage between Snelson and Ricroft. *Printed below, p.* 61.

143 bk. (P.'s 80). **Will.** Deposition concerning the Will of Agnes Sutton.

144 (P.'s 81). **Nuncupative Will.** Depositions concerning the Nuncupative Will of Humphrey Barneshau.

145. **Libel.** Isabella Nicolson *v.* Henry Nicolson, for calling her 'hoore,' and saying she was with child.[2]

*w*ith child before any other, in-somuche that the said Collen made his bost, that 'whosou*er* beate the bush, Joh*n* Dutton shall have the bird*es*.'" Also "this deponent saies the said Kat*e* had a child before / and she hath hard it reportid in the towne of Holt, that Peter Rodon had to do *w*ith the said Kate."

Joseph, in the *Coventry Plays* (No. XII, l. 82), uses *bough* for *bush*, when telling his wife Mary that no Angel was the father of the child in her womb:

It was su*m* boy began þis game,
þat clothyd was clene and gay;
& ȝe ȝeve hym now an aungel*e* name!
Alas! alas & welaway,
þ*at* evyr this game betydde!
A, dame! what thought haddyst þou?
her*e* may aƚƚ men þis proverbe trow,
þ*at* many a man doth bete þe bow,
Another man hath þe brydde.

At the Trial of Joseph and Mary (No. XIV, l. 276-9) the first Detractor makes the old suggestion of a Snow-father:

In Feyth, I suppose þat þis woman slepte
W*ith*owtyn aƚƚ coverte, whyll*e* þ*at* it dede snowe;
And a flake þ*er*of into hyr*e* mowthe crepte;
& þ*er*of þe chylde in hyr*e* wombe doth growe.

[1] 22nd July, 1563°. Elizabeth Moels, of Ormskirk, aged 57, [3]saies, that the p*ar*ties libellate did make a contract of m*at*rimony on the backside of W*illi*am Asmall, clark, of Ormiskirk, this depon*ent* beynge p*re*sent, and beynge callid bie Gilb*er*te Wright, to be there for that purpose; and the co*n*tract was made apon a sonday, about Lent viij yeres shalbe the sonday afore Lent next. she sais, she cann not reherse the word*es* well; but the said Gilberte, holdinge M*ar*gery bie the hand, said, "I, Gilb*er*te, take the, M*ar*gery, to my weddid wief." & the said M*ar*gery said likewise, she holding the said Gilb*er*te by the hand. and they witnes, seynge them handfast and trought-plightid, thought it ynoughe; but Gilb*er*te wold be more sure, and sware apon a boke w*hi*ch the clark, at the instance of the said Gilb*er*te, send for. and the said M*ar*gery and Gilb*er*te sware apon the boke; & the said Gilb*er*t swore he wold neu*er* tak other woman; & the said M*ar*gery swore she wold neu*er* [4]wedd any other man but the said Gilb*er*te. and after that, they kissed, and so went in to the clark*es* house, and Dined together after. beynge exa*mine*d, 'howe she remembres the day of the co*n*tract, & the yere'; she sais, 'biecause her husband died about the same tyme a little before.' Ad iij, nescit depon*ere*. Ad iiij, this depon*ent* sais, that 'all the cuntry therabout Ormiskirk, that knewe the p*ar*ties, repute them for man & wief afore god.' Ad v, dicit eunde*m* fore ver*um*. Ad vi, credit eund*em* fore ver*um*. Ad vlt*imum*, dicit p*re*deposit*a* p*er* ea*m* fore vera, &c.—W. H. P.

[2] Roderick Lowe, on 21 Oct. 1563, "says that he neu*er* hard Henry Nicolson nor Alis Wilcokson call the said Isabell 'hoore,' or els say she was *w*ith Child, or any

[3] leaf 141, back (Piccope's No. 77). [4] leaf 142.

LEAF
146 (P.'s 82). **Child-Marriage.** Deposition concerning the marriage of Roger Massey and Jane Somner, minors. *Printed below, p.* 25.

146 bk.-147. Copulation of Margery Mutchell with Geffrey Brerton.[1]

147 bk.-148 bk. **Affiliation.** John Thirlewind and Elizabeth Crosse: her 7th child is his. *See extract below, p.* 99.

148 bk.-149 (P.'s 83). **Tithe.** Depositions concerning the refusal of Tythe in Farndon Parish.

149 bk.-150 (P.'s 84). **Nuncupative Will.** Depositions concerning the Nuncupative Will of Margaret Swetnam.

150 bk.-151. **Trothplight.** Hugh Pollett *v.* Elizabeth Eccles, spinster, alias Burton, widow. Contract of Marriage.§ *Printed below, p.* 62.

151 bk.-152 (P.'s 85). **Tithe.** Deposition (16 Dec. 1563) concerning the tything of Hay in Eccleston Parish.

152. **Will.** Depositions as to the character of Laurence Swetnam's witnesses in a Will case.[2]

A.D. 1564.

153 (P.'s 86). **Tithe.** Depositions (18 Jan. 1563-4) concerning the refusal of Tythe Corn, and the custom of Tything, in Wigan Parish.

153 bk.-154 bk. **Trothplight.** § Further Depositions in Hugh Pollett *v.* Elizabeth Eccles alias Burton. (See lf. 150 bk.) *Printed below, p.* 62.

such thinge tendinge to the diffamac*i*on; but saies that the said Isabell was bigg & gret in the belly, in so much that she was thought to be w*i*th Child, of her ney-bo*ures*. and after, she fell sick; and w*i*thin iij or iiij[or] daies after, was of small belly againe; and her swellinge was gone, & [she] came abrode: vpon w*h*ich occasion, Henry Nicolson desired M*aste*r Hide, one of the best in their p*ar*ish, to knowe what was the cause of her sicknes, and whie the dores were made. and this deponent hard Mr. Hide say to the said Henry Nicolson, that he wold declare nothinge till he were callid before som*me* that hath auc*tori*tie to examyn hym."

[1] On 29 Oct. 1562, Richard Brerton "sais he sawe M*ar*gery Mitchell sins sonday last; and he hath sene Geffrey Brerton, esq*uie*r, in company w*i*th the said M*ar*gery since the last assises at Chester . . . [and] at meate, drink, and in bed togethers, [and] he hath sene the [said] m*ar*gery in Tatton Hall diu*er*se tymes sins the said assises" . .

Edmund Dudson "saies he hath sene the said Geffrey and M*ar*gery in bed together at Tatton Hall sins the tyme articulate, and hath sene them eatinge and drinkinge together . . And he saies he hath brought the said M*ar*gery meate & drink dyverse tymes." There is nothing to show why this suit was brought.

[2]Examinacio testium in ca*usa* testa*men*taria producta*rum* ex parte Laurenc*ii* Swetna*m*, sub c*er*t*is* excepc*io*nibus oblatis con*tra* testes Thomae Swetnam, capt*a* die et an*no* p*re*d*ictis*. [16 Dec. 1563.]

Richard Ridgway, of the parish of 'P*re*sbury,' aged 28, "thinketh Eliz*abet*h Tailio*ur* is an honest woman; but her husband is tenaunt to Tho*mas* Swetna*m* . . . dicit, that Joan Newall is seru*au*nt to the said Tho*mas*, and hath bene a good while . . . . . think*es* Sir Rob*er*te Plant much favoreth the p*ar*te of Tho*mas* Swetna*m*; yet he think*es* he wold not, for his friendship, breake his othe . . . saies that M*ar*garet Ball hath had iiij[or] Children, gotten out of wedlock, and is w*i*th child w*i*th y[e] v[th] . . . . that M*ar*garet Burges is nowe s*er*uant to Tho*mas* Swetna*m*, & hath had a child in fornicac*i*on [lf. 152 bk.] . . . that Elein Hethcote was s*er*u*au*nt to Tho*mas* Swetna*m* ij[o] or iij yeres ago, & she had ij[o] children out of wedlock" . . . "bie one Norman Sill." Edward Claiton, 22, of Presbury, gives like evidence.

LEAF

154 bk.-156 (P.'s 87). **Tithe.** Further Depositions concerning the above Tithing in Wigan. (lf. 153.)

156. **Will.** Declaration by Richard Leigh that certain words were not in his Father's Will.

156 bk.-157 bk. (P.'s 88). **Child-Marriage.** Depositions concerning the marriage of John Somerforth and Jane Brereton. *Printed below, p.* 25.

158-159 (P.'s 89). **Tithe.** Depositions concerning the custom of Tything in Davenham Parish.

160-162 (P.'s 90). **Tithe.** Further Depositions concerning the above.

162 bk.-164 (P.'s 91). **Trothplight.** Depositions concerning a contract of marriage between Alex. Winstanley and Ellen Sonkie. *Printed below, p.* 198.

164 bk.-165. **Libel.** Constance Frost *v.* Wm. Ball and others, for saying she had 2 husbands, and was 'a very hoore.' (*See 3rd Exam., p.* 122.) *Printed below, p.* 208.

165 (P.'s 92). **Child-Marriage.** Further Depositions concerning the marriage of Jn. Somerford and Jane Brereton. *Printed below, p.* 27.

166 (P.'s 93). **Will.** Deposition concerning the Will of William Jenkinson, alias Fletcher.

166 bk.-167. **Libel.** Constance Frost *v.* Wm. Ball and others. Further Depositions. (*See the 3rd Exam., p.* 122.) *Printed below, p.* 208.

168-170. **Adultery.** Wm. Eiton *v.* Mary Eiton. *Printed below, p.* 82.

170. **Affiliation.** Robert Walton *v.* Anne Doxie,[1] Copulation with John Cliff.§ *See below, p.* 100.

171 (P.'s 94). **Child-Marriage.** Deposition concerning the marriage of Lawrence Parker and Jenet Parker, minors.* *See Extract below, p.* 28.

171 bk.-176 (P.'s 95). **Tithe.** Depositions concerning the Tythe of Geese in the Parish of Lowe; and a dispute between Sir Thos. Gerrard and Sir Tho. Langton as to the Tythe.

176 bk. (P.'s 96). **Child-Marriage.** *Further Depositions concerning the marriage of Lawrence Parker and Jenet Parker. *See Extract below, p.* 28.

177-178. **Affiliation.** Robert Walton and Anna Doxie. Two men 'burnid' or poxt by Anna: others have had her. *See below, p.* 100.

[1] Depo*sicio*nes testiu*m* in ca*usa* reclamac*ionis* purgac*ionis* ex p*ar*te Rob*er*ti Walton, cont*ra* An*nam* Doxie; capte cora*m* *M*agis*t*ro Cheta*m*, p*ri*mo Junij 1564.

Margeria Wagge, of the Parish of Astbury, aged 30, "saies that she, being *seru-aunt* (and yet is) at the house of Rob*er*t Walton, about the Thursdaie after the Roode daie was xij moneth, did se John Cliff in a secrete Chamb*er* of the house bie hym self. but this depon*ent* saies, she did se no bodie w*i*th hym; but this depon*ent* saies that Ann Doxie was spin*n*inge there at that tyme." . . .

Ellen Coke of 'Asbury,' aged 20, "saies that she, being*e* seru*au*nt vnto Rob*er*t Walto*n*, as yet she is, was send about her M*ist*ris busines, as she rememb*er*s, the Thursdaie afore Midsom*er* daie shalbe xij moneth. And when this depon*ent* came home in the night, this depon*ent* went into a Chamb*er* of the said house, where seru*aunte*s were wont to Resort; and there she found*e* lienge apon a bed, Joh*n* Cliff and Anne Doxie; and a coue*r*let cast oue*r* them. but what they did, this deponent cannot tell /"

LEAF

178 bk.-179. ‡**Libel.** Constance Frost *v.* Wm. Ball and others. Further Depositions. *Printed below, p.* 122.

179-181 (P.'s 97). **Will.** Depositions concerning the Will and Inventory of Lawrence Rope.

181. §**Affiliation.** Robert Walton and Anne Doxie (Non-committal Answers of John Cliff and Oliver Vaudrey). *See below, p.* 101.

181 bk. 182 (P.'s 98). **Child-Marriage.** Depositions concerning the marriage of Henry Whittacres and Margaret Hawcks, Minors. *Printed below, p.* 29.

183. ‡**Libel.** Constance Frost *v.* Wm. Ball and others. Further Depositions. (See p. 208 below.) *See below, p.* 123.

184 (P.'s 99). **Will. Low Valuation of Goods of Testator.** Further Deposition in the matter of Lawrence Rope. *Printed below, p.* 133.

184 bk.-186 (P.'s 100). **Seat in Church.** Depositions concerning a form or Kneeling place in Malpas Church, claimed as belonging to Buckley Hall.§

186-187 (P.'s 101). **Tithe.** Depositions concerning the refusal of Tythes to the Rector of Middleton.

188. **Affiliation.** Thomas Underwood and Ellen Key. *Printed below, p.* 101.

189 (P.'s 102). **Nuncupative Will.** Deposition concerning the Nuncupative Will of William Birchall.

189 bk.-192 (P.'s 103). **Seat in Church.** Further Depositions concerning the form in Malpas Church.§

192-193. **Adultery.** Wm. Eiton (Heyton) *v.* Mary Eiton (Heyton, See lf. 168). Further Depositions. *Printed below, p.* 84.

193 bk. ‡**Libel.** Constance Frost *v.* Wm. Ball and others. Further Deposition. *Printed below, p.* 123.

193 bk.-194. **Libel.** Jone Ashley *v.* Margaret Stele and others. *Printed below, p.* 123.

195 (P.'s 104). **Child-Marriage.** Depositions concerning the marriage of Robert Mason and Margaret Dudgale, Minors.* (See No. 104, lf. 97.) *Printed below, p.* 30.

196. **Libel.** †Elizabeth Basnet *v.* Anna Venables, for calling her 'hoore.' *Printed below, p.* 209.

197. **Child-Marriage and Divorce.** Answer of Margaret Mason (born Dugdale).* *Printed below, p.* 31.

197-8. (P.'s 105). **Trothplight.** Depositions concerning a Contract between Rich. Pickforth and Katherine Man. *Printed below, p.* 63.

199. †**Libel.** Elizabeth Basnet *v.* Anna Venables. Further Depositions. *Printed below, p.* 209.

200. ‡**Libel.** Jone Ashley *v.* Margaret Stele. *Printed below, p.* 124.

201. **Will.** Depositions as to the right of Margaret Crowshawe, and her husband William Crowshawe, to property (2 houses) under a Will.§

LEAF

201 bk.-202. **Identity.** Deposition, that Jas. Chadwick's daughter has married Robert, the son of John Butterworth, the elder, who is uncle of Charles Butterworth.

202-203 bk. ‡**Libel.** Joan Ashley *v.* Margaret Stele and others. Further Depositions (7 Dec. 1564). *Printed below, p.* 125.

A.D. 1565.

203 bk.-204. **Will.** §Margaret and Wm. Crowshawe's right to 2 houses under a Will. Further Depositions.

204-205 bk. (P.'s 106). **Child-Marriage and Divorce.** Depositions concerning the marriage of Thos. Bentam and Ellen Bentam (born Bolton), Minors. *Printed below, p.* 32.

206. **Libel.** Ellen Gillam *v.* Agnes Gillam, for calling her a 'hoore.'§ *Printed below, p.* 126.

206 bk.-207. **Libel.** Isabell Pattel *v.* Rafe Hare, for calling her 'a hoore and a thief.' *Printed below, p.* 128.

207 bk.-209 (P.'s 107). **Tithe.** Depositions concerning the refusal of Tithes in Whitegate Parish.‖

209 bk. §**Libel.** Ellen Gillam *v.* Agnes Gillam. Further Depositions. *Printed below, p.* 127.

210 (P.'s 108). **Sanity and unexecuted Will of Testatrix.** Depositions concerning the sanity of Alice Broadhurst, a Testatrix. *Printed below, p.* 134.

211-213 (P.'s 109). ‖**Tithe.** Further Depositions concerning the Tithe of Whitegate.

213 bk.-214. §**Libel.** Ellen Gillam *v.* Agnes Gillam. Further Deposition, Eliz. Walley's. *Printed below, p.* 127.

214 bk.-215 (P.'s 110). **Child-Marriage.** Depositions concerning the marriage of Rafe Fyshe and Kath. Bolton, Minors. *Printed below, p.* 33.

215 bk.-220 bk. (P.'s 111). **Chapel in a Church.** Depositions concerning the right of Ed. Leigh, Esq[re], to a Chapel in Bowden Church.

221. §**Libel.** Ellen Gillam *v.* Agnes Gillam. Further Depositions. *Printed below, p.* 127.

221-222 (P.'s 112). **Inventory.** R. Ithell *v.* W. Horton. Depositions concerning Mrs. Warbara [? Werburgh: St. Werburgh] Horton, widow of John Horton, deceased, having made a false Inventory.†

222 bk.-224 (P.'s 113). **Trothplight.** Depositions concerning the marriage of Tho. Sothworth and Margaret Ward. *Printed below, p.* 65.

224 bk.-225 (P.'s 114). **Child-Marriage.** Depositions concerning the marriage of Alex. Osboston and Margaret Hothersall, Minors.‡ *Printed below, p.* 34.

225 bk. (P.'s No. 114*). **Inventory.** R. Ithell *v.* Warborow. Deposition as to a bull, brass, and pewter.†

LEAF
226 (P.'s 115). **Child-Marriage.** ‡ Further Depositions concerning the above case, marriage of Alex. Osboston and Margaret Hothersall. (lf. 224, P.'s No. 114). *Printed below, p.* 183.

226 bk.-227 (P.'s 116). **Trothplight.** Depositions concerning a marriage between Roger Bybbye and Ellen Manwaring. *Printed below, p.* 67.

228-238 (P.'s 117). **Will.** Depositions concerning the making of the Will of William Coke.

239-240.§ **Libel.** Ellen Gillam *v.* Agnes Gillam. Further Depositions. *Printed below, p.* 127.

240-242 (P.'s 118). **Child-Marriage.** Depositions concerning the marriage of William Westby and Ann Southworth, Minors. *Printed below, p.* 35.

242 bk.-244 bk. (P.'s 119). **Child-Marriage.** Depositions concerning the marriage of George Spurstowe and Brigitt Dutton, Minors. *Printed below, p.* 38.

245-246 bk. (P.'s 120). **Child-Marriage.** Depositions concerning the marriage of Roland Dutton and Margaret Stanley, Minors. *Printed below, p.* 41.

247-248 (P.'s 121). **Child-Marriage.** Deposition concerning the marriage of Wm. Spakman and Lettice Unsworth, Minors. *Printed below, p.* 43.

248 bk.-249 (P.'s 121*). **Child-Marriage and Divorce.** Wm. Westby and Ann Southworth. Further Deposition. *Printed below, p* 37.

249-250 bk. (P.'s 122). **Child-Marriage.** Depositions concerning the marriage of James Ballard and Ann Ballard.§ She gives him 2 apples to marry her. The Curate acting is punisht. *Printed below, p.* 45.

250 bk.-251 (P.'s 123). **Nuncupative Will.** Deposition concerning the Nuncupative Will of John Olton. *Printed below, p.* 135.

251 bk.-252 bk. (P.'s 124). **Child-Marriage.** Depositions concerning the marriage of Wm. Stanley and Ann Dutton, Minors. *Printed below, p.* 47.

253 (P.'s 125). §**Child-Marriage.** Further Depositions concerning the marriage of James Ballard and Ann [here cald Jane] Ballard. *Printed below, p.* 47.

253 bk.-255 bk. (P.'s 126). **Trothplight.** Depositions concerning a contract of Marriage between Tho. Middlehurst and Ellen Carter.‡ *Printed below, p.* 200.

256-257. **Libel.** Thomas Grenehalgh's adultery with Jane Nuttall: Depositions 6 Dec. 1565. *Printed below, p.* 129.

A.D. 1566.

257 bk.-259 (P.'s 127). **Tithe.** Deposition (16 Jan. 1565-6) concerning the refusal of Tithe in Haigh in Wigan Parish.||

260-261 (P.'s 128). **Inventory.** Depositions concerning a false Inventory of the effects of Rich. Bentam.

261-264 (P.'s 129). **Tithe.** Further Depositions concerning the refusal of Tithe in Haigh.||

LEAF

265-267 (P.'s 130). **Trothplight.** Depositions concerning a contract of Marriage between John Brotherton and Alice Ince. *Printed below, p.* 68.

267-268 (P.'s 131). **Will.** Deposition concerning the Will of John Oulton. *Printed below, p.* 136.

268. **Affiliation.** Sibil Blackhurst and Randle Ramshae.† (See p. 69-71.) *Printed below, p.* 210.

268 bk. (131*), ‡**Contract of Marriage.** Thos. Middhurst and Ellen Carter. Further Depositions as to the Character of Witnesses. *Printed below, p.* 210.

269 bk.-271. †**Affiliation.** Sibil Blackhurst and Randle Ramshae. Further Depositions. (See also p. 69-71.) *Printed below, p.* 210.

271 (P.'s 132). **Will.** Deposition concerning the witnessing of the Will of James Moss.

271 bk.-276 (P.'s 133). **Tithe.** Depositions as to the liability to pay Tythe for the first crop from newly enclosed land, in Capenhurst, near Chester.

277, 278 front, blank, lf. 278 bk. end (P.'s 134). **Mortuary.** Deposition as to a Mortuary due to the Rector of Davenham (incomplete).

Child-Marriages at 12, *in France in the* 13*th Century.* Prof. W. P. Ker kindly sends me the following extract (with englishing) from the 13th century portion (that in Alexandrines) of *Aiol,* a chanson de geste, ed. Jacques Normand and Gaston Raynaud; *Soc. Anc. Textes,* 1877.

l. 1704 Nus hom ne prendoit feme, s'avoit .xxx. ans passé,
Et la pucele encontre aussi de bel aé ;
Quant venoi[en]t al terme qu'aloient espouser,
Avoient il tel honte, ce sachiés par verté,
1708 Quidoient tous li puples les deust esgarder.
Dont estoit fois el siecle, creanche et loiautés :
Mais puis est avarisse et luxure montés,
Mavaistiés et ordure, et faillie est bontés ;
1712 L'uns compere ne vient a l'autre foi porter
Ne li enfes al pere, tant est li maus montés !
Ou fait mais .ii. enfans de .xii. ans asanbler :
Prendés garde qués oirs il peuent engenrer !
Por chose est tous li siecles a noiant atornés
1717 Et si amenuisiés com chi oir pores.

No man took a wife till he was past thirty years, and the maiden also of right age: when it came to the time of marriage, they were shamefaced as tho' all the world were witnesses: there was good faith, and trust and loyalty in the world; but since then, luxury and avarice are grown up, naughtiness and filthiness, and goodness has failed. Gossip will not trust his fellow, nor will child trust his father, so is the mischief mounted! They mate together two children of 12 years: think what sort of heirs they are like to gender. So is the whole world turned to vanity, and enfeebled, even as I tell you.

NOTES TO FOREWORDS, &c.

p. xxii. *Robert Parre* v. *Elizabeth Rogerson*. See *Wirral Notes and Queries*, ii. 81-7 (1893).

p. xxxviii. Child-Marriage in 1477: Boy 4, girl 6. In 1477, 17 Edw. IV, a Petition to Parliament (*Rot. Parl.* vi. 168 *a*) says that the King has married 'his seid intierly belovid secunde Son, Richard [Duke of York,[1] at 4 years old] to Anne [Mowbray], Doughter and Heire to John, late Duc of Norff*olk* . . And . . the same Anne is but nowe of the age of vi yere. and the lyf of every creature is uncertayn, and specially of tho that be of such tender age.'

p. xxxix. *Evasion of the Sovereign's Guardianship.* But see *Prerogativa Regis* in vol. i. of the Record Office edition of the Statutes, p. 226: "If a Woman, before the Death of her Ancestor that held of the King in chief, be married before she be marriageable [12 years old], then the King shall have the Ward of the Body of the same Woman until she be of Age able to consent; and then she may chuse whether she will have him to whom she was first married, or him that the King will offer her." The date is uncertain, tho the Act 'is inserted in all the Printed Copies as a Statute of 17 Edw. II.,' A.D. 1323-4. Kings' Prerogatives were no doubt modified as Time ran on.

p. xli, note 2. *Knighthood to prevent Wardship.* But see *Magna Carta*, § III. Wardship. As to the infant heir of a tenant-in-chief of the King: "if such an Heir, being within Age, be made Knight, yet nevertheles his Land shall remain in the keeping of his Lord unto the term aforesaid," his Age of one and twenty years.—Record Office Statutes, i. 115. I suppose that this Prerogative gradually dropt.

p. xlii, note 1. *Forcible carrying-off of Women.* See the case of 'Isabell that was the wife of John Boteler, of Bransey in the Shire of Lanc*aster*, Knyght,' in 1436, 15 Hen. VI, *Rot. Parl.* iv. 497-8. 'William Pulle, late of Wyrall in the Shire of Chestre' (with many *oth*er Felons and Distourbours of the King's peace, 498 *a*) broke into her house, and there, her 'felonousely and moste horribely rauysshed, and her naked, except hir Kirtyll and hir Smokke, ledde with him into the wylde and desolate places of Wales.' He brought her back 'unto Birkhede (Birkenhead) in the Countee of Chestre,' kept her in prison till the Tuesday after, then took her to the 'Parysh Kirk of Bidstone' and there, forst her to marry him, 'havyng with hym a Prest of his aune assent,' took her back to Birkhede, 'and then putte hir in a stronge chaumbre till nyght; and *th*en *th*ere *th*e said William, felonousely and flesshly knewe and ravysshed *th*e said Isabell' again.

p. lxxi. *Stanlow Abbey.* See extracts from these Depositions, in *Wirral Notes and Queries*, ii. 14—15 (1893), by Mr. W. F. Irvine. Also Mr. E. W. Cox's history of the Abbey in the *Birkenhead News*, Nos. 122 and 124, October 1892.

[1] He was the younger Prince murderd in the Tower by Richard III's order.

[To tell the Chester folk of this volume of the Society's issues, the following Notice was circulated by the City publishers, Phillipson and Golder, with the Title-page, Dedication, and p. 26 below as a Specimen of the Text.]

NOTICE.

THIS book is believd by the Editor to be the most light-giving and interesting volume ever publisht on the social life of the Diocese of Chester in 1561-6, and some score years before. It ranges over the whole middle-class of its area, from the Stanleys and mansion-owning squires to the little alehouse-keepers, farmers and cobblers, the maids and the men. It tells of the birth and nursing of babies, their marriages to one another in friends' and nurses' arms. It shows us a girl giving a boy two apples to marry her, and another boy turning his back on his child-wife all night in bed. It tells of boys at school, of children at Christmas merriments; of maids and men at service, at work, and at naughty pranks. It gives us women tricking men, and more men tricking women. It contains quarrels and abuse of all kinds, exprest often in homely, racy words. It shows the farmer's wife trying to palm off her worst lame goose on the tithe-collector; the scholar writing letters in a loft; the Bishop visiting his gentry; the parson his plague-struck parishioners; the chaplain doctoring ladies; and one improper cleric amusingly illustrating a joke of Shakspere's. Death-beds are in the book as well as births; marriages by torch-light, candle-light, and moon-light. One man buys a mare of the gipsies; another chivies a woman with an axe; a third, another man, with a drawn sword, to 'mark' him. The City-authorities look after the meals and morals of the citizens, settle their disputes, and put those who infringe the City-privileges, in gaol.

To all folk in the county and diocese, whose minds can call up the scenes detaild or alluded to in these records of Tudor trials in the Chester Bishop's Court, this volume is full of interest and life. As the Editor can make no money out of it—for his colleagues and he always work, and work hard, for nothing,—he can honestly recommend the book to Cheshire and other men. But if they don't buy it, their neglect is of no consequence; the loss 'll be theirs: the Text is to be issued in March by the Early English Text Society to its Members in advance for the year 1897. So let everybody please himself, and then we shall all be happy.

F. J. F.

3 Feb., 1894.

Depositions taken in the Ecclesiastical Court of Chester,

from Nov. 1561 to March 1565-6.

I. CHILD-MARRIAGES.

§ 1. DIVORCES.

1. Elizabeth Pole (born Tilston) *v.* Wm. Pole (she 8 (?) at marriage, he 11).

(Depositions made in Nov. 1561.)

[1] Deposition 2, leaf 3, begins with the evidence of the child-wife Elizabeth Pole (once Tilston). The words left[2] seem to say that she was 8 years old when she married William Pole in 'Marburie[3] Churche,' 'no bodie, to her knoledge, beynge p*resen*t at the same, but onlie the father of her p*rete*nsid husband.' The boy-husband 'was aboue xj yeres of age'; 'and . . they were bothe so ignoraunt, they knewe not what the matter meanid; and forther she sais, that they neue*r* dwellid together, or had any carnall copulac*io*n together, nor neue*r* lay together. forther, she sais, that she, beynge pe*r*swadid bie the Counsell of Ric*hard* Pole, father of her p*rete*nsid husband, and of Agnes Tilston, this *respo*ndent*es* suster, went on*e* night p*ri*velie from her graundmothers house, and came to the house of the said Ric*hard*, and from thense was brought to the churche, and so maried; and then returnid home to her graundmothers house againe the same night, no bodie knowinge of hit but the pe*r*sons above rehersid; nor no*n* of her frend*is* knewe of hit bie the space of iij' yeres after, to her [. . .] or bie her meanes.' and [they [4]'neuer] ratified the said marriage . . . bie kissinge, or sendinge' [tokens, &c.] &c.

The next tatterd evidence is that of Richard Pole, the father, who 'sais that his sonne Wi*llia*m' and Elizabeth Tilston were married about the Feast of St. Valentine—there being 'no banes askid, but a License

[1] Piccope's No. 2.

[2] Ad p*rimam* pos*itio*nem, This r*espo*ndent [. . .] this p*rese*nt about the age of [x . . .] she hathe bene married to [. . .] yeres viij yeres at the tym[e . . .] feast of sainte Valentyne. [3] Near Whitchurch in Cheshire. [4] leaf 3, back.

had,—in a morninge about Cock*es* crowinge, with Torche light and Candell-light, in the parishe churche of M*ar*burie . . . bie Sir Wi*lliam* Bedoe, curate of M*ar*burie; there beynge p*resen*t at the said mariage, the said Sir Wi*lli*am Bedoe, the said parties beynge maried, and this depone*n*t; and no*n* other, to this depone*ntes* knoledge.'

'Ad iij ar*ticu*lu*m*, This depone*n*t sais, that the said Wi*lli*am Pole, his sonne, at the tyme of his mariage was aboue xj yeres of age; and he saith that they neu*er* dwellid together, lye together, nor neu*er* had carnall dole; and that, to this depone*ntes* knoledge, they neu*er* consentid together in kissinge, gevinge tokens, or in any other thinge, to his knoledge. Wherbie he might coniecluid that eu*er* they favored either other as man & wief.'

Christopher somebody's evidence follows, but gives no new facts.

2. Humfrey Winstanley *v.* Alice Worsley (he under 12 at marriage, she over 17).

[1] Exa*min*acio testiu*m* in ca*usa* divorcij inter Homfridum Winstanley, p*ar*tem act*ricem*, & Alicia*m* Worsley, p*ar*tem rea*m*, capt*a* cora*m* m*agist*ro Robe*r*to Leche, &c., xxviij° die mensis novembris, a*nno* do*mi*ni 1561.

Jacobus Worsley, p*a*rochi*e* de Wigan, ibi*de*m oriundus, etat*is* circiter xxvij annos, nouit p*a*rtem act*ricem* a n*ativitat*e, et p*a*rtem rea*m* si*mi*liter.

Ad p*r*imu*m* ar*ticu*lu*m*, this deponent, askid off the age off Homfrey Winstanley, answareth, that the said Homfrey is above xiiij*tene* yeris off age, and vnder xv*tene* /

Ad ij*d* ar*ticu*lu*m*, this depone*n*t, beynge demau*n*ded wher, when, and what tyme off the daye, and the yere, and bie whos procure[ment], and howe longe agoe, the said Homf[ray was] maried / answareth, that the said Ho[mfray [2] was marie]d att a chapell off S*ir* Thomas Gerrard, [callid] the Brynn,[3] in the parish off Winwick, [last M]ydsom*er* was toe yeres, abowt x*te* or xj*te* [off the] clock off the daye, bie the procureme*n*t of the said S*ir* Thomas Gerrard, gardian to the said Homfrey.

Ad iij' ar*ticu*lu*m*, this deponent . . . sais, the said Homfrey maried one, Alice Worsley, sister to this depone*n*t, then beynge off the age off xvij' yeres and above.

Ad iiij*tum* ar*ticu*lu*m*, this depone*n*t, beynge asked whether, to his knolege, the said Homfrey had ratefied this pretensid mariage, bie expresse word*is* off consent, or anye other meanes; this depone*n*t sais, that he has been a meane to winne the fauo*ur* off the said Homfrey to his pretensid

[1] leaf 7 (Piccope's No. 4). [2] leaf 7, back. [3] Brynn Hall, Sir T. Gerrard's seat.

wiff, both afore the said Homfrey came to the yeres off discreccion, and after; and he cold neu*er* gett hym to grant his good will to his pretensid wiff. Wherfore this depone*nt* verilie belevis that the said matrimonie was neu*er* ratefied. and forther he sais, that they neu*er* dwelled together this yere and halff; and neu*er* sawe the one the other, off that space: and this, depone*nt* sais, is true, bie cause the said Homfrey went to the scole viij or x^te myle off the howse off this depone*nt*, wher the said Alice remayned till she went owt of Lancashire a greatt way [1]forther off the said Homfrey.

Joannes Sothworth . . . [etatis] xxix annor*um* . . . sais that Homf[rey] Winstanley is att this p*rese*nt, above xi[iij] yeres off age, and viij wekis, and hath bene ward to S*ir* Thomas Gerrard eu*er* syns his fathers deth, bie a bargen. and the said Homfrey was maried, bie the constreynt of his said gardiañ, to Alice Worsley, the said Alice then beyng abowt the age off xvij', and the said Homfrey vnder xij' yeres, more then toe yeres agoe, as moch as syns mydsom*er*, in a chapell w*i*thin the howse of S*ir* Thomas Gerrard, bie one S*ir* Oswalde Key, chapleñ singing att Aston chapell / And forther, this deponent sais, that he is able to saye that the said Homfrey wold neu*er*, bie the allurement off this depone*nt*—beyng oft in this deponentis howse, as w*ith* his frend, bie cause this depone*nt* had maried his awnt,—grante or consent vnto the said mariage, bie word or dede; and yett this depone*nt* hath done the best he cold, to p*er*swade hym to the same / And this depone*nt* forther sais, that the said Homfrey and Alice did [not] dwell together this yere and a halff; nor the one sawe the other bie that [space, as they [2]have] bene asonder, su*m* tymes xx' or viiij' myles [att] the lest. all the p*rem*isses, this depone*nt* knowis [to be] true, bie cause he is Vncle-in-lawe to [the sai]d Homfrey, and hath hym oft tymes att his howse; and nowe, after the decesse off his awntc, this depone*nt* and the said Homfrey be beedfelowes / when the said Homfrey comes from the scole to this deponent*es* howse /

R*esp*onsio*nes* p*er*so*na*les Alicie Worsley, sup*ra* exc*epcio*nib*us* et ar-*ticu*lis in ca*usa* divorcii, ex p*ar*te Homfrid*i* Winstanley, ei*us* p*ret*ensi mariti, oblat*is*; capte cora*m* Ve*nerabi*li viro Rob*er*to Leche, &c., xj° die decembr*is* 1561.

Ad p*ri*ma*m* p*osit*ionem, This r*esp*ondent sais, that Homfrey Winstanley is, at this p*rese*nt, about the age of xiiij^tene yeres, and vnder xv^tene.

Ad ij^d, this r*esp*ondent sais, that Homfrey Winstanley and she were maried together at a chapell of S*ir* Tho*mas* Gerrard*es* callid the Brinne,

[1] leaf 8. [2] leaf 8. back.

in a morninge about ix' or x' of the clocke, about Midsom*er* was two yeres, bie the p*ro*curem*en*t of S*ir* Thom*as* Gerrard, gardian of the said Homfrey, against the mynd of the said Homfrey, as she think*es* . . .

Ad iiij p*ositi*onem, This r*espo*ndent, beynge askid whether the said Homfrey had ratified the p*re*t*e*nsid mariage, bie expresse word*is*, [1]bie consent, or bie [any other meane, this respondent sais] she could neu*er* p*er*[swade the said Homfrey to shew her] good will, love or [*MS. torn*, nor] he neu*er* came in bed w*i*th her [nor did he euer carnally] knowe her. And forther she [sais that] she will neu*er* refuse hym, but he shall Refuse her first. and nowe she desirethe, that he may ether take or refuse her before a Judge, biecause he is at the yeres of Consent /

3. Eliz. Hulse *v.* George Hulse (she 4 at marriage, he 7).

[2](7) R*es*p*o*nsio p*er*so*na*lis Eliza*bethe* Hulse, in c*ausa* Divoricii sup*er* sum*m*aria petic*io*n*e* inter no*minat*am et Georgiu*m* Hulse, capt*a* cora*m* ve*nera*b*i*li viro, Robe*r*to Leche, in L*egibus* Bacc*alaureo*, xij° die Decemb*ris*, A*nn*o 1561

This r*espo*ndent sais, that George Hulse and she were maried together in the chappell of Knotisford, what tyme she knowis not, bie reason hit was done when she was but three or iiij^or^ yeares old; and beynge asked howe she knowithe they were maried in Knottisford, she sais she knowis not, but bie the sayenge of her father & mother. forther, she sais, she was married to hym biecause her frend*es* thought she shuld have had a lyvinge bie hym; but after the mariage, the said George was bounden prentise in Congleton for the space of x' yeres; and after x' yeres, the said George came to her mothers house; but she said she cold neu*er* fansie or cast favo*ur* to hym, nor neu*er* will do; and she sais thei neu*er* dwellid together sins this r*espo*ndent was sixe yere old, and neu*er* had any Carnall act together.

R*es*p*o*nsio p*er*so*na*lis Georgii Hulse, capt*a* cora*m* m*agist*ro Robe*r*to Lech*e*, cancell*ario*, die et a*nn*o p*re*d*ictis*. [12 Dec. 1561.]

This r*espo*ndent sais, that he was about vij yere old, & Eliza*beth* Hulse about iiij^or^ yeres old, at the tyme of the mariage betwixe them; & that he can nowe find in his hart to have her, yf she wold have hym; but he sais he cold neu*er* have favo*ur* at her, nor neu*er* had any Carnall dole w*i*th her; & that makis hym to thinke that they shuld neu*er* do well yf they were not dyvorsed; & he beinge nowe a poore wast*es* man,

[1] leaf 9. [2] leaf 12, back (Piccope's No. 7).

she despisethe hym, & dothe set little bie hym; & forther he sais, they have bene absent, one from an other, this x' yeres; & nowe he is about xxiij yeres old, & neu*er* had any token from her, wherbie he cold eu*er* pe*r*ceyve that she lovid hym as his wief.

[1]Depo*sitio*nes testiu*m* capt*e* m*agist*ro [*MS. torn*] et anno p*re*dicto.

Jacobus Browne, p*ar*ochie de Witton,[2] etat*is* xl an*norum*, nov*it* p*ar*te*m* act*ricem* a puericia, et p*ar*te*m* rea*m* xv^cim^ an*n*os. Exa*minatus* sup*er* sum*m*aria peticione, ex p*ar*te p*ar*t*is* act*ricis* oblat*a*. This depone*n*t sais, that Eliz*abeth* Hulse and George Hulse were maried together in the churche of Knotisford, the saied Eliz*abeth* beynge about the age of iiij^or^ yeres: and he sais he knowis well her age, biecause he had maried her mother a little afore, and was bounden in obligac*io*n[3] to one Mr. Leghe of the Ridge, to marie them bie a certen day; and they were maried accordinge to the effect of the band, about xiiij^t^ yeres agoe. and forther, this depone*n*t sais, they neu*er* dwellid together, nor the said Eliz*abeth* neu*er* did ratifie the said mariage, or did eu*er* fansie or love the said George, especiallie after that he had lost his lyvinge, w*hi*ch was thought shuld have bene his enheritaunce. Reddend*o* racione*m* sui d*icti*, sais that, for the space of this x' yeres, the said george hath bene absent, and hathe sought his lyvinge in an other cuntrie; and the said Eliz*abeth* hath continuallie bene w*i*th this depone*n*t in house, so that this depone*n*t is certen the one kissed not the other this x' yeres, or eu*er* shewid any signe of Consent: tho this Depone*n*t be her stepfather, he can bringe a C witnes [? MS.].

Rob*er*tus Wright, p*ar*ochie de Gostre,[4] etat*is* xxxiiij an*norum*, nov*it* Eliz*abetham* Hulse x an*n*os, et p*ar*te*m* rea*m* xiij^cim^ an*n*os, et vltra. Exa*minatus* sup*er* su*m*maria petic*io*ne &c, This depone*n*t sais, that Eliza*beth* Hulse & George Hulse were maried together in the churche of Knotisford, the said Eliz*abeth* beynge at that tyme about the age of iiij^or^ yeres: and [5]he knowis this to be true, biccause he, this depone*n*t, was maried to the mother of the said George xiij^tene^ yeres ago, & he well remembrith that George Hulse did marrie Eliz*abeth* the same yere; and forther, he sais, when the said Eliz*abeth* came to the yeres of consent, and afore, she neu*er* did fansie or love the said George, for bie-cause the said George had lost his lyvinge a good while afore, and was not able to mentaine her, but for necessitie was driven to binde hym-self a prentice to a shomaker in Congleton, callid Rondull Hankinson, where he servid his prentiship out, and hath continued Jorneman sins: in all the space of

[1] leaf 13. [2] Northwich, Cheshire. [3] by Bond, in a penalty.
[4] Goostrey, Cheshire, 10 m. from Witton. [5] leaf 13, back.

ix' yeres. and this deponen*t* sais, he knowis they neue*r* came together sins the tyme the said Eliz*abeth* came to yeres of discrecion, nor neue*r* had carnall copulacion together, thoughe George was lothe to part w*i*th her, but wold have Lovid her yf she wold have bene co*n*tent: of the w*hi*ch premisses, all the pa*r*ishe talk*is*, & can be witnes in hit /

4. John Bridge *v.* Elizabeth Bridge (born Ramsbotham). He 11 or 12 at the marriage, she ? 13-14.

(Beginning lost. Depositions taken on Dec. 1561.)

[[1]Elizabeth Bridge, born Ramsbotham, answers the Bill or Petition of her husband John Bridge, & says that after their child-marriage he never treated her] "lovinglie, insomoche that the first [night they] were maried, the said John wold Ea[te no] meate at supper. and whan hit was bed ty[me], the said John did wepe to go home w*i*th his father, he beynge at that tyme at her brothers house. yet neue*r*theles, bie his fathers intreating, and bie the pe*r*swasion of the priest, the said John did com*m*e to bed to this Re*spo*ndent far in the night; and there lay still, till in the morninge, in suche sort as this depone*n*t might take vnkindnes w*i*th hym; for he lay w*i*th his backe toward her all night; and neither then, nor anie tyme els, had carnall dole w*i*th her, nor neue*r* after came in her Companie, more then he had neue*r* knowne her."

"Ad iij a*rticulum*, This re*spo*ndent sais, that the said John did neue*r* ratifie the mariage w*i*th her. neue*r*theles, this re*spo*ndent wold yet be co*n*tent to take hym yf he wold have her; nor neue*r* did vse hym vnkindlie."

Depo*sici*ones testiu*m*, capte in ca*usa* predi*cta*, capt*e* xij° Decembr*is*, a*n*no 1561.

Edmu*ndus* Kay, pa*r*ochie Burie,[2] etat*is* xxxij', no*vi*t pa*r*te*m* act*ricem* ab infancia, et pa*r*te*m* rea*m* a puericia.

Ad p*r*imu*m* ar*ticu*lu*m*, This depone*n*t sais, that Johñ Bridge and Eliz*abeth* Ramsbotham were maried together in the parishe Churche of Burie, this depone*n*t beynge p*resent*; but what tyme of the [3]yere, this depone*n*t knowis not; the said John beynge, at the tyme of the said mariage, about the age of xiij^{tene} yeres, and vnder xiiij^{tene}. Reddend*o* racion*em* sui D*i*cti / biecause he was his neybo*u*r and his kinseman, and therfore he dothe well remembre [his] age; for when the said John Bridge was but two yeres old, his graundfather and the father of the said Eliz*abeth* Romisbotham made a bargaine of mariage; and the monie was

[1] leaf 11 (Piccope's No. 6). [2] Bury, Lancashire. [3] leaf 11, back.

paid bie the father of the said Eliz*abeth*, to bie a pece of land: and therfore the said John was maried vnder age, after the deathe of his graundfather, bie the Executo*urs* of his said graundfather, to the said Eliz*abeth*, to save the monie /

Ad ij[d] ar*ticulum*, This depone*nt* sais, that the said John cold neu*er* love or favo*ur* the said Eliz*abeth*; but hathe often tymes desired this depone*nt* to speake to his father to get them asonder.

Ad iij *articulum*, This depone*nt* sais, that the said John and Eliz*abeth* neu*er* dwellid together sins ther said mariage, nor neu*er* lay together; but the first night they were maried, bie the p*er*swasion of a priest, the said John went to bed to the said Eliz*abeth*, w*i*th much ado; and neu*er* after came in her Companie, so that this depone*nt* think*es* in his Conscience they had neu*er* carnall copulacion together.

Ad vltim*um*, dicit p*re*deposit*a* p*er* eu*m* fore vera, et fama*m* sup*er* h*ujus*mo*di* laborare. no*n* est doct*us*, no*n* conduct*us* &c.

[1] Joh*anne*s Key, p*ar*ochie de Burie, etatis x [? annorum, novit partes a] puericia.

Ad p*rimum* ar*ticulum*, This depone*nt* sais, [that John Bridge] and Eliz*abe*th Romisbotham were m[aried to]gether in the parishe churche of Burie, apon a Mighelmas even, iij yeres passid sins Mighelmas; and that the said John was, at the tyme of the said mariage, aboue the age of xiij yeres, and vnder xiiij[tene]. and beynge askid of his just age, he sais, he is well Remembrid that he was borne about Candelmas;[2] and beynge his neybo*ur*, is well remembrid of the yeres. This depone*nt* sais he was not p*rese*nt at the mariage; but the same morninge he was maried, he came ou*er* this depone*ntes* ground, and wept gretlie, and said, "John, / I wold I might go w*i*th you to the milne" . . . . . .

Ad iij ar*ticulum*, This depone*nt* sais, the first night the[y] lay together bie the Compulsion of the priest of the Chapell; for he[3] wold have gone home w*i*th his father the same night, but his father wold not suffer hym. & yerlie[4] in the morowe he went from her brothers house, & neu*er* came in her Companie sins, nor had any Carnall dole together, nor wold eu*er* drawe to her, or love her, bie any Counsell . . . . . .

[5] Fact*a* fuit sequens exa*minacio* testiu*m* in ca*usa* Divorcij inter Joh*anne*m Bridge, p*ar*te*m* act*ricem*, et Elizabeth[am] Bridge, p*ar*te*m* rea*m*, capt*a* cora*m* m*agist*ro Rob*er*to Leche, &c, xvj° Januarij 1561[-2].

[1] leaf 12. [2] Feb. 2: the Purification of the Virgin Mary. [3] the boy-husband, John Bridge. [4] early. [5] leaf 18, back (Piccope's No. 10).

Jacobus Hardcar, p*a*rochie de Burie, etat*is* liij' anor*um*, no*vi*t p*ar*tes ab Infancijs earund*em* /

Ad p*ri*mu*m* ar*ticu*lu*m*, dicit eunde*m* fore veru*m*. Reddend*o* rac*i*on*em* sui d*ic*t*i*, he sais, that Johñ Bridge & Eliz*abeth* Bridge, al*ia*s Romisbotham, were maried together in the p*a*rishe Churche of Burie, about thre yeres passid, apon a Michelmas even.

Ad ij^{d} ar*ticu*lu*m*, This depone*n*t sais, that he knowithe that Johñ Bridge was vnder age of xiiij yeres when he was married. Reddend*o* racion*em* d*ic*t*i* [sui], this depone*n*t sais, he was in the Churche, when the said Johñ was christnid; w*hi*ch day was a weddinge in the Churche; and bie that, he well dothe beare the yere in mynd. and forther, he [1]sais, that when the said Johñ came to the full ag[e of] xiiij^{t} yeres, he did neu*er* agre to the said mariage, b[ut] alwais did dissent. and all this, he knowis to be true, biecause he is a next neybo*u*r; and the said Johñ hath told hit dyverse tymes to this depone*n*t /

Ad iij ar*ticu*lu*m*, This depone*n*t sais, that the said Johñ and Eliz*abeth* did neu*er* dwell together, or lye together, but onlie the first night: and that night he had no carnall Copulac*i*on w*i*th her. Reddend*o* rac*i*on*em* d*ic*t*i* [sui], he saithe, that the said Johñ was maried in the Churche, for savinge of a band;[2] and that tyme he said he wold go to Churche, and say the word*es*, for savinge his father of a band; but he said he wold neu*er* consent to them in his hart. and the first night, he went to bedd w*i*th the said Eliz*abeth*; but he told this depone*n*t that he neu*er* touchid her bare skin, bothe afore he came to the age of xiiij, and xx^{tie} tymes sins. forther, he sais, that he dare make good on a boke, that they did neu*er* ratifie the mariage bie any meanes, as sendinge of tokens, or kepinge Companie, or any suche like sort, wherbie they shuld favo*u*r one another.

Ad vltim*um*, dicit p*re*deposit*a* p*er* eu*m* fore vera: and hereof, he sais, the said Johñ might bringe a C witnes, yf he might for cost.

Thom*as* Bridge, p*a*rochie de Burie, etat*is* lij' annor*um*, no*vi*t p*ar*tes ab infancijs earund*em* /

Ad p*ri*mu*m* ar*ticu*lu*m*, This depone*n*t sais, that Johñ Bridge was compellid bie his father to marrie the said Eliz*abet*h Romisbotham, sore against his w[ill], [3]beynge but a child, and vnder the age of xiiij yeres, havinge no mynde of mariage. and beynge demaundid 'whie his father enforcid hym to the said mariage'; he sais, that 'his father was bound

[1] leaf 19.
[2] Bond, given by his Father, to make the marriage, with a penalty if he did not.
[3] leaf 19, back.

in suche a band, that yf he had not gone to the Churche, and there have spoken the word*es* after the priest, his father had bene vndone.'

Ad ij[d] ar*ticu*lu*m*,—beynge askid, howe old, John Bridge is nowe, and whether he did dissent from the mariage streyghtwais, before he was xiiij, This depone*n*t sais, that Johñ Bridge is nowe about the age of xviij'. beynge askid 'what tyme of the yere he was borne'; he [Thos. Bridge] sais he knowis not pe*r*fittlie biecause he was not p*res*ent at his christninge in the Churche, but he see when he went to christninge, for they came by this depone*n*t, beynge at his worke when they went to church / And forther, he sais, that the said Johñ neue*r* agreid to the said mariage. reddend*o* rac*io*ne*m* sui d*i*c*t*i; biecause the said Johñ told this depone*n*t C tymes, that he wold neue*r* consent, love, or have the said Eliz*abeth* as his wief.

Ad iij ar*ticu*lu*m*, This depone*n*t sais, that the said John and Eliz*abeth* neue*r* dwellid together sins the said mariage; but before, they did. then the said Eliz*abeth* beynge a bigge woman, and the said John but a child, she delt shrewdlie w*i*th hym: and that made hym to cast his love so from her; that yf hit had not bene [1]for savinge of the band, he wold neue*r* have maried her. & sins that tyme he neue*r* dwellid w*i*th her, nor did lye w*i*th her, but the first night; and then, this depone*n*t thinke*s* in his Conscience, that he had neue*r* any Carnall dole w*i*th her. and further, this depone*n*t, beynge ther neybo*u*r, did neue*r* here word spoken, or Token sent, betwixe them, or any suche familiaritie betwixe them, wherbie he might iudge that they vsid them self as man and wief, or eue*r* ratified the mariage.

Ad vlti*mu*m, dicit p*re*deposit*a* pe*r* eu*m* fore vera, et fama*m* sup*er* h*u*j*us*mo*d*i laborare, ... in the Cuntrie thereabout. [2]no*n* est doct*us*, &c.[2]

5. Andrew Haworth *v.* Constance Entwisell: boy 9 at marriage; girl 11.

[3]Exa*mina*cio testiu*m* in ca*usa* Divorcii inter Andrea*m* Haworth, paroch*ie* de Bolton, p*ar*te*m* act*ricem*, con*tra* Custancia*m* Entwisell, p*ar*te*m* rea*m*, capt*a* cora*m* m*agist*ro Robe*r*to Leche, in legib*us* baccall*aureo*, &c v° die M*ar*tii 1561[-2].

Jacobus Sharplus, p*a*rochie de Bolton,[4] ib*id*em oriund*us*, etat*is* circite*r* lxvj' an*n*os, no*vi*t p*ar*te*m* act*ricem* a pue*r*icia sua, et Custancia*m* Entwisell, ex quo fuit sex an*n*os.

[1] leaf 20. [2—2] The MS. puts this before 'in the Cuntrie thereabout.'
[3] leaf 40 (Piccope's No. 16). [4] Bolton-le-Moors, Lancashire.

Ad *primum* ar*ticu*lu*m*, This Depone*nt* sais, that he was p*re*se*nt* in the p*ari*she church of Bolton, at the m*at*rimony solempnized betwixe Andrewe Haworth (then beynge, to his Estimac*io*n at that tyme, ix' yeres of age), and Custance Entwisell, then beynge about xj yeres of age; and that, this depone*nt* knowes well to be true, biecause he was neybo*ur* dwellinge nere to the said pa*r*ties, and knowes the same to be true; but what tyme of the yere the said m*at*rimony was celebratt, this depone*nt* can*n*ot tell. Interrog*atus* de compuls*ione* et impulsion*e* p*a*rentu*m* et amicor*um* suor*um*, This depone*nt* sais, that Andrewe Haworthes father, p*er*ceyvinge the father of Custance Entwisell dep*ar*tid when the said Custance was of the age of xj yeres as abovesaid, did obteyne the Landlord*es* goodwill of the Teneme*nt* wherein the father of the said Custance did dwell, and so maried the said Andrewe his sonne, & the said Custance, together; and so the said Andrewe & Custance did dwell at the said Teneme*nt*. al*ite*r quoad ar*ticu*lu*m* nescit depon*er*e . . . . . .

[1]Robertus Wodde, p*a*rochie de Bolton, ib*ide*m oriund*us*, etat*is* circit*er* xlij an*no*s, nov*i*t p*a*rte*m* act*r*ice*m* a na*tiuita*te, et p*a*rte*m* rea*m* simil*ite*r.

Ad p*rimu*m ar*ticu*lu*m*, This depone*nt* sais, that Andrewe Haworth, then beynge about the age of viij yeres, or there-about, bie the p*er*swasion of his father & mother, & other his frend*es*, did marrie in the som*er* season, in the p*a*rishe churche of Bolton, Custance Entwisell, (then beynge about the age of xj[2] yeres), about xiiij[t] yeres past. and that, this depone*nt* well knowis, beynge a nere neybo*ur* to the said p*ar*ties. al*ite*r nescit depon*er*e.

Ad ij[d] ar*ticu*lu*m*, this depone*nt* sais, that Andrewe Haworth & Custance Entwisell, after the said m*at*rimony, did dwell together in the house of the father of Andrewe Haworth bie a c*er*ten space; but howe longe, or whether they did lye together, or had carnall dole together, This depone*nt* can*n*ot tell.

Ad iij ar*ticu*lu*m*, dicit, q*uod* nescit depon*er*e, an volu*n*tarie coh*ab*itarunt, aut carnale*m* copula*m* invice*m* h*ab*uer*un*t; but this depone*nt* sais, he hath sene them go and come from the church together, as man and wief. al*ite*r nescit depon*er*e . . . . . .

[3]R*esp*onciones p*er*so*na*les Custancie Entwisell, sup*er* po*sicio*nib*us* et ar*ticu*lis li*bel*li ex p*ar*te Andrei Haworth oblat*i*, capt*e* die et an*no* p*re*d*ic*tis [20 March, 1561-2].

Ad p*rima*m po*sicio*nem, This re*sp*ondent sais, that Andrewe Haworth & she were maried together in the p*a*rish church of Bolton about xij

[1] leaf 40, back. [2] Alterd from xij. [3] leaf 53, back (Piccope's No. 20).

yeres ago, the said Andrewe beynge betwene ix & x yeres old, and this *respondent* betwene xj or xij; and she sais they were maried together bie the Compulsion of their frend*es*.

Ad ij^d^ posic*io*nem, dicit eand*em* fore vera*m*; and they neu*er* consentid or lovid together, as man and wief, after they came to yeres of discrec*io*n.

Ad iij, This *respondent* sais, bie vertue of her othe, that they have dwellid together in a house of the said Andrewe bie the space of two yeres, about two yeres ago; and afore that tyme, they dwellid together in the house of the said Andrewe Haworthes father about tenne yeres; but she sais, bie vertue of her othe, that duringe all that tyme they neu*er* had carnall dole, nor neu*er* vsid themselfe famylierlie together as man and wief, althoughe, bie the compulsion of their frend*es* they were kept so longe together; nor neu*er* consentid to the same . . . . . .

6. Peter Haworth *v.* Margery Haworth, born Heydocke: girl 8 at marriage; boy less.

[1] *Respo*nsi*o*nes p*er*sonales M*ar*gerie Haworth*e*, al*ias* Heydocke, sup*er* allegac*i*o*n*e ex p*ar*te Petr*i* Haworth con*tra* ipsam, in ca*us*a Divorcii oblat*a*, capt*e* die et an*no* p*re*d*i*c*t*is / [8 May, 1562].

Ad content*a* allegac*io*n*i*s sive ma*ter*i*e* p*er* Petru*m* Haworthe oblat*e*, this *respondent* sais, that Peter Haworthe and this *respondent* were maried together in the p*ar*yshe churche of Blagburne about xviij yeres ago, the said Peter beynge young*er* then this *respondent*; & this *respondent* sais she was, at the tyme of the said m*ar*iage, about viij yeres of age; and that she is, at this p*resen*t, about xxvj yeres old: and that the said mariage was made bie the advise and Compulsion of this *respondent*es freind*es*, apon her p*ar*te; but howe hit was apon his [Peter H.'s] p*ar*te, this *respondent* knowes not. and forther, this *respondent* sais, that when she came to the age of consent, she did not agre to the said mariage, and that she did neu*er* ratifie hit bie Consentinge therevnto; nor that she had eu*er* p*ar*te of his bodie; but that she is a good maide, for hym; & that they neu*er* dwellid together sins they were of the age of xij yeres: but then dislove fell betwene them. and this R*espo*ndent sais, that sins that tyme she hathe dwellid w*i*th her frend*es*; & he hath bene eu*er* sins w*i*th his frend*es*, and abroade at Service. beynge askid howe hit ch*a*uncid that they have not got a divorce this xviij^tene^ yeres; she sais, ther was a discord betwene them, & a sute in this Cowrt, about xvj^t^ yeres ago; but howe hit endid, this *respondent* knowes not.

[1] leaf 59, back (Piccope's No. 23).

7. Joan Whittall, born Leyland, *v.* Rafe Whittall.

(Each between 11 and 12, at marriage. Depositions made, 25 Sept. 1562.)

[1] When 'the said Joan was . . . a xj yere old, and vnder xij, and the said Rafe was iij wekes young*er*,' the children were married 'in the *pa*rishe church of Leyland,' Lancashire, about Candlemas, [2] 'biecause the said Rafe had about xl *s* a yere of land.' [3] He staid at her fathers house for less than a month, then went to his mother's till he was 15 or 16, & then returnd to her father's for two years, but (as he says) he 'neu*er* lay w*i*th her, biecause he was ordred [treated] worse then any s*er*u*au*nt in her fathers house; & biecause he p*er*ceyvid she neu*er* lovid hym, he went away, and neu*er* came there sins; and so she hath bene at service abroad; and the one neu*er* sent the other, token. and biecause she dealid so vnkindly with hym, he will neu*er* have her, for whie, she eu*er* lovid oth*er* boies (to his knoledge) as well as hym. and forther, he sais he neu*er* lay w*i*th her, or had carnall Acte w*i*th her.'

Thomas Pincok says [4] that 'when the boy came to xv' or xvj' yeres, he was entysed away bie the stepfather and mother of the said Raffe, bie reason the one fansied not the other.'

[5] Joan's father, Rafe Leyland, 71 years old, 'sais that they were maried biecause she shold have had bie hym a p*re*ty bargane, yf they cold have lovid, on the other.' When 'the said Rafe [Whittall] came to the age of xvj yeres,' he 'came to this Depone*ntes* house, and there remayned at bedd and bord bie the space of ij yeres; nor neu*er* came in bed, the one w*i*th the other, nor the one cold not fansy the other.' [6] 'beynge askid whie the said J[o]ane did not begin her sute afore, he sais that she was poor, and had no money; and nowe she hath gotten somwhat in S*er*uice, and nowe spende*s* hit in triall of the Lawe.'

8. Ellen Dampart *v.* John Andrewe. (Her 2 Sisters put between them in bed on the wedding-night.) Girl under 8 at marriage, boy 10.

[7] Exa*min*a*c*io testiu*m* in ca*usa* Divorcii sup*er* li*be*llo ex p*ar*te Elene Damp*ar*t[8] con*tra* Joh*ann*em Andrewe oblat*o*, capt*a* cora*m* m*agis*t*ro* Rob*er*to Leche &c., xxij° die Octobr*is* 1562° /

Galfrid*us* Tailiour, parochie de Chedill, no*vi*t p*ar*te*m* act*ricem* et p*ar*te*m* rea*m* a puericiis. Testis p*ro*duct*us*, Jurat*us* et exa*min*at*us* sup*er* Allegac*io*ne

[1] leaf 73, back (Piccope's No. 33). [2] leaf 74. [3] leaf 74, back.
[4] leaf 74. [5] leaf 73, back. [6] leaf 74. [7] leaf 79 (Piccope's No. 36).
[8] The country shortening of "Davenport."

sive summaria peticione ex parte partis actricis oblata, dicit, in vim Juramenti sui, that, by the report of the Cuntry, Elen Dampart[1] and John Andrewe were maried together in a Chambre at Widford;—howe longe sins, or what tyme of the yere, this deponent knowis not, bycause he was not present by at the solempnizacion of the said matrimony;—but they were maried vnder age, as he hard say, [2]not past ix or x yeres old. And forther he sais, that the cause of their mariage was, that John Dampart of Widford, and William Andrewe, fathers of the said parties, beinge at contencion and sute, and havinge a Tenement wherein John Andrewes father dwellid, devided betwixe the said Andrewes father, and one James Smith; and the said James Smith toke a Lease of his part of the Tenement, and set-in the said Ellin to have hit after his decesse; and the said Mr. Dampart and John Andrewes, for that entent, to wyne the house together, thought it convenient to marry the said Ellin and John Andrewe together; and so they did; but yet the said parties neuer consentid thervnto; in-somuch, that William Andrewe, perceyvinge the mynde of his sonne, who said to hym, "Father! gyve me your blessinge, and I will go into an other Cuntry, to seke my Livinge; for I will neuer take her as my wief." And his father answerid and said, "he wold spend half a score of Nobles, but he wold have them divorcid." And this, he [Geoffrey Tailiour] knowes to be true, bie the report of John Andrewe and other neigboures / And forther, this deponent sais, that at the last beyng of Sould[i]ers at Lithe, this deponent and John Andrewe beynge souldiers together, and the said John lyenge at the point of death, very sicke, said to one Roberte Williamson, "I pray the, yf euer thou comme in the Cuntry, say & declare that he [my Son] neuer toke Ellin Dampart for his wief, nor neuer wold do, in this world or in another." And forther, he sais, they neuer dwellid together sins they were of yeres of consent; for the said Ellin went to London; and John Andrewe, articulate, went abroad, to seke his Livinge and to do service; wherby this deponente thinkes, and knowes to his knoledge, or for euer any thinge that this deponent cold here or know of, that they neuer had carnall Act together, or vsid either other as man and wief ought to do, forbiecause this deponent hath hard Ellin Dampart say oftentymes, that 'she had rather dy, then she cold take hym [Jn. Andrewe] as her husband, and forsake all that she had or shuld have' /

Carolus Worthington, parochie de Presbury, etatis xxix annorum, norit partem actricem et partem ream a puericiis earundem. Examinatus

[1] The country shortening of "Davenport."
[2] leaf 79, back.

super allegacione &c, dicit, that as he, beynge a new neibour, [1]hath hard say[1] that Ellin Dampart and John Andrewe were maried together about xiij or xiiij yeres ago, come Christmas next, in a Chamber at Widford; and for this cause, that William Andrewe, father to the said John Andrewe, and one James Smith, had a house on the Landes of John Dampart of Widford, esquier, devided betwene them; and the said James Smith had gotten a Lease of his parte, and in the same had put Ellin Dampart, a base doughter of the said Mr Dampartes, to have hit after his decesse. and the said William Andrewe, fearinge lest he shuld lose his parte of his Lyvinge, and to wyne all the tenement together againe, made a mariage with the said Ellin Dampart to his sonne John, against the consent of both parties, at that tyme, and euer sins; for he hath hard John Andrewe say many tymes, that 'he had rather dye, or he wold have her as his wief': and the said Ellin hath said no lesse by the said John; wherby hit appereth that they neuer lovid either other. And forther, this deponent sais, that they neuer dwellid in one house together sins they came to yeres of Consent, biecause they agreid so evill. and sins they came to yeeres of consent, the said Ellin went to London; and John Andrewe went to service abrode in the Cuntry; and neuer vsid either other as man and wief, or euer had Carnall dole together, to this deponentes knoledge; &, as this deponent hath hard say, the said John hath desired his father of his blessinge, and said to hym that 'he wold rather forsake all, or he wold take the said Ellin as his wief.' beynge askid howe [he] knowis they were maried together, he sais, biecause this deponent was a nere neibour, within a fieldes broade to them /

Willelmus Bridge, etatis xxiiij^or annorum, novit partes vj annis, quia est servus partis ree / Examinatus super allegacione &c. This deponent sais, that, by report of the neighboures thereabout, the said parties were maried together, beynge but Children. sins the tyme he hath dwellid with John Andrewe, he neuer se them vse either other as man and wief, which is above vj yeres ago: but that they wold avoid the Company & speakinge, [2]the one of the other, nor neuer did consent or agre together by any waies. and forther he sais, that by report, the said John Andrewe askid his father his blessinge after he was maried, & said he wold go out of the Contrey or euer he wold take her as his wief. And for the cause of their mariage, he sais, per relacionem aliorum, that hit was vt precontestes sui deposuerunt. and forther, he sais, he hath hard the said John say he wold neuer take her as his wief. And to this deponentes

[1—1] Struck out, and "doth knowe" written over by another hand.
[2] leaf 80, back.

knoledge, they neuer dwellid together; biecause the said Ellin went to London, and the said John) went to the warres, & abrode to service. and as for Carnall Act, this deponent thinkes veryly, for any thinge that euer he hard or se, they neuer had carnall dole together, or euer vsid either other as man & wief, to his knoledge; but euer did discent /

[1]Responsiones personales Johannis Andrewe, super positionibus et articulis Libelli ex parte Elene Dampart contra ipsum oblati, capte coram magistro Roberto Leche, in Legibus baccallaureo, v° die Novembris 1561° /

Ad primam positionem, This deponent sais, that Elein Dampart & he were maried together vnder age,—this deponent then beyng about x yeres old, & the said Ellin somewhat vnder viij,—in a Chamber at Widford Hall, by one Sir John) Handford, who servid Mr. Dampart of Widford at that tyme, xiij yeres ago, or there-aboutes. beyng askid 'who was present by'; he knowes not. beyng askid whether, sins he came to age, he euer fansied her, he saies 'no; neither sins nor afore, nor neuer in his hart toke her for his wief'; for, at the tyme of their mariage they knewe not what they did; or els this respondent wold neuer have had her. beynge askid whether he euer lay with her, he answeris, that 'the first night they were maried, they lay both in one bed, but ij of her sisters lay betwene hym & her; and sins that tyme, he neuer Lay with her in bed, nor neuer had carnall dole with her.' beynge askid whether he did euer ratify the mariage by sending her tokens,[2] or kissinge, or mutuall Cohabitacion; he saies 'neuer.' beyng askid 'where they have dwellid asonder,'—he sais, 'she hath dwellid sommetyme at Middlewich, sommetyme with Mr Duncalf, and sommetyme at London. and this deponent dwellid in Presbury, with his sister, iij yeres, & was in the North part iij yeres' / forther, beyng askid, 'howe hit chauncid the[y] sewid not a dyvorse afore nowe, seynge they could not agre,' he sais that 'they began to sewe a dyvorse afore, about v' yeres ago; & the matter, to his remembraunce, was brought to witnes; and then he went

[1] leaf 88 (Piccope's No. 39).

[2] In April 1540, Thomas Brevokes deposes, that 'on a Monday last month, about sunset . . he heard John Yenne ask William Cupper whether there was any contract of marriage between him and Elisabeth Yenne.

'Said he': "She hath a napkyn of myne in token of maryage, and condicionally that she shulde be my wyffe; and upon the same, she hath my fayth and troth; and I have hirs. And I have a ryng of her, and a napkyn, upon the same condicion; and in case this be no bargen, and if she will take the parcell upon her, discharging mee, I ame well contented; and she shall have parte of my goodes."

'But, said Elisabeth': "I will not discharge you: a bargen hit ys; and a bargen yt shall be; and I will goo therow the lande with you."—*Old Ways in Olden Days, down West.* Exeter, 1892.

to Scotland, & he thought he wold se his comyng againe, or euer he sewid any forther'; & so, they beyng asonder till they were detectid in the visitacion for the same, neuer did sewe the matter, but did let it slippe till nowe, for Lack of ability to followe the Lawe. beyng askid whether she doth fansy hym, or wold have hym to her husband; he sais 'no'; and therfor he cannot fansy her, nor neuer did /

9. Grace Boyes *v.* Robert Talbot.

(She 9-10 at marriage; he about 13. Depositions taken, 6 Nov. 1562.)

One of the three Deponents, Thomas Pope, of the parish of Ribchester, 43, who had known the parties from childhood, says [1]'that Grace Boyes, beynge somwhat aboue ix yeres old, & vnder x', was maried about iiij^or^ yeres past to Roberte Talbot, at that tyme .... about xiij yeres old, in the parish church of Blagburne; .... he neuer hard they euer lye together, biecause the said Grace Boys was taken away from her Grandfathers house by a wile, to comme lye at Master Talbot house, half-brother to Roberte Talbot; and when she was there, without consent of her frendes, was maried to the said Roberte in the night season, as he hath hard; but he sais she neuer fansied hym as her husband, nor neuer had carnall dole together, or vsid either other as man & wief, by kissinge, speakinge, or such like; but the said Grace did euer dissent, as she dothe at this present, by reason of her sute of divorce commensid against hym. & this deponent hath hard her say xl' tymes, that she wold neuer take hym as her husband /'

Richard Dewhurst, of Ribchester, aged 44, deposes that 'the cause' of these children's marriage 'was, that mistris Talbot, wief to John Talbot, esquier, halfebrother to the said Roberte, desired of graundfather of the said Grace, where she dwellid, to haue her homme to her house, to make mery. and when she had her there, she maried her to Roberte Talbot, against the consent of the will of the said Grace, who, this deponent hath hard say many tymes, that she wold neuer take hym to her husband.'

10. Margery Vernon *v.* Randle More (she 9-10 at marriage, he 7-8).

[2]Examinacio testium in causa Divorcii super allegacione ex parte Margerie Vernon contra Randulphum More, oblata, capta coram magistro Roberto Leche &c, xj° Februarij 1562°[-3].

[1] leaf 88, back (Piccope's No. 40). [2] leaf 117, back (Piccope's No. 58).

Thom*as* Pole, paroch*ie* de Bartumley, etat*is* l an*norum*, no*vit* p*ar*tes ab infancijs earund*em* . . . . dicit, that M*ar*gery Ve*r*non and Ran*dle* More were maried together in the chapell of Hasslington in the p*ar*ishe of Bartumley, somwhat above x yeres ago, almost xj: and this, he knowes to be true; for this depone*n*t dwellid with Robe*r*t Ve*r*non esquier, father vnto M*ar*gery Ve*r*non at the same tyme; the said M*ar*gery at that tyme beyng*e* above ix yeres old, and vnder x; and *the* said Ran*dle* more above vij, and almost viij. beynge askid whether they eu*er* dwellid together in one house, he saies 'no.' and forther he saies, that the said M*ar*gery did, at merrimente*s* in Christmas; and at such tymes wold go to M*aste*r Mores house, and there lye a night or two at seue*r*all tymes; but the said Randle did neu*er* lie al night at M*aste*r Ve*r*nons house, to this depone*nte*s knoledge; neither had *th*ei any carnall copulac*i*on [1]together, to his knoledge. beynge askid howe long it is sins the p*ar*ties dissentid, he answeres, 'thre quarters of an yere sins, & not afore, to this depone*ntes* heringe.' but he saies, he cold neu*er* pe*r*ceyve any Love nor affection betwixe the p*ar*ties libellate. and forther he saies, that the said Randle did go and com*m*e to M*aste*r Ve*r*nons house many tymes, to dinn*er* and supper, but went home alwaies against night. beyng askid what is the cause they p*ar*ties cannot agre, and that the said M*ar*gery doth sue a divorce, he saies hit is for som*m*e Imped*i*me*n*t that the said Randle hathe longe bene on hym. and forther, this depone*n*t saies he neu*er* se any token or signe of Love betwixe them, or that the one wold kisse the other; and yet this depone*n*t hath bene much conve*r*saunt in the house w*i*th the said M*ar*gery Ve*r*non /

(Richard Poole, of Bartumley, aged 43, confirms Thomas Pole, tho' he knows less of the parties than Thomas does.)

[2]Joh*annes* Damp*ar*te, paroch*ie* de Bartumley, etat*is* xxx an*norum*, aut circite*r*, no*vit* p*ar*tes a pуericiis eorund*em* / Exa*minatus* supe*r* allegac*ionem* &c / This depone*n*t saies, he was p*re*sent by, when M*ar*gery More al*ias* Ve*r*non, and Ran*dle* More, were maried together in the Chappell of Hasslington above x yeres ago, the said M*ar*gery then beyng*e* about ix or x yeres old, and the said Randle about ij° yeres young*er*. beyng*e* askid whether they eu*er* dwellid together, he saies 'no,' to his knowledge; for the said Randle dwellid at the Hall of the Heath w*i*th his father, and the said M*ar*gery w*i*th her father, not far asonder. forther he saies, he did neu*er* knowe that the said Randle did lye any night at his father-in-Lawe his house; & tho he did resort nowe and then thither, he did neu*er*

[1] leaf 118. [2] leaf 118, back.

shewe any token or signe of Love toward ye said M*a*rgery, to his knoledge or sight. beynge askid whether the said M*a*rgery did resort and lye at M*aste*r Mores house any night, he saies 'no,' to his knoledge. but he saies, he hath hard it reportid that she wold com*m*e thither nowe and then at a Christmas tyme to make mery, and p*er*adventure lye there a night, & then go home; but she did not lye w*i*th the said Randle, to his knoledge / beynge askid whether eu*er* they eu*er* had carnall dole together, he saies 'no,' to his knoledge; and he think*es* in his Conscience they neu*er* had carnall act together, biecause the said Randle is very sickly, and hath som*m*e gret Impedim*en*te apon hym, w*h*ich causeth this depon*ent* to iudge that, by reason of the said infirmity, the said M*a*rgery can*n*ot fansy the said Randle. and forther he saies, he neu*er* se them kisse, or call ether other 'man and wife,' or shewe any token of Love, thone to thother, sins they came to discrec*io*n . . . . . .

Robert Short, of the parish of Bartumley, aged 46, confirms the last deponent in all particulars. After the children's marriage, [1] "he saies that they did neu*er* agre as man and wief sins they came to they[r] yeres of discrec*io*n, biecause he neu*er* did se any token of Love betwixe them, nor did neu*er* se hym [kisse] her sins they were maried. beynge askid whether the said Randle vsid to come to his father-in-Lawe his house, he saies he was wont to com*m*e thither, but, to this depone*ntes* knoledge, he did neu*er* lye there al night, but wold go home againe, biecause his owne fathers house was not far distant thens. and the said M*a*rgery wold go to M*aste*r Mores house at merime*ntes* in Christmas, or at gestninges, as he hard reportid; and he hath sene her go that way; but he neu*er* se her [there]. interrogat*us* de carnali: forther he saies, he think*es* in his Conscience they neu*er* Lye together, or had carnall act betwix them, biecause [MS. betwix] he is a sickly young man, and hath as yet small mynd of such matters, as this depone*nte* think*es*. and forther he saies, he hath hard w*i*thin this twelf month, the said m*a*rgery say she cold not fansy hym, and not agre. and forther he saies, he neu*er* se them shewe any token of Love, or Lovinge Counten*au*nce the one to the other . . . . est tenens Rob*er*ti V*er*non, p*at*ris p*arti*s act*rici*s . . . . and that it is supposid they may be divorsed, biecause they were vnder age; and he hath had a gret Impedim*ent* betwix them."

11. Peter Hope *v.* Alice Ellis (? both of Hawarden), (he nearly 13 at marriage, she 9).

[1] leaf 119.

[1] Examinacio testium super materia excepta et oblata ex parte Petri Hope, contra Libellum Alicie Ellis, alias Hope, capta coram magistro Roberto Leche, in *Legibus* baccalaureo &c iiij° Martii 1563° /

[2] Johñ ap Johñ, parochie de Hawarden, etatis circiter lx annos, novit Petrum Hope a puericia, et Aliciam Ellis, alias Hope, xvj annis et vltra / . . . . saies, he thinkes, by vertue of his othe, that the said Peter neuer gave his Cònsent to the said matrimony . . . . for he, the said Peter, told this deponent & his wief, the night afore he was maried, that he wold neuer call the said Alis Ellis his wief; the said Peter beinge at the tyme of his mariage, about xiij yeres old, and somwhat older, not xiiij by iij quarters. and forther he saies, that sins the tyme of his said mariage, the said Peter neuer gave his Consent to the said Alis, to take her as his wief, to his knoledge. reddendo certitudinem sue etatis, this deponent saies, he was nursid by this deponentes wief, who gave hym suck; and he knowes he was no elder, bie the age of his owne children /

[3] Ad iij Articulum, This Deponent saies, that he neuer knewe or hard that the said Peter Hope wold recognise or take Alis Ellis to his wief; but euer wold dissent, and say he wold neuer take her so. and as for their Cohabitacion, this deponent thinkes the matrimony cannot be ratified, biecause, at the same tyme as this deponent hard their frendes report, the said Alis was but ix yere old. and they dwellid together the next iij yeres after that, in house with the mother of the said Peter. and the said Peter went abroade to Schole,—to what place this deponent knowes not;—but this deponent verely thinkes the said Peter neuer consentid to take her as his wief, neither afore their mariage, nor sins . . . . . .

Agnes, *videlicet* Johñ, parochie de Hawarden, etatis xlviij annorum, novit Petrum Hope, ab infancia, et partem Aliciam Ellis, xv annis . . . .

Ad ij^d^ articulum, This deponent . . . . forther she saies, the said Peter neuer gave his consent to marry the said Alis Ellis (in her conscience), nor did not promise the same, nor the banes (as is articulate,) to be askid, biecause the said Peter was, at the tyme of his said marriage, but a boy, somwhat about xiij yeres old, in iij or iiij^or^ wekis, or therabout. reddenda racionem sui dicti, this deponent saies, she knowes well his age, biecause she was his nurse, after that he was a quarter of a yere old.

Ad iij articulum, This deponent saies, she knowes not certenly whether Peter Hope knewe of the said mariage; but she saies he, euer sins and

[1] leaf 119 (Piccope's No. 59).
[2] Read the last Deposition first, and the second, the Nurse's, second.
[3] leaf 119, back.

afore the said mariage, did dissent to take the said Alis to his wief. and this deponent diuerse tymes hath movid hym to take her, and vse her as his wief; and he wold euer answere, "she is non of my wief; and I will neuer take her so." and forther she saies, that they dwellid in house together with the mother of the said Peter about ij or iij yeres next after their mariage; but this deponent saies she thinkes they neuer consentid together, or had carnall dole together; for the said Alis was little past ix yeres old, tyme of the said mariage. And forther, this deponent saies, that she had a boy somwhat younger then the said Peter, who did lye with the said Peter at the same tyme when he and Alis Hope, alias Ellis, dwellid with Peter Hopes mother / which boy told this deponent, that the said Alis [1] wold comme and bringe the said Peter his sheetes to bed; and this deponentes sonne wold say to hym, "Peter, whie do not you take your wief to you?" and he wold answere, "Peace! she is non of my wief": wherby this deponente thinkes ther was neuer good will or lovinge consent shewid to the said Alis by the said Peter / . . . . . .

Edmundus Watkinson, parochie de Dodleston, etatis lix annorum, novit Petrum Hope ab infancia, et Aliciam Hope articulatam, xv annis / . . . . . .

Ad ij articulum, quoad primam partem eiusdem, nescit deponere; but he sais, that he well knowes Peter Hope was neuer the causer that he was maried to Alis Ellis, nor neuer gave his Consent therto. but he saies the marriage was consentid of betwix the mother of the said Peter, and the father of the said Alis; but what was the cause, this deponent knowes not. and the said Peter was, at the tyme of the said marriage, somwhat above xiij yeres old, & vnder xiiij.

Ad iij articulum, this deponent saies, that he knowes not whether euer the said Peter did remember the said mariage; but he saies, he thinkes verylie, that the said Peter did neuer consent to take the said Alis as his wief. reddendo racionem sui dicti, he saies, the said Peter told this deponent and John ap John his foster-father, the night afore he was maried, that he wold neuer take the said Alis as his wief. but he said, biecause it was his mothers mynde, he durst not displease her. and forther, this deponent saies, he neuer hard tell that the said Peter did consent to the said matrimonye; but he saies, they dwellid together about iij yeres next after their mariage, with the mother of the said Peter, beynge both but children; for the said Alis was little past ix yeres old when the said Peter & she were maried.[2] and after the said mariage, this

[1] leaf 120. [2] MS. marided.

deponent came to Peter Hopes mothers house, where she dwellid together, many tymes, yet he did neuer se or perceyve that the said Peter bere any Love or affection to his said wief; wherby he thinkes ther was neuer carnall dole betwixe them / . . . . . .

[1]Examinacio Testium in causa Matrimoniali ex parte Petri Hope contra presentem (?) Libellum ex parte Alicie Mathue, alias Ellis, oblatum, capta et medijs (?) eorum Juramentis, coram Johanne Chetam, notario publico examinatorum, xvij° Die martii 1562° /

Willelmus Sefton, parochie sancti Martini, civitatis Cestrie, ibidem morans traxit xvj annis, etatis lxvj annorum, novit Petrum Hope xx' Annis et vltra, et Aliciam Hope, alias Ellis, [*blank in MS.*].

Ad primam excepcionem / this Deponent saies, about xvj^tene^ yeres ago, as he remembres, he was seruaunt with Master Richard Hope, commynge & goynge; at what tyme Peter Hope was about xiiij yeres of age, & then was maried, by the Counsell of Christian Hope, his mother, vnto Alice Mathue, alias [Ellis *struck out*] Hope, then beynge about thage of xij yeres, in the parishe church of Saint Maries in Chester; but what tyme of the yere, this Deponent cannot well remember.

Ad ij^d^ excepcionem, this deponent saies, that after this Matrimony had and solempnizate, he hard the mother of Peter Hope, callid Christian Hope, say to Peter Hope, that yf he and Alice Ellis, alias Mathue, cold not agree when they comme to Lawfull age, that the said Peter shuld be at Libertye, and the Matrimony shuld be void; and that his mother did cause Alice Ellis to reache the said Peter drink, which he refusid to take at her handes . . . . . .

Richardus Burgenye . . . saies, that Peter Hope, as he hard say, ([R. B.] beynge then seruaunt with the mother of the said Peter Hope), was maried to Alice Ellis at Saint Maries in Chester, bie the perswasion of Mathue Ellis, father vnto Alice Ellis, and Christian Hope, mother to the said Peter, about xvj yeres ago, the said Peter then beynge about xij yeres of age, and the said Alice beynge then about x yeres of age, or vnder, as this deponent thinkes; but what tyme of the yere, this deponent cannot well remember . . . . . .

[2]Ad iij excepcionem, this deponent saies, that he, beyng at that tyme seruaunt at Mistris Christian Hopes, did neuer here the said Peter call the said Alice his wief; nor did lye together, to this Deponentes knoledge; nor made signe of Love betwixe them; nor did voluntarylie dwell

[1] leaf 124 (Piccope's No. 61). [2] leaf 124, back.

together as man and wief, to this Depone*ntes* knoledge; although they were in one house together, bie the space of almost iij yeres, or thereabout, after the said ma*tr*imony . . . . . .

12. Elizabeth Dampart (born Page) *v.* Thos. Dampart. (Boy under 10 at marriage. Wife leaves Husband.)

[1] Re*spon*siones pe*rsona*les Thome Dampa*r*t supe*r* ce*r*t*is* a*r*t*icu*lis sive Interrogatoriis sibi ex offic*io* mero obiect*is*, capte cora*m* ve*nera*b*i*li viro, M*agis*tro Robe*r*to Leche, in Le*gibus* baccall*aureo*, Vica*rio*, &c, xviij° Ma*r*tii 1562[-3].

Ad p*rimum* A*r*t*iculum* sive Interro*gatorium*, this re*spo*ndent saies, that this is the first othe that eue*r* he made before a iudge; neue*r*theles, he wold be lothe to breake it; and saies he stande*s* in state of dampnac*i*on yf he breake his othe; and that he is above xx, and vnder xxi yeres old.

Ad ij[d], he saies, he was maried, beyng vnder x yeres old, to Elizabeth Page.

Ad iij, This re*spo*ndent saies, that he hath laine w*i*th his wief, and ratified the mariage.

Ad iiij, This re*spo*ndent saies, that he did Cohabit w*i*th his wief about viij yeres. and he saies forther, he neue*r* put her away, nor gaue her cause to goe away, but would fayne haue had her to haue taryed in howse w*i*th him, this re*spo*ndent. And farther, this re*spo*ndent thinketh that her father was the cause that she went away; and sayth moreoue*r*, that where she is, it is vnto this re*spo*ndent not knowne; and this re*spo*ndent would gladdly come to the knowledge thereof.

Ad v[t], negat that he vsid her otherwise than a man ought to do his wief; and he saies she can p*ro*ve non otherwise; and sais he neue*r* had any knef [knife] in bed to do her hurt w*i*th-all; and that she doth misreport hym; and yf ther was any such thing*es*, it was rather of her doynge then of his; and that he doth take it apon his othe.

Ad vj[t], he saies he neue*r* vsid the Company of any woman besides his wief suspiciously, neither in the parishe of Werington, nor w*i*thout.

13. Thomas Fletchar *v.* Anne Whitfield (he between 10 and 11 at marriage, she about 9).

(He bargaind away, to pay his father's debts.)

[1] leaf 123.

[1]Examinacio testium in causa divorcii, super allegacione ex parte Thome Fletchar contra Annam Whitfield, capta coram magistro Roberto Leche, xxvj° Maii Anno predicto (1563).

Robertus Mercer, parochie de Walton,[2] etatis lvj annorum, novit partem agentem a nativitate, et partem ream vj annos, &c.

Ad contenta in allegacione, dicit, that he knoweth well the parties Libellate—Thomas Fletchar, the sonne of John Fletchar, and Anne Whitfield, the doughter of William Whitfield;—and saies they were maried together in the parish church of Childwall,[3] betwene Candlemas and Lent, about ix yeres nowe past. the said Thomas, at tyme of the said mariage, was about x yeres & vnder xj; & thage of the said Anne, he knowes not certenly, but, to his Judgment, she was about ix yeres old at the same tyme / beynge askid howe it Chauncid they were maried so younge, this deponent sais, that John Fletchar, father of the said Thomas, was in debt; and, to get somme money of William Whitfield, to the discharge of his debtes, maried and bargained his sonne to the said Whitfeildes doughter. Interrogatus de Cohabitacione, this deponent saies, that the said Thomas dwellid with his father duringe his lief,—in which house he still dwelleth;—and the said Anne dwellid in Childwall with her mother & father duringe their lief; and after, dwelled with master Fazakerley; and nowe, with a suster of her owne; so that the said Thomas and Anne were neuer cohabitant together, to his knoledge. but when the said Anne was younger, she came, a gestwise, to make mery with the mother of the said Thomas; where she taried not past a day or a night. Interrogatus de carnali copula, this deponent saies, that he neuer perceyvid, or knewe, or hard of, any Love betwixe them; wherbie he thinkes ther was neuer any carnall dole betwixe them,—bie vertue of his othe,—nor any ratifienge bie other Consent; but he hard say, they wold neuer agree together, but euer did dissent, sins the tyme they came to perfitt age of consent, and before / reddendo racionem scientie sue, he saies, he knowis the premisses to be true, biecause he is a nebour.

[4]Johannes Wolfall, parochie de Walton, etatis xxx^a annorum, novit partem actricem, et partem ream, ab infanciis earundem. Examinatus, &c / This deponent saies, bie voice of the Cuntry he knowes Thomas Fletchar and Anne Witfield were maried together (but he was not present at their said mariage,) about Candlemas, ix or x yeres ago, in the church of Childwell; the said Thomas beynge, at tyme of the said mariage, about

[1] leaf 130, back (Piccope's No. 68).
[2] Walton-on-the Hill, near Liverpool, part of it now.
[3] Near Liverpool.
[4] leaf 131.

ix or x yeres old, and the said Anne was somwhat young*er*, to this depon*entes* Judgm*ent*. and after the said mariage, the said Thom*as* dwellid w*ith* his father, & went to schole; and the said Anne dwellid w*ith* her father duringe his lief; and sins then, she dwellid w*ith* her suster, so that they neu*er* dwellid together, except the one came ou*er*, a gestwise, to the other, when she was not past xij yeres old, to this depon*entes* knoledge; wherby, this depon*ent* verylie think*es* that they neu*er* had carnall dole together; for he neu*er* p*er*ceyvid, or hard of, that the one fansied the other. beynge askid whie they maried so younge, he saies, biecause the father of Tho*mas* Fletchar was in debt, he maried his sonne to Wi*lliam* Whitfield*es* doughter for a peice of mony, for discharge of his said debt*es* w*ith* the said mariage good*es*. and further he saies, he neu*er* hard that the one sent the other any Tokens sins the[y] came to Consent; but the neibo*ures* were sory that they were maried soe younge, biecause the said Thom*as* wuld not agree to take the said Anne as his wief /

Rob*ertus* Fletchar, p*ar*ochi*e* de Walton, eta*tis* xl an*norum*, no*vit* p*ar*te*m* act*ricem* a puericia, et p*ar*te*m* rea*m* iiij^{or} a*nnis* / Exa*minatus* sup*er* allegac*io*ne &c, This depon*ent* saies, that he, beynge a neibo*ur*, hard say, and knewe bie the vooice of the Cuntry, that Tho*mas* Fletchar and Anne Whitfeild were maried together in Childwall church, about ix or x yeres ago, as he hard say, about Candlemas, to his knoledge; the said Thom*as* beynge at that tyme about x yeres old: and thage of the said Anne, he knowes not; but he think*es* she was not so old as the said Thom*as*. and after the said mariage, the said Thom*as* dwellid w*ith* his father still; and the said Anne, w*ith* her father, as this depon*ent* well remembres. but he is assured that they neu*er* dwellid together; but on gestwise, p*er*chaunce, Tho*mas* wold go to play at Anne Witfield father for a day or two, when he was not past xj yeres old; but sins he came to yeres of Consent, he neu*er* wold take the said Anne as his wief, but eu*er* did dissent, as this depon*ent* hath hard ser*uaun*te*s*, that dwellid w*ith* Anne Whitfeild*es* father, report. Wherbie this depon*ent* think*es* verylie, ther was neu*er* carnall dole betwixe them: and besides that, this [1]deponent hath hard the said Tho*mas* say, that at xiiij^{tene} yeres old, it was lawfull for hym to Choose hym a wief; and that he thought he might refuse the said Anne, biecause he was maried vnder age. as for any tokens betwixe them, he neu*er* hard of [any]. et de ca*usa* Ma*t*rimonii, consentit cu*m* ceter*is* /

[1] leaf 131, back.

14. Jane Sommer *v.* Roger Massy.

(He says he was "borne in a mans armes" at the Marriage; according to her, he was 7. Her age is not stated.)

[1]*Responsiones* per*sonales* Rogeri Massy, capte super allegacione sive summaria peticione in causa Divorcii ex parte Jane Sommer, contra ipsum oblatum, xxj° Octobris 1563°.

Ad Contenta allegacionis sive summarie peticionis oblate ex parte partis actricis / respondet virtute Juramenti sui prestiti, that he was in the parish Church of Deasbury [Daresbury, by Warington,] a good while sins, longe before he came to any Judgment or discrecion; and whether he was then maried to Jane Sommer or no, he knowes not, for he was borne in a mans armes. beynge askid howe Longe he did cohabit [dwell] together, he saies, not this iij yeres; and howe longe Afore, he saies he cannot tell, biecause he is yet little past xiiij yeres old. beynge askid whether he did euer lye with her, or consentid to the mariage, he saies 'no'; for she refusid this deponent above a yere and half ago, which was afore he came to his age [of discretion, 14]. and sins that tyme he neuer Lovid her, nor yet knowes not what Love meanes: vt patet per aspectum eius corporis /

Responsiones personales dicte Jane, capte eodem die.

Ad contenta allegacionis, she saies, it is about vj yeres ago sins they were maried. quoad carnalem copulacionem, she saies, [2]he neuer had carnall dole together, neither did they euer take either other as man and wief, nor did euer lye together /

15. John Somerford *v.* Jane Somerford (born Brerton): boy 3 at marriage, girl 2; carried in friends' arms, who spoke the words of Marriage for them.

[3]Examinacio testium in Causa Divorcii super Allegacione sive summaria peticione oblata ex parte Johannis Somerford, generosi, contra Janam Somerford alias Brerton, Capta coram [M]agistro Roberto Leche, in *Legibus baccalaureo*, &c, xv° die Aprilis, 1564 /

Johannes Somerforth of[4] Asbury, generosus, etatis xxviij annorum, novit partes ab infanciis. Examinatus super allegacione sive summaria peticione ex parte Johannis Somerforth oblata, dicit, that he was present bie, when John Somerforth and Jane Brerton were maried together in the parish Church of Brerton about xij yeres ago. Reddendo racionem

[1] leaf 146 (Piccope's No. 82). [2] ? they
[3] leaf 156, back (Piccope's No. 88). [4] of, not *de*, in MS.

sc*ient*ie sue h*ujus*mo*d*i, he saies that he carried the said Johñ in his armes, beinge at tyme of the said Mariage about iij yeres of age, and spake som*m*e of the word*es* of M*at*rimonye, that the said Johñ, bie reason of his younge age, cold not speake hym self, holdinge him in his armes all the while the word*es* of M*a*trimonie were in speakinge / And one James Holford caried the said Jane in his armes, beinge at the said tyme about ij° yeres of age, and spake all, or the most p*ar*te of, the word*es* of m*at*rimony for her; and so held her still in his armes. Interrogat*us* de etat*e* p*ar*tiu*m* te*m*por*e* exa*minac*ionis sue; he saies that the said John) is above xv, and vnder xvj' yeres of age; and the said Jane is about one yere young*er* then the said Johñ. And further, beinge required whether the said marriage was eu*er* ratified bie carnall Copulac*io*n or other meane, Answereth that, in his Conscience, it was neu*er*. Reddend*o* rac*io*n*em*, he saies, that this depon*ent*, beinge vncle to the said John), did, in his behalf, saie to the frend*es* of the said Jane to have [1]had the Mariage ratified betwixe them, and p*ro*cured the Counsell*es* l*ett*res theranend*es*: notw*i*thstandinge, ratificac*io*n cold neu*er* be had; whereapon the said Johñ Som*er*forth doth sue the divorse, because of her vnkindnes, and other weightie Causes . . . . . .

Joh*anne*s Holford, gen*erosus*, parochi*e* de Davenh*a*m, etat*is* † an*no*ru*m*, novit p*ar*tes ab infanciis. Exa*minatus* sup*er* Allegacione &c., This Depon*ent* saies, that 'he was p*rese*nt in the p*ar*ish churche of Brerton when Johñ Som*er*forth was Maried vnto Jane Brerton, beinge then both Infant*es*. the said John) was holden in th[e] armes of one then p*rese*nt, and this depon*entes* brother held the said Jane in his Armes, scarse able to speake.' And this depon*ent* think*es* the said Jane was spoken for. and further he saies, 'it was the youngest Mariage that eu*er* he was at.' Exa*minatus* de ratificacione M*at*rimonii inter p*ar*tes fact*a*; he saies he cannot depose; but he saies he neu*er* hard that they did, or were eu*er* like to, Consent; and he thinkes the p*ar*ties ar*e* yet scarsly at the yeres of Consent.

Examinacio Janæ Smith, Mater [*so*] part*is* ree. Exa*minata* sup*er* Allegacione &c., This Depon*ent* saies, that John) Som*er*forth and Jane Brerton were maried together in Brerton Church xij yeres ago, beinge both infant*es*; the said John) beinge at that tyme vnder iiij^or^ yeres old, and the said [2]Jane was vnder iij yeres of age. Interrogat*a* de Consensu p*ar*tiu*m*, she saies that they neu*er* have consentid together, nor did neu*er* lie together sins the tyme of consent. Interrogat*a* de ratificaci*o*ne, this

[1] leaf 157. [2] leaf 157, back.

deponent saies, that the said Jane hath declarid that she wold neuer have the said John; and the said John is of the same mynd also.

[1]Examinacio testium ex parte Johannis Somerford generosi, et contra Aliciam Brerton, in causa Divorcii predicti, capta coram [M]agistro Johanne Chetam, notario publico, per mandatum reverendi patris Domini Willelmi, Episcopi Cestrensis, xv° die Aprilis 1564.

Johannes Parkinson, parochie de Asbury, ibidem oriundus, etatis circiter lx annos, testis in causa predicta productus, Juratus, et examinatus: Interrogatus primo de noticia partium, dicit, quod novit Johannem Somerford, generosum de Natiuitate sua; et novit Janam Brerton alias Somerford, vxorem Johannis Somerford, ex quo fuerant invicem maritati in ecclesia parochiali de Brerton, xij annis elapsis, et vltra. Interrogatus de etate dicti Johannis Somerford, tempore solempnizacionis matrimonii, dicit, in virtute Juramenti sui prestiti, that 'Mr John Somerford was about iij yeres and a half, at the tyme of the said Matrimony.' Interrogatus de causa scientia sua, this deponent saies, that 'his wief Elizabeth Parkinson was nurse to the said John Somerford the first yere that he was borne. And then, after that, the said John Somerford was sent for, home to his owne fathers house'; & then, after that, within ij yeres and a half, Sir William Brerton and William Somerford, father vnto John Somerford, made mariage together betwixe the said John Somerford, and Jane Brerton, doughter of the said William Brerton. And howe the said John and Jane did agree, after they came to Lawfull age, this deponent [2]cannot tell. and this deponent saies, that John Somerford is nowe about thage of xv yeres and vpward, as this deponent verelie knowes. et de etate alterius partis, nescit deponere. Aliter nescit deponere . . . . . .

Elizabetha Parkinson, parochie de Asbury, ibidem morans traxit xxx annis et vltra, etatis circiter lx annos, novit Johannem Somerford a natiuitate sua, et Janam Brerton a Matrimonio inter dictum Johannem Somerford et dictam Janam Brerton, xiij annis elapsis. Interrogata de etate partium tempore matrimonii, dicit, quod Johannes Somerford fuit etatis iij annorum et vltra, eodem tempore; et etatem Dicte Jane eodem tempore, nescit. Deponente Interrogata de causa sciencie, this deponent saies, that sone after the said John Somerford was borne, he was send to this deponent to nurse; which this deponent did norishe a Twelf moneth; and after that, the said John was send for, homme to his Parentes, and there continued

[1] leaf 165 (Piccope's No. 92). [2] leaf 165, back.

two yeres and a half. And then S*ir* W*illiam* Brerton and W*illiam* Som*er*ford, father vnto the said Johñ Som*er*ford, did agree of Mariage betwixe the said John Som*er*ford and Jane Brerton; *which* were then maried together, and dwellid together at Brerton, after the Mariage betwixe them, the space of x yeres. sed de Consensu, assensu, Carnali Copula, et aliis post pub*er*tatem, Dicit *quod* nescit Depon*er*e. et vlterius dicit, q*uod* Joh*annes* Som*er*ford e*st*, in p*re*senti, circit*er* xv' sue etat*is* annu*m* constitut*us* . . . . . .

16. Jenet Parker *v.* Laurence Parker.

(She 5 at marriage; he 9-10.)

[1] 1 June 1564, Henry Parker the elder, of Holt House in the parish of Colne, about 52 years old, & father of the child-husband, deposes that the children were married about 12 years before, in the Church or Chapel of Colne, outside the diocese of Chester, his boy Laurence being between 9 & 10 years old, & Jenet (*Lat.* Joana) 5, or more. "And he saies, that after the M*at*ri*mo*nie had betwixe the said p*ar*ties, the said Laurence and Jenet dwellid with Alex*ander* P*ar*ker, father vnto the said Jenet, about iiij[or] yeres, or there-about. And after that, the said Alex*ander* P*ar*ker, father vnto the said Jenet, cold not agre; and so the said Lau*rence* went from hym̄, & dwellid in sundrie places, the space of iiij[or] yeres, and came not at his wief after, to his knoledge."

[2]On 15 June 1564, James Shackilton of Colne, aged 46, who was present at the children's marriage, confirms the facts of it & their ages &c, and the boy's running "his way from the said [Alex Parker's] house . . . biecause he cold not agree with his father-in-Lawe." Shackilton also "saies he neu*er* hard that eu*er* they consentid sins they came to yeres of discrec*io*n; and he verilie think*es* in his Conscience, the said Jenet and Laurence had neu*er* carnall act together."

Henry Mitton of Colne, aged 38, who "was in the towne of Colne the same daie that Jenet P*ar*ker and Laurence P*ar*ker were maried together in Colne Church," confirms all the foregoing statements, & that the boy & his father-in-law "disagreed, in so much that the said Laurence went away from Alex*ander* P*ar*kers house, the said Jenet beinge not xj yeres old. and they dwellid neu*er* after that, together, to this depon*entes* knoledge . . . [&] he hath hard it reportid bie the Neibo*ures* there about, that the said Jenet, both before she was xij yeres old, and after, that alwaies she neu*er* wold Consent to take the said Laurence as her husband; wherbie he think*es* in his Conscience they neu*er* had carnall act together."

[1] leaf 171. [2] leaf 176, back.

17. Margaret Hawke or Whittacres *v.* Henry Whittacres (girl 11, boy 10, at marriage).

[1] Exa*minac*io testiu*m* sup*er* allegacione*m* ex p*ar*te M*ar*garete Hawke, al*ias* Whittacars, con*tra* Henricu*m* Whittacars, in ca*usa* divorcii, capt*a* die et an*no* p*re*d*ictis* [30 June 1564].

Edmund*us* Starkie, paroch*ie* de Whalley, etat*is* xxvj an*n*oru*m*, no*vi*t p*ar*te*m* act*ricem* et p*ar*tem rea*m* xiiij an*n*is. Exa*minatus* sup*er* allegac*ion*e &c. This depon*ent* saies, that he was p*rese*nt in the chappell of Church [? New Church in Pendle, or Church Kirk] when the said M*ar*garet and Henry were Maried togeth*er* [2]bie the Curate there, then beinge about x' of Clock afore none; the said M*ar*garet beinge at that tyme about xj yeres old, and vnder xij, as this depon*ent* certenly knowes / and the said Henry, one yere and a half young*er*. Interrogat*us* de Coha*b*itac*ion*e, consensu, et carnali copula; he saies, they dwellid neu*er* much together; for, for the most p*ar*t, till w*i*thin this ij° yeres, for the said Henry was at schole in diu*er*se places; and she was at her fathers. and, to his knoledge, they neu*er* consentid together, nor the one neu*er* lovid thother; but always they mislyked one the other. and for carnell dole, he saies, he think*es* ther was neu*er* no*n* betwixe them, to his knoledge, that eu*er* he cold eu*er* here tell of, or p*er*ceyve. P*rese*ntib*us* te*m*po*r*e solemnizac*io*nis p*re*d*icti* m*at*rimonii, Nic*olao* Ashton, gen*er*oso, Tho*ma* Catly, isto deponen*ti*, et mult*is* alijs . . . . . .

Thom*as* Rily, p*a*roch*ie* de Castill in Clidroe,[3] etat*is* xxx an*n*oru*m*, no*vi*t p*ar*tes ab infancijs . . . . . . saies that, for the space of this vij yeres last past, this depon*ent* hath bene tablid in house w*i*th the father of the said M*ar*garet, where she still dwellid; & the said Henry nowe and then resortid thither; and yet he neu*er* p*er*ceyvid any Love betwixe them, but rather, mislykyng, as he hath heard them forty tymes say that they would neu*er* contynue together as husband & wyfe; [4]and he think*es*, if eu*er* ther was any cohabitac*io*n, it was bie Compulsion of frend*es*, and not for any love . . . . . .

Chr*isto*pherus Dicconson, p*a*roch*ie* de Clidroe, etat*is* xxxj an*n*o*rum*, no*vi*t p*ar*tes a pu*er*icijs . . . saies . . . for any thinge that eu*er* he cold here, beinge a neibo*u*r hard bie, the said M*ar*garet and Henry neu*er*

[1] leaf 181, back (Piccope's No. 90). [2] leaf 182.

[3] Clitheroe, now a municipal borough, township, and market-town, in Whalley parish, N.E. Lancashire, on the river Ribble, and at the foot of Pendle Hill, 10¼ miles N.E. of Blackburn, 35 miles N. of Manchester, and 220 miles N.W. of London by rail. Clitheroe was a borough by prescription as early as the 11th century.—Bartholomew. [4] leaf 182, back.

agreed together, especiallie sins they came to yeres of consent; nor thone cold not fansy thother, but euer did dissent; wherbie he thinkes in his conscience ther was neuer carnall act together; and they neuer dwellid together but by stertes, in the house of the father of the said Margaret; for the said Henry went to schole, somtymes being tabled at Donham[1] and somtyme at Padiam.[2] And, as he verelie thinkes, they neuer lay together . . . . . .

18. Robert Mason *v.* Margaret Mason or Dugdale (he 9, she 10, at marriage).

[3]Examinacio testium super libello sive allegacione oblata ex parte Roberti Maison contra Margaretam Maison alias Dugdale, capta coram magistro Roberto Leche, &c, xij° Octobris 1564.

Georgius Sherington, parochie de Preston,[4] etatis † annorum, norit partes a puericijs. Examinatus super allegacione ex parte Roberti Maison oblata, dicit, in virtute Juramenti sui prestiti, that he was present when the said Roberte and Margaret were maried together in the parish Church of Preston, apon a Sondaie, about x of clock afore none, bie one Van Banester, Clark, then curate there, in the presence of this deponent, Johñ Maison, John) Hardman, and many others, about ix yeres ago; the said Roberte beinge, at that tyme, not past ix yeres of age, and the [said] Margaret was vnder xj. Interrogatus de Cohabitacione, carnali copula, et ratificacione huiusmodi matrimonij, this deponent saies, that he[5] wold not tarry or dwell with the said Margaret after the said mariage, but went and dwellid with his frendes. and further he saies, he verely knowes ther was neuer carnall acte betwixe them, nor the[y] neuer consentid together. and further, this deponent saies, that diuerse & many tymes sins the said Roberte came to Lawfull age, he hath hard hym saie he wold neuer take her as his wief, nor wold euer dwell with her. reddendo racionem sui dicti, he said he cold neuer fansy her, nor her father; biecause he kept the mother of the said Roberte to paramour, afore he maried her, & consumed the said Robertes gooddes, and for diuerse suche causes / . . . . . .

[1] Downham, a township in Whalley parish, N.E. Lancashire, on the river Ribble, 3 miles N.E. of Clitheroe.

[2] Padiham, now a manufacturing town and township, with railway station, in Whalley parish, N.E. Lancashire, 3 miles W. of Burnley, and 8 miles N.E. of Blackburn.—Bartholomew.

[3] leaf 195 (Piccope's No. 104).

[4] Now a parliamentary and municipal borough, &c., in N. Lancashire, on the Lancaster Canal, and river Ribble, near the head of its estuary, 28 miles N.E. of Liverpool, 31 N.W. of Manchester, and 209 from London by rail.—Bartholomew.

[5] The boy Robert Mason.

Johannes Mason, patruus partis eum producentis, parochie de Kirkham,[1] etatis lviij annorum, novit partem actricem a Nativitate; et partem ream, a Matrimonio &c. Examinatus super Allegacione &c / this deponent saies, that he was present when the said Roberte and Margaret were maried together in Preston church, about ix yeres ago; the said Roberte beinge at that tyme betwixe ix and x yeres old, & the said Margaret vnder xj. & the bridall was kept at the fathers of the said Margaret; & there the said Roberte remaynid lesse then a yere, and, immediatlie after the said Mariage, went from his father-in-Lawe, and neuer came in house with the said Margaret to dwell, sins that tyme; but hath euer sins disagreed from the said mariage, & hath often tymes told this deponent, beinge his vncle, both afore he was xiiij, & alwaies sins, that he wold neuer have the said Margaret to wief, nor agre to the said mariage; and he hath Continued in the same mynde still euer, wherof this deponent hathe certen knoledge: wherbie he [uncle Jn. Mason] verelie knowes they neuer had carnall acte together, nor bie any other meanes euer Ratified the said Mariage. reddendo racionem premissorum, This deponent saies, that he, beinge his vncle, hath bene privye to all his doinges in that behalf.

[2] Responsiones personales Margarete Mason, partis ree, super posicionibus et articulis Libelli, capta coram magistro Roberto Leche vicario [generali] &c, die et anno predictis. [26 Oct. 1564.]

Examinata super allegacione sive summaria peticione ex parte partis actricis oblata, dicit, that she and Roberte Mason were maried together in Preston Church about x yeres ago, the said Roberte beinge at that tyme above ix and vnder x; and this deponent was somwhat elder, vnder xj yeres of age. and the said parties dwellid together, imediatlie after the solempnizacion of the said Mariage, for the space of half a yere, or there about, and not a xij moneth. And after, when the said Roberte came to Lawfull age, he dissentid from the said Mariage, and neuer did cohabitt with her, nor neuer ratified the same bie carnall act or otherwise, but euer dissentid, and callid her before my Lord Archbishop of York his grace; and hath put her to gret trouble and sute.

19. Thos. Bentam *v.* Ellen Bentam (born Bolton): he 12, she 10, at marriage.

[1] In N. Lancashire, 9 miles N.W. of Preston. [2] leaf 197 (Piccope's No. 101).

[1]Exa*minac*io testiu*m* in ca*usa* divorcij ex p*ar*te Tho*m*e Benta*m* con*tra* Elena*m* Bentam, *alias* Bolton, oblat*a*, capt*a* p*ri*mo Februarij, Anno p*re*d*icto*. [1564-5.]

Dauus Haydock*e*, paroch*ie* de Brimley,[2] etat*is* xlv an*noru*m, no*vit* p*ar*tes xvj an*n*is.

[3]Ad p*ri*mu*m* ar*ticu*lu*m*, This depon*en*t saies, that the said Thom*as* Benta*m* and Elene Benta*m* were maried together at Engleton[4] above xij yeres past, the said Thom*as* beinge at that tyme vnder xiij yeres of age, and the said Ellin somwhat young*er*: and this, he knowes to be true, beinge a nere neibo*ur* there, and one of the same p*ar*ishe with the said p*ar*ties. And further, he saies, he neu*er* knewe that they lay together; but eu*er* did dissent, and neu*er* dwellid together. beinge askid howe he knowes that they dissent, he saies, the said Thom*as*, p*er*ceyvinge her to be a light woman, cold neu*er* fansie her; and she, not fansienge hym, fell to lightnes.

Ad ij[d] et iij[tium] ar*ticu*los, Credit in se contin*er*e ver*ita*te*m*; and saieth, she hathe iij Children bastard*es*; ij° bie one man, and one bie an other man, and no*n* bie Bentam; for this Depon*en*t think*es* they neu*er* had carnall copulac*io*n together / . . . . . .

Ad vlt*imum*, dicit p*re*d*icta* p*er* eu*m* fore vera. no*n* est doct*us* &c / reddend*o* ca*usa*m scienc*ie* sue h*ujus*mod*i*, he sais his father was Executo*ur* to the graundfather of the said Elene; and therefore he hath had cause to knowe her misdem[e]no*ur*.

Ricardus Dickson, p*a*roch*ie* de Sondell,[5] ebor*acensis* dioc*ese*, etat*is* xliiij[t] an*norum*, [novit partes] xvj an*n*is.

Ad p*ri*mu*m* ar*ticu*lu*m*, This depon*en*t saies, that the said Tho*mas* and Elene were maried together [6]at Engleton about xij yeres passid, the said Thomas beinge about thage of xiij yeres,[7] and the said Ellein somwhat younger. beinge askid whie they were maried in their minoritie, he saies, that Ric*hard* Benta*m*, graundfather vnto the said Eleine, was a very welthie man; and [it] was supposed that he wold have bene good vnto them, and bestowid som*m*e good ferme apon her; but, or he died, the said Tho*mas* and Ellein disagreed, and she plaid manie light points. the graundfather, takinge displeasure, left her nothinge. and further saies, the said p*ar*ties neu*er* agreed, but were eu*er* asonder, and neu*er* dwellid

[1] leaf 204 (Piccope's No. 106).
[2] or 'Brunley,' for Burnley, near Whalley; ? Brindley, a township in Acton parish, W. Cheshire, 4 miles N.W. of Nantwich. [3] leaf 204, back.
[4] ? Ingleton, in the parish of Bentham, in the Northern division of the West-Riding of Yorkshire.
[5] ? what and where ? [6] leaf 205. [7] MS. yeres of.

together; wherbie he thinkes, nor neuer cold here tell, that the Marriage was euer consummate bie carnall acte, or otherwise, betwixe them.

Ad ij et iij articulos, dicit eosdem fore veros; et dicit quod mulier est fame lese, et male conversacionis, ac vulgati Corporis, insomuch that she hath had diuerse children bie diuerse men, as William Saiger & John Michell; and fame goth, she burned[1] the said Saiger, and one Miles Ashton / . . . . . .

Ad vltimum, dicit predicta per eum fore vera. non est doctus, non conductus &c. and gevinge cause of the Notice[2] thereof, he saies he was seruaunt with her graundfather, and was in howse with her duringe her mynoritie, and well knewe her Conuersacion, and hath Maried her Aunte.

Responsiones personales Elene Bentam, capte eodem die /

Ad primum, This Respondent saies, she was Maried vnto Thomas Bentam in Engleton churche; but howe longe ago it is, she knowes not, biecause she was very younge, about x yeres old, or xj at the most, the same tyme; & Thomas Bentam somwhat elder then she. and further, she saies, that after the said mariage, they neuer lay together, nor dwellid together in one howse; but euer did dissent, and were continuallie euer asonder; she with her mother, and he x miles of, or thereabout, with Richard Bentam or Thomas Walmesley in Service; nor euer ratified the mariage after they came to yeres of consent &c.

Ad ij et iij posiciones, fatetur contenta in dicta posicione fore vera. and further she saies, she is very sory for her offencis.

20. Rafe Fishe *v.* Katherine Fishe (born Bolton). He under 14 at marriage.

[3] Examinacio testium, capta coram Ricardo Grenehalghe, clerico, super libello ex parte Radulphi Fishe contra Katerinam eius vxorem, virtute cuiusdem commissionis, &c.

Willelmus Barker of Churche,[4] of thage of xl yeres, sworne and examined, deposeth and saieth, that Raffe Fishe was maried vnder thage of xiiij yeres, and at the parishe of Blagburne / the said William Barker saieth, that the said Rafe and Katherine Bolton, alias Fishe, did not, at any tyme after they were maried, accompanie together as man and wief. the said William Barker, sworne and examined, saieth, that the [5]said Raffe and Katherine had neither child nor children, nor, to his knoledge,

[1] poxt. [2] his knowledge. [3] leaf 214, back (Piccope's No. 110).
[4] ?Church Kirk, about 4 miles from Darwen, N.E. Lancashire. [5] leaf 215.

had any carnall dole or confederacy at any tyme together / the said *William* Barker, sworne and examined, saieth, that the said Rafe and Katerin have bene asonder, and not conversaunt, to his knoledge, about xix yeres / The said *William* Barker, sworne and examined, deposeth and saieth, that the said Kattrin Bolton, alias Fishe, hath, sins she was Married to the saide Raffe, had a child bie one Roberte Forrest; and that she hath behaved her self in suche sort as is not thought honest amonge her Neiboures.

John Walshe of Darwen, of thage of xl^{ty} yeres, sworne and examined, saieth to all and euery the said articles, as the said *William* Barker hath afore said.

Henry Walmesley, of Meller,[1] of thage of xxxvj yeres, sworne and Examined, deposeth and saieth to all and euery the said articles conteynid in the saide Commission, in all and euery thinge and thinges, as the said *William* Barker hath afore saide, &c /

(signd) Per me, Ricardum Grenehalgh curatum de Preston.

21. Alexander Osboston (Osbaldiston) *v.* Margaret Osboston (born Hothersall): he nearly 11 at marriage, she 6 or 7, partly borne in arms, and partly led to Church.

[2]Examinacio testium ex parte *Alexandri* Osboston[3] contra [*blank in MS.*] capta die et anno predictis. [4 May 1565.]

Robertus Harrison, parochie de Kirkham,[4] etatis xxx annorum, novit partem actricem x annos, et partem ream a tempore hujusmodi presentis matrimonii. Examinatus super allegacione sive summaria peticione ex parte partis actricis oblata, This deponent sais, that Alexander Osboston was married to the said Margaret iij or iiij^{or} daies afore the death of Richard Osboston, father to the said Alexander. and imediatlie apon the death of his father, by an Excheqvoures quest, was found to be of the age of x yeres and xj monethes. and the same tyme, videlicet, at the said marriage, the said Margaret was about thage of vj or vij yeres, as it semed to this deponent, bie reason she was partlie borne in armes, and partlie Led to Lowe-church, where they were Maried bie Sir Thomas French, then Curate there / and after the said Marriage, the said Alexander went to Cuerdo[n],[5] to his graundmothers, where he dwellid

[1] Mellor, an ecclesiastical district and township in the parish of Blackburn, N.E. Lancashire, 2½ miles N.W. of Blackburn.—Bartholomew.

[2] leaf 224, back (Piccope's No. 114). [3] The local contraction of Osbaldistone.

[4] In N. Lancashire, 9 miles N.W. of Preston.

[5] ? Cuerden Hall, in Cuerden, a township in Leyland parish, N. Lancashire, on the river Lostock, 5 miles N.W. of Chorley.—Bartholomew.

duringe her lief; and the said M*ar*garet, at Hothersall[1] w*i*th her father, where she dwelt still yet, and hath done sins. And further, he saies, that the said Alex*ander*, after and before he came to thage of xiiij yeres, did eu*er* disagre and dissent from the said Marriage; and bie open word*es* declared [2]that he wold neu*er* have the said M*ar*garet to his wief. and also he saies, they neu*er* dwellid together; neither by any other meanes ratified the said marriag*e*. reddend*o* rac*i*on*em*, saies, that he, this deponent, hath bene seru*aunt* w*i*th my said Ladie Osboston, and eu*er* knewe of all the doing*es*. no*n* est doct*us*, no*n* Conduct*us*, no*n* curat &c /

Henricus Colthurst, p*ar*och*ie* de Preston in Amu*n*dernes,[3] etat*is* xxx an*noru*m, nov*i*t p*ar*te*m* act*ricem* ab infanc*ia*, et p*ar*te*m* rea*m* a m*atri*mon*i*o &c. Exa*mina*t*us* &c, This Deponent saies, that Alex*ander* Osboston was married at Lowe-church, to M*ar*garet Hothersall, bie S*i*r Thom*as* French, cur*ate* there, in the p*rese*nce of certen pe*r*sons, to the nomber of vij or viij at the least, the said Thom*as* [*that is*, Alexander] beinge at that tyme vnder xij yeres, and the said M*ar*garet about vj or vij yeres of age. Inter*rogatus* De co*habi*tac*io*ne, carnali copulac*io*ne, et ratificac*io*ne, he saies, they neu*er* dwellid together in one house; for he dwellid w*i*th my Ladie Osboston, his graundmother, during her lief; and the said M*ar*garet, with her father at Hothersall, where she yet dwelleth. and further, he saies, to his knoledg*e*, or that he cold p*e*rceyve, the[y] had neu*er*[4] carnall act together, or ratified the said Marriage bie tokens, in word*es*, or otherwise, but did eu*er* dissent; nor the said Alex*ander* cold eu*er* to be content to take her as his wief. no*n* est doct*us*, no*n* tenens, no*n* aff*i*nis, &c. [*See the further Depositions on page* 183 *below.*]

22. Wm. Westby *v.* Anne Sothworth; boy under 10 at marriage, girl under 11.

[5]Exa*mina*cio testiu*m* sup*er* su*m*maria Peticione ex p*ar*te Will*elm*i Westbye, generos*i*, con*tra* Anna*m* Sothworth, capt*a* cora*m* M*agist*ro Rob*er*to Leche, in L*egibus* bacc*alaureo*, xxv° die Octob*ris*, 1565.

Thom*as* Harrison, p*ar*och*ie* de Sampsbury,[6] etat*is* xlviij an*noru*m, vel vlt*ra*, nov*i*t p*ar*te*m* acta*m* vij an*n*is, et p*ar*te*m* Rea*m* a Na*tiuita*te / Exa*mina*tus &c, dicit in vi*rtute* Jura*men*ti sui, that he was p*rese*nt at the solempnizac*io*n of the mariage of Will*ia*m & Anna in the libelle

[1] A township in Ribchester parish, N. Lancashire, on the river Ribble, 6½ miles N.E. of Preston.—Bartholomew. [2] leaf 225.

[3] Amounderness, a Deanery including Preston, Ribchester, Lancaster, Kirkham, &c. [4] MS. neu*er* h [5] leaf 240 (Piccope's No. 118).

[6] Samlesbury, in Lancashire, on the Ribble, near Preston.

mencioned; and sayth *that* the same mariage was solemnized in the church of Samsbury about seven yeres agoe, the said Will*iam* being, at the tyme of the said solempnizac*i*on, vnder the age of ten yeres, and the said Anne, at the same tyme, being vnder thage of xj yeres, About the feast of thassumpc*i*on of the Virgin Marie. Reddend*o* rac*ion*em sui d*icti*, sayth, that he was the same tyme dwelling in the howse of the father of the said Anne, and caried her vpon horseback behinde him to the said churche to be maried. And further sayth, that the said Will*iam* and Anne did neu*er* cohabite, or dwell in one howse togethers, sythence the tyme of the said solemnizac*i*on. Reddend*o* rac*ion*em sui dict*i*, sayth, that the said Will*iam* hathe ben*e* tabled much abrode, at schole, and most p*ar*te ben at his awne fathers howse, vnder a scholem*aster*, And neu*er* at the howse where the said Anne dwelled or dwelleth, but as a strang*er*. [1]Int*er*rogatus de carnal*i* copula et ratificac*ione* d*icti* m*at*rimonii, sayth, *that* after the tyme he, the said Will*iam*, came to the xiiij[th] yere of his age, or theraboute*s*, he neu*er* ratified y[e] said mariage by any way or meanes, as this depon*ent* iudgeth & thinketh in conscience. / Reddend*o* rac*ion*em sui d*icti* hu*ius*mod*i*, sayth, *that* when the said p*ar*ties, Will*iam* & Anne, came to that age *that* their frende*s* & parente*s* thought their discrec*i*on s*er*ved them to agree together & to ratifie the said mariage, or els to disagre and dissent from the same, John Westbie, father to the said Will*iam*, came to the howse of Sir John Southworth, knight, father vnto the said Anne, about one yere and half sythence, to enquire and dem*m*and of the said Anne, what she could finde in heart to doe conc*er*ning the said mariage. And after the said Anne was dema*u*ndid that question of her owne father, she answered that 'she could not phansie the said Will*iam*; and that she would not consent to take him, the said Will*iam*, to her husband.' Whervpon, the said John Wesbye dep*ar*ted home againe. and about one twelvemonthe after, the said Will*iam* was demaunded by the father of the said Anne, 'what liking he had of her, and whether he could so well phansie her as to haue her to wief'; who made answere in the p*rese*nce of diu*er*se worshipfull, *that* 'he would not haue her to wief, nor ratifie mariage w*i*th her in any wise.' no*n* est doct*us*, no*n* Conduct*us*, no*n* Consang*uineas*; est Seruiens D*omi*ni Joh*ann*is Sothworth, p*at*ris p*re*d*ict*e Anne, no*n* curat &c.

[2]Will*elmus* Preston, paroch*ie* de Sampsbury, etat*is* circit*er* xliiij an*no*-*rum*, nov*it* p*ar*tem act*ricem* circit*er* x a*n*nos, et p*ar*tem Rea*m* a N*atiuitat*e. Exa*minat*o &c dicit, that he, beinge Seru*au*nt to S*ir* John Sothworth, was attendaunt apon W*illiam* Westby when the mariage was Solempnizate in

[1] leaf 240, back. [2] leaf 241.

Sampsbury churche, bie one S*ir* Ric*hard* Percevall, betwene the said Will*iam* and Anne Sothworth, about thAssumpcion of the blessid Virgin S*aint* Mary, and also about vij yeres ago; at w*hi*ch Mariage, this depon*ent* was p*resen*t, the said Wi*llia*m beinge at the same tyme somwhat above thage of ix yeres, and vnder tenne, as this depon*ent* hard Johñ Westby, father to the said Wi*llia*m, declare the same tyme, and as this depon*ent* did also iudge bie the sight of his bodie; and the said Anne was somwhat above x, and vnder thage of xj yeres, as this depon*ent* did certenly knowe, beinge conversaunt very much w*i*th the said Anne, and having knowne her from her Nativitie. Interrogat*o* de carnali copula, vel ratificac*ione* h*ujus*mod*i* m*at*rimonii post pub*er*tatem p*ar*tiu*m*, This depon*ent* saies, that the said Wi*llia*m and Anne did neu*er*, either afore they came to yeres of consent, or after, cohabitt and dwell together,—as this depon*ent*, beinge houshold S*er*ua*u*nt to S*ir* Johñ Sothworth, well knowes,—nor eu*er* vsed either other, as man and wief, in word*es* or otherwise. And further this depon*ent* saies, that about a yere and a half ago, Johñ Westby, [1]father to the said Will*iam*, in the p*rese*nce of S*ir* Johñ Sothworth, k*night*, and the Ladie Mary Sothworth his wief, parent*es* to the said Anne, and of diu*er*se others, did demaund of the saied Anne, whether she cold be co*n*tent to take the said Wi*llia*m as her husband; and the said Anne answerid that 'she wold not take hym as her husband; nor she cold not fansy hym, or consent to the said Mariage.' And S*ir* Johñ Sothworth, her father, askid her the same question, & she answerid as before; whereapon Mr Johñ Westby dep*ar*tid. And after that, about S^t^. James day last past, at my L*ord* Bushops beinge at Sampsbury, the said Wi*llia*m, in the p*rese*nce of diu*er*se Worshipfull, was demaundid by S*ir* Johñ Sothworth and others, 'whether he cold be content to fansy the said Anne, and take her as his wief': who answerid that 'he wold not take her as his wief, biecause she had afore refusid hym': whereby this depon*ent* verily belevis in his conscience, the said Mariage was neu*er* Ratified betwene them.

[On lf. 242. Thomas Walmesley, another household servant of the said Sir Jn. Sothworth, deposes to the same effect, and often in the same words.]

[2]Exa*minacio* testis in ca*usa* Westby con*tra* Sothworth, in ca*usa* Divorcii, capt*a* cora*m* m*agist*ro Rob*er*to Lech*e*, &c, viij° Novemb*ris* 1565 /

Joh*anne*s Wodhouse, p*a*roch*ie* de Poton,[3] etat*is* circit*er* lviij an*norum*, novit p*ar*te*m* act*ricem* a N*atiuitat*e, et p*ar*te*m* rea*m* a M*at*rimonio &c.

[1] leaf 241, back. [2] leaf 248, back (Piccope's No. 121).
[3] ? Poolton in Lancashire, or Poulton ?

Exa*m*i*n*at*o* supe*r* allegac*i*o*ne* &c, dicit, that he was not p*re*se*n*t at the Mariage had and Solempnized betwene the said Wi*ll*i*a*m and Anne; but he saies he well knowes they were maried together. reddend*o* rac*i*o*nem* sui d*i*c*t*i, he saieth that he, this depon*ent*, was household Se*r*u*au*nt to M*a*s*te*r Johñ Westby, father to the said Wi*ll*i*a*m at the same tyme. and further he saieth, that he well knewe thage of the said Wi*ll*i*a*m, that he was vnder x yeres of age at tyme of the said Mariage; and the said Anne, as he hard it reportid of her fathe*r* and frend*es*, was vnder xj the same tyme / Interr*ogatus* de cohabit*acione* carnali copula, et ratificac*i*o*ne* h*uius*mo*d*i M*at*rimonii, This Deponent saieth, that they neue*r* dwellid together after the said Mariage; for the said Wi*ll*i*a*m went hom*m*e to his father, and the said Anne remaynid w*i*th S*i*r Johñ Sothworth her father. And further he saies, he think*es* in his Conscience they neue*r* consentid together sins they came to yeres of Consent; for he, this depon*ent*, hath diue*r*se tymes hard the said Wi*ll*i*a*m say, sins and afore this sute [1]begonne, that he wold neue*r* take her as his wief; in somuch that the said Wi*ll*i*a*m, being at Whalley at Schole, w*i*thin theis two monethes last, send a *lett*re to his mother-in-Lawe, beinge suster to S*i*r Johñ Sothworth, and aunt to the said Anne, that if his father wold have hym to take her as his wief, he wold rather be banished out of *th*e Cuntrey: w*h*i*c*h *Lett*re, this Deponent hard red / wherfore this depon*ent* verely think*es* that the said Wi*ll*i*a*m neue*r* consentid to the said Mariage, or that ther was eue*r* any carnall dole betwene the said Wi*ll*i*a*m and Anne; but that eue*r* they have dissentid, as they do at this p*re*se*n*t . . . . . .

23. Brigitte Dutton *v.* George[2] Spurstowe (she 4-5 at marriage, he 6).

[She could not perfectelie speake the wordes of matrimonie after the priest, because she was, at that tyme, in yeares tender and younge.[3]]

[4]Exa*minac*io testiu*m*[5] in ca*usa* Divorcii ex p*ar*te Brigitte Dutton con*tra* Rad*ulphum* Spurstowe, capt*a* xxvij Octobr*is*, A*nno* 1563.

Rob*er*tus Large, p*a*roch*ie* de Wau*er*ton, etat*is* lvij an*norum* aut circite*r*, nov*i*t p*a*rt*em* act*ricem* a Na*tiuita*te, et p*a*rte*m* rea*m* a M*at*rimonio inter p*ar*tes / Exa*minatus* in vim iura*men*ti sui, dicit, that the said Brigette & George, in the libell mencioned, were maried togethers in a p*r*ivate

[1] leaf 249.

[2] He is cald *George* by all the Deponents, but *Rafe* (*Radulphus*) in the heading, the latter name being probably got from the bride's father, Rafe Dutton.

[3] End of Robert Large's evidence. [4] leaf 242, back (Piccope's No. 19).

[5] Brigitte's nurse, Margaret Cawkin, gives evidence.

chapell belonging to the dwelling house of Rafe Dutton esquier, called the Hall of Hatton, about seven yeares past, or somwhat aboue; [1]the said Brigitte beinge at the tyme of solempnizac*i*on of the said marriage, vnder the age of fyve yeares, and the same George beinge at the same tyme aboute thage of sixe yeares. And further sayeth, that the said Brigitte and George did neu*er* ratifye the said mariage. reddendo rac*io*n*em* sui dicti, sayeth, that the same Brigitte is, at this p*rese*nte, aboue thage of twelue yeares, and vnder thage of threttene / and the said George, by this deponentt*es* estimac*i*on, aboue thage of xiiij^{e} yeares / And this deponent sayeth, that allmost for the space of too yeares last past, the said George and Brigitte were not in house together, nor neu*er* sawe ether other, synce / for he sayeth, that im*m*ediatlie after the deceasse of Randull Spurstoo, grandfather to the said George, Ric*hard* Spurstoo, father to the said George, did take the said Georg*e* secretlie from the Hall of Hatton, where the said George had before (for a certeyn*e* space) ben*e* kept at scole / sythens the tyme of w*hi*ch conveyaunce, the said Brigitte hathe misslyked of the said George, and playnelie declared to this depo*n*-*en*t, that she would neu*er* haue the said George to her husband / et reddendo ratio*n*em e*or*und*em*[2] d*ict*orum suorum, sayethe, that he hathe of long tyme bene reteyninge to the house of Hatton / and was p*rese*nte when the said mariage was solempnized in the said Chapell / and saythe further, that, at that tyme, the said Brigitte coulde not p*er*fectelie speake the word*is* of matri*m*onie after the priest, because she was, at that tyme, in yeares tender and younge.

[3]Margaret Cawkin, vxor W*illel*mi Cawkin, p*a*roch*i*e de Tattenall, Cestren*is* dioc*ese*, etatis circiter xlvj annorum, testis product*a*.[4] dicit, q*uo*d nouit Brigittam Dutton per spacium xij^{a}' annoru*m*. bene nouit et Georgium Spurstou a temp*or*e matrimonij &c. / Exam*in*at*a*, in vim iura-*men*ti sui, super allegac*i*o*ne* al*i*a*s* in causa p*r*incipali porrect*a*, dicit vt se-quit*ur* / That mariage was solempnized betwene the said p*ar*ties, vi*delicet*, Brigitte and George / about Mydsom*er* w*hi*ch was seven yeares ago, at Midsom*er* laste / the said Brigitte beinge at the same tyme aboue the age of fowre yeares, and not fyve. and as conc*er*ninge the age of the said George, she, this depo*nen*t, cannot certenlie depose; but he semed to her at that tyme, veraie younge / And further sayeth, that the said p*ar*ties were maried in the p*ri*uate Chapell of the Hall of Hatton, by a p*ri*est that then s*er*ued at Wau*er*ton / And further sayeth, that the said Brigitte was twelue yeares oulde at the feaste of Michaelmas last past; for she, the

[1] leaf 243. [2] MS. eūn or eñn [3] leaf 243, back.
[4] This refers to Margaret, I suppose, tho her husband is 'productus' too.

said Brigitte, was bo*ur*ne vppon Michaelmas daye was twelue yeares / Reddendo ratio*n*em d*ict*orum suorum, sayethe, that she, this deponent, was nurse to the said Brigitte, and gaue vnto her first soucke; and therefore she remembreth her age veraie well / et quoad Ratificatio*n*em d*ict*i matri*m*onij, sayethe, she veralie thinketh in her conscience, that the said mariage was neu*er* ratified betwene the said p*ar*ties, because the said George was taken from Hatton imediatlie after the deceasse of his grandfather / and the said Brigitte, hath at diu*er*s tymes, for the space of this twelmoneth last past, denied to this depo*nent* that she would haue the said George vnto her husband. Et dicit, q*uo*d est tenens Radulphi Dutton, p*at*ris d*ict*e Brigitte, &c.

Will*el*m*us* Calkin, p*a*roch*ie* de Tatnall, etat*is* circit*er* xlvj an*n*or*um*, Dicit, q*uod* nov*it* Brigitta*m* Dutton a N*ativitat*e, et p*ar*te*m* Rea*m* vij an*n*is, aut circit*er*. Exa*minatus*, in vi*m* Jura*men*ti sui, sup*er* allegac*ione* al*ias* ex p*ar*te p*ar*tis act*ricis* &c, dicit, that Brigitt Dutton and George Spurstowe were maried together in a p*ri*vate chapell of the Hall of Hatton, bie a p*rie*st that then Servid at Waue*r*ton, Seven yeres ago, and as much as sins Midsom*er* last. beinge demaundid whether he was p*resen*t at the said mariage, he saies 'no'; but he saieth, he knowes well it was so; for this depon*ent* was, and is, ten*au*nt to M*aste*r Raffe Dutton, father to the said Brigitt, and dwell*es* nere vnto Hatton Hall. And further he saieth, that the said Brigitt was about v yeres old, tyme of the said mariage; and the said George, to his iudgment, was much about the same age; and he well knowes th~ey were both very younge / Interr*ogatus* de etat*e* d*ict*e Brigitte, he saies, she was twelf yere old at Michaelmas last. reddend*o* rac*io*ne*m* sui d*ict*i, he saies, he well knowes her age, biecause this depon*entes* wief was the first that gave her suck*e*, and nursid her. Interr*ogatus* vlteri*us* de consensu et Ratificac*ione* h*ujus*mo*d*i M*at*rimonij, this depon*ent* saies, that he verily think*es* they neu*er* consentid to the said Mariage; and this Depone*nt* saies, he hard the said Brigitt, somwhat afore Midsom*er*-day last, report in the house of this depon*ent*, that she wold neu*er* take the said George as her husband. and the said George was taken from Hatton im*m*ediatly after the death of his graundfather; sins w*hi*ch tyme the said Brigitt neu*er* se hym, as this depon*ent* verylie supposeth.

Jacobus Blundell, p*a*roch*ie* de Waue*r*ton, etat*is* circit*er* xxxvj an*n*os et vlt*ra*, nov*it* p*ar*tem act*ricem* a N*atiuitat*e; et p*ar*te*m* Rea*m*, circit*er* vij an*n*is bene nov*it*, v*idelicet*, a te*m*p*or*e M*at*rimonii &c. Exa*minatus* sup*er* allegac*ione*, al*ias* ex p*ar*te D*ict*e Brigitte oblat*a*, Dicit, in vi*m* Jura*menti* sui p*re*stiti, that the said Brigitt and George were maried together vij yeres ago, and as much as sins Midsom*er* last; the said Brigitt beinge at that tyme betwene thage of iiij^or or v yeres; and the said George much about the same age, or rather older, to this Depon*entes* Judgm*ent*. Reddend*o* rac*ion*e*m* sui d*ic*t*i*, he saies, he was p*resen*t at the said mariage, and is a neybo*u*r nere Hatton Hall, where the father of the said Brigitt dwelleth. Interr*ogatus* de consensu et ratificac*ion*e &c, This Depone*n*t saieth, that apon the death of the graundfather of the said George, the same George, by his father was taken from the said Howse of Hatton; & Brigitt & he were neu*er* together sins. et al*it*er nescit Depon*er*e.

[The same 3 witnesses depose in the next suit for the divorce of Roland Dutton, Brigitt's brother.]

24. Roland Dutton *v.* Margaret Dutton (born Stanley): he 9 at marriage, she 5.

[1]Exa*m*i*na*cio testiu*m* sup*er* Allegac*io*n*e* sive Sum*m*aria petic*io*n*e*, ex p*ar*te Roland*i* Dutton, con*tra* M*a*rgareta*m* Stanley, oblat*a*, capt*a* cora*m* *m*ag*ist*ro Rob*er*to Lech*e* &c, xxvij° Oct*o*b*ris* 1565.

Robertus Larg, p*a*rochi*e* de Wau*er*ton,[2] etat*is* circit*er* lvij an*n*os, no*v*i*t* p*a*rte*m* act*ricem* a Nat*ivitat*e, et p*a*rte*m* rea*m* a M*a*trimonio &c. Exa*m*i*n*at*us* sup*er* allegac*io*n*e* &c, et in vim Jura*men*ti sui, dicit vt sequit*ur*: that Roland Dutton and Margaret Stanley, al*ia*s Dutton, in the Allegac*io*n menc*io*ned, were maried together in the chapell w*i*thin the howse of the Hall of Hatton[3] / aboute the feaste of Christmas last past was fower yeares; &, as this deponent thinketh, vppon the Sondaye next after the said feaste of Christmas; The said Roland beinge at that tyme aboue the age of Nyne yeares, and not tenne / and the said Margaret beinge at that tyme (by this deponentt*es* estimac*io*n) young*er* than the said Roland / and sayethe further, that the said Roland, eu*er* synce the solempnizac*io*n of the said mariage, remayned at Hatton / and the said Margaret hathe remayned els-where from Hatton; and neu*er* remayned at Hatton but onlie as gesteweyes / and further sayeth, that the said Roland is of the age of xiiij yeares, and vnder fyftyne; and for the space of this twelue-moneth last past, or therabout*es*, the said Roland and Margaret were neu*er* in house togither, to this deponentt*es* knowledge / and this depon*ent* sayethe moreou*er*, that the said Roland, w*i*thin a smale while after he

[1] leaf 245 (Piccope's No. 120).

[2] A parish, township, and village (now with railway station), 4 miles S.E. of Chester.

[3] The Stanleys' place, in the parish of Waverton, N. Cheshire, 6 miles W. of Tarporley.

was xiiij^e^ yeares of age, did, before his ordenarie, declare, that he would refuse to take the said Margaret to his wief; and that he would not consent to the said mariage w*h*ich was solempnized in his minoritie / wherbie this deponent iudgeth in conscience, that the said mariage was neu*er* ratified by anie meanes betwene the said Roland and Margaret. Reddendo ratio*n*em d*ict*orum suorum, sayeth, that he was p*rese*nte at the solempnizac*i*on of the said mariag*e*, and hathe ben*e* conu*er*saunt w*ith* the said Roland synce the infancie of the same Roland. Et dicit q*uo*d non est Doctus, nec conductus, sed est tenens Radulphi Dutton, patris d*ict*i Rolandi Dutton /

[1]Margareta Cawkin, vxor Will*el*mi Cawkin, P*ar*ochie de Tattenall,[2] Cestren*sis* Dioc*ese*, etat*is* circiter xlvj annorum / dicit q*uo*d Rolandum Dutton, a na*tivita*te bene nouit; et M*ar*garat*am* Stanley, p*er* spacium quatuor annorum nouit // Examinat*a* in vim iura*men*ti sui, dicit, That Roland Dutton is of the age of xiiij^tene^ yeares and more, asmuche as synce Lente last past; and that he was maried to the said Margaret Stanley in the Chapell of the Hall of Hatton / aboute fyve yeares agoo / as she, this deponent, supposeth; for she sayeth that she was not at the solempnizac*i*on of the same, but harde it certenlie reported / And beinge demaunded de ratificatio*n*e matri*m*onij, Dicit, That sythence this two yeares last past, she, this deponent, neu*er* sawe the said p*ar*ties together; nether dothe she knowe of anie token, or signe of loue that the saide Roland hathe shewed or delared vnto the said Margaret, synce the tyme that the said Roland came to thage of xiiij^tene^ yeares; and therefore in conscience she thincketh the said mariage was not ratified. Et quoad etatam d*ict*e Margarete Stanley, dicit, that she supposethe her to be about thage of twelue yeares / but thage of Roland, she knoweth ce*r*tenlie to be as before she hath deposed /

[3]Will*el*mus Calkin, p*ar*ochi*e* de Tatnall, etat*is* circit*er* xlvj an*n*os, nov*i*t p*ar*te*m* act*ri*ce*m* a Na*tivita*te, et p*ar*te*m* Rea*m* circit*er* v an*n*is. Exa*min*ato &c, dicit, in vi*m* Jura*men*ti sui, &c, that Roland Dutton and the said M*ar*garet libell*ate* weie maried together in a p*ri*vate Chapell of Hatton Hall, abovt fyve yeres ago, in the Christmas tyme; the said Rowland beinge at the same tyme aboue thage of ix, or x; for this depon*ent* well knoweth that he is nowe not xv yeres old. Reddend*o* ra*t*io*n*em, he saieth, that this depon*entes* wief was nurse vnto the said Roland; and that this depon*ent* is the nebo*u*r vnto the said Roland,

[1] leaf 245, back.
[2] A market-town, parish and township (now with railway station), 7½ miles S.E. of Chester. [3] leaf 246.

and ten*au*nt to his father; and therfore he well knowes his age / et quoad etate*m* D*ict*e M*ar*garete, this depone*nt* saieth, she semeth to be of thage of xij or xiij yeres; et al*ite*r nescit depone*re* certitudinalite*r* de etat*e* D*ict*e M*ar*garet*e* &c. Interro*gatus* de consensu et coh*abi*tac*io*ne et Carna*li* copul*a* &c, this Depone*nt* saies, that the said M*ar*garet was neue*r* at the Hall of Hatton, where the said Rowland dwelleth, but for a night or two in a yere on gestwise; and for the space of more then a yere nowe last past, the said M*ar*garet was neue*r* in the companye of the same Roland, to this deponent*es* knoledge. and this Depone*nt* ver[i]ly think*es* in conscience, the said mariage not to be of any force betwene them, but that it may be lawfully dissolved.

[1]Jacobus Blundell, Parochie de Waue*r*ton, etat*is* circiter xxxvj an*n*os, novit p*ar*te*m* act*ri*ce*m* ab infancia; et M*ar*gareta*m* Stanley, dicit q*uod* no*vi*t illa*m* a te*m*po*r*e m*at*rimonii. Exa*m*i*natus* supe*r* allegac*io*ne al*ias* ex p*ar*te D*ict*i Rolandi Dutton oblat*a* &c / Dicit, in vi*m* Jura*menti* sui, that he was p*resen*t at the solempnizac*i*on of Mariage betwene the said Roland and M*ar*garet, w*hi*ch was Celebratid and done at Hatton in a p*ri*vate Chapell there, apon a Sondaie in the *Christ*mas tyme iiij^{or} yeres ago, and as much as sins *Christ*mas last, the said Roland beynge then vnder x yeres old, and the said M*ar*garet (in this Depone*ntes* Judgment) vnder viij yeres old. Interrogat*us* de consensu, &c, dicit, that the said Roland hath continued at Hatton, for the most p*ar*te, sins the said Mariage, & dwellid neue*r* in any other place; and M*ar*garet hath continued els-where, insomuch as this depon*ent*,—beinge a neybo*u*r to the Hall of Hatton, and vsing*e* very often, almost dailie, to come to *th*e said Hall,—neue*r* se the said M*ar*garet there passinge ons, sins tyme of the said Mariage, to this depone*ntes* Remembraunce. and therfore this depone*nt* think*es* verely, the said Mariage was neue*r* ratified betwene them / And further he saies, he demaundid of the said Roland, whether he wold take the said M*ar*garet as his wief; who answerid 'he wold neue*r* have and take the said M*ar*garet as his wief, nor consent to the said Mariage.'

25. Wm. Spakeman *v.* Leticia Unsworth: he about 10 at marriage; she about 11.

[2]Exa*minac*io testiu*m* in ca*usa* Divorcij ex p*ar*te Will*elm*i Spakeman con*tra* Leticia*m* Vnsworth, capt*a* cora*m* *M*agi*st*ro Joh*anne* Chetam, No*ta*rio pu*bli*co, ex Man*da*to D*omi*ni Judic*is* xxv^{o} Octob*ris* 1565 /

[1] leaf 246, back. [2] leaf 247 (Piccope's No. 121).

Thomas Kilshae, p*a*roch*ie* de Winweke,[1] cestr*ensis* dioc*ese*, ibi*de*m Mora*ns*, traxit vij an*n*is, oriund*us* infra paroch*iam* de Leghe,[2] dict*e* dioc*ese*, etat*is* circit*er* xxiij an*n*is, no*vi*t p*ar*te*m* ac*tricem* ix an*n*is, et p*ar*te*m* Rea*m* p*er* illud Spaciu*m*. Interr*ogatus* de M*at*rimonio, Habi*ta*-*cione* et Celebra*cione*, inter Wi*llelmu*m Spakeman, p*ar*te*m* Act*ricem*, et Leticia*m* Vnsworth, p*ar*te*m* Rea*m* / This depon*en*t saies, *tha*t he hath hard say, by neibo*ures* of Winweke p*ar*ish, that Wi*llia*m Spakeman was Maried vnto Letice Spakeman, al*ias* Vnsworth, in the p*ar*ish Church of Winweke, quu*m* d*icta* Alicia fuit circit*er* vij [i. e. xj^m] sue etatis Annu*m*; sed de etat*e* Will*elm*i Spakeman tunc t*em*po*r*is, Nescit depon*er*e / et de etate p*ar*tiu*m* tunc t*em*po*r*is nescit depon*er*e; et de etat*e* p*ar*tiu*m* nu*n*c t*em*po*r*is nescit depon*er*e / Interr*ogatus* de consensu et assensu post Pub*er*-tatem, dicit, q*uod* no*n*unq*ua*m Coh*ab*ita*ve*runt in domo p*at*ris p*ar*tis ree, tribus an*n*is elaps*is*; sed, an concenserunt post pub*er*tatem, nescit depon*er*e: al*ias* nescit depon*er*e. no*n* est doct*us*, no*n* Consang*uineus*, no*n* aff*in*is, no*n* tenens, non curat &c /

Chr*isto*pherus Gest, p*a*roch*ie* de Winweke, ibi*de*m oriund*us*, etat*is* circit*er* lxxj an*n*os, novit p*ar*te*m* ac*tricem* a Na*tiuita*te, et Letic*iam* Spakeman, al*ias* Vnsworth, simil*ite*r. Interr*ogatus* de M*at*rimo*nio* [3] inter ip*s*os celebrat*o*, dicit, q*uod* p*er*sonalit*er* fuit p*resen*s in eccl*esia*m paroch*ie* S*anct*e Trinit*atis* iux*ta* Holcrofte, circiter x an*n*os elaps*os*, quu*m* m*at*ri-mo*niu*m fuit celebrat*um* et Solempnizat*um* inter p*ar*tes, quu*m* dict*us* Will*el*m*us* Spakeman fuit circit*er* x sue etatis annu*m* eod*em* t*em*po*r*e, et Leticia Vnsworth fuit etat*is* x annor*um* et vlt*ra*. Dicit q*uod* Do*m*in*us* Will*el*m*us* nu*n*c attingit xx sue etat*is* annu*m*, et Leticia est circit*er* dict*am* etatem et vltra. Interrog*atus* De Consensu, assensu, mutua Cohabitacione, et Carnali Copula post pubertatem, dicit, in vim Jura-*men*ti sue prestiti, that, to his knoledge, they neu*er* Consentid together after they came to p*er*fitt age; but that the One wold not Continue there as the other was. and ther was diu*er*se daie-holding*es* to get them to abide together; wh*i*ch they neu*er* cold bringe to passe . . . . . .

Thomas Vnsworth, p*a*roch*ie* de Winweke, ib*ide*m oriundus, etatis circit*er* lx an*n*os et vlt*ra*, novit partes a puericia. Interrogat*us* de M*at*ri-monio celebrat*o* inter partes / [4]This deponent saies, that about tenne yeres ago, afore Christmas, bie Counsell of his frend*es*, he causid his Doughter, Letice Vnsworth, to be Maried vnto Will*ia*m Spakeman, in the

[1] Winwick, a village on the turnpike-road midway between Warrington (3 miles off, N.) and Newton in Mackerfield (2 miles off, S).—Hamilton.

[2] Leigh, a market-town in the hundred of West Derby, Lancashire, 7 miles S. of Bolton, 15 from Manchester, and 193⅓ from London.—Hamilton.

[3] leaf 247, bk. [4] leaf 248.

church of the Trinitie: w*hi*ch Will*iam* Spakeman was, as this Deponent iudgid, vnder x yeres of Age; and his doughter, Letice Vnsworth, was then about xj yeres old. Et dicit q*uod*, isto te*m*po*r*e, dict*us* Will*elm*us Spakman est circit*er* xix sue etat*is* annu*m*, et d*ict*a Leticia est circit*er* vigint*as*. Interrogat*us* de consensu, mutua Coh*ab*itac*ion*e, et carnali Copula post pub*er*tatem, This depon*ent* saies, by vertue of his othe, that after the said p*ar*ties came to Lawfull age, neither the said Wi*lli*am Spakeman wold agre to take the said Letice to his wief, and to vse her as he ought to do, nor the said Letice wold take the said Will*ia*m to her husband, nor consent to hym; but eu*er* the one hath, and do at this instant, reclaime against the other; nor neu*er* did lye together, nor had Carnall Copulacion, to this deponent*es* knoledge. al*ias* nescit deponere. no*n* est doct*us*; est p*ate*r p*ar*tis ree, &c.

26. James Ballard *v.* Anne Ballard. She gives him, when 10-11, two apples to marry her. The curate acting, is punisht.

[1]Exa*min*acio testiu*m* sup*er* Allegacione ex p*ar*te Jac*obi* Ballard con*tra* Anna*m* Ballard, capt*a* Die et Anno p*redictis* / [8 Nov. 1565].

Jacobus Hartley, p*ar*och*ie* de Clidroe,[2] etat*is* xl an*norum*, aut circit*er*, no*vi*t p*ar*te*m* act*ricem* a N*atiuita*te, et p*ar*te*m* rea*m* x an*n*is. Exa*m*i*nat*us sup*er* Allegacione oblata ex parte &c / Dicit, that he hard say that the said James and Anne articulate, were Maried in the p*ar*ish Church of Colne, apon the xijth even in the *Christ*mas shalbe v yeres, com*m*e the Twelfth even next, about x of the Clocke in the night,—the said James at that tyme beinge about xj or vnder xij yeres of age,—w*i*thout the consent of any of his frend*es*, bie one S*i*r Roger Blakey, then curate of Colne. Reddend*o* rac*io*ne*m* sui [3]d*ict*i, he saies, that the same night, this deponent was in the house of *Christo*fer Hartley of Wwller,[4] vncle to the said James libellate, and sawe when the said James [Ballard] was brought into the said house about Midnight bie ij^{o} fellowes, w*hi*ch (as this Depon*ent* supposethe) had bene at the said Mariage. And in the morowe after, the same James [Ballard] declarid vnto his said Vnckle, that the said Anne had intised hym w*i*th two Apples, to go w*i*th her to Colne, and to marry her. w*hi*ch word*es*, or the like in effect, the said James spake then in the p*rese*nce and heringe of this Deponent / And further he saieth, that the said Curate was ponished by the Archbushop of York his grace, for marieng at inconvenient tymes and vnlawfull p*er*sons,

[1] leaf 249 (Piccope's No. 122). [2] Clithero. [3] leaf 249, back.
[4] Wooler? ? MS. Wicoller.

after the tyme of the Solempnizacion of *th*e said mariage. Et quoad ratificac*i*on*em* h*ujus*mod*i* M*at*rimonii, he saies, that i*m*mediatly after the said Mariage, v*idelicet*, the Morninge after, he repentid the said Mariage, when he p*er*ceyvid what he had done; and eu*er* sithence hath dissentid from the same, and neu*er* remained in her Co*m*pany for any space. Reddend*o* rac*i*one*m* sui d*i*c*ti*, he saies, that the said James hath remaynid and dwellid in the house of the said *Christo*fer, together w*i*th this depon*ent*, being brother to the said *Christo*fer; and therfore he hath knowne his doing*es* in and concerning the p*re*misses from tyme to tyme.

[1]Joh*an*nes Smith, paroch*ie* de Colne,[2] etat*is* xxx an*n*or*um* et vlt*ra*, novit Jac*obum* Ballard xij an*n*is, et p*ar*te*m* Rea*m* circit*er* v an*n*os / Exa*m*in*a*to sup*er* allegacione &c, Dicit in vi*rtute* Jura*men*ti sui p*re*stiti / that, by the report, this Depon*ent* hard that Mariage shuld be Solempnized betwene the said James and Anne, Libellate, at an inconvenient tyme of night, apon the twelf even, bie the Curate there, callid S*i*r Rog*er* Blakey. And further he saieth that he hard the said James, w*i*thin iiij^or daies after he had maried the said Anne, say that he was intised therto by the said Anne; and saies it shalbe v yeres, com*m*e the xij^th even next, sins the said mariage; and that he is not yet xvij yeres old, to this depon*entes* Judgm*ent*, who hath knowne the said James longe, and is well acquainted w*i*th hym. And further he saieth, that the said James declarid to this depon*ent*, at Sundry tymes, that he wold neu*er* have the said Anne to his wief; and as far as this depon*ent* cold eu*er* p*er*ceyve, he hath bene of that mynd eu*er* sins this Depon*ent* eu*er* talkid w*i*th hym concerninge the said mariage / and he saies that the said James and Anne neu*er* coh*ab*ited together, nor kept Companie, thone w*i*th other, sins the said tyme. Reddend*o* rac*i*on*em* sui d*icti*, he saieth, that he is neibo*ur* to the said James and his frend*es*, and is akin (as he think*es*) afar of, to the said James, but he know*i*th not in what degre / and therfore he hath knowne James mynd and his doing*es* in this matter, from tyme to tyme.

[3]Barnard P*ar*ker, etat*is* xxiiij an*n*or*um* et vlt*ra*, novit p*ar*te*m* act*ricem* xij an*nis*, et p*ar*te*m* rea*m* simil*iter*. Exa*minatus* &c quoad M*at*rimon*ium* &c, concordat in o*m*nibus et p*er* o*m*nia cu*m* Joh*anne* Smith, p*re*conteste suo; et Dicit, q*uod* audivit, ex relac*i*o*ne* alior*um*, provt ceteri testes deposuerunt quoad h*ujus*mod*i* Allegac*i*on*em*; et al*ite*r nescit depon*er*e, &c.

[1] leaf 250.

[2] A market town and township, now with railway station, in the parish of Whalley, N.E. Lancashire, on an affluent of the Calder, near the Liverpool and Leeds Canal, 26 miles N. of Manchester, and 204 N.W. of London: is a place of great antiquity, and as early as the 14th cent. was a seat of the woollen manufacture.—Bartholomew.

[3] leaf 250, back.

[1]Ex*aminac*io*n*es testiu*m* sup*er* allegac*io*ne ex*hibita* ex p*ar*te Jac*obi* Ballard con*tra* Jana*m*[2] Holden, capt*e* cora*m* m*agist*ro Cane, die et An*no* p*redictis* / [22 Nov. 1565. leaf 250, back.]

Barnardus Emmot, p*ar*och*ie* de Colne, etat*is* xxiij an*noru*m, no*vi*t p*ar*te*m* act*ricem* ab infanc*ia*; et p*ar*te*m* [rea*m*] no*n* novit sed de facie / Interrog*ato* &c, This depon*en*t saieth, that the said James Ballard was Maried in the night season, de facto, betwene iiij[or] and x of the Clock, apon the xij[th] even, or xij daie at nyght, w*hi*ch shalbe v yeres, come the said tyme next, the said James beynge at that tyme vnder thage of xij yeres; and the said Jane beyng a bigge damsell & mariage*a*ble the same tyme, by one S*ir* Roge*r* Blakey, then curate of Colne / Interr*ogato* de ratificac*ione*, &c, This deponent saieth, that eu*er* sithence, the said James hath dwellid and continued w*i*th his vncle *Chrisť*ofer Hartley, at Wooller [*or* Wwller]; and the said Anne hath remayned far from that place: this depon*en*t well knowes not where / And further he saies, that the said James hath declared to this depon*en*t sundry tymes, that he wold neu*er* take the said Anne to his wief; & forther declared, howe he was entysed, w*i*thout consent of any of his frend*es*, to say & do, he cold not tell what. and therfore this depon*en*t think*es* the Mariage was neu*er* ratified betwene them / no*n* est doct*us*, no*n* consang*uineus*, no*n* affi*ni*s &c; but he saies he is a neybo*u*r, & knowes all the p*r*emises to be true.

[3]Chr*ist*opherus Hartley, p*ar*och*ie* de Colne, etat*is* xxix an*noru*m . . . concordat in o*mn*ib*us* et p*er* o*mn*ia cu*m* Barnard*o* Emmot . . . Et reddendo, dicit, that he hath dwellid this v yeres in Wwller, where the said James hath dwellid, and knowes the said James hath still dwellid w*i*th his vncle there, and yet this depon*en*t neu*er* sawe the said Anne in the said Towne, nor neu*er* knewe of her beinge there /

27. William Stanley *v.* Anne Stanley (born Dutton), (he 12 at marriage, she 10).

[4]Ex*aminac*io testiu*m* super li*bel*lo ex p*ar*te Will*elm*i Stanley oblat*o*, capta cora*m* m*agist*ro Rob*er*to Lech*e*, Die et an*no* p*redictis*. (22 Nov. 1565.)

Rogerus Poll*e*, p*ar*och*ie* de Estam,[5] etat*is* xxvj annor*um*, no*vi*t p*ar*te*m* act*ricem* a pue*ri*cia, et Anna*m* Dutton a M*at*rimonio. Exa*mi*n*atus* sup*er*

[1] leaf 253.
[2] She was cald Anna in the first Depositions: see last page, and page 45.
[3] leaf 253, back. [4] leaf 251, back (Piccope's No. 124).
[5] Eastham, a parish in the higher division of the hundred of Wirrall, in the county palatine of Chester, 5 miles N.E. of Great Neston, and 9 N.W. of Chester.—Hamilton.

allegac*io*ne &c, Dicit, that he was p*re*sent when Mariage was had and Solempnized betwene the p*ar*ties Libellate, at a Chapell at Hatton,[1] in the Christmas tyme, five yeres com*m*e *Christm*as next; the said Wi*lli*am beinge at that tyme about thage of xij yeres, or thereabout, as this Depon*en*t hard his m*aste*r, S*ir* Rowland Stanley, report at the same tyme; and the said Anne was about thage of x yeres, to this Depon*ent*es Judgment, at the same tyme / and he saies he think*e*s the said Wi*lli*am is nowe much about xvij yeres old. Interr*ogatus* de carnal*i* Copula, coh*a*bitac*io*ne, et ratificac*io*ne hui*us*mo*d*i M*at*rimo*n*ij &c, This Depon*en*t saieth, that to his Knoledge, beynge household seru*au*nt & attendaunt vpon S*ir* Rowland Stanley, father to the said Will*ia*m, he think*es* ther was neu*er* carnall act betwene them. Reddend*o* rac*io*ne*m* scien*tie* sue h*uius*mo*d*i, This depo*n*ent saieth, they neu*er* dwellid together, nor neu*er* came together, but on gestwise; and for the said Wi*lli*am hath for the most p*ar*te bene, sins the said Mariage, bene at Lathum,[2] at schole there, and in S*er*vice w*i*th therle of Derby, and remaynid there for the most p*ar*te. And the said Anne hath dwellid at hom*m*e w*i*th her father, or els-where out of the company of *th*e said W*illia*m. [3]And further, this depon*en*t sais, he hath hard the said Wi*lli*am diu*er*se tymes say he wold not take her as his wieff; wherby he verely think*es* the Mariage was neu*er* consum*m*ate betwene them /

Oliverus Totty, p*a*roch*ie* de S*an*cta Maria, ci*vi*t*a*tis Cestr*ie*, etat*is* l an*no*ru*m*, no*vi*t p*a*rte*m* act*ri*ce*m* ab infanc*ia*, et p*ar*te*m* [ream] a te*m*p*or*e M*at*rimonij &c. Exa*min*ato sup*er* allegac*io*ne &c, This Depon*en*t saies, that he was p*rese*nt at the Mariage betwene the p*ar*ties libellate, in a chapell at Hatton Hall, in *Christm*as tyme, w*hi*ch shalbe v yeres at *Christm*as next ensuynge; the said Wi*lli*am beinge at [the] tyme, somwhat above xij yeres old, and vnder thirtene, as he well knowes, biecause this depon*en*t hath knowne hym from his infancy. and the said Anne, as he think*es*, was much about thage of x yeres, in his iudgment / Interr*ogatus* de coh*a*bitac*io*ne, carnali copul*a* &c, This depon*en*t sais, that the said Wi*lli*am hath bene at Schole at Lathum,[2] w*i*th one Doct*ou*r Standish, and w*i*th therle of Derby in S*er*vice, for the most p*ar*te, sins tyme of the said Mariage; and the said Anne hath bene sep*ar*atid from the said Wi*lli*am, in such places as her father hath appointed her; and they haue neu*er* com*m*e together, but on gestwise, sins the same tyme. and he well knowes they have neu*er* Lyen together; wherby he verely think*es* the

[1] In Waverton parish, W. Cheshire, 6 miles W. of Tarporley.
[2] Lathom, in Lancashire, parish of Ormskirk.
[3] leaf 252. See an abstract of this Stanley case, in one of Mr. Irvine's books.

Mariage was nev*er* consum*m*ate betwene them by carnall act, or any other Lawfull Meanes /

[1]Oliverus Tarleton, paroch*ie* de Estham, etat*is* lxvj an*norum*, nov*it* p*ar*te*m* actr*icem* a pue*r*icia, et p*ar*te*m* Rea*m* iiij^or^ an*n*is et vlt*ra*. Exa*mi*-*n*ato sup*er* allegac*ione* &c, This Depon*ent* saieth, that he came to Hatton Hall w*i*thin two daies next after that,—as he hard it reportid by diuerse worshipfull and others, that were p*resen*t at the said Mariag*e*,—that Mariag*e* was Solempnized betwene the p*ar*ties Libellate, in a chappell there, in *Christm*as tyme, which shalbe v yeres ago, com*me* *Christm*as next; the said Wi*lli*a*m* beinge the same tyme vnder[2] thage of xiij yeres; and the said Anne, to this depon*entes* Judgm*ent*, was much about thage of xij yeres. Interrog*atus* &c, This depon*ent* saies, that the said p*ar*ties have eu*er* dwellid in sonder, sins tyme of the said Mariage; for the said Wi*lli*a*m* hath bene, for the most, at Schole and in S*er*vice, at Lathum; and the said Anne hath bene at her fathers appointment. Et quoad cetera, concordat cu*m* Rob*er*to [? Olivero] Totty, p*re*conteste suo /

§ 2. RATIFICATIONS.

1. John Starkie and Alice Dutton.[3] Depositions as to the parties' ages: both now 14; married at 10.

Depositions of 1. the Man who fetcht the Midwives to the boy's Mother; 2. a Midwife, the Boy's Nurse; 3. the Girl's two Nurses.

[4] Exa*min*acio testiu*m* sup*ra* ratificac*ione* m*at*rimonii inter Joh*ann*em Starkie, *generosum*, et Alicia*m* Dutton, capt*a* cora*m* m*agist*ro Rob*er*to Leche, &c, iij° die februarii, 1561.

Henricus Boswell, p*a*roch*ie* de Wrenburie,[5] vbi mora*ns*, trax*i*t xxx^ta^ an*n*os, novit Joh*ann*em Starkie, *generosum*, a n*ativitat*e sua, et Alicia*m* Dutton nu*n*q*uam* vidit vsq*ue* in istu*m* die*m*. Exa*minatus* de etate Johan*n*is Starkie, *respo*ndet in vi*rtute* iura*men*ti sui, that the said John Starkie is xiiij yeres of age, and as muche as sins Whitsonday-Monday last past. Interrogat*o* de c*ausa* scien*tie* sue h*uius*mod*i* / This depone*nt* sais, that he dwellid w*i*th James Starkie, beynge father vnto the said Joh*n* Starkie; and, at tyme of the birthe of the said Joh*n* Starkie, went

[1] leaf 252, back.
[2] MS. beinge vnder.
[3] The parents being gentlefolk, the Ratification was doubtless made to prevent any question rising as to the heirship to the family property.
[4] leaf 24 (Piccope's No. 12).
[5] Wrenbury, a parish, township, and village (now with a railway station), in Cheshire; the village, on the river Weaver, 5 miles S.W. of Nantwich.

to fetche midwyves vnto the mother of the said Johñ Starkie, *whi*ch did beyre the said Johñ Starkie w*i*thin the p*ar*ishe of Bu*n*burye,[1] at a house of James Starkies, beynge in Terton,[2] then beynge ten*au*nt vnto S*ir* Laurence Smythe, knight, and the said Johñ Starkie was christned the xv[th] day of June in the yere of *our* lord god, a Thousand, fyve hundrethe, fortie and sixe; as, bie bill exhibitid bie this deponent, doth more plainelie appere recordid in the registie boke w*i*thin the p*ar*ishe of Bu*n*burye / and as for the age of the woman, this deponent knowes not . . . . . .

Elena Wilbram, p*ar*ochie de Bu*n*burye, etat*is* xl an*norum*, no*vi*t Joh*ann*em Starkie a na*tiuitat*e, et Alicia*m* Dutton non no*vi*t vsq*ue* in istu*m* die*m*. Exa*minat*a sup*ra* etate Joh*ann*is Starkie, re*spon*det in vir-*tute* Jura*men*ti sui, that the said John Starkie is xiiij[tene] yeres old, and as muche as sins Whitsonmonday last past. [Interrogata] de c*ausa* scien*cie* sue h*uius*mo*di* / This deponent [sais that she] [3]was sent for to be nurse vnto the said Joħn, and was bye at his birthe, at the house callid the Hall of Holgreve,[4] w*i*thin the p*ar*ishe of Bu*n*burie, the father of the said Johñ beynge then ten*au*nt vnto S*ir* Laurence Smithe. and this deponent was p*rese*nt at the christninge of the said Johñ in the p*ar*ishe churche of Bu*n*burye, at the same tyme as before she hathe deposed / . . . . . .

Katarina Kirfote, p*ar*ochie de Waue*r*ton, ib*ide*m mora*ns*, trax*it* p*er* spaciu*m* xx' an*norum*, etatis circite*r* xl an*no*s, no*vi*t Joh*ann*em Starkie a m*a*trimo*nio*, vi*delicet*, ad iiij[or] an*no*s elaps*os* circiter festu*m* N*atiuitatis* d*omi*ni, in domo h*a*bitac*io*nis Rad*ulphi* Dutton de Hatton, ar*migeri*. Exa*mina*t*a* sup*ra* etat*e* Joh*ann*is Starkie tunc temporis, Dicit q*uod* fuit circite*r* x[mum] sue etat*is* annu*m*, eode*m* te*m*po*re* / Exa*minata* sup*ra* etate Alicie Dutton, dicit, that she is xiiij[tene] yere old, and asmuche as sins Alhalowtide last. reddend*a* rac*io*ne*m* sui d*icti*, she saies that she was p*rese*nt at her birthe, and gave her first sucke; and after that, was p*rese*nt at her christninge in the p*ar*ishe church of Waverton; and therbie she knowes verylie that she is of the same age. and as for the age of Johñ Starkie, she knowes not p*er*fittlie, biecause she was not p*rese*nt at his birthe. . . . . .

Margeria Coke, p*ar*ochie de Tatnall, vbi mora*ns*, traxit xj[m] an*no*s,

[1] Bunbury, a parish and township in W. Cheshire, 3½ miles S.E. of Tarporley, 8 N.W. of Nantwich.

[2] Turton is a town and township, in the parish of Bolton-le-Moors, S.E. Lancashire, 4 miles N. of Bolton, by rail; but Mr. Price says Terton here must be intended for Tiverton, a township in the parish of Bunbury, Cheshire: it evidently is so.

[3] leaf 24, back.

[4] Not mentiond under Bunbury in the present Post Office Directory, Kelly's.

etat*is* circit*er* xxxiij an*nos*, no*vit* Joh*anne*m Starkie a m*at*rimo*nio*; but howe longe the mariage was sins, she knowes not [as she] was not p*rese*nt at hit. Exa*minat*a de etate Alicie Dutton, dicit, that she is at this p*rese*nt, xiiij yere old, and asmuche as sins Alholloweday last. reddend*a* rac*ione*m sui d*ic*ti, she sais that she was not p*rese*nt at her birthe, but [1]she sais she came w*i*thin two daies after she was borne, and enquired the day of her birthe; and was sent for to her father, M*aste*r Rafe Duttons house, where she nursid the same m*ist*res Alicie Dutton; wherbie she knowes her age p*er*fittlie. And as for the age of Johñ Starkie, she sais she knowes not, biecause she was not p*rese*nt at his birthe . . . . . .

2. Elizabeth Culcheth and Rafe Culcheth, A.D. 1562. (She had 4 Children by him.)

[2]Elizabeth Culcheth deposes 'that Rafe Culcheth and she were maried together in the p*ar*yshe churche of Eccleston,'[3] when 'she was but a child, and the said Rafe but a child.' Then she seems to contradict flatly her first statement as to the place of marriage, saying "but she wel remembers that she was maried out of Eccleston,[3] [in] Master Doct*our* Piers Bradshawe house. & the said Doct*our* Bradshawe maried them." Further "she think*es* the said mariage to be good and effectuall; neu*er*theles she knowes not what age the said Rafe was of at the tyme of the solempniza*cio*n of the said mariage; but this she sais, that the said Rafe had iiij[or] children gotten in lawfull marriage, bie this re*spo*ndent, after he came to ripe age; & that was token of co*n*sent, in this re*spo*ndent*es* iudgm*en*t. . . . she sais she is of the p*ar*yshe of Bolton of *the* dioc*ese* of Chester."

3. Thos. Wicksted (16-17, married at 9-10), and Ellen Wicksted (15-16, born Ball, married at 8-9).[4]

[5]Exa*minac*io testiu*m* super Ratificac*ione*m m*at*rimonij inter Tho*mam* Wicksted et Elena*m* Wicksted, al*ias* Ball, ei*us* vx*orem*, capt*a* cora*m* m*agist*ro Rob*er*to Leche, in L*egibus* bacc*alaureo*, xij° Die Maij, 1563°.

[1] leaf 25.

[2] leaf 64, back (Piccope's No. 27).

[3] No doubt Eccleston in Lancashire, on the river Yarrow, 4½ miles W. of Chorley; not the Eccleston near Chester. (The township of Eccleston is in Prescot parish, N. Lancashire, now partly in the town of Prescot, but mostly in the municipal borough of St. Helens. In N. Lancashire are also the townships of Great Eccleston (in the parish of St. Michael on Wyre, 5½ miles S.W. of Garstang), and Little Eccleston with Larbreck, in the parish of Kirkham, 6 miles N.E. of Kirkham.)—Bartholomew.

[4] No doubt the families of the parties were landed folk, and wisht the Ratification to be on the Records of the Bishop's Court.

[5] leaf 125, back (Piccope's No. 65).

[*Unsignd slip stuck into the Deposition-book:*]

"To the ryght worshipfull master Chavncelar of Chester.

"My dewtye moaste humblye p*re*mised, thys shalbe to certyfye your mastershippe, that I Wylliam Beddow, curat at Merburye,[1] did solemnise matrimonye betwixte Thomas Wycsted, this bearer, and Elync, the doughter of Thomas Baulle of Biclaye,[2] in the p*re*sence of a great multytude of people, the syxte daye of June, in the yere of oure Lorde god, A thousand fyve hundred fyftye and fyve" /

[*Depositions*]

Joanna Ball, mater Elene Ball, se Jurat*a* medio eius Jura*men*to, saies, the mariage was solempnizate betwix Tho*mas* Wicksted and Eleine Ball, her doughter, about Midsom*er* seven yere, com*m*e the tyme,—the said Thom*as* beynge, at the tyme of the said marriage, about the age of x, and the said Eleine about thage of ix yeres old,—in the Chappell of M*ar*bury, bie S*ir* Wi*lliam* Bedoe, Curate there, at due tyme of the day, the banes beyng Lawfully askid: p*rese*ntib*us* tunc ib*ide*m, *Chris*tofero Holford gene*r*oso, M*ar*garet*a* ei*us* vx*ore*, Joh*ann*e Gravenou*r*, gene*r*oso, et Alicia ei*us* vx*ore*, cu*m* alijs. and forther she saies, the said Tho*mas* is, at this p*rese*nt, above xvj, and the said Eleine above xv^{tene} yeres old. . . . . .

(The facts stated above are, with slight variations, also deposed by John Wicksted of Marbury, aged 40 and upwards; Thomas Donne of Marbury, aged 33; and Thomas Golburne of Bickley in the parish of Malpas, aged 50 and upwards, tho' the last-named didn't know the children's ages at their marriage, or the boy's age on May 12, 1563.)

§ 3. RESTITUTION OF CONJUGAL RIGHTS.

Child-Marriage, but of lawful age. Suit for Restitution of Conjugal Rights.

Margaret Stanley *v.* Thomas Stanley. She 16 at marriage; he 14-15. She starvd by his Parents.

[3]Exa*mina*cio testiu*m* in ca*usa* restitucio*n*is sup*er* Li*bel*lo ex pa*r*te Ma*r*garete Stanley, con*tra* Tho*mam* Stanley, ei*us* viru*m*, oblat*o*, capt*a* cora*m* m*agist*ro Rob*er*to Leche, die et anno p*re*d*ictis* / [19 Nov. 1562.]

[1] Marbury, a parish and village in Cheshire, 7 miles S.W. of Nantwich. (The township of Marbury is in Great Budworth parish, Cheshire, on the Grand Trunk Canal, 1½ miles N. of Northwich.)

[2] Bickley, a township in the parish (and 3 miles N.E.) of Malpas, W. Cheshire.

[3] leaf 95, back (Piccope's No. 44).

Rogerus Isherwod, *parochie* de Blagburne,[1] etat*is* lx an*norum* et vltra, novit p*ar*tes a puericiis. Exa*minatus* sup*er* sum*maria* petic*ione* ex p*ar*te p*ar*t*is* act*ricis* oblat*a* / Dicit, in vi*rtute* Jura*men*ti sui, that M*ar*garet Stanley he knowis well, and Thom*as* Stanley; that they dwell in Blagburne p*ar*ish, the said M*ar*garet in a towne callid Pleddington,[2] & the said Tho*mas* in a towne callid Mello*ur*,[3] a mile asonder, or there-about. and forther he sais, the said M*ar*garet & Thom*as* were maried both together in Blagburne Church, by a priest servinge there as vic*ar* or Curate: the name of the p*ri*est, he knowis not, biecause ther were iij or iiij^or^ that tyme / and the mariage was about M*ar*timas or Michaelmas, like xiij or xiiij yeres ago, in the p*re*sence of S*i*r John Sothworth and many other gent*lemen* mo, & yoman to the nomber of a hundreth, apon a workday, about x' of Clock afore None, this depone*n*t beynge p*rese*nt at the mariage, and bid to it, and to the dinn*er*, w*hi*ch was in Peirs Stanley, father to the said Thom*as*, in Mello*ur* aforsaid. and forther, this depone*n*t saies, by v*er*tue of his oth, that Thom*as* Stanley, at the tyme of the mariage, was elder then the said M*ar*garet; and she, at that tyme, was xvj yeres old. reddend*o* rac*i*on*em* sui d*i*c*ti*, he sais, for M*ar*garet Stanley her age, this depone*n*t knowes it well, biecause he hath a doughter borne the same weke that she was, callid Anne; and he hard it recknid at the tyme of the making*e* vp of the mariage among*es* ther frend*es*, that Thom*as* Stanley was elder, for he was mariageable, and a cleane striplinge, and knew what Love ment, as it semid bie his stature, and by suche Clipping*e* and kissing*e* as this deponent hath sene betwene the p*ar*ties before they were maried. and forther, he saies, that the two p*ar*ties did cohabit and dwell together in the house of Peirs Stanley, father to the said Thom*as*, a yere and a half, & somwhat more; and, [4]to their neighbo*urs* Judgm*ent*, delt quietly & lovingly together, as man and wief, beynge suche young Cowples as they were. & forther, this depone*n*t saies, that he hath hard say they were sep*ar*ated before the p*ar*son of Bury; but he hath no c*er*tenty therof; but he think*es* they have no good proof therof, nor good cause of sep*ar*ac*i*on, consideringe the p*re*m*i*sses. And forthe*r* he saies, the said Tho*mas* and M*ar*garet wold yet agre, and love either other, were it not the mother of the said Tho*mas*, who was a straite woman, at that tyme, to the said M*ar*garet; and, afore the said

[1] Blackburn, now a big borough in N.E. Lancashire, 9 miles E. of Preston, and 210 miles N.W. of London by rail.

[2] Pleasington, a township, and village (now with railway station), in the parish (and 3 miles S.W.) of Blackburn, N.E. Lancashire.

[3] Mellor, in the parish (and 2½ miles N.W.) of Blackburn, N.E. Lancashire.

[4] leaf 96.

Divorce, did not allowe her meate and drink sufficient, in somuch that M*ar*garet*es* father gave her meate, as bred, cheese, & other victualles, w*hi*ch she for a tyme kept lockt in *th*e chest, till they, beyng ware of it, convaid the kay away from her, & so toke away her victualles, and fell worse out w*i*th her, that her father was faine to fetch her home, for feare she shuld be Clem*m*id [starvd]. and moreou*er* he saies, that Peirs [*that is*, Thomas] hath eu*er* sins that tyme kept hymself sole & vnmaried, and so hath the said M*ar*garet, who neu*er* consentid to the said divorce.

Georgius Cowburne, p*ar*och*ie* de Blagburne, etat*is* lxx an*norum*, nov*i*t p*ar*te*m* act*ricem* xxx' an*n*os, et p*ar*te*m* rea*m* xxj an*n*os. Exa*minatus* sup*er* allegacio*nem* &c. This depone*n*t saies, that M*ar*garet Stanley and Thom*as* Stanley, he knowis well, and was p*re*s*e*nt at ther mariag*e* and bridall in the p*ar*ish church of Blagburne, one a work-day, in the p*re*sence of S*ir* John) Sothworth & many other mo; but howe long sins, this depone*n*t dois not well remembre; nor the p*r*iest*es* name he knowes not, biecause ther was iij or iiij[or] p*r*estes servinge then in Blagburne; the said M*ar*garet beynge, at that tyme, above the age of xvj' yeres, and the said Thom*as*, bie the sayeng of frend*es*, was somwhat elder. and their ages he knowes well, biecause he hath a child callid Rafe, w*i*thin iij daies of the age of the said M*ar*garet: & Thom*as* age he knowes well, biecause he is a nere naybo*u*r vnto hym. and further, this depone*n*t sais, that the said Tho*mas* and M*ar*garet dwellid, after the said mariag*e*, almost ij[o] yeres w*i*th Peiers Stanley, father to the said Thom*as*, and were taken and reputid in all the Contry there as man and wief, and vsed them-selves as Lovingly and as familerly together as any two such young*e* Cowples cold do, till the father & [= or] mother, or both, of the said Peirs [*that is*, Thomas] beyng*e* a heady follk [*over* foman *struck out*] toke a folish opinion against her, that they almost clem*m*id her for default of meate, as this depone*n*t hath hard say bie the neigbo*ures* there. and when her father gave her a chest and victuall*es* in it, they, among*es* them, stale the kay away from her; [1]and her father seyng that, toke her home to hym, where sins she hath lyved, sole & vnmaried; and so likewise the said Peirs [*that is*, Thomas] hath done. and, as this depone*n*t hath hard say, that they were divorcid before the p*ar*son of Bury; but he think*es* they have no good profe that the divorce is Lawfull /

Laurencius Walmesley, paroch*ie* de Blagburne, etat*is* xt an*norum*, nov*i*t p*ar*te*m* act*ricem* ab infancia, et p*ar*te*m* rea*m* xx an*n*os et vltra / [confirms the two former deponents, and then varies slightly, saying that

[1] leaf 96, back.

the young maried folk] "he knowes c*er*tenly lyved together, and vsed either other as man and wief shulde do. and this depon*en*t hath sene them at the said Peter Stanleys house many tymes, beyng their nere neigbo*ur*; and they were reputid and com*m*only taken for man & wief through-out the hole Cuntry, till after the father & mother of the said Thom*as* cast a dislove vnto the said M*ar*garet, and, bie the report of the neighbo*ures*, almost famished her for want of meate; in somuch that her father toke her home to hym, where she hath eu*er* sins remayned, sole and vnmaried; and so likewise the said Thom*as* hath done. and for the divorce that shuld be betweene them, he saies he cannot depose of, biecause he knowes nothing of it; but as he hath hard say, they were divorcid before the p*ar*son of Bury. but what was the cause, this depon*en*t knowes not; but he think*es* the said M*ar*garet neu*er* consentid to the said divorce /" [No such pretended Divorce could be legal, though it might be good as an Agreement for a Separation.]

[1] Exa*min*acio testiu*m* sup*er* allegac*ion*em oblat*am* ex p*ar*te M*ar*garete Stanley, con*tra* Tho*mam* Stanley, capt*a* cora*m* m*agistr*o Rob*er*to Leche, die et an*n*o p*re*d*ictis* [2 December, 1562].

Georgius Wadington, etat*is* circit*er* lx an*n*or*um* . . . dicit, that he was p*rese*nt in the parish church of Blagburne, when Tho*mas* Stanley and M*ar*garet Stanley were maried together bie a p*r*est that servid there, in the presence of xl p*er*sons & mo, at a conveni*en*t tyme of day, the same M*ar*garet at that tyme beynge xvj[2] yere old, as he remembrith, for he hath a doughter about the same age; the said Thom*as*, to his Judgm*en*t and thinking*e*, beyng*e* the same tyme above xiiij yeres old, as he cold gesse by his stature, or more. and forther, this depon*en*t saies, that the said Thom*as* and M*ar*garet continued together in one house w*i*th the father and mother of the said Thom*as*, after their sayd mariag*e*, a yere and more; and that, to this depone*n*t*es* knoledge, beyng*e* a neighbo*u*r by, they agreid well together, & lovid either other, for any thing*e* he knewe, during*e* the said yere. howe they went asonder, or howe they did disagre, this depon*en*t doth not well knowe /

[1] leaf 103 (Piccope's No. 49). [2] ? xvij or xviij turnd into xvj or xv.

II. TROTHPLIGHTS.

1. Jane Walkden *v.* Richard Lowe. A girl born.

[A first contract of Marriage, followd by issue, invalidates a later Marriage.]

[1]Re*spon*sio*n*es pe*rsona*les Ric*ardi* Lowe sup*er* *certis* [articulis (*MS. torn off*)] sibi ex offic*i*o mero obiiciend*is*, capt*e* D[ie et] an*n*o infrascript*is* [12 Dec., 1561].

This res*pon*dent sworne and Exa*mine*d, sais, bie vertue of his othe, that he hathe drawen to the Companie of Jane Walkden bie the space of iiij^or^ yeres; and, bie reason this res*pon*dent was a widoe, cast his love to her, and p*ro*mised her mariage; and she likewise p*ro*mysed hym, secretlie betwene them self, and thereapon had carnall dole together. then Jane Walkden desired this res*pon*dent to make her a p*ro*misse before witnes; and so he did. and beynge askid whether he had made any p*ro*mysse to any other, afore he made that p*ro*mysse to her, he sais and answeris 'no; but stode as fre from all, as he was the first day he was borne.' and forther he sais, he had Issue, a wenche, bie the said Jane. and beynge demaundid whie he maried her not, he sais her frend*es* p*ro*mysed hym a pece of good, and wold not p*er*forme hit, so that this res*pon*dent was lothe to marrie, and not well able to kepe her, except he had had that mariage good. and forther, he think*es* in his Conscience, he can neu*er* marie any other but her, and she hym. and this res*pon*dent, askid whether he made any p*ro*messe after;—he sais he contract after w*i*th on Ellin Stones, and maried her; but she, vnderstandinge the mariage is vnlawfull, is partid from hym, and refusethe to take hym as her husband. and he said he made the contract w*i*th Jane Walkden thre quarters of a yere before he maried Helen Stonis. and forther he saith, he is hartelie sorie that he hath disceyvid [2]them bothe; and will do any thinge for the health of his soull*e*.

Chr*ist*opherus Aynsworth, parochie de Blagburne, sworne and exa*mine*d apon a contract betwixe Ric*hard* Lowe and Jane Walkden, sais, bie vertue of his othe, that Ric*hard* Lowe made a contract w*i*th Jane Walkden about three yeres ago, in the presence of this depone*n*t, Henrie Cowburne, Tho*mas* Holden, & others in the Towne of Blagburne, in a house of Tho*mas* Sharplus; and there they two p*ar*ties did take ether other bie the hand*is*, and plight their trouthe, either to ether; and they had carnall dole together, and had Issue, a wenche, betwixe them, yet lyvinge. and

[1] leaf 14 (Piccope's No. 8). [2] leaf 14, back.

after, the said Ric*hard* maried an old woman [Helen Stonis]; w*h*ich this deponent and all the Cuntrie were offendid w*i*th hit, and did thinke that the said marriage was nought, & this pore maid Jane Walkeden to have grett wronge, biecause she is not able to followe sute against hym.

2. Christian Grimsdiche *v.* John Smith.

[1]Re*spon*siones *per*so*na*les Joh*ann*is Smith in *causa* contract*i* sup*er* li*bello* ex p*ar*te *Chris*tiane Grimsdiche cont*ra* i*psum* oblat*o*, cora*m* m*agist*ro Rob*er*to Leche, artiu*m* m*agist*ro, et in L*egibus* bacc*alaureo*, &c, xv° Junij, A*nno* Do*mi*ni 1562°

Ad p*r*ima*m* po*sitio*nem / This *res*p*o*ndent sais, that he was free from mariage; but what *Chris*tian Grimsdiche was, this *respo*ndent cannot tell; but he saies that he had no Co*mmun*icacion of mariage w*i*th her, though the said *Chris*tian wold com*mune* w*i*th this *respo*ndent, nowe & then, of mariage; but this *respo*ndent wold neu*er* graunt his Consent thervnto /

Ad ij^d po*sitio*nem, This *respo*ndent denieth that eu*er* he p*ro*mysed her any mariage. et ad cetera content*a* in d*ic*t*a* po*sitio*ne, *respo*nde*n*t negat, savinge that he sais he hath had carnall dole w*i*th her, & kissed her, dyu*er*se tymes; but neu*er* apon *the* condic*io*n of marriage /

Ad iij^d po*sitio*nem, he sais, that he hath lett *Chris*tian Grimsdiche have a pece of mony; and he hath had of her a sate [a sute, ? MS.] of silu*er* and a handcheuerchef*e*. beynge askid what he said at the receyvinge of them, he sais, she gave them to this *respo*ndent frely. beynge askid, what she me*n*t by gevinge them, this *respo*ndent sais she had a better thinge of hym. beyng askid what: he sais she had of hym, at two or iij tymes, about x s. or a m*ar*ke. beynge askid, for what intent, this *respo*ndent gave so much money to the said *Chris*tian, beynge but a poore man, he sais, because he had, and wold have, to do w*i*th her, & knewe her Carnally; & not for that he wold mary her. as for any other token, he sais ther was no*n* sent from hym, or receyvid from her, by any messeng*er*, as far as he remembres . . . . . .

3. Anne Yate (Victualler) *v.* George Johnson (married after).

[2]On 18 March, 1562-3,—Oliver Foxe deposes "that, to his thinkinge, and for any thinge that eu*er* he knewe, Georg*e* Johnson and Anne Yate were free from all Contract at the tyme that they did make a contract in the p*r*esence of this Depone*n*t. and forther he saies, that, by reason the

[1] leaf 68 (Piccope's No. 29). [2] leaf 121 (Piccope's No. 60).

said Anne did kepe a vittaylinge house, he resortid often thither, and did, diu*erse* tymes, before the co*n*tract made, com*m*en and talke of mariage to be made betwixe theis two p*ar*ties.

"Ad ij^{d}, this Deponent saies, that George Key, of the p*ar*ish of Davenh*am*, nowe dep*ar*tid, did, apon a Thursday, a fornight before Christmas, like sixe yeres ago, Did com*m*e to the house of Anne Yate, and there did finde George Johnson had co*mmun*icac*i*on of mariage; and so concludid that they shuld call witnesses of the co*n*tract. and thereapon, this Depone*n*t was sent for, out of his owne shop, to beare witnes. and when he came to the house, ther was Georg*e* Johnson, Anne Yate, George Kay, and Cicilie Key, w*i*th this depon*ent*. and before the said Georg*e* Kay, Cicily, and this depon*ent*, the said Georg*e* Johnson did take the said Anne by the hand; [and] [1] when they held hand in hand, George Kay said, "art thou, Georg*e*, contentid to take Anne to thie wief, & so to vse her?" and George Johnson answerid, "Yea, by my faith and trowth." and likewise the said George Kay said, "Anne, art thou co*n*tentid to take George Johnson to thi husband, and so to vse hym?" and she answerid, "Yea, by my faith and trouth*e*." and thereupon they did drinke together; but he doth not remember they kissed. & this co*n*tract was made toward eveninge nere the fireside. and when they had done, this depone*n*t eate a cowple of wodcok*es* w*i*th them.

"Ad iij, this depone*n*t saies, that he dothe well kno that the said Georg*e* hath had out of Anne Yates purse, above xl^{s}, w*h*ich this deponent was p*r*ivy vnto, w*h*ich the said Anne did Lend vnto the said Georg*e* /

"Ad iiij, This Depone*n*t saies, that they were reputid and taken for man and wief amonge their neighbo*ures*. reddend*o* rac*i*one*m* sui d*i*c*t*i, [he] saies, that Georg*e* libellat*e* did daylie and howrely vse the house; and did nightly Lye ther; and brought his dogg*es*, his horse, and his hawkes thither; w*h*ich thinge*s* wold not have bene suffrid, but that the parrish thought they were man and wief before God; for they did lye in one house, and nothing*e* betwix them but a broken wall and a paintid clothe /" . . . . . .

Cecilea Key confirms the fact of the Contract, and "saies that George hathe sent Anne tokens and a l*ett*re sins the said Contract; and well she remembres he send her a Spanish vj^{d}. and as for any token gevin by Anne to hym, she saies he had of her, when he nedid, by xx^{s} at once /

"Ad iiij, This depone*n*t saies, the neigbo*ures* thereabout did take them as man and wief, in somuche that they have Laine together in bed, and so

[1] leaf 121, back.

vsed them selfes as man & wief. and forther she saies, George Johnson was maried suspiciously, or els he cold not have bene maried there, w*i*thout banes askinge, & not in due tyme, as she think*es*, fewe witnes by " . . . .

4. Ellen Ricroft *v.* Thomas Snelson. Banns askt. A Child born.

[1]Exa*min*a*c*io testiu*m* in Ca*usa* contract*i* inter Elena*m* Ricroft, p*ar*te*m* act*ricem* ex vna, et Tho*mam* Snelson, p*ar*te*m* rea*m*, capt*a* Die et an*n*o p*r*edic*tis*. [28 May, 1563.]

Ran*ulphus* Mainwaringe, parochi*e* de Rostorne, etat*is* lxvj an*norum*, no*vi*t p*ar*tes ab infanciis /

Ad p*r*imu*m* ar*ticu*lu*m*, This deponent saies, that he neu*er* was p*rese*nt at any word*es* of Contract made or spoken betwene Eleine and Thom*as*, articulate.

Ad ij[d] ar*ticu*lu*m*, this depon*en*t saies, he did neu*er* carry any Tokens betwixe them hymself, but he hard say ther hath bene Tokens sent betwixe them; and this depon*entes* wief caried one from Thom*as* [2]Snelson to the said Elleine, w*hi*ch was a xij[d], on Midsomm*er* Even last was.

Ad iij, This depon*ent* saies, that the banes were askid betwene the said Tho*mas* and Eleine twise or thrise, and the day of mariage set and apointed; and further saies, that Thom*as* Snelson, havinge gotten Eleine w*i*th Child, desired this deponent to take her into his house for a fortu[3]-night, and p*r*omysed, bie his faith and treuth, that w*i*thin that fortnight he wold marry her, for, in his Conscience, he cold marry no*ne* other; or els this depon*en*t wold not have taken her to his house, but that he thought they were man and wief before God. and at the fortnight end, he maried her not, but toke her away thens; and after her deliue*r*aunce, desired this depon*en*t to go w*i*th hym to speake w*i*th her; and in the p*r*esence of this deponent, desired her to release hym, and he wold geve her xx[i] nobles. and she answerid 'she wold not'; & said 'she passid not for his gooddes, but for hym.' "Well," q*uod* the said Thom*as*, "yf thou will not release me, I have gone so far w*i*th my frendes in talk w*i*th an other woman, that it is best for you to get out a Cita*ci*on, and call me before the Ordinary." and she said, "I am a seru*aun*t, and cannot followe the Lawe." "Well," q*uod* the said Thom*as*, "then I will"; and so p*r*ocurid out a Cit*acion* against hym-self, paid for it, and convaide it to her frend*es* &c. & further he saies 'the child was got ij[o] yeres after the banes were askid' / . . . . . .

[1] leaf 131, back (Piccope's No. 69). [2] leaf 132. [3] so, or 'nn' in MS.

Alicia Manwaringe, parochie de Rostorne, etatis † annorum, novit partes xvj annis.

Ad primum articulum, This deponent saies, she was not present at any solempne Contract made betwene the parties articulate; but she saieth, that the said Thomas brought the said Eleine to the house of this Deponentes husband, and then, before this deponent and her husband, and the said Eleine standing in presence, promysed to marry the said Eleine [1] bie his faith and trouth; and said he cold not marry any other; for he said his Conscience shuld prick hym yf he did so. and further this deponent saies, that after the said Eleine was deliuered, Thomas Snelson causid a metinge of frendes to be had, and did offer her a piece of mony to release hym; and she answerid 'she wold not release hym for no gold,' "for I am your lawfull wief; and so take me." "Well," quod he, "sticke to *that*, and I will neuer Leave the."

Ad ij^d^, this deponent saies, that apon Midsomer even last, the said Thomas send a Token, videlicet a xij^d^. to the said Eleine, bie this deponent. As for any other Tokens, this deponent knowes not, for she caried non betwixe them, but the said xij^d^; which xij^d^ she [Eleine Ricroft] toke thankfully.

Ad iij, this deponent saies, that "the said Thomas hath had a child bie the said Eleine, after the banes were askid betwixe them; which banes were askid afore he gate her with child, or els, as the voice of the Cuntry is, she was so honest, he cold not bringe his purpose about; for, after that the banes were askid, he toke her as his wief afore God, and so [she] consentid to his follye" . . . . . .

[2] Examinacio testis intra Elenam Ricrofte et Thomam Snelson, capta coram magistro Roberto Leche, in Legibus baccalaureo, &c, v^to^ Junii 1563° /

Hugo Holme, parochie de Codington, etatis lij annorum, novit partem actricem x annis, et partem ream iiij^or^ annis / . . . . . .

Ad iij, This deponent saies, that Elein Ricroft was in this deponentes service above iiij^or^ yeres ago; and Thomas Snelson came to this deponent, and desired to be a suter to the said Eleine in the way of mariage; and this deponent gave hym Licence, because it was honest. and longe after this, this deponent was desired to be at the mariage of one that was suster to Eleine Ricrofte. and this deponent, walkinge furth on a grene by the place where the said mariage was, Thomas Snelson came to this deponent, and bade hym welcomme into those partes, and desired hym to be good

[1] leaf 132, back. [2] leaf 133.

to hym concerninge the said Eleine; for the said Snelson said "she is my wief, afore god and man; for I have trouthplightid her, and was askid in the Churche with her, or euer I ouercame her and gate her with child." and that this was true, he sware to this deponent, bie his Christendome. and further he said to this deponent, "helpe, I pray you, that Eleine may get a Citacion to call me to the Lawe. I have geven her xij^d^. to pay for it / and I will beare her other Chargis, and will Confes before the Ordinary that she is my wief, and I have Contracted her; and I can marry non other woman to be my Lawfull wief. I am waide[1] by masters and frendes to marry a wido, which I can neuer do, yf Eleine forbid the mariage" / . . .

[2]Responsiones personales Thome Snelson, capte xxiij° Septembris 1563° /

Ad primam posicionem / This Respondent saies, that ther hath bene a talk of mariage, and communicacion movid by frendes, betwixe hym and Eleine Ricrofte; but he saies that ther was neuer any Contract of mariage as it is libellate, at any tyme / further beynge demaundid, whether he toke her bie the hand afore witnes, and spake the wordes as the articulate, or the like in effect; answereth, bie vertue of his othe, 'no' / and beynge put in mynd of Roberte Wethers house, he saies he was neuer there for such purpose.

Ad ij^d^, This Respondent saies, that he hath send diuerse tokens to the said Eleine; not as to his wief, but as to other he hath done / and hath Received others from her againe, biecause he was a suter to her /

Ad iij, this Respondent answereth, that he did neuer make any contract as above expressid, or on this sort / "I will take the for my wief," with entent to marry her; neuertheles, he denieth not but he hath had carnall Copulacion with her. and saies further, the banes were askid, as he hard say,—but not through hym, or any frend of his,—bie her procurement. beynge demaundid whether he had carnall Cognicion after the banes askid, he saies he cannot certenly tell, biecause the banes were askid without his consent or knoledge, but bie heresay, vt supra. further he saies, the banes were not askid in the church wherto he doth resort, but in the parish church of Presbury, beynge iiij^or^ miles of from hym. altho he be in that parishe, he resorteth to Chelford[3] [by Crewe] whereat mariage is solempnized /

Ad iiij, he saies he [workes] in Presbury, and dwell[es] in Capisthorne[3] [near Crewe] . . . [See the further Depositions on page 196 below.]

[1] urged [2] leaf 143 (Piccope's No. 79).

[3] Chelford and Capesthorne are townships in the parish of Prestbury; and each township had a chapel of ease to the mother church of Prestbury.—W. H. Price.

5. Hugh Pollett *v.* Elizabeth Eccles (spinster), alias Burton (widow).

[1]2 Dec. 1563 Randle Fowdon, about 43, of the parish of Wilmysloe,[2] "sais he was *present* abowt mychaelmas last, att the request off Hugh Pollett, in the howse off Elisabeth Burton, when Hugh Pollett did declare to the said Elisabeth, that she hade made hym a contracte, as is speciefied in the said [2nd] article. And the said Elisabeth vttirlie denyed the same."

[3]John Burton, of Wilmyslowe, about 76, "sais that abowt toe yeris agoe, and dyverse tymes syns, this deponent offerid *Master* Damp*ar*te and other, to marie *with* the said Elisabeth Burton, al*ias* Eccles; and at all tymes the said Elisabeth gave hym answare ageyne, 'that she was nott for no ma*n* to marie, but onlie w*i*th Hugh Pollett.'"

> [4]Exa*minac*io testis in ca*usa* contract*us* inter Hugone*m* Pollet et Eliz*abetham* Pollet, capt*a* cora*m* Joh*anne* Cheta*m*, no*tario* pu*blico*, man*dato* d*omi*ni canc*ellarij*, xvj° Dece*mbris*, a*nn*o 1563.

Agnes Cash, p*a*roch*ie* de Wilmeslowe, Cestr*ensis* dioc*ese*, ib*idem* oriund*a*, etat*is* circit*er* lxx an*n*os, et no*vi*t p*a*rte*m* act*ricem* vj an*n*is, et Eliz*abetham* Burton al*ias* Eccles, x an*n*os et vltra.

Ad p*ri*mu*m* ar*ticulum* dicit, q*uod* nescit depon*er*e /

[5]Ad ij[d] ar*ticulum*, dicit, q*uod* nu*n*q*uam* talia v*er*ba spe*cif*icat*a*, nec hijs si*mi*lia, in ar*ticu*lo sic recitat*a*, inter p*ar*tes audivit; nec vnq*ua*m vidit d*ictu*m Hugone*m* Pollet in domo d*ic*te Eliz*abethe* Eccles, al*ias* Burton. al*ite*r quoad D*ictu*m ar*ticulu*m et content*a* in eod*em*, nescit Depon*er*e /

Ad iij ar*ticulu*m, Dicit, q*uod* nescit depon*er*e prors*us* aliquid ad content*a* in eod*em*.

Ad iiij, dicit, q*uod* nu*n*q*ua*m audivit Hugone*m* Pollet et Eliz*abetham* Eccles, al*ias* Burton, infra p*a*roch*iam* de Wilmeslowe,[6] aut alibi inter vicinos, reputat*os* et no*mi*nat*os* vt vir et vx*or*. al*ite*r quoad ar*ticulu*m nescit depon*er*e /

Ad v[t], dicit eund*em* fore veru*m*.

Ad vj dicit, q*uod* querelat*a* e*st* ex p*ar*te D*ic*ti Hugonis: an le*giti*m*e*, nescit depon*er*e /

Ad vlt*imum* dicit, q*uod* p*re*deposit*a* p*er* ea*m* sunt vera. no*n* e*st* doct*a*, no*n* consang*uinea*, no*n* affinis, no*n* Conduct*a*, no*n* curat &c

[1] leaf 150, back.
[2] Wilmslow in Cheshire, on the river Bollin, 5 miles S.W. of Stockport.
[3] leaf 151. [4] leaf 153, back. [5] leaf 154. [6] Wilmslow, Cheshire.

Ad *primam positionem* addicionalem.

Ad *primam*, dicit, *quod* nescit deponere, *quia* nunquam talia audivit.

Ad ij[d], this Deponent saies, that Elizabeth Burton, alias Ecles, within one moneth space after her husband Edmund Burton was buried, what for thoughtes, and for that she had bene sick after the birth of ij[o] Children, she send her water bie this deponent to a phisicion at Chelford,[1] to knowe his opinion, what was good for her: which bade her take spice, nutmegges, ginger, and old Ale, and drink them, and she wold mend; for it was no sicknes, but that her braine was wastid with takinge thoughtes.

Responsio personalis Elizabethe Burton, partis ree, super positionibus et articulis libelli in causa predicta, capta coram magistro Chetam &c, xx[o] Januarij anno predicto (1563-4).

Ad *primam positionem*, non credit eandem continere in se veritatem; nec vnquam talia verba inter eosdem fuerant prolata de Matrimonio.

Ad ij[d] positionem, negat eandem continere in se veritatem; nec vnquam talia verba protulit, aut hijs consimilia.

Ad iij posicionem, this respondent saies, that of loane she had x[s] of gold, and viij[s] of monie, which this respondent toke of hym of loane; and this respondent hath gevin the same to George Dicon, bailie to Mr Trafford, her landlord, to geve againe to the said Hugh Pollet; but whether the said Hugh Pollet hath received the same, or no, this respondent cannot tell. and also this respondent saies, she had a siluer ringe of the said Hugh at that tyme likewise; and the said Hugh desired this respondent to kepe the same, for that intent, that he might shewe his master, Mr Trafford, that ther had bene tokens goinge betwixe them, but apon no contract; and so this respondent likewise did geve the said ringe likewise to the said George Dicon, to geve againe to the said Hugh; but whether the said Hugh hath, as well the monie and the ringe againe, this Respondent cannot tell / . . . . . .

6. Katherine Man *v.* Richard Pickforth. (She had a child by him.)

[2]Examinacio testium super libello ex parte Katerine Man contra Richardum Pickforth, capta coram magistro Leche, ix[o] Novembris, 1564.

Willelmus Pierson, parochie de Limne,[3] etatis xl annorum, novit partem actricem ab infancia, et partem ream xx annis /

[1] See p. 61, note 3. [2] leaf 197 (Piccope's No. 105).

[3] Lymm in Cheshire, on the Bridgwater Canal, 5 miles S.E. of Warrington, in Lancashire, just across the Mersey.

Ad p*rimum* ar*ticulum*, This depon*en*t saies, that Ric*hard* Pickforth and Kat*herine* Man articulate, did talk*e* of mariage to be had betwixe them w*i*thin a fortnight, after Easter next com*m*ynge shalbe iij yeres; but whether they were then free from all other Contract*es*, this Deponen*te* knowes not /

[1]Ad ijd ar*ticulum*, This deponent saies, that the same tyme, Ric*hard* Pickforth, in the p*rese*nce of this deponent, did take Kat*herine* Man bie the hand,—not in his house, but in the Towne field of Warburton,[2]—and said this vnto her: "Katari*ne*, bie my faith and trouth, I will marry the: put no dout of it. I p*ro*mes the here, before thie frend here," inuendo this deponent. al*iter* nescit depon*er*e; but that he think*es* the said Kat*herine* was w*i*th child at the same tyme.

Ad iij, this depon*ent* saies, that she brought furth a Child; and the said Ric*hard* toke it as his owne. w*hi*ch child, this depon*en*t think*es* was gotten before the wordes of Contracte afore named; for she then semed to be w*i*th Child.

Ad iiij, this depon*ent* saies, that the said Kat*herine* was supposid to be gotten w*i*th Child w*i*th the said Ric*hard*; but there was no thought they were assured as man and wief together . . .

Johñ Huet, p*a*roch*ie* de Witton,[3] husbandman, etatis xlvj an*no*r*um*, nov*it* p*ar*te*m* act*ricem* a pue*r*icia, et p*ar*tem rea*m* ij an*n*is.

Ad p*rimum* ar*ticulum* et ijd, This depon*en*t saies, that 'Ric*hard* Pickforth and Kat*herine* Man came to this Depon*entes* house about Easter was twelf moneth; and the said Ric*hard* declared to this depon*en*t that he had made a Contract w*i*th the said Kat*herine*, this depon*entes* kinswoman; and willed this depon*entes* fartheraunce, beinge vncle vnto the said Kat*herine*. and this depon*ent* therapon went to his suster, mother vnto the said Kat*herine*, and required her to be good vnto the said Kat*herine*, as she was vnto her other suster. and whereas her said mother appointid gooddes to the value of xiij Nobles towardes her said doughters Mariage, this depon*ent* was content to make it vp xix nobles bie his owne meanes . . . . . .

Ad iij, this depon*en*t saies, the Child was borne, w*hi*ch was supposid to be the said Ric*hards*, before the tyme before menc*ion*ed in the further articles.

[1] leaf 197, back.
[2] Warburton, a Cheshire village on the rivers Mersey and Bollin, 5 miles N.W. of Altrincham.
[3] ? Witton, near Northwich, Cheshire; not Witton, a township in the parish of Blackburn, N.E. Lancashire, on the W. side, and now mostly within the borough of Blackburn.

Ad iiij^{tum}, he saies, they were not taken as man and wief; and therfore, when they came to this deponentes house, he wold not suffer them to Lye together / . . . .

Peter Man, *frater* partis actricis, parochie de Limne, novit partem Ream xiij annos.

Ad primum et ij^{dum} articulos, This deponent saies, that about Easter shalbe ij° yeres, the said Richard came to this deponent, and told hym that he had made a contract with Katherine Man, his suster, and desired hym to be good vnto her. he answerid, "one of my suster is maried alreadie, and I have gevin her xx^{s}; and I wilbe as good vnto my suster Katherine, sins you have made a Contract, and can marry non other woman." and further touchinge the Contract, this deponent cannot depose /

Ad iij, he saieth that the said Katherine bare a Child bie the said Richard, which he toke as his owne, and set it to nurse; which child was borne, as he [P. Man] supposid, afore the Easter above mencionid ./

7. Thos. Sothworth *v.* Marg. Sothworth. (Runaway Match.)

[1] Examinaciones testium super libello ex parte Thome Sothworth contra Margaretam Sothworth, alias Ward, oblato, capte coram magistro Randulpho Cotgrave, notario publicco, iiij° Maij, 1565.

Georgius Haydock, parochie de Blagburne, etatis xxviij, novit partem actricem xx annis, et partem ream per annum et dimidium, et vltra /

Ad primum et ij^{d}, This deponent saies, that the said parties, beinge free from all precontractes, as this Deponent thinkes, did drawe together in way of Love or marriage. and Thomas Sothworth articulate, perceyvinge that the frendship and good will of the parentes of the said Margaret cold not be had, did, on a certen [2] night, videlicet, apon Michaelmas daie at night,—howe longe sins, this Deponent knowes not perfittlie—repaire to the fathers house of the said Margaret, and then and thens toke her away with hym, bie her free consent, and convaide her to the Chamber of one of Sir Edmound (what his syrname was, this deponent knoweth not), a priest that syrved at Balderston Chappell:—which Chamber standeth about ij or iij bowshoot from the said Chapell; and the said priest is now deade:—and when they were comme thither, one Edmund Leyver did open the dore, and did let them in: and ther was a boke of Service, which the said Sothworth (as this deponent thinkes) brought thither from the house of Roger Smalley, a neybour of the priestes. and

[1] leaf 222, back (Piccope's No. 113). [2] leaf 223.

then the priest, sittinge vp in his bed, apon his pillowe, (beinge a very old and a sicklie man,) did marry them together, as this Deponent thinketh. beinge askid of the tyme, the wordes, and the maner of the doinge; and who were present by; he saieth, hit was about midnight: and what wordes were spoken betwene the parties, he certenlie cannot declare, biecause he did not marke them well; but he saies he hard the said Thomas say to the said Margaret, "I take the, Margaret, to my weddid wief"; and hard the said Margaret say to the said Thomas, "I take the, Thomas, to my weddid husband": and of more wordes, he cannot certenlie depose. And further he saies, gold and siluer was put on the boke / and a ringe put on her finger bie the priest. and saieth further, that, to his knoledge ther was no bodie by, but this deponent, the parties, & the prest.

Ad iij, This deponent saies, that after they had bene at the priestes chamber, they went to Thomas Irelandes house, of the grene, the same night; and there had meate and drinke; and the parties went to bed together. and further he saies, that after that, the morninge following, the said Thomas brought her to his owne house, where they cohabited & continued as man and wief about half a yere together, to this deponentes remembraunce.

[1] Ad iiij et v, credit eosdem continere in se veritatem.

Ad vj, he saies, he thinkes she is within the diocese; and he knowes not in what parish . . . . .

Edmundus Leyver, parochie de Blagburne, etatis xliij annorum, novit partem [actricem] xxvj annos, et partem ream a puericia, de facie /

Ad primum et ij^d articulos, This Deponent saies, that George Haydock, apon Michaelmas Day at night, as this deponent thinkes, about iiij yeres ago, did, when it was far in the night, knocke at this deponentes dore; who, beinge awaked bie the knockinge, after this deponent knewe who it was, rose and opened the dore, and did let hym and the said Thomas and Margaret into his house. and after communicacion had, perceyvinge it was her mynd to mary with the said Thomas, notwithstandinge this deponent (beinge her kinsman,) did then move her to the contrary, praid the said Thomas to make much of her. And then [2] incontinent, the said George, Thomas, and Margaret, went into the priestes chamber, which was at thend of this deponentes howse, wherof the Inner dore stode open (biecause the priest was an impotent man); and then this deponent, beinge desirous to knowe what was done, followed in short while to the Chamber / and when he came in, the first thinge he sawe,

[1] leaf 223, back. [2] leaf 224.

was, the p*r*iest toke them both sworne that they were free to marry w*i*th either other; and then said, S*i*r, certen service apon the co*mmun*ion bok*e*. And further saieth, that he hard the p*r*iest reade the word*es* of M*at*rimony; and first, Thomas, after the p*r*iest, said, "I, Thomas, take the, M*ar*garet, to my weddid wief" &c; and she said the same likewise. and all thother word*es* of M*at*rimony vsed in the church in that cause, was spoken betwene them. and then he se her hold vp her fing*er*, when the priest put on the ring*e*. and then this depon*ent* dep*ar*tid, and, being*e* somwhat offendid w*i*th the matter, wold not suffer them to be in his house the rest of the night; and so the[y] went to Thom*as* Ireland*es* house, of the Grene, as they said they wold do. and further saieth, that he was not required to go w*i*th them to the p*r*iest*es* chamber; but, on his owne mynd, went to se the same /

Ad iij, This deponent saies, that they have dwellid together as man and wief in Sothworth house; & were so reputed & taken / . . . . . .

8. Eleanor Manwaring *v.* Roger Bybbye. (Going to Sea.)

[1]Exa*minac*io testis sup*er* li*bel*lo oblat*o* ex p*ar*te Elenore Manwaring*e*, Capt*a* cora*m* *magist*ro Rob*er*to Leche, p*r*imo Junij, 1565.

Thomas Port, p*ar*ochi*e* de Walton, etat*is* xl an*norum*, nov*it* p*ar*te*m* act*ricem* fere p*er* annu*m*, et p*ar*te*m* rea*m* xvj^{cim} an*n*os.

[2]Ad p*r*imu*m* et ij^{d} ar*ticu*los / This deponent saies, that apon a monday in the morning*e*, about S*ain*t Andrewes day Last past, as he remembres, this depon*ent* beinge especially required bie Rog*er* Bibbye articulat*e*, repaired to the house of Alex*ander* Garnet, nowe Maior of Liu*er*pole, and there hard and se as followeth, vi*delicet*: this deponent and the said Rog*er*, com*m*ynge together thither, mett Ellin Manwaringe com*m*yng furth of the dore of the said house; who declared vnto them, that she had lefte her mynd w*i*th the said Maior. then the said Rog*er* requestid her to tarrye, and said he must have more talk w*i*th her; and she did so. whereapon the said Rog*er*, beinge desirous to have her to wief, and to kepe his house, beinge toward a voiag*e* (for he is a Travailer bie the Seas) / requestid the said Maior to take hym, the said Rog*er*, and her, the said Ellin, contractid together. to whom the said Maior answerid thus; vi*delicet* / "Rog*er*, it is best to take delib*er*aci*o*n in the matter, and knowe what frend*es* the said Ellin hath, and what they will do for her"; and such like counsell &c. whom the said Rog*er* answerid, "I have a voiage beyond the sea, toward Ireland, and wold have one in the meane season

[1] leaf 226, back (Piccope's No. 116). [2] leaf 227.

to loke to thinges in myne house; and therfore, I pray you, let her be made my wief, and then I trust you will suffer her to be my housekeper without suspicion." at whose earnest request, the said Maior consentid so to do; and the said Alexander toke the said parties and this [1]deponent with hym on his backside[2]; and there the said Roger and Ellin, in the presence of this deponent and the said Alexander, toke handes together; and the said Roger said, after the said Alexander, to the said Ellin, beinge present: "I, Roger, take the, Ellin, to my weddid wief, for better, for worse, for richer, for porer, in sicknes and health, till death vs depart;" and all such wordes as the prest vseth in Contractinge Matrimonye. and then the[y] drewe handes; and the said Ellin toke the said Roger bie the hand, and said: "I, Ellin, take the, Roger, to my weddid husband, for better for worse, till death vs departe," &c; and afterward kissed together, and callid together man and wief, and dronke a Cuppe of ale together in the Maiores house; and so departid / . . . . . .

9. Alice Ince *v.* John Brotherton.

(Two Forms of Words for the Trothplight. Child born after it.)

[3]Examinacio testium in causa Contracti super libello ex parte Alicie Ince, contra Johannem Bretherton oblato, capta coram Magistro Roberto Leche, &c, Die et Anno predictis. [17 January, 1565-6].

Galtherus Coller, parochie de Winweke,[4] etatis xxx annorum, novit partem actricem iij annis, et partem ream circiter xx annis.

Ad primum et ij^{d} Articulos, This Deponent saieth, that much about this tyme two yeres, John Bretherton articulate came to this deponentes house, beinge his neibour, and requested hym to go with hym to the house of Richard Haie, an other neibour of his; who so did. and when the[y] so came thither, the[y] found Alice Ince in the said house; and John Bretherton desired the same tyme, that he and the said Alice might be Contractid together the same tyme. and the said Richard Haie answerid, and desired them to take an other then hym for witnes; for he said he was a lame man; and if occasion servid, he was not able to travaile. whereapon the matter staid at that tyme, and they all went home. And then about a fortnight or thereabout after, Galther Thelwall, of Holme[5] in the parish of Winweke, came, in the name of the said John, and willid this deponent to comme speake with hym at the house of the said Galthere. and this deponent repaired to the house of the said Galthere, and

[1] leaf 227, back. [2] The back of his house. [3] leaf 265 (Piccope's No. 130).
[4] Winwick, Lancashire, across the river from Warrington.
[5] Winwick with Hulme.

there found the said John and Alice sittinge together bie the fire in the eveninge tyme at after Evensonge, afore dailight was done. And the said John toke this Deponent and the said Galther Thelwall out of the [1]house, biecause ther was other Company in the said house. And so this depon*ent*, Galther Thelwall, John and Alice, came furth out of the said house, and stode before the strete dore apon the grene. And then the said John toke a boke out of his hose,—w*hi*ch this depon*ent* did not open, and therfore he knowes not what boke hit was, but he thinkes hit was a Psalter-boke,—and gave the said boke to this depon*ent* to hold in his hand; who did hold the said boke: and then the said John toke the said Alice bie the right hand, and said, "I take the, Alice, to be my wief, and no*n* other woman, so God me helpe, and the Content*es* of this boke" / then the said Alice said those word*es* were not well and sufficient. Then the said John said, "Here I take the, Alice Ince, to my wief, before all other women: so God me helpe, & holidame! and bie this boke," and kissed the boke, holding*e* her hand still in his; and the said Alice likewise said, "here I, Alice, take the, John Bretherton, to my husband, before all other men: so God me helpe, and holidame, and by this boke!" and likewise kissed the boke, having*e* ther right hand*es* ioyned together: and then the[y] losid hand*es*; and the said John and Alice went awaie together, w*i*thout other Companye; but whether [= whither] they went, this depon*ent* knowes not.

[2]Ad iij, This deponent saieth, he think*es* this article is true; for he saieth that, sins the tyme of the said Contract, the said John begott a man child of the bodie of the said Alis. Reddend*o* ra*cio*ne*m*, he saieth, that while the said Alis lay in, she was kept in John Bretherton his fathers house, & the child was there borne. And when the child was borne, he toke hit to be his owne, and still kepeth hit as his owne; and this depon*ent*, beinge his neib*our*, neu*er* knewe hym refuse hit.

Ad iiij, he saieth, they ar*e* supposed to stand in such case, that they neither of them can marry any other p*er*son duringe their liues.

Ad v et vj, dicit et credit eosd*em* fore veros.

Ad vlt*imum*, dicit p*re*d*icta* p*er* eu*m* fore vera.

10. Sybil Blakhurst *v.* Randle Ramshae.

(In it, a walk home from Saturday's market at Nantwich. See first, p. 210 below.)

[3]Exa*mina*cio testiu*m* sup*er* li*bel*lo ex p*ar*te Sibille Blakhurst con*tra* Ran*dulphu*m Ramshae oblat*o*, capt*a* cora*m* M*agist*ro Rob*er*to Leche, &c. vlti*mo* Februarii 1565[-6].

[1] leaf 265, back. [2] leaf 266. [3] leaf 269, back.

Johannes Newton, generosus, parochie de Acton,[1] etatis xlviij annorum, novit partem actricem xij annis, et partem ream iij annis. Ad primum et ij^d articulos, This deponent saieth, that bie reason that this deponent was lefte one of the ouerseers in the testament of Richard Blakhurst, father to the said Sibill articulate, the said Randull Ramshae havinge, as this deponent supposeth, a good affeccion in the waie of Mariage toward the said Sibill, thought good to Request the good will of this deponent in that behalf. And so, about the latter end of Somer was iij yeres, as this deponent was goinge homeward from the Nauntwich, after the market tyme apon a Saterdaie—which daie this deponent doth not otherways remembre at this present,—Randull Ramshae, articulate, did ouertake this deponent; and after Salutacion had, this deponent said to the said Randull / "I vnderstand ther is good will betwene you and this maide," meaninge Sibill Blakhurst, who was then present, and had then come in Company from the said Nauntwiche, after this deponent, with the said Randull. And the said Randull answerid, that 'ther was [2]good will betwene hym and the said Sibill'; & thereapon Requestid this deponentes good will therin. apon which request, this deponent demaundid of hym to knowe his habilitie, forasmuch as this deponent knewe that the said Sibill shuld have an honest porcion of gooddes to marry her withall. who answerid, saienge, "I trust my father will let me have half of his house duringe his tyme; and the whole after hym"; or such wordes in effect. And then this deponent askid of hym 'whether they two, videlicet, the said Randull and Sibill, were concludid or agreed apon Mariage to be had betwene them.' whervnto the said Randull made answere, that 'they were so agreed.' And thereapon this deponent wished well vnto them. et aliter, ad primum et secundum articulos, nescit deponere / savinge, that this deponent hard say that frendes did mete and commen [= commune] together touchinge marriage to be had betwene the said Sibill and Randull; and savinge also, that this deponent saieth that a child was begott of the bodie of the said Sibill, and borne about Michaelmas was two yeres, as far as this deponent nowe remembres; which Child, the said Randull hath acceptid, and kepeth as his owne child; which tyme of the birth of the child induceth this deponent to think, by conference of the tyme of the talk had betwene this deponent and the said Ramshae, that the said child was begott after that the said Ramshae had declarid to this deponent, that they two, videlicet, the said Randull and Sibill, were concludid apon Mariage betwene them /

Ad iij, nescit deponere /

[1] Near Nantwich, Cheshire. [2] leaf 270.

Ad iiij, credit hunc ar*ticu*lu*m* fore veru*m*.

Ad v^t^, this depon*en*t saieth, that if this cause be iust, this Cowrt is to Complaine in /

Ad vlt*imum*, dicit p*r*ede*posita* p*er* eu*m* fore vera, &c.

(signd) Joh' Newton.

[1]Margareta Gravenou*r*, p*a*roch*ie* de Auldlem,[2] etat*is* xxx an*norum*, est soror p*ar*t*is* act*ricis*; no*vi*t p*ar*te*m* Rea*m* vj an*nis* /

Ad p*ri*mu*m*, credit hunc ar*ticu*lu*m* fore veru*m*; and saieth, that the said Ran*dull* was a Suter to the said Sibill for the space of two yeres afore the child was borne, w*hi*ch she bare to the said Ran*dull*, as this depon*ent* iudgeth.

Ad ij^d^ ar*ticu*lu*m*, This depon*en*t saieth, that the said Ran*dull* and Sibill standinge free (as this depon*ent* think*es*) from any contract of Mariage w*i*th others, did p*r*omes mariag*e*, eche to others, diu*er*se tymes in the p*rese*nce of this depone*n*t, and in sundrie places; as ons, this depon*en*t is remembrid, in the house of Jone Blakhurst, about Michaelmas was iij yeres, w*i*th theis word*es*, or the like in effect: Ran*dull* Ramshae saienge to the said Sibill, "I will marry the, if eu*er* I marry any." And the said Sibill likewise answerid, "I will marry you, if eu*er* I marry any." And an other tyme, vi*delicet*, about the feast of all S*aintes* then next followinge, this depon*ent*, the said Ran*dull* and Sibill goinge from Buerton to Aldlem church togethers in company, [3]the said Rand*ull* spake vnto the said Sibill, in the p*rese*nce and heringe of this depon*ent*, the same word*es* that wer spoken afore, or the like in effect; v*idelicet*: "if eu*er* I marry any, I will Marry the"; and the like was done and spoken bie the said p*ar*ties an other tyme, in the waie as the[y] all three were com*m*inge from the fathers house of the said Ran*dull*, to the house of the Mother of the said Sibill. And further, this deponent saieth, that about *Christ*m*as* next after theis p*r*omesses so made and spoken, the said Ran*dull* begat the said Sibill w*ith* Child. Reddend*a* Rac*io*ne*m* sui d*ict*i, she saieth the child was borne about Michaelmas was two yeres; and the said Ran*dull* taketh and kepeth hit as his owne /

Ad iij, nescit despone*re* / (&c &c)

[1] leaf 270, back. [2] Audlem, near Nantwich, about 18 miles from Chester. [3] leaf 271.

[See the other Trothplight cases in the Supplement, p. 184-201, 210 below.]

III. ADULTERIES.

1. Mr. Rafe Holden. (Adultery and Bigamy.)

[1]Mr. Rafe Holden, a man of property, married Gile Bilsbie, and had at least one daughter by her, who married a Hull man, Simon Danbie, "then a riche march*a*unt man, and nowe [11 Dec. 1561] is fallen in decay, and gone to his Cuntrye." With her daughter, Mrs. Holden spent her 'latter daies,' and her husband sent her some 'rent*es*' by his servant Roger Romisbotham. Being thus free of his old wife, Rafe Holden married a new one, 'Isabell Houghton [in Northamptonshire, in Haselbishe[2]], in the last yere of the reigne of Kinge Henrie the Eight, betwene the feast*es* of M*ar*tinmas [11 Nov.] and St. Andrewe,' [30 Nov.] 1546. His old wife "thought he had bene vp at London in the Cowrt," & was never told of this second marriage by Christopher Hindill who saw her, "biecause he wold get no displeasure on neyther side." A nice-temperd old body—see below—she must have been, for she sent her husband's sisters, Sibell and Lettice, tokens, 'a paire of Flemynge knyves, and a Ribon' (leaving him out only because she thought he was in London), and chatted with Hindill, a workman, who "bie reason that the said M*is*tres Gile was of this Cuntreie, for Cuntreies sake drewe acquaintau*n*ce [w*i*th her] and often tymes reportid to her." He was there, with "diverse others, to make one bulwarke & two blockhouses for the defence of the Towne."

He saw Mr. Holden and his 2nd wife (?), Isabell Houghton, at a tenant's of his at Duckworth, 'for Mr. Holden was about, at that tyme, to build a newe house.' His first wife died about Easter, in 1 Edward VI, A.D. 1547. But before her death comes a nice little bit about her. Nicholas Baron, of Whalley, aged 40, knew her and her son-in-law Mr. Danbie of Hull. He heard of her husband's second marriage; and when askt how he knew that she was then alive, "he sais, that bie reason he is an occupide [man], and draweth pack*es* of Cloth from Holifaxe to Hull, and ther lodethe hymself home againe w*i*th stockfishe, red hering*es* and such marchaundrie wares; and bie that occasion was well acquaintid w*i*th one M*aste*r Danbie, a m*er*ch*a*unt man, and hath bestowid, bie tymes, aboue on C^{li} w*i*th hym. and so apon a tyme hit was this depone*ntes* fortune to se m*is*tres Gile, whom he well knewe, and often tymes had sene her, and she hym; and she axid hym whether he knewe M*aste*r Holden; and he said 'yes.' and she said, "have me comended to

[1] leaf 4, back, and 9. [2] Hazelbeach, near Northampton.

my husband; and say I am glad that he is merie; and geve hym this bendid grote"; and she paid for this deponentes supper. and so this deponent came home, and did his message, and delivered Master Holden his token. and beynge askid whie he wold not tell her of Master Holdens other wief, he answerith, 'biecause he wold not discomforth an old auncient gentlewoman' /" (Well said, Mr. Cloth- and Fish-carrier.)

Ad ij^d^ articulum, This deponent sais, that Master Holden did knowe of his forther[1] wief beynge on lyve, bie reason of the bended grote deliverid to hym from her as a token. and forther he [*next leaf of the MS. is gone.*]

2. Margaret Alatt *v.* Richard Pierson.

Suit for Divorce for Husband's alledgd Incompetence and Wife's alledgd Adultery.

[2]facta fuit sequens examinacio testium, in causa divorcii, super libello ex parte Margarete Alatt contra Ricardum Pierson, eius maritum, oblato, capta coram magistro Roberto Leche &c, xvij° die Martij 1561[-2].

Ricardus Birchwodde, parochie de Weram [Weaverham], novit partem actricem et partem ream a pueriicis; et [est] etatis xliij annorum /

Ad primum articulum / This deponent sais, that he was present bie, when Margaret Alat and Richard Pierson were maried together in the paryshe church of Weuerham, about Candlemas was twelfmonthe.

Ad ij^d^ articulum, This deponent sais, that Margaret Alat hath told this deponent, that she hath done what she could to have children bie Richard Pierson, her husband.

Ad iij articulum, putat eundem continere in se veritatem, sed nescit pro certo deponere. et interrogato plenius de primo articulo, vtrum Ricardus Pierson sit frigide naturæ, vel maleficiatus, This Deponent sais, that Richard Pierson hath told this deponent, that he neuer had carnall dole with Margaret Alat, his wief. what the cause shuld be, this deponent sais he knowes not; but ther was gret love betwene them before the said mariage, insomuch that this deponent was desired of both parties, to be a meane that they might marie before the day appointid, lest Margaret Alat father had not continued in the same mynde: which thinge, this deponent & other their frendes brought to passe.

Ad iiij^t^ articulum, dicit eundem fore verum /

Ad v^t^ articulum, nescit deponere /

Ad vltimum, dicit predeposita per eum fore vera et famam supe huiusmodi laborare. non est doctus, non conductus &c. /

[1] former, earlier [2] leaf 46, No. 19 in Piccope's Index.

[1]Edwardus Amery, parochie de Weuerham, etatis xliiij' annorum, novit partes ab infanciis eorundem.

Ad primum articulum, This deponent sais, that Margaret Alat and Richard Pierson were maried together in the parysh church of Weuerham apon a Saturday, about Candlemas was twelfmonth; and that, he perfittlie remembres, biecause he was present bie at the same; & they were maried bie Sir William Holcrofte, vicar there; and a gret nombre was present bie els, bisides this deponent. and forther, this deponent sais, that he cannot certenly tell whether ther be any Impediment wherbie the mariage shuld not continue; but he sais that he hard bie Report, Richard Peirson to be a man vnable to have children; & he hath hard, bie the mouth of the said Richard, that the said Richard had neuer carnall Acte with the said Margaret Alat, his wief; and that he had had counsell to go to phisike, to seke remedye for the same. Moreouer, this deponent, beynge askid what the cause shuld be of Richard Pierson his infirmitie, answeris, that 'whether hit came of a hurt, or els of somme naturall Impediment, he cannot Judge.' beynge forther demaundid, whether ther was no displeasure taken betwene the two parties maried, wherfore he will not cast his love to his wief for a wilfull stubburnes, rather then for any Impediment; sais, that the[y] lovid very well at the begininge, for the space of viij wekis; and then this Deponent hard say that the said Margaret laid this fault vnto her husband, that he was vnable &c / what displeasure hath growen betwene them sins, this deponent knowis not; but this he well remembres, that a learnid man councelid the said Richard to seke Remedie betwene Whitsonday last till Michaelmas last; but when Michaelmas day was past, & his wief perceyvinge [2]that he could not do any more then afore, she comensid a sute, and sekid for a divorce to be had bie the lawe betwixe them; wher-of Richard Pierson was so ashamid, that he wold have runne his way; and had gone xxx^tie^ mile on his way, and was fett againe bie his frendes, and bound to abide the award of the lawe / and forther, this deponent,—beynge askid whether Margaret Alat did not fansye some other man more then her husband; and for that she wold have an other, and hath laid this faut to her husbandes charge wrongfullie;—answeris, that in his Conscience he knowes non that she fansied so, at the first when she did alledge Impediment against her husband: but what may be sins, this deponent knowis not.

Ad ij^{d} articulum, credit eundem continere in se veritatem.

Ad iij^{t} articulum, credit eundem fore verum.

Ad iiij articulum, dicit eundem fore verum.

[1] leaf 46, back. [2] leaf 47.

Ad v[t] ar*ticu*lum, credit eundem fore verum.

Ad vltim*um*, dicit p*re*deposite per eum fore vera, et famam super huiusmodi laborare[1] in parochiis circum vicinis. non est doctus, non conductus, non affinis, non consanguineus, non curat de victoria &c /

Responsiones personales Ricardi Pierson, capte coram *magistro* Roberto Leche &c, eodem die /

Ad primum articulum, This respondent sais, that he & Margaret Alat were maried in Weuerham church, about Candlemas was twelfmonth, bie the vicar there, bie the consent of their frendes, who made vp the mariage betwixe them. and forther, this Respondent sais, that he thinkes the said Margaret toke this respondent for verye love. beynge askid 'howe longe the same love did continue'; he sais "but a while; [2]for the said Margaret sclaundrid this respondent, that he was not able to do as man ought to do with his wief, within viij wekis after the mariage." beynge askid whether hit was a sclaunder, he sais "Yea; and a very false sclaunder"; for he sais, 'he is able to have children, and hath provid hit by an other woman; & hath a child, which in his conscience he thinkes to be his owne.' beynge askid, 'howe hit chauncid he wold medle with an other, havinge a wief'; he sais, 'he wold neuer have done so, but that she had reysid suche a sclaunder; which all the Cuntrie shuld knowe to be false by this meane.' beynge askid 'whether he hath had carnall copulacion with his wief,' he answeris 'no.' beynge askid the cause whye; he sais, 'the first night he was maried, he wold have had his pleasure of her; and bie chaunce hurt hym before he could have his pleasure; and thereapon, thinkinge he shuld have mendid, he absteynid from her Companye. then she, in the meane season, before he cold be perfitle amendid, sclaundrid hym with the lacke of [Membra, *struck out*] that which a man shuld have. afterward, this respondent perceyvinge that without Remedye he did not amend, askid councell of one Sir Roberte Swan, who dwellith in Rostorne paryshe; which Sir Roberte sawe this respondentes water; & told hym he might be easilie holpen, & gave hym a drinke, which he dranke eveninge & morninge, bie the space of ix[t] daies, & so was curid, and perceyvid hym self lustye.' beynge askid, 'whie he went not then, when he was lustie, to his wief, and vsid her companye in bed': he answeris, 'biecause his wief vsid [3]the companye of one Thomas Pawton, and one Jane Sidebotham, who is knowne to be a naughtie woman.' and forther, beynge demaundid 'whether he will hereafter fansie his wief, as he ought to do'; he sais,

[1] MS. s. h. laborare super huiusmodi. [2] leaf 47, back. [3] leaf 48

'he will neu*er* loue her, biecause she hath so sclaundrid hym.' beynge demaundid forther, 'whether eu*er* his wief did desire hym bie gentle word*es* to shewe that he lovid her, in vsinge her as a husband shuld his wief'; he sais that 'she did desire hym two or thre tymes, before he was amendid, to have dole w*ith* her; but neu*er* sins': to w*hi*ch word*is* he made answere, that 'he was not well, but he thought he shuld amend in co*n*tinuance of tyme.'

Ad ij^d / credit p*ar*s act*a* cupit de m*arito* [? MS.], et p*ro*creare filios.

Ad iij^t ar*ticu*lu*m*, negat eund*em* fore veru*m*.

Ad iiij^t, dicit eundu*m* fore veru*m*.

Ad v^t nescit depon*er*e.

Ad vltim*um*, credit credit*a*, et negat negata; et sup*er* no*n* credit*is* et negat*is*, credit fama*m* no*n* laborare /

3. Henry Price *v.* Mawde Price or Gregorie.

(Adultery: Divorce on account of Precontract of Marriage.)

[1] Re*spo*nsio p*er*sonalis Matilde Gregorie al*ia*s Price, capt*a* sup*er* li*bel*lo ex p*ar*te Henrici Price, in ca*usa* Diuorcij contra eandem Matildam oblat*o*, exa*mi*n*at*a medio suo ra^to [? MS.], cora*m* ma*gist*ro Rob*er*to Leche &c, viij° die mensis maij 1562°.

Ad p*ri*ma*m* po*siti*onem, credit dicta*m* po*siti*onem fore vera*m*, q*uia* matrimon*ium* fuit solempnizatu*m* inter ista*m* re*spo*nd*ent*e*m* et Henricu*m* Price, in eccl*es*ia p*a*roch*ie* de Bu*n*burie, citra festu*m* omn*ium* S*anct*or*um*, xxj annis, vt recolit, elapsis.

Ad ij^d po*siti*onem, credit dict*am* po*siti*onem continere in se v*er*itatem. reddendo racio*n*em sui dicti; that abowt a twelmonde afore this re*spo*ndent was maried to Henrie Price,—afore sufficient recorde, callid Rob*er*t Wilson, Thomas Spark, Alice Dood & other,—she was contracted to one Rondall Gregorie, off the p*a*rich of Bu*n*burie, in the howse off Hugh Gregorie, in thes wordis, vi*delicet*: "I, Rondall, take the, Mawde, to mye wiff, from this daye forthward, till death vs dep*a*rte; and therto I plight you mye troth." and so likewise she,[2] this re*spo*ndent, said: "I, Mawde, take the, Rondall, to my wedded husbonde, from this daye forthward, till death vs dep*ar*te; and therto I plight you mye troth," manibus iunctis, et disiunctis, et sic osculati su*n*t (?). and after that, this re*spo*ndent hade toe children bie the said Rondall, after that this re*spo*ndent hade maried the said Henrie Price, then the said Henrie beyng in s*er*uice w*ith* certen gentilme*n* / and this re*spo*ndent sais, that she

[1] leaf 55, back (Piccope's No. 21). [2] MS. the

was abowt xviij^tene^ yeres off age when this contracte was made *with* Rondall Gregorie, and free then from all other me*n* /

[1]Ad iij' po*siti*onem, dicit content*a* in dicto ar*ticu*lo fore vera, q*uia* necq*ue* habuit carnalem copula*m* cu*m* dicto Henrico, nec q*uia* ex p*ar*te sua necq*ue* ratificauit hoc matrimo*nium* re aut ve*r*bo / post hoc p*r*esens matrimo*nium* solempniza*tum*.

Ad iiij^tam^ p*ositio*nem, credit content*a* in dict*a* p*ositio*ne fore vera; et q*uia* compuls*a* fuit pe*r* parentes et amicos suos, ipsa invita, ad contrahend*um* matrim*onium* cu*m* dict*o* Henrico Price . . . . . .

Exa*mina*cio testiu*m* in ca*usa* p*r*edict*a*, die et an*no* p*r*edictis . . .

Alicia Doode, p*a*roch*ie* de Bu*n*bure, ib*ide*m oriunda, etat*is* circiter xl annos, nouit p*ar*tem actricem xxj annos, et nouit p*ar*tem rea*m* a puericia sua.

Ad prim*um* ar*ticu*lu*m*, this deponent sais, that Henrie Price and Mawde Price were maried together in the p*a*rich church off Bu*n*bure, abowt the fest off Mychaell the arcangell, xxj yeres past; and that, she knowis well, beyng a neybo*ur* dwelling ther adioneng, nere vnto Hugh Gregorie, father vnto the said Mawde Gregorie, al*ia*s Price /

Ad ij^d^ ar*ticu*lu*m*, this deponent sais, that betwixe the fest off Estur and the Roode daye, xxij annis elapsis, she, this deponent, was bie, when one Rondall Gregorie, and the said Mavde Gregorie, al*ia*s Price, made a contracte together in the howse of Hugh Gregorie, father vnto the said Mavde Gregorie, in thes wordis, vi*delicet*: "I, Rondall, take the, Mawde, to my weddid [2]wiff, in sekenes and in helth, till death vs dep*ar*te; and therto I plight you my troth." And the said Mavde saide vnto the said Rondall: "I, Mavde, take the, Rondall, to mye weddid husbonde, in sikenes and in helth, till death vs departe; and therto I plight you mye troth"; manibus iunctis et disiunctis; p*rese*ntibus tunc ib*ide*m, Thoma Sparke et Robe*r*to Wilson. al*ite*r q*u*oad ar*ticu*lu*m* nescit depone*re* / but *tha*t Rondall Gregorie had toe children bie the said Mavde Gregorie, after the said mariage.

Ad iij^tium^ ar*ticu*lu*m*, this deponent sais, after this matrimonie, to her knolege, the said Henrie [Price] did neue*r* lye *with* the said Mavde, nor did cohabete volu*n*tarie together, nor did consent together as ma*n* & wiff.

Ad iiij^tum^ ar*ticu*lu*m*, dicit, q*uod* dict*a* Matilda compulsa fuit pe*r* parentes et amicos eorunde*m*—ipsa invita,—ad contrahend*um* matrimoni*um* cu*m* dicto Henrico Price, prout ista deponens be*ne* sciuerit. . . .

Matilda Broke, p*a*roch*ie* de Bu*n*bure, ib*ide*m mora*ns*, traxit xviij

[1] leaf 56. [2] leaf 56, back.

annos; etat*is* circiter xlvij^tem annos; nouit p*ar*tem act*ricem* xxx^ta annis, et Matildam Gregorie a natiuitate sua.

Ad p*r*imu*m* ar*ticu*lu*m*, this deponent sais: as she reme*m*bres, Henrie Price and Mavde Gregorie were maried together in the p*ar*ich church off Bu*n*bure, abowt the fest off mychaell the arcangell, xxj^ti yeres past; and that, she knowis, bie cause she was one that dressid the dyn*er* the same day*e*.

[1]Ad ij^d ar*ticu*lu*m*, this deponent sais, that, as she harde saye, Rondall Gregorie hade made a contracte w*ith* the said Mavde Gregorie afore the mariage celebrate and solempnized betwixe the said Henrie P*r*ice and the said Mavde; and that after the said contracte made, the said Rondall Gregorie hade bie the said Mavde toe children, a boye and a wench; wich this deponent well knowis to be true.

Ad iij^tium a*rticu*lu*m*, dicit, in vim iuramenti sui, that she verelie knowis that the said Henrie Price did not ratifie the said matrymonie bie carnall copulacion; for the said Henrie hade told hyr[2] bie a secrett frende, that the said Mavde was w*ith* childe; and therapon wolde haue no thinge to do w*ith* hyr; and itt proved not so; and so, apon that, they fell owt, and dwellid not together; but the said Henrie went to s*er*uice, and dwellid abrode w*ith* gentilme*n*, so that this deponent thenk*is* verelie they neu*er* consented together /

Ad iiij^tum ar*ticu*lu*m*, this deponent sais, that the said Mavde was compellid bie her parent*is* and other hyr frendis to marie the said Henrie, for bie cause she wept the same daye that she shuld be maried, afore this deponent, and said, "bie hyr owne mynde, she wold rather haue drowned hyr, then maried the said Henrie Price." . . . . . .

[3]R*es*p*o*nsio*n*es p*er*so*na*les Henrici Price, capte Die et loco p*r*ed*ic*t*is*.

[8 May, 1562, is the last date given, on leaf 55, back.]

This r*es*p*o*ndent sais, by vertue of his othe, that he did not here of any p*r*econtract made by Mawde Gregory, his p*r*ete*n*sid wief; for yf he had, he sais he wold neu*er* have maried her. beyinge askid howe & by what meane he hard hit, for that the said Mawde had made a p*r*econtracte, he answerid, he came to the knowledge [of] hit by one, Rob*er*te Wilsons wief, about half a yere after the mariage betwixe the said Mawde & hym; who said, that 'she cold have told hym that afore.' beynge askid whether he had eu*er* carnall Act w*i*th the said Mawde; he answeris, bie his othe, 'no.' reddend*o* rac*i*on*em* sui d*ic*ti, he sais, that the first night that this r*es*p*o*ndent & the said Mawde laid-bye together,

[1] leaf 57. [2] MS. hym [3] leaf 61 (Piccope's No. 25).

he wold have had his pleasure apon her; and she answerid & said, that 'he should not have any pleasure of her of vij yeres.' whereapon this *respondent*, *perceyvinge* and iudging that she lovid an other man better then hym, fell into such sorowe that he was not his owne man; & went out of the Cuntrey to *Service*. & sais, he hard tell that she had two children by Rondull Gregory; *which* hath causid hym to cast his mynd from her, & to forsake her Company, & to repent the mariage /

[1]Exa*mina*cio Ran*dulphi* Gregory in *causa* divorcij inter Henricu*m* Price et Matilda*m* P*rice*, capt*a* cora*m* *magistro* Ro*berto* Leche, &c, xxix° die Maie, 1562° /

This depone*nt* confesseth that ther was a full and *perfitt* co*n*tracte betwixe Mawde Gregory & this depone*nt*, of mariage, before that she maried Henry P*rice*; and that this depone*nt* sais he was at that tyme fre from all women, and the said Mawde free from all men, to his knoledge. and further he sais, that he did not forbid the banes askid betwixe the said Henry P*rice* & Mawde Gregory, biecause he hard men say that the said Mawde & this depone*nt* were to nere akinne to marry in those daies, forbiecause this depone*ntes* father was brother to the said Mawdes grandfather. but afterward, he *perceyvinge* the marriage cold not stand betwixe the said Mawde & Henry; & *perceyvinge* that *the* first co*n*tract shuld stand / had carnall dole *with* the said Mawde sins the said mariage of Mawde & Henry; & by her had two children. & further this depone*nt* beleves, & takes hit in his Conscience, that the said Mawde & Henry had neu*er* carnall Acte together. Reddend*o* ra*cionem* d*icti* sui, he sais, that the said Henry compleynid to dyverse of his frend*is* that she wold not accept hym as her husband. & also this depone*nt* sais, that yf he thought they had carnall dole together, she shuld neu*er* be his wief; & nowe this depone*nt* tak*es* her to be his wief; & where there hathe bene dyverse better mariages offred to hym, he hath alwaies refusid to marry any, biecause he cold not marry any other in his Conscience; nor neu*er* will, duringe her lief; for that the vic*ar* of Bu*n*bury, a learnid man, beyng gostly father to this depone*nt*, Mawde, & Henry, hath counselid this depone*nt*, either to take her, or to absteyne from mariage duringe her lief, for that hit is a full p*re*contract, by Godd*es* lawe, betwixe this depone*nt* & the said Mawde /

[1] leaf 63, back (Piccope's No. 25*).

4. Elizabeth Shuttleworth's Confession.

(Has refused her Husband for Peter Hartley, and past off Hartley's child as her Husband's.)

[1]Res*po*nsiones pe*r*so*na*les Elizabeth*e* Shotilworth sup*er* ce*r*t*is* ar*ticu*lis, sibi pe*r* Laurenc*ium* Shotilworth obiect*is*, capte cora*m* m*a*g*is*tro Robe*r*to Lech*e* &c ix° die Octobris, 1561°.

This Res*po*ndent sais, that she was Lawfully maried vnto Laurence Shotilworth w*i*thout any Lawfull Impedim*en*t betwixe them; & that she was, and is, his Lawfull wief, and hath had vj or vij Children by the said Laurence. further beynge demaundid why she did, contrary to her p*ro*messe made, & contrary to the Lawe of wedlocke, play the hoore: she answeris, 'her grace was no better' / beynge askid who was the Adulter w*i*th her, she sais, 'one Peter Hartley of the pa*r*ish of Colne; and they were neibo*ures* together; and the said Peter had a child bie this res*po*ndent, yet Livinge, w*hi*ch was the last child this Res*po*ndent bare of her body' / beynge askid, 'howe longe sins the said Peter drewe into her Company vnlawfully'; she sais 'it is about iiij^or yeres ago; & to discharge her Conscience, this Res*po*ndent [confesses that she] had a child supposid to be her husband*es*, callid Jone, bie the said Peter Hartley: and Peter Hartley hath had oftener to do w*i*th her w*i*thin this iiij^or yeres, then her husband.' beynge askid 'howe this matter first apperid to her husband*es* knoledge:' she sais, 'she lovid Peter Hartley so well, that she wold not suffer her husband to lye w*i*th her; and so, whan he pe*r*ceyvid this Res*po*ndent to be w*i*th child, he pe*r*ceyvid her noughtie lief and misdeameno*ur*; & biecause he did not lye w*i*th her, he knewe certenly it cold not be his.' beynge demaundid 'whether she can burthen her husband w*i*th his mislyvinge w*i*th women'; she answeris, 'she can*n*ot truly burthen or suspect hym' / beynge askid 'whether any other had to do w*i*th her, but Peter Hartley, sins she was maried,' she sais 'no'; and that, she may depose on the Sacram*en*t. beynge askid, 'whether she was compelld by force, or alurid by faire p*ro*mysses, to confesse so much against herself'; she sais 'no! for she doth hit only to save her othe, and discharge her Conscience; biecause hit is a matter of Truthe.' beynge askid 'howe she will lyve hereafter, sins she can*n*ot mary, and her husband hath refusid her'; she sais 'she knowis not, but as God will p*ro*vide for her.' beynge threatnid to do pen*aun*ce, she desires [the Chancellor] to be good to her, and she will do what she shalbe assigned to do /

[1] leaf 77, back.

5 *b.* Jane Downes *v.* Reginald Downes. (See 5 *a*, p. 202-3.)

Adultery and Separation. (A Child-Marriage: see p. 202-3.)

[1] R*esp*onsiones p*er*son*a*les Reginaldi Downes, sup*er* po*sitio*nibus et ar*ticu*lis Li*bel*li oblat*i* ex pa*r*te Jane Downes, capt*e* cora*m* ma*gis*tr*o* Robe*r*to Leche, in l*egibus* bacc*alaur*eo, &c., die et an*n*o p*redictis*. [17 Dec. 1562.]

Ad p*r*ima*m* po*sitio*nem / This r*esp*ondent saies, that Jane Downes and he were maried together, and lyved together as man and wief, and had Issue together; and this r*esp*ondent saies, he loves her as a man ought to do his wief.

Ad ij, this r*esp*ondent saies, he had neu*er* mariage good w*i*th the said Jane; for this r*esp*ondent*es* father sold hym as his heire [? sold his heritable land], and had the good to hym self, to his knoledge, wherfore this depon*en*t spent no*n* suche. and forther he saies, that the said Jane and this r*esp*ondent neu*er* dwellid together; but she remayned at her mothers house, wherevnto this r*esp*ondent had free accesse at all tymes. and about xv' yeres ago, this r*esp*ondent had a child by one Ellin Coke, w*hi*ch child is somwhat young*er* then his owne child he had by his wief. and sais, the tyme the said Jane had knoledge of that child vnlawfully begotten, she, the said Jane, wold neu*er* graunt her good will to contynue w*i*th this r*esp*ondent as his wief. but he think*es* that stubbornes rather came of her frend*es*, then of the said Jane. and forther he saies, he hath sins had a child by one Sibill Pott.

Ad iij . . . beynge askid whether he hath had any more children vnlawfully begotten, this r*esp*ondent saies he will not answere; for he saies he is not bounden so to do by the Lawe /

Ad iiij, This r*esp*ondent saies, he knowes not what the said Jane is afraide of; but he saies he will put in sureties to vse her as an honest man ought to do his wief. and yf she be afraide of his children illegitimate, he saies he wilbe bounden also to put them away from hym. and as for the kepinge of any women, he saies he will kepe no*n*, nor hathe kept no*n* this iij or iiij^or yeres, or there about. and yf ther be any other thing that she is afraid of, or stand*es* in feare of her lief, this r*esp*ondent saies the cause therof shalbe taken away, as shalbe thought reasonable by Lawe or by frend*es* /[2] . . . . . .

[1] leaf 107 (Piccope's No. 51).

[2] Mr. W. H. Price has shown me the enrolment of the Decree by which Jane Downes got her Separation from bed and board (*a mensa et thoro*, preserving the nominal marriage), on March 4, 1562-3.

6. William Eiton *v.* Mary Eiton.

(A Chaplain, as a Doctor, has a Woman's water sent to him for the disease of *Mother.*)

[1]Exa*minac*io testiu*m* in ca*usa* Divorcii, sup*er* lib*ell*o ex pa*r*te Will*elm*i Eiton, ar*migeri*, con*tra* Maria*m* Eiton oblat*o*, capt*a* cora*m* Do*m*ino Ep*iscopo* et *Magist*ro Rob*er*to Eblethwaite, in absenc*ia* Do*mi*ni Canc*ellarii*, p*ri*mo Junij, 1564 /

Simon Bradshawe, *Cler*icus, Cap*ell*anus Joh*ann*is Vrmeston, *generosi*, etat*is* lx an*noru*m aut circite*r*, no*v*it pa*r*te*m* act*ricem* v an*n*is, et pa*r*te*m* rea*m* pe*r* anno*s*. . . . . Interrogat*o* de adulterio pe*r*petrat*o* cum Georgio Haughe a*rticula*to pe*r* eande*m* Maria*m*, et an vsa e*st* medicament*is* / This Depon*ent* saies, that 'he neue*r* knew of any evill Com*m*itted betwixe the said George Haugh and Mary Heiton, Articulat*e*.' And further he saies, that 'a woman came vnto this depon*ent*, beinge a man havinge skill and practize in Phisick, in the Name of the said Mary, w*i*th the Water of the saide Mary, (as she said,) to knowe of this Depon*en*t what disease the said Mary had; and to his Judgm*ent*, she that ought that water, had a disease callid the Mother, and no*n* other'; but this Depon*en*t think*es* it was not the water of the said Mary, biecause she came, about vj wekes after, to this Depon*ent* bie chaunce, the said Marie beinge at that tyme about xxx wekes or more gone w*i*th Child, to his knoledge or Judgm*ent*; and told this Depon*ent*, she sent one to this Depon*en*t not longe afore w*ith* her water: ali*te*r nescit depone*re* . . . . . .

[2]Seath Man, pa*r*och*ie* de Deane, ætat*is* xxx an*noru*m, no*v*it pa*r*te*m* act*ricem* xx an*n*is, et pa*r*te*m* rea*m* xij an*n*is. Ad p*ri*mu*m* ar*ticu*lu*m*, quoad p*ri*ma*m* pa*r*te*m* eiusde*m*, putat fore veru*m*; et quoad adulteriu*m* com*missu*m cu*m* Georgio Haugh, et de p*r*ocreat*io*ne p*r*olis, This Depon*ent* saies, that 'about S*ain*t George daie was a xij moneth, this Depon*en*t rid w*i*th his M*ist*ris, Marie Eiton, from Deane to Stoforth,[3] where the mother of Wi*llia*m Heiton dwellid; and bie the waie, betwixe Deane and Manchester, when the said Marie and this depon*en*t were but a verie little from one Irlames house, one came to the said Marie out of the said house, and said to her, "Here is a frend of yo*u*rs wold faine speake w*i*th you"; and she returnid, and went into the house or eue*r* this Deponent came to her. and this depon*en*t scarslie rested walkinge the horses at the doore, half or quarter of an howre, when one callid hym in to his M*ist*ris. and he com*i*nge in, she gave hym drinke.' beinge askid, 'Who was drinkinge w*i*th her,' he saies, 'one George Haughe, and two or iij others; but for any evill signe or Token betwixe the said George and Mary, he did

[1] leaf 168. [2] leaf 168, back. [3] Stofforth.

not se nor p*er*ceyve. and after he, this depon*ent*, had dronk, he went, and cold gird but one horse, when his M*ist*ris came out; wherbie he think*es* in his Conscience, ther was no carnall act com*m*itted betwixe them.' Cetera nescit . . . . . .

[1]Jac*obus* Eiton, *par*och*ie* de Deane, etat*is* xxxiij an*n*or*um*, no*v*i*t* *par*te*m* act*ricem* xx an*n*is, et *par*te*m* rea*m* simil*iter* . . . . This depon*ent* saies, that somewhat afore Candlemas last, about ij or iij daies, this depon*ent*, ridinge toward*es* London w*i*th Marie Eiton, apon Candlemas even, or thereabout, the said Marie, in Totceter,[2] was deliu*er*id of a Man Child, havinge all his right and livelie Limmes, and beinge borne out of the Accompt*es* that Eiton acountid apon, about xij wekes; which Child, in his Conscience he beleves not to be W*illia*m Heitons, for that Cause / but whose it was, he knowes not; or whether Haugh and the said Marie had carnall act together, this Depon*ent* knowes not. And further he saies, as touchinge Medicines, he knowes not she toke any to the entent*es* spec*if*ied in this Article / Al*iter* nescit depon*ere* / . . . . . .

[3]Agnes Holme, *par*och*ie* de Deane, etat*is* circit*er* xl an*n*os et vltra, no*v*i*t* *par*tes xij an*n*is . . . . . . Interrogat*a* de Medicament*is* articulat*is*, This depon*ent* saies, that 'betwixe St Ellin daie and Whitsondaie was a xij moneth, Mary Eiton send this depon*ent* w*i*th her water to S*i*r Simon Bradshawe, who lokid apon the same, and declarid, to his knoledge, she had a disease callid the Mother; and for the same, he told this Depon*ent* what he shuld get her for the same, beinge a herbe callid Muggwede.' Ali*as* ? Alit*er* nescit depon*er*e . . . . . .

[4]Elizabeth Winstanley, *par*och*ie* de Wigan, etat*is* xix' an*n*or*um*, no*v*i*t* *par*tes iiij an*n*is.

Ad p*ri*ma*m* *par*te*m* p*ri*mi Ar*ticu*li, concordat cu*m* p*re*contestibus suis: et quoad reliqua*m* *par*te*m* huius Ar*ticu*li, nescit deponere; but apon St Ellin daie was a xij Moneth, this depon*ent* did helpe Mary Eiton, her M*ist*ris, w*i*th whom she then dwellid, to make a Posset, and bredd of a herbe callid Mugge-wede, for that (as she think*es*) that she had the Mother, as this Depon*ent* hard her said M*ist*ris saie . . . . . .

[5]Exa*minac*io testiu*m* sup*er* Excepc*ion*ib*us* oblat*is* ex *par*te Marie Heyton, con*tra* testes p*ro*duct*os* ex *par*te Will*elm*i Heyton ar*migeri*, ei*us* mariti, capt*a* cora*m* m*agist*ro Rob*er*to Leche, &c, xxix° Septem*bris* 1564.

[1] leaf 169. [2] Towcester, Northamptonshire.

[3] on leaf 169, back. The evidence of Elizabeth Partington, at the top of this page, is in short Latin paragraphs, and amounts to little. Her husband (like Agnes Holme's) is a tenant of the party producing her, evidently Wm. Eiton. See below.

[4] on leaf 170. [5] leaf 192.

Petrus Winstanley, par*ochie* de Wigan, etat*is* l an*norum*, no*vit* p*artem* act*ricem*, Wi*llelmum* Heiton, ar*migerum*, xxiiij an*n*os, et p*artem* rea*m* xij an*n*is.

Ad p*rimum* ar*ticul*u*m* excepcion*um*, nescit depone*re*, sed refert se ad Jura in ea p*ar*te; but that the said S*ir* Simon is a sp*eci*all frend of Wi*lliam* Heiton /

Ad ij[d], this depon*ent* saies, that the said Seath Man articulate, was seru*aunt*, and is Ten*aunt* nowe, to Wi*lliam* Heiton esq*uie*r; and therefore this depon*ent* saies, he think*es* he wold favo*ur* his m*aste*rs p*ar*tie /

[1] Ad iij ar*ticul*u*m*, this deponent saies, that James Heiton articulate, and the said Wi*lliam* Heiton, are cosin germains: and this depon*ent* think*es* he dothe favo*ur* Wi*lliam* Heitons p*ar*te gretlie, and is a gret berer w*i*th hym in the same.

Ad iiij[or] et v[t], this depon*ent* saies, that the said Elizabeth Partington is wief vnto a Ten*aunt* of the said Wi*lliam*; and therfore he think*es* she wold [favo*ur*] her said M*aste*rs p*ar*tie. & Elizabeth Holme is either a ten*aunt*, or a ten*aunte*s wief,[2] to the said Wi*lliam*.

Ad vj, he saieth, that the said Elizabeth Winstanley, at the tyme of her Exa*mina*cion, was seru*aunt* to the said Wi*lliam* Heiton, and is doughter to this deponent, beinge ten*aunt* of the said Wi*lliam*; and therfore he think*es* she wold favo*ur* her M*aste*rs p*ar*tie /

Ad vlt*imum*, dicit p*redicta* p*er* eu*m* fore vera. no*n* e*st* doct*us*, no*n* instruct*us*; e*st* tenens Wille*lm*i Heiton, ar*migeri*; no*n* Curat [de victoria] &c.

Wille*lmus* Chadock, p*ar*och*ie* de Wigan, etat*is* xliiij an*norum*, no*vit* p*ar*te*m* act*ricem* xvj an*n*is, et p*ar*te*m* rea*m* xij an*n*os /

Ad p*rimu*m ar*ticul*u*m* nescit depone*re*, sed refert se ad Jura in ea p*ar*te: and he saies, S*ir* Simon Bradshawe is an honest priest; & whether he favo*ur*s M*aste*r Heitons p*ar*tie, or no, he knowes not.

[3] Ad ij[d], this depon*ent* saies, he knowes th[e said] Seath Man very well, who is Ten*au*nt to the said Wi*llia*m Heiton; & therfore he think*es* he favo*ur*s the cause of the said Wi*lliam*; but he think*es* he wold not go against his othe.

Ad iij ar*ticul*u*m*, This depon*ent* saies, that James Heiton and Wi*llia*m Heiton esq*uie*r ar cosin germans; and the said James was a gret doer in following of this Matter, as the Cowrt can testifie /

Ad iiij, this depon*ent* saies, he knowes on, P*ar*tingtons wief, whose husband is ten*aunt* to the said Wi*llia*m Heiton, w*hi*ch this depon*ent* think*es* is she that is articulate.

[1] leaf 192, back. [2] She stated herself that her husband was the tenant. [3] leaf 193.

Ad v[t] nescit depon*ere*, q*uia* no*n* novit mulier*em*.

Ad vj, this depon*ent* saies, that Elizabeth Winstanley, at the tyme she was sworne & Exa*min*ed in this cause, was seru*au*nt vnto Wi*lliam* Heiton esquier, and yet is a ten*au*nt*es* doughter of the said Wi*lli*am, callid Peter Winstanley.

Ad vlt*imum*, dicit p*redicta* p*er* eu*m* fore vera. no*n* est doct*us*, no*n* Conduct*us*; est tenens p*ar*t*is* act*ricis*; no*n* Curat de victoria, &c /

IV. AFFILIATIONS.

1. Anne Wadesworthe *v.* John Whitwham. 19 Feb. 1561-2.

[1]Christabella Bridge, al*ia*s Hope . . . etat*is* circit*er* xlviij an*n*os . . . [2] . . . sais that she, with others, were at the birth of a woman child, w*h*ich Agnes Wadesworth brought forth into this world about the feast of the Ascenc*i*on of o*u*r lord last past; and at that tyme this depon*ent* sais, that the said Agnes toke hit apon her charge, that John Whitwh*am* was the father of that child, & no*n* other, in the presence of Jenet Pollet, midwyve, Agnes Estwodd, M*ar*garet Smith, Benet Aspden, this depone*n*t, & M*ar*garet Wadesworth, & other . . . . . .

Margareta Wadesworth, alias Smithe . . . etat*is* circit*er* xl[ta] an*n*os et vltra . . . sais that she did knowe that Joħn Whitwh*am* did go a woeinge to Agnes Wadesworth, & drue into her Companye; but whether he was taken any tyme in bed w*i*th her, this depon*ent* can*n*ot tell. /

Ad iij ar*ticu*lu*m*, this depon*ent* sais, that she, w*i*th other, were at the labo*ur* of Agnes Wadesworth, beynge w*i*th child, in the house of Joħn Wadesworth, the monday afore the Ascenc*i*on of o*ur* lord[3] last past; where the said Agnes then brought forth into the world a woman child, w*h*ich she toke, apon her charge & Conscience, to be the child of John Whitwh*am*, & no*n* other: beynge there p*rese*nt, Jenet Pollet, mydwyve, Agnes Estwood, M*ar*garete Smith, Isabel Shore, Christable Bridge, vnacu*m* ista deponen*te* . . . . . .

2. Randle Fradsam *v.* Margaret Wilkinson.

(Suit for Disproof of Affiliation.)

[4]Exa*mi*n*a*cio testiu*m* in *causa* Reclamac*io*n*is* purgac*io*nis, sup*er* li*be*llo ex

[1] leaf 30, back. [2] leaf 31.

[3] Ascension-day, or Holy Thursday, is the Thursday following the fifth Sunday after Easter-day, Thursday in Rogation week, *i. e.* the week following Rogation Sunday. [4] leaf 49, back.

parte Ranulfi Fradsam contra Margaretam Wilkinson oblato, capta coram magistro Roberto Leche, &c, xix° die Martii 1561[2].

Anna Billinton, parochie de parva Budworth, etatis lx' annorum, novit partem actricem a natiuitate, et partem ream iiij[or] annis.

Ad primum articulum, This deponent sais, that Margaret Wilkinson came to the Vicar of Budworth with a filiacion; & that the Vicar gave no warninge, but proceded to owninge of hit the same day / but after that hit came to the knoledge of the said Randall Fradsam, he reclaymed the same; but the same day that the child was ownid,[1] he was not in the churche, nor knewe not of hit.

Ad ij[d] articulum, This deponent sais, that the said Margaret Wilkinson brought v' women, and her self vj', and they were all her nere kinswomen.

Ad iij articulum, nescit certitudinaliter deponere.

Ad iiij[t] articulum, This deponent sais, that Margaret Wilkinson is of an evill name and fame, and of evill Conversacion. Reddendo causam sciencie sue huiusmodi, This deponent sais, that she had a child before by one Darlington. aliter nescit deponere.

Ad v[t], dicit eundem fore verum.

Ad vltimum, dicit predeposita per eam fore vera, et famam super huiusmodi laborare. non est docta, non conducta, non consanguinea, non affinis, non curat de victoria &c /

Margeria Wilkinson, statim de Budworth minori[2], etatis xli annorum, novit partem actricem a natiuitate, et partem ream v, annis /

[3]Ad primum articulum, nescit certitudinaliter deponere, nisi ex relacione aliorum, qui retulerunt huic deponente dictum articulum fore verum.

Ad ij[d] articulum, This Deponent sais, that, as she hard say, the said Margaret brought certen women thither,—the nombre she knowes not,— to make her filiacion, who were all her nere kinswomen, as she also hard reportid; but she knewe them not.

Ad iij' articulum, nescit certitudinaliter deponere ad contenta in eodem; but she sais, she hard the said Margaret say, the said Randall was father of her child, about two monethes before she was deliured.

Ad iiij' articulum, This deponent sais, that the said Margaret had a child before, with one Darlington; and that she is of evill name and fame. aliter nescit deponere.

Ad v', dicit eundem fore verum.

Ad vltimum, dicit predeposita per eam fore vera, et famam super huiusmodi laborare. non est docta, non conducta, non consanguinea &c /

[1] was sworn or attributed to him. [2] Little Budworth. [3] leaf 50.

Margareta Bellin, p*a*rochie de Torporley, etat*is* xxij an*norum*, nov*it* p*a*rte*m* act*ricem* a pue*r*icia, q*ui*a est soror eiusd*em*; et p*a*rte*m* rea*m* v' an*n*is /

Ad p*r*imu*m* ar*ticu*lu*m*, nescit certitudinal*ite*r depone*re*, sed ex rela-c*io*ne alior*um*, q*ui* retuleru*n*t huic deponen*ti* d*ictu*m ar*ticu*lu*m* fore ver*um*.

Ad ij^d ar*ticu*lu*m*, This depone*n*t sais, that she, beynge in the towne of Budworth, did here hit reportid, that the same day M*a*rg*a*ret Wilkinson shuld have fatherid her child, that she brought thither a certen of wyves, whose names she knowes not, who were nere kynswomen to the said M*a*rgaret articulate.

Ad iij ar*ticu*lu*m*, This depone*n*t sais, that M*a*rgaret articulate, sit-tinge in her house in Eton, in the p*a*rysh of Torporley, declared to this depone*n*t, that she counted her goynge w*i*th child to be till the later Lady-day in harvest; and she was not brought to bed till Alhalowtide after, w*h*ich is about viij weke distant; and forther, declared to this depone*n*t, [1] that yf the child were not borne at o*u*r Lady day, hit were not Ran*dall* Fradsams; but she, this Depone*n*t, think*es* her said brother to have had carnall act w*i*th the said M*a*rgaret Wilkinson.

Ad iiij^t ar*ticu*lu*m*, nescit certitudinal*ite*r depone*re* ni*si* ex auditu; but this Depone*n*t sais, the said M*a*rgaret had a child bie one Rondull Darlington before this tyme. cetera nescit.

Ad v^t, dicit eund*em* fore ver*um*.

Ad vlt*imum*, dicit p*r*edeposit*a* p*er* ea*m* fore vera. no*n* est doct*a*, no*n* conduct*a*; est soror p*a*r*tis* act*ricis*; no*n* curat &c.

[2] Katarina Okis, p*a*rochie de Oue*r*,[3] etat*is* xxxviij an*norum*, nov*it* p*a*rte*m* act*ricem* a pue*r*icia, et p*a*rte*m* rea*m* vij an*n*is.

Ad p*r*imu*m* ar*ticu*lu*m*, nescit depone*r*e.

Ad ij^d ar*ticu*lu*m*, nescit depone*r*e, sed ex auditu.

Ad iij ar*ticu*lu*m*, This depone*n*t sais, that she and the said M*a*rgaret Wilkinson, beynge seru*a*unt*es* in house w*i*th S*i*r Phelippe Egerton, hit chauncid that on a night the said M*a*rgaret and this depone*n*t shud have lyen together,—bitwixe Christmas and Alhalowtide, was twelfmonth,—one Henry Hilton, when they were bothe a bed, came into bed to them; and this depone*n*t p*er*ceyvinge that, did ryse, and went into an other bed in the same chambre; & the said Henry Hilton & M*a*rgaret Wilkinson did so continue in bed together, half the night; but who shuld be father of the child, she knowes not; but she eu*er* fathered hit apon Ran*dall* Fradsam, from the tyme she appearid to be w*i*th child; but whether the

[1] leaf 50, back. [2] on leaf 50, back.

[3] Over near Winsford, which is in the neighbourhood of the parties.

said Ran*dall* had carnall acte w*i*th her, or no, she [Kat. Okis] cannot certenlye depose.

[1] Ad iiij ar*ticu*lu*m*, concordat Anna Billington, p*re*conteste sue.

Ad v', dicit eund*em* fore ver*um*.

Ad vlt*imum*, dicit p*re*deposit*a* p*er* ea*ndem* fore vera. no*n* est doct*a* &c.

Robertus Russell, p*a*rochie de Malpas, etat*is* lx[t] anor*um*, no*vi*t p*a*rte*m* act*ricem* a nat*ivitat*e, et p*a*rte*m* rea*m*, iiij[or] an*n*is.

Ad p*ri*mu*m* ar*ticu*lu*m* nescit depon*e*re.

Ad ij[d] ar*ticu*lu*m*, dicit eund*em* fore ver*um*, p*ro*vt audivit ex relac*io*ne alior*um*.

Ad iij ar*ticu*lu*m*, This depone*n*t sais, that one Ric*hard* Weld, beynge seru*a*unt to his m*aste*r, S*i*r Phelip Egerton, reportid before this depone*n*t & dyverse others at Olton,[2] about Candlemas day last, that he had had carnall acte w*i*th M*a*rgaret Wilkinson; but the tyme he named not. al*ite*r quoad dic*tu*m ar*ticu*lu*m* nescit depon*e*re.

Ad iiij' ar*ticu*lu*m*, concordat cu*m* Kat*erina* Okis, p*re*conteste sue.

Ad v', dicit eund*em* fore ver*um*.

Ad vlt*imu*m, dicit p*rede*pos*i*t*a* p*er* eu*m* fore, vera, &c.

Edward ap Robin, p*a*rochie de Budworth,[3] etat*is* xxij an*no*r*um*, no*vi*t p*a*rte*m* act*ricem* et p*a*rte*m* rea*m* ij an*n*is.

Ad p*ri*mu*m* et ij[d] ar*ticu*los, nescit depon*e*re ni*si* ex relac*io*ne alior*um*, q*ui* retuler*unt* huic deponen*ti* d*ict*os ar*ticu*los fore ver*os*.

Ad iij ar*ticu*lu*m*, This depone*n*t sais, that he and one Rog*er* Egerton, havinge a suspic*io*n that one Henry Hilton shuld lye w*i*th M*a*rgaret Wilkinson, about alhalowtide was twelfmonth, to his Remembr*a*unce; and this depone*n*t, goynge to a chambre w*i*thin the house of S*i*r Phelip Egerton, found the said Henry Hilton and M*a*rgaret Wilkinson lyenge together on a whele bedd[4]; and this depone*n*t returnid to his fellowe, Rog*er* Egerton, & declarid to hym that the [5]said Henry Hilton was not w*i*th her [Margaret], for els, yf this depone*n*t had told hym the truth, the said Rog*er* wold have taken hym [H. Hilton] there; but what he wold have done, he knowes not / and forther he saies, he think*es* Ran*dall* Fradsam, articulate, to have had carnall Acte w*ith* the said M*a*rgaret; but whether he be father of her child, or no, he ca*nn*ot depose.

Ad iiij ar*ticu*lu*m*, dicit p*ro*vt audivit, ar*ticu*lu*m* contin*e*re in se verit*a*tem.

Ad v[t], dicit eund*em* fore ver*um*.

Ad vltim*um*, dicit p*re*deposit*a* p*er* eu*m* fore vera &c. no*n* est doct*us* &c.

[1] leaf 51. [2] Oulton, in the parish of Over. [3] about 20 miles N. of Chester.
[4] The little truckle bed that ran on wheels and was put under a big bed.
[5] leaf 51, back.

3. Wrongful Affiliation. Oliver Leghe *v.* Rose Sworton.

Deposition as to Rose Sworton's bastard Child.

[1]Exa*min*acio testis in ca*usa* Reclamac*ion*is purgac*ion*is sup*er* li*bel*lo ex p*ar*te Oliveri Leghe con*tra* Roseam Sworton oblat*o*, capt*a* cora*m* mag*ist*ro Rob*er*to Leche &c, die et an*no* p*redict*is / [8 May, 1562, on leaf 55, back].

Will*el*m*us* Duckworth, p*ar*ochie de Nauntwich, etat*is* lx[ta] an*norum* et vltra, no*vi*t p*ar*tem act*ricem* xviij[cim] an*n*is, et p*ar*te*m* rea*m* iiij[or] an*n*is /

Ad p*r*imu*m* ar*ticulu*m, credit Oliver*um* Leghe no*n* fore p*at*rem p*r*olis p*er* Roseam Sworton genita*m*.

Ad ij[d], This depone*nt* sais, that he hathe hard Rose Sworton say, dyverse tymes, that 'there was not any weddid man that shuld have the Child in her belly.' but she namid neu*er* any man to this depone*nt*, but only Oliver Leghe articulate; & that was bothe sins the child was borne, & afore. and forther he sais, he thinkethe that Roger Crockett is not father of the same child; nor she neu*er* namid hym as father vnto this depone*nt*; but this depone*nt* sais that ther*e* was a rumo*ur* of hit that the child shuld be his; but this depone*nt* think*es* hit came of Rose Sworton, that said hit in an anger or pride, biecause Crockett was a handsom*me* man; but after she was exa*min*ed of hit, she denied hit.

Ad iij nescit c*er*titudinal*ite*r depone*r*e, (&c &c . . . . . .).

[2]Exa*min*acio testiu*m* in ca*usa* Oliveri Legh*e* contra Rosea*m* Sworton, capt*a* cora*m* m*agist*ro Rob*er*to Lech*e*, &c, xix° Novemb*ris* 1562°.

Rogerus Crocket de Vic*o* Malba*no* [Nantwich], an*norum* xx, no*vi*t Oliver*um* Leg*h* p*er* iiij[or] an*nos* familiar*iter*, et p*ar*te*m* rea*m* p*er* vij an*nos*.

Ad p*r*imu*m*, credit co*n*tin*ere* in se veri*tate*m, sed p*ro* certo nescit.

Ad ij[d], this depone*n*t saies, he neu*er* hard the said Rose, or any other p*er*son, name or affirme hym, this depone*nt*, to be the father of the child borne of the said Rose; neu*er*theles, sins the said Oliuer did call this depone*nt* to witnes, c*er*ten, in the way of mirthe, have said to this depone*nt*, "God send you no p*ar*te therof!"

Ad iij, nescit c*er*titudinal*ite*r depon*ere* /

Ad iiij, this depone*nt* saies, that Rose, articulate, had an other child before this infant articulate, supposid to be gotten of W*illia*m Crofte, in whose house the said Rose was dwelling*e* as s*er*u*au*nt, for *th*e space of ij° or iij yeres. & beynge nere the tyme of travaile, she was convaid from her said m*ast*ers house. and after she was deliverid, came

[1] leaf 60, back. [2] leaf 99, back.

to dwell againe w*i*th the said Crofte; & at the said house was gott w*i*th child the secound tyme. and forther, this depone*n*t saies, that when the said Rose was first knowne to be w*i*th child, the wief of Crofte aforsaid did beate Rose very sore; whereapon it was rumorid, that the said Rose was found bie the said wief, in bed w*i*th the said Crofte. Moreoue*r*, the said Rose, beyng demaundid of this Depone*n*t, who was the father of her secound child, answerid "a younge maried man in the Aspell strete": w*hi*ch ansswere, altho it did not declare any certen man knowne to this depone*n*t, yet it concludeth that Oliue*r*, articulate, cold not be [1]father of the child;[1] as well for that he was not lately maried, as that he dwellid not in the same strete. But the said Wil*lia*m Crofte was lately then maried to his secound wief, albeit he dwellid not in the said strete. And further, this depone*n*t saies, that no*n* in *th*at strete, at the tyme of the said demaund, was lately maried /

[2]Ad v', this depone*n*t saies, that the said Rose is, and hath bene, reputid and taken for a woman of light demeanou*r* . . . . . .

Wille*l*mu*s* Duckworth of the Nauntwich, an*n*oru*m* lxiij, no*vi*t p*ar*te*m* act*ricem* pe*r* an*n*os xiiij aut xv^cim^, et p*ar*te*m* rea*m* pe*r* iij or[3] iiij^or^ an*n*os.

Ad p*ri*mu*m* ar*ticu*lu*m*, he saies, that Oliue*r* Leigh may be the father of the child articulate, & may not be, for any thing that he certenly knowes; but he rather iudgeth Wil*lia*m Croft to be father therof, by theis reasons: the said Rose was dwellinge in Croft*es* house; &, beynge w*i*th child, went to one Awcock*es* in Hurleston;[4] & there was d*eliver*id of a child, supposid to be the said Croft*es*, for that she neue*r* fatherid it of any; and afterward came to dwell againe w*i*th the said Crofte. and beynge w*i*th child againe, was by the said Croft*es*—somwhat before her lyenge downe, placid in a void house oue*r* against the house of Crofte, and had such thing*es* as bedding, fire, Candle &c, as were nec*essari*e for her, at the hand*es* of the said Crofte. and when she was small againe, she was set to one Ric*hard* Croft, brother to Wil*lia*m Crofte forsaid; and there abiding vj or vij wekis, at the last did not like [= please] there, but fell at word*is* w*i*th the wief of the house, vsinge this talke: "Well, yf p*ro*myses be not kept, he shall have w*hi*ch is his; and I will go where I may do better": w*hi*ch word*is*, this depone*n*t did here, lyenge in his bed, very nere vnto them. further, w*i*thin a while after, the said Rose came to this depone*n*t, desiring hym to do so muche for her as to speake w*i*th Wil*lia*m Crofte forsaid,—who mynded to go from home, and to tarry

[1–1] Struck out, and 'therof' put instead. [2] leaf 100.
[3] so in MS. (not *aut*). [4] In the parish of Acton, by Nantwich in Cheshire.

ij or iij wekis away,—that she and her child might in the meane tyme be p*ro*vided for, according as he had p*ro*messid her, 'both *tha*t she and it shuld not want; and that she shuld have as good raym*en*t as eu*er* she did weare.' So this depon*en*t, reasoninge with her, did p*er*ceyve in his iudgm*en*t that the said Croft shuld rather be the father of her Child than any other. neu*er*theles, he went not to hym [W^m. Crofte], for other busines that he had. And he saies moreou*er*, that the said Rose hath burthenid many w*i*th the said Child; somwhile sayeng a Lanc*ashire* man shuld have it; somwhile, Crocket forsaid; somwhile, Oliu*er* Lee forsaid, &c /

4. Suit for Cancellation of Affiliation. John Cotgreve *v.* Margaret Monelay.

(She slept with John Barnes. But Cotgreve confesses copulation with her once.)

[1] Exa*mina*cio testiu*m* in ca*usa* reclamac*io*nis purgac*io*nis, ex p*ar*te Johannis Cotgreve, sup*er* li*bel*lo con*tra* M*ar*garet*am* Monelay o[b]lat*o*, capt*a* cora*m* m*agis*tro Rob*er*to Leche, &c, xxiiij° die Octob*ris* 1562°.

Maria Haselwall, paroch*ie* de Worthinbury,[2] etat*is* xix an*norum*, nov*i*t Joh*ann*em Cotgreve vij an*n*is, et p*ar*te*m* rea*m* iij an*n*is /

Ad p*ri*mu*m* ar*ticulum*, This depon*en*t sais, that she cannot certenly depose; but she think*es* Joh*n* Cotgreve is not the father of M*ar*garet Monelays child.

Ad ij^d ar*ticulum*, this depon*en*t sais, that for any thinge she knowes, Joh*n* Cotgreve did not lie w*i*th M*ar*garet Monelay; & for any thinge she knowes, he might lye w*i*th her. and this depon*en*t sais, she knowes not certenly when the child was borne / or whether hit be the said Cotgreves or no /

Ad iij ar*ticulum*, quoad p*ar*te*m* ad carnale*m* copula*m*, deponit vt prius. quoad confess*io*nem M*ar*garete Monelay cora*m* non*n*ullis matronis, nescit depon*er*e. Interrogat*a* de carnale Copula cu*m* Joh*ann*e Barnes / This depon*en*t sa*i*s, that M*ar*garet Monelay, beynge w*i*th child, was tablid at George Garratt*es* house, then m*aste*r vnto this depon*en*t, wherby hit fortunid the said M*ar*garet and this depon*en*t did lye nightly together. and after that the said M*ar*garet had bene at that house the space of vj or vij wekis, apon a night the said M*ar*garet did secretly leave the bed of this depon*en*t, & did steale to the bedd of the said Joh*n* Barnes, who had [bene] and was comynge & goynge to that house about x or xj wekis or M*ar*garet came thith*er*. [3] And this depon*en*t,—p*er*ceyvinge that ther had bene, a gret tyme, suspic*io*n betwene the said M*ar*garet & Joh*n*, &

[1] leaf 80, back. [2] Just in Wales, near Malpas, Cheshire. [3] leaf 81.

felinge her to go p*ri*vely out of the bed,—did lye still for a while, to knowe what M*ar*garet ment; & in p*ro*cesse of tyme, this depone*n*t might here the said M*ar*garet & John Barnes talke together. whereapo*n* this depone*n*t gate vp, and put on her clothis, & drewe nere them: & so did plainly p*er*ceyve, by many tokens, that they were nought together; & lay together the space of ij° houres & more. the said M*ar*garet, cominge from his [John Barnes's] bed, to her owne, found this depone*n*t vp; & this depone*n*t did aske her 'what she did all that while from her; & whie she wold go to that Pocky knaves bed (for this Depone*n*t hath hard that he hath the Pock*es*).' the said M*ar*garet answerid 'she was but talkinge w*i*th hym.' "Well," q*uod* this depone*n*t, "thou & I will neu*er* lye together againe; and I shall tell thie noughtines, howe thou fatheris thie Child apon an other, & go to bed to an other." & whan hit was day, M*ar*garet Monelay [1]wold have gevin this depone*n*t[1] a paire of shoes that she ware apon her feete, to have held her counsell close; & she refusid them. & then she wold have gevin her a peticote; & she refusid hit likewise. & the same day, this depone*n*t told hit to Joh*n* Cot*greve* & his fellowis apon Dye [Dee] bridge; and then one of his fellowis callid Rondull Jerratt, came the next day after, to Garrett*es* house, & found the said Garrett, his wief, & the said Barnes, at din*er* together; & so told them howe M*ar*garet & Barnes were nought to-gether; & they denied hit. & he did aske for the said M*ar*garet; & the[y] said she was in the kitchin. & then the said Rondull Gerrard askid her whether she lay w*i*th Barnes; & she cold not deny hit; & the said Joh*n* Barnes, after he hard tell that she had told, said to her, 'he wold be her death.' and apon that, for fere of hurt, this depone*n*t went away from her m*aste*r, biecause the said Barnes is but a desperate fellow . . . . . .

[2]Exa*min*acio testiu*m* in ca*usa* reclamac*ionis* purgac*ionis*, ex p*ar*te Joh*ann*is Cotgreve con*tra* Margareta*m* Monelay &c, vl*timo* Octob*ris* 1562°.

Will*el*m*us* Washington, paroch*ie* s*anc*te Brigitte,[3] etat*is* xxxvj, no*vi*t p*ar*te*m* act*ricem* xij an*ni*s, et p*ar*te*m* rea*m* p*er* vnu*m* annu*m*, et vltra /

Ad p*ri*mu*m* ar*ticulu*m, This depone*n*t sais, that he think*es* that Joh*n* Cotgreve is not the father of M*ar*garet Monelaes child, biecause, this depone*n*t & he beynge bedfellowes, and dailie conv*er*saunt together, yet he neu*er* se him so much as kisse her mouth, nor to be eu*er* in her Company suspiciously.

Ad ij^d, this depone*n*t think*es* verely in his Conscience that, for any

1—1 Repeated in MS. 2 leaf 84, back. 3 In Chester.

thinge that euer he se or hard of, [John Cotgreve] neuer had carnall dole with her.

Ad iij articulum, this deponent sais, he thinkes this Article to be true for the gettinge of the child. Reddendo racionem sui dicti, this deponent sais, that when Margaret Monelay did name Cotgreve to be the father of her child, the said Cotgreve hard say that one Fazakerleys wief had questionid with her about the gettinge of the same; wherfore he send for her to comme, to say what she hard, before this deponent & dyverse others. and the said Fazakerleis wief declarid then, that the said Monelay, commynge apon a tyme to her house, when she was with child, the said Fazakerleis wief askid her who was father of her child; and she answerd & said, 'hit was Cotgreves.' and she askid when hit was gotten; & she answerid, 'in the Later end of Christmas.' "Then," quod she, "thou maist work all harvest, & gett a gret dele." and the said Fazakerleis wief beyng at that tyme gret with child, as she is yet, said, "I pray God let neuer parte with this betwene my sides, yf this be not true." and the said Monelaies child was borne about Midsomer last. wherby this deponent thinkes verely, that the said Cotgreve cannot be father of her child, for that it came above a quarter of an yere of out[1] the account / . . . . . .

[2]Elena Prince, parochie Sancte Marie,[3] etatis xli annorum et vltra, novit partem actricem vj annis; et partem ream non novit sed de facie /. Ad primum et ij[d] articulos, nescit certitudinaliter deponere; but she thinkes verylie that he [John Cotgreve] is not father of Margaret Monelaies child; for this deponent durst depose for Cotgreve, yf the child were his, that he wold take it /

Ad iij articulum, this deponent sais, that apon a tyme, she, this deponent, Owen Otye, and one Margaret Isherwod, sittinge together in one Ledsams dore, in company of Fazakerleis wief, the said Fazakerleis wief, amonges other talke, told this deponent & the others, that Margaret Monelay, apon a tyme came to her house, beyng gret with child; & she askid her who was father of her child; & she answerid that 'Cotgreve was father of hit' / and she said "When was it gotten?" she said "the later end of Christmas last." "Mary!" quod Fazakerleis wief, "sins thou was so vnhappy, yet it is well, because thou maist labour all harvest, & get a gret deale of mony," biecause she had so long to go / toward her keping in childbedd. & this, the said Fazakerleis wief told of a truth, beynge at that tyme with child. aliter nescit deponere . . . . . .

[1] out of. [2] leaf 85. [3] In Chester.

[1]Examinacio testium in causa reclamacionis purgacionis super libello oblato ex parte Johannis Cotgreve, contra Margaretam Monelay, capta coram magistro Roberto Leche, &c, x° die Novembris 1562° /

Ranulphus Jerrat, parochie Sancti Martini,[2] etatis xlv' annorum, novit partem actricem a puericia, et partem ream circiter duos annos /

Ad primum articulum et reliquos articulos, credit Johannem Cotgreve non esse patrem prolis parte per Margaretam Monelay. Reddendo racionem sui dicti, he sais, Mary Haselwall told this deponent & William Washington, that Margaret Monelay did go from her owne bed prively to John) Barnes bed prively, and plaid the nought with hym. whereapon this deponent came to George Garrattes house, where the said Margaret lay, & founde the said Garret, John) Barnes, & Garrettes wief, at dinner together / & after a little reasoninge, this deponent said in thes wordes: "it is told me that Margaret Monelay did rise from her owne bed prively in the night, & go to an other mans bed," meaninge John) Barnes. Whereapon, Garret denied, and said: "I think it is not so." "Yes," quod this deponent, "let me comme to hir face, & she shall not deny hit." then this deponent went into the kitchin where she was; & before Garrettes face, his wief, & the said Barnes, she did neither say 'yea' nor 'nay' / then quod Garret to his wief, "we had nede to loke better about vs, yf this be so." forther, beynge askid whether euer he se any suspicion betwixe them, he sais, 'none that euer he cold perceyve, to his knoledge, althoughe he was daily conversaunt with hym' / cetera nescit deponere.

Philippus Prince, parochie Sancte Marie,[2] etatis xl annorum et vltra, novit partem actricem xj annos et vltra; et partem ream, de facie novit ij annos et vltra /

Ad articulos omnes et singulos, nescit deponere; sed interrogato de familiaritate inter partes, he sais, beynge fellowe to Cotgreve, & contynually conversaunt together, yet he neuer se any Token of suspicion of Love or favour betwixe Margaret Monelay & hym; nor neuer hard of any familiarytie betwixe them, till it was noysed, her to be with child with hym. and Garrat, with whom Margaret Monelay dwellid, said to this deponent, that 'yf Cotgreve wold have bene rulid by hym, & lovid hym as he lovid hym [Cotgreve], he shuld have had a small part of the child, or no part at all; but sins he [Cotgreve] was stout against hym [Garret], he shall have it; and no man els' / aliter nescit deponere /

[1] leaf 90. [2] In Chester.

[1]Examinacio testis in causa reclamacionis purgacionis, ex parte Johannis Cotgreve contra Margaritam Monelay predictam, capta coram magistro Roberto Leche, &c, xvj° Decembris 1562° /

Margareta Fazakerley, parochie de sancta Maria, novit partem actricem x annos, et partem ream iij annos / . . . . . . Ad iij articulum, This deponent saies, that apon a tyme, Margaret Monelay beynge with child, came to this deponentes house, to desire this deponentes husband to get her in favour with her brother, to be good to her, and to helpe her to a place to lye in childbed. and this deponent askid her, 'who was the father of her child'; and she said 'Cotgreve.' and this deponent demaundid her, 'what tyme he had to do with her'; and she answerid "about Christmas." [2]"Then," quod this deponent, "thou art happy; thou may have a pece of harvest to get somwhat in." but this deponent cannot tell when the child was borne. but this that she hath spoken, this deponent (beynge with child, and not countinge past iiij^{or} daies, or little more,) doth say, as God shall helpe her to her deliveraunce in safety, that it is true. aliter nescit deponere.

Ad iiij, nescit deponere; but she saies she was of Saint Michaelles parishe . . . . . .

[3]Examinacio testium super materia exceptiva, oblata ex parte Margarete Monelay contra Johannem Cotgreve, capta coram magistro Roberto Leche in Legibus baccalaureo, die et anno predictis [4 March 1562-3].

Jana Wright, parochie de Westkirkby,[4] etatis xl annorum et vltra, novit Margaretam Monelay ab puericia; et Johannem Cotgreve non novit sed de facie /

Ad primam excepcionem, non novit Mariam Haselwall, ideo nescit cuius sit condicionis; but she saies she was midwief to Margaret Monelay when she was deliuered; and she confessed in her extremes, that John Cotgreve was father to her child, & non other; beinge very sore chargid, bie reason that this deponent & others were troublid with an other but a little afore /

Ad reliquos articulos nescit deponere, quia non novit dictos testes per Johannem Cotgreve productos; sed ad famam, she saies that she neuer hard but that Margaret Monelay was a maid of honest name & fame before this dede; and therfore she dois think in her Conscience, the said Margaret doth not father it on hym without a cause.

[1] leaf 105. [2] leaf 105, back. [3] leaf 120, back.
[4] West Kirby, near Birkenhead, Cheshire.

M*ar*gareta Monelay, paroch*ie* de Westkirkbe, etat*is* xlij an*norum*, no*vi*t M*ar*gareta*m* Monelay xv an*nos*, et Joh*ann*em Cotgreve a S*anct*o Ph*ilippo* [et] S*anct*o Jaco*bo*, Ap*r*ili / Ad ar*ticul*os o*mn*es et sing*u*los, This depone*nt* saies, that she was p*rese*nt at the Childinge of M*ar*garet Monelay; and the said M*ar*garet did take it apon her charg*e*, when she did not knowe whether she did lyve or dye, that she neu*er* did offend w*i*th man, but w*i*th John) Cotgreve; and that he was father of her child, and no*n* other: and this she confessid to the midwiefe, and the other wieves there p*rese*nt. for the midwief did ask*e* her the question, when she was in her grettest paine. and as for the fame, she saies she is, and hath bene, of honest name and fame, to her knoleg*e*, but for this dede w*i*th John) Cotgreve /

[1]Joh*ann*es Huntington, paroch*ie* S*anct*i Oswaldi, ci*uitatis* Cestr*ie*, etat*is* xxxix an*norum*, no*vi*t M*ar*garet*am* Monelay p*er* duos aut tres an*nos*, et Joh*ann*em Cotgreve vj an*nos*.

Ad p*ri*ma*m* excepc*ion*e*m* / This depone*nt* saies, for any thing*e* that this depone*nt* knowes, Mary Haselwall is an honest damoysell. and forther, this Deponent saies, That he, this depone*nt*, and George Garrat, were sent by Henry Monelay, brother vnto M*ar*garet Monelay, to John) Cotgreve, to knowe the certenty and truth of hym, whether that he wold deny or confesse the Act. and at the first, he did stoutly deny it; but afterward he confessid that he had carnall act w*i*th her ons; and shewid them the place vbi ea*m* carnall*ite*r cognoue*r*it / And forther he saies, the said Cotgreve said he neu*er* had to do w*i*th her but ons carnally /

Ad reliquos ar*ticul*os, Dicit se nihill scire, nec pot*est* excipere con*tra* testes; sed de fama, ait, that she is taken for an honest wenche, but for that one Dede. and forther, this Depone*nt* hearith it comenly reportid that the said Cotgreve is father of the Child.

[2]Exa*minac*io testis sup*er* mate*r*ia exceptiva M*ar*garet*e* Moneley con*tra* Joh*ann*em Cotgreve, capt*a* p*ri*mo Ap*r*ilis 1563°.

Georgius Garret, paroch*ie* s*anct*i Mich*ael*is, etat*is* xl[ta] an*norum*, no*vi*t M*ar*garet*am* Moneley vij, et Joh*ann*em Cotgrave xij an*nos* et vltra /

Ad p*rimam* Excepc*ion*e*m*, This depone*nt* saies, that Mary Haselwall is a light p*er*son, both of her tonge and of her dede; w*hi*ch this depone*nt*, beynge ons her m*aste*r, doth well knowe, and entendith to have remedy against her for her evill demeanou*r* in his house, & for her goynge away in the night season w*i*th-out Leave takinge / not w*i*thout som*m*e of this depon*entes* good*es*. And further, this Deponent saies, that he and John)

[1] leaf 121. [2] leaf 124, back.

Huntunston were sent by Henry Moneley, brother to M*ar*garet articulate, to comen w*i*th John Cotgreve, and bade hym be advised. and they both did aske hym howe he wold vse the woma*n* and the child in tyme to com*me*. and he answerid and said, 'the child was no*n* of his.' "Yes," q*uod* this depone*n*t, "by the same token, it was behind the Milne dore." "Cock*es* woun*des*," q*uo*d John Cotgreve, "can a man get a child standinge? for I neue*r* had any thinge to do w*i*th her but standinge."

Ad reliquos ar*ticu*los et testes, nihil h*a*bet q*uod* dicat con*tra* testes; but for the com*m*en fame, he saies that it is thought that John Cotgreve is to blame for doynge such wronge; for she was an honest maide afore, and in good servise, and of good fame.

5. Wm. Clare *v.* Ellen Gardiner. Suit for Cancellation of Affiliation.

The Child is said to be Hugh Holt's. But "Clare hath a house, & Holt hath non; & therefore, Clare shalbe father of my Child."—p. 98.

[1]Exa*minac*io test*iu*m in ca*usa* reclamac*ionis* purgac*io*nis, capt*a* cora*m* mag*is*tro Rob*er*to Lech*e*, die et an*n*o infrascript*is*[2] [19 Nov. 1562] inter Wi*llelmu*m Clare et Elena*m* Gardin*er* /

M*ar*geria Bradburne, p*a*roch*i*e de Budworth, etat*is* lx an*norum*, nov*i*t p*ar*te*m* act*ricem* et p*ar*te*m* rea*m* ab infanciis /

Ad p*rimam*, nescit c*er*titudinal*ite*r depon*er*e /

Ad ij^{d}, this depone*n*t sais, she knowith two women, Ellin Okell, and John Dichfeld*es* wief, that were w*i*th Ellin Gardin*er* at her purgac*i*on / Ellin Okell was 'suspiciose fame' biecause she had children before she was maried, whom she gave to beggers; and Dichfeld*es* wief had a child before she was maried. but sins she was maried, she was taken for an honest woman, w*hi*ch is viij yeres.

[3]Ad iij Ar*ticu*lu*m*, This depone*n*t saies, that the said Ellin was taken for an honest wenche and a good laborer, before she came to Will*iam* Holt*es* house, of the p*ar*ishe of Rostorne [Rostherne] where she was iij or iiij^{or} yeres before she was gotten w*i*th child.

Ad iiij ar*ticu*lu*m*, This depone*n*t saies, that the said Ellin, p*er*ceyvinge her-selfe to be w*i*th child, came to this depone*ntes* house, beyng her nere kinswoman, in the iij^{e} and ij^{d} degre, to moue her case, and told this depone*n*t that she was w*i*th child, and required her that she might be deliue*r*ed in her house; and this depone*n*t toke her for mere pitty, w*hi*ch she was loth [to] do, but for that she was her kinswoman. and the said

[1] leaf 93. [2] for suprascriptis [3] leaf 93, back.

Ellin, when she cold go abroad much, did repair to W*illia*m Holt*es* house and was but goyng and co*m*myng to this depone*ntes*. so apon a tyme, when she drewe toward her travaile, she came to this depone*ntes* house from Holt*es* house, where she had bene the most part of the day before, & fell on wepinge; whereat this depone*nt*, m*er*valinge, askcd her what was the cause she did so lament: the said Ellin answerid, "Alas! I am vndone; for he whom I wold father my Child on, will forsake it." Then said this depone*nt*, "Who is that?" She answerid, "W*illia*m Clare." This depone*nt* askid, Whi he will[1] forsake [it]. She answered, "Biecause he hath hard say that I have offended w*i*th Hugh Holt." "Well," q*uod* this depone*nt*, "hath he so in dede?" "Yea," q*uod* she; "yf you will kepe my Counsell, I shall tell you: he did offend w*i*th me about Midsom*er*, or sone after." "Wel," q*uod* this Depone*nt*, "then thou hast nede to count thie tyme well, and take hede apon whom thou fathers thie child." "Nay," q*uod* Ellin, "Clare hath a house, & Holt hath no*n*; & therefore, Clare shalbe father of my Child." & forther, this depone*nt* saies, that the said Ellin was d*eliuere*d apon Ester even was xij moneth, in this depone*ntes* house; and beynge in her Travaile & paines, she fathered her child apon W*illia*m Clare; but she semid lothe to vtter it at the first tyme when she was askid the Question, biecause, as this Depone*nt* thinkes, she stode in gret dout.

Ad v, credit omne fore ver*um*.

Ad vlt*imum*, dicit p*re*deposit*a* p*er* ea*m* fore vera. et fama est incerta: for som*m*e think Clare to be father, & som*m*e thinke Holt to be father, for the said Holt was in way of mariage w*i*th the said Ellin; and betwene [2]Alhollowtide & Christmas, next afore her delivery, went vnto her frend*es* w*i*th her to get mariage good*e*; & Ellin Gardin*er* shuld have maried Hugh Holt; & her suster, Holt*es* elder brother / no*n* est doct*a*, no*n* Conduct*a*; for she saies she was loth*e* to beyre witnes, biecause this depone*nt* is Holt*es* aunt, and kinswoman to Ellin; & the said Ellin and Holt are also akinne; but that she was servid w*i*th p*ro*ces.

Thom*as* Steele, paroch*ie* de Restorne, etat*is* xxx' an*norum*, n*ovi*t p*ar*te*m* act*ricem* xx' an*n*is, et p*ar*te*m* rea*m* viij an*n*is.

Ad p*rimu*m ar*ticulu*m, nescit depon*ere* /

Ad ij[d], nescit depon*ere* /

Ad iij ar*ticulu*m, This depone*nt* saies, that the said Ellin was taken, before the birth of her child, but a woman of Lighte behaveo*ur*, biecause she dwellid in a little peltinge alehouse, vi*delicet*, W*illia*m Holt*es* house.

[1] MS. he will he will. [2] leaf 94.

and forther, he saies, that he, this deponent, dwellinge with one Agnes Lough, widowe, in a somer morning yerly, about Midsomer, went to the said alehouse to fetch a Cole of fire, and did therein se Hugh Holt in bed with the said Ellin. Reddendo racionem, saieth thes house is ruynous, & the walles & dores ar not close; and forther, this deponent saies, at that tyme he said nothinge to her; but after, this deponent examined her, and she said that as she was goynge for Turves, he [Hugh Holt] pullid her to bed to hym.

Ad iiij', nescit certitudinaliter deponere.

Ad v[t], credit eundem continere in se veritatem /

Ad vltimum, dicit predeposita per eum fore vera. beynge askid whether Ellin Gardner shuld mary Hugh Holt, he sais he dwellid nere them, & ther was spech of such thinges, but he toke no hede of them.

Henricus Bowne [? Browne], parochie de Budworth, etatis xxiij annorum, novit partem actricem a tempore noticie sue, et partem ream vj annis /

Ad primum et ij[d] articulos, nescit deponere /

Ad iij articulum, This deponent sais, that he, beynge susters sonne vnto Hugh Holtes mother, who kept an Alehouse in the parish of Rosterne in Swinhed, went apon a [1]Sonday in the somer season to se his aunt; and as they fell in talke, Hugh Holt willed his mother to get Ellin Gardiner out of the house; who answerid, "thou may hold thie peace, knowinge what thou hast done to her; for yf she had fatherid the Child a-right, thou shuld have had it" / cetera nescit deponere; but he sais he is akinne to Hugh Holt & Ellin Gardiner, & wold wish them to do well.

6. Jn. Thirlewind and Elizabeth Crosse. 3 Nov. 1563.

[2]Alicia Holland, parochie de Eccles, etatis lxviii annorum, novit partes ab infanciis earundem.

Ad primum articulum, This deponent saies, that she, beynge Midwief vnto Elizabeth Crosse at the tyme of her deliverye of the last child, did aske her in her extremes, who was the father of her said child; and she answerid that 'it was the Child of John Thirlewind, as euer it and she shuld parte, and non other mans' . . . This deponent saies, that the said Elizabeth hath had diuerse Childer bie on, Master Radcliff, and ij[o] bie the said Thirlewind; but she saies, the said Elizabeth was neuer put therfore out of the parish of Eccles, &c /

Cecilea Sedden, of 60 and more, "saies that she hard bie the midwief that was present with Elizabeth Crosse at the delivery of her last child,

[1] leaf 94, back. [2] leaf 147, back.

that it was John Thirlewind*es*. and in her Conscience she think*es* it to be his, biecause he hath vsid her Company so much, as this depon*ent*, beynge next neibo*u*r to the*m* both, very well knowes / . . . This deponent saies, that the said Eliz*abeth* hath had vij Children."

Jeneta Gee, p*ar*och*ie* de Eccles . . . saies, that she was p*rese*nt in the tyme of Travaile of the last Child of Eliz*abeth* Crosse; and when the said Eliz*abeth* was in her extremes, the midwief askid her who was the father of her child; and she answerid, 'as god shuld helpe her to p*ar*te with it, hit was Joh*n* Thirlewind*es*, and no mans els' / and this Depon*ent*, in her Conscience think*es* it to be his / . . . the said Elizabeth hath had vij Children.

7. Robert Walton *v.* Anne Doxie. Affiliation-Cancelling.

[1] Exa*min*acio testiu*m* inter Rob*ertu*m Walton et Anna*m* Doxie, capt*a* cora*m* m*agist*ro Leche, Die et an*n*o p*re*d*ictis* [15 June 1564].

Roger Walmesley, of the parish of Asbury, aged 55, "saies that he, being*e* a practisione*r* of surgery, the said Joh*n* Smith articulate came to hym; and this Depon*ent* found he was burnid[2]; and he exa*min*ed hym, of whom; and he answerid, of Anne Doxie. . . . This Depon*ent* saies that he hath hard it crediblie reportid that the said Anne is a woman of very evill lief; and that she hath vsed the vnlawfull Companie of one Wi*lli*am Galliomoure, and of many others."

John Smith, of the parish of Asbury, aged 26, "saies he hath hard it reportid that she hath vsid Company very evill w*i*th Joh*n* Cliff . . . [and] that Oliue*r* Vaudrey hath Confessid hym self to have had carnall Act w*i*th Anne Doxie / . . . This Depon*en*t cannot deny but he hath [had] carnall Act w*i*th Anne Doxie, and bie her was grevouslie plagid in his bodie, and was shewid bie Roge*r* Walmesley, his surgeon, that he was burnid.[2] w*hi*ch Roge*r* healed hym of the said disease . . . this depone*n*t saies that he hath hard George Sharmon of Spenne grene report that he hath had Carnall act w*i*th the said Anne . . . [and] he knowes she is a very evill woman of lief, and hath vsed the Companie of many men / "

[3] George Sharmon of the parish of Asbury, & township (ville) of Smalewod, dwelling in Spenne grene, aged 26, says he has heard John Cliffe and John Smith report that they've had 'carnall dole w*i*th Anne Doxie diu*er*se (and 'Manie') tymes'; and "that he hym self hath vsed the evill Companie of Anne Doxie about iij or iiij^or^ yeres afore the Child was gotten, that is nowe in sute about . . . [and he] knowes she is

[1] leaf 177. See earlier Depositions, p. lxxxii, n. 1. [2] poxt. [3] leaf 178.

a woman of very evill Conu*er*sac*i*on; and, as report is, she hath vsid the evill Companie of Wi*lli*am Gallimo*ur*, and many others / "

Lastly, George Sharman of Asbury, aged 24, "saies that he himself hath had carnall act w*i*th her diu*er*se tymes."

On leaf 181, John Cliff and Oliver Vaudrey answer as little as they can, and make no confessions. To the 2nd article, Cliff "saies he think*es* he is not bounden to thanswere therof, biecause it toucheth his owne accusac*i*on."

8. Thos. Underwood *v.* Ellen Key. To cancel Affiliation.

(The Child said to be John Amery's.)

[1]Depo*sitio*nes ex p*ar*te Thome Vnderwod con*tra* Elena*m* Key, in ca*usa* reclamac*ionis*, capt*e* xxvij° Julii, 1564.

Rob*er*tus Heisha*m*, p*a*roch*ie* de Weu*er*ha*m*, eta*tis* lx an*noru*m, n*ovi*t p*ar*te*m* act*ricem* de pu*er*icia, et Elena*m* Key simil*it*er.

Ad p*r*imu*m* ar*ticu*lu*m*, nescit depon*er*e.

Ad ij^d^ ar*ticu*lu*m*, This depon*ent* saies, that Elene Key, articulate, Did ride[2] behinde a young man about Corpus Ch*risti* daie was xij monethe; and when they came to a suspicious place, the[y] light both; and ther horse was rayned in the midest of the Lane; and they went both ou*er* a stele[3], and backside a hedge, very suspiciously, [&] did Continue together for the space of a quarter of an howre & more; but what they did ther, this depon*en*t can*n*ot certenlie tell; but he suspectid it was for no good purpose. And further, this depon*ent* saies, the said Heline told this depone*nt*, it was Joh*n* Amery that she rid behinde, that daie.

Ad iij, credit hunc ar*ticu*lu*m* fore veru*m*, p*ro*vt audivit ex Relac*ione* alio*rum*. And further, he saies, she hath a very evill Name in the Cuntrye /

Ad iiij^t^, he saieth, that she hath burthenid Vnderwod wrongfullie, but [the father of her child is] rather Joh*n* Amery; biecause, if Amery had to do w*i*th her that tyme above-said in the ij^d^ article, it shuld seme to be Amery child bie Computac*i*on; but he will not depose that Amery had to do w*i*th her / . . . . . .

[4]Ran*dulphus* Wilbram, p*a*roch*ie* de Witton, eta*tis* xxxv an*no*r*um*, no*vi*t p*ar*te*m* act*ricem* xxx an*n*is, et p*ar*te*m* rea*m* vij an*n*is.

Ad p*r*imu*m* ar*ticu*lu*m*, This depon*ent* saieth that the said Heleine dwellid at this depon*entes* house, [&] was demaundid, beinge w*i*th Child,

[1] leaf 188. [2] On a pillion. [3] stile, still cald 'stele' in Cheshire.
[4] leaf 188, back.

who was father of it; and she answerid, *that* Thom*as* Vnderwod was father, and begatt her w*i*th Child such a daie; and if it came not at that daie, he shuld not have it; and it was not borne w*i*thin vj wek*es* of that daie; therfore this depon*ent* think*es* Thom*as* Vnderwod is not father of it. and this tale she told this depon*ent* & his wief, and an othir woman called Eleine Fazakerley /

Ad ij[d], nescit Certitudinal*iter* depon*ere*; but he hath hard reportid they have had evill Company together /

Ad iij, this depon*ent* saies she is an evill woman before, and hath had ij[o] Children before, by a maried man / . . . . . .

V. LIBELS.

1. Jane David *v.* Robert ap David, and *v.* John ap John (for calling her 'a strong hoore'). And John ap John *v.* Jane David.

Robert ap David calls Jane David 'a strong whore.'[1]

[2]fact*a* fuit sequens exa*mina*cio testiu*m* in ca*usa* diff*amacionis* sup*er* lib*el*lo ex p*ar*te Jane, v*idelicet* Dav*i*d, con*tra* Rob*er*t*um* ap Dav*i*d oblat*o*, capt*a* cora*m* m*agis*tro Rob*er*to Leche, &c, xxix[o] Januarii 1561[-2].

Joh*ann*es Rondull, p*a*rochie de Hanm*er*,[3] etat*is* xxviij' an*noru*m, nov*i*t p*ar*te*m* act*ricem* x' an*n*os, et p*ar*te*m* rea*m* simil*iter* /

Ad p*rimu*m ar*ticu*lu*m*, credit eunde*m* contin*ere* in se veri*ta*tem.

Ad ij[d] ar*ticulum*, This deponen*t* sais, that betwene o*ur* Lady day Last in harvest, and Michaelmas, this deponen*t* hard Rob*er*te ap D*avi*d articulate, call the said Jane, v*idelicet* Dav*i*d, "stronge hore"; and forther said, "I will p*r*ove the a stronge hoore"; but apon what occasion, this deponen*t* sais he knowes not: and thes word*es* were spoken bie the said Rob*er*te in the town [4]of Haleghden, in the p*a*rishe of Hanm*er*, p*rese*ntib*us* tunc ib*ide*m, vnacu*m* isto deponen*te*, te*m*p*ore* p*r*olac*io*nis istor*um* verbor*um*, knaurand [or Katherine] v*idelicet* Dav*i*d, [et] Roger v*idelice*t Dav*i*d, husband to the said Jane v*idelicet* Dav*i*d, articulate. as for any other thinge concerninge the said article, he ca*nn*ot depose.

[1] So Henry Fazakerly calls Margaret Wirrall 'stronge hoore and provid hoore,' p. 117. There are other cases: See below.
[2] leaf 20.
[3] In Flintshire, close by Overton.
[4] leaf 20, back.

Ad iij et iiij[t] *articulos*, This deponent sais, that for any thinge that euer he hard, the said Jane, *videlicet* David, afore the same sclaunder begon, was of honest name and fame, and yet is, to his knoledge.

Ad v[t], dicit eundem fore verum.

Ad vj[tum], credit eundem fore verum.

Ad vltimum, dicit predeposita per eum fore vera; and that this matter is talkid of about in all the Cuntrie. non est doctus, non conductus; est consanguineus vtrique parti.

Katarina alias Knaurand, *videlicet* David, parochie de Hanmer, etatis xlix' annorum, novit partem actricem xx' annos, et partem ream a puericia, quia est soror eiusdem.

Ad primum articulum, credit eundem fore verum.

Ad ij[d] articulum, This deponent sais that Roberte ap David articulate, did call Jane, *videlicet* David, "stronge hoore" in the presence of this deponent, somwhat about Michaelmas last, in the house of Joħn Rondull, the said Joħn Rondull and his wief beynge present: apon what occasion, this deponent knowis not, but onlie that the said Roberte lackid grace. and forther, this deponent sais, the said Robert David callid his brother Roger, husband to the said Jane, "cuckolid" [*so*] in the presence of this deponent; but this deponent toke little hede of hit, biecause she thought hit wold neuer have comme in Controversye.

[1]Ad iij et iiij[t] articulos, this deponent sais, that she, with all the rest of her neyboures, thinke the said Jane to be of honest name before the said sclaunder; and sais that they neuer hard otherwyse bie her.

Ad v[t], dicit eundem fore verum.

Ad vj[tum], credit eundem continere in se veritatem.

Ad vltimum, dicit predeposita per eam fore vera, et famam super huiusmodi laborare. non est docta, non conducta, est affinis parti acte, et soror partis ree; non curat de victoria, dummodo fiat iusticia &c.

[2]Examinacio testium in causa diffamacionis super libello ex parte Jane, *videlicet* David, contra Johannem ap John oblato. [on or after 12 June 1562, on the preceding page.]

Homfridus ap Howell, parochie de Hanmer, etatis xxx[ta] annorum et vltra, novit partem actricem et partem ream x annis et vltra.

Ad primum articulum, credit eundem fore verum.

Ad ij[d] articulum, This deponent sais, that he hard John ap John talkinge with David ap Griffith, and one other woman, and said to them, that 'Jane, *videlicet* David, was a hoore & a strong hoore, and had

[1] leaf 21. [2] leaf 65.

hoorishe castes with her.' and theis wordes were spoken about Lent last,—the day, he remembres not,—in the village of Halghton[1]; the persons above namid beyng present. ad cetera in dicto articulo nescit deponere /

Ad iij articulum, he sais her good name is gretly hindred bie theis sclaunderous wordes, for any thing that he knowes.

Ad iiij articulum, This deponent sais, that the said Jane was, and is, taken and reputid for an honest woman, for any thing that euer he knewe bie her / . . . . . .

David ap Griffith, parochie de Hanmer, etatis xl^ta annorum, et vltra, novit partes circiter xv' annis.

Ad primum articulum, dicit eundem fore verum.

Ad ij^d articulum, This Deponent sais, that hit chauncid John ap John to have bought a mare above a Twelfmonth sins; and the said mare fortunid to breake into a close of Roger David, husband to the said Jane, videlicet David; and the said Roger turnid [2]the said mare out of the Close; and when the said John ap John knewe of hit, he required this deponent and Roger ap John to go to the said Roger David, and said, "bid that foule cuckold, seke me for my mare againe"; presentibus tunc ibidem, Elena Lloide [et aliis multis *struck out*]. and further, this deponent sais, that the said John hath, to this deponentes face, said that Jane, videlicet David, was 'a hoore and a stronge hoore'; and that, he hath reportid to hym many tymes /.

Ad cetera contenta in dicto articulo, nescit deponere.

Ad iij^t articulum, This deponent sais, that, by reason of theis sclaunderous [wordes], the gode name and fame of the said Jane is impaired gretly; and that there is very grett talke of hit in all the Cuntry thereabout.

Ad iiij articulum, This deponent sais, that the said Jane was an honest woman afore this sclaunder rysen; and yet is so taken; for he sais he hath dwellid hard by her house this xv^tene yeres, and cold neuer here or se any dishonesty by her . . . .

Rogerus ap John, parochie de Hanmer, etatis lij annorum, novit partem actricem vij annis, et partem ream similiter . . . . . .

[3]Ad iiij, This deponent sais, that he, beynge a neybour by her, neuer hard but that she was, and is, a woman of honest name and fame, to his knoledge, and so is taken & reputid in the Country and paryshes thereabout . . . .

[1] About 8 miles from Chester, Malpas way. [2] leaf 65, back.
[3] leaf 66.

John ap John *v.* Jane David.

Roger is cald 'Cuckold,' as he spread the Report that his Wife got between him and another man in bed.

[1]Exa*mina*cio testiu*m* sup*er* ma*teri*a oblat*a* ex p*ar*te Joh*anni*s ap John, con*tra* Jana*m*, v*idelicet* Dav*i*d, capt*a* cora*m* Mag*ist*ro Rob*er*to Leche &c, viij° die Octobr*is* 1562° /

Oliuerus Lowther, p*ar*ochie de Hanm*er*, etat*is* liiij an*norum*, nov*i*t Joh*anne*m ap John vj an*n*is et vltra, et p*ar*te*m* act*ricem* simil*it*er /

Ad p*ri*ma*m* excepc*i*on*em* ma*teri*e, putat eund*em* contin*er*e in se verit*a*te*m*.

Ad ij[d] excepc*i*on*em*, This depone*n*t sais, he neu*er* hard John ap John call Rog*er* Dav*i*d 'Cuckold,' or his wief 'stronge hoore'; but he sais that Rog*er* Dav*i*d hath reportid Jane, v*idelicet* Dav*i*d, his wief, to be hoor w*i*th John Leigh, and to have lyen in bed w*i*th hym. And this depone*n*t sais, this matter was in exa*mina*cion w*i*th hym and his wief; and they thought to have agreid Roger Dav*i*d and his wief; and in exa*mina*cion of the matter, the said Jane cold not deny, but that John Leigh, and she and her husband, were all iij in bed together, and she lay in the middest; and forther, she cold not deny but that she came to bed after her husband and John Leigh were a bed; where-as she might have lyen in bed w*i*th her maid, as she did before. moreou*er*, the said Jane said to her husband in the p*re*sence of this depone*n*t and his wief, that 'he, the said Rog*er* Dav*i*d, came of Cuckold*es*, and wold be knowne for a Cuckold.' Where-apon the said Jane and her husband cold not then be agreid together.

Ad iij excepc*i*on*em*, This depone*n*t sais, that Jane, v*idelicet* Dav*i*d, and John Leigh, have bene sene in suspicious placis together, as in the Rye[2] and others placis; and ar vehemently suspectid in the matter, in the Cuntry. And as for Thom*a*s Puleston, he hath hard say that he hath followid John Leigh w*i*th a nakid sword; but that, he referris to Tho*mas* Puleston exa*mina*cion.

Ad iiij, continet in se veri*tatem*, p*ro*vt credit; for John Leigh & his wief be nowe in sute together; but Rog*er* Dav*i*d and Jane his wief, bie report, dwell together in house; but she hath not had p*ar*t of his bed, this iij yeres, as this depone*n*t hath*e* hard reportid.

Ad v[t] excepc*i*on*em*, This depone*n*t sais, she is reputid to be of evill name; and was w*i*th child or eu*er* Rog*er* Dav*i*d maried her.

Ad vj[tum], This Depone*n*t think*es* the witnes brought in by Jane, v*idelicet* Dav*i*d, be not sufficient, but very poor, and have p*ar*t of their

[1] leaf 75 (see leaf 20, back). [2] Compare 'Comin' thro' the Rye.'

Lyvinge at her handes; and are also suspectid persons; for they cold not depose her to be of honest name, biecause they have hard theis thinges bie her husband &c /

[1]Ad vij excepcionem, nescit deponere /

Ad viij excepcionem, This deponent sais, that he neuer knewe of any mare that John ap John bought, sins one that he bought of the Egiptians[2] about iij or iiij^or^ yeres ago; and that mare, to this Deponentes thinkinge, was turnid out of Roger David Close full iij yeres ago / and so left for a tyme.

Ad ix', nescit deponere.

Ad x, refert se ad libellum.

Ad vltimum, dicit predeposita per eum fore vera. et quod eadem Jane est male et suspecte fame ac opinionis, cum Johanne Leigh predicto.

Jana ap Thomas, parochie de Hanmer, etatis xxx annorum, novit Johannem ap John xx' annis, et Janam, videlicet David, xij annis.

Ad primam excepcionem, refert se ad Jura in ea parte.

Ad ij^d^, This deponent sais, that Roger ap David refusid his wief; and did report that John Leigh and his wief were in bed together; et per omnia, concordat cum preconteste suo, quoad istum articulum.

Ad iij articulum: quoad istum articulum, nescit certitudinaliter deponere.

Ad iiij^t^ excepcionem, nescit deponere certitudinaliter; but as for John Leigh, he came not nere his wief this twelf-month, but one night that he was in house with her, to this deponentes knoledge.

Ad v^t^, This deponent sais, that sins the disagreinge of Roger David and his wief, the said Jane hath had no good name . . . .

[3]Thomas Puleston, parochie de Hanmer, etatis xxvj annorum, novit Johannem ap Joh̄n et Janam David xij^cim^ annos.

Ad primam[4] excepcionem, refert se ad Jura in ea parte.

Ad ij^d^ excepcionem, This deponent sais, bie the report of the parish there, Roger David did say plainely that John Leigh was in bed with his wief; and thereapon, within a while after, he turnid her away, and they were asonder a moneth or iij wekis, to this deponentes remembraunce.

Ad iij excepcionem, This deponent sais, that many tymes John Leigh and the said Jane many tymes have been talkinge together suspiciously; and apon a tyme, above iiij^or^ yeres ago, at the same tyme the Souldiers went to St Quintins,[5] about Whitsonday, this deponent, walkinge in the way by a ry field, he was ware of Jane, videlicet David, sodenly comme

[1] leaf 75, back. [2] gypsies. [3] leaf 76. [4] MS. primum.
[5] Battle, 10 Aug. 1557: Spanish and English beat French in Low Countries.

out of the rye towardes the way, and runne home; and was ware also of Johñ Leigh ronnynge further into the Ry, belike to hide hym-self. and this deponent followid hym with a sword in his hand; and yf he cold have taken hym, he wold have gevin hym a marke.

Ad iiij, This deponent sais, that Jane, *videlicet* David, and her husband, and John Leigh, dois not agre with hes wief;[1] wherfore he iudgid the matter to be more suspicious betwene Jane & John.

Ad v[t], This deponent sais, that sins the said Report risen by her husband, the said Jane hath bene but of evill name & fame.

Ad vj[t], nescit certitudinaliter deponere; but he thinkes Jane, *videlicet* David, witnes, be not lowable for many causes, especially biecause they must nedis here of her evill report, for all the parish knowes it . . . . . .

Ad vltimum, dicit predeposita per eum fore vera, et famam super hujusmodi laborare; and he thinkes, yf Johñ ap John shuld be ponished for this matter, he shuld have gret wronge, biecause all the parish knowes it.

[2]Thomas ap John, parochie de Hanmer, etatis xxvj' annorum, novit partes a tempore noticie sue /

Ad primam excepcionem, nescit deponere, sed refert se ad Jura.

Ad ij[d] excepcionem, This deponent thinkes that Johñ ap Johñ is not worthie to be ponished for speakinge any thinge against Jane *videlicet* David; for Roger, *videlicet* David, her owne husband, did report plainely, that John Leigh and she did lye together; and told this tale to Knaurade [or Katherine] *videlicet* David, suster to Jane, *videlicet* David, husband, that John Leigh and Jane, *videlicet* David, did lye in bed together. Reddendo racionem sui dicti, biecause this deponent was seruaunt to the said Knarad at that tyme; and so he har[d] the said Jane, *videlicet* David husband, tell hit his dame. and forther he sais, the said Roger ap David put away the said Jane from hym; on which, gret talk rise on hit /

Ad iij, nescit deponere /

Ad iiij[t] excepcionem, This deponent sais, the said Jane and her husband do dwell together nowe; but they were a gret while a-sonder. and as for John Leigh and his wief, they ar at sute, the one against the other.

Ad v[t], This deponent sais, that the sayenges be bad by her &c . . . .

Willelmus Gilberte, parochie de Hanmer, etatis xxxij annorum, novit partes xvj[im] anos [*so*].

[1] Neither R. ap David nor John Leigh agrees with his wife. [2] leaf 76, back.

Ad prim*am*, nescit depon*ere*.

Ad ij[d], This depone*nt* think*es* that John) ap John) is not worthie ponishme*nt* for callinge Rog*er* ap D*avi*d 'cuckold,' biecause he, this depone*nt*, hathe hard hym so callid viij or x yeres ago. And forther he sais, it is comenly taken for a truth, that Rog*er* ap D*avi*d pleynly said, that John) Leigh & his wief Jane, v*idelicet* D*avi*d, [1]were in bed together; whereapon they have bene asonder.

Ad iij excepc*ion*em, This depone*nt* sais, that he hath hard reportid that John) Leigh*e* and Jane, v*idelicet* D*avi*d, have met together dyverse tymes suspiciously in inco*n*venient placis.

Ad iiij, nescit depon*ere* de concordia inter Roger*um* ap D*avi*d et Jon*am*, ei*us* vx*orem*. but as for John) Leigh*e*, [he] and his wief ar at Lawe together.

Ad v[t] dicit, that she hath but an evill name in the Cuntry.

Ad vij[t], This depone*nt* sais, that the witnes 'p*ro*duct*e* p*er* Jan*am*, v*idelicet* D*avi*d,' cold not depose truly that she was of honest name, biecause they hard of her evill Report, as other her neighbo*ures* did.

Ad vij et viij nescit depon*ere* /

Ad ix', he sais he knowes one Ellin Lloid; but he neu*er* hard her speake any thinge that John) ap John) shuld report of Jane, v*idelicet* D*avi*d.

Ad x', refert se ad li*bell*u*m*.

Ad vlt*imum*, dicit p*re*deposit*a* p*er* eu*m* for*e* vera; et fam*am* sup*er* h*ujus*mo*d*i Laborar*e* in p*ar*ochiis circu*m* vicinis.

Joh*ann*es Carison, p*ar*och*ie* de Hanm*er*, etat*is* liiij an*norum*, no*vi*t p*ar*tes xij an*n*is.

Ad p*ri*mam, refert se ad Jura.

Ad ij[d], This depone*nt* sais, that he think*es* John) ap Joh*n* is not worthie to be ponished for callinge Rog*er* ap D*avi*d 'Cuckold,' biecause the report goeth that he is one, in all the Cuntry; for, as this man hath hard, the said Rog*er* was the first that rysed this tale hym-self, that he was a Cuckold.

Ad iij excepc*ion*u*m*, Refert se ad fam*am*; for he sais that she hath but an evill name in the Cuntrye.

Sup*er* ceteris excepc*ion*ib*us*, no*n* exa*m*in*atur*, quia nescit Lingua*m* Anglican*am* /

[2]Exa*m*in*a*cio testiu*m* in ca*usa* Diff*amacionis* sup*er* replicac*ionibus* ex p*ar*te Jane, v*idelicet* D*avi*d, con*tra* Joh*ann*em ap John) oblat*a*, capt*a* cora*m* M*agist*ro Rob*er*to Leche &c v° Novemb*ris* 1561° /

[1] leaf 77. [2] leaf 86, back.

Willelmus David, parochie de Wems in comite Salopie, etatis lij' annorum, novit [partem actricem] xxiiij^or annos, et partem ream similiter.

Ad primam, nescit omnino deponere . . . . . .

Ad iij', this deponent sais, that John ap Johns wief mother, and the said Puleston articulate, were cosin germains, to his knoledge. aliter[1] nescit deponere . . . . . .

Ad vltimam, dicit predeposita per eum fore vera. and beynge askid 'on what point of the matter he came hither to testyfie,' he answeris, that, after tyme of the contencion arysen betwixe Jane, videlicet David, & John ap John, the said Jane went away from her husband vnto her brothers house; and then her said brother send this deponent & Jenkin Evans to her husband, to knowe of hym, whie he put his wief away; and the said Roger David answerid, "for her owne wordes, and for her vnrulines. I bade her not go; but she might have taried yf she wold." Aliter nescit deponere /

Jankin Evans, parochie de Hanmer, etatis circiter lx annos, novit partem actricem xxviij annis, et partem ream vj annis /

Ad primam, he sais he knowes no dishonesty by Oliuer Lowther; & that the wief of Oliuer Lowther and of John ap John ar a-kinne in the third and iiij^th [degrees]; but the two [Lowther & John ap John] ar not akinne; but he sais, he knowes hym not either to be dronkard, or such like . . . . . .

[2]Ad vj^tum, this deponent sais, that Jane, videlicet David, was from her husband about a fortnight, iiij^or yeres ago: the cause, this deponent knowes not; but this deponent sais that Edward, brother to the said Jane, send this deponent & one William David to her husband, to knowe whie he put his wief away from hym; & he answerid, that 'it was longe of her tonge'; & 'he bade her not go away, nor he wold not bid her comme againe'; and said 'it was longe of his father' / . . . . .

Ricardus Lloid, parochie de Hanmer, etatis xxx annorum, novit partem actricem xij annis, et partem ream x annis.

Ad primam, dicit Oliverum Lowther fore virum bone fame; for so he hath knowne him this viij yeres ago; for the said Oliuer & he, this deponent, have bene in house both together; but he neuer se but honesty by hym. & forther he saies, that the wieves of Oliuer and John ap John ar akinne, as he thinkes, but he knowes not howe /. . . . . .

Ad iij, dicit that Thomas Puleston is an honest man, and is but little of his wordes; but he knowes of no kinred betwene John ap John and hym.

[1] ? MS. alias. [2] leaf 87.

Ad iiij, this depone*nt* sais, that he knowes not Tho*mas* ap John. and as for Wi*lliam* Gilb*ert*, he knowes nothing of hym, but that he is ten*aunt* to Mr Dimock, who is Landlord to John ap John.

Ad v, dicit q*uod* nescit depone*re*, but that Key articulate is ten*aunt* to Mr Dimock.

Ad vj^t, this depone*nt* sais, that Jane, v*idelicet* Dav*i*d, was oway from her husband iiij^or yere ago, for a space; but what was the matter, this Depone*nt* knowes not. al*iter* nescit depone*re* . . . . . .

Dav*i*d ap Edward, paroch*ie* de Hanme*r*, etat*is* xxxvj an*norum*, nov*i*t p*ar*tes xx an*n*is /

Ad p*rimam*, this depone*nt* sais, that he knowes no*n* other, but that Oliver Lowther is an honest man. al*ite*r nescit depone*re* /

[1] Ad ij^d, this depone*nt* sais, he knowes Jane Thom*as* to be a honest [wo]man, & seru*au*nt to Oliver Lowther; but of any kinred betwene her & John ap John, he knowes not.

Ad iij, this depone*nt* sais, that he knowes Tho*mas* Puleston to be an honest young man. al*ite*r nescit depone*re*.

Ad iiij, dicit, q*uod* nov*i*t Tho*mam* ap John et Wi*llelmu*m Gilbe*r*t fore bone fame, quoad auditu*m* et noticia*m* sua*m*; & that Wi*llia*m Gilbe*r*t is ten*au*nt to Mr Dimock, Landlord to John ap John . . . . . .

Ad vj, dicit, that he hath hard say that Jane, v*idelicet* [David], & her husband wer asonder; but what was the matter, this depone*nt* knowes not / . . . . . .

Rogerus Dav*i*d, maritus p*ar*tis act*ricis*, exa*minatus* medio suo Jura*mento*, dicit, that 'his wief Jane, v*idelicet* Dav*i*d, hath gone from him twise: one tyme she was away iij or iiij^or daies; & an-other tyme, about a moneth.' beynge askid 'what was the cause?' this depone*nt* sais, 'biecause his father & she did not agree; and likewise this depone*nt* was away from his wief iiij^or or v' daies, & lay in John ap Johns house iiij^or night*es*, biecause of a little debat betwix this depone*nt* & his father.' beynge askid of the Conue*r*sac*i*on of his wief and John Leigh, he sais, that 'John Leigh did neue*r* lye in bed w*i*th hym & his wief, sins he was in mans state; but about xiij or x[i]iij yeres ago, beynge a boy, he lay w*i*th them; but this depone*nt* think*es* that there was no suspic[i]ous delinge betwix them, biecause the said John was very younge.'

It*em*, beynge askid 'what tyme he turnid John ap John mare out of his close,' he sais 'hit was iij or iiij^or yeres ago'; and apon that occasion his neighbo*ures* told this depone*nt*, the said John callid this depone*nt* 'cuckold,' & reviled hym; but he neue*r* hard hym say so.

[1] leaf 87, back.

2. Wade *v.* Rile. Libel: Alledgd Adultery of Custance Wade (wife of Randle Wade) with young Robert Rile.

Depositions-book 1561-6, Chester [between 4 and 19 February, 1561-2]. lf. 25.

[1]Rob*er*tus Capp*er*, p*a*rochie de Mynshull, ib*id*em mora*ns* trax*i*t duob*us* an*n*is; oriund*us* infra p*a*rochia*m* de Bu*n*burye,[2] cestren*sis* dioc*ese*; etat*is* circit*er* xx^t^ a*n*nos; no*vi*t p*ar*te*m* act*ricem* ab infancia sua, et Custancia*m* Wade iij^t^ an*n*is. Interrogat*us* ad merita ca*us*e, et ad o*mn*ia et sing*u*la content*a* in li*bel*lo, et quid pot*erat* depon*er*e in ca*usa*, This depone*n*t sais, that 'he was s*e*ru*au*nt to Rondull Wade about Michelmas was twelfmonthe; and about that tyme, this depone*n*t came rydinge bye whereas Alis Rile, wief vnto Rob*er*te Rile the elder, was mylkinge; and the said Alis Rile callid this depone*n*t to her, & askid hym howe his m*aste*r, Rondull Wade, and his dame Custance Wade, did agre. and this depone*n*t answerid againe, that they did agre well, for any thinge that he did knowe. and the said Alice said to this depone*n*t, that she had thing*es* to tell hym, yf he wold say nothinge. and this depone*n*t said he wold kepe counsell, yf they were hurtfull. and then the said Alice said and told this depone*n*t, that her sonne, Rob*er*te Rile the younger, and Custance Wade, this deponent*es* dame, did love together; and said that the said Custance Wade wold come to the said [3]Rob*er*te her sonne, dyverse tymes. and this depone*n*t askid the said Alis what tyme they were; and the said Alis said, 'apon one saturday in the morowe afore that tyme, w*hi*ch was a snowe morowe, the said Custance came to the said Rob*er*te Ryles, her sonnes, chambre; and the said Alis said that she lokid throwe a hole of a dore at them into a chambre; and there the said Alis said she did see them as homelye as eu*er* her husband and she were, or had bene'; and the said Alis Rile said that 'she spake to the said Custance Wade, and said to her that she thought she had bene at the Nauntwiche;' and the said Custance answerid that 'she had other busines in hand.' and the said Alice then answerid and said, "so me thinke."' al*ite*r nescit depon*er*e / Interrogat*us* qu*i* fuera*n*t p*res*entes t*em*po*r*e p*ro*lac*i*onis h*uius*mod*i* verbor*um* / This depone*n*t sais, 'there was no bodie bye, but the said Alice and this depone*n*t.' Vlterius, this depone*n*t sais, that 'the said Custans Wade, for any thinge that eu*er* he knewe, was of good name and fame afore that tyme this depone*n*t hard thes word*es* bye her.' Ad fama*m*, this deponent sais, 'this sclaunder is brutid abroad all the Cuntrie; but afore this, he neu*er* hard evill bie the said Custance.' no*n* est doct*us*, no*n* conduct*us*, no*n* consang*uineus*, no*n* affinis, no*n* curat &c.

[1] leaf 25. [2] Near Tarporley. [3] leaf 25, back.

Agnes Hardinge, parochie de Mynshull, ib*ide*m mora*ns* trax*it* xv[im] an*n*is, oriund*a* infra p*a*roch*ia*m de Over,[1] Cestren*si* Dioc*esa*, etat*is* circit*er* li an*n*os, no*vi*t p*ar*te*m* act*ricem* a na*tiuita*te, et p*ar*te*m* rea*m* iij' an*n*is. Exa*minata* super merit*is* ca*us*e, et content*is* in d*ict*o li*bell*o, et ad o*mn*ia et sing*u*la co*n*tent*a* in eode*m*,—This depone*n*t sais, that 'afore Michalmas was twelfmonth, she came from mylkinge in company w*i*th Alis Rile, wief vnto Rob*er*te Rile the elder, who told this depone*n*t, that there was as bodelie dole betwixe her sonne, Rob*er*te Rile, and Custance Wade, wief vnto Rondull Wade, as was betwixe the said Alis Rile and her husband Rob*er*te Rile. and said that she, the said Alice Rile, had [2]sene the said Custance Rile [*that is,* Wade] and Rob*er*te Rile, her sonne, vnconvenie*n*tlie together in the said Rob*er*te Riles chambre.' and the said Alice Rile said, that 'she had spoken to the said Custance, and taken her downe for the same, betwixe them twaine; and said that the said Custance gave her no*n* answere againe, but made her a countenaunce to bite apon a barlye corne.' al*ite*r quoad merita ca*us*e, nescit depon*er*e. Interrogat*a* q*ui* fuerant p*re*se*n*tes *tempor*e p*r*olac*io*nis h*uius*mod*i* ve*r*bor*um*, this depone*n*t sais, 'there was no bodie bie, but the said Alice and this depone*n*t.' Vlterius, this depone*n*t sais, that 'she neu*er* hard but the said Custance was of good name & fame, afore theis word*es* were reportid bie her.' Ad fama*m*, this depone*n*t sais, that 'bye reason of thes word*es*, the said Custance is sclaundrid all the Cuntrie ou*er*, where she dwell*es*.' no*n* *est* doct*a*, no*n* consang*uinea*, no*n* affinis, no*n* tenens, no*n* conduct*a*, no*n* curat de victoria &c.

M*ar*geria Tottie, p*a*rochie de Minshull, vbi oriunda, etat*is* circit*er* xxx[t] an*n*os, no*vi*t p*ar*te*m* act*ricem* ab infancia sua, et p*ar*te*m* rea*m* xij[t] an*n*is. Interrogat*a* sup*er* merit*is* ca*us*e, et content*is* in d*ict*o li*bel*lo,—This depone*n*t sais, that 'in Lent tyme shalbe two yere, Alis Rile, wief vnto Rob*er*te Rile the elder, came vnto this depone*ntes* house, and, among*es* other co*mmu*nicac*io*n, she told this depone*n*t that her sonne, Rob*er*te Rile, and Custance Wade, did love together'; and said, that 'apon a saturday afore that tyme, beynge a gret snowe, she, the said Alis, did here two whisper together in a chambre of the said Rob*er*te Rile, her sonne'; and the said Alice Rile said, that 'at that tyme she had a p*ri*vie hole into the said chambre, and lokid into the Chambre at the said hole, and did se the said Rob*er*te, her sonne, and the said Custance, stand together as famylierlie as and[3] they had bene man and wief.' al*ite*r nescit depon*er*e. Interrogat*a* q*ue* fuera*n*t p*r*ese*n*tes t*em*p*or*e p*r*olac*io*nis h*uius*mod*i* v*er*bor*um*,—

[1] Over, a small market-town and parish, 4¼ m. W. from Middlewich, and 15 E. from Chester. [2] leaf 26. [3] an, if.

This deponent sais, 'there was no bodie bye but little children'; & sais that, 'afore this sclaunder, the said Custance was of good name & fame, for any thinge that euer this deponent hard.' Ad famam,—this deponent sais, that 'many thinke that the said Alis Rile [1]did say suche wordis bie the said Custance, for the evill will that she had to the said Roberte Rile, to whom she was stepmother.' Non est docta, non conducta, non consanguinea, non affinis, non tenens, non curat &c.

Agnes Lowther, parochie Medii Vici,[2] ibidem morans, traxit xiij^cim^ ebdomadas; antea, infra parochiam de Minshull, cum Randulpho Wade, per spacium xiiij^ci^" annorum; etatis xl annorum, et vltra, novit partem actricem xvj annis, et partem ream tribus annis. Examinata super meritis cause, et contentis in dicto libello,—this deponent sais, that 'about Easter was twelfmonthe, Alis Rile, wief vnto Roberte Rile the elder, came vnto the house of this deponent, and amonges other communicacion they talkid of Custance Wade, wief vnto Rondull Wade'; and the said Alis, then and there, did report vnto this deponent, that 'the said Custance Wade lovid Roberte Rile, her husbandes sonne, in somuche' (the said Alice told this deponent) 'that apon a saturday in the snowe tyme afore that, the said Custance Wade came to the house of Roberte Rile her husband, and there was privilie with Roberte Rile the younger in a chambre'; and that the said Alice said 'she did se at that tyme the said Roberte makinge his bed; and when he had done, he putt to the dore, and the said Alis lokid in at a tote[3] hole, and se the said Roberte shutt the windowes,[4] and went to the said Custance, and vsed her as famylierlie as she had bene his wief; and that the said Custance neuer warnid hym.' aliter nescit deponere. Interrogata qui erant presentes tempore prolacionis huiusmodi verborum,—this deponent sais 'there was no bodie bye, but the said Alis and this deponent.' Vlterius dicit, that 'the said Custance was of good name and fame afore this sclaunder, for any thinge that euer this deponent hard, or did knowe bie her.' [5]Ad famam, this deponent sais, that 'the name[6] is, as she thinkes, the said Custance is wrongfullie sclaundrid.' non est docta, non conducta, non tenens, non consanguinea, non affinis, non curat &c.

Elena Kenworth, parochie de M[i]nshull, ibidem oriunda, etatis circiter xxxiij annos, novit partem actricem ab infancia sua, et partem ream xij^cim^ annis. Examinata super meritis cause, et contentis in libello: in virtute Juramenti sui prestiti,—This deponent sais, that in the Lent last past, in

[1] leaf 26, back. [2] Middlewich, about 16 miles of Chester. [3] ? peep, spy.
[4] wind-dores, shutters. Compare Shakspere's *Venus & Adonis*, l. 482.
[5] leaf 27. [6] opinion in the neighbourhood.

the house of Alis Rile in Mynshull, she hard the said Alis Rile report and say to this deponent, that 'her sonne Roberte Rile was homelie with Custance Wade, wief vnto Rondull Wade, as yf they were man and wief together; and said that her husband Roberte Rile had warnid Roberte Rile, his sonne, from the Cumpanye of Custance Wade; and the said Roberte would not leave her companie': aliter nescit deponere. and that 'there was no bodie present at the Reportinge of thes wordes'; and forther she sais, that 'the said Custance Wade, to her knoledge, was of gode name and fame afore thes wordes were spoken.' Ad famam, dicit famam laborare indifferenter. non est docta, non conducta, non consanguinea, non affinis, non tenens, non curat de victoria &c.

Johannes Hefeild, parochie de Medio Vico [Middlewich], ibidem morans traxit xviij annos; etatis circiter xliiij^or annis; novit partem actricem xxxv^t annos, et partem ream viij annis, vel circiter. Interrogatus super meritis cause, ac ceteris circumstancijs in libello,—This deponent sais, that about Midsommer last, Rondull Wade had hard that Alis Rile had sclaundrid his wief Custance Wade, that she shuld be of evill conversacion with Roberte Rile the younger; and thereapon the said Rondull Wade put the said Custance out from his cohabitacion & Cumpanie; and then Thomas Brinley, beynge frend vnto the said Custance Wade, went to Yorke, & purchasid a Comaundment[1] for the said Alis Rile; whereapon the said Alis Rile send for this deponent bie Ellin Mynshull, which came to the said Alis Rile; & the said Alis desired this deponent, that he wold go vnto Custance Wade, wief vnto Rondull Wade, [2]and to deliuer from her a crosse of gold, which was the said Custance owne afore, and say she send her that, bie the same token she callid the said Custance into her lower brue house, and to tell her that she had said vnto hir there, she had told certen of her neyboures, and they had betold hir, and published hit abroade; and said, that 'yf the said Custance wold not geve ouer her sute at Yorke, she, the said Alis, wold declare hit openlie in the court, apon her boke othe, yf she were callid; and till then she wold beyre with her.' and moreouer this deponent sais, that 'the said Alis at that tyme did declare vnto this deponent and Ellin Mynshull, that Custance Wade had bene in hir sonne Robertes chambre; and that she did se hym tyne the windowes, and putto the dore with his fote'; presenti tunc ibidem, tempore prolacionis huiusmodi verborum, Elena Mynshull, vnacum isto deponente. Ad famam, dicit quod nescit deponere. non est doctus, non conductus, non consanguineus, non affinis, non curat &c.

[1] Citation. [2] leaf 27, back.

Elena Mynshull, *par*ochie de Mynshull, ib*ide*m oriund*a*, etat*is* circit*er* xxx' an*n*os, nov*it* p*ar*te*m* act*ricem* a discrec*io*ne sua, et p*ar*te*m* rea*m* p*er* spaciu*m* octo an*n*or*um*. Exa*min*at*a* sup*er* merit*is* ca*use*, et co*n*tent*is* in lib*el*lo exhibit*is* in Judicio, dicit, in vi*rtute* Jura*men*ti sui p*re*stiti, 'dicit et concordat in o*mn*ib*us* et p*er* o*mn*ia cu*m* Joh*ann*e Hefield, p*re*conteste suo'; and 'afore that tyme, for any thinge that eu*er* this depone*n*t hard, the said Custance was of good name and fame.' ad fama*m*, dicit q*uod* nescit depon*er*e quomodo volat aut laborat sup*er* h*uius*mo*di* ca*us*a. est consang*uinea* · p*ar*tes[1] ca*use* p*re*d*icte*, noeñ (? MS.) in quo gradu nescit depon*er*e. no*n* est doct*a*, no*n* co*n*duct*a*, no*n* tenens, no*n* curat &c.

[2]R*es*pons*io*n*es* p*er*so*n*ales Alicie Rile, capt*a* cora*m* m*agist*ro Rob*er*to Leche, artiu*m* m*agist*ro, &c', xix°, M*ar*tii 1561[-2].

Ad p*ri*mu*m* ar*ticu*lu*m*, negat penitus.

Ad ij^d^ ar*ticu*lu*m*, negat eund*em* penitus.

Ad iij ar*ticu*lu*m*, simil*ite*r negat eund*em*.

Ad iiij^t^, dicit, q*uod* n*ov*it Rob*ertu*m Capp*er*, et q*uod* est seruus Ran*dulphi* Wade; and that she neu*er* spake w*i*th hym concern[i]nge any evill demeanou*r* of Constance Wade.

Ad v^t^ ar*ticu*lu*m*, dicit, q*uod* novit Agnete*m* Hardinge; but she sais, she neu*er* talkid w*i*th her concerninge that matter of Custance Wade; but she said to Agnes Hardinge, that hit was vnhonestlie done of Custance Wade to com*m*e to any younge mans chambre w*i*thout Cumpanye; and this that [3]she said to her, was more then a twelfmonth ago, in som*er* tyme, as they went on mylkinge; & the occasion of this talke was, forbiecause Ran*dull* Wade lovid not his wief Custance Wade; & more, touching her dishonestie, she said not.

Ad vj^t^, dicit, q*uod* novit Agnete*m* Lowther; and that she was se*ruau*nt to Ran*dull* Wade xj yeres, to her reme*m*braunce; & she said she neu*er* spake any other word*is* but such as she hath spoken to Agnes Hardinge / and forther she sais, she knowis Jankin Heyghfeld; and that she remembres well she spake to Jenkin Hefeld about Custance Wade, apon this occasion: This Depone*n*t sais, she had a guilt crosse of silu*er*, of the said Custance, & desired the said Joħn Heighfeld to deliu*er* the same crosse to Custance Wade, bie the same token that this depone*n*t and Custance Wade came into a chambre of this depone*ntes*, where stode a secke of barlye; & this said Custance there chewid barlye corne; and bie that token, this depone*n*t desired Jankin Hefeld to deliu*er* her that crosse, w*h*ich was Custance Wad*es* her owne. and the said John deliu*er*ed not

[1] so in MS. [2] leaf 48. [3] leaf 48, back.

the same; wherfore this re*spo*ndent desired & had the crosse of hym againe. beynge demaundid, apon what occasion she had that same to kepe; sais, that the said Custance had deliu*er*ed this re*spo*ndent afore tyme, iij silu*er* peces of a girdill, a silu*er* pinne, & the same crosse, for feare lest the husband of the said Custance wold have broken her Coffer, & have taken hit away;[1] & so, after a certen tyme, the said Custance toke all away but the same crosse. beynge askid 'howe hit Chauncid that she left the said crosse behind her'; she sais that 'when the other Jewell*es* were askid, hit ch*a*uncid she had lent the crosse to a younge woman callid Anne Barker, to go to a weddinge or a wake; and bie that [2]hit chauncid that she had the same crosse so longe in her kepinge, after the other Jewell*es* were d*eliuered*.' and forther, she grauntith that she said to the said Jenkin Hefeld, that 'Rob*er*te Rile putto a dore of a Chamber where the said Custance & he were talkinge; & the said Custaunce im*m*ediatlie pullid hit oppen againe.' beynge askid of the shuttinge of windowes, she said that 'a grett windowe in the same chambre was shutt afore the said Custance came thither; & the other be little glasse windowes, & cannot be shutt.'[3] beynge askid whether she knowes Ellin Minshull, she sais 'Yea, biecause she is doughter to one of her neybo*uris*; and she desired the same Ellin to go to Jenkin Hefeld to carrye the said Crosse to Custance Wade; and the said Ellin was p*rese*nt bie, when she spake the word*is* aforsaid to the said Jankin Hefeld.'

Ad vij^um^ ar*ticulum*, This re*spo*ndent sais, that 'apon a certen tyme Custaunce Wade was sicke; and this re*spo*ndent, as one neybo*u*r wold do to an other, did bringe her chickens, spice, and other thing*es* to comfort her; and after that, hit chauncid to this re*spo*ndent to be sicke; and the said Custance brought this re*spo*ndent a little quantite of befe, to release her mouth, and said, 'bie her trouth, she was ashamid that she had not some better thinge to bringe her.' also she brought the same tyme a little salt Eele[4] w*i*th her; and no more befe or elis, neither sins nor afore.' and as touchinge the crosse, she answerith vt sup*ra*. cetera negat.

Ad viij ar*ticulum*, This Re*spo*ndent sais, that 'Rob*er*te Rile the young*er* neu*er* p*ro*mysid her any pease of the lease of the house where her husband nowe dwell*is*, nor nothinge els: neither doth she loke for any thinge at the hand*is* of the said Rob*er*te, except her m*aste*r, Mr Minshull, helpe her to somwhat duringe her widowhodde.'

1 ? From his Protestant hatred of the emblems of Popery.

2 leaf 49.

3 shutterd ?, so as to stop folk seeing thro them.

4 *Snigge* struck out in the MS., and *Eele* substituted.

3 *a.* Margaret Wirrall *v.* Henry Fazakerley.

xxv die Maij, 1561.

[1]Willelmus Plumpton . . . saies, that Henry Fazakerley, before the dore of one Ric*hard* Wolfall of Darbye [West Derby, near Liverpool], in the p*re*sence of this depone*nt* & dyverse other, did call M*ar*garet Wirrall 'stronge hore' and 'provid hoore,' and said that 'all the p*ar*ysh knewe her to be M*aste*r Mores provid hoore': and thes word*es* were spoken about M*ar*tinmas last, in an Eveninge, or aundert[2] [*so in MS.*] after none . . . [leaf 52] . . . he sais . . . that he stode at a corner of a house out of the sight of M*ar*garet Wirrall & Henry Fazakerley; & so hit chauncid that, beyinge at such word*is* as 'thou hoore,' and 'thou thief,' Fazakerley, workinge at a pale[3] *with* an Axe, followid M*ar*garet Wirrall, to have smit her w*ith* the axe; and she Run*ne* into Wolfall house; and Topping*es* wief, who stode by when they were at thes word*is*, shutt the dore against Fazakerley; & so hit fortuned that he hitt her not. and he confessid, in that tene, he carid not yf he had knockid her downe. and then this depone*nt* com*m*ynge then in sight, the said M*ar*garet desired hym to beyre witnes howe she was ordered. [All the abuse and row arose] apon this occasion: the said M*ar*garet desired vij' grotes of the said Henry Fazakerley, w*hi*ch she had lent hym about iij yeres afore; & he made answere and said 'he owid no*n*'; and she said he did; and apon that occasion they fell i*m*mediatelie to thes sclaunderous word*es*. and forther he sais, that the said Henry callid the said M*ar*garet 'M*aste*r Mores hore'; and she, answering, callid hym 'grinn*in*ge thief'; and apon that, he callid her 'M*aste*r Mores provid hore'; so that he callid her 'hore,' before she callid hym 'thief' . . . &c &c. [See 3 *b*, below, p. 204-7.]

4. Mrs. Katherine Claiton *v.* Margaret Tauliour (for abusing her).

(In it, a man goes to a high loft to write a letter; women drink with men at an inn.)

[4] Exa*mina*cio testiu*m* sup*er* li*bel*lo ex p*ar*te Kat*erine* Claiton, p*ar*t*is* act*ricis*, con*tra* et adu*ersus* M*ar*gareta*m* Tailiou*r*, p*ar*te*m* rea*m*, capt*a* cora*m* m*agist*ro Robe*r*to Leche, &c, xj° die Ap*ri*lis, 1562.

Laurencius Manwaringe, p*ar*ochie Vici-Malban*i*,[5] etat*is* xxxv^t^ an-

[1] leaf 51, back.

[2] *aunder* or *undern*, 1. the time from nine to twelve o'clock in the morning—see Bradley's Stratmann;—then shifted to 2. the afternoon: 'the time between, the time between sunrise and noon, between noon and sunset, a mealtime.'—Mayhew and Skeat.

[3] A paling, a fence of wooden stakes. [4] leaf 54.

[5] Witch-Malbank, or Nantwich, near Crewe. See Jas. Hall's *History of Nantwich*, 453, 458.

norum, *novit partem actricem* a *matrimonio* inter *Willelmum* Claitton et ipsam, et *partem ream* a *natiuitate* /

Ad *primum articulum*, credit *eundem* fore *verum*.

Ad ij^d *articulum*, nescit *deponere nisi* ex auditu. Reddend*o racionem* sui *dicti*, this *deponent* sais, that apon a Saterday in Septembre last, at an after-none, this *deponent* beinge required bie one Browne, newly *comme* from Barwicke, to write hym a *lettre*, went to the house of *Richard* Wright of the Bell[1]; and there, in a hye lofte, this *deponent* beynge writinge the said *Lettre*, *Mistres* Claiton came in to the said chambre, and brought *with* her thither, on, John Ma*ist*erson, and the said Brownes wief; and the said *mistres* Claiton seid, "cosin Ma*ist*erson, I have brought you hither, to here what this gent*leman* sais about suche sclaunderous word*es* as he hard spoken by me." and then she, desiringe the said Mr Browne to report the same talke, that he had hard the night before: and the said Browne said, that the night before, he enquired of the said *Margaret* Tailiour, 'what *maner* a man Mr Cleyton was'; and she answerid & said, 'he was an evill man.' & the said Browne said, 'He hath report to be an honest gent*leman*,' & she answerid & said, that 'he was a very evill & noughtie man.' & the said Browne said, 'what is his wief then?' & she answerid and said, that 'like as the one, like the other'; *presentibus* tunc *ibidem*, *tempore prolacionis hujusmodi verborum*, vnacu*m* isto deponent*e*, Joh*anne* Maisterson, the said Browne & his wief, & a brother of Browne, *Mistres* Claiton, et alijs, quor*um* no*mina* no*n* recolit. cetera ad co*ntenta* in *dicto* li*bel*lo nescit depon*ere* /

Ad iij^t *articulum*, nescit depon*ere* *certitudinaliter*.

Ad iiij *articulum*, dicit et credit eund*em* fore veru*m*.

Ad v^t, dicit eund*em* fore ver*um*.

Ad vj^t, refert se ad Jura in ea *parte*.

Ad vlt*imum*, dicit *predeposita per* eu*m* fore vera, &c.

(signd) *per* me lavrence maynwaryng.

[2]Joh*annes* Ma*ist*erson, de Vico Malbano [Nantwich], *generosus*, etat*is* xxxij an*norum*, no*vit* par*tem* act*ricem* xvj^cim an*n*os, et *Margaretam* Tailio*ur* a pu*eri*cia.

Ad *primum* ar*ticulum*, credit eund*em* fore ver*um*.

Ad ij^d ar*ticulum*, This Depon*ent* sais, that about Septembre last, he was sent for by M*ist*res Claiton articulate, to com*me* to drinke w*ith* her in the Bell, w*ith* dyverse of her husband*es* frend*es*, in his absence; and

[1] In the great Fire at Nantwich, on Thursday, 10 Dec. 1583, Richard Wilbraham says, that among the 150 houses burnt, including seven "Innes for loging, & very ffayre," was "the bell, Richard Wright."—Jas. Hall's *History of Nantwich* (1883), p. 105.

[2] leaf 54, back.

com*m*ynge thither, into an hye lofte, she said "Cosin M*aister*son, I have sent for you hither to beyre witnes what this gent*leman*, Ma*iste*r Browne, hath hard reportid sclaunderouslie spoken of me." & the said M*aiste*r Browne beynge in the said chambre afore his com*m*ynge, and Lawrence Manwaringe, and dyverse others, w*it*h hym; and the said Browne declarid *that* he, beynge in the Bell the night before, & M*ar*garet Tailio*ur* beynge drinkinge w*it*h hym, the said Browne enq*ui*red of her 'what man*er* of man Mr Claiton was'; and she answerid and said he was 'an vnthrifte, and spent all that eu*er* he had.' and he answerid & said, he thought he was 'a good gent*leman*'; and askid her then, 'what his wief Kat*herine* Claiton was.' and she answerid and said, "suche one, such is the other." as for any other sclaunderous word*es* that he hard spoken bie the said Browne, to be reportid of the said M*ar*garet Tailo*ur*, this depone*n*t knowes not / beynge p*resen*t at that tyme, Laurence Manwaringe, Roger Crocket, & others. cetera ad co*n*tent*a* in d*ict*o ar*ticu*lo nescit depon*er*e /

Ad iij, credit eund*em* fore veru*m*.

Ad iiij^t^, nescit depon*er*e.

Ad v^t^ ar*ticu*lu*m*, credit eund*em* fore ver*um*.

Ad vj^tum^ ar*ticu*lu*m*, refert se ad Jura in ea p*ar*te.

Ad vltim*um*, d*i*cit p*re*deposit*a* p*er* eu*m* fore vera, &c. & forther he sais, as concerninge the secound article, that the said Browne said, he hard M*ar*garet Tailio*ur* say, that 'Mr Cleyton & Ric*hard* Wright had fought together in London.' but what was the cause, this Depone*n*t knowes not.

[1]Rogerus Crocket, de Vico Malbano [Nantwich], etat*is* xx' an*norum*, nov*i*t p*ar*te*m* act*ri*ce*m* vij an*n*is, et vltra, et p*ar*te*m* rea*m* sim*ili*ter /

Ad p*ri*mu*m* ar*ticu*lu*m*, credit eund*em* fore ver*um*.

Ad ij^d^ ar*ticu*lu*m*, This depone*n*t sais, that he hath hard the said M*ar*garet Tailio*ur* speke evill and sclaunderous word*es* bie Kat*herine* Cleyton, in the house of the father of the said M*ar*garet, apon a Saterday afore none, apon the occasion of rehersall of word*es*. The word*es* w*h*ich he did here M*ar*garet Tailio*ur* speake, were theis / "Ric*hard* Wright had gevin W*illi*am Cleytons wief a paire of damaske sleves, w*h*ich W*illi*am Clayton burnid afore his wiefes face." and as for any other sclaunderous word*es*, he hard not the said M*ar*garet speake: p*resen*tibus tunc ib*id*em, te*m*po*r*e p*r*olac*i*o*n*is h*u*j*us*mod*i* verbor*um*, the father of the said M*ar*garet, Rondull Santley, one M*ist*res Griffin, & the mother of the said M*ar*garet. beynge askid 'who made the rehersall of word*es* spoken of afore'; he answeris, that 'on, Browne, a Barwicke, came into this contrye, and with his wief, as hit is supposid; w*h*ich Brownes wief came

[1] leaf 55.

into Margaret Tailiours fathers house, at the request of Katherine Claiton, to knowe whether the said Margaret wold stand to the wordes she had spoken bie the said Katherine, in the house of Richard Wright.' & the said Margaret answerid, that she wold not deny any wordes that she had spoken; and she grauntid that she had spoken those wordes about the damaske sleves, & non other /

Ad iij articulum, credit eundem fore verum.

Ad iiij[t] articulum, dicit et credit eundem fore verum.

Ad v[t], dicit eundem fore verum.

Ad vj, credit eundem fore verum.

Ad vltimum, dicit predeposita per eum fore vera. non est doctus, non conductus; duxit sororem Willelmi Claiton, mariti partis actricis; non curat de victoria, &c.

(signd) Roger Crokett.

5. Margery Morgan *v.* Philip Jenkin.

[1]Willelmus Colly, generosus, parochie de Malpas,[2] etatis xl[ta] annorum, novit partem actricem x annis, et partem ream vij annis. [1562.]

Ad primum articulum, credit eundem fore verum.

Ad ij[d] articulum, This deponent sais, that he was required to comme to a field nere vnto Kidden Hilles,[3] about a mariage, to this deponentes thinkinge, betwixe Margery Morgan and John Gam. and in debatinge the matter, John Gam said vnto Margery, that she was sclaundrid with one William Bathoe; for Phelippe Jenkin told the said John, that William Batho had laine bie her fortie nightes, or suche like, to this deponentes remembraunce; and that he wold have her to clere her-self of that matter; and so ther was no promes of mariage made at that tyme. whereapon, the said Margery spoke to the said Phelip Jenkin, there beynge present, and said, "thou hast reportid suche wordes bie me" / and the said Phelip answerd, "that I have said, William Bathoe told hit vnto me; and I told hit John Gam, for good will; and I will stand to hit, that William Bathoe told hit vnto me." but for that Act, this deponent is a straunger to the matter, & knowis no more /

Ad iij articulum, nescit deponere.

Ad iiij[t] articulum, credit eundem fore verum.

Ad v[t], dicit eundem fore verum.

Ad vj[tum], credit eundem fore verum.

[1] leaf 58, back.

[2] Malpas, a town about 12 miles S.E. of Chester. Part of the parish is in the detacht portion of Flintshire. [3] ? MS. Riddenhilles

Ad vl*timum*, quoad fama*m*, nescit depon*ere*, bicause this Depone*nt* is not muche at home /

[1] Exa*minacio* testi*um* sup*er* li*bello* oblat*o* in ca*usa* Ma*r*ggerie Morgan con*tra* Ph*ilippum* Jenkin, capt*a* die et an*no* p*redict*is (15 June 1562).

Joh*anne*s Phineus, p*a*rochie de Malpas, etat*is* xx' an*norum*, no*vi*t p*a*rte*m* act*ricem* ij an*n*is, et p*a*rte*m* rea*m* te*m*po*re* memorie sue / . . . . .

Ad ij / This depone*nt* saies, That M*a*rgery Morgan, beynge of honest name afore, for any thinge that eu*er* he hard afore the tyme of this sute come*n*sid, was reportid bie the mouth of Phelip Jenkin, to have lyene sondry nightes, and in sundry places, w*i*th Wi*llia*m Bathoe. reddend*o* rac*ione*m sui d*ic*ti, he saies, he came from the Malpas, and mett w*i*th Phelip Jenkin, who demaundid whether he had bene to se howe M*a*rgery Morga*n* did. this depone*nt* answerid, he had not bene w*i*th her. "well," said Philip Jenkin, "I have told thie m*aste*r, Joh*n* Gam,—in*n*uendo vt sup*r*a—that Wi*llia*m Bathoe had laine, bothe in this Cuntry & othere, w*i*th M*a*rgery Morgan diu*er*se night*es*." . . . . . .

Alicia Gam, parochie de Malpas, etat*is* xxix' an*norum*, nov*i*t p*a*rte*m* act*ricem* et p*a*rte*m* rea*m* xij^cim annis et vltra / . . . . . .

[2] Ad ij^d ar*ticulum*, This depone*nt* sais, that Phelip Jenkin come apon a certen tyme to the house of the mother of Joh*n* Gam,—this depone*nt* then beynge only w*i*th his mother,—and there did plainly tell this depone*nt* & her mother, that M*a*rgery Morgan had lyen w*i*th Wi*llia*m Bathoe xx' night*es*; and the said Wi*llia*m had had the Company of her, xx' tymes. cetera ad co*n*tent*a* huius ar*ticu*li, nescit depon*er*e /

6. Matilda Holme *v.* Elizabeth Tilston, widow, for calling her 'Roberte Soundes hoore.' [21 Nov. 1562.]

[3] Widow Tilston said 'she had so callid her, & wold so call her'; & when put 'in mynd of the daung*er* of the Lawe, neuertheles she wold not call back these wor*des*; but [said] that she [Maude Holme] was an arrant hoore, and Roberte Soundes*es* hore, and like vnto Mawde Scottabout, who was a most notorious hoore.' So deposes Rafe Golburne of Christleton, near Chester, aged 42. Thomas Edge of Christleton, aged 30, who went with Rafe Golburne to Widow Tilston, deposes that she said that Maude Holme 'was as arrant a hoor as eu*er* went abrode'; and, 'as this deponent think*es*, she likned her to Mawde Scotabout, and said she was Rob*er*te Sound*es* hoor, & had bene his hore vij or viij yeres.'

[1] leaf 68, back. [2] leaf 69. [3] leaf 98.

[1]On 17 Dec. 1562, Rafe Bostok deposes that Widow Tilston answers him about Mawde Holme: "What, wold you have me to say she is an honest woman? No; she is my sonne Roberte Sonnd*es* hoore; and had causid hym to spend many a pound."

[2]And Randle Roland says, that Widow Tilston cald Mawde Holme 'a stronge hoore.' "and as they wer*e* talking*e*, it chauncid Mawde Holme to come vp the strete; and the said Eliz*abeth* bade a boy [a son] of Rob*er*te Sound*es*, beynge w*i*th her, "call her thy fathers Scattabout," & so the boy did. and then the said Eliz*abeth*, beynge as it were but in dout afore lest it wer*e* she, said 'Yes, in faith, it is that stronge hoore, that made my sonne-in-Lawe to sell his land to M*aste*r Cholmeley, and had kept her this viij yeres':" . . . .

On the other hand, Mathew Lithgo deposes [3]that he "said to Mawde Holme," "Mawde, thou hast begonne a mad matter against Eliz*abeth* Tilston, widowe, for thou hast reported as ill by her. 'whie?' q*uod* she. 'one foule word askis an other.' q*uod* this depone*n*t: 'thou hast reportid that the said Eliz*abeth* thelder said to [3][her] husband 'com*m*e, Roger, and pull Rob*er*te Wright out of Elizabeth thie doughter.' and the said Mawde answerid and said 'she wold stand to that, afore my L*ord*[4] and M*aste*r Chauncel*our*, whensoeu*er* she was callid.'"

Richard Penk also deposes, that he "came into the house of Mathue Lithgo, and found Mawde Holme there. And this deponent wold have kissed her; and she said 'Beware! for I will make an end of my matter, and prove my self an honest woman, or any man touche me; or I will spend my mothers field of barly, and all that eu*er* I haue, but I wilbe revengid on Tilstons wief.' 'well,' q*uod* the forsaid Mathue, 'thou hast a mad matter; for thou hast spoken as ill by Eliz*abeth* Tilston the young*er*.' 'well,' q*uod* the said Mawde, 'that I spoke, I will stand to; that the said Eliz*abeth* Tilston, widowe, said to her husband, 'Rise, Rog*er*; and thou may take Rob*er*te Wright in Eliz*abeth* thie doughter, in the lofte.'"

7 *b.* Constance Frost *v.* Wm. Ball and others.

(Third Examination of Witnesses: see leaves 164 back—165, and 166 back—167, pages 208-9 below, for the 1st and 2nd.)

[5]Exa*m*i*n*acio testiu*m* in ca*usa* diff*amacionis* inter Custanc*iam* Frost art*iculatam*, con*tra* Wi*llelmum* Ball et al*ios*, capt*a* xxj° Junij, 1564.

Cicilea Strete, of the parish of St Mary's, Chester, aged 50, "saies, that the same Daie after that the Cit*ation* was servid apon Eliz*abeth*

[1] leaf 105, back. [2] leaf 106. [3] leaf 106, back (A.D. 1562). [4] The Bishop.
[5] leaf 178, back.

Brerewod, this depon*ent* and Eliz*abeth* Willi*a*mson came from the Church w*i*th the said Eliz*abeth* Brerewod: the said Eliz*abeth* Bre[re]wod said to them, "What say you bie that queane that hath put me in younder thinge?" "In what thing?" this depon*ent* and Eliz'. [Williamson] askid her. "I cannot tell," said the said Eliz*abeth* [Brerewod]; "but what-soeu*er* thing*e* it is, that knave yo*ur* sonne—inn*u*endo this depo*nentes* sonne—made it, & brought it to the Church." Then said this deponent, "Yea, a very knave in dede, if he either make or meddle with it." 'No,' said Eliz*abeth* Will*ia*mson, 'it is a Cit*acion* com*m*es out of the sp*irit*uall Court; it com*m*es not out of the castell nor the Exchequer.' then said the said Eliz*abeth* Brerewod, "had the Jawde no-bodie to put in but me? if the hoore Jawde wilbe a hoore Jawde, let the hoore Jawde be a hoore Jawde. if the hoore Jawde will plaie the hoore Jawde, let the hoore Jawde play the hoore Jawde; and let me alone bie her."

[1]On 1 July 1564, Elizabeth Will*ia*mson gives the above speeches as, "howe say you, that I am servid w*i*th a Cit*acion*?" 'bie whom?' q*uod* this depon*ent*. "Mary," q*uo*d the said Eliz*abeth*, "bie yonnder Jawde,"—inn*u*end*o* Custance Frost, as she think*es*.—and further she said, "if she be a Jawde, let her be a Jawde for me! what I have [? have I] to do w*i*th her, or she w*i*th me?" Joan Gittin reports it as [2]"had the Jawde no bodie to set in but me? if the Jawde wilbe a hoore Jawde, let the Jawde let me alone! I will neither make nor medle with her." Joan "think*es* her [Constance Frost's] good name is not hurt, biecause the word*es* were spoken in a furye."

[3]On 3 Oct. 1564, Richard Barker of St. Oswald's parish, Chester, aged 70, says "he think*es* she, the said Custance, is an honest woman."

8. Joan Ashley *v.* Margaret Stele and others, for saying she was with Child by John Jackson. [3 Oct. 1564.]

[4]Depo*sicio*nes testiu*m* inter Joanna*m* Ashley, p*ar*tem act*ricem*, et alios /

Ricardus Haiton [? Halton], p*a*roch*ie* de Rostorne, ib*id*em mora*ns*, trax*i*t a n*ativita*te (?) etat*is* lxxviij an*nos*, no*vi*t Joanna*m* Ashley a p*ue*ricia, et M*a*rgaret*am* Stele cir*citer* xx an*n*is, Cicilia*m* Ingh*a*m trib*us* an*nis*, et Petru*m* Johnson duobus an*n*is / . . . .

Ad ij^d^ ar*ticu*lu*m*, This depon*ent* saies, that apon midlent sondaie last past, about iiij^or^ of the clock after none, this depon*ent* went to one W*illi*am Stelis [5]house; and immediatly ther came in M*ar*garet Stele,

[1] leaf 183. [2] leaf 183, back. [3] leaf 193, back. [4] leaf 193, back. [5] leaf 194.

suster to the said W*illia*m Stele, into the said house; and the said M*ar*garet in bourd said to this depon*ent*, that she wold declare vnto the said W*illia*m, her brother, howe this depon*ent* did sitt w*i*th his wief. and the said M*ar*g*ar*et further said, that such old men as this depon*ent* was, were not to trust; for, the said M*ar*garet said, 'there is a man in this Towne, as old as this deponent was, had gotten a woman w*i*th Child.' and this depon*ent* askid the said M*ar*garet, who that shuld be; and the said M*ar*garet bade this deponent reade [= guess] if he cold. and this depon*ent* saied it was likest to be John Jackson. and the said M*ar*garet said it was the same. and this depon*ent* askid the said M*ar*garet who the woman was. and the said M*ar*garet said it was Jone Ashley . . . . . .

Alexander Lineye, p*ar*och*ie* de Rostorne, ib*ide*m mora*ns*, trax*i*t vj an*n*is, oriund*us* infra p*ar*och*ie* Mancestre, etatis circiter xxiiij an*n*os no*vi*t p*ar*te*m* act*ricem* iiij[or] an*n*is, M*ar*gareta*m* Stele, Cicilia*m* Ingh*a*m p*er* spaciu*m* an*n*i, et Petru*m* Johnson p*er* dimidiu*m* an*n*i, &c . . . . . .

Ad ij[d] ar*ticulum*, This depon*ent* saies, that about viij wekes ago, as this depon*ent* was in Companie w*i*th Peter Johnson, he hard the said Peter saie and report to this depon*ent*, that he, the said Peter, was by in Companie about a quarter of a yere ago, when the said Peter, and John Jackson, and Jone Ashley, came from Arley,[1] S*i*r John Warburtons place, together; when the said Jone Ashley shuld say vnto the said John Jackson, that the said John Jackson shuld p*ro*vide a place for her, for she was w*i*th child w*i*th hym; and if her father & her mother did knowe, she most be driven out of the Cuntrie: et hec audivit ex Relacione Petre [*so*] Johnson . . . . . .

[2]Joh*anne*s Aspshawe, p*ar*och*ie* de Rostorne . . . etat*is* lx an*norum* . . . saies, that about a quarter of a yere ago, he hard Peter Johnson report to this depon*ent* and Alex*ande*r Liney, that the said Peter Johnson came from Arley in Company w*i*th John Jackson and Jone Ashley, when the said Jone Ashley said to the said Johñ Jackson, that she was w*i*th child w*i*th hym, & willed hym to p*ro*vide a place for her; for if her father did knowe it, she shuld be driven out of the Cuntrie . . . . . .

[3]Exa*mina*cio testiu*m* sup*er* Excepc*ion*ib*us* ex p*ar*te Petri Johnson et al*iorum* oblat*is*, capt*a* xxiij° Novembr*is*, cora*m* *magist*ro Rob*er*to Leche, &c 1564.

Rob*er*tus Leighe, paroch*ie* de Rostorne, etat*is* xxx[a] an*norum*, no*vi*t Joanna*m* Ashley iij an*n*is, et Petru*m* Johnson xij an*n*is.

[1] Arley Hall, in Great Budworth parish, Cheshire, 4¼ miles N.E. of Northwich. The Warburtons have it still. [2] leaf 194, back. [3] leaf 200.

Ad *primam* excepcion*em*, this depon*ent* saies, that Alex*ander* Liney is a very poore man, and hath bene lately arrestid of felonye, and hath confessid the same /

Ad ij[d], this depon*ent* saieth, the said John Aspshawe is a very poore man, and Liveth apon his neib*ours*, and is a thatcher; and his wief and children go on begginge; and he hym-self hath no certen dwellinge place, to this depon*entes* knoledge. and further saieth, he hard it reportid that John Jackson brought the said Joan Ashley to one Will*ia*msons house, an Alehouse, there to be tablid; but the wief wold not suffer her. . . . .

Galfridus Bretton, p*a*roch*ie* de Pever inferior*i* [Lower Pever, near Rostherne and Knutsford, Cheshire], etat*is* xxxiiij . . . saieth, Alex*ander* Liney is a very poore [man], and hath no certen abidinge place; and this depon*ent* think*es* he is of small credite; and he hard a priest declare that he was a suspectid fellowe.

[1]Ad ij[d], this depon*ent* saieth, that John Aspshawe is a very poore man, yet he knowes no dishonestie bie hym. and further this depon*ent* saies, that John Jackson came to the house of Rafe Will*ia*mson, and com*m*oned w*i*th the wief of the house, and went his way imediatlie. after whose dep*ar*ture, Will*ia*msons wief askid this depon*ent*, beinge her neib*our*, whether she might kepe a woman of John Jackson; 'for,' said she, 'he hath bene here about that purpose.' this depon*ent* answerid, 'yonder old man hath no woman; and if he have, it is not best for you to kepe her.' w*i*thin a weke after, the said Jackson and Joan Ashley came to the said house; and this depon*ent* found them there; and after they were gone, the wief said: "younder is the woman that Johñ Jackson wold have had me to have kept; but through thie Counsell, I have turned them awaie." . . . . . .

[2]7 Dec. 1564. John Barlowe of Stretton,[3] clerk, aged 56, "saies that Alex*ander* Liney is a light p*er*son; and nowe latelie it was p*r*ovid before S*ir* Rafe Leycet*our*, k*night*, a Justice of peace, that he did consent to the Convaieng away of c*er*ten butter & cheese from this depon*ent*, deliu*er*ed to the said Alex*ander* & his wief, bie one Ellin Brodley; and for the same, both he & his wief were ponished in the stock*es* /"

[4]Ad ij[d], he saieth, that John Aspshawe is a light p*er*son, and a fugitive, and hath flitted twise w*i*thin this half yere. And further, this depon*ent* saieth, that he did demaunde of John Jackson whie he wold have tabled

[1] leaf 200, back. [2] leaf 202.

[3] A township and village in Great Budworth parish, Cheshire; the village is 3½ miles S. of Warrington. Another Stretton, a township, lies to the S.W., in Tilston parish, Cheshire, 4 miles N.W. of Malpas.—Bartholomew.

[4] leaf 202, back.

Jone Ashley at Williamsons house; & he, this deponent, said further that men wold Judge evill of it. and Jackson answerid, "what if I did so? yet she provid not with child." . . . . . .

Richard Hatton of Rostorne, aged 77, "saieth that Alexander Liney is a poore man, an[d] getteth his Livinge bie his sore workinge; and he thinkes he wold depose nothinge but truth."

Ad ij^d^, this deponent saieth that John Apshawe is a very poore man, and doth rest little in one dwellinge place . . . . . .

Ad iij, This deponent saies, that John Jackson came apon a tyme to the wief of this deponent, and desired her to let hym have a Chamber, to talk with Jone Ashley in an Eveninge; and she answerid, [1]she cold do nothinge without her husband, this deponentes, consent. and within ij° Daies after, he came to this deponent, and demaundid the same of hym, that he might have a chamber where he might talk with Jone Ashley in an eveninge; "for," said Jackson, "she is content to speake in secrete with me; & so I am with her." to whom, this deponent answerid, beinge Jacksons kinsman, that he shuld have non there; and it was vnsemelie for his age: and so the said Jackson departid; & this deponent hard no more of hym.

William Urmiston, of the parish of Knottisford, aged 38, "saies, that apon a tyme John Jackson came to this deponent, and willed to have a Service for a maide; and an other tyme he willed this deponent that his wief shuld take her into service, if she nedid a seruaunt; which this deponent denaide, but said she shuld be with her till he had provided for her, if she were an honest woman. after that, the said Jackson brought the said Jone Ashley vnto this [2]deponentes, beinge then not in his owne house, and lefte her with this deponentes wief. and this deponent came in, a while after; and finding her there, demaundid what she was, and what acquaintance was betwixe Jackson and her. and she answerid at first, she had a poore woman to her mother; and after, in talke, she said she was Henry Ashley his doughter. and biecause this deponent misliked her, he commaundid his wief to geve her meate and drinke of the best she had, and so lete her departe; for this deponent said he mynded not to kepe her." . . . . .

9. Ellen Gillam *v.* Agnes (or Anne) Gillam, for calling her a 'hoore.'

[3]14 Feb. 1564-5, Elizabeth Seaton, of the parish of St. Peter's, Chester, aged 38, "saies, that Anne Gillam spake theis wordes, that 'Ellin Gillam

[1] leaf 203. [2] leaf 203, back. [3] leaf 206.

was nought *with* Roger Brine; and yf nobodie wold say nothinge to her, she herself wold go to the said Roger Brines wief, & tell her of hit, that she might lay in waite for them, and take them together.' and further saieth, that thone chidinge *with* thother about thinges throwne out of a windowe, the said Anne said to Thom*as* Gillam, com*m*ynge out of his owne howse, 'go vp, and take a hoore bie the Nose,' inue*n*do, the said Thom*as* his wief, to this depon*en*tes Judgm*ent*."

[1]On 1 March, 1564-5, Matilda Gillam, of the parish of St. Peter's, Chester, aged 50, "saies, that about the beginninge of harvest last, in talk *with* Agnes Gilla*m*, amonges other thinges, the said Agnes said to this depon*ent*, that Ellin Gilla*m* was a hoore; and that the child in her bellie was Roger Brians. and this depon*ent* said it was shame for her so to report. and many tymes sins, this deponent hath hard the said Agnes report that the said Ellin was a hoore."

"Ad iij et iiij[t], this deponent sais, she belevis theis articles to be true, and that Ellin Gillams husband put her awaie from hym above a Moneth, bie reason of this sclaunder."

[2]On 16 March 1565, Elizabeth Walley "saieth, that she hard Ellin Gilla*m* say thus to Agnes Gilla*m*, 'thou liest like an arrant howre as thou art.' beinge demaundid [on] what occasion theis wordes were spoken, she saies, she thinkes it was in quarelling about some thinge that was throwne out of Ellin Gillams windoe."

"Ad ij et iij, This Deponent saies that she thinkes the good Name of Agnes Gilla*m* is not hurt herebie, biecause the wordes were spoken in anger; & she was, & is, accountid and taken for an honest woman /"

[3]On 30 March, 1565, Jane Clough, of St. Peter's parish, Chester, says "that she neue*r* hard Agnes Gilla*m* speake any sclaunderous wordes bie Ellin Gilla*m*."

[4]On 28 Sept. 1565, Ellen Price, of St. Brigit's parish, Chester, aged 46,—in answer to the Exceptions taken by Agnes Gillam to Ellen Gillam's witnesses,—"saies she thinkes that Mawde Gilla*m* [the 2nd witness above] is an honest woman / and she thinkes that the said Mawde wold depose no*n* other thinge then truth. and further she saies, she takes her for no schold, nor an vnhonest woman /"

"Ad ij[d], this deponent saies, that she hath hard bie report that the said Eliz*abeth* articulate [E. Walley, the 3rd witness above] had a child bie one Pe*r*cevall; but she knowes nothing therin but by heresay. as concerninge the chanse that concerneth John) ap Res, this depon*en*t saieth, the said John) is her husband, and saies that she knowes nothing but by

[1] leaf 209, back. [2] leaf 213, back. [3] leaf 221. [4] leaf 239.

heresay: and this depon*ent* her-self, to knowe the truth, made serche for triall therof; but she knowes nothing certenlie; for if she had, she, this depon*ent*, wold have complained apon her, the said Eliz*abeth*. and further saies, that the said Agnes wold have gevin her ij s to have testified som-what against the said Eliz*abeth* in this matter, which this depon*ent* refusid, altho she be very poore / as concerninge Joh*n* Seaton, this depon*ent* saies, that the said Eliz*abeth* and Joh*n* rid in a cart[1]; but therin she think*es* they had extremitie; for the said Joh*n* & Eliz*abeth* were trouthplight together afore, & maried im*me*diatlie after."

[2]Jane Bolton of the parish of St. Mary's [on the hill] Chester, aged 50, "think*es* that Mawde Gilla*m* articulate is an honest woman, and will depose nothing*e* but truth, to this depon*entes* Judgment, or for any thing*e* that this depon*ent* knowes of."

"Ad ij[d], this depon*ent* saies that the said Eliz*abeth* articulate [E. Walley] had a child bie Peter P*er*cevall articulate; but this depon*ent* saies hit was in way of Mariage; for this depon*ent* was at the trouthplightinge of them before the child was gotten; & he shuld have maried her if he had lived. quoad Joh*ann*em ap Rice, nescit depon*er*e. et quoad Joh*ann*em Seaton, she saies that the said Eliz*abeth* [Walley] was cartid bie extremitie and wrongfullie; for as much as the said Seaton was trouthplightid to the said Eliz*abeth* aefore she was cartid, and they were maried w*i*thin ij[o] daies after. al*ite*r nescit depon*er*e [3]but that the said Agnes wold have gevin this depon*ent* xij[d] to depose that Eliz*abeth* Bailie was nought; w*h*ich she refusid, and wold not do it / . . . . . ."

10. Isabell Pattele *v.* Rafe Hare, for calling her 'a hoore and a thief.'

[4]Exa*mina*cio inter Isabell*am* Pattele [? MS.] et Rad*ulphum* Hare, capt*a* xv[o] Februarii 1563-4.

Homfrid*us* Steele, cl*er*icus, cur*atus* de Prise, Coven*trie* et Lich*feldie* dioc*ese*, etat*is* xxiij an*norum*, nov*it* p*ar*tes ij a*nnis* / . . . . . .

Ad ij[d] ar*ticulum*, This depon*ent* saies, that about Michaelmas daie last, he hard Raffe Hare, before S*ir* Hugh Cholmeley, k*night*, say vnto the mother of Isabell Pattel (?) that 'she, vid*elicet* the said Isabell, was a hoore and a thief; and that M*aste*r Bromley had put cloth, tenne yard*es*, to the said Isabell, to make sheet*es* of; and she made smok*es* & sheet*es* to lapp her hoore ars in.' and the same night, this depon*ent*, havinge

[1] Drawn about in a cart, as a punishment for incontinency.
[2] leaf 239, back. [3] leaf 240. [4] leaf 206, back.

one other honest man in compan[i]e, did exhorte the said Raffe to geve ouer those sclaunderous wordes; and in debatinge the matter, the said Rafe affirmed that she the said Isabell was a hoore; & that, he wold stand to, and prove it . . . . . .

[1] William Bebington, parochie de Wrenbury, etatis xlvj annorum . . . .

Ad ij[d] articulum, dicit eundem fore verum. reddendo racionem sui dicti, this deponent saieth, that abowt Michaelmas daie last past, he was in Companie with diuerse others appointid bie Sir Hugh Cholmely, Knight, apon certen occasions; and in wordinge betwixe the mother of the said Isabell & the said Rafe, the said Rafe said to her, that 'her doughter Isabell was a hoore and a thief; and that she had x yardes of cloth, of one Master Bromley, and she cutt it in sheetes and smockes to lapp her hoores ars in' / and the same eveninge, Sir Homfrey Steele [the curate, above], in the presence of this deponent did exhort the said Rafe to leave such noughtie wordes, for he had vndone the poore wench. and he answerid againe she was a hoore, & he wold stand to hit / . . . . . .

11. Thos. Grenehalgh *v.* Fras. Grenehalgh for saying he committed Adultery.

Examinacio testium super libello ex parte Thome Grenehalghe vj° Decembris [1565].

[2] Ad Ecclesiam.

Johannes Key, parochie de Bury,[3] etatis xxxv' annorum, novit partes xvj[cim] annis /

Ad primum articulum, credit eundem fore verum.

Ad ij[d], This deponent sais, that he, beinge a wright bie his occupacion, and, apon [or] about the tyme libellate, workinge with Francis Grenehalgh, sawe Thomas Grenehalghe goinge toward the house of one Thomas Nuttall, husband to Jone Nuttall articulate; and amonge other talk of and by[4] the said Thomas Grenehalgh, the said Frauncis said, that 'Margaret Bradley, mother to the said Jone, came to, and was at, the house of her doughter Jone Nuttall; and the doughter went vnto the house of the said Margaret her mother; and thone remayned at the house of the other, vntill the said Thomas Grenehalgh had plaid the nought with the said Jone, in the house of the said Margaret, her mother.' And at the same tyme in talk, the said Anne Grenehalgh,[5] libellate, affirmed the same to be true.

[1] leaf 207. [2] leaf 256. [3] In Lancashire, now in the diocese of Manchester.
[4] about, against. [5] Wife of Francis Grenehalgh, the libeller of Thomas Grenehalgh.

[1] Ad iij^t^, dicit; that, bie occasion of theis sclaunderous word*es*, the said Thom*as* Grenehalgh his good Name is empaired and gretly hurt therby . . . . . .

Thom*as* Lomas, paroch*ie* de Bury, etat*is* xx an*n*or*um*, no*vi*t p*ar*te*m* act*ricem* et p*ar*te*m* rea*m* x an*n*is.

Ad p*ri*mu*m*, credit eund*em* contin*er*e in se veri*tate*m.

Ad ij^d^ ar*ticu*lu*m*, This Depon*ent* saies, that about the tyme libellate, this deponent, workinge at the house of one Fraunc*i*s Grenehalgh, Thom*as* Grenehalgh, articulate, walkid toward the house of Thom*as* Nuttall, husband to Jone Nuttall articulate; and when they sawe hym goinge toward the said [2]Thom*as* Nuttall*es* house, they began to com*m*en & talk of the said Thom*as* Grenehalgh; and among*es* other thing*es*, the said Fraunc*i*s spake theis word*es*, or the like: "M*ar*garet Bradley went to her doughter Jone Nuttall*es* house; and she, on the contrary wise, went to the house of the said M*ar*garet, her mother; and there plaid the nought w*i*th the said Thom*as* Grenehalgh articulate, while the mother was at her house." And the said Anne Grenehalgh, wief to the said Fraunc*i*s, beinge p*rese*nt at this talk, and affirme[d] the same that the said Fraunc*i*s her husband had said, to be true; and said the like bie Thom*as* Grenehalgh, in effect /

Ad reliquos Ar*ticu*los, concordat in o*mn*ib*us* cu*m* Joh*anne* Key, p*re*conteste suo /

VI. WILLS.

1. [3]Jn. Crompton *v.* Isabella Crompton, testator's widow, and Jn. Crompton.

(Widow steals the testator's Will and money. The 2nd of the 2 Depositions made on 22 June 1562.)

Rogerus Bradshawe, p*ar*ochie de Bolton, etat*is* xxxj an*n*or*um*, no*vi*t p*ar*te*m* act*ricem* xx' an*n*is, et Isabella*m* a m*at*rimo*ni*o suo cu*m* Jankin Cromptom.

Ad p*ri*mu*m* ar*ticu*lu*m*, This Depone*n*t sais, he was p*rese*nt when Jenkin Crompton, the tes*ta*to*ur*, desired John) Crompton, his brother, to be a father & an ou*er*seer to his children. quoad cetera, refert se ad testa*mentu*m . . . . . .

Ad v^t^, This depone*n*t sais, that Isabell Crompton[4] told this depone*n*t

[1] leaf 256, back. [2] leaf 257. [3] leaf 69, back-70,
[4] The testator's wife: later, his widow.

that she had lost the key of a chest, & desired hym to pull out the nayles of the hindges, and open hit on the other side, co*n*trary to the locke; and then he sawe her take out the will, and a box w*i*th a drawinge coue*r*, and certen writing*es* w*hi*ch lay not in the box: what they were, this depone*n*t knowes not; neither what was in the box. and after that done, the said Isabell brought hym newe nailes, and made hit close againe, as yf hit neue*r* had ben*e* openid. & then this depone*n*t, pe*r*ceyving hit to be done for a pollicy, his conscience accusid hym, and he declarid hit to John Crompton. and forther, this depone*n*t sais, that the testato*u*r, before his death, confessid he had about xj^{li} in gold & silue*r* in the house; which was not found, nothinge like. and this depone*n*t think*es* that Alis Aynsworth had hit, biecause he hard the said Alis say she had a som*m*e of gold w*hi*ch Isabell Crompton brought her, either when her husband John Crompton lay on his death bed, or sone after his death . . . . . .

2. A Deposition as to Richard Pendleton's Will.

(Taken 2 Sept. 1563.)

[1]Roger Burges, p*a*roch*i*e de Hyton,[2] etat*is* xlviij an*norum*, nov*i*t Rica*r*-*dum* Pendleton a te*m*po*r*e noticie sue /

Exa*minatus* &c, This Depone*n*t sais, that Ric*hard* Pendleton, beynge in his pe*r*fitt memory, about half a yere afore his death*e*, made his last will, w*hi*ch was written by S*i*r Ed*ward* Lowe, Vica*r* of Hyton, and no*n* other, that eue*r* this depone*n*t hard of. and after that will made, he went to church, and after seconnd[3] againe; and, beynge in his pe*r*fitt memory, cold tell of thing*es* don*e* lxxx' yeres ago, and knewe his neighbo*u*r*es* well, and did talke to them discretly. and forther, he sais, that he was w*i*th the testato*u*r at the day of his death, and taried w*i*th hym when the breath went out of his mouth; and all this while neue*r* revokid his testame*n*t, and did sticke still to hit, and desired all the neibo*u*r*es* p*res*ent to testify the same / and beynge demaundid of his [the testator's] tacke of ground in Whiston, [4]he sais he knowes that tacke, and namid hit, vi*delicet* the Lowe field, the Rye hay, and the Kilne crofte: w*hi*ch tacke and ground, he gave to the children of his doughter Emme, equally to be devided among*es* them, as well to the younge*r* as to the eldest. and as for Thom*as* Barnes, this depone*n*t sais, that he neue*r* had any p*a*rte of that tacke lefte vnto hym; but he well remembres that Thom*as* Barnes laborid to have hit; for this depone*n*t was w*i*th the Testato*u*r, the Aunderth[5] that the testato*u*r died, and went home

[1] leaf 71, back (Piccope's No. 31). [2] Huyton in Lancashire, near Liverpool.
[3] sickend [4] leaf 72. [5] undern, afternoon: see p. 117, note 2.

againe to se his busines; and was sent for as he was goynge; and come to the testatour, and said, "Eame[1] Richard, will you have any thinge alterid in your will?" and he answerid and said, "no, neiboures." and therapon, this deponent was goynge home againe, and yet was callid backe; and so askid hym as he did afore: and he answerid and said, "I will nothinge, neiboures; but go home, and attend your busines." yet this deponent taried still. and in the meane season, this deponent hard Thomas Barnes repeat that 'the Testatour had gevin the Tacke of ground in Whiston, as well to his susters, as to his aunte Emme her children.' and this [deponent] answerid and said: "yf I here the testatour speake, I will testify hit: otherwise I will not." Et sic concordat cum precontestibus suis, quod nunquam dictum testamentum variebatur per dictum testatorem: et in eodem testamento, dictum Thomam Barnes et Johannem Williamson nominavit executores /

3. Nuncupative Will of Roger Hodson.

[2]Examinaciones testium super viribus testamenti nuncupativi Rogeri Hodson, defuncti, capte coram magistro, Roberto Leche, in *Legibus* baccalaureo, &c, x° die Februarii, 1563°[-4].

Johannes Bostoke, parochie de Warmengham, etatis xlviij annorum, Examinatus super viribus testamenti asserti nuncupativi Rogeri Hodgson defuncti, dicit, in vim Juramenti sui prestiti, that he came to the house of Roger Hodgson, decessid, to se howe he did; and after the parson had gevin hym the rites of the church, he askid hym whether he wold make his testament; and whom he wold make his executour: and he answerid, "my brother John, the parson of Warmengham." [and this deponent] said, "thie brother John is sick, and cannot well comme: therfore it is best to put John thie sonne in with hym, or somme other honest man." and he answerid and said, "no body shal-be my Executour, but my brother John." et dicit se non fuisse requisitum per testatorem ad interemendum tempore prolacionis huiusmodi verborum; and saies forther that he hard nothinge bequeathid. and so this deponent left them for that tyme, and came that day in the Eveninge againe; and then he drewe nere his death. and this deponent hard say, he gave a maid of his, xl^s^. cetera nescit deponere /

[3]Thomas Halsall, parochie de Warmengham / etatis xl' annorum et vltra / Examinatus super viribus testamenti asserti nuncupativi Rogeri

[1] Uncle: tho he was Grandfather. [2] leaf 116, back (Piccope's No. 56).
[3] leaf 117.

Hogson def*uncti*, dicit, in vi*m* Jura*men*ti sui p*re*stiti, that he came to the house of the testato*ur*, vnsent for be the said testato*ur* and in this depone*ntes* p*re*sence, the p*ar*son of Warmengh*a*m did put the testato*ur* in mynd to make his Will; and the said testato*ur* said, "I will do nothinge till my brother com*m*e; for he shalbe the doer of all; and no*n* but he." beynge askid whether he said "I ordeine, name, and make, Johǹ my brother my executo*ur*," he saies, he had not knoledge to speake them so plainely; but when the p*ar*son told hym that his brother was sick, and cold not com*m*e; and therefore it were good to ioyne his sonne, or som*m*e other man w*i*th hym, he answerid, "no body shuld meddle w*i*th his goodd*es* but his brother." then his sonne said, "alas, father, wherein have I offendid you, that you will not make me yo*ur* Executo*ur*?" and he said, "thou shall not meddle." and forther he saies, that in this depone*ntes* p*re*sence he did bequeth*e* iij s iiij d to the church, and iij s iiij d to the poore, and no more, to this deponent*es* remembr*a*unce. but this depone*n*t hard say, he gave xl s to a maid of his, callid Katarin Newall. and forther, this depon*en*t saies, that the testato*ur* send for the said Johǹ his brother, who, by reason of his sicknes, came not so sone as he shuld have done; for the testato*ur* died afore he came /

Matheus Halsall, paroch*ie* de Warmengh*a*m, etat*is* xliij an*norum*, Exa*min*at*us* sup*er* virib*us* testa*men*ti Rogeri Hodgson def*uncti*, dicit, that the p*ar*son of Warmengh*a*m, after the rites gevin to the testato*ur*, they fell at an argument about a little dett betwixe them; but the p*ar*son wold not disquiet hym about such a smale trifle, but willid hym to p*ro*cede and make his will. and the p*ar*son writt p*ar*cell of his debt*es*, and then demaundid of the Testato*ur*, who shuld be his executo*ur*. and he answerid, his brother Johǹ. and the p*ar*son said, "yo*ur* brother is sick*e*, and can*n*ot com*m*e. ioyne yo*ur* sonne, or som*m*e other honest man w*i*th hym." and he answerid, "my brother shalbe the doer of all my matters; and no*n* els." and men m*ar*vailed whie he put not in, his sonne. and he answerid, he trustid hym not /

4. Thos. Pole *v.* Randle Rope, executor of Laurence Rope.

Valuation of property under will.

[1]Exa*min*acio testis in ca*usa* inter Tho*mam* Pole, gen*er*o*sum*, con*tra* Ran*dulphum* Rope, gen*er*o*sum*, Exe*cutorem* Lau*rencii* Rope def*uncti*, capt*a* cora*m* *M*agi*st*ro Rob*er*to Lech*e*, xij die Julij 1564.

Elenora Pole, paroch*ie* S*anc*ti Joh*ann*is, nuper vx*or* Lau*rencii* Rope,

[1] leaf 184 (Piccope's No. 99).

testat*oris* def*uncti*, no*vi*t p*ar*te*m* agente*m* v an*n*is, et p*ar*te*m* rea*m* xx' an*n*is et vltra / . . . . . .

Ad iiij : p*ro* p*ri*ma p*ar*te ar*ticu*li, credit eund*em* contin*er*e in se veri-tate*m*. reddend*o* rac*ion*em sui d*ic*ti ; biecause the goodes ar not p*r*aysed as they were worthie, vi*delicet*, a nagge articulate, preysed to xij d : this depon*en*t saies she knowes hym to be at that tyme worth vj s viij d ; also the Mare articulate, she think*es* was worth xx s. ; the field of wheate and Rye was worth, to her estimac*io*n, better then xxx s ; the fetherbedd and the Coueringe*s* was well worth v' me*r*ke*s* / the diap*er* table clothes, she saies ther worth xiij s iiij d / the oxen, she saies she think*es* in conscience were well worth xx' m*er*ke*s* ; the chales, worth xxx s., & the silu*er* salt was worth xl s. ; the silu*er* spones were better worth then xl s / as she well knowes.

Ad v[t], this depon*en*t saies, that she hath hard Rondull Rope say diu*er*se tymes, that the gold and monie Articulate, was in the hand*es* of Homfrey Manwaringe. and for the Lease articulate, she saies she hath hard her husband, the testat*or*, say many tymes he wold not geve the same for an C ti.

Ad vj, she knowes this article to be true, for it appereth bie the will of the same dett*es*.

[In the first Register of Wills at Chester, Mr. W. H. Price finds one of Laurence Rope of Wybunbury, in 1551, with a List of Debts. He appoints as executors Alice Rope, his mother, Laurence Woodnet, the Rev. Mathew Woode, vicar of Wybunbury, and Randle Rope his cousin.]

5. As to the Sanity and unexecuted Will of Alice Brodhurst.

[1]Exa*mina*cio testiu*m* sup*er* ce*r*t*is* Inter*rogatoriis* test*iu*m et vlt*ra* volun-t*atem* Alicie Brodhurst, capt*a* cora*m* D*omi*no Ep*iscopo*, viij° M*ar*tij 1564[-5].

Rogerus Hough, cl*er*icus, cur*atus* de Wilmeslowe, etat*is* lxvj, no*vi*t testat*ricem* a pue*ricia* ist*ius* deponen*tis*.

Ad p*ri*mu*m* Interrogat*orium*, dicit, in vi*m* Jura*men*ti sui p*re*stiti, that he neu*er* knewe, or eu*er* p*er*ceyvid, that the testatrixe was Lunatike at any tyme. reddend*o* rac*io*n*em* sui D*ic*ti, he saies, that she receyvid the Co*mmun*ion very Reverentlie about vj daies afore she died /

Ad ij[d] et iij, this depon*en*t saies, that the testatrixe was hard of hear-inge ; and that he, this depon*en*t, made a certen note of her Will, w*hi*ch

[1] leaf 210 (Piccope's No. 108).

he red not afore her, afore she died, biecause, as he saies, she was so deafe, she cold not here hym. and after she was dede, this exa*min*ant made it formallie. and he made the said notes, the Friday in w*hi*ch she receyvid the co*mmun*ion, about ix of clock*e* afore none, in her owne dwellinge house.

Ad iiij, dicit, q*uod* fue*r*ant p*re*sentes tunc tempore [? MS.], Ric*ard*us Kelsall, M*ar*geria Piers, and a doughter of Ric*hard* Kelsall, callid Kat*herine* Kelsall, & one Ric*hard* Eccles: but he think*es* they were not Req*ui*red; but were there p*re*sent bie chaunc*e* /

Ad v[t], he saies, that M*ar*gery Piers wold have dep*ar*tid from Ric*hard* Kelsall about the tyme testatrixe made her Will; and he willed her to tarry, & he wold be good vnto her. al*ia*s nescit depon*ere*.

Ad vlt*imum*, negat penitus.

[1]M*ar*garie Piers, p*a*roch*ie* de Wilmesly, etat*is* xxiiij an*norum*, novit testat*ricem* a pue*r*icia isti*us* deponen*tis*.

Ad p*rimum* Interrogat*orium* et ij[d], this depon*ent* saies, that she, beinge se*ruaunt* w*i*th the testatrix, did neue*r* knowe that eue*r* she was Lunatike or furiouse; but that she was deafe till she died.

Ad iij, this depon*ent* saies, that Roge*r* Hough, clark, made her Will apon a Friday, about x of clock afore none, sixe daies afore she died: in w*hi*ch daie she receyvid the co*mmun*ion.

Ad iiij, she saieth, ther were p*re*sent, Roge*r* Hough, clark, Kat*herine* Kelsall, Ric*hard* Kelsall, and Ric*hard* Eccles; but she saies she was not req*ui*red to testifie of the said Will, nor any of thother p*re*sent, bie the testatrix, to her knoledge.

Ad v, negat penitus; but that Ric*hard* Kelsall hath p*ro*mysed her to be good vnto her, to tarry w*i*th the testatrixe; & he wold geve her a Cowe and a panne, and som*m*e furniture toward a bed /

Ad vlt*imum* dicit, q*uod* *est* famula D*i*cti Ric*ardi*, p*ar*t*is* ea*m* p*ro*du-cen*tis*. and forther beinge exa*mi*n*e*d, she saies the Will was not redd afore the testatrix, after the said Will was made.

6. Robert Olton *v.* R. Dod and the other Executors of John Olton's Will.

(Losing his father's house, he claims a Child's share in his father's goods.)

[2]Exa*min*acio testis sup*er* li*bel*lo oblat*o* ex p*ar*te Rob*er*ti Olton con*tra* Executo*res* Joh*ann*is Olton def*uncti*, capt*a* cora*m* M*agist*ro Rob*er*to Lech*e*, xxij° Novem*bris*, 1565.

[1] leaf 210, back. [2] leaf 250, back (Piccope's No. 123).

Anna Sharman, p*a*roch*ie* de Ou*er*, etat*is* xlij', no*vi*t p*ar*te*m* act*ricem* xix an*n*is, et p*ar*te*m* Joh*ann*is[1] Olton simil*iter*.

Ad ar*ticu*los o*mn*es et sing*u*los, This depon*ent* saieth, that she hard John) Olton decessid, father to the nowe pl*aintiff*, apon his deathbead, when he said theis word*es*, or the like in effect: "if Rob*er*te my sonne cannot enioye and have the lease,—meaninge the lease of *th*e house & Tenem*ent* wherin the said John) then dwellid,—that he, the said Rob*ert*, shuld have a child*es* p*ar*te of goodd*es*, as other of his children. interr*ogata* de te*mpo*re et alijs circu*m*stanciis, she saieth, the question was askid by Rondull Dod, one of thexecut*oures*, as [2]far as she nowe remembres; w*hi*ch Randle askid the testat*ou*r this question, or the like in effect, vi*delicet*: "what shall yo*u*r sonne Rob*er*te have?" & the testat*ou*r answerid thus, or the like: "Mary, he hath the lease of my house, w*hi*ch, if he may enioye, it is a better p*ar*te then any of the rest." then said one that then was p*resent*,—w*hi*ch she supposeth was the said Ran*dle* Dod / "what if he cannot enioye the said Lease quietly?" then the said testat*ou*r answerid as afore / And forther saies, that after the death of the testat*ou*r, the said Rob*er*te held possession in the said house till he was, bie order of Lawe, dispossessed, as appeirs bie an order taken before the quenes Ma*jesties* Counsell in the M*ar*ches of Walles in that behalf, bie this depon*ent* nowe p*resen*tly shewid. And further saies, that she, this depon*ent*, neu*er* gave hym any thing*e* for his good will of the said Lease, or any thing*e* in recompence therof . . . . . .

[3]R*esp*onsio personalis Rond*ull* Dod sup*er* li*bel*lo oblat*o* con*tra* ips*u*m et alios Exec*utores* Joh*ann*is Olton, def*uncti*, capt*a* cora*m* Ma*gist*ro Rob*er*to Leche, &c, vlti*mo* Januarij 1565[-6] /

. . . Ad iij, This r*esp*ondent saieth, that when the testament was redd bie one Rob*er*te Riley, that writt the same, to the testat*our*, in the p*res*-*e*nce of this r*esp*ondent and others, to be allowid of hym, the said testat*our*: when this r*esp*ondent hard this clause, vi*delicet*: "and thother p*ar*te to geve and bequethe vnto my Children, beinge not Maried, and not otherwise Competentlie p*re*ferred," this r*esp*ondent askid the testat*ou*r this question, vi*delicet*: "what waie do you take for Rob*er*te yo*u*r sonne?" and the said testat*ou*r answerid and said: "you knowe he hath an assignement from his brother John), of this house; and he shall have, to beginne with, all the bark house and the bark-house yerd; and other thing*es* he shall have after the death of Isabell my wief; w*hi*ch, if he have a ben*e*fite by, hit shall stand hym in sted of a Child*es* p*ar*te.

[1] MS. Johis [2] leaf 251. [3] leaf 267 (Piccope's No. 131).

and if he have no benefite [1]by hit, then he shall have his child*es* pa*r*te. whie shuld he not?" And further he saieth, the said Rob*er*te is put by the house, and hath no b*en*efite therof, to his knoledge / Interrogat*us* whie theis word*es* were not put in the testament, this *respo*ndent saieth, that the testament was written before this talk, and was then in readinge. And this *respo*ndent think*es* this talk was not put in, biecause no*n* thought but he shuld have had the house; or els this clause, "not beinge competentlie p*re*ferd" wold have holpen hym. Et ad cetera Content*a* hui*us* ar*ti*c*u*li, dicit eade*m* fore vera /

Ad iiij, negat eande*m*.

Ad v[t], this *respo*ndent saieth, that he and thother Executo*ures* p*ro*ved the true will of the testato*ur*; and had, bie ve*r*tue therof, Admi*ni*stracion grauntid them / et cetera in ist*a* po*sitio*ne content*a*, w*hi*ch burthen hym and thother executo*ures* with vntruth or dishonestie, negat penit*us* /

Ad vj, he saieth*e*, that Rob*er*te Olton, iij or iiij[or] yeres after his fathers decesse, did demaund his childes p*ar*te of goodd*e*s bequeathid to hym. and this r*espo*ndent answerid, that 'he had a house in liue[2] of his child*es* p*ar*te; and that he knewe not whether he ought to have any child*es* p*ar*te or not, biecause he claymed it not as when devision was made of the good*es*; and for that cause, he wold not pay it, but by order of lawe, for his owne discharg*e*.' . . . . . .

VII. MISCELLANEOUS MATTERS.

1. Henry Blagburne's Answer to his Wife's Exceptions to his suit about an Impediment in her body.

[3]R*espo*nsi*o*nes p*er*so*na*les Henrici Blagburne, capt*e* die et an*no* p*re*d*ictis* (2 Dec. 1562).

Ad p*r*ima*m* excepc*io*ne*m*, this depone*n*t saies, it is twelve yeres sins he maried Joan Blagburne articulate; and he neu*er* complayned to any ordinary before my L*or*d*es* [Bishops] tyme nowe beynge; but he saies he hath sought helpe of Phisic*io*ns [for his wife's Impediment]; but she wold not suffer her self to be curid that way, for feare of daung*er*.

Ad ij[d], this r*espo*ndent saies, that for that space of xij yeres, they [he and his wife] have dwellid together in one house, and did neu*er* p*ar*te from bed or bord; but about iiij[or] yeres past they partid, & then the Justices of peace compellid hym to take her againe till the Sp*irit*uall

[1] leaf 267, back. [2] lieu [3] leaf 102.

Lawe had ordrid it. and he saies, by v*ir*tue of his othe, that he neu*er* carnally deale w*i*th her, as a man shuld w*i*th his wief naturally, biecause of the Impedime*nt* alledgid.

Ad iij, this re*spo*ndent saies, that before his said mariage, he did love her well, and had the vse of her body, insomuch that the said Joan did pe*r*swade this re*spo*ndent that she was w*i*th child by hym. whereapon, this re*spo*ndent did mary her the soner, not thinking she had the said Imped*i*me*nt*.

Ad iiij^tum^, this re*spo*ndent saies, that he had a child by one M*ar*garet Radcliffe, w*hi*ch he toke, and kept it for his; and also he hath offendid w*i*th one Parnell Somersbee; but he takis it [her child] not yet to be his.

2. The Tithing of Pigs and Geese in Whalley, Lancashire.

[1]On Dec. 17, 1562, John Billinge, of the parish of Clidroe (Clitheroe, a chapelry of Whalley), deposes, in a Tithe suit of Rafe Ashton against Henry Duckworth & Christopher Hargrevis, "that the man*er* of tiething pigge and gose is, yf one have vij^th^, to pay one; and likewise yf he have x, to pay one ane." And "this depone*nt* saies, that he went at michaelmas to *Christ*ofer Hargrevis house, and demaundid a tieth goos*e* of his wief, who had ix geese this yere; and she wold have gevin him non*e* but one that haltid, and tralid the winge. and this depone*nt* wold not take it, biecause the vse is, to have the best, saving*e* two; and that was the worst, to this depone*ntes* Judgm*ent*. and after, the said ferm*our* send an other of his men to demaund a tieth goose there againe; and it was denied."

This deponent cannot state "the value of the tieth pigge," but "the tieth goose w*i*tholden was worthe vj^d^:"

[2]Roger Hey, of the parish of Clidro, "saies that the man*er* of tiethinge pigge and goose w*i*thin the *pari*she of Whalley is, to pay one of vij, and one of x; and two of xvij &c." And "This depone*nt* saies, that Henry Duckworthe had vij pigg*es* this yere, and refusid to pay one. and the said ferm*our* send his seru*au*nt for one; and he had it denied againe. and as for *Christo*fer Hargrevis, this depone*nt* spake w*i*th his wief to pay her tieth goose, for she had ix; and she wold not; but said she was comaundid to kepe hit, and wold pay no*n*." He also "saies that he think*es* the tithe pigge w*i*thelden, was worth*e* xx^d^,—for so they sell;—and the tieth goose was worth vj^d^, w*hi*ch was w*i*tholden likewise," & "that Henry & *Christ*ofer were dem*a*undid vt sup*ra*, et recusaru*nt*."

[1] leaf 108. [2] leaf 108, back.

3. 1562. Depositions under Commission.

John Legh, clerk, the rector of Northenden, in Cheshire, visits the Sick diligently. The Baguley[1] folk are to stick to their parish-Church at Bowdon,[2] and not to come to Northenden[3] church.

Here is a bit of one: "[4]Rob*er*te Tatton, esq*ui*er, of thage of lx yeres, or there about, sworne & exa*mi*ned, deposeth and saieth that, about xlviij yeres past, he came to Schole to Northerden, beynge then about the age of xij yeres, and tablid at W*i*thinshawe,[5] w*i*th James Barlowe, then fermo*ur* there; and so continued at schole there about iiij^or or v' yeres; and for the most p*ar*te of this xxvj yeres last past, hath bene com*m*orant w*i*thin this p*ar*ish of Northerden, at his mansion house of W*i*thinsawe aforesaid . . . . . this depon*en*t saieth that, about v' yeres past, when *th*e newe sicknes[6] was hote and extreme w*i*thin this p*ar*ishe, so that John Leigh, clark, vncle to the said Edward Leigh,[7] and then p*ar*son there, havinge, at that p*rese*nt, no curate, but forsed to m*i*n*i*ster hym self, was so continually travaylid in visitinge of his p*ar*ishion*er*s, that as he, the said John Leigh, reportid to this Deponent, he gave warninge to thinhabitant*es* of Baguley, in Bawden p*ar*esh, that they shuld resort to their owne p*ar*ish churche of Bawden, there to receyve their right*es* and duties of *th*e church, for *tha*t he cold not bothe, serve them, and discharge his duty and cure to his owne p*ar*ishion*er*s. And moreoue*r*, this depon*en*t forther saieth, that in Lent before Easter was twelvemonth, Rob*er*te Vaudrey,[8] gent*lema*n, fermo*u*r of the vicariage of Bawden, sent his l*ett*res to this depon*en*t, requiringe hym therby to cause warninge [to] be gevin to thinhabitant*es* of Baguley in Bawden p*ar*ishe, that they shuld resort to their owne p*ar*ish churche of Bawden, there to receyve & have their duties, and likewise to answere and pay their duties accordingly; who so did, altho it was muche against their will*es*, consideringe the eases & pleasures they had at Northerden church of gentill sufferaunce. And for the household of the said Ed*ward*

[1] A township, in Bowdon parish, Mid-Cheshire, 3¼ miles N.E. of Altrincham.

[2] Bowdon, a large and important parish (containing Altrincham) and township, in Bucklow Hundred, Mid-Cheshire.

[3] Northenden, an important parish in Macclesfield Hundred. Northenden church is much nearer to Baguley than Bowdon church, and although in the parish of Bowdon, the inhabitants generally frequented Northenden church.

[4] leaf 113, back.

[5] Wythenshawe Hall, a fine old gabled mansion, partly black and white, in Northenden parish; for generations the seat of the Tattons, one of the oldest families in the county.

[6] This was probably a local visitation of the Plague.

[7] This was Edward Legh of Baguley Hall, Esquire, the representative of a family long resident there. He was nephew of the then rector of Northenden (see Earwaker's *East Cheshire*, vol. i. p. 291).

[8] Of the Riddings in Bowdon parish.

Leigh, he, the said Edward made desires to this deponent, to license them to receyve the Communion at Northerdon, who grauntid [1] to the same request at that tyme."

VIII. CLANDESTINE MARRIAGES.[2]

1. Phillipe Mainwaringe and Jane Serjant. 1588.

24th May, 1588. Thomas Tomstall, of the Parish of Winwick, aged 34, deposes "that he was presente in the howse of the said Jane, when matrimonie was solempnized betwyxe the said Phelippe & Jane, by Sir Roberte Bradshawe, Clarke, Curate att Newton chappel, aboute one yeare sins, in order, & accordinge to the book of Common prayer, with a ryng, and according to the lawes of this realme of England; saving that ytt was in a howse, & the banes nott asked iij tymes. and further sais, they haue cohabited togeather as man & wief, & doe; and shee is with childe, as the reporte is: Present [at the said Marriage], this deponent, William Blackborne, George Ainsworth, and Margaret Christofers."

William Blackborne, of the Parish of Winwick, aged 50, also deposes to the above.

2. Thomas Walker and Isabella Walker, *alias* Bamford. 1609.

13th September, 1609. Isabella Walker, "being demaunded when, where, and by whom, shee was maried to thaboue named Thomas Walker, saith: 'the saide Thomas Walker & this respondent [Isabella Walker], in the moneth of Auguste laste paste, were maried together in a field neare to the towne of Ashton-vnder-lyne, in the nyghte tyme, by moone lighte, by one Syr John Ward, Clarke.' And saith 'they were maried accordinge to the booke of Common praier in all pointes, and accordinge to the Ceremonies of the Church of England.' And saith shee beleeveth 'there was no Impediment, saueinge there was no lycence firste obteyned, neither were the bannes of matrimonie thrice lawfully asked or published in the Church: Presente att the same mariage, William Winterbothom, Edward Bramall and William Stansfield.' And saith, 'they haue lyne together in one bedd; & saith hee hath intreated this respondent like a louenge wief, & shee him like a loueinge husband.'"

[1] leaf 114.

[2] Mr. W. H. Price found, and kindly sent me these. They are separate single documents.

William Winterbothom 'saith he dwelleth in Stockporte Parishe, in the dyoces of Chester, Aged aboute xliij' [years]. And 'that he was presente when tharticulate Thomas Walker and Isabell Bamford, alias Walker, were maried together in the moneth of Auguste laste paste, in a meadowe neare the towne of Ashton under Lyne, in the night season, by the lighte of the moone'; & saith 'the same mariage was solemnized by one Syr John Ward, Clerke, accordinge to the booke of Comon praier, & the Ceremonies of the Church of England.' And saith, 'hee beleeveth there was noe Impediment betwixe the parties, saueinge the bannes of matrimonie were omitted; neither was there anie lycence procured from the Ordinarie, for the solemnizinge of the same mariage.' And saith, 'the saide Thomas & Isabell are reputed for lawfull man & wief amoungeste theire neighbours. presente att the same mariage, Edward Bramall, William Stansfield, and this deponent.'

3. Richard and Anne Stockley.

26 March, 1621[-2]. Thomas Woofall, of the Parish of Walton, age 29, deposes "that two or three yeares sithence, or thereabouts, vpon a Saboth daie, [he] this deponent, goeinge to sooke [seek] a Malche,[1] found Master Kendricke solemnizinge matrimonie betweene the said Richard and Anne, in the heighe waie that leadeth to Mellinge meadowes; and sayth he married them, ye said Richard and Anne, accordinge to ye forme layd downe in the booke of Common prayer, with the vse of a ringe. and further sayth, by vertue of his othe, that he dyd not knowe of there[2] beinge there, butt came acciedentally" * * * And "he, this deponent, findeinge the said Kenricke marryeing them as aforesaid, he stayed with them, and was presente vntill he had married them. Presente: James Woods, Joane Weste."

[1] Milch Cow.
[2] their: see the converse spelling below, in Fazakerly *v.* Wirrall, Supplement, p. 206.

[There are other Clandestine Marriages—if those in a Church can be cald so—in the Trothplight cases above and below: see pages 56, 59, 65-7, and also John David's Deposition in Elizabeth Bird *v.* Morgan Edmund in the Supplement, p. 187.]

Notes to Pages 47, 100, 106, 129.

p. 47. Wm. Stanley. See the Rev. F. Sanders's Life of him in *Wirral Notes and Queries*, ii. 1—22 (1893).

p. 100. *burnid*, poxt. Compare Shakspere, in the *Comedie of Errors*, IV. iii :—

Enter a Curtizan.

Dromio of Siracusa. Master, is this Mistris Sathan?

Antipholus of Siracusa. It is the Divell.

Dromio of Siracusa. Nay, she is worse ; she is the Divels Dam : And here she comes in the habit of a Light Wench ; and thereof comes, that the Wenches say 'God dam me'! That's as much as to say, 'God make me a Light Wench'! It is written, 'they appeare to men like Angels of Light.' Light is an effect of Fire ; and Fire will burne : *ergo*, Light Wenches will BURNE. Come not neere her.

p. 106. *The Souldiers went to St. Quintins.* Lord Pembroke (who had then lately saved Calais for a time) commanded the English contingent. To oblige her husband Philip, and provoked by Sir Thos. Stafford's seizure of Scarborough Castle with French help, Mary got the English (under Pembroke's command) to join the Spaniards against France. The Spaniards invaded "Picardy, and invested the town of St. Quentin." The French took the field with 20,000 men, "the reserved force of the kingdom—princes, peers, knights, gentlemen, with their personal retinues, the best blood in France. It was such an army as that which lost Agincourt ; and a fate not very different was prepared for it. . . . Mistaken movements caused a panic in the opening of the battle, and the almost instant result was a confused and hopeless rout" of the French . . . "the defeat was irretrievably complete, and to the (Spanish) victors almost bloodless. The English did not share in the glory of the battle, for they were not present ; but they arrived two days after, to take part in the storming of St. Quentin, and to share, to their shame, in the sack and spoiling of the town. They gained no honour ; but they were on the winning side. The victory was credited to the Queen as a success, and was celebrated in London with processions, bonfires, and *Te Deums*."—Froude, *Hist. England*, vol. vi. (Reign of Mary), p. 482-3, ed. 1870.

p. 129. *he wold stand to hit*, adhere to, stick to it : See the many uses of this phrase by Shakspere, in the Cowden Clarkes' *Shakspere Key*, p. 394. Here are a few :—

Now I'll *stand to it* ['maintain'] the pancakes were naught.—*As you like it*, I. ii.

And yet you will *stand to it* ['stick to the same story,' 'maintain it to be truth]' : you will not pocket up wrong.—1 *Hen. IV*, III. iii.

I beseech you, *stand to me* ['befriend me'].—1 *Hen. IV*, II. i.

I'll back with you ; and pray you *stand to me* in this cause.—*Coriol.* V. iii.

And call them Pillars that will *stand to* ['abide by, remain firm to'] us.—3 *Hen. VI*, II. iii.

To this point I *stand* ['I stick to this point,' 'I remain firm on this point'].—*Hamlet*, IV. v.

Sir John *stands to* ['keeps,' 'abides by'] his word.—1 *Hen. IV*, I. ii.

We *stood to't* ['remained firm'] in good time.—*Coriol.* IV. ii.

SOME ENGLISH ENTRIES FROM THE MAYORS' BOOKS, CHESTER.

A.D. 1558-9, 1591, 1597-8, 1598-9, 1600.

Notes to Pages 145, 146-9, 150, 156-8.

[1] p. 145. The Barber's Bond. The unlawful Games named in 27 Hen. VIII, c. 35 (A.D. 1535-6: An Acte for punysshement of sturdy Vacabundes and Beggers,) § 8, are "commen bowling, dysyng, carding, closhe, tenys." To these, 33 Hen. VIII, c. 9 (A.D. 1541-2), § 8, adds "Coytinge [quoits], Cayles, half bowle, Table [backgammon], and any unlaufull newe game nowe invented or . . . hereafter to be invented." The Act 2 and 3 Philip & Mary, ch. 9, (A.D. 1555) mentions another game, "White & Blacke Making & Marryng." In 1477-8, the 17th of Edw. IV, c. 3, enacted that any body suffering any person to use and occupy the 'ungracious and incommendable' 'new-imagined Games called Closh, Kailes, Half-bowl, Hand-in and Hand-out, or Queekboard, or any of them,' should be imprisond for three years, and forfeit 20£. 'Dice, Coits, Tennis, and such like Games' are also declared unlawful. See my note in *Ballads from MSS.* p. 531, and Halle's *Chronicle*, 1548, ed. 1809, p. 712.

p. 146-9, 156-8. *Bastards.* The law about their keeping was then containd in 18 Eliz. ch. 3, 'An Acte for the setting of the Poore on Worke, and for the avoyding of Ydlenes,' A.D. 1575-6, Record edition, Vol. IV, Pt. i, p. 610:

Firste, concerning Bastard*es* begotten and borne out of lawfull Matrimonye (an Offence against God*es* Lawe and Mans Lawe,) the said Bastard*es* being now lefte to bee kepte at the Chardg*es* of the Parishe where they bee borne, to the greate Burden of the same Parishe, and in defrauding of the Releife of the impotente and aged true Poore of the same Parishe, and to the evell Example and Encouradgement of lewde Lyef: It ys ordeyned and enacted . . . That two Justis*es* of the Peace, whereof one to bee of the Quorum, in or nexte unto the Limit*es* where the Parishe Churche ys, *w*ithin *wh*ich Parishe suche Bastarde shalbee borne, (upon Examinac*i*on of the Cause and Circomstance,) shall and maye, by their discretion, take Order for the kepinge of everye suche Bastarde Childe, by chardging suche Mother or reputed Father *w*ith the paymente of Monie Weekely, or other Sustentac*i*on for the Releefe of suche Childe, in suche wise as they shall thincke meete and convenient: And yf, after the same Order by them subscribed under their Hand*es*, any the said p*er*sones, viz. Mother or reputed Father, upon Notyce thereof shall not for their parte observe and p*er*fourme the said Order, That then everye suche partye so making Defaulte in not p*er*fourminge of the said Order, to bee committed to Warde to the Co*m*mon Gayle, ther to remaine, *w*ithout Bayle or Maineprise, excepte hee, she, or they shall put in sufficient Suretye to p*er*fourme the said Order, or els p*er*sonally to appeare at the next Generall Sessions of the Peace to be holden in that Countye . . . and also to abyde suche Order as the said Justices of the Peace, or the more part of them, then and there shall take in that Behalfe" . . .

Two Justices of Peace enabled to make Orders for Punishment of the reputed Parents of Bastard Children, and for the maintenance of such children by their Parents:

Parents not obeying such Order shall be committed.

p. 150. Recorders. Mr. J. P. Earwaker writes: "The Chester Archæological Society is fortunate in possessing one of the finest sets of Recorders known to be in existence. They are four in number, and are in excellent preservation."

(Mayor's Book, Chester. Book much rotted.)

(?) 10 Dec. 1558, 1 Eliz. Bond by Jn. Church of the City of Chester, and John Rodorye, fisher, to bring their grain into the City, and not carry any out of it. Penalty £40.

The condic*i*on of this Recognisaunce is suche, that if John Rodorye do not at any tyme on this side & before the feast of the natyvitie of St. John baptyst next ensuyng the date hereof, nether by hym-self, nor by any other, by his cause, consent, or p*ro*curement, carye, transporte, bagge, or bring away, any mann*er* of corne or grayne, out of the Citie of Chester, or the porte & creke*s* to the same belonging, w*i*thout spe*c*iall license thervnto obteyned of the mayor of the same Citie; And also do bring vp into this Citie, all suche corne and grayne as p*rese*ntlye is & remayneth w*i*thin his ship or vessell now w*i*thin the Ryver, on this side the xth daie of this p*r*esent dece*m*ber, That then &c or ell*is* &c.[1]

21 Dec. 1558. Bond of Thos. Mercer, barber, not to play at unlawful Games, or let them be playd in his house.

(Rotted Mayor's-Book, 1 Q. Eliz.)

[Memorandum quo]d Thom*as* Me*r*cer, ciuitatis Cestr*ie*, in Com*ite* Cestr*ie* de[2] barbor, [venit in propria] persona sua, xxj die Dece*m*br*is*, Anno regin*e* p*r*efat*e* d*omi*ne [Eliza]bethe Regine primo, &c, coram Lauurencio Smith, [milit]e, maior*e* C*iuitatis* Cestr*ie*, & Recogn*ovit* se tunc ib*ide*m debere [x libras] p*r*efate Regine, Soluendas &c.

The condic*i*on of this Recognisaunce is such, that if the aboue-bounden Thom*as* Merser, on this side and before the feast of the Epiphany of o*ur* lord, next ensuyng the date hereof, do, nether in his house in the Citie of Chester, nether w*i*thin iiij myle compas vnto the same Citie, play at any vnlaufull gamez prohibeted by any act, law, or statute of this Realme, nor suffer the same to be vsed ne played at, by any other, w*i*thin his said house; And also if the said Thomas do not at any tyme hereafter, during the mayoraltie of the said Sir Lauure[nce] Smith, knight, play in any place ell*is*, at any of the said vnla*u*full games p*r*ohibited, but shall vtterly refuse the same, That then &c, or ell*is* &c.[1]

[1] The full clause is seen at the end of John Barker's Bond, p. 147. [2] ? MS.

4 Dec. 1590. Bond to secure Hy. Gibbons his Sword, on payment of 3*s*. borowd on it, and 3*d*. interest.

4 die Decemb*ris* Anno R*egni* Regine Elizabethe xxxiij°, Ricard*us* Holford et Robe*r*tus Leene de Ciuitate Cestr*ie*, Tailers, vener*unt* cora*m* p*r*efato Maiore [Wm. Massy], et recog*noverunt* se debere Henrico Gibbons, de Cowfild in com*ite* Leicestr*ie*, yoma*n*, xx s. Soluendas &c.

The condicion of this Recognizans is suche, That whereas the said Ric*hard* Holford heretofore borowed vpon a sworde of the said Henr*y* Gibbons, for the same Henr*y*, of one Robe*r*t Kirks, tailer, iij s. for the gaine of iij d, w*hi*ch Sword, the said Rich*ard* Holford hath now redemed & recurid[1] into his hand*is*, That yf the said Henry Gibbons shall & Maie haue the said Sword as his owne, paiing the said iij s iij d, That then &c or el*is* &c.

(Mayor's Book, Chester, 1590-1.)

2 Jan. 1591. Surrender by a Mason of his Patent to keep the City Walls in repair.

2 Januarij 1590(-1).

Thom*as* Wiswoll of the Citie of Chester, mason, having by patent vnder the Seale of this Citie, A graunte, for terme of his lief, of xl s. and a lyverey gowne, for the Mainten*a*uns of the wall*es* compassing rownde about the said Citie, hath surrendred and deliue*r*ed vp to the Maior & Citizens of the said Citie, the said Patent, & made voide the same, in respect that he was not hable to kepe the rep*ar*ac*i*ons of the said wall*es*, or to p*er*forme the coven*a*untes menc*ion*ed in the said Patent, which, vpon his p*ar*tie are to be done; & for & in consid*eracio*n of the some of xxx s. to him truly paied by the said Mr Maior in p*rese*nce of Mr Edmund Ganull (?) & Will*iam* Knight /

12 Jan. 1591. Jn. Barker's Bond to secure the due Nursing and keeping of his Bastard Baby till Michaelmas.

xij^{mo} die Januarii, Anno R*egni* Reg*i*ne Eliza*bethe* &c xxxiij^{cio}, Johannes Richardson de Hanbridge, infra libe*r*tat*em* Ciui*tatis* Cest*r*ie,

John Barker. Tanner, et Dauid Richardson de ead*em*, fishmonger, vener*unt*, in propriis p*er*sonis suis, Coram Will*el*mo Massy, Maiore Ciui*tatis*, p*r*ed*icte*, in Interiori Penticio eiusdem Ciui*tatis*, et ad tunc et ib*id*em recognover*unt* se debere d*icte* d*omi*ne Regine xx^{li}, Soluend*as*, &c.

[1] recoverd.

The condic*io*n of this Recognizaunce is suche, That, whereas ther is a child borne in Bastardy vpon the bodie of *Mar*garet Collyns, & late *ser*u*a*unte to thaboue bounden Joħñ Richardson w*i*thin the p*ar*ish of St Marye vpon the hill, in the Citie of Chester, whereof the said Joħñ Richardson (vpon exa*m*i*n*ac*io*ns in that behalfe) is the reputed father, w*h*i*c*h Child the said John hath requested maie be deliu*er*ed to the said Dauid Richardson; and that he wolde sufficiently Maintaine & finde it all necessaries sufficiently, which is granted to him; Therfore, if the said John Richardson, vpon his owne proper costes doe cause the said Bastard Childe to be sufficiently nursed, founde, Mayntained and kept, with app*ar*ell, Suck, attendinge, and all other necessaries nedfull or belonging to such a childe, from time to tyme hensforth vntill the Feeste daie of St. Michaell tharchang*e*ll next ensuinge the Daie of the date of these *pre*sent*es*, except other order in that behalf be taken by the said Maior in this meane while before the said feaste; And also if the said John Richardson, at the same feaste daie of St. Mich*ael* tharch*angel* next com*m*inge, doe p*er*sonally app*er*e before the Maior of the said Citie for the tyme beinge, and vpon his app*er*auns doe not dep*ar*te without the special lycens of the said Maior; And in the meane while doe at all tymes honestly behaue him-selfe, and as becometh an honest man, That then this p*re*sent Recognizaunce to be void & of none effect, or ell*is* yt to stande, be, and remaine in full power, force and vertue.

13 Jan. 1591. Award of the Mayor, Wm. Massie, in a Dispute about a Lease of a house in Northgate St., and a Bond for due keeping of its Covenants.

(A.D. 1591) Apud Ciuitat*em* Cestr*ie* xiijto die Januarij, Anno R*egni* R*egi*ne Elizab*ethe* &c. xxxiijcio.

At w*h*ich daie, matter of varyaunce was in question betwene Rob*er*t Whitby, gentl*eman*, vpon thon p*ar*tie, and Robert Laton, m*er*ch*a*unt, vpon thother p*ar*tie, for and conc*er*ninge one mess*uage* or Tenem*ent*, with thapp*ur*ten*au*ns, in the Northgate streete w*i*thin the said Citie, wherein the said Rob*er*t Laton doeth now inhabite: w*h*i*c*h p*re*misse*s* were lately p*ur*chesed by the said Rob*er*t Whitby of one Rauff Wytter / and the same were before demised to the said Rob*er*t Laton, by and from the said Rauff Witt*er*, for xxj yeres for c*er*taine yerely Rent, with a forfeiture for no*n*-paym*ent* at daies appointed, menc*io*ned in that leas thereof; as also a bande [= Bond] made by the said Rob*er*t Laton to the said Rauff Witter in xvli for p*er*formaunce of all coven*a*unt*es* in that indenture /

And whereas the said Rob*er*t Whitby alledgeth the said leas forfeited, & band also; and the same band, vpon suite in the pentice Court w*i*thin the same Citie against the said Rob*er*t Laton, recou*er*ed, savinge only destet*es* (or desteth) for iudgm*ent*; albeit the said p*ar*ties haue willingly compromitted them selues to the order of M*ast*er W*illia*m Massy, maior of the said Citie / wherevpon he, the same Maior, by assent of both p*ar*ties, doeth order and award, that the said Rob*er*t Laton, his wief & famely, on the feaste day of thannu*n*ciac*io*n of Blessed Mary the Virgen next cominge, departe from the quiet occupac*io*n of the said mess*uage*; and, at no time afterward*es*, chalenge, claime, or demaund, any right, title, or interest thervnto, nor to any p*ar*te or p*ar*cell thereof; and at the same feaste, to deliu*er* to the said Rob*er*t Whitby, quiet possession thereof, & all suche good*es* & implement*es* remaininge therin, wherof p*ar*ticuler mencion is made in a Scedull now agreed vpon or made knowen. And further, he the said maior doeth, by like assent, order that it shalbe leafull, & at the pleasur of the said Rob*er*t Whitby, his s*er*vant*es* & workmen, at all tymes before the [1] said feaste, to enter into the said mess*uage* or Tenem*ent*, and to haue free corse and recorse into, throw, and from the same, for the amend*me*nt, repairinge, and putting of it in sufficient repairs, and for all other necessarie vses in the betteringe of it, w*i*thout the lett, suite, or disturbans of the same Rob*er*t Laton, his wief or family, or any other by his or ther meanes, act, deed or p*ro*curem*ent*. In considerac*io*n whereof, the said M*aste*r Maior doe, by like assent, award that the said Rob*er*t Whitby shall paie to the said Rob*er*t Laton foure pounds, Tenne shilling*es*, in forme folowinge: vi*delicet*, xx s. in hand, and thother iij^{li} x s. at the said avoidinge of the said Rob*er*t Laton, his wief & famely, from the quiet occupac*io*n of the said mess*uage* & other the p*re*misses, & deliu*er*y of the said good*es* & implement*es* menc*io*ned in the said inventory as aforsaid / for payme*n*t whereof, the said Rob*er*t Whitby hath yelded vnto, the rather, in respect of the grete yeres and disabilitie of the said Rob*er*t Laton & his wief, & for quietnes sake, and to cause them to be thankfull vnto him for the same.

Also it is ordered that the said Robert Laton shalbe discharged of all Rent*es* heretofore due for the same / & *tha*t the said Rob*er*t Laton shall p*re*sently deliu*er* vp the indenture & bande which he hath thereof, of & from the said Rauff Witter, vi*delicet*, of the said mess*uage*, & quiet occupac*io*n thereof.

(Signed by) Will*ia*m Massie
Maior

Robert Lawton. p*er* me Rob*er*tu*m* Whitbrid

[1] back of leaf.

20 Jan. 1591. Rd. Porter's Bond to secure the due Nursing and Keeping of his Bastard Baby for a year.

M*emorandum* q*uod* xx^{mo} die Januarii, Anno R*egni* Reg*i*ne Eliza*bethe* &c xxxiij^{cio}, Ric*ard*us Porter de Ciui*ta*te Cestr*ie*, Tailer, et Joh*anne*s Sele de ead*em*, Tailer, Vener*unt*, in proprijs p*er*sonis suis, Coram Will*el*mo Massy, maiore Ciui*ta*tis p*re*di*cte*, in Interno Penticio Ciui*ta*tis p*re*di*cte*, et recognover*unt* se debere d*ic*te D*om*i*ne* Regine xx^{li}, Soluend*as* &c, Et nisi &c.

The condic*i*on of this Recognizaunce is suche, That whereas the aboue-bounden Ric*hard* Porter is the Reputed father of a man childe, borne in Bastardie, vpon the body of Mawde Ratcliff,—Iff the same Ric*hard* Porter, vpon his owne p*ro*per Cost*es* and charges, doe cause the said childe, suffic*i*ently to be nursed and Maintained with all necessaries duringe one whole yere next ensuinge the date hereof; and at that yeres ende, p*er*sonally to app*er*e before the maior of the said Citie for the tyme beinge, and Not dep*ar*te thens w*i*thout Licens of the said Maior for the tyme beinge, & p*er*forme truly suche order towchinge the said Childe as shalbe taken by the same such Maior, That then this p*re*sent Recogniz*aunce* to be voide, or ell*is* it to stand in force /

[*note at side*] 12^{d}: John Sele to pay it at Est*er* next.

11 Ap*rilis* 1591

note. Mr. Joħn Glasior (is said) to vnd*er*take, for his work, Adam Hunt.

Ric*hard* Wilson vndertaketh for the furth-coming of Rob*er*t Kirks.

Mr Paull of Chauntrell[1] vndertaketh for the furthcoming of Mich*ael* Vrmeston.

21 Aprilis 1591 (Agreement as to the payment and re-payment of a Rentcharge on a house.)

Then Agreed, betwene Joħn Throp, Tailer, and *Christo*fer Conwaie, towching a Rent issuing out of the howse wherin the same Throp now dwelleth, that the said Joħn Throp shall paie the same yerely Rent to the said *Christo*fer, according as the same was graunted to Mr W*illia*m Mutton / and to thassuraun*c*e thereof, the[2] said *Christo*fer Conway p*ro*miseth to discharge the said Joħn Throp of as much money as the same *Christo*fer shall receive of him, the said John) Throp /

[1] Mr. Earwaker suggests 'Mr. Paul Chauntrell.'

[2] MS. & the

Primo Maii, 1591. Commitment to Gaol, of a County Bailiff who arrested a man in the City Market-Place.

note. a warrant shewed, dated the vth of December laste, from & vnder the hand & Seale of John) Milner, Bailiff Itinerant of this Countie Palantine of Chester, authorizing Thomas Smith, & Richard Donne his Deputy bailiff, by vertue of a writt of attachment out of theschequer of Chester, to attach the body of Roger Dod, & to fane his body ther, the xij^th^ day of June next cominge. the said Smith, by vertue of the said warrant, did arreste the said Roger Dod in the open market place of this Citie, this present daie; and beinge charged to be a wronge, & contrary to the liberties & charters of this citie, iustifieth to be lawfull; & therfor, beinge a moste Manifest wronge, & contrary to the Grauntes, chartres & privileges of this Citie, is Comitted to the Gaile of the Northgate of the said Citie.

28 May 1591. Agreement as to the Ownership of the Hautboys, Recorders,[1] Cornets and Violins, of the City Waits.

Apud Ciuitatem Cestrie, xxviij° die Maii, Anno Regni Regine Elizabethe &c. tricesimo tercio, Coram Willelmo Massy, maiore Ciuitatis Cestrie.

At which day, matter was in question betwene Ales Williamz, late wief of Thomas Williamz, late one of the waytsmen of the said Citie, vpon thone party, and Christofer Burton and William Madock, the other waitsmen of the said Citie [of the other party], for and Concerninge their instrumentes of musick, videlicet, the howboies, the Recorders, the Cornetes and violens, whereof the said Ales Claymeth a parte, as to her said late Husband, in his lief tyme belonginge / which they deny to yeld vnto; But are Contented, and soe are now Agreed,—and it is now fully ordered by Assent,—that the said instrumentes shall from hensforth forever remayne, Continue, and bee, the owne proper goodes of the said Waitesmen, and of the survivour of them, and of William Williamzs, late sonne of the said Thomas Williamz, and of Henry Burton, sonne of the said Christofer, when they shall haue served out their Yeres as Apprentices to the said exercise, and to the svru[iv]our of them, and the survivour of euery of them, and of the survivinge sonne of euery of them experienced, or to be experienced in the said exercise, and Apte and fitt for the same, servinge within the said Citie, or ellis to remayne foreuer to the said Citie, At the

[1] A kind of Flute.

Appoyntm*en*t and Admittance of the Maior of the said Citie for the tyme beinge.

10 July 1591. Bond of a Slater to buy Slates only for his own use and Buildings.

"*Memorandum* that the tenneth daie of July, Anno . . . Elizabethe xxxiij^{cio}," Robert Fazakerly of the City of Chester, slater, was bound in a penalty of £10 to the said Queen:

"The condic*i*on of this Recognizauns is suche, That if thaboue-bounden Robert Fazakerley, by him-self, nor by any other p*er*son or p*er*sons, at any time or times hereafter, doe not buy any kinde or sorte of slates, directly nor indirectly, but only for his owne proper vse in slat-inge, & for slates to Cover, and therw*i*th doe cover, his owne howses & buldinges. That then this Recognizaunce to be voide, or els yt to stand in force."

9 die Augusti 1591 (Acknowledgment of a Debt, to be paid at Michaelmas.)

Memorandum, that Thom*as* Case, s*er*iant [of Chester], doeth acknow-ledge him-self indebted to Jeffrey Cooke of the same, fishmong*er*, xxx s. of leafull money of England, to be paied to the same Jeffrey Cooke, his executo*rs* or assignes, at, in, and vpon, the feaste daie of S*ain*t Michaell tharchangell next cominge. Et nisi &c; and to paye to Mr Maior x s. at M*aste*r Maiors comandem*en*t.

16 Augusti 1591. Acknowledgment of a Debt. On default of payment, Debtor to be sent to Prison.

(A loose two-leaf, put into the Mayor's Book. The paper was loose in the book, and I got Mr. Johnson to stick it in its proper place.)

Memorandum that the xvjth day of Auguste 1591, John Rathburne of the Citie of Chest*er*, Iremonger, doeth acknowledge himself to be indebted, and to owe, to Thom*as* Thornton of the same Citie, Iremong*er* and M*ar*ch-aunte, the som*m*e of fourtene pound*es*, tenne shilling*es*, of good and lawfull money of England, To be paid to the same Thom*as* Thornton, his executors or Assignes, in mann*er* and forme followinge, That is to say, att, in, and vpon Saturday next Cominge, xl s; and w*i*thin fourtene daies then nexte, and ymediatlie followinge, v^{li}; and, vpon the feaste daie of S*ain*t Michell tharchangell then nexte folowing, all the reste and residue of the said som*m*e of xiiij^{li} x^{s}. And vpon eu*er*y defalt of paym*en*t, that M*aste*r Maior shall send for the said John Rabon, and Comitt him to warde, and there detayne him vntle[1] the said whole som*m*e be payde.

Certificate of a Statute Merchant of £800.

Apud Ciuita*tem* Cestr*ie* xxx° die Januarii, Anno p*re*d*ic*to.
(33 Eliz. A.D. 1591)

At w*hi*ch daie, at the requeste of John Poole thelder, of Poole in the countie of Chester, esquier, & of Thomas Bunbury of Stanney in the same countie, esquier, a certificat of A Statute me*r*chant of viij C^li^, dated the xxij^th^ daie of Septembre, Anno R*egni* Regine Elizabeth*e* &c xxxiij^cio^, acknowledged to them by John Hocknell of Hocknell in the countie of Chester, esquier, Thom*as* Brymestoich (?)[2] of Hadham in the countie of Hartford, esquier, & Henry Brymestoich (?)[2] of Halies in the countie of Essex, gentl*eman* / before Will*ia*m Bird, late maior of the citie of Chester, & Richard Birkhenes,[3] esquier, Record*er* & Clerk &c / was certified Excelent*issimo* princip*i* Do*mi*ne n*ost*re Elizab*ethe*, in sua Cur*ia* cancella*rii* Angl*ie* sine bri ? Bri*tannie*.

Censure of an Alderman for sueing a Fellow-Citizen and late Sheriff for damages. Friendly arrangement as to the Debts.

xvij° die Maii, 1591

At which daie / Rob*er*t Amery of the Citie of Chester, Iremong*er*, Complained him againste Dauid Lloid of the same Citie, Alderman, for that he, the same Dauid Lloid, doeth sue him in thexchequer of Chestre for a supposed escape, the time of his Office of Sheriffwick, aswell for xx s. debt, iiij d dam*age*, of Ric*hard* Bird, Tann*er*; and for xxviij s vj d debt, and iiij d dam*age*, of James Wilkinson :[4] wherevpon, M*aste*r Maior called before him the said Dauid Lloid, and declared vnto him the said complaint, &c, m*ar*veld that he, beinge of the best callinge w*it*hin this Citie, shuld doe any suche attempt, tendinge to the preiudice of the ancient ord*er*s thereof / wherevpon, by Assent, it is ordered that the said Robert Amery, by Saint James tide next com*m*inge, shall satisfy to the said David Lloid the said seu*er*all dett*es* & damag*es*; and that, in the meane while, he, the said Rob*er*t Amery, shall, vpon his owne cost*es* & charg*es*, sue out severall fier*i* faci*as* against the said Ric*hard* Birt & James Wilkinson, to revive the said recon*izances* (?), & to doe his beste to p*ro*cure thexecucion (?), serves, & satisfacion (?) made for his helpe therin.

[1] until [2] Brymestich. [3] Birkened.—Earwaker.
[4] See the further Order as to this debt of 28*s*. 10*d*., at p. 159 below.

Acknowledgment of Debt for Rent.

25 Feb. 1590-1

M*emorandum* that the 25th daie of Februarij, Anno R*egn*i Regine Elizabeth*e* &c xxxiijcio, Roger Horton, of the Citie of Chester, sherman, came in p*er*son before the said Maior, and acknowledged him-selfe to owe to Jane Blackston al*ias* Smith, wedow, xxvj s. viij d, of lefull money of England, for the Rent of the howse wherin the said Roger now dwelleth, To be paied to the same Jane in man*er* & forme folowinge, vi*delicet*, at Thanu*n*ciac*i*on of bleassed Mary the Virgen, and the Na*tiui*tie of S*ain*t John Baptiste next ensuinge the date hereof, by equall porc*i*ons. Provided, that, if before the said payment*es*, ther shalbe such sufficient mat*er* shewed to M*aste*r Maior, that the said Rent doeth not belong to the said Jane, then all the said paym*entes* to ceasse.

xth April 1591

further day, by assent geven for ye said firste payme*n*t vntill ye xth of Aprill 1591 inst*an*t &c.

[1] Chester. Mayors' Books. 1591.

Oath of the Butchers in Chester. A.D. 1591.

Oct. A List of the 33 Butchers in Chester is given, and their oath follows:

Carnificesium Ciuitat*e* Cest*rie*.

Godfrid*us* Wynne
Joha*nn*es Wade } Alderman*ni* art*is* p*redicte* Jur*ati*
&c &c &c.

The othe.

All suche kinde & sorte of victuall as hereafter yow shall slaughter & kill, or cause to be slaughtered & killed, vttered & sold, shalbe good & holsome: And yow shall make sufficient p*ro*vic*i*on of suche Victuall, accordinge to yo*ur* facultie, to serue the citie with-all / And all suche yo*ur* victuall *tha*t yow shall vtter & sell, yow shall vtter & sell, to poore & Riche, at reasonable p*ri*ces / And that yow doe not follow, vse, nor make, nor consent to be made, any order or orders, or other ordinances, from hensforth amonge*s* yo*ur* selues, concerninge *th*e sellinge of yo*ur* Victualls, againste the comen we[l]th of this Citie. Soe god yow helpe, & by Jesus Christe!

[1] leaf 4.

Oath of the Bakers in Chester, 1591.

[1]Chester. Mayors' Books. 1591. Oct. List of the 30 Bakers.

No*mi*na Pistor*um* in Ciuitate Cest*rie*.

Willelmus Kinge senior, Alderman*nus* art*is* pred*icte*, &c &c.

The Othe.

All suche kinde & sorte of bread as yow hereafter shall bake or cause to be baken, vttered & sold, shalbe altogether sufficient & holsome bred & paste for mans sustenans; And also haue sufficient prouision of suche good, and holsom, & seasonable Bread & paste to se*r*ue this Citie w*i*th-all from time to time, & at all times hereafter, w*i*thout denyall. So helpe your god, & by Jesus Christe!

A Chandler's Bond to sell Candles at 4*d*. a Pound.

[2]23 die novemb*ris* 1591.

Thomas Case, de Ci*vita*te Cest*rie*, chandler, Tenet*ur* d*omi*ne Regine in x[li] bone et legal*is* monet*e* Anglie.

The condic*i*on of this Recognizaunce is such, That if the above-bounden Thom*as* Case, by him-self, or by any other pe*r*son or pe*r*sons for him, at any time hereafter, doe not vtter nor sell any pounde of Candles aboue iiij d eue*r*y pounde; and also at all times hereafter doe make sufficient p*r*ovis*i*on of Tallow, and se*r*ue this Citie & all others by retaile, w*i*th sufficient Candell*es* at iiij d the pounde, & not aboue, w*i*thout deniall, That then &c or ell*es* &c.

Hugh Hine, Tallowchandler, in x[li], Sub cond*itione* Id*em*, mutat*is* mutand*is*.

Bond by Sellers of Meat, to bring the animals' Skins and Tallow for sale too, and charge only 3*s*. 4*d*. for the Tallow.

[3]Mayors' Books. Chester. 1591.

27 die Novemb*ris*, Anno R*egni* Regine Elizab*ethe* &c xxxiiij[to]: Radu*lphus* Haselwall de Hanbridg, infra libe*r*tates Ciui*tatis* Cest*rie*, ven*it* in p*ro*p*ria* pe*r*sona sua cora*m* prefat*o* maior*e*, et recogn*ovit* se debere x[li] d*icte* d*omi*n*e* Regine, &c, Soluend*as*, &c, Et nisi &c.

The Condic*i*on of this Recognizaunce is suche, That if thaboue bounden Rauff Haselwall, at any time hereafter, doe not bringe to the m*ar*ket w*i*thin the Citie of Chester, any kinde or sorte of victuall but such as shalbe good and holsome, and of all such victuall doe bringe to

[1] leaf 4, back. [2] *Ib.*, leaf 11. [3] leaf 12, back.

this Citie the skins, fells, heds and Tallow; and all the same, within the same Citie, vtter & sell at resonable *pr*ice; & all his tallow thereof doe vtter & sell for iiij s iiij d, & not aboue that, then &c or ells &c.

Robertus Willes de Happesford David Barker de Holt Thomas Bithell de Holt *Christo*ferus Low de Farndon Will*el*m*us* Pulford de Farndon	quilibet in x[li] Sub condic*ione* pred*icta*. *pro* quolibet p*er*umpt*ione* [? MS.] x[li] separatim, mutat*is* mutand*is*.

Bond by a City Merchant to keep and produce 6 Butts of Sack—belonging to Outsiders, which are enterd in his name in the City Customs' Book—or pay £50.

[1]1591. Mayors' Books, Chester.

Memorandum, q*uo*d nono die Decembris, Anno R*egni* Regine Elizabeth*e* &c xxxiiij[to], Joh*anne*s Aldersay, de Ciui*ta*te Cestr*ie*, m*er*cator, venit in propria p*er*sona sua Coram Thoma Lynyall, maiore eiusdem Ciui*tatis*, in Interiori Penticio Ciui*tatis* p*r*ed*icte*, et adtunc et ib*ide*m recognovit se debere dict*e* d*omi*ne Regine, Quinquaginta libras Legal*is* monet*e* Angl*ie*, Soluend*as* eid*e*m d*omi*ne Regine, hered*ibus* vel Successor*ibus* suis &c, Et nisi &c.

John Aldersey

The Condic*i*on of this Recognizauns is, that where-as the aboue bounden Johñ Aldersay hath Cellered w*i*thin the Citie of Chester, as his owne good*es* (as he Affirmeth / Sixe Butt*es* of Seck, lately transported [2]into the Ryver and porte of Chester, aborde a Barque Called the Meyden, of the Towne of Airre in Scotland, whereof was M*aste*r, Dauid Killymer / And whiche wines, Ralphe Allen and Richard Broster, Sheriff*es* of the Citie of Chester, haue seased vpon as forfeited, because they were sold w*i*thout, and before they were gauged; and besides, yt app*er*eth by A note shewed, that the said wines (amongest others) were transported into the said River vpon the m*er*ch*a*unt strang*e*rs adventure, & yet entred in the Custome booke of the said Citie in the name of the said John Aldersay, therby nerely towchinge the said John Aldersay in Othe / Iff the said John Aldersay doe well, and in good saffetie, p*re*serue and kepe all the said sixe Butt*es* of Seck in As good plite and sorte as now they are, and haue them and eu*er*y of the same Vj Butt*es* Seck furthcum*m*inge, and all the same such vj Buttes Seck, in such good sorte & safetie, doe, frank and free, deliu*er* vnto the said Sheriff*es* vpon the demaund of the said Maior & Sheriff*es*, or eny of them, or

[1] leaf 15, back. [2] leaf 16.

vpon warninge lefte at the now Dwellinge howse of the said John Aldersay *wi*thin the said Citie, in suche man*er* and forme, and in suche order, as he the same Maior shall lymite or appointe, *wi*thout fraude, guile, deceipt, or contradicc*i*on, Or ells, well and truly contente and paie vnto the said Sheriff*es* the Som*me* of fiftie pound*es* of good and lawfull money of England, vpon the resonable demaund of the said Sheriff*es*, or eth*er* of them, in one whole & entier paym*ent*, *wi*thout fraud or desept, in lue or satisfaction of the said wines, That then this p*re*sent Recognizans to be voide, or ell*es* yt to stande in force and vertue.

Bond by the Father of a Bastard Child, to provide for the Child, and marry its Mother. A.D. 1591.

[1] M*emorandum*, q*uo*d xiij° die decembr*is* Anno R*egni* Regine Elizab*ethe* &c, xxxiiij^to^, Joh*ann*es Title et Georgius Title de Ci*vit*a*te* Cestr*ie*, Brickm*aker*s (?), et Fulco Carter [or Carler] de ead*em*, Baker, vener*unt* in p*ro*priis p*er*sonis suis coram Thoma lynyall, maior*e* Ciui*tatis* p*re*d*icte*, et recogn*overunt* se deber*e* d*icte* d*omi*ne Regine xx^li^, Soluend*as* &c, et nisi &c.

George Title.

A bastard childe.

The Condic*i*on of this Recognizaunce is suche, that whereas there is one Ellen, Bastard daughter of Jane Davies of the Citie of Chester, borne *wi*thin the same Citie, whereof thaboue bounden George Title is the reputed father, whoe confesses himselfe to be the father of the said Childe // if therefore the said george Title doe p*re*sently take into his Custody the said Ellen, and her at all times hereafter well and sufficiently Maintaine, p*ro*vide for, norse, and kepe *wi*th all thing*es* as beseemeth, and so as thencorporac*i*on of the said Cyty shall not be in any wise Charged nor burthened with her kepinge; And also if the said George Title, [2] before the feaste daie of thappostles Phillipp and James next com*m*inge, shall espowse, wed, and take to his wief, the said Jane, doing accordinge to the ecclesiasticall*e* Lawes of this Realme,—if the Lawes of holy Church will it p*er*mitt & suffer, and that the said Jane will therewith consent and Agree,—That this &c Or ell*es* &c.

Bond by a Sadler to pay his Fine for putting red and white Harness in his Shop before taking it to the Common Hall.

[3] 1591. Mayor's Books, Chester.

M*emorandum*, q*uo*d xv^to^ die decemb*ris*, Anno R*egni* Reg*i*ne Elizab*ethe*, &c, xxxiiij^to^ / Ric*ard*us Ince de Ciui*ta*te Cestr*ie*, Sadlor, ven*it* in

Ricardus Ince.

[1] leaf 16, back. [2] leaf 17. [3] leaf 26.

comparuit / propria persona sua, coram Thoma lynyall, Maiore, Ciuitatis predicte, et Recognovit se debere dicte domine Regine, quinque libras, Soluendas eidem[1] domine Regine, heredibus vel Successoribus suis &c, et nisi &c.

The Condicion of this Recognizaunce is suche, That whereas thaboue bounden Richard Ince hath receyued into his howse diuers parcelles of Red and white harnes northenwardes within the said Citie, which came thither to be sold, before the same cam to the comen hal, contrary to the orders of the said Citie in that behalfe / Iff the said Richard Ince doe personally appere before the said Maior, the Aldermen, Sheriffes & comen Councell of the same Citie, At the next Assemble there to be holden, and then and ther contente and paie soe muche of the Appointed Paine in that behalfe, as by that Assembly shalbe Lymited & Agreed vpon, That then &c Or elles &c.

Bond by a young Goldsmith to provide for his Bastard Child when born, and for its Mother till a month after its birth. 1592.

comparuit et relaxatur per maiorem

John lingley

[2]*Memorandum*, quod nono die mensis Februarii, Anno Regni Regine Elizabethe &c xxxiiij^to^: Johannes Lingley, Junior, de Ciuitate Cestrie, goldsmith; Ricardus lingley, de eadem Ciuitate, shomaker; Robertus leeche, de dicta Ciuitate, Barbor; Johannes Farrow de dicta Ciuitate, lynen-draper, et Johannes Hutchens de Ciuitate Cestrie predicte, hatter, venerunt, in propriis personis suis, Coram Thoma Lynyall, maiore eiusdem Ciuitatis, in Interiori Penticio eius[3] predicti, et recognoverunt se, et quemlibet eorum, pro se debere dicte domine Regine, Quadraginta libras legalis monete Anglie, Soluendas eidem[1] domine Regine, heredibus vel Successoribus suis, &c, Et nisi, &c.

The Condicion of this Recognizance is such, That whereas one Elizabeth Phillips, spinster, is greate with Childe by the aboue bounden John Lingley, begotten by him in Basterdy, whereof provicion is made, as well for her maintenaunce, as keepinge of the Childe when it shall be borne / Therefore, if the said John Lyngley, vpon his owne propper Costes and Charges, doe well and sufficientlie mayntene and kepe the saide Elizabeth Phillips with sufficiente meate, drinke and lodginge, at all tymes hereafter, vntill she shall be deliuered of the saide Childe, and duringe the

[1] The scribe 'rightly held Elizabeth to be of the masculine gender.' [2] leaf 26.
[3] Till lately there were Pentice and Portmote Courts. The Pentice Court was for the admittance of Freemen.

space of one monethe nexte after she shalbe deliue*r*ed of her such Childe, if she, the same Elizabeth Phillips shall Accepte of such her mayntenans by the saide John) Lyngley, [1]or if she shall refuse the same such mainten-*au*nce, then vpon knowledge thereof, to be geven by her to *th*e saide John,[1] he the said John) Lyngley, duringe all the said terme and tyme thensfurth, vntill she shalbe deliue*r*ed of her saide Childe, and duringe the said terme of oone whole moneth then nexte folowinge, doe Content and paie, or Cause to be trulie Contented and paide, to the vse of the said Elizabeth Phillips, weekelie and every weeke, two shillinges of leafull money of England towarde*s* her mayntenance and keepinge; And alsoe doe, at all tymes from the birth of the said Childe, take to it, and the same Childe sufficientlie, vpon his owne propper Costes and Charges, Cause to be Nursed, found and mayntened at all tymes thensfurth, and thereof fullie and Clierly discharge the said Elizabeth and all her frendes; And alsoe if the said John) Lingley doe p*er*sonallie App*er*e at the nexte gen*er*all sessions of her highnes peax*e*, to be houlden and kepte w*i*thin the said Citie before the Maior and Justice*s* of peax*e* thereof, and then and there abide such further order as shalbe taken by the said maior and two other iustices of the peax*e* w*i*thin the said Citie, towchinge the said Childe, accordinge to the statute in that behalfe, and vpon his App*er*ans doe not departe without the speciall lycence of the said maior, That then this recongnizaunns to be voide, or el*les* yt to stande in force &c.

Bond to secure a debt of 50*s*. to a City Servant. 1592.

[2]1591 (and 1592). Mayors' Books, Chester.

Vacatur M*emorandum*, quod decimo die m*ar*cii, Anno R*egni* Reg*i*ne Elizabe*the* &c xxxiiij^{to}, Joh*anne*s Ridley, s*er*uiens ad panem Ciui*tat*is Cestr*ie*, venit in propria persona sua coram Thoma lynyall, maiore Ci*uitatis* p*redicte*, in Interiori Penticio eiusd*em* Ciui*tatis*, et tunc et ib*id*em recognovit se debere d*icte* d*omi*ne Regine, Quinq*ue* libras legal*is* monet*e* Anglie, Soluend*as* eid*em*.

John) Ridley eisdem die et Anno p*redictus* Joh*anne*s Ridley cognovit se debere Ran*dulpho* Caton, vni ex s*er*uien*tibus* ad clavas Ci*uitatis* Cestr*ie* p*redicte*, V^{libras}, Soluend*as* eidem Ran*dulpho*, aut suo c*er*to Attor*nato*, executor*ibus* vel Administrator*ibus*, siue Assignat*oribus* suis, Et nisi &c.

The condic*i*on of this Recognizauns is such, that if thaboue bounden John) Ridley, his executors, Admin*ist*rators or Assignes doe well and

[1—1] Interlined. [2] leaf 30.

trulie Content and pay, or Cause to be trulie Contented and paid, vnto thaboue-named Randle Caton, his executors, Administrators or Assignes, the some of Fiftie shillinges of good and leafull money, At, in, and vpon the feaste day of thappostles Phillipp and Jacob nexte ensuinge the date hereof, in one whole and entier payment, *w*ithout fraud, guile, deceipte or Contradicc*i*on, that then this present Recognizaunce to be voyd and of none effecte, Or ell*es* it to stand, be, and remayne, in full power, force and vertue.

Censure of two men for entering an Innholder's, a Freeman's house, and arresting him.

[1]Apud Ciuitat*em* Cestr*ie*, die solis, vi*delicet*, ix^mo^ die Aprilis Anno R*egni* John) miln*er* Reg*i*ne Elizabethe, &c, xxxiiij^to^. (1592.)

At w*hi*ch daie, the wief of Thom*as* Barker of the said Citie, inholder, cam in proper p*er*son, before the said maior, Edward Halsall, esquier, Vicechamb*er*len of the countie Palentine of Chester, and others, Justices of peaxe within the said*e* Citie, and complayned Againste Joħn Miln*er*, pursivant, for that he, the same miln*er*, yesterdaie night laste, accompaned *w*ith Joħn Burton, seru*au*nte to Mr. Joħn Dutton, of dutton, esquier, entred into the Dwelling Howse of the said*e* Barker *w*ithin the said Citie, and arested him, and drew him out of his howse to or toward*es* the Castle of Chester, and detained him prison*er*, and as yet so remaineth, Wherevpon, beinge hear[d]e & exa*m*i*n*d, forasmuch as this mann*er* of entrinnge into a freemans howse, and his arreste thervpon, is againste the liberties of this Citie, a*n*d not sufferable, the said areste is voide, & the p*r*ison*er* to be restored to his owne howse, & the said Miln*er* rebuked for his such iniuryous dealinge in that behalfe disliked, & caused to be reformed by the said Mr. Halsall, Vicechamb*er*lains, consent & good likinge.

[2]comp*a*ruit et relaxatur p*er* maior*um* ex assensu p*ar*tiu*m*.

Order on the late Sheriffs to pay 28*s*. 10*d*. for an Execution Debt and costs. (See p. 152, above.)

[3]1592. Chester. Mayors' Books.

[2]Apud Ciuitat*em* Cestr*ie*, xiiij^to^ die April*is*, Anno R*egni* Reg*i*ne Elizab*ethe* &c, xxxiiii^to^. (1592.)

Rob*er*t Amery and Ric*hard* Knee, late sheriff*es*, beinge complained vpon by Mr. Dauid lloid for xxviij s vj d^t^ debt [&] iiij d dam*ages* for the debt of James Wilkinson, vpon execuc*i*on when they were sheriff*es*,

[1] leaf 36. [2] ? Don't apply to the case above. [3] leaf 36, back.

whervpon it is now ordered that they, the said Robert Amery & Ric*hard* Knee, shall contente and paie to the said D*auid* lloid the seid xxviij s x d. vpon to-morow fortenight next com*m*inge, or ell*es* to be comitted.

Certificate by the Mayor of the due payment of £400 secured by a Statute Merchant.

19 Aug. 1592. ([1]1591-2. Mayor's Book, Chester.[2])

To all Christen People to whom this present wrytinge shall Come to be seene, heard, or redd, Thomas Lynyall, maior of the Cittie of Chester, Send greetinge. Knowe yow, me, the sayd Maior, to haue seene, and throughlie redd, A Certen note entred in the Booke of the maioraltie of Will*iam* Hamnet, Alderman deceassed, late maior of the sayde Citie, and in the tyme of his maioraltie, and before him as maior: the tenor of w*hi*ch note, soe entred in the saide booke, doeth followe in these p*rese*nt*es* :—

"Apud Ciuitatem Cestr*ie*, xv^to^ die Julij, Anno R*egni* R*egi*ne Elizab*ethe* &c, xxxj°, Coram Will*el*mo Hamnet, maior*e* Ciui*tatis* p*redicte* / whereas the xiij day of October, A*nno* R*egni* R*egine* Eliz*abethe* &c, Vicesimo nono / John) Dutton, of Dutton in the Countie of Chester, esquyer, And Peter Dutton, gent*leman*, sonne and heire Apparant of the same John), haue knowledged A statute m*er*ch*a*unt of viij C^li^ the same thirtenth of October, to Nicholas Looker of Waterford, w*i*thin the Realme of Ireland, m*er*ch*a*unt, and Rob*er*t Cutt, Citizen and Iremonger of London, vpon Certen Defeizaunce for payment of iiij C^li^ / Edmund Gamull of the said Citie, Alderman, this present xvj^th^ of July, preserued[3] vnto me, the said Maior, the said Statute and defeizaunce, as Atturney to and for the sayd Nicholas Looker and Robert Cutt, and acknowledged that the sayd foure hundreth pound*es* was iustlie and trulie payd and satisfied, according to the said defeizaunce, and Affirmed the Agreement of the said p*ar*ties; And in token thereof, hath now deliu*er*ed and Cancelled the said Statute and Defeizaunce, to thend that the Recognizaunce thereof may be Adnihilated and voyd, and a vacat therevpon to be entred. Will*iam* Hamnet, Maior, Edmund Gamull[4] / And further knowe yow, that the day of the date of these p*rese*nt*es* the said Edmund Gamull Came before me, the said maior, And willinglie of himself, w*i*thout Compulsion, hath deposed vpon the holie Evangelist of god, that all and singuler the matter menc*ion*ed in mann*er* and forme aforesaid recyted, be true, and were trulie sett downe according to the truth; And that he, the said Edmund

[1] leaf 56, back. [2] On leaf 56 is an entry of 4 Sept., 34 Eliz. (A.D. 1592).
[3] ? presented. [4] MS. Gannull.

Gamull was deputed and Aucthorised by the said Nicholas Looker and Robert Cutt, to receave the som*m*e of One hundreth pound*es*, the rest and last payment of the said Som*m*e of iiij C[li], of the said John Dutton, w*hi*ch C[li] he sayth he did receave accordinglie, and the same truly payd over to the vse of the sayd Nicholas Looker and Rob*er*t Cutt; And also he had Aucthoritie therevpon to deliu*er* the said Obligac*i*on or wryting Obligatory of the sayd Statut to be Cancelled, which was donne [1] Accordinglie; And that, in testemony thereof, the said note was entred into the said Maiors booke; and that this deponent did subscrybe his name thervnto, in further testymony thereof." All w*hi*ch to be true, I, the said Thom*as* Lynyall, Maior, doe by these p*re*sent*es* Certefie. And to thintent, the more Credicte may be herevnto geven, I, the said Thomas Lynyall, maior, haue to these present*es* Caused to be Affixed and set, the Seale of myne office of Maioraltie of the said Citie. Dated at the sayd Citie of Chester, the Nynetenth day of August Anno R*egni* Reg*i*ne Elizabeth*e*, &c, tricesimo quarto.

[2] 1597-8. Mayor's Book, Chester.

The names of those who haue the keies of the Thresure howse, and Chestes therin. /

Mr Maior, 2 hanginge Locks, & of the ch*ar*tres the middest.
Mr Greene, the fourth ther folowinge southward.
Mr Birde, the second of the Coffer wherin the charters coffer is /
Mr Ric*hard* Bavand*e*, firste vpon the right hande.
Mr Brerewod, the furthest sowth side of the chest adioning to the dore.
Mr Broughton, of the longest coffer.
Mr Gamull [MS. Gannull], the first and next to the door.
Mr Will*iam* Walle, seconde of the cofer wherin the ch*ar*tre cofer is.
Mr Dauid Lloid, the second next to Mr Gamull.
The Sheriff*es*, the furmost but one southward.
Thrēs.

[3] List of 29 Bakers of Chester (Will*elmus* Kinge senior / Alderman*us* art*is* p*re*d*ic*t*e* ju*ratus* /) with the Othe, as in 1591 Book. (1597.)

[4] List of 27 Butchers of Chester ("but Tho: Bebinton—dead") with the Othe as in 1591 Book. (1597.)

"Godfridus Wynne }
Thom*as* Holbrok } Alderman*i* art*is* p*re*d*ic*t*e*

[1] leaf 57. [2] leaf 1. [3] leaf 3, back. [4] leaf 4.

[Bond by a Merchant not to sell 70 Bushels of Rye without leave of the Mayor. A.D. 1597.]

[1]1597-8. Mayor's Book, Chester.

Coram Thoma Greene, Ald*ermano* et Justic*ia* pac*is* Ciui*tatis* Cestr*ie*.

M*emorandum*, q*uo*d vicesimo nono die Octobris, Anno R*egni* R*egin*e Elizabeth*e* &c tricesimo nono, Thomas Thropp, Junior, de Ciui*ta*te Cestr*ie*, mercator, venit in propria p*er*sona sua Coram prefat*o* Thoma Greene, Ald*ermano* et Justic*ia* pacis Ciui*tatis* pred*icte* in interior*i* Penticio eiusdem Ciui*tatis*, et adtunc et ib*id*em recogn*ovit* se debere d*ict*e d*omi*ne Regine quadragint*a* Libras bone et legalis monet*e* Anglie, Solvend*as* eidem d*omi*ne Regine, hered*ibus*, vel Successoribus suis, in festo Omni*um* Sanctor*um* prox*imo* futur*o*, Et nisi, &c.

The Condic*i*on of this Recognizaunce is such, That whereas the abouebounden Thomas Thropp hath bought of one Will*ia*m Watson, servant to one Mr Brererey of York, marchant, the quantetie of threescore and tenne busshells of Rye of the good*es* of the said Mr Brererey and Henry Thompson of the Citie of Yorke, m*er*chant, his Cop*ar*tene*r*, w*i*th intent, as is supposed, to sell the same againe at a deerer rate then he bought the same; Therefore, yf the said Thomas Thropp, by him self, nor by any other p*er*son or p*er*sons for him, or to his vse, doe not vtter or sell the said threescore and tenne busshells of Rye, nor any parte or p*ar*cell thereof, to any manner of p*er*son or p*er*sons, w*i*thout the speciall lycens of the maior of the said Citie of Chester for the tyme being, first hade and obtayned, That then &c, or ells &c /.

[Bond by a Searcher of Tand Leather and Leather-ware, for his due Fulfilling of his Office. A.D. 1597.]

[2]1597-8. Mayor's Book, Chester.

Willelmus Hulton / Thomas Newp*arte* / Thomas Tilston / Ric*ard*us Woodcock / Serch*ers*, Sealers & Regesters.

M*emorandum*, q*uo*d xxij^{do} die decembris, Anno R*egni* Regine Elizabeth*e* &c Quadragesimo: Will*el*m*us* Hulton, Ran*dulph*us Ince senior, et Will*el*m*us* Vrmeston de Ciui*ta*te Cestr*ie*, shomakers, Vener*unt* in prop*riis* p*er*sonis suis cora*m* Thoma*s* Fletcher, maior*e* Ci*uitatis* p*redicte*, in Interior*i* Pentic*io* Ci*uitatis* pre*dicte*, et adtunc et ib*id*em recognover*unt* se debere d*icte* d*omi*ne Regine quadragint*a* libr*as* legal*is* monet*e* anglie, Soluend*as* eidem d*omi*ne Regine, vel Successor*ibus* suis, &c, Et nisi &c.

[1] leaf 5. [2] leaf 12, back.

The condic*i*on of this Recognizauns is such, that whereas thaboue bounden Will*iam* Hulton is admitted by the aboue-Named Maior, one of the Se*r*che*r*s, seale*r*s & Regesters of all Tanned lether and made wares of leth*er* in the county of the citie of chester, Accordinge to one pointe or article of one Estatute thereof, made in the firste yere of the Raigne of the quenes Ma*ie*stie that now is / And where also it is p*ro*vided by the same estatute that if any defalt or negligens in do[i]nnge of Dutie in that behalfe be made or founde in any of the Serche*r*s, Seale*r*s, or Regeste*r*s of such lether & made wares w*hi*ch so yerely shulde be chosen, That then the Maior & othe*r*s Admittinge such officers to that charge shulde forfeit for eu*ery* defalt in not doinge their duties accordinge to the same estatute, fortye shillinge*s*, as by the said estatute thereof made, more plainly appe*r*eth. / If the said Will*iam* Hulton doe iustly and truly, w*i*thout favour, Affection, concelem*ent*, mallice, collusion or displeasure, exercise, occupie, discharge and doe the said Office as one of the Se*r*che*r*s, Seale*r*s & Regeste*r*s of Tanned Lether and made wares of leth*e*r in the Countie of the Citie of chester from time to time & att all times hereafter, so longe as he shalbe charged or chargeable therw*i*th, or shall remaine in that Office & charge, Accordinge to the tenor, p*ur*port, effect & true meani*n*ge of the same estatute, And doe also accomplishe, p*er*forme, oversee & put in execuc*i*on hensforth all man*er* of thinge & thinge*s*, Acte and Actes belonginge or appe*r*tayn*i*nge to the said Offices accordingly / And also if the said W*illi*am Hulton, his executors, administrators & Assignes, from time to time, & at all & eu*er*y time and times hereafter for Ever, Doe well and truly exone*r*ate, acquite, discharge, save, and Harmeles kepe, the said Thom*as* Fletcher, Maior, his executors and administrators, of, for, & from all fines, forfeitures, ame*r*cem*entes*, troubles, suite*s*, Coste*s* and charge*s*, as the said Thom*as* Fletcher, Maior, shall happen to incurr, sustaine, have or endure, by [1] the admittaunce of the said Will*iam* Hulton into the said Offices, That then this Recognizauns to be Voide, Or elle*s* it to stande in full power, force & Vertue.

[Agreement by a Hatmaker, that, on his failing to pay £12, by 3 instalments, his Creditor may take possession of his Shop, Tools, and Goods.]

[2] 1597-8. Mayor's Book, Chester.

Apud Ciuitat*em* Cestr*ie* sec*un*do die Januarij	Anno R*egni* R*egi*ne Elizab*ethe* &c Quadragesimo. (1598.)

[1] leaf 13. [2] leaf 13, back.

At w*hi*ch daie and yere, John) Allen, of the Citie of chester, Hatmaker, cam in his owne proper p*er*son before me, the maior of the same citie, And acknowledged him-self to be indebted vnto Rob*er*t Fletcher, one of the sheriff*es* of the said Citie, for money owing to him, and of him to be taken vp, Twelue pound*es* of good & lawfull money of england ;—And for want of other securitie to assure the payment thereof at Easter, midsom*er*, & michelmas next com*i*nge, or w*i*thin 3 daies en*suing* of the same feast*es* ensuinge, by equall porc*i*ons, Graunted that the said Rob*er*t Fletcher shall p*re*sently, vpon any defalt, enter into the Shop scituate in the northgatestret w*i*thin the said citie now in his occupac*i*on, of the land*es* of Humffrey Houghton of Manchester in the countie of lanc*aster*, m*er*ch*a*unt, and quietly enioye thensforth the same, being tennau*n*t at will*e* to the said Humfrey Houghton, and to haue as his owne all the implem*entes* of good*es* therin, and all the interest thereof, of the said John) Allen ; and thervpon the said Rob*er*t Fletcher deliu*er*ed to me, the maior, A l*ett*re vnder the hand and Seale of the said Humfrey Haughton, of his assent & good will of the acceptans of the said Rob*er*t Fletcher to be his ten*au*nte at will of the said shop, payinge the accostomed due Rent therefore, if any defalt of paym*en*t were made / And thervpon it is now, befor me, fully agreed by the said p*ar*ties, That if the said John) Allen, his executors, administrators or Assignes, doe well & truly content and paie, or cause to be truly contented and paied, vnto the said Rob*er*t Fletcher, his executors or assignes, the said Som*m*e of Twelve pound*es* of good and lawfull money of England, in man*er* & forme aforesaid, That then the said John) Allen thensforth to continue tenna*n*t at will of the said shop to the said Humfrey Haughton, as now he doeth, pa[i]nnge the yerely Rent thereof, and to retaine the said implem*entes* as his owne good*es* ; And in defalt of any of the said seu*er*all paym*entes*, in p*ar*te or in all, over or after any of the said seu*er*all Feastes daies of paym*en*t thereof, [1]and after the space of three daies, eu*er*y of the said seu*er*all feast*es* daies next folowing, That then he, the said Rob*er*t Fletcher, shall enter into the said shop, and all the implem*entes* therin, And i*m*mediatly from any such defalt of any such paym*ent*, quietly to enioie the same shop as ten*a*nt at will to the said Humfrey Haughton, at the vsuall Rent thereof, and haue to his owne vse for ever, all the said implement*es*, w*i*thout the lett or disturba*n*s of the said John) Allen, his executo*rs*, or Assignes ; And also fully Agreed by Assent, that the maior of the said Citie of chester for the time beinge, shall Cause p*er*formans of this agrem*en*t to be had vpon eith*er* side, of the said John) Allen & Rob*er*t Fletcher, w*i*thout any suite in lawe.

(signd by) Tho : Fletcher maior
Robart Fletcher

[1] leaf 14.

[The Stewards of the Fishmongers' Company sent to Gaol, for buying Ling and Cod for their Company, instead of letting the Mayor buy it for the Citizens.]

[1] 1597-8. Mayor's Book, Chester.

28 die Marcii 1598.

eod*em* die

Whereas M*aste*r Maior of this Citie, as clerk of the m*ar*ket w*i*thin the same / hath bene in hande to buy certaine newland fishe, Linge and Cod, for a Com*m*on bargaine, to the vse of this Citie: Thomas Lynaker the yong*e*r and John Scons, Stewarde*s* of the fishmongers, haue, vnknowen unto[2] the said Maior, and Vnder hand, Boght the said fish for their owne vse, & of their Compeny, out of M*aste*r Maiors hand*es*, w*hi*ch they confesse to be true: Therefore it is fully agreed by the Aldermen and Justices of pea*c*e whose names are subscribed, That the said Steward*es*, for ther said Offence and abuse, shall p*re*sently be comitted to the gaile of the northgate w*i*thin the said Citie: ther to remaine vntill they shalbe thens deliue*r*ed by Assembly.

Mr Grant Warb*ur*ton	Mr Valen*tine* Broughton
Mr Tho: Greene	Mr John Fyton
Mr Will*iam* Bird	Mr Dau[i]d lloid
Mr Ric*hard* Bavand	Mr fulk Aldersey

[Award of the Mayor as to the possession and use of a Table and Frame.]

[3] 1597-8. Mayor's Book, Chester.

7 die Marcii (1598).

Whereas Matter of Controu*e*rsie Came in question this day before me, Thomas Fletcher, Maior of the Citie of Chester, betwene Katheryne Whitched, spinster, and Margaret Coldock, wief of Ric*hard* Coldock, shomaker, for and conce*r*ning the right of and vnto a table and frame in the possession of the said Katheryne, wherevnto the said Margaret Claymeth prop*er*tie,—I, the said Maior, doe, by Consent of both the said p*ar*ties, order that the said Kath*eryne* shall, during her naturell lief, haue the possession and vse of the said table & frame; and after the decesse of the said Katheryne, that the said Margaret shall haue and enioy the said table and frame to her owne prop*er* vse for euer; and that in the meane tyme, the said Katheryne shall not alter, sell, exchange, or dep*ar*te w*i*th the same.

Tho: Fletcher, maior.

[1] leaf 21, back. [2] MS. vnunto. [3] leaf 24.

[1] 1597-8. Mayor's Book, Chester.

[1598. Letter from Lord Burleigh to the Officers of the Port of Chester, authorising them to enter, without tax, the Gascony wines of a City Merchant's Widow.]

After my hartie Commendac*i*ons, Whereas I vnderstand that yow haue made scruple to take entrie of certeine Tonnes of Gascoine wynes broughte into that port in december laste, beinge the proper good*es* of Ales Massy, wydowe, late wife of william Massy, merchant, of *that* Cittie, deceassed, as also of certein other Tonnes of Gascoine wynes, brought in thither by william Massey his sonne, late merchant and free citesin of *that* Cittie, also deceassed, whose administratrix the said Ales Massy is. For-as-much as I fynde by a graunte by privy seale, from hir ma*ies*tie, dated the xxjth daye of maye in the ninthe yeare of hir raigne, that her pleasure is, (for good Considerac*i*ons in the said pryvye seale specified,) That all merchant*es* inhabitant*es* and Free Citisins of *that* Cittie shalbe freed and discharged from payment of any Imposte for such wynes as they bringe into that port / And Forasmuch as also I haue receyved a L*ett*re from the Maior and Aldermen of that Cittie, whereby they doe certifye vnto me, that all Free-mens wydowis of that Cittie, during theire wydowhood, by the Custome of the said Cittie Have Vsed, and ought to have and enioie, all [such] trades, Fredomes, & liberties as their husband*es* vsed in their life tyme, w*hi*ch Custome hath bene vsed and allowed of tyme out of mynde / Therefore, Theise are to will and require yow to take entrie of all the aforesaid wynes of the said wydow massies, as well those that she hath as administratrix to W^{m}. Massey, as of hir owne proper wynes, w*i*thout takinge or demaundinge Imposte for the same wynes. And this shalbe yo*ur* discharge in *that* behalf / From my howse at westm*inster* the xiiijth of Apr*il* 1598.

directed this — Yo*ur* lovinge frende

To my lovinge frend*es*
ye Officers of ye port — W: Burgheley.
of Chester.

in thend of that Let*ter*, this:
Officers of ye port of
Chester ./ — Tho: Fletcher
written in that l*ett*re this also: — Maior

Recepta p*er* nos, viij die Maij, p*er* man*us* Richardi Massie.

[1] leaf 28.

S : Coles
Edw : Kitchin *pro* /
Cust*ode*.

Truly copied out and exa*min*ed, the xiij[th] daie of May 1598, by the comaundm*en*t of M*aste*r maior; by me, Will*iam* Knight.

/T/ /r/ x

[1] 1597-8. Mayor's Book, Chester.

[Fine for not bringing Brass for Sale in the Common Hall.]

11 : Maij 1598.

Whereas Thom*as* Simon of the Citie of Chester, Butcher, Lately bought w*i*thin the same Citie, c*er*tain Bras w*hi*ch cam from beyond sea, out of Ireland, by way of Marchundizes, before the same was brought to the com*m*on hall of the said Citie, contrary to the orders of this Citie in that behalf, wherby he hathe forfeited xl s to this incorporac*i*on,—whose falt being duly exa*min*d, the same is p*ro*ved to be true, w*hi*ch he doeth not denie; whervpon It is now ordered

Tho: Simon by M*aste*r Maior, that he shall pay the whole xl s. as by the said ordre is appointed; and that in regard of his confess*i*on and submiss*i*on, he shall haue thereof retorned to him as forgeven, Twenty shilling*es*, & the [? that] by intreaty of his good frend*es*.

[Receipt and Forwarding of Letters by Post.]

[The 7th and 6th leaves from the end of this 1597-8 Mayor's Book, have entries of the receipt and dispatch of Letters—of which I copy the first and last two :]

Post *Lett*res hoc Anno.

15 Novemb*er* 1597, 8 in the eveninge

Then receaued a pacquet of L*ett*res from Bewmarres by the hand*es* of Richard Makin, directed for her Ma*iesties* affayrers to the right ho*norable* S*ir* Rob*er*t Cecyll his ho*use* :

20 : decemb*er* 1597,—6 in the eveninge
& gave it to the poste

Then Rece*aued* out of Ireland, a pacquet directed for her Ma*iesties* speciall Affaie*rs*, to the right Ho*norable* S*ir* Rob*er*t Cecill, knight, principall Secretory, &c., indorsed "post hast, hast, post hast": Dublin 17 : decemb*ris* Ad dublin*iam* (?)

* * * * * * * * *

[1] leaf 28, back.

21th of Septembre 1598. 11 : in Ye night

Bewmarris from ye Maior ther. Then receved thens, inclosed in Mr Thomas Bulkely, maior ther, his Lettre: 2 packetes, both directed for her Maiesties affaiers to the lords and others of her Maiesties moste Honorable privey councell, with post haste, whereof thon[1] indorsed "per Adamum Dubliniensem" &c, which were maintenaunt per Mullinex', Master Maior of this Cities appointment, deliuered to Mr. John Francis to be posted hens ./

29 September, 6 in the eveninge.

Receaued out of Ireland 3 seuerall lettres, whereof thone for her Maiesties affayres, directed to the Erle of Essex, Earle Marshall of England, and to Sir Robert Cecyll, with 'hast, post hast' Adam Dublin; one other to the said Sir Robert Cecyll, & the other to Capte Francis Stafford.

[Gifts of Money by the Mayor and Common Council, 1597-8 :]

[2]1597-8. Mayor's Book, Chester.

viijo novembris 1597

Then, by the appointment of Mr Smith, Mr Greene and Mr Wm. Aldersey—geven to Doctor Canon his wife, to depart this City to Ipswich, where she was borne, with her children, vpon her promis never to retorne hither to be troublesom to this Citie ... ... } vj s viij d

13 november

Then geven, by the appoyntment of the said aldermen & the reste, to xj soldiers of therle of Essex men, their ship being Caste awaie in Walles, fourteene shillinges vj d, per Dalby ... ... } xiiij s vj d

25 November

Then by the appoyntment of Mr Greene, to a poore man, one Frances Throgmorton ... ... } xij d

7 December 1597

Then, to Mr. Greene, for the burial of Margaret Huntington ij s

[1] the one. [2] 3rd leaf from end.

14 Decemb*er*

Then geven to the burial of Ric*hard* gunn*er*s Childe, him self lying bed Rotton ... ... } xij d

17 December

Then, by thappoyntm*ent* of Mr Maior, for the Buryall of the said Rich*ar*d Gunner ... ... } iij s iiij d

Then more to a soldier into lancaster ... ... xij d

24 Decemb*er*

Then more to a gent, p*er* man[1] ... ... xij d

Then to Rob*er*t p*er*sivall, p*er* man[1] ... ... iii s iiij d

Then to Peter Buxy [or Bupy], p*er* man*um*[1] ... ... iij s iiij d

Then to the late crier his sonne, p*er* ma*num*[1] ... ... xij d

Then to cicely Gaymestral (?), p*er* man[1] ... ... xij d

To nicolsons lame wench ... ... xij d

To wedow Richardson, 7 Jan*uary* (?) 1597(-8) ... ... xij d

To John Nemor 12 Jan*uary*, per man*um*[1] ... ... xij d

To Ric*hard* Evans, soldier, one Arme, 16 Jan*uary* (?) per man*um*[1] ... ... } xij d

To m*ar*gare*t* stanley, lame, the 24th Jan*uary* per man*um*[1] xij d

To wm Smithyman, p*er* Ridley, 27 Jan*uary* ... ... xij d

To the sonne of James Banestr, to send him vp to london, p*er* man*um*, 7 s Fe. 8 159(8) ... . } v s.

[2]14 Feb. 1597(-8)

Then to Tho*mas* Slater, p*er* Throp ... ... vj d

18 Feb. 1597(-8)

Then to 2 fleminge*s* ... ... vj d

21 Feb.

Then to a lame soldier, to london ... ... xij d

22 Feb.

Then to A maid of hanbridg vp A Wusnipne (?) per manum (?) ... ... } vj d

10 Marcij 1797(-8)

Then geven to a poore wom*an* & child*e* ... ... xij d

14 April [1598]

Then geven to the swordberer for Rob*er*t Richardson, Tho*mas* Richardson elder, his son ... ... } xij d

[1] ? All these contractions in the MS. Mr. Price and Mr. Davies read as Mai*orem*.
[2] back of leaf 3, from end.

15 April

Then, by Mr Maiors appoynt*ment*, geven to aldersey Davies, the woman of s*aint* peters & others ... ... } V s

3 maij

Then, by dalby, to 3 yorksh*ire* soldiers ... ... ij s

Then geven to a lame boy to travell into Lancasher for cuer, having a sore legg ... ... } ij s

5 May.

Then geven to one Joħn Gold & Will*iam* Barrat, souldiers, ij s

8 Maii

Then geven to one Coth (?) Stone, a frend of W*alter* Halsalls, at maiores (?) appointm*ent* ... ... } ij s

27 Maii

Then geven to John Hall, Erle of Essex man ... ... ij s

3 Junii

Then geven to John Hill, of London, lame ... ... ii s

5 Junii.

Then geven to Edmund Brickhill ... ... ij s

25 Junii

Then geven to Jo: Hollenbury ... ... ij s

27 Junii

Then geven to Fletcher the sho*m*ak*er*s daught*er*: going vp to London ... ... } iij s iiij d

Then gevin to the buryall of Benet*es* wife ... ... xij d

Then geven to a poor crepple ... ... vj d

3 July

To the wief of Robert Foxall ... ... ij s vj d

[1]7 July 1598

Then to Cranes wife, her Legg broken ... ... iiij d

13 July 1598

Then to Rob*er*t Wilson, Smith, & his wife, dangerus sick vj d

[1] last leaf but 2.

23 July 1598

Then to the Buryall of Henry Prinros his wives suster, at Mr Maiors appoint*ment*, & mot*i*ons of Mr Wm Wall to his litle apprentice	V s.

2 Septem*ber* 1598

Then to a poore soldier having a canker & pox; by the L*ords* Justices Warrantt	xij d

12 Sept*ember* 1598

To a woman, for to Cary her to Hardn, whom.[1] ... xij d

13 Sept.

Then to a sick soldier of Chery Norton ... ... xij d

22 Sept*ember*

Then to a messinger, being porkigell from bewma*ris* (?) iij s iiij d

27 Sept*ember*

Then to 3 soldiers, p*er* Ridley ... ... xij d

28 Sep*tember*

Then paid to 3 soldiers p*er* cast. ... ... iij s.
more to 2 poore soldiers ... ... xij d

20 octob*er*

Then to Ric*hard* Brostr thelder ... ... xij d

[Description of men for the "Hue and Cry."]

[2]28 Sept*ember* 1598.

hue & crie

John Whitlock, a tall man, w*i*th a yelow beand & greene bretch*es*, & white canvas dublet, lev[a]nd in norpold (?) vnd*er* cap*ten* Bingh*am* (?), rune away

4 Sep*tember* 1598

Bark [shire ?] Will*iam* Yeves, *Christ*ofer Beyman, Vincent Clifford — ran away sonday, monday, tewsday & this day

5 Sept*ember*

Th*omas* Hurst, lodging at Ric*hard* Callis (?), went away before supp*er*, being A big black man, w*i*th litle heare on his face, blew coat, faste[3] w*i*th yelow.

[1] Hawarden, home. [2] last leaf. [3] faced

Edward Cott*es*
John Phrary
John Reames } of S*ir* Rich*ard* Bingham his comp*any* (?)
John Morris
Henry Gosely

Will*ia*m Roal*es*, w*i*th a yeulwish heare & beard, & a long lock tyed vp.

John Sharpe, a tall bigg fellow w*i*th a col (?) meis cheek his Colouree.

John Bassel of meane stature,[1] well set, & a paier of whitish hose, all luste (?) about his pocket.

Henry Hove, levid out of Tinstwick in Buck*ingham*, vnd*er* captane Rich*ard* Evans.

13 Oct*ober*

Buckingh*am* Richard Gardener of Wendover } cap^r^ Stafford
William Squire of Wickham

[Distribution of Lady Savage's and Robert Offlee's Gifts to the Poor.]

[2]1597-8. Mayor's Book, Chester.

23 Decemb*er* 1597

The Lady Savage, her guifte among*es* the poore

Theis.

St Mari*es* ward	xxx s.	Thestgate ward	xxx s
St Ola*ves* ward	xxxv s.	North	xx s.
St Brid*es* ward	xx s.	S^t^. Thom*as* ward	xxx s.
St Mich*aels* ward	xv s.	St Oswald*es* ward	xxx s.
St Johns warde	xl s.	Trynitie ward	xxv s
St Giles ward	xxxv s.	S^t^ M*ar*tens ward	xxx s.

note, xx.s. in Mr Maiors hand*es* besid*es* this.

note, Margaret Hocknell, al*ias* m*ar*ten, had iij s iiij d, w*hi*ch I deliu*er*ed to Mr Maier of Mr Offles money, but it must be said of my lady Savage guifte.

[3]23 Decemb*er* 1597.

Then the Distribution of Mr Rob*er*t Offle*es* Device of x^t^ to 20 poore people having bene free of this Citie for 20 yeares at the least.

S^t^ marys ward + (1) John Bingley x s & (2) Raff Jenson x s.

St Oswald ward + (3) Hugh Stockt*on* x s, (4) Thom*as* Poole x^t^ (5) Will*ia*m Kirk*es*.

[1] MS. statut. [2] 11th leaf from end. [3] back of 11th leaf from end.

St Johns ward + (6) Raff Baxt*er* x s & Ind (?) (7) Ric*hard* Bird
St Giles ward + (8) Ric*hard* Broster thelde*r* x s.
Thestgat*e* ward + (9) Will*iam* Greene + (10) Edward allen (?), (11) wedoue Wilcok & (12) Ric*hard* Anion
St Olas (13) Rob*ert* Sleves x s.
St Brid*es* (14) Henry Puners (?) x s
St Thom*as* (15) wedew Coventree [x s.]
S^t mich*aels* // (16) Geoff*rey* Dod x s
north + (17) m*is*tr*is* Sedgwick
S^t m*ar*te*n*s + (18) wedow Ru*es* & (19) wedow loy
Tri*nit*i*e* + (20) Rog*er* Bryne

[Order by Justices of the Peace, at Sessions, that a well-off Son shall pay his poor old Father 20*s*. a Quarter, and give him a Gown.]

1598-9. Mayor's Book, Chester.

[Sessions of 24 Oct., 27 Oct., and 6 Nov. 1598.]

M*emorandum*, that At the same Sessions, Richard Broster thelder, of the Citie of Chester, Tann*er*, wholy decaied and in greate yeares, is become humble suter vnto the said Justices of peax*e* for his sustenauns and reliff, accordinge to the Laste estatute thereof made / Wherevpon, his state, yeres, and former Callinge and Countenaunce beinge deliberately wayed and Considered, and the welth and habilitie of Richard Broster, of the said Citie, Tann*er*, his sonne and heire, Likewise knowen, and the pointe also of the said estatute in that behalf, well p*er*vsed, and suche his smale yerely paym*en*t*es* which the said Ric*hard* Broster thelder hath, & have had, besid*es* this his humble suite / both of the said Ric*hard* his sonne, for his interest of his lands, as that come of the Curtesy of Thom*as* Antrobus, gent*leman*, to be bestowed vpon him, allowed & considered, It is fuly Concluded, ordered and appointed at this, her Ma*ies*t*ies* gene*r*all Sessions, by the said Justices in their open Sessions and full sittinge, That the said Ric*hard* Broster, the yonger, shall geve and paie yerely vnto the said Ric*hard* Broste*r*, thelder, duringe the Lief of the said Ric*hard* Broster theld*er*, Twentie shillinges of leafull money of England, quarterly, whereof the firste quarter to be paied in hand, over & besid*es* his forme*r* allowances & paym*en*t*es*, and shall also geve vnto him A convenient gowne, as so ordered by the said Justices, vpon the paine menc*i*oned in the said estatute. [39 Eliz. ch. 3 : see extract, p. 182.]

Ric. Rathburne Maior
Thomas Grene
Will*iam* Bird
Rob*er*t Brerewod*es*
Davyd Lloyd.
Will*iam* Aldersey.

[Order against a Plaintiff for not being ready for the Trial of his Cause.]

[1]1600. Mayor's Book, Chester.
(After an entry of 14 July, 1600.)

It is ordered, att this court of Portmote, by the saied court, that in respect, will*iam* Alcocke, Elizabeth Jeffereyes, widowe, and George Heath, defendants, att the suite of will*iam* Dunsterfield, in a plainte of eiectio*ne* ferme, had warninge to be ready for triall of the saied cause att this Portmote court, & are ready with their counsell learned; & the saied p*laintiff* not ready, & not furnished for tryall; that the saied p*laintiff* shall either paie vnto the saied def*endant*s the som*m*e of x s. for their chardges of their counsell learned, for this daie, or els the saied cause not to be tryed vppon the writt*es* already oute for the Jury, sued oute by the pl*aintiff*, butt the def*endant*s to sue oute a writte of veing far[2] & other writt*es*, with a provisoe that if twoe writt*es* come, thone shalbe only executed. And the cause, if either the x s. be paied, or els, if the same not paied, & the saied writt*es* be sued oute by the def*endant*s, to be tryed vppon mondaie, beinge the viijth daie of Septem*ber* next.

[Bonds to produce, on warning, Patrick Ford, a Dublin Merchant come to Chester, and not let him leave without the Mayor's license.]

[3]1600. Mayor's Book, Chester.

Cora*m* Henrico Hardware, ar*migero*, Maiore ciuitat*is* Cestr*ie*, xiiij^{o} August*i* 1600, Anno R*egni* Reg*ine* Elizabethe &c xlij^{do}.

[*In margin:*] comp*aruit*e et relaxatur p*er* Maior*em* sup*ra* script*us* obligator sequen*s* in hoc libro.

Patrick Foord, de Ciuitate Dublyn in regno Hib*er*nie, mercator, Rob*ertus* Bennett, de Ciuitate Cestrie, drap*er*, et Ran*dulfus* Ince de eadem, drap*er*, Cognove*runt* se debere d*omi*ne R*eg*ine Centu*m* libras legalis monete Anglie, sub Condicio*ne* sequen*ti* / viz.

[1] leaf 43, back. [2] ? venire facias [3] leaf 50.

That the said Pattrick Foord shall not dep*ar*te out of this Citie of Chester, w*i*thout the specciall licence of Henry Hardware, Esquire, maior of this Cittie of Chester; and alsoe that the said Pattrick shalbe ready to appeare w*i*thin xij howres before the said maior, vppon warninge geuen at any of the houses of the said Rob*er*te Bennett & Randle Ince, scituate in the said Cittie of Chester, and not to dep*ar*te without licens.

Coram maiore xiiij August*i*, 1600.

[*In margin:*] Comp*aruit* et relaxatur vt sup*ra* d*ictum*.

Alex*ander* Cappock, de Ciuitate Dublyn, in regno hib*er*nie, mercator, Will*elmus* Denwall de Ciuitate Cestr*ie*, drap*er*, et Thomam [*sic*] Tomlynson de eadem, Cowp*er*, tenend*i*, d*omi*ne R*egi*ne in C[li] sub Condic*ione* sequent*i*, vi*delicet*:

The Condic*i*on is, that the said Alex*ander* Cappock shall not dep*ar*te out of the Cittie of Chester w*i*thout the licence of the maior of Chester; and alsoe that the said Cappock shalbe ready—w*i*thin xij howers after warning geuen at any of the howses of the said Denwall & Thomlynson scituate in the Cittie of Chester—to apeare before the said Maior, and not to depart w*i*thout licence.

[Entries of Writs of Error.]

[1](Portmote Plea., Monday, 25 Aug. 1600.)

A writt of error pro Joh*ann*e Anderton u*ersus* Humfred*um* Stubbes, dated att Chester the xviij[th] of August xlij[do] &c primo die prox*i*me Session*is*.

A writt of error pro Henrico Manley, generoso, u*ersus* Henricu*m* Hamnet, defen*dentem*, dated att Chester the xix[th] of August xlij[do] &c primo die prox*i*me Sessionis.

[Bond to secure the appearance of Patrick Ford, on his return to Dublin, before the Lord Deputy of Ireland.]

[2]1600. Mayor's Book, Chester.

Nou*er*int vniu*ersi* per p*re*sentes, nos, Patricino Foord, de ciuitate Dublin, in regno Hib*er*nie, m*er*cator, et Alex*ander* Cappock, de ciuit*ate* Dublin p*redicte* in d*ict*o regno Hib*er*nie, m*er*cator, teneri et firmiter obligari Serenissime et excellentissime princess*e* Elizabethe, dei gracia, Anglie, Fraunce et Hib*er*nie R*egi*ne, fidei defensori, &c, &c in Quingent*is* libris bone et legalis monet*e* Anglie, Solvend*is* eid*em*

[1] leaf 53. [2] leaf 55.

d*omi*ne Re*gi*ne, aut suo cert*o* attornat*o*, hered*ibus* vel successor*ibus* suis. Ad quamquid soluc*ion*em bene et fidel*iter* faciend*am*, Obligamus nos, et vtrumque n*ost*rum per se, pro toto et in solid*o*, heredes, executore*s* et administratore*s* n*ost*ros, et heredes, executores et administratore*s* vtriusq*ue* n*ost*rum, firmiter p*er* p*re*sentes. Sigillis n*os*-*t*ris sigillat*ur*. Datum tertio die Septembr*is*, Anno regni d*omi*ne n*ost*re Elizabethe, dei gracia, Anglie, Fraunce, et Hib*er*nie Re*gi*ne, fidei defensor*is*, &c, Quadragesimo secundo /

The condic*io*n of this obligac*io*n is such, That yf the aboue bounden Patrick Foord doe, within one daie next after his arrivall att the citty of Dublin in the realme of Ireland, personally appeare before the Lo*rd* Mountioye, Lo*rd* deputie of the saied realme of Ireland, to aunsweare to such matters as on her Ma*ies*t*ie*s behalf shalbe obiected against him, and then & there doe attend, & not dep*ar*te withoute license, yf he, the saied Lo*rd* deputie, shalbe then att the saied citty of Dublin; And yf he, the saied Lo*rd* Deputie, shall not then be att the saied citty, Then, yf the saied Patrick Foord doe p*er*sonally appeare before the saied Lo*rd* Deputy within one daie next after his, the saied Lo*rd* deputies comminge vnto the saied citty, to aunsweare to such matters as shalbe obiected against him as aforesaied, and then and there doe attend, & not dep*ar*te withoute licence; Yf he the saied Lo*rd* deputy shalbe att the saied citty within one moneth next after the saied next arryvall of him the saied Patrick Foord att the same citty; And yf itt happen the saied Lo*rd* Deputy not to be att the saied citty of Dublin att the saied next arryvall of him, the saied Patrick Foord, as aforesaied, nor within one moneth after, Then, yf he the saied Patrick Foord doe p*er*sonally appeare before the Queeines ma*ies*t*ie*s counsell of the saied realme of Ireland, att the end of the saied moneth next after the saied arryvall of him, the saied Patrick Foord, att the saied citty of Dublin, then & there to aunsweare the causes & matters aforesaied, and then & there doe attend, & not dep*ar*te withoute license, That then this p*re*sente obligacion to be voied & of none effect, Or els to stand & abide in full force & vertue /

The like bond from the aboue-bounden Alex*ander* Cappocke, wherein the aboue-bounde*n* Patrick Foord is also bounde*n* for him as his surety, in the like penalty vnto her ma*ies*tie for his app*er*aunce, mutat*is* mutand*is*.

[Order for Stay of a Trial till Counsel are appointed on each side.]

[1] 1600. Mayor's Book, Chester.

xxv° die Augusti, 1601 (? 1600 : other dates after, as well as before, are 1600).

Att which Portmote it is ordered by Mr Maior & Mr Recorder, that the matter betweene James Banester, plaintiff, and John Langdale, clerke, Def*endant*, adm*inist*rator of the goodes & cattells of Thom*as* Whalley deceased, beinge putt on for tryall this Portmote, shalbe stayed as well this court, as other court*es* hereafter, vntill that there be counsell Learned to speake & pleade on both sides, because that the Yssue ioyned is a plene administrauit, and requireth counsell to sett forth the cause on both sides, soe as neither p*ar*tie be wronged therein.

[Order that the Keeper of the Conduit shall let the Stalls near it and take their rents, he cleaning the Street thro it, and paying 8*s.* a year.]

[2] 1600. Mayor's Book, Chester.

Sec*und*o die Octobr*is* 1600. Anno R*egni* R*egi*ne Elizabethe &c xlij^do^.

Memorand*um*, that the daie & yeare aboue written, yt was ordered betweene Richard Woodcocke, cryer of this Citty, and Jasp*er* Gill*am*, yeoman of the Pentice of this citty, by Henry Hardware, esquier, Maior of this citty, & Will*iam* Aldersey, Alderman, by & with the assent & consent of the saied p*ar*ties, That the saied Jasp*er* Gill*am* shall from henceforth, dur*i*nge soe longe time as he shall continewe in his office of keepinge the conduyt, haue the settinge & lettinge of the stalls att the conduyt of the saied citty of Chester, And yearely to haue & take to his owne vse, the rent, benefite & proffitt thereof, withoute gainesayinge or clayme of the saied Ric*hard* Woodcocke therevnto; In consideraci*on* whereof, it is ordered, by assent as aforesaied, that the saied Jasp*er* Gill*am* shall yearely, duringe the time aforesaied, keepe & make cleane the streete anidest the saied conduyt vnto the chanell, And shall also yearely, att the feastes of the Natiuity of S^t^. John Baptiste & St Michaell the Archaungell, paie or cause to be paied vnto the saied Ric*hard* Woodcocke, for & duringe soe longe time as he shall continewe in his saied office, the yearely rent of viij s, by even & equall porci*o*ns. And it is further ordered by assent as aforesaied, That if the saied rent be behinde

[1] leaf 55, back. [2] leaf 59.

& vnpaied, in p*ar*te or in all, by the space of iiij[or] daies next over or after either of the saied feaste daies in which the same ought to be paied, That then, & from thenceforth, it shall be lawfull to & for the saied Ric*hard* Woodcocke to haue the settinge & lettinge of the saied stalls, and to haue & take the rent, benefite & proffitt thereof to his owne vse.

H. Hardware
maior

Will*iam* Aldersey

[Promise that a Mariner and his Bark and Crew shall be ready by 25 July 1600, for the Queen's service.]

[1]1600. Mayor's Book, Chester.

xj° Julij 1600.

Memorand*um*, that the daie and yeare aboue saied, Thomas Revington of the cittie of Chester, bearbruer, did geve his word & promisse vnto Henry Hardware, esquior, Maior of the citty of Chester, and becamd*e* suerty that *Christ*ofer Hood of the citty of Chester, Maryner, shalbe ready with his barque, & himself & his servant*es*, the xxv[th] of this instant July, ffoor to be ymployed in her ma*ies*ties service as occasion shalbe mynistred.

[Receipt of 9*s.* 8*d.* for the Highway-rate.]

Vlti*mo* Septem*bris* 1600

[2]Receaved by me, Ellis Will*ia*ms, of Will*ia*ms Sare, constable of Trinity ward, the som*m*e of ix s. viij d, p*ar*cel of the money collected for the mendinge of the high waies, sessed in Mr Smithes Mayralty, ix s. viij d.

[Receipt and Forwarding of Letters by Posts.]

[3]1600. Mayor's Book, Chester.

Post L*ett*res hoc Anno.

3 December, 5 in the evening, geven to the post 8.

R*eceiued* by the hand*es* of Thomas Lynaker, one pacquet of l*ett*res dyrected for her Ma*iesties* affayres, to the right honorable the L*ordes* and others of her Ma*iesties* moste ho*norable* priuey Counsayle, w*i*th an other L*ett*re dyrected to the l*ord* high Thre*sure*r of England, for her Ma*ies*ties seruice, both subscrybed by S*ir* George Cary, knight, w*i*th 'post haste,'—which were sent away by poste.

[1] leaf 166. [2] leaf 178. [3] leaf 181.

6 of December 1599, at 9 in the night.

Receiued, one pacquet of L*ett*res p*er* poste dyrected to Mr. Maior, wherein was enclosed a pacquet dyrected for her Ma*iesties* affayres to the L*ordes* Justices of Ireland, sent over by *Christ*ofer Hoole.

26 of December 1599, at in thafter noone.

Receiued one pacquet directed for her Ma*ies*ties se*r*uice to the Lo*rd* Mountioy.

29 of December 1599, at iij[e] in thafter-noone: geven to the poste vj.

Receiued one pacquet of L*ett*res by thand*es* of Robert Gill, directed for her Ma*ies*ties affayres to the L*ordes* of her Ma*iesties* moste ho*norable* priuey Counsayle.

31 December, at 1 afternoone geven to the poste.

Receiued then a pacquet of l*ett*res by the hand*es* of Will*iam* Griffeth, a pacquet of l*ett*res dyrected for her Ma*iesties* affayres to the L*ordes* of her Ma*iesties* moste ho*norable* priuey counsayle, subscrybed by S*ir* George Cary, knight.

17 December, at 2 in *th*e afternoone.

Receiued one pacquet of l*ett*res by *th*e hand*es* of the post of Chester from Sir George Cary to *sir* Rob*er*t Cecyll; another from the sheryfe of Chesshyre to the lord*es* of the pryvy Counsell.

30 December 1599.

Receiued one pacquett of L*ett*res dyrected for her Ma*iesties* speciall affayres to S*ir* George Carey, knight, one of the Lo*rdes* Justices and Thres*urer* at warres in Ireland, w*hi*ch was deliu*er*ed vnto one Mr. Rob*er*t Lenoster, seru*a*nt to the Lo*rd* Chauncellor of Ireland.

B. Leycester.

[1]xxxj[mo] Maij 1600, att one of the clocke in the Afternoone.

Receiued one packquet by the handes of John Ellart of Washford in Ireland, which was deliu*er*ed him by Sir Arthur Chichester att Carrickfergus, to be conveyed by the poste to Sir Rob*er*te Cecill; which was, p*rese*ntley vppon the receipt thereof, deliu*er*ed to the postm*an* to be conveyed accordingly.

iiij[to] Junij 1600, from the Lo*rdes* of the counsell.

Receiued one pacquet of l*ett*res directed to Sir Henry Dockwra, Knight, att Lough foile; & deliu*er*ed to Guyle to be conveyed accordingly.

[1] leaf 181, back.

xxiij° Augusti 1600, from the L*ordes* of the counsell.

R*eceiued* one pacquet of l*ett*res directed to the Lo*rd* Mountioie, Lo*rd* deputie of Ireland; & deliu*er*ed to Will*ia*m Fräuncis the Postboie.

eod*em* die et anno.

R*eceiued* one l*ett*re from the lo*rd* Thres*urer* directed to the Lo*rd* deputie of Ireland, & deliu*er*ed the same daie to the saied Postboie.

1578?

[1]The names of those that have landes w*i*thin the Countie of Chester, and do not dwell w*i*thin the same.

In primis, the Quenes ma*jes*tie, bothe of the Erledome of Chester and Duchie of Lancaster, and the Forrest of Macclesfelde & Dalamere.

Item, the Earle of Darbye.
Item, S*i*r Christofer Hattoñ.
Item, S*i*r Gilbert Jerrarde [Gerrard].
Item, S*i*r Edmonde Trafford.
Item, S*i*r John Ratclif.
Item, S*i*r Arthure Manwaringe.
Item, M^r^. Talbot.
Item, M^r^. Neadame of Shentone [Shevington].
Item, M^r^. Gratwood.
Item, M^r^. Corbet.
Item, M^r^. Meverill.
Item, M^r^. Willoughbie.
Item, M^r^. Leighe of Shorleye.
Item, M^r^. Stanley, sonne and heire to S*i*r Thomas Stanleye.
Item, M^r^. Maker.
Item, M^r^. Butler.
Item, M^r^. Mordaynte.

Note, that Chessheire is but in lengthe Fyftie miles; and xvj. in bredth in ye brodest place.

[The Queen's Cheshire Wards in 1578?]

Theis vnder writteñ are the quenes ward*es*.

Bothe of Dunhame.
Daniell of Tableye.
Newton of Pewnal [Pownall].

[1] From State Papers, Domestic, Elizabeth, Vol. cxxvii., No. 89.

Hassall of Hankelowe.
Gravenour of Eaton.
Marie Somerforde.
Starkeye of Wrenburye, lunaticke.

[*Endorsed:*] Names of suche as have landes in Chesshyre, and dwell not there.

1549 (June ?), Petition of the Men of Staines, Middlesex, that their Bridge over the Thames may not be wholly broken down.

[State Papers, Domestic, Edward VI., Vol. vii., No. 46.]

To the right honorable lord*es* of the King*es* Ma*ies*ties moost hon*or*able p*ri*vie Counceill.

In their moost humble wise, besechen and shewen vnto yo*ur* good lordshippes, yo*ur* Orato*ur*s Thinhabitaunt*es* of the Towne of Stanys in the Countie of Midd*lesex* / That where yo*ur* said Orato*ur*s haue receyved Comaundement from*m*e my lorde P*ro*tecto*ur* [Somerset], in the King*es* grac*es* name, to pluck vpp the Comen bridge at Stanys, for the saufgarde of the Realme, as they allege, frome enymyes,[1] whiche ys and wilbe to thutter vndoyng and distruccion*e* of alle the hoole Towne and Countrie therabowt*es* / And the saide Bridge is yett staied, p*ar*te of it, vpon*e*[2] that the saide Towne of Stanys hathe p*ro*mysed to sende owte a Scowte, to discrye yf any Armye be comyng that waie / In consideracion*e* wherof, it maie please yo*ur* good lordshipps to signifie vnto yo*ur* said Orato*ur*s, yo*ur* lordshipp*es* pleaso*ur*s herin, and what yo*ur* said Orato*ur*s shall do therein / And yo*ur* said Orato*ur*s shall dailly praie vnto almightie Jhesu for the p*ro*sperous p*rese*r*u*acione of yo*ur* good lordshippes. /

[*Endorsed:*] The supplicac*i*o[n] of the men of Stanes.

[This Petition is not lugd in here because Staines has anything to do with Cheshire; but because I was born at Egham, two miles from Staines, and have often crost the present bridge, and (I believe) the old one before it, further down the river. Also, as Dee Bridge is mentiond above,

[1] The rising in the West. Cp. (June 24) Instructions to Lord Russell (Lord Privy Seal) for the government of the Western counties of Devon, Cornwall, Somerset, and Dorset, and for suppressing the disaffection and commotions there.—*ibid.* June 29. Guildford, Henry Earl of Arundel to Sir Wm. Petre. The country remains "in a quavering quiet."—*ibid.* See my *Ballads from MSS.*, p. 116-117.

[2] For the reason, because.

p. 92, I think this Petition shows how the Chester folk, if they were never actually cald on to destroy their Bridge, may well have feard that they would be, in times of trouble in Wales.[1] At any rate, the Staines incident is an illustration of the lively times of the 16th Century in England.]

[1] But the ordinary incursion from Wales would be further South, I suppose.

Note to Page 173.

p. 173. *The Laste Estatute.* This is the 39th of Elizabeth, chapter 3, A.D. 1597-8, 'An Acte for the Reliefe of the Poore.' § 7 has the later side-note "Parents or Children shall maintain their Relations; Penalty, 20*s.* per Month," and is "And be yt further enacted, That the Parents or Children of every poore, olde, blynde, lame, & impotent p*er*son, or other poore p*er*son not able to worke, beinge of sufficyent Ability, shall, at their owne Chardges, releive & maintayne every such poore p*er*son, in that manner & accordinge to that Rate, as by the Justices of Peace of that County where such sufficyent p*er*sons dwell, or the greater nomber of them, at there gene*r*all Quarter Sessions shall be assessed; upon payne that every one of them to forfeit xx s. for every monethe which they shall fayle therein."

The Statute ends: "Provided allwayes, That this Acte shall endure no longer then to the ende of the nexte Session of Parlyament."—Record edn., Vol. IV, Pt. ii, p. 897-9. The Act was enlarged and re-enacted by 43 Eliz., c. 3, which is the only one given by Pulton in his edition of the Statutes, 1636, a folio that often disappoints the searcher for old enactments.

SUPPLEMENT

OF

DEPOSITIONS LEFT-OUT IN THE TEXT.

COPIED AND SENT BY MR. W. H. PRICE.

I. CHILD-MARRIAGES. § 1. Divorces. No. 21 *b*.

Alexander Osboston *v.* Margaret Osboston or Hothersall.

[*This should have followd the former Deposition on p. 35 above.*]

[1] Exa*minaciones* testiu*m*, capt*e* cora*m* M*agist*ro Leche, xvij Maij, sup*er* sumaria petic*ione* ex pa*r*te Alex*andri* Osboson con*tra* M*ar*gareta*m* Hothersall. 1565.

Georgius Coke, parochie de Lowe, etat*is* xlij an*norum*, nov*it* pa*r*tes a pu*er*icijs earunde*m*. Exa*minatus* sup*er* allegac*ione* sive sumaria petic*ione*, &c, Dicit, that he well knowes that the said Alex*ander* and M*ar*garet were maried together in the pa*r*ish churche of Lowe, about ix yeres ago, bie S*ir* Thom*as* Frenche, M*inister* there; the said Alex*ander* beinge at the same tyme about thage of xi yeres,—w*hi*ch he knowes well, bie thage of a child of his owne, borne about the same tyme; and also this depon*ent* was then seru*au*nt w*i*th the Ladie Osboson, w*i*th whom the said Alex*ander* then remayned, at tyme of the said mariage,—and the said M*ar*garet was about or vnder vij yeres of age, to this depon*entes* iudgment, w*hi*ch well knewe her, and viewed her bodie; and the said M*ar*garet was borne in a womans armes to the churche to be maried. And further, this deponent saies, that the said pa*r*ties did neu*er* cohabitt together, nor neu*er* [2] had carnall act together, or thone fansied thother; insomuche, that this depon*ent*,—bothe afore he came to Lawfull age, and sins,—hath hard the said Alex*ander* report and say, 'he cold not fansye the saide M*ar*garet, nor cold not Love her as his wief'; wherbie he [George Coke] verilie think*es* the marriage was neu*er* ratified betwene them. no*n* e*st* doct*us*, no*n* conduct*us*, no*n* consang*uineus*, no*n* aff*in*is, no*n* curat &c.

[1] leaf 226 (Piccope's No. 115). [2] leaf 226, back.

Thomas Smith, parochie de Sampsbury, etatis xxxij annorum, novit partem actricem xv annis, et partem ream vij annis. Examinatus, &c, This deponent saies, that he was seruant with the Ladie Osboson, where Alexander Osboson then remayned, at the tyme the said Alexander and Margaret Hothersall were maried together in Lowe churche. et quoad efficium dicte allegacionis, concordat in omnibus et per omnia cum Georgio Coke, preconteste suo. non est doctus, non tenens, &c.

II. TROTHPLIGHTS.

11. Katherine Strete *v.* Nicolas Jepson.

[1]Responsiones personales Nicholai Jepson, super positionibus et articulis libelli ex parte Katerine Strete contra ipsum oblati, capte coram Magistro Roberto Leche, Artium Magistro, &c, xv° Januarij 1561[-2].

Ad primam positionem, This respondent sais, that he and Katerine Strete have bene in the house of John Aynsworthe, and after, Richard Aynsworth house, in companie eche with other, twise or thrise, bie Reason that this Respondent was a neybour bie, and Katherine Strete was suster vnto Richard Aynsworthis wief. and apon a tyme, this respondent, beynge fullie mynded at that season to marrie the said Katherine, did, bie his faithe and trouthe, takinge the said Katherine bie the hand, promysse that he wold marrie her in the face of the churche hereafter, as the tyme wold serve; thes beynge present, William Siddall, Antonie Bowker, and Richard Aynsworthe: And this respondent sais, he remembres not perfittlie whether Richard Aynsworthe wief was present or not. and forther beynge demaundid, 'what answere Katherine made hym againe'; he sais, she said 'bie her faithe and trouthe'; but whether she said any more wordis, this respondent knowis not; neyther dothe this respondent remembre whether they losid handes, and toke handes together againe; but he said, they ons toke handes together, and held hand in hand. and forther beynge askid 'howe longe hit was sins; and what age he is nowe of'; he sais, that 'hit was done somwhat nere the tyme of Christmas last save one, apon a holiday or Sunday in the Eveninge; and he is nowe above xviij yeres of age.' and forther, beynge enquired 'whether he had euer made any contracte to any other person afore that tyme'; he answerithe that 'he had made non' / beynge demaundid, 'whether he did [2]kisse her, or shewe her any such token of love, after the wordes spoken': he answeris 'to his thinkinge no.' and forther he sais, 'to his knolidge, he sent her neuer token, or receyvid any

[1] leaf 15 (Piccope's No. 9). [2] leaf 15, back.

token from her, sins nor afore the said tyme of Contract.' Moreou*er* he sais, that 'the Contract was made in a worke-house, w*hi*ch is an outhouse.' beynge askid, 'whie they went into such an Inconvenie*n*t place'; he sais, that 'his nor their mynd*es* was [for] any to here of theire talke and co*mmun*icacion, lest hit shuld be vttrid abroade' /. and forther he sais, that 'to his thinkinge, at the tyme of the forsaid contract, the said Kat*herine* was free from all Contract; but sins he hathe hard *tha*t the said Kat*herine* hathe made a p*re*contract, but he hathe no certayne knoledge of hit.'

Ad ij[d] po*sitio*nem, Credit in se contin*er*e vere*ta*tem.

Ad iij, po*sitio*nem, nescit depon*er*e, sed refert se ad predeposit*a*.

Ad Vltima*m*, credit credita et negat negata; et sup*er* no*n* creditis et negatis, credit fama*m* no*n* laborare.

Fact*a* fuit sequens Exa*min*acio testiu*m* in ca*us*a p*re*d*ict*a, capt*a* cora*m* M*agis*t*r*o Rob*er*to Leche, &[c], die et a*nn*o p*re*d*ict*o [MS. o, not *is*] [15 Jan. 1562].

Willi*elm*us Sidall, p*ar*ochie de Mancestr*e*, etat*is* xlix' annor*um*, no*vi*t p*ar*tes ab infancijs ear*und*e*m*.

Ad p*r*imu*m* a*rticul*u*m*, This depone*n*t sais, that the mother of Kat*herine* Strete articulate, and other of her frend*es*, were myndid that she shuld have gone to London to service; and this depone*n*t, [1]bie reason he had his brother-in-lawe, on Andrewe Mathewe, a grocer of London, lyenge at his house at that tyme bie the space of a forthnight, had spoken to hym to take the said Kat*herine* to service; whereapon, the said Kat*herine* and her frend*es* were fullie purposid that the said Kat*herine* shuld go w*i*th hym. but after a while, the suster of the said Kat*herine*, Alice,—beynge then the wief of Ric*hard* Aynsworthe, & beynge nowe wief to Nic*holas* Jepson,—came to this depone*n*t, as he was co*m*mynge from even songe w*i*th the mother of them bothe, and told hym, that 'yf Kat*herine* articulate might tarie at home in that Cuntrie, Nic*holas* Jepson wold be content to marie her'; and thereapon, bothe the mother & the doughter Alis willid this depone*n*t to go to Ric*hard* Aynsworthis house, and there he shuld find them bothe. and so, at their request, this depone*n*t went thither, and there found them bothe. and this depone*n*t sais, he toke Nic*holas* Jepson aside to fele his mynd; wherein the [said] Nic*holas* was well pleasid, and said he was contentid to do any thinge that the frend*es* of Kat*herine* Strete shuld thinke mete for the p*er*formaunce of a mariage, so that hit might be kept close from

[1] leaf 16.

the father of the said Nic*holas*. and thereapon, in like case, this depone*nt* sais, he toke forthe Kat*herine* articulate for the same purpose; and *per*ceyvinge she was well content to agre to the mariage, did lett them bothe go into a house w*hi*ch is secrete and sep*ar*atid from the house where the meynie and companie resort. and then,—in the p*re*sence of this depone*nt*, Antonie Bowker, and Ric*hard* Aynsworthe, and the wief of the said Ric*hard* Aynsworthe,—Nic*holas* Jepson did take Kat*herine* Strete bie the right hand, and said, "Kat*herine*, bie my faithe and trouthe, I will marrie th[ee] [1]in the face of the Churche when the tyme shall serve"; and so drewe hand*es*. then Kat*herine*, takinge the said Nic*holas* bie the hand, likewise said, "Nic*holas*, bie my faithe and trouthe, I will marrie the in the face of the churche": whether she said, 'when tyme will serve,' as Nic*holas* said, this depone*nt* remembres not; but they did kisse apon this p*ro*messe made. forther, this depone*nt* beyng*e* askid, 'whether any man did speake thes*e* word*es* before them'; he sais, that 'he spake thes word*es*, and the said Nic*holas* followid hym, and repetid word bie word as this depone*nt* had said afore; and so did the same Kat*herine* in like case.' moreou*er*, this depone*nt* beynge askid, 'how hit chauncid that he spake not the word*es* of mariage de p*rese*nti'; he sais 'he is vnlernid, and knewe not thos word*es*; but, he said, yf he had knowne any other word*es* of more effecte then the above written were, he said at that tyme he wold have spoken them; for this depone*nt* sais, his mynd was to have made them as sure as he cold.' and forther he sais, that 'ther was brought a boke to have sworne them; and he had like to have sworne them; but he was afraid to take an othe, biecause he had no suche com*m*ission. whereapon, when all the word*es* of contracte was finished, he gave them an exhortac*i*on to love well one an other, and to avoid all other Cumpanie; and so this depone*nt* went home [2]to the mother of the said Kat*herine*, and told her what had bene done.' Moreou*er*, this depone*nt* sais, that 'he did not remembre at the tyme of the Contract above written, that the said Kat*herine* had made any p*re*contract to any other; but he sais he well remembres sins, that before that tyme he had hard that the said Kat*herine* had made a contract to one Kay of Yorkshire.' and forther he sais, that 'the contract betwixe the said Nic*holas* Jepson and Kat*herine* Strete was made about*e* this tyme twelfmonthe, on a sonday or holiday, in an eveninge.'

Ad ij[d], credit eunde*m* fore veru*m*.

Ad iij [et iiij'] ar*ticu*la, credit hanc curia*m* et foru*m* *ess*e competitu*m*; sed nescit an sit iuste querelat*um*, an no*n*.

[1] leaf 16, back. [2] leaf 17.

Ad vultimum, dicit predeposita per eum fore vera, et famam vehementer laborasse super matrimonio Nicolai Jepson contracto cum Alicia, sorore Katerine articulate, sed nunc magna ex parte sepositam esse [? MS.].

12 *a.* Morgan Edmund *v.* Elizabeth Bird.

[1]Examinacio testium in causa contractus, super libello ex parte Morgani Edmound, generosi, contra Elizabeth Brid, alias Dilon, capta coram Magistro Roberto Leche, &c, xxvij° die Octobris, Anno Domini, 1562°.

Edward Griffiths, Paintor, infra ecclesiam cathedralem cestriensem, etatis lxxii' annorum et vltra, novit partem actricem x annis, et partem ream xxxiij annos.

Ad primum articulum, This deponent sais, that he supposeth Morgan Edmound, & she, the said Elizabeth, were both free when they were contractid together: and this deponent sais he neuer hard otherwise.

Ad ij articulum, This deponent sais, that in Ellin Mercers house, in a parlour there on the backside, about a fortnight afore midsommer last past, as he remembres, ther was a communicacion about a Jointure that Morgan Edmound had promysed Elizabeth Brid, beynge xl yerely, to be set apon the said Elizabeth. and when they were agreid that she shuld have so muche duringe her lief, he askid her, 'whether she wold be content to geve hym her faith and trouthe before such as were there'; and she said she wold. and there-apon, the said Elizabeth did geve the said Morgan her right hand, and said to hym: "I take you for my husband; and I will marry you when you comme back againes: I will neuer marry non but you." & then they vnlosid handes; and she said, "you shalbe bound to me as I am to you": and then he gave her his hand likewise, [2]& said, "I take you for my wief, with all my hart, & I will marry you, by my faith & trouthe": & so the[y] losid handes, & kissed together. beynge askid, 'whether ther was any man that pronounced the hole wordes of matrimony betwixe them'; he sais, 'no, but[3] ther owne selvis.' and forther, this deponent sais, that 'Morgan toke this deponent with hym for that only purpose, to witnes with hym; and that causid hym to marke so much as he hath said.' beynge askid, 'whether the one gave the other any token at that tyme'; this deponent sais, 'no, to his knoledge.' but he sais, 'the next morninge after, Mistris Brid send the said Morgan a Ringe of gold by this deponent, with a blewe stonne in; and the said Morgan gave her gret thankes; but

[1] leaf 82 (Piccope's No. 37). [2] leaf 82, back. [3] except.

he send nothinge by this deponent at that tyme.' but he sais, that 'after that, she, the said Elizabeth, send to this deponent a pece of gold worth iiij[l], to this deponentes Iudgment, bie her suster Marget, willinge hym to bringe that pece of gold to Morgan, in sted of the ringe, biecause hit was a trifle.' & this deponent answerid, 'he wold not go againe with any more tokens; wherfore, whether the gold came to hym or no, this deponent knowes not certenly.'

Ad iij articulum, respondet vt prius deposuit; and forther, he sais, 'he hard say that, after Morgan was gone into wales, the said Morgan send the said Elizabeth a Ringe of gold; & she sent hym a hart of gold by one Richard Morgan of Beaumaris.' alias nescit deponere.

Ad iiij articulum, This deponent sais, that he belevis the contentes of this article to be true; for 'he thinkes that handes trouthe, with such wordes as he hard spoken, shuld make them man & wief before god.'

Ad v[t], dicit eundem fore verum.

Ad vi[t], credit iuste fuisse querelate.

Ad vltimum, dicit predeposita per eum fore vera, et famam super huiusmodi Laborare; and that he hath hard xx say, that 'Henry Dilon mariage was nought, biecause of this precontract.'

Johannes David, sacrista infra ecclesiam cathedralem cestriensem, etatis liiij annorum, novit partem actricem vij annos, et partem ream xx annis.

Ad primum articulum, credit eundem fore verum, quoad noticiam suam, that bothe parties articulate were fre from all precontractes.

[1] Ad ij[d] Articulum, This deponent sais, that he came into one Ellin Mercers house, not knowinge of this matter afore; and then hering them commen of a mariage, stode still, and went not away, bycause his frendes were there, videlicet: Edward Griffiths,[2] Res Adder, and the said Master Morgan, whom he had knowne afore. and when this deponent came thither, they [Eliz. Bird and Morg. Edmund] were holdinge the one hand in the other; & the said Elizabeth said: "I wilbe your wief, and take you for my husband from hense forth, by my faith and trouth, with all my hart." and he, the said Morgan, likewise toke the said Elizabeth by the hand, and said: "I wilbe your husband from hensforward, with all my hart"; and then they kist; and he said she shold have x[l] land Joynture. and they said, one shuld go se the land; and pointed a day to marry: at which day the said Morgan apointid to be here again with her, and fell sick in the meane season. and this deponent sais, he hard say that the said Morgan was dead, or els he wold have forbid the mariage

[1] leaf 83. [2] The last Deponent but one.

betwixe the said Eliz*abeth* and Henry Dilon. but altho he wold have done so, he cold not, biecause they did steale a mariage w*i*thout banes askinge. and forther, this deponent sais, 'when they made the said contract, holdinge hand*es*, the said Eliz*abeth* said, "I will neu*er* marry other; but take you for my husband duringe lief." & he answerid her likewise.' and forther, this depone*nt* sais, that 'the morrowe after the said contract, the said Eliz*abeth* send Morgan a gold ringe w*i*th a blewe stonne in hit; & he sent her another ringe.' beynge askid, 'in what place of the house this co*n*tract was'; he sais, 'hit was in a p*a*rlo*u*r, on the backside, betwixe xi and xii a clock afore none.' beynge askid, 'apon what occasion he came thither'; he sais, 'he came thither to get som*m*e threde; & so hard tell of his forsaid frend*es*; and taried there still.' and forther, [beynge askid] 'where Morgan was, when the Ring w*i*th the blewe ston was delivered hym'; he sais, 'at M*ist*ris Ormisdich, in Chester, where the said Morgan tablid, at his bedside.' beynge askid, 'whether ther was any more spoken by any other man concerninge the w*or*d*es* of contract': 'no*ne*, for any thinge that he hard.'

Ad iij ar*ticu*lu*m*, re*spo*ndet provt p*ri*us deposuit; and he sais, 'he hard say there was a token of a pece of gold of iiij[li] send betwene them; but he knowes not *cer*tenly.'

Ad iiij ar*ticu*lu*m*, this depone*nt* sais, that 'they that were p*rese*nt by, thought them to be man & wief afore god. & they had bene mar[i]ed together before, at the day appointed, yf the said Morgan had bene in health, &c, to this depone*ntes* thinkinge.'

[1] Ad vj, credit eund*em* fore ver*um*.

Ad vlti*mum*, dicit p*re*deposit*a* p*er* eu*m* fore vera, et fama*m* sup*er* h*uius*mod*i* laborare. no*n* est doct*us*, no*n* conduct*us*, &c.

Margareta Fradsam, vid*ua*, p*a*roch*ie* S*anct*i Oswald*i*, nov*i*t p*a*rte*m* act*ricem* a festo Pasche sup*ra*, et est soror p*ar*t*is* ree. &c.

Ad p*ri*mu*m* ar*ticu*lu*m*, beyng demaundid 'whether Morgan was a suter to Eliz*abeth* Brid, her suster, or no, in the way of mariage'; this depone*nt* answerid "yea." beynge askid, 'what frend*es* he made, & howe oft he came to her'; she answerid, that 'he wold have had one M*aste*r Will*i*ams, and M*aste*r Moston, Esq*ui*ers, to have com*m*e w*i*th hym, and 'spoken w*i*th her.' and the said Eliz*abeth* was somwhat bashfull, & said 'she wold have no such men to come to her.' & the said Morgan did com*m*e almost dalie to this depone*ntes* suster; for he tablid at M*istre*s Grimsdiches, not far from her.' beynge askid, 'whether the said Eliz*abeth* was free from all p*re*contract*es* afore that day'; she saies,

[1] leaf 83, back.

'yea; & so she durst depose; for she knowes her counsell & secrett*es* more then any other.'

Ad ij^d^, this depone*n*t sais, that 'the said *par*ties, Morgan Edmond & M*ist*ris Brid, made a full contract, & a *per*fitt, of mariage, hand in hand, plightinge to ech other faith*e* and trouth*e*: *pre*sentib*us* tunc ib*idem*, Edward Griff*iths*, John D*avi*d and a beadman callid Res. & this co*n*tract was made about a fortnight afore Midsom*er* day last, in a *par*lo*ur*, behind the house of Ellin M*er*cer.' beynge askid, 'by what word*es* they did make the contract'; she sais, 'by the word*es* of Wedlock—as nere as they cold hit those word*es*,—*tha*t ar spoken at the church dore: "I take the for my weddid husband," & "I take the for my weddid wief, for better & for worse, &c." and when the word*es* were spoken, they kissed.' & forther, she sais, 'the said Eliz*abeth* shuld have had x^li^ land*es* set apon her, in Anglysey, as she think*es*, w*hi*ch came by his [Morgan Edmund's] mother; for he cold not [1]set any that came by his father, biecause he made such p*ro*messe at the mariage of his heire.' beynge askid, 'when this co*mmun*icacion was'; this depone*n*t sais, 'hit was afore the co*n*tract. & after and when they had agreid apon the co*n*tract, then they wold have had one to go se the Land*es*; and he [Morgan] bade her send any frend that she wold. & so she desired Mr Robe*r*te Brock to take the paines, who can testify the same.' beynge askid, 'whie the said Eliz*abeth* wold marry Dilon, and havinge made a co*n*tract afore': she sais, 'she hard say that the said Morgan Edmond was dead; and dyverse did bear her in hand so; and she was temptid by daily sute of the said Dilon, & did forget her forther[2] p*ro*messe.' and beynge askid, 'whether any Ringe, or any other token, was gevin, the one to the other, at tyme of the said co*n*tract'; she sais, "no: but after, the said Eliz*abeth* send the said Morgan a ringe by D*avi*d Griff*iths*, the morning after; who said it was not good ynough; but yet he deliu*er*ed hit. and afterward the said Eliz*abeth* send a better token to the said Edward, to geve the said Morgan; and he said that ringe shuld suffice." beynge askid, 'whether morgan send her any thinge'; this depone*n*t answeris and sais, 'he send her an other ringe of a blewe turques. and when it was sent, she dothe not remembre; but she sais hit was fairer then her susters, beynge of the same kind.' beinge askid 'whether she send hym any more tokens'; this depone*n*t sais, 'she send hym a hart of gold by one, M*aste*r Morgan, a s*er*u*an*t of S*ir* Ric*hard* Duckleis,' &c.

Ad iij, dicit vt p*ri*us deposuit.

Ad iiij ar*ticulum*, this depone*n*t sais, that 'they were taken and

[1] leaf 84. [2] earlier.

reputid as man & wief afore god, by this depone*n*t, and of all other that were p*resen*t by, & of the neighbo*ures* thereabout that knowe of it.'

Ad v, credit contin*ere* in se verit*atem*.

Ad vj, credit eund*em* fore ver*um*.

Ad Vltim*um*, dicit p*re*deposit*a* per ea*m* fore vera; forbiecause this depone*n*t hath hard her suster often tymes lament, for that she maried the said Dilon, after she knewe the said Morgan to be on lyve; & said 'it was a scourge for her nowe in her old daies.' & this depone*n*t think*es* in co*n*science, that she hath iust cause to repent for this purpose only.

[1]Res*ponsi*ones p*er*son*a*les Elizabeth Brid al*ia*s Dilon capt*e* sup*er* Li*bel*lo ex p*ar*te Morgani Edmound, gen*er*os*i*, cont*ra* ipsam oblat*o*, in ca*usa* contract*us*, capt*e* cora*m* M*agist*ro Rob*er*to Leche, &[c], iiij[o] die Novemb*ris*, 1562[o].

Ad p*ri*ma*m* pos*itio*nem, this R*espo*ndent, beynge put in mynd of her othe to say the truthe w*i*thout respect of any thinge, sais, that she hath a soule to kepe, & that she is not like longe to lyve; & now in her old age she wold not hurt her soule, & refuge Christ, that hath bought her, in speakinge any thinge apon her othe but the truthe: wherfore she sais, that in her conscience she was free from all men when she made the contract w*i*th Morgan Edmound; and for any thinge that this R*espo*ndent knowes, the said Morgan was also free.

Ad ij[d], This R*espo*ndent sais, that somwhat afore midsom*er* last past, in a p*ar*lo*ur* of Ellen M*er*cers, w*i*thin the p*ar*ish*e* of S[t] Oswald*es* in Chester, she, this R*espo*ndent, & Morgan Edmound, did make a co*n*tract of mariage, speakinge the word*es* of mariage (as nere as this R*espo*ndent cold remember the same), saynge: "I take the, Morgan, to my husband, from this day forward; and therto I plight the my trouthe"; and held hym by the hand, sayeng these word*es* aforesaid, w*i*th other, in full mynd to have hym for her husband duringe her lief: and likewise Morgan toke this R*espo*ndend by the hand, and said: "I take the, Eliz*abeth*, for my wief from hensforth; and therto I plight the my trouthe": & so they drewe hand*es*, & kissed either other. It*em* she sais, 'she send hym a Ringe by Edward Grif*fith*s, who thought the Ringe was not good ynough; neu*er*theles he d*elivere*d hit; and after, this depone*n*t [Respondent] wold have sent, by the said Edward, a gret pece of gold to the said Morgan Edmound: w*hi*ch pece came to this R*espo*ndent*es* hand againe, & was not d*elivere*d, as she think*es*, biecause the said Morgan was gone out of the towne.' and forther she saies, that 'the said Morgan send her a ringe

[1] leaf 85, back (Piccope's No. 38).

w*i*th a stonne in hit, better then this R*espo*ndent*es* ringe was.' beynge askid whether ther was any more tokens sent betwixe them; she sais, that 'she sent hym a little hart of clene gold, by a gent*leman* of Bewmarris, who said he was cosin to the said Morgan; but she Receyvid no*n* againe of hym again.' beynge askid 'howe it chauncid that she, havinge made suche a co*n*tract w*i*th Morgan Edmound, wold wed Henry Dilon': she answeres, that 'hit was told her by certen Walshmen, that Morgan was dead; w*hi*ch [1]thinge, this R*espo*ndent belevid, bicause she hard nothing from the said Morgan after she had sent hym the said hart.' and further, this R*espo*ndent sais, that 'she was in trouble in the Lawe about a certen Lyving; and therefore she was counselid to take a hesband to followe her sutes & matters. for w*hi*ch cause, & for others, she was seducid by one Henry Dilon to forget her other p*ro*messe made vnto Morgan; for w*hi*ch she is hartely sorey; for she did neu*er* any thing*e* that hath grevid her conscience so muche.' & forther, she sais, apon her othe, that 'ther is no collusion wrought; but that in conscience she is Lawfull wief, afore god, to Morgan, & he her husband; & wisheth that either Morgan had bene dead indede, or els had gevin her knoledge rather.'[2] and forther she sais, that 'she shuld have had x*li* yerely during her lief, made vnto her by the said Morgan for her Ioynture, in Anglisey; and Mr Brock was desired to go se it; but he had other busnies,' &c.

Ad iij, dicit vt p*rese*ns deposuit.

Ad iiij', this R*espo*ndent sais, that in her conscience she thought she was Morgans wief; but what the neighbo*ures* did think*e* therein, she knowes not; but she sais, the neighbo*ur*es thought they shuld be maried together.

Ad v, dicit eand*em* fore vera*m*.

Ad vi, dicit eand*em* fore vera*m*.

Ad vltima*m*, credit credita et negat negat*a*; et sup*er* no*n* creddit*is* et negat*is*, credit fama*m* no*n* laborare.

28 Nov., 1562. Deposition of Thomas Bildon, Junior, aged 24. [3]"This depone*n*t . . . beynge demaundid apon what he was brought, sais, that 'for as much as this depone*n*t stand*es* suerty for Morgan concerninge an action dependinge before the Sherieves of Chester, the said Morgan vttrid his mynd vnto hym concerning this case, sayenge vnto hym, that he wold neu*er* marry the said Eliz*abeth*, biecause she was a priest*es* hoore: and at the said tyme, and the same day, the said Morgan told this depone*n*t, that yf the Lawe wold geve Eliz*abeth* vnto hym, he

[1] leaf 86. [2] sooner, earlier: Milton's '*rathe* primrose,' &c. [3] leaf 98, back.

wold agre w*i*th Dilon, and abide this depone*ntes* award, and not marry her.' and forther, he told this depone*nt*, 'he was afeard lest, yf he shuld obteine her by the Lawe, lest he cold not be divorsid from her.' & forther, this depone*nt* sais, for Morgans abode in Chester, he sais it appens[1] by two actions in the shryreves boke.[2]

(signed) p*er* me, Tom*a*s Byldon."

Randulph Manwaringe, of the City of Chester, Alderman, aged 57, deposes, [3]"that at the tyme the suite was com*m*ensid by Morgan against the said Elizabeth, this depone*nt*, havinge a house for w*h*i*ch* he shuld pay rent vnto the said Eliz*abeth*, did meryly aske the said Morgan 'whether he or Dilon shuld be his Landlord': he answerid no*n* answere to the purpose. then this depone*nt* earnestly askid hym, 'what Title he had to the said Eliz*abeth*.' "marry," said he, "I have a p*ro*myse of her; and she had a token of me; and I receyvid an other from her." "Then," q*uod* this depone*nt*, "will you marry her that hath maried an other in the face of the churche, and hath lyen w*i*th hym?" then Morgan answerid, that 'he wold neu*er* marry priest*es* hoore, as longe as he lyved.' "whie," q*uod* this depone*nt*, "whie do you make suche Title vnto her?" and he answerid, "mary, to make Dilon to pay me suche mony and plate as he had of hers in his hand*es*." q*uod* this depone*nt*, "you cannot so do, yexcept you p*ro*ve the co*n*tract, and marry her." and Morgan answerid and said, "I will neu*er* marry her, biecause she hathe plaid the hoore, & com*m*itted adultery; and therfore I may iustly refuse her by the order of the Lawe."

(signed) p*er* me, Rondull Maynwaring."

Charles Blackstonne, of the Parish of Saint Oswald's, Chester, aged 23, deposes, that 'beynge askid of Morgans beynge in towne, and whether ther was any co*n*tract betwixe Morgan Edmound & the said Eliz*abeth*'; he sais, 'Morgan was at this depone*ntes* house, w*i*th Mr. Will*i*ams, and Griff*ith* of London, about barthelewne tide last,[4] or somwhat before. and as for co*n*tract made betwixe them, he can say nothinge, but that talke was, one Pole and Morgan were suters to the said Eliz*abeth*.' . . .

(signed) Charles Blackeston.

[1] ? apperes. [2] ? Cote, for Court. MS. not plain.—W. H. P.
[3] leaf 99. [4] St. Bartholomew's Day is Aug. 24.

[12 *b.* Cross-suit. Hy. Dillon, Elizabeth Bird's Husband, *v.* Morgan Edmund.]

[1]Exa*mina*cio testiu*m* in ca*us*a Contractu*s* sup*er* excepc*io*nib*us* oblat*a* ex p*ar*te Henrici Dilon, mariti Eliz*abethe* Brid, con*tra* Morganu*m* Edmound capt*a* cora*m* M*agist*ro Leche, &c, ij^do^ die Decemb*ris*, 1562°.

Rob*er*tus Pole, *gener*os*us*, serviens re*uerend*i p*at*ris Willi*elmi*, cest*ri*en*sis* epis*co*pi, etat*is* xxvij an*n*or*um* et vltra, no*ui*t Morganu*m* Edmound p*er* an*nu*m, et Eliz*abetham* Brid sim*i*l*ite*r, et Henricu*m* Dilon ex t*em*po*r*e m*at*rimonij inter ip*su*m et Eliz*abetham* Brid.

Ad p*r*ima*m* excepc*io*n*em*, this depone*n*t sais, that he hard that Morgan Edmound & Eliz*abeth* Brid, al*ias* Dilon, made a co*n*tract of mariage, and that Tokens were sent, the one from the other. and forther, he sais, that he se a ringe w*hi*ch the said Eliz*abeth* had send Morgan,—before Dilon was any suter to the said Eliz*abeth*,—apon the said Morgans finger: he supposith it was a Turques; but what the word*es* of co*n*tract, or els the substaunce of the said co*n*tract was, this depone*n*t knowes not, biecause he was neu*er* callid as witnes. but beynge a suter hym-self, this depone*n*t sais, he hard the said Elizabeth say, and her suster M*ar*garet Fradsam also, that the day of mariage was apointed, yf the said Morgan had kept pointment: and all this was sene, hard, and knowne bie report to this depone*n*t, afore Dilon was talkid of, or hard of, in this towne.

Ad ij^d^, this depone*n*t saies, he knowes not certenly; but saies he hathe hard say that Alis Pery, who was a suter for Dilon, did demaund of the said Eliz*abeth*, whether the said Eliz*abeth* was free from all men; and that she answerid 'yes'; but there the said Eliz*abeth* answerid not truly, as this depone*n*t well knoweth.

Ad iij po*sitio*nem, nescit depone*r*e, sed refert se ad Jura in ea p*ar*te, whether the co*n*tract be good or bad.

Ad iiij, credit testes p*r*oduct*os* p*er* Morganu*m* Edmound, fore honestos et discretos.

Ad v', refert se ad Jura in ea p*ar*te.

Ad vj', this depone*n*t sais, 'he think*es* the mariage of Henry Dilon and Eliz*abeth* Brid to be nought, for that he stale her away, and maried her out of this Dioces, w*i*thout banes askinge, & contrary to the Com*m*aundm*en*t of the Ordinary. and for that, the shrief of the citty of Chester, at the request of this depone*n*t, did com*m*e to the said Dilons house at ix of clock in the night, or ther about, to take them as adulteres, for that they were not knowne to be maried. and then the said Dilon

[1] leaf 100, back (Piccope's No. 47)

said, that 'tho she was in house w*i*th hym, yet she was not in bed w*i*th hym: whereapon the said Shirieve toke suerties of hym; or els he shuld have gone to ward for his misdeamenou*r* in that behalf.' and this depone*n*t sais, 'for any thinge he knowes, they be not reputid as man and wief.' And forther, this depone*n*t beynge [1]demaundid and exa*min*ed apon this one point, 'whether that he did require the said Morgan Edmound, at the tyme of his sute dependinge before the ordinary, co*n*cerning a *p*re*con*tract supposid to be made betwixe this depone*n*t & the said Eliz*abeth*, to be a witnes therin, yf nede so req*ui*red'; this depone*n*t sais, 'he neu*er* instantly req*ui*red hym, biecause his matter came not to *p*roduc*ere* test*im*o*nium*; and so they were neu*er* there in Company together; for they were both suters at ons; and this depone*n*t wrought closely for his p*ar*t; and the said Morgan did like wise for his. yet this depone*n*t doth graunt that, in company & talke at the tyme of this depone*ntes* sute against the said Eliz*abeth*, this depone*n*t did colourably declare (for the maintenaunce of his matter) that he had sondry witnesses. but what they wold depose, he knowes not, biecause hit neu*er* came to the profe: among*es* the said witnes, he might name Morgan, w*hi*ch cold say nothinge; rac*ionem*-q*ue* sup*r*adi*xit*.'

Ad vlt*imum*, dicit p*r*edeposit*a* p*er* eu*m* fore vera, et fama*m* sup*er* &c.

(signed) By me
Robart Poole.

Joh*anne*s Gayton, serviens D*omi*ni Epi*scopi*, etat*is* xxiij. an*norum*, no*vi*t Morg*anum* Edmound cu*m* Eliz*abetha* Brid, p*er* annu*m*, et Henricu*m* Dilon xiiij hebdomad*as*.

Ad p*r*ima*m*, nescit depon*er*e.

Ad ij[d], simil*iter* nescit depon*er*e.

Ad iij', nescit depon*er*e.

Ad iiij', credit testes p*er* Morganu*m* Edmound [productos] fore honestas p*er*sonas.

Ad v', refert se ad Jura in ea p*ar*te.

Ad vj', credit that Henry Dilon and Eliz*abeth* Brid be taken & reputid as man and wief by the neighbo*ures* thereabout. beynge askid, 'what he can sey in this case either p*ro* aut con*tra*'; saieth, that 'he hard Rob*er*t Pole, at the tyme of his sute com*m*ensid before my L*ord*, sey that Morgan Edmound wold be one of his witnes.' whereapon, this depone*n*t told Dilon, that Pole had a good matter against M*ist*ris Brid; for that she had said, that yf she eu*er* maried, she wold marry no*n* but Pole: w*hi*ch word*es*, Morgan wold testify, as this depone*n*t hard by

[1] leaf 101.

Pole; but whether he wold have testified this or no, this depone*n*t knowes not; but as Pole told hym, one fellowe wold tell an other.

(signed) p*er* me, John Gayton.

4 *b*. Ellen Ricroft *v*. Thomas Snelson.

[These further Depositions should have followd those on pages 59--61. The case is one of attempted Evasion of Trothplight (by a secret marriage with another woman in another parish), like those of George Johnson (p. 57), Richard Lowe (p. 56), and Hy. Dilon (p. 194, at foot).]

18th March, 1562-3. [1]R*esp*onsiones p*er*son*a*les Joh*ann*is Willy.

This r*esp*ondent saies, that Thom*as* Snelson req*ui*red hym to go w*i*th hym to his mariage, w*hi*ch was solempnized by one S*i*r Rob*er*t—the other name he knowes not,—betwene hym and Joan Willy in Rishton Chappell, in Staffordshire, as this r*esp*ondent think*es*. and the mariage [2]was solempnized about the dawninge of the day, sins Candlemas last [2 Feb. 1562-3]: the tyme, day, nor weke, he remembres not: p*re*s*e*ntibus t*em*po*re* Solempnizac*on*is eiusde*m* m*at*rimonij,[3] Rad*ulph*o Barker, vnacu*m* isto deponen*te*, et alijs, quo*rum* no*m*ina ignorat.

[4]R*esp*onsio*n*es p*er*son*a*les Joanne Wily, al*ia*s Snelson, capt*e* cora*m* M*agist*ro Rob*er*to Lech, &c, p*ri*mo Ap*ri*lis, 1563°.

This r*esp*ondent sais, that she was married to Tho*mas* Snelson betwene Candlemas [2 Feb.] and Shrovetide[5] last,—the day nor weke she remembres not; but it was—in Rishton, in an other Dioces, (what priest it was, she knowes not; whether he was curate or not); in the p*re*sence of Rafe Barker, and John Willy, and another, whose name this r*esp*ondent knowes not, and Edward Lowe of Staffordshire. beynge askid, 'whie she was maried in an other Dioces'; she answeris, 'it was throughe the procurement of Thom*as* Snelson; and she thought it was not so gret daung*er* as she think*es* it nowe be.' and forther she saies, 'the banes were askid twise; and the iij^d tyme Ellin Ricrofte forbade the same.'

13. Alice Wodfall *v*. Thomas Torbock.

(Daysmen or Referees chosen, who order a proper Trothplight, which is made.)

[6]Exa*minac*io testiu*m* in ca*usa* contract*us* ex p*ar*te Alicie Wodfall con*tra* Tho*mam* Torbock oblat*a*, capt*a* cora*m* M*agist*ro Rob*er*to Leche, in L*egibus* Bacc*alaureo*, Die et an*no* p*re*dic*tis* [25th June, 1563].

[1] leaf 123, back. [2] leaf 124. [3] MS. adds 'p*rese*ntibus contra seu (?).'
[4] leaf 125 (Piccope's No. 62).
[5] Shrove Sunday, or Quinquagesima Sunday, is the seventh Sunday before Easter day. [6] leaf 136 (Piccope's No. 73).

Ric*hard*us Bowre, paroch*ie* de Prescot, etat*is* l an*norum*, no*vi*t p*ar*te*m* act*ricem* xx annos, et p*ar*te*m* rea*m* a puericia.

Ad p*ri*mu*m* ar*ticu*lu*m*, This Depon*en*t sais, that diu*er*se tymes Alice Wodfall and Thom*as* Torbock talkid of a mariage to be had betwixe them; and, as he think*es*, they were free from all p*re*contract*es*.

Ad ij[d], this depon*en*t saies, that after co*mmun*icacion had of the mariage had betwix the p*ar*ties Libellate, they agreid that the said Alis shuld take a daiseman for her p*ar*te, & the said Tho*mas* an other for his p*ar*te. [1]she, the said Alis, chose this deponent; and the said Tho*mas* chose Ric*hard* Parre, of the P*ar*ish of P*re*scot, for the said Daiesmen; who met on day at her house, and eate a pigge, and cold not agree. and afterward, at an other day, they mett, & agreed of ce*r*ten coven*aunt*es conce*r*ninge mariage. and when they were agreed apon the Coven*ant*es, this depon*ent* said to thother Daiesman, "howe shall we make them sur[*e*] together, that mariage may p*ro*cede?" and the said Ric*hard* Par answerid, 'they shuld be sworne either to other, hand in hand.' Interrogat*us* de mod*o* [et] forma co*n*tract*us*, et verbis; this depon*ent* sais, the said Ric*hard* toke the said Alis bie the Right hand, and said, "by my trouth, I will marry the bie such a Day,"—& did no*min*ate the day (w*hi*ch day was not a moneth of)—"yf god spare me healthe." and then they losed hand*es*; and she, the said Alis, said, "and[2] I be woman on lyve, I will mete you (inuendo dict*um* Tho*mam*) at the day appointid, at the Church dore or before." and apon this, the said Alis toke Par bie the hand; and the said Tho*mas* toke this depon*en*t bie the hand. Interrogat*us* de verbis content*is* in d*ict*o ar*ticu*lo; he sais, that 'thes word*es* articulate were not spoken bie either of the p*ar*ties, but the word*es* that he hath deposid, or the like in effect, and no*n* other.' and further he sais, 'he knowes not whether they kist; but Par bade them kisse; and they had good chere after.'[3]

Ad iij, this depon*en*t sais, he knowes not of any Tokens sent or Recyvid betwix them; but this depon*en*t saies, that he had a ce*r*ten Lease, w*hi*ch he p*ro*mysed to deliu*er* the said Tho*mas*, as sone as the Ring was put ou*er* her fing*er*.

Ad iiij, he sais he knowes not what other men ment bie it; but this depon*en*t thought a truth in it.

Ad v, dicit fore ver*um*.

[1] leaf 136, back. [2] an, if

[3] Do you notice, that the Daiesmen could not agree over their food, that is, 'a pigge'? But on their second meeting, when the 'good chere' was held over until they were agreed, they would seem to have soon polished off the business for which they met.—W. H. Price.

Ad vj, credit fore ver*um*.
Ad vlt*imum*, dicit p*re*deposit*a* per eu*m* fore vera.

14. Alexander Winstanley *v.* Ellen Sonkie.

(3 or 4 weeks after her Trothplight, she married another man; and this Suit is not brought till 20 years later.)

[1]Exa*mina*cio testiu*m* sup*er* p*re*tenso Contract*u* Ma*trim*on*ii*, fac*ti* inter Alexand*rum* Winstanley et Ellena*m* Sonkie, capt*a* cora*m* D*omi*no Canc*ellario*, xxviij° Ap*ri*lis, 1564.

Georgius Holland, p*ar*och*ie* de Wigan, vbi nat*us est*, etatis xlj an*n*or*um*, no*vi*t Alex*andrum* Winstanley xxxvj an*n*os, et Elena*m* Sonkie xxvj an*n*os. Interrogat*us* de h*ujus*modi p*re*tenso contract*u*, This depon*ent* saies, that 'apon Thursdaie at night, before Alhalontide, about xix or xx' yeres ago (and, as this depon*ent* well remembres, about iij wek*es* or a moneth afore the marriage of the said Eleine and Rob*er*te Gidlowe), Alex*ander* Winstanley did require this depon*ent* to go w*i*th hym to the fathers house of the said Eleine. and when this depon*ent* and the said Alex*ander* came thither, the father of the said Eleine was in bed. Then the said Alex*ander* said: "Eleine, I here say you must be maried; but so you cannot do, biecause you & I have bene sworne apon a boke together afore now." she answerid, that 'what she had sworne, she wold not go against'; & said, "I will neu*er* marrie no*n* but you." "then," said Alex*ander*, "yf you be so determynid, let vs make the matter sure, before this man and theis ij° women": and thereapon he callid, as witnes, this depon*ent*, Eliz*abeth* Winstanley, and M*ar*garet Waite. then the said Alex*ander* toke the said Eleine bie the hand, afore the said witnes, and said: "I, Alex*ander*, take the, Eleine, to my weddid wief, to have and to hold, for better & worse, [2]for richer and poorer, in sicknes & in health, till death vs dep*ar*te; and therto I plight you my trouth." and so, vnlosing hand, the said Eleine toke the said Alex*ander* bie the hand likewise, and spake the like word*es* in effect to hym. and afterward, the said Alex*ander* and this depon*ent* tarried there ij° howres, and dronk, and so dep*ar*tid back againe to the said Alex*ander* his fathers house' / beynge askid 'what cause the said Alex*ander* had to take this depon*ent* w*i*th hym'; he sais, that 'he this depon*ent*, beinge a Tailio*ur*, was workinge at the fathers house of the said Alex*ander*, and was requestid to go w*i*th hym, but he knewe not to what intent till he came thither. no*n* est Doct*us*, no*n* conduct*us*, no*n* iurat*us*, &c.'

[1] leaf 162, back (Piccope's No. 91). [2] leaf 163.

Margareta Waite, parochie de Wigan, vbi nata est, novit Alexandrum Winstanley et Elenam Sonkie a pueriiciis eorundem. Examinata de huiusmodi contractu, &c, This deponent saies, that 'she well remembres the mariage of Roberte Gridlowe and Eleine Sonkie, which is about xx' yeres ago. and about a moneth or iij wekes afore that tyme, Alexander Winstanley and George Holland came to the house of William Sonkie, father to the said Eleine, in the night season, when Sonkie and his wief were a bed. and then fallinge in talk and communicacion, Alexander said vnto Eleine, "I heresay you must be maried." she answerid, "I am readie to be maried to no man livinge, except it be to you." Then said he, "I think you can marry non but me; seinge we are sworne to be true, one to an other." she answerid, "I will neuer go against my othe, if you be the same man" / Then said Alexander: "ar you content to be contractid, and make all thinges sure?" and she answerid, "yea." then the said Alexander callid George Holland, Elizabeth Winstanley, and this deponent, to here & see what they saied and did; and takinge the said [1]Eleine bie the hand, said: "I, Alexander, take the, Eleine, to my weddid wief, to have and to hold, for better for worse, till death vs departe; and therto I plight you my trouth." and the said Eleine said: "I, Eleine, take the, Alexander, to my weddid husband, to have and to hold, for better for worse, till death vs departe; and therto I plight the my trouth." after which wordes spoken, the said Alexander toke her in his armes, and kissid her, and said, "I will take thee for my wief from this daie forward"; and so tarried a while after, drinkinge, and departid. beinge askid, 'whether theis were the wordes of contract, or whether ther were more spoken'; she saies, 'theis and all the wordes vsid to be spoken bie the priest, were spoken, altho nowe she hath forgotten them: then she had them in memory.' Reddendo racionem scientie sue huiusmodi, she saies she was hired there to spinne; and sais, she is not remembrid of the nomber of the yeres perfittlie; but she well remembers it was done afore she went to London, which is almost xx' yeres ago.' further beinge demaundid, 'whether euer she hard they were sworne together'; she sais, 'no, afore that night that the said Alexander said so, and the said Eleine denied it not.' non est docta, non conducta, &c.

Elizabeth Winstanley, parochie de Wigan, etatis xliiij annorum, novit partes ab infanciis. Interrogata de mente (?) cause; This deponent sais, that the said Alexander,—perceyvinge that the father of Eleine Sonkie was offendid that he came to his house,—did therfore comme in the

[1] leaf 163, back.

night [1]season customablie; and apon a certen Thursday at night, afore the mariage of Gidlowe and the said Elene, about iij wek*es* or a moneth, w*h*ich is about xix' or xx yeres ago, Alex*ander* came, and brought George Holland w*i*th hym, to the said house. and when he was com*m*e thither, he said to Eleine, "It is told me you ar bound to be maried"; and she said "nay." said Alex*ander* againe, "remember what you have done; and be well advised of the oth that you have made vnto me." "well," said Elein, "that I have said and sworne, I will p*er*forme and stand to." Alex*ander* answerid, "if you be so determyned, let vs make the matter sure before witnes"; and thereapon callid the said George Holland, M*ar*garet Waite, and this depon*ent*, to beare witnes what was said and done. and so, taking the said Eleine bie the hand, said vnto her, "I, Alex*ander*, take thee, Eleine, to my weddid wief," and so furth, all the rest of the word*es* as the p*r*iest vseth to say; and the said Eleine answerid the same word*es* againe. and so, vnlosinge hand*es*, they kissed, as she remembers; and so they tarried together somwhat more then an houre after that; and the said Alex*ander* and George Holland dep*ar*tid away. being askid de consanguin*itate* inter illa*m* et p*ar*te*m* illa*m* pro-ducen*tem*, she sais she is cosin germaine to the said Alex*ander* in ij^{do} et ij^{do} consanguin*itatis* grad*ibus*. beinge askid 'howe she knoweth it was done apon a Thursdaie'; she saies, 'bie her supp*er*; and biecause they made an end of flesh meat that night for that weke.' no*n* e*st* doct*a*, no*n* conduct*a*, &c.

15. Ellen Carter *v.* Thomas Middlehurst.

(Middlehurst is an inconstant man, and is therefore cald on to make a formal Trothplight before witnesses, which he does.)

3rd Dec. 1565. [2]Robert Brok, of the Parish of Saint Mary, 35, "saies, that about penticost, in an*no* d*omi*ni 1564, he was requestid bie Ellin Carter articulate, to be p*rese*nt w*i*th her, to talk of mariage to be had betwene her and Tho*mas* Midlehurst articulate, in the house of Edward Tomson articulate. and this depon*ent* com*m*inge thither at her request, and after longe co*mmun*icacion had among*es* them,—concerninge the same [3]matter, and a certen lease to be made of the house wherin the said Ellin dwelles, by this deponent, and the said Ed*ward* Tomson; he, this deponent, after agrement of mariage to be had betwene them, know-inge the inconstancye of the said Thom*as* Midlehurst,—biecause he had bene diu*er*se tymes at intreaties of mariage to be had betwene them, the said p*ar*ties, and the said Tho*mas* wold eu*er* shrink from the same—

[1] leaf 164. [2] leaf 255. [3] leaf 255, back.

willed the said Thom*as* to take the said Ellin bie the hand. and the said Tho*mas*, holdinge her bie the hand, this deponent askid hym, and said theis word*es* at the least: 'Thom*as*, will you have this woman?' . . . and the said Tho*mas* answerid 'yea.' and then this deponent askid the said Ellin, ther hand*es* beinge still ioyned, and said: 'Ellin, will you have this man' (meaninge the said Tho*mas*) 'to yo*ur* husband?' and she answerid 'yea.' and therapon they plightid their trouthes together, and kissed together, and after dronk, & made mery. but whether the word*es* were spoken in suche forme as is menc*ion*ed in the boke of com*mon* praier, and w*i*th such circ*um*stances, this depon*ent* can not certenly depose; neu*er*theles he think*es*, as far as he remembres, *that* he, this depon*ent*, spake the word*es* of mariage that the priest speaketh; and the[y] spake the same after; [so] That the p*ar*ties libellate, in his conscience were lawfullie contractid as man and wief together; and so he taketh them to be, before god. and further he sais, that sins tyme of the said Contracte, hit hath bene told this depon*ent*, that they have vsid either other at bed and board, as man and wief."

Edward Tomson, of the parish of St. Peter, Chester, aged 42, and Randulph Thornton, Senior, of the Parish of St. John's, in the same City, aged 59, also depose in like effect to Robert Brok.

27th February, 1565-6. [1]Thomas Yokin, "saieth, that he thinks (1) Edward Tomson is an honest man, and is landlord to the said Ellin; but he thinkes he will depose nothinge but according to truth; (2) That Rafe Thornton is an honest neighbo*ur*, and such one as this deponent verily think*es* will depose nothinge in this cause but that he knowes to be true; and (3) That he well knowes Robert Brok to be an honest man, and landlord to the said Ellin; yet he think*es* he will depose nothinge in this cause, but that he knowes to be true."

Richard Middlehurst, of the Parish of Roncorne, aged 30, "saieth, that he knowes Edward Tomson articulate, and thinke*s* he is an honest man, and is landlord to the said Ellin; and therfore he think*es* he somwhat favors her. yet this deponent belevis that he will depose nothinge but truthe in this cause betwene them, by vertue of his othe. That he think*es* that Raffe Thornton is an honest man, and gretlie favors the said Ellin; yet he think*es* he will not hurt his conscience in this cause, in deposinge otherwise than truth. And that he knowes Rob*er*t Brok by sight, and think*es* he is an honest man, and landlord to the said Ellin, and som*w*hat favo*ur*es her p*ar*tie for that cause: yet he think*es* he will, apon his othe, say nothinge but truth. and this depon*ent* saieth

[1] leaf 268, back.

that he wold put the cause, if hit were his, to the othes and deposic*i*on of the said Robe*r*t and *Edward* Tomson."

III. ADULTERIES.

5*a*. Jane Downes *v*. Reginald Downes. (A Child-Marriage.)

[*This should have come before the Adultery-and-Separation Case on p.* 81.]

[1]Exa*minacio* Testiu*m* in ca*usa* divorcij sup*er* li*bel*lo oblat*o* ex p*ar*te Jane Downes cont*ra* Reginald Downes, capt*a* cora*m* M*agist*ro Robe*r*to Leche, &c, xxiiij° Septembr*is* 1562°.

Laurencius Geslinge, paroch*ie* de Taxall,[2] etat*is* lxx an*norum*, no*vi*t p*ar*te*m* ac*tricem* a m*at*rimonio inter ip*s*am et p*ar*te*m* arti*culatam*,[3] [et] p*ar*te*m* rea*m* a puericia.

Ad p*rimu*m a*rticulu*m, This depone*n*t sais, that 'Regina*l*d Downes and Jane Downes were maried together in the face of the churche, and ar taken & reputid as man & wief.' and forther he sais, that 'he neu*er* knewe of any hate that the said Reginald owid his wief; but was eu*er* willinge and contentid to take her, love her, & cherishe [her] as his wief.' cetera nescit depon*er*e ad co*ntent*a in d*ict*o ar*ticu*lo; but he sais 'the said Reginald wold be very faine to take he[r] againe, whether she have Land*es* or no' /

Ad ij[d] a*rticu*lu*m*, nescit certitudinal*it*er depon*er*e; but he sais he [Reginald Downes] hath kept dyverse women at sondry tymes.

Ad iij' a*rticu*lu*m*, This deponent sais, that 'against his Soull health, the said Reginald hath had iiij[or] children by one Ellin Coke, and iij children by one Sibill Pott; w*hi*ch childre*n*, those that be on lyve, he kepis still at his charges. and as for Ellin Coke, [she] lyveth in her fathers house from his Company; and Sibill Pott is maried in Burton apon Trent. as for any other women that he hath kept, this depone*n*t knowes no*n*.' he think*es* that 'he [R. Downes] neu*er* put his wief from hym, biecause she was neu*er* dwellinge w*i*th hym.'

Ad iiij, nescit depon*er*e; but this depone*n*t sais, he think*es th*at yf she [Jane Downes] were w*i*th her husband, he wold vse her aswell as any man in England wold do his wief.

Ad v', dicit eund*em* fore veru*m*.

Ad vj', refert se ad Jura in ea p*ar*te, q*u*od nescit depon*ere*.

Ad vlt*imum*, dicit p*re*deposit*a* p*er* eu*m* fore vera. no*n* est doct*us*, no*n* conduct*us*, no*n* affinis; est Tenens p*ar*te ree; no*n* curat, &c.

[1] leaf 72, back (Piccope's No. 32). [2] Taxal, Cheshire, near Stockport.
[3] The MS. is smudged here.

[1]Homfri*d*us Downes, p*a*rochie de Tacksall, etat*is* xxx' an*norum*, no*vi*t p*ar*te*m* act*ricem* xvij' an*n*os, et parte*m* rea*m* a na*tivitat*e: est fr*ater* eiusd*em*.

Ad p*rimum* ar*ticulum*, This depone*nt* sais, that 'Reginald Downes and Jane Downes were maried together beynge children; and when they did com*me* to the yeres of Consent,[2] did lye together as man and wief, and had a child together, and at the same tyme, the said Reginald had one Ellin Coke w*i*th child, insomuch that he think*es* his wife and his Leman[3] lay in childbed at on tyme: by w*hi*ch did growe an vnkindnes betwene them. and the said Jane, after yt, wold not company w*i*th hym as her husband; but he sais he neu*er* hatid her, but lovid her as his wief, and wold be contentid to love and cherish her as his wief, although she had no Land*es* fallen vnto her.'

Ad ij^d ar*ticulum*, This depone*nt* sais, that he think*es*, apon the vnkindnes growen betwene the said Jane and her husband, he did wast and consume in folly and adultry,—in kepinge of noughtie women, and the children that he had by them,—suche Land*es* as he had for his owne p*ar*te; biecause the said Jane had the one half that he had duringe his fathers lief.

Ad iij' ar*ticulum*, *res*p*o*ndit p*ro*vt p*rim*us [testis] deposuit. and forther, he sais, that 'the cause of the viciouse lief of the said Reginald was, after he had a child by Ellin Coke, his wief wold not co*m*pany w*i*th hym; whereapon, frend*es* bound the said Reginald, that he shuld neu*er* claime the said Jane as his wief, but yf she were pleasid and co*n*tent; and she was likewise bound to hym, not to claime hym as her husband, except he were co*n*tent; and then he, seying he cold not have her, but he shuld breake his boond*es*, fell to such folly, and had other iij children by the said Ellin Coke, and by one Sibill Pott iij childre*n*, two at a birth, and was suspectid w*i*th one Agnes Turn*er*, to have had a child by her; but he cold neu*er* knowe of his said brother, or of the said Agnes, that hit was the said Reginald*es*. and the children that he had, & be on lyve, the said Reginald kepes nowe. and as for any women that he doth kepe nowe, this depone*nt* knowes of no*n*.'

[4]Ad iiij' ar*ticulum*, This depone*nt* sais, he think*es* that 'the said Jane Downes nedis not to feare to be poysoned or slaine by any secreate meanes; biecause this depone*nt* think*es*, that the said Reginald wold be bounden to vse her as a man ought to do his wief, and not to hurt her by suche meanes.'

[1] leaf 73. [2] Girl 12, boy 14: the copulation may well have been later. [3] Concubine, Ellin Coke. [4] leaf 73, back.

Ad v' ar*ticu*lu*m*, dicit eund*em* fore ver*um*.

Ad vj, nescit depon*ere*, sed refert se ad Jura in ea p*ar*te.

Ad vlt*imum*, dicit p*re*deposit*a* p*er* e*um* fore vera, et fama*m* sup*er* hu*jus*mod*i* laborare. no*n* est doct*us*, no*n* conduct*us*; est fr*ater* p*ar*t*is* ree; no*n* curat de victoria &c.

V. LIBELS.

3 *b*. Henry Fazakerley *v*. Margery Wirrall.

[*Should have followd the case on p.* 117 *above.*]

[1]Exa*min*a*c*io Testiu*m* in ca*usa* diff*amacionis*, sup*er* excepc*io*nib*us* ex p*ar*te Henrici Fazakerley con*tra* M*ar*geria*m* Wirrall, oblat*is*, capt*a* die et a*nn*o p*redic*t*is* [8th May 1562].

Ric*hard*us Wolfall, p*ar*ochie de Walton, etat*is* l annor*um*, no*vit* M*ar*geria*m* Wirrall xxx' an*norum*, et Henricu*m* Fazakerley ab infancia sua.

Ad p*ri*ma*m* excepc*io*n*em* quoad W*illia*m Plumpton, p*ri*mu*m* test*em*, he sais he cannot say anythinge of his honesty, of nor fro[2]; but he sais, he hathe hard say that 'he varyed in his talke in this matter, tellinge one gent*leman* this, and an other gent*leman* a tale cleane contrary, as he hard say; but he is not able to prove hit.' and forther he sais, that 'M*ar*garet Wirrall, apon occasion came to this depone*ntes* house, where she found Henry Fazakerley; but she had knoledge that he was there afore; & that made her more willinge to co*mm*e to this deponen*tes* house, biecause she had enquired of this depone*ntes* syruent (who told her that the said Henry was there afore). & when she came thither, she said bie Fazakerley, "yonder fellowe hathe entrid me into the Cowrt for a pece of mony; & he owes me som*m*e," & namid the sume, as he think*es*, to be iij^s^ ij^d^.' and he said, that 'yf he owid her any thinge, she might [3]also demaund the mony there where he had done his, and she might have right.' and the said M*ar*garet answerid & said, "dost thou denay hit? then thou art a false thief!" and apon *that*, Fazakerley answerid & said, "thou art as like a hoore, as I a thief." and therapon she said, "thou art a thief; and I am able to prove the for a thief; & thou art a thief!" and to his knoledge she spake of all his kin; and so ther was angry word*es* betwene them; but she callid hym 'thief' afore he called her 'hoore'; & that, this depone*nt* is sure of, for he was p*rese*nt by. & forther he sais, that 'Topping*es* wief was by; but as for Rob*er*te Wolfall, he was set to threshe in an old house; but at that tyme he was gone out to seke beast*es*, & might fortune to come againe or eu*er* theis angry

[1] leaf 61. [2] for or against. [3] leaf 61, back.

wordes were endid; but yf he were, there was no body knewe of hym, to this deponentes knoledge, nor ther was no mencion made of hym.' and further he sais, that 'the said Roberte Wolfall was requestid bie Margeret Wirrall to go with her to her Master, Sir Richard Molinex; who answerid, that 'he wold go with her any whether els, to spend xx^s in her cause; but as for thither, he wold not go with half a tale, biecause he was not present at the begin[i]nge.' 'and as touchinge William Plumpton, ther was no body see hym at that present, to this deponentes knoledge, nor had anythinge to do at this deponentes house, where Fazakerley was workinge, nor cannot prove hym self to be there, nor what place he stode by, when he hard the said wordes; but yf he were present, hit was for no good to this deponent.' & as for 'Master Moores hoore,' this deponent sais he neuer hard Fazakerley call Margaret Wirrall so, to his remembraunce.

Ad ij^d excepcionem, This deponent sais, that 'Katherine Walley was present all the tyme of the talke, from the begin[i]nge to thendinge.' & further he sais, that 'Roberte Wolfall did say one a certen tyme, that he wold do as much for the said Margaret as for his mother, in this cause.' & further he sais, 'the said Roberte is of the iij or iiij^th degree [of kin] to the said Margaret; and he, this deponent, standes in the same degree, to his remembraunce; & this deponent, he wold do for her what shuld lye in hym, but for his othes sake, & conscience.' & he sais moreouer, that 'Roberte Wolfall was this [1]deponentes seruaunte at that tyme; but sais he is entysed away bie the said Margaret & her houseband; whereas he was thes deponentes hired seruant for all the yere; & therfore hit is to be muche suspectid, biecause, contrary to his bargaine, he is gone away from hym.'

Ad vltimam, dicit predeposita per eum fore vera.

Jana Wolfall, parochie de Walton, etatis xxxvj' annorum, novit Margaretam Wirrall xij' annos et vltra, et partem ream similiter.

Ad primam excepcionem, dicit Willielmum Plumpton esse honestum virum, quoad noticiam suam; but this deponent see hym not at the wordes spoken betwene Margaret Wirrall & Henry Fazakerley; nor non about her house se hym, as far as she cold enquire of, nor had any thinge to do about this deponentes house. & further, this deponent sais, that 'the said Margaret callid the said Henry "thief," dyverse tymes before he callid her "hoore"; & he namid her not any mans hore, neither Mr Mores, nor noman els, to this deponentes heringe; & she thinkes that the said Henry wold not have callid her "hoore," but that she first callid hym "thief," & said "he was nought, & all his kinne."' & further, this

[1] leaf 62.

deponent sais, 'the occasion began about a mony matter.' & beynge askid, 'apon what occasion the said Margaret came to this deponentes house'; she said, 'apon this occasion: this deponent send to her for mony, & by her syruant; & the said Margaret enquired of the said syruant whether the said Henry was at her Mistreses house; & she answerid "yea." then Margaret Wirrall said, "then I will go with the myself." wherfore this deponent thinkes she came thither to scould.' and further, she sais, for Roberte Wolfall, that 'he shuld have gone for beastes; but whether he went for them or no, she cannot tell; but yf he were threshinge, she shuld have hard hym; & therfore he might stand prively to heare them; but he was not knowne to be their[1] of any man; but that he came in after.'

Ad ij[d], This deponent sais, that 'Katherine Walley was present by, at all the talke; but that she went downe to fetche a baskett full of Turves, where she might here all the talke, commynge & goynge.' & this deponent hath hard Roberte Wolfall say dyverse tymes, that 'he wold do as muche for Margaret Wirrall as for his owne mother in this cause.' [2]and further, this deponent sais, she hath hard hit recknid that 'Margaret Wirrall & the said Roberte were nere akinne in the iij[d] or iiij[th] degre'; & that 'Roberte Wolfall was Richard Wolfall hired syruant, & went away before his covenant, & was well vsed of his brother; but whether he be gone away through the entysement of the said Margaret Wirrall & her husband, or for what occasion, she cannot tell; but it is to be suspectid that hit was so biecause he was honestly entreatid of his brother, & did not mynd[3] to go away before.'

Ad vltimam, dicit predeposita per eam fore vera.

Katarina Toppinge, parochie de Walton, etatis xxx' annorum et vltra, novit Margaretam Wirrall xiiij annis, et partem ream similiter.

Ad primam excepcionem, dicit quod novit Willimum Plumpton fore virum bone fame. & further, this deponent sais, that 'in wordinge betwixe Margaret Wirrall & Henry Fazakerley, the said Margaret callid Henry "thief," before he callid her "hoore"; and said "he was a thief; and all his kine was nought." & the reasonynge was about a pece of mony, quemadmodum deposuit Richardus Wolfall. & when she callid hym often tymes "thief," he said "she was as like a hoore, as he a thief."' and this deponent sais, that 'she thinkes the said Henry wold not have said hit, but in his chafe, because she callid hym "thief" dyverse tymes.' & as for William Plumpton, she sais, 'she neither se nor knewe hym to be there; but as she was goynge homeward with Wirralles wief, they mett

[1] for 'there.' See the converse, p. 141. [2] leaf 62, back. [3] intend.

Wil*lia*m Plumpton a stones cast from the old house, com*m*ynge from Kirkbe or Darby, & goynge to his owne house, as this depone*n*t supposeth; but well she knowes he had nothinge to do about the house at that tyme. and as for Robe*r*te Wolfall, she se hym not; but as this depone*n*t & M*ar*garet Wirrall were goynge homeward, they se Robe*r*te Wolfall in the old house; [1]but what he was about to do, or had bene doynge, this depone*n*t knowes not.'

Ad ij[d], This depone*n*t sais, that 'Kat*herine* Walley was p*resen*t at all the talke betwixe the said M*ar*garet & Henry, & hard all the talk; but that she went for a baskett full of Turves, where she might here all the talke, com*m*ynge & goynge.' and further, she sais, 'Rob*er*t Wolfall is akinne to M*ar*garet Wirrall; & was hired sy*ruan*t to Ric*hard* Wolfall, his brother, till this chidinge & contenc*io*n begon; & after that, this depone*n*t thinke*s* that M*ar*garet Wirrall & her husband have sins entised hym away; for he was well vsed w*it*h his brother, &c.'

Ad vltima*m*, dicit p*re*deposit*a* p*er* ea*m* fore vera.

Katarina Walley, p*ar*ochie de Sefton, etat*is* xxx[ta] an*n*or*um*, nov*it* p*ar*tes ab infancia istius deponen*tis*.

Ad p*ri*ma*m* excepc*io*ne*m*, dicit, q*uod* nov*it* Wi*lliel*m*um* Plumpton fore viru*m* bone fame. and further, this depone*n*t sais, that 'apon occasion risinge about a mony matter, M*ar*garet Wirrall callid Henry Fazakerley "hard, strong thief," and "gryninge thief"; and said he was "a p*ro*vid thief, & all his kinne"; and apon that, he callid her "p*ro*vid hoore," & said "she was as like a p*ro*vid hoore as he a thief"; & so thus they fell to "thief & hoore." and as for Wi*llia*m Plumpton, this depone*n*t sais that she se hym not at theis word*es*, nor knewe not of hym; but after the word*es* endid, the said M*ar*garet Wirrall & Topping*es* wief goynge homeward, they found Wi*llia*m Plumpton in a hye way, a flight shote from the place where the word*es* were spoken, half an howre after.' quoad Rob*ertu*m Wolfall, concordat cu*m* Rich*ardo* Wolfall, p*re*conteste suo.

Ad ij[d], This depone*n*t sais, that 'she was p*rese*nt by at the word*es* spoken, as before she hath deposid. as for Rob*er*t Wolfall, wher he was, this depone*n*t knowes not; but she sais he was not p*rese*nt by in sight at that tyme. & further, as for goynge to Mr. Molinex, concordat cu*m* Ric*hard*o Wolfall. [2]and forther, she sais, that Robe*r*te Wolfall is akin in the iij[d] or iiij[th] degre to M*ar*garet Wirrall, et a hired sy*ruan*t to his brother. Et quoad cetera, concordat cu*m* Ric*hard*o Wolfall, p*re*conteste suo.'

Ad vltima*m*, dicit p*re*deposit*a* p*er* ea*m* fore vera.

[1] leaf 63. [2] leaf 63, back.

7 *a.* Constance Frost *v.* William Ball and others.

(For saying that she was 'a very hoore,' and had 2 Husbands.)

[These Depositions should have come before those printed on p. 122-3 above.]

28th April, 1564. [1]Robert Johnson, of the Parish of Saint Bridget, Chester, 'sais, that apon a tyme, he and one Ric*hard* Barker, com*m*ynge through a rowe in the bridge Strete, Ric*hard* Derwall, standinge at his owne dore, came vnto them, and said to this depon*ent*: "I had thought Custance [2]Frost had bene an honest woman; but she is a very hoore, and hath ij° husband*es*; and it [= this] is reportid of them that have borne worship in Chester, who will stand to it." and so all iij went to Ric*hard* Barkers house, and dronke, eithe[r] of them a peny; and had there the talk there about the same matter.' and further saies, 'he neu*er* hard it reportid other wise but she was an honest woman, afore this tale reasid; but sins, he think*es* her good name is much empaired therby.'

16th May, 1564. [3]Thomas Burges, of the Parish of St. Bridget, Chester, aged 53, deposes, 'that in co*mmun*icac*i*on betwixe Wi*lli*am Ball articulate, and this depon*ent*, the said Wi*lli*am declared, among*es* other thing*es*, that Custance Frost had made hym chalenge, for that he shuld have reportid her to have ij° husband*es*.' and further he said: "I said so, but I care not. I do not care; for I knowe where I hard it: when I was at the Counsell." . . .

[4]John Whitheadd, Junior, of the Parish of Saint Michael's, Chester, aged 38, Baker, 'saies, that in certen talk apon a tyme had betwixe Wi*lli*am Ball Articulate, and this depon*ent*, Custance Frost came vnto them; and after salutac*i*ons done, she said vnto the said Wi*lli*am: "ar you one of them that bringe word from the Counsell that I have two husband*es*?" he said "yea, mary, that I am." "then," q*uod* she, "will you stand to it?" "yea, mary," said [William Ball], "that, I will stand it, that I hard it." "then," q*uod* she, "you may better bringe them furth that spake." "nay," q*uod* Wi*lli*am Ball, "I will not bring them furth: bring you them furth, & you will have them." q*uod* she, "*per*ch*a*unce I shall make you bring them furth, or els the lawe shall faile me." and so she dep*ar*tid, and willed this depon*ent* to beare her witness . . . he sais, he think*es* she is an honest [woman], both sins and before . . .'

[5]Richard Orton, of Chester, deposes, "that somwhat afore Christmas last, he was at brekfast, w*i*th Elizabeth Brerewodd in company, and

[1] leaf 164, back. ? [2] leaf 165. [3] leaf 166, back. [4] leaf 167.
[5] leaf 166, back.

others, and he made haste away. the question was askid, 'whie he hastid so away.' and this depon*ent* answerid, 'he went to the Castell to paie his fees.' then Elizabeth Berewod said: "if you go thither, you may call Frost*es* wief 'sister'; and she may call you 'brother'; biecause, if it be as I here say, she hath ij° husband*es*, and you have two wieves." . . . He think*es* her good name is not impaired therbie, bicause no man beleues it." [See the Depositions continued at p. 122 above.]

12. Elizabeth Basnett *v.* Anne Venables.

(For calling her 'a hoore' with Anne's late Husband. Daiesmen or Referees appointed; their decision rejected by Defendant.)

26th October, 1564. [1]Cicilea Litlo*ur*, wife of Thomas Litloure, of the Parish of Budworth, aged 40, "saieth, that about Lent last past, as this depon*ent* nowe remembres, the said Anne Venables, Landladie to this Deponent*es* husband, came into this deponent*es* house, beinge her nere neybo*ur* and Ten*nan*t. after whom, a little space after, came Eliz*abeth* Basnett. and so they fell apon reasoninge together, and amonge other scoldinge word*es* betwixe them, the said Ann Venables said, 'she, the said Eliz*abeth*, was a hoore, and had plaid the nought w*i*th Raffe Venables, her [Ann's] husband decessid.' and the said Eliz*abeth*, the said daie or the daie after, willed this depon*ent* to testifye the same she had hard, when she shuld be callid therto."

[2]Elizabeth Litlo*ur*, of the Parish of Budworth, aged 18, 'sais, that about Lent last, as she remembres, the said p*ar*ties, viz. the said Eliz*abeth* and Ann, came into this depone*ntes* fathers house—apon what occasion she knowes not,—and amonge other scoldinge word*es* had betwixe them, the said Anne said to the said Eliz*abeth*, "thou art a hoore; and hast bene nought w*i*th Raffe Venables, my husband." and w*i*th that, the said Eliz*abeth* rushed furth, and willed this depon*ent* and her Mother, the said daie, to beare witnes what she said.'

19th November, 1564. [3]Homfri Holford, of Witton, in the Parish of Budworth, aged 50, "saieth, that for such sclaunderous wordes as it was alledgid that Anne Venables shuld saie against Elizabeth Basnet, the said Anne Venables and Eliz*abeth* Basnet toke Daisemen, to make an end of the same. and this depon*ent* stode by, when the daiesme*n* of Anne Venables did p*ro*mes vnto the daiesme*n* of Elizabeth basnet, that Anne Venables shuld com*m*e afore a dosen or xvi pe*r*sons, in a place and daie appointid, & there aske forgevenes of Eliz*abeth* Basnet for such word*es* as

[1] leaf 196. [2] leaf 196, back. [3] leaf 199.

she had wrongfullie spoken by Eliz*abeth* Basnet. and at the daie & place appointid, the said Anne Venables did refuse, and wold not com*me* to ask the said Eliz*abeth* Basnet forgevenes; but came not there at all."

[1]Thomas Bromfeld, of the chapelry of Witton, and Parish of Budworth, deposes to the same effect as Homfri Holford.

II. 10 *b*. Sybil Blakhurst *v*. Randle Ramshae.

[This should have come before the Depositions on p. 69-71 above.]

[2]R*es*p*on*sio*n*es Perso*na*les Ran*dulphi* Ramshae sup*er* p*ositi*onib*us* et Ar*ticu*lis li*bel*li oblat*i* ex pa*r*te Sibille Blakhurst, capt*e* Die et A*nno* p*r*ed*ictis* [31 Jan. 1565(6)].

Ad p*r*ima*m* p*ositi*onem, This re*spo*ndent saieth, that after he had begotten Sibell Blackhurst w*i*th child, about a moneth or sixe wekes afore she was deliu*er*ed, the frend*es* of this R*esp*ondent did talk and com*m*en together w*i*th the frend*es* of the said Sibell, concerninge mariage to be had betwene the said Sibill and this re*spo*ndent; at w*hi*ch tyme this R*esp*ondent stode free from all contract*es*.

Ad ij[d] p*ositi*onem, negat eand*em* penitus, that either he hath made the said Sibill any contract or p*r*omes, p*er* verba de p*r*es*e*nti aut de futuro, &c.; neu*er*theles, he confesseth that he kepeth a child borne of the bodie of the said Sibell, w*hi*ch he think*es* to be his owne; but he saieth, he made her not any p*r*omes of mariage, vt sup*ra* deposuit.

Ad iij, he saieth, he neu*er* either send the said Sibell any token in waie of mariage, or receyvid any from the said Sibell [[3]but one handcherchief, w*hi*ch this re*spo*ndent plucked from her].

Ad iiij', fatetur eand*em* fore vera*m*.

Ad v', this re*spo*ndent saies, he think*es* the said Sibell hath no iuste cause to complaine; or els, this Cowrt is for her iust remedie.

Ad vlt*imam*, credit credita et negat negata; et sup*er* no*n* creditis et negat*is*, credit &c.

[1] leaf 199, back. [2] leaf 268.
[3] The words bracketed are struck out in the MS.—W. H. P.

INDEX OF NAMES OF MEN AND WOMEN.

BY MR. W. H. PRICE.

Abdiah, xxix.
Accars, Harrie and Jane, xxii, xxiii.
Adder, Res, 188, 188 *n*, 190.
Ahab, xxix.
Ahaz, King, xxvii.
Ainsworth, George, 140 (*see also* Aynsworth).
Alatt (Alat), Margaret (wife of Richard Pierson), 73, 74, 75; liv, lxxiii, lf. 46.
Albericus, xxix.
Alcocke, William, 174 (*see also* Awcockes).
Aldersey, F[o]ulk, 165.
„ John, 155.
„ William, 168, 174, 177, 178.
Allen, Edward, 173.
„ John, 164.
„ Ralph, 155.
Allerton, Richard, of Swyne, in Holdernesse, Yorkshire, xxiv, xxvi.
Amery, Edward, 74.
„ John, 101; lxxiv, lxxv.
„ Robert, 152, 159, 160.
Anderson, Christopher, xxiii *n*.
Anderton, John, 175.
„ Mr., xlvi.
Andrew, Ellen (born Dampart), 12, 13, 14, 15; lxxiv, lxxv.
„ John, 12, 13, 14, 15.
„ William, 13, 14.
Anglesey, Lord, xxi, xxxi, xxxii.
Anion, Richard, 173.
Antrobus, Thomas, 173.
Apshawe (Aspshawe), John, 124, 125, 126, lx.
Arderne, William, lxxx.
Arlington, Lord, xxxiii.
Arrowsmith, Alice, lxxviii, lf. 128.
Arundel, Henry, Earl of, 181 *n*.
Aschams, xxxvii *n*.
Ashley, Henry, 126.
„ Joan, 123, 124, 125, 126; lxxxiii, lxxxiv.
Ashton, Miles, 33.
„ Nicholas, 29.
„ Rafe, 138.
Asmall, William, lxxix, lxxx *n*.
Aspden, Benet, 85.
Aspshawe (*see* Apshawe).
Aston, Hugh, li.
Austin, Mr. T., xiii.
Awcocke [ ], 90 (*see also* Alcocke).
Axon, Mr. W. E. A., xxxi.
Aynscoe, Ellen and John, xxiii.
Aynsworth, Alice (Alis), 131, 184, 185, 186, 187.
„ Christopher, 56.
„ John, 184.
„ Richard, and his wife, 184, 185, 186.
„ *See also* Ainsworth.

Bacon, Sir N., xli *n*.
Badcocke, Alson, xlix *n*.
Baigent, Mr., lxix.
Bailie, Elizabeth, 128.
Ball (Baulle), Ellen (Elene, Elyne), (married Thomas Wicksted), 51, 52; lxxviii.
„ Joanna, 52.
„ Margaret, lxxxi *n*.
„ Thomas, 52.
„ William, 122, 208; lx, lxxxii, lxxxiii.
Ballard, Ann (born Holden), 45, 46, 47; lxxxv.
„ James, 45, 46, 47; lxxxv.
Bamford (Walker *alias* Bamford), Isabella, 140, 141.
Banester, James, 169, 177.
„ Van, 30.

Barcumbe, Richard, xlv *n.*
Barker, Ann, 116.
„ David, 155.
„ John, 145 *n.*, 146.
„ John H., lxix.
„ Randulph, 196.
„ Richard, 123, 208.
„ Thomas, 159.
„ William, 33, 34.
Barlow (Barlowe), James, 139.
„ John, 125.
Barnes, John, 91, 92, 94, lv.
„ Thomas, 131, 132.
Barneshaw, Humfrey, lxxx.
Baron, Nicholas, 72.
Barrat, William, 170.
Bartholomew, 29 *n.*, 30 *n.*, 34 *n.*, 35 *n.*, 46 *n.*, 51 *n.*, 125 *n.*
Barton, Margery, lxxviii, lxxix, lxxx.
Basnet, Elizabeth, 209, 210; lx, lxxxiii.
Bassel, John, 172.
Bath and Wells, The Bishop of, xxx *n.*
Bathoe, William, 120, 121.
Bavande, Richard, 161, 165.
Bawdry, lvii *n.*
Baxter, Raff, 173.
Bebington (Bebinton), Thomas, 161.
„ William, 129.
Beddow (Bedoe), Sir William (Wylliam), 2, 52.
Belen, Alice, (Belen *alias* Gidlowe), li.
„ Thomas, li.
Bellin, Margaret, 87.
Bennett (Benet), 170.
„ Robert, 174, 175.
Bentam, Ellen (born Bolton), 31, 32, 33; lxxxiv.
„ Richard, 32, 33; lxxxv.
„ Thomas, 31, 32, 33; lxxxiv.
Berkeley, divers Earls, xxvii, xxviii, xxxix, xli *n.*
Bersher, lxii.
Beyman, Christopher, 171.
Beyne, Agnes, xlv *n.*
Bildon, Thomas, junior, 192, 193.
Billinge, John, 138.
„ Catherine, lxxviii and *n.*
Billinton, Anna, 86, 88.
Bilsbie, Gile (married to Rafe Holden), 72.
Bingham, Captn. Sir Richard, 171, 172.
Bingley, John, 172.
Birchall, William, lxxxiii.
Birchwood (Birchwodde), Richard, 73.
Bird, Elizabeth, 187, 188, 189, 190, 191, 192, 193, 194, 195; xliv *n.*, xlvi, lxxv.
„ Mr., 161.
„ Richard, 152, 173.
„ S. R., xlix *n.*
„ William, 152, 165, 174.
Birkenhead (Birkenes), Richard, 152, 152 *n.*
Bithell, Thomas, 155.
Blackburne (Blagburne, Blackborne), Henry, 137; lx, lxxv.
„ Joan, 137, 138.
„ William, 140.
Blackhurst, Sibil, lxxxvi.
Blackston, *alias* Smith, Jane, 153.
Blackstone, Charles, 193.
Blakey, Sir Roger, 45, 46, 47.
Blakhurst, Jone, 71.
„ Richard, 70.
„ Sybil, 69, 70, 71, 210; xlviii, lxxxvi.
Blundell, James, 40, 43.
Bodley, Ellen, lx.
Boich, Henry, xxix.
Bolton, Ellen (Eleine, Elene, Ellein, Ellin), (married Thomas Bentam), 31, 32, 33; lxxxiv.
„ Jane, 128.
„ Katherine (married Rafe Fishe), 33, 34; lxxxiv.
Bond, Elizabeth, 145.
Bonner, B., lxviii.
Booth (Bothe), , 78.
Borde, Andrew, lviii *n.*
Boscawen, Mr. St. Chad, lxiv.
Bostock (Bostoke, Bostok), John, 132.
„ Rafe, 122.
Boswell, Henry, 49.
Boteler, Jn. Bransey, Lancashire, lxxxvii *n.*
„ Isabell, lxxxvii *n.*
Bowes, Sir William, xxiv *n.*
„ Margery, xxiv *n.*
Bowker, Antonie, 184, 186.
Bowne (? Brown), Henry, 99.
Bowre, Richard, 197.
Boyes (Boys) Grace, (married to Robert Talbot), 16; lxxv.
Bradburne, Margaret, 97.
Bradley, Margaret, 129, 130.
(Bradley's Stratman's Dict., 117 *n.*)
Bradshawe, (Master Doctour) Piers, 51.
„ (Sir) Robert, 140.

Bradshawe, Roger, 130.
„ (Sir) Simon, 82, 83, 84.
Braine, Roger, 127.
Bramall, Edward, 140, 141.
Brand, lvii *n.*
Brandlyngs, Sir Robert, lviii.
Brererey, Mr., 162.
Brereton (Brerton), Alice (? Jane), 27; lxxxii.
„ Geffrey, lxxxi, lxxxi, *n.* 1.
„ Jane (married to John Somerford), 25, 26, 27, 28; lxxxii.
„ Richard, lxxxi, top.
„ (Sir) William, 27, 28.
Brerewood (Brerewod, Brerewode), Elizabeth, 123, 208, 209.
„ Mr. , 161.
„ Robert, 174.
Bretherton (*see* Brotherton).
Bretten, Sir Rich., lxxiv *n.*
Bretton, Galfrid, 125.
Brevokes, Thomas, 15 *n.*
Brians (Brine, Briens, Bryne), Roger, 127, 173.
Brickhill, Edmund, 170.
Bridge, Christabella (Christable Bridge *alias* Hope), 85.
„ Elizabeth (born Ramsbotham), 6, 7, 8, 9; lxxi, lxxii.
„ John, 6, 7, 7 *n.*, 8, 9; xviii, xix, lxxi, lxxii.
„ Thomas, 8, 9.
„ William, 14.
Brindley, Thomas, 114.
Broadhurst (Brodhurst), Alice, 134; lx, lxi, lxxxiv.
Brock, Robert, 190, 192, 200, 201, 202.
Brodley, Ellin, 125.
Bromfeld, Thomas, 210.
Bromley, Master, 128, 129.
Brooke (Broke), Matilda, 77.
Brooke, Richard, xxii.
Broster, Richard, 155, 171, 173.
Brotherton (? Bretherton), John, 68, 69; xlvi, lxxxvi.
Broughton, Mr. , 161.
„ Valentine, 165.
Browne, Allison, xlix *n.*
„ Henry, 99.
„ James, 5.
„ Maister , 118, 119; lix.
Brydge, lxii.
Brymestich (Brymestoich), Henry, 152.
Brymestich, Thomas, 152, 152 *n.*, 156.
Bryne (or Brians), Roger, 127, 173.
Buccleugh, Countess of, xxxii.
Bulkely, Thomas, 168.
Bunbury, Edward, xxii.
„ Thomas, 152.
Bupy (or Buxy), Peter, 169.
Burgenye, Richard, 21.
Burges, Margaret, lxxxi, *n.* 2.
„ Roger, 131.
„ Thomas, 208.
Burkill (*see* Brickhill).
Burleigh (Burgheley), Lord W., 166; lxiv.
Burn, J. S., xxxvi *n*, xxxix, xlv *n.*
Burns (Ecclesiastical Law), xxxii.
Buron, Humphrey, Curate of Chedill, lxxvi.
Burton, Christopher, 150.
„ Edmund, 63.
„ Elizabeth (Burton *alias* Eccles), 62, 63; lxxxi.
„ Henry, 150.
„ John, 62, 159.
Butler, Mr. , 180.
Butterworth, Charles, lxxxiv.
„ John, lxxxiv.
„ Robert, lxxxiv.
Bybbye, Roger, 67, 68; lxxxv.

Cadogan, Sarah, xxxiii.
„ Wm. (1st Earl of), xxxiii.
Calderwood, xxxi.
Calkin (Cawkin), Margaret, 38 *n.*, 39, 42.
„ William, 39, 40, 42.
Callis, Richard, 171.
Cally, Thomas, 29.
Canon, Doctor, 168.
Canterbury, Archbishop of, xxxi, xxxii.
Capper, Robert, 111, 115.
Carison, John, 108.
Carr, Robert, xli.
Carter, Ellen, 200, 201; xliv *n.*, lxxxv, lxxxvi.
Carter (? Carler), Fulco, 156.
Cary, (Sir) George, 178, 179.
Case, Thomas, 151, 154.
Cash, Agnes, 62.
Catly, Thomas, 29.
Caton, Randle, 158, 159.
Cecill, Sir Wm., xli.
Cecyll, (Sir) Robert, 167, 168, 179.
Chadderton, Joan, xxii.

Chaderton, Wm., Bp. of Chester, xxii, xxxviii, lxxvi.
Chadock, William, 84.
Chadwick, James, lxxxiv.
Chamber, Henry, xl.
Chambers, xxxii.
Chaucer (Poet), xl.
Chauntrell, Mr. Paul, 149 *n.*
Chester, City Conduit Keeper, lxiv.
„ City Waits, lxiv.
„ Deputy Bailiff of the County Exchequer, lxiii.
„ Mayors of (Mr. Maior, &c.), 145—182; lxiii, lxiv.
„ Sheriff of, 192, 195; xlvi, lxiii, lxiii *n.*
„ William, Bishop of, 27, 195; lxxvi.
Chetam, John, 21, 27, 43, 62, 63.
Chichester, (Sir) Arthur, 179.
Cholmondeley (Cholmely), (Sir) Hugh (Knight), 128, 129; lxxvi.
„ Master, 122.
Christofers, Margaret, 140.
Church, John, 145.
Claiton (Claitton, Cleiton, Cleyton), Edward, lxxxi, at foot.
„ Katherine, 117, 118, 119, 120; lxxiii.
„ William, 117, 118, 119, 120; lix.
Clare, William, 97, 98; lvi, lxxv.
Clark, Mr. Chas. J., xxxiii.
Clarke, Bridget, xxxiii.
„ John, lxxvii, and *n.*
Cleaver, xlviii *n.*
„ Robert, xlvii *n.*
Cleveland, Duchess of, xxxiii.
Cliff, John, 100, 101; lxxxii, lxxxii *n.*
Clifford, Elizabeth, d. of Thomas, Lord Clifford, xxxii.
„ Thomas, Lord, xxxii.
„ Vincent, 171.
Clopton, Ann, xxx.
Clough, Jane, 127.
Cockayne, xxiv *n.*
Coke, Ellen, 81; lxxxii *n.*, 202, 203.
„ George, 183, 184.
„ Margeria, 50.
„ Sir Richard, Curate of Eastham, lxxii.
„ William (as to his Will), lxxxv.
„ *See also* Cooke.
Coldock, Margaret, 165.
Coldock, Richard, 165.
Coles, S , 167.
Collen, Edward, lxxix, *n.* 2, lxxx.
Coller, Galtherus, 68.
Collins, Dr., lxvii.
Colly, William, 120; lxxiii, lf. 58 bk.
Collyns, Margaret, 147.
Colson, Helinor, xlix *n.*
Colthurst, Henry, 35.
Connell, Claude, lxix.
Conway (Conwaie), Christopher, 149.
Cooke, Jeffrey, 151.
„ *See also* Coke.
Cope, Sir William, xxxiii.
Coppock (Cappock), Alex., 175, 176.
Corbet, Mr. , 180.
Cotgrave, lix *n.*
Cotgreve, John, 91, 92, 93, 94, 95, 96, 97; lxxiv, lxxv, lxxvi, lxxvii, lxxviii.
„ John, clerk, of St. Peters, Chester, li, lv, lxiii.
„ Randulph, 65.
Cottes, Edward, 172.
Cotton, Mr. Jas. Sutherland, xxxiii.
Coventree, Widow (Wedew), 173.
Cowburne, George, 54.
„ Henry (Henrie), 56.
„ Rafe, 54.
Cowdale, Robert, lxxvi, *n.* 2.
Cowper, Roger, lxxi, *n.* 2.
Cox, Mr. E. W., lxxxvii.
Cragge, John, xlix *n.*
Cranes Wife, 170; lxiv.
Cranmer, xlviii *n.*
Crockett, Roger, 89, 91, 119, 120.
Croft (Crofte), Richard, 90.
„ William, 89, 90, 91.
Crompton, Isabella, 130, 131; lx, lxxiii.
„ Jenkin, 130; lxxiv, lf. 69.
„ John, 130, 131.
Cromwell, Thomas, xlviii *n.*
Crosse, Elizabeth, 99, 100; lxxxi.
Crowshawe, Margaret and William, lxxxiii, lf. 201; lxxiv, lf. 203 bk.
Culcheth, Elizabeth, 51; lxxiii.
„ Rafe, 51; lxxiii.
Cumberland, Earl of, xli.
Cupper, William, 15 *n.*
Cutt, Robert, 160, 161.

Dakyn, Dr. John, xxvii.
Dalby, , 168.
Dalton, Michael, xxxvi *n.*, xxxix *n.*
Dampart (*see* Davenport).

Danbie, Simon, 72.
Daniel, , 180.
Darcy, Dowsabel, xxiv *n.*
„ Lord, xxi, xxii, xxiii, xxiv, xxiv *n.*, xxv, xxvi, xxvii.
„ Mary, xxiii, xxiv, xxv, xxvi, xxvii.
Darlington, Rondull, 86, 87.
Davenport (Dampart, Damparte), Elizabeth (born Page), 22; xx, lxxiv, lxxvii.
„ Ellen (married to John Andrewe), 12, 13, 14, 15; lxxiv, lxxv.
„ John, 13, 14, 15, 17.
„ Master, 62.
„ Thomas, 22; xx, lxxvii.
„ Thomas M., lxviii.
David, Jane, 102, 103, 104, 105, 106, 107, 108, 109, 110; lviii, lxxii, lxxiii, lxxiv, lxxv.
„ John, sacristan, 188, 190; xliv *n.*
„ Katherina (Knarad, Kanaurand, Knawrade), 102, 103, 107.
„ Robert ap, 102, 103, 104; lxxii.
„ Roger ap, 102, 103, 104, 105, 106, 107, 108, 109, 110; lviii.
„ William, 109.
Davies, Aldersey, 170.
„ Jane, 156.
„ Phil, xv.
Decies, Vicount, xxxii.
„ Vicountess, xxxii.
Delavall, John, xliii *n.*
de Lisle, Lord, xxviii.
de Merlay, Roger, xxiii *n.*
de Montford, Simon, xl *n.*
Denwall, William, 175.
Derby (Darbye), the Earl of, 48, 180; xviii, xxii.
Dering, Edward, lxii.
Derwall, Richard, 208.
de Syde, William, xli.
de Tuenge (Thweng), Marmaduke, xxiii *n.*
de Umfraville, Gilbert, xl *n.*
D'Ewes, Sir Simonds, xxi, xxix, xxx.
Dewhurst, Richard, 16.
Dicconson, Christopher, 29.
Dichfelde, John, 97.
Dickson, Richard, 32.
Dicon, George, 63.
Diconson, Mistris, lxxii *n.*
Dilon, Henry, 188, 189, 190, 191, 192, 193, 194, 195, 196; xliv *n.*, xlvi, lxxv.
Dimock, , 110.
Dockwra, (Sir) Henry (Knight), 179.
Dodd (Dod, Dood), Alice, 76, 77.
„ Bartime, li.
„ Geoffrey, 173.
„ Roger, 150.
„ Rondull, 135, 136.
Donne, Richard, 150.
„ Thomas, 52.
Donnyng, Margaret, xlvii *n.*
Downes, Humfrey, 203.
„ Jane, 81, 202, 203.
„ Reginald, 81, 202, 203; liv, lxxiv, lxxvi.
Doxie, Anne, 100; lxxxii, lxxxiii.
Dublin, Adam, 168.
Duckley, Sir Richard, 190.
Duckworth, Henry, 138.
„ William, 89, 90.
Dudson, Edmond, lxxxi *n.*
„ Elizabeth, lxxvii.
Dugdale, Margaret (married to Robert Mason), 30, 31; xviii, lxxxiii.
Duncalf, Mr. , 15.
Dunn (*see* Donne).
Dunsterfield, William, 174.
Dutton, Alice (married to John Starkie), 49, 50, 51; lxxii.
„ Ann (married to Wm. Stanley), 47, 48, 49; lxxxv.
„ Brigitte (married to George Spurstowe), 38, 39, 40, 41; lxxxv.
„ John, 159, 160, 161; lxxix and *n.*, lxxx *n.*
„ Margaret (born Stanley), 41, 42, 43; xx, lxxxv.
„ Peter, 160.
„ Rafe (Rondull), 38 *n.*, 39, 40, 42, 50, 51.
„ Roland, 41, 42, 43; xx, lxxxv.
Dymoke, Sir Edward, xxiv *n.*

Earwaker, J. P., 139 *n.*, 142 *n.*, 149 *n.*, 152 *n.*; xiv, xiv *n.*, xvii *n.*, xix *n.*, xxi *n.*, xxiii, xxv, xxxviii, lxi, lxv *n.*, lxxiii *n.*
Eastwood (Estwood), Agnes, 85.
Eaton (Eiton, Heiton, Heyton), James, 83, 84.
„ Mary (Marie), 82, 83, 84; liv, lxxxiii.
„ Richard, 123.

Eaton, William, 82, 83, 83 *n.*, 84, 85; liv, lxxxii, lxxxiii.
Eblethwaite, Robert, 82.
Eccles, Elizabeth (Eccles *alias* Burton), 62, 63; lxxxi.
„ Mr., xxxiv, xxxv.
„ Richard, 135.
Edge, Margaret, lxxvii, and *n.* 2.
„ Thomas, 121.
Edmund, Morgan, 187, 188, 189, 190, 191, 192, 193, 194, 195; xlvi, lxxv.
Edward, David ap, 110.
Egerton, (Sir) Philip (Phelippe), 87, 88; lv, lxxii *n.*
„ Roger, 88.
Eiton, Katherine, lxxviii and *n.*, lxxix, lxxx.
„ Mary, lxxxii, lxxxiii.
„ William, lxxxii, lxxxiii.
„ *See* Eaton.
Eliakim, King, xxvii.
Ellart, John, 179.
Ellis, Alice (Alis Mathue *alias* Ellis, married to Peter Hope), 18, 19, 20, 21; xviii—lxxvii.
„ or Edge, Margaret, lxxvii, *n.* 2.
„ Mathue, 21.
Emery (*see* Amery).
Emmot, Barnard, 47.
England, Earl Marshall of, 168.
„ Lord High Treasurer of, 176.
Entwistle (Entwisell), Constance (married to Andrew Haworth), 9, 10; lxxii, lxxiii.
Essex, Earl of, 168, 170; xxix.
„ Wm., xxxiii.
Evans, Jenkin (Jankin), 109.
„ Richard, 169, 172.
Eurye, Lord, xix, xix *n.*, xxi, xxiii, xxiv, xxv.
„ Mary (born Darcy), xxiii, xxiv, xxv, xxvi, xxvii.
Ezechias, xxvii, xxix.

Farefaxe, William, of Alne, Yorkshire, xxiv.
Farmer, Mr., lxvi *n.*
Farrow, John, 157.
Fazakerley (Fazakerleis), Ellen (Eleine), 102.
„ Henry, 102 *n.*, 117, 204, 205, 206, 207; lxxiii, lf. 41, lf. 61.
„ Margaret, 93, 95; lxxiii, lf. 41, lf. 61.
Fazakerley, Master, 23.
„ Robert, 151.
Fernhed, John, Rector of Limme, lxxvi.
Fishe, Katherine (born Bolton), 33, 34; lxxxiv.
„ Rafe, 33, 34; lxxxiv.
Fisher, Joanna, lxxix *n.*
Fitton, (Sir) Edward, xlii.
„ Mary, xlii.
Fitzgerald, Catherine, xxxi.
Fitzherbert, xxxvi *n.*
Flamock, Wm., xl.
Fletcher (Fletchar), 170.
„ Anne (born Whitfield), 22, 23, 24; lxxix.
„ Captn., xlix *n.*
„ John, 23; xliv *n.*
„ Robert, 24, 162, 164.
„ Thomas, 22, 23, 24; lxxix.
„ Thomas (Mayor of Chester), 162, 163, 164, 165, 166.
„ William, lxxxii.
Foot, William, xlii *n.*
Ford (Foord), Patrick, 174, 175, 176.
Forman, Dr., xxix, xxx.
Forrest, Robert, 34.
Foster, lviii.
Fowdon, Randle, 62.
Fowler, Mr., xlvii *n.*
Foxall, Robert, 170.
Foxe, Oliver, 57.
Fradsam, Margaret, 188, 189, 194; lxxiii.
„ Randle, 85, 86, 87, 88; lxxiii.
Francis (Frauncis), John, 168.
„ William, 180.
French, (Sir) Thomas, 34, 35, 183.
Frost, Constance, 122, 123, 208, 209; lx, lxxxii, lxxxiii.
Furnivalls, The founder of the Yorkshire Branch, xl.
Fyton, John, 165.

Gallimour (Gallimoure), William, 100, 101.
Gam, Alice, 121.
„ John, 120, 121; lxxiii, lf. 58 bk.
Gamon, Mr. John, xv, lxvi, lxvi *n.*
Gamull (? Gamull), Edmund, 146, 160, 160 *n.*, 161.
Gardener, Ellen, 97, 98, 99; lv, lvi, lxxv.
„ Richard, 172.

Garnet, Alexander, 67, 68.
Garrat (Garrate, Garret), George, 91, 92, 94, 96.
Gates, H. N., lxviii.
Gaymestral, Cicely, 169.
Gayton, John, 195, 196.
Gee, Jenet, 100.
Gerrard (Jerrarde, Jerratt), Elline, xxiii *n.*
„ (Sir) Gilbert, 180; xxii.
„ Rondull, 92, 94.
„ (Sir) Thomas, 2, 3, 4; lxxv, lxxxii.
Geslinge, Laurence, 202.
Gest, Christopher, 44.
Gibbons, A., lxviii.
„ Henry, 146.
Gidlowe, Alice (Bellin *alias* Gidlowe), li.
„ Eleine, 198.
„ Robert, 198, 199, 200; l.
Gilbert, Sir Humphrey, xli *n.*
„ William, 107, 110.
Giles, xxxvii *n.*
Gill, Robert, 179.
Gillam, Agnes (or Anne), 126, 127, 128; lix, lxxxiv, lxxxv.
„ Ellin, 126, 127; lxxxiv, lxxxv.
„ Jasper, 177.
„ Matilda (or Mawde), 127, 128.
„ Thomas, 127.
Gittin, Joan, 123.
Glasior, John, 149.
Glyn, Henry, lvii *n.*
Golburne, Rafe, 121.
„ Thomas, 52.
Gold, John. 170.
Goodman, Rafe, lxxix.
Gosely, Henry, 172.
Gottschalk, Pastor, xlii *n.*, xliii *n.*
Grafton, Duke of, xxxiii.
Gratwood, Mr. , 180.
Gravenour, of Eaton, 181.
„ John, 52.
„ Margaret, 71.
Greene (Grene), Mr. , 161, 168.
„ Thomas, 162, 165, 174.
„ William, 173.
Greenhill, Thomas, xliii *n.*
Gregory (Gregorie), Hugh, 76, 77.
„ Matilda or Mawde Price, *alias* Gregory, 76, 77, 78, 79; li *n.*, liii, lxxiii.
„ Rondall, 76, 77, 78, 79; liii, lxxiii.
Gregory, Saint, xxix.
Grenehalgh, Ann, 129, 130.
„ Frauncis, 129, 130.
„ Richard, 33, 34.
„ Thomas, 129, 130; lxxxv.
Griffin, Mistris, 119.
Griffith, David ap, 103, 104, 190.
„ Edward, 187, 188, 190, 191, 193.
„ William, 179.
Grimsdiche, Christian, 57, lxxiv.
„ Mistres, 189.
Grondye, George, xliv *n.*
Grosvenor (*see* Gravenour).
Guest (*see* Gest).
Gunners, Richard, 169.
Guyle, , 177.

Haie, Richard, 68 (*see also* Hey).
Haiton, Richard, 123 (*see also* Eaton).
Haliwall, Henry, lxxvi *n.*
Hall, James, 117 *n.*, 118 *n.*
„ John, 170.
„ Mr., xli.
Halle, liv *n.*
Halsall, Ann, lxxii.
„ Edward, 159.
„ Henry, lxxii, lf. 21, lf. 45.
„ Matthew, 133.
„ Thomas, 132.
„ Walter, 170.
? Halton, Richard, 123.
Hamilton, 44 *n.*, 47 *n.*
Hamnet, Henry, 175.
„ Randle, lxxii *n.*
„ William, 160.
Handford, (Sir) John, 15.
Hankinson, Rondull, 5.
Hardacre (Hardcar), James, 8.
Harding, lxii.
Hardinge, Agnes, 112, 115.
Hardman, John, 30.
Hardware, Henry, 174, 175, 177, 178.
Hare, Rafe, 128, 129; lxxxiv.
Hargreves (Hargrevis), Christopher, 138; lxi.
Harington, Sir John, xxii.
Harris, Mr., lxix.
„ Richard, lxviii.
Harrison, xv, liv *n.*, lxii.
„ Robert, 34.
„ Thomas, 35.
Hartley, Christofer, 45, 46, 47.
„ James, 45.
„ Peter, 80; liii.

Haselwall, Mary (Maria), 91, 94, 95, 96.
„ Rauff, 154; lxiii.
Hassall (of Hankelowe), 181.
Hastings, Sir Hugh, xxiv *n.*
Hatton, (Sir) Christopher, 180.
„ Richard, 126.
Haughe, George, 82, 83.
Haughton, Humfrey, 162.
Haweis, Mrs., lxv.
Hawke, Margaret (married to Henry Whittakers), 29, 30; lxxxiii.
Haworth, Andrew, 9, 10, 11; lxxii, lxxiii.
„ Custance (born Entwistle), 9, 10; lxxii, lxxiii.
„ Margery (born Heydocke), 11; lxxiii.
„ Peter, 11; lxxiii.
Haydocke, David, 32.
„ George, 65, 66.
„ *See also* Heydocke.
Heath, George, 174.
Heaton (*see* Eaton).
Hefeild (Hefeld, Heighfeld, Heyghfeld), lxxvii.
„ Jenkin (Jankin), 115, 116.
„ John, 114, 115; lxxvii, lxxvii *n.*
Heisham, Robert, 101.
Hellard, William, xli.
Herbert, William, xlii.
Hervey, Lord Arthur, xxx *n.*
Hethcote, Ellein, lxxxi, *n.* 2.
Hewett, of Dunton Basset, xxxii.
„ *See* Huet.
Hey, Roger, 138 (*see also* Haie).
Heydocke, Margery (married to Peter Haworth), 11; lxxiii. *See also* Haydocke.
Heyton (*see* Eaton).
Hide, Master, lxxxi *n.*
Hill, John, 170.
Hilton, Henry, 87, 88; lxxii *n.*
Hindill, Christopher, 72.
Hine, Hugh, 154.
„ John, lxxi, *n.* 2.
Hocknell, John, 152, 156.
„ Margaret, 172.
Hodgson, Edmund, xlix.
Hodson (Hogson), John, 133.
„ Roger, 132, 133; lxi, lxxvii.
Holbrok, Thomas, 161.
Holcrofte, (Sir) William, 74.
Holden, Anne (? Jane, married James Ballard), 45, 46, 47.
Holden, Gile (born Bilsbie), 72.
„ Lettice, 72.
„ Rafe, 72, 73; liii, lxxi.
„ Sibell, 72.
„ Thomas, 56.
Holford, Christofer, 52.
„ Humfrey, 209, 210.
„ James, 26.
„ John, 26.
„ Richard, 146.
Holland, Alice, 99.
„ George, 198, 199, 200.
Hollenbury, John, 170.
Holme, Agnes, 83, 83 *n.*
„ Elizabeth, 84.
„ Hugh, 60.
„ Matilda (or Mawde), 121, 122; lxxv, lxxvi.
Holt, Hugh, 97, 98, 99.
„ William, 97, 98.
Holte, John, xli.
Hood, Christopher, 178.
Hoole, Christopher, 179.
Hoothorne (Hothorne), Peter, xxiv, xxv.
Hope, Alice (Alis, born Ellis *alias* Mathue), 18, 19, 20, 21; xviii.
„ Christian, 21.
„ Christabella (Bridge *alias* Hope), 85.
„ Peter, 18, 19, 20, 21; xviii, lxxvii, lxxviii.
„ Richard, 21.
Horton, John, lxxxiv.
„ Richard, lxxviii, lf. 148.
„ Roger, 153; lxxix, line 1 (*see also* Houghton).
„ Warbara, lxxxiv.
„ William, lxxxiv.
Hostiensis, xxix.
Hotersall, John, lxxiv and *n.*
Hotham, William, xxv.
Hothersall, Margaret (married to Alexander Osbaldiston or Osboston), 34, 35, 183, 184; lxxxiv, lxxxv.
Hough, Roger, 134, 135.
Houghton, Lady Ann, lxxiv, lxxiv *n.*
„ Humffrey, 164.
„ Edward, lxxxiv *n.*
„ Isabell, 72; lxxi.
„ Sir Richard, and Lady, lxxiv, lxxiv *n.*
„ *See also* Horton.
Hove (? Houe or Howe), Henry, 172.

Howarth, Andrew, lxxii, lf. 40; 9, 10, 11.
„ Custance (born Entwistle), lxxii, lxxiii.
Howell, Humfri ap, 103.
Huet, John, 64.
Hulse, Elizabeth, 4, 5, 6; xiv, lxxi.
„ George, 4, 5, 6; xiv, xviii, lxxi.
Hulton, William, 162, 163.
Hunt, Adam, 149.
Huntington, John, 96.
„ Margaret, 168.
Hurst, Thomas, 171.
Hutchens, John, 157.
Huyton, Thomas, lxxvi *n.*

Ince, Alice, 68, 69; xlvi, xlvii, lxxxvi.
„ Randle (Randulph), 162, 174, 175.
„ Richard, 156, 157.
Ingham, Ciscilia, 124.
Ireland, Lord Chancellor of, 177.
„ Lord Deputy of (Lord Mountjoye), 175, 176, 179, 180.
„ Lord Justices of, 177.
„ Thomas, 66, 67; xliv.
Irlam, one, 82,
Irvine, Mr. W. F., 48 *n.*; xxii, l, lxxxvii.
Isherwood (Isherwod), Anne, 53.
„ Margaret, 93.
„ Roger, 53.
Ithell, R., lxxxiv.

Jackson, John, 123, 124, 125, 126.
Jardine, John, xlii *n.*
Jeafferson, Mr. Cordy, xiii.
Jefferyes, Elizabeth, 174.
Jenkin (Jankin), Philip (Phelippe), 120, 121; lxxiii, lf. 58 bk., lxxiv.
„ Kate, lxxix, lxxix *n.*, lxxx *n.*
Jenkinson, William, lxxxii.
Jenson, Raff, 172.
Jepson, Nicolas, 184, 185, 186, 187; xlvi, lxxi.
Jerome, St., xxviii.
Jerrarde (*see* Gerrarde).
Jerrat, Randulph (Rondull), 92, 94 (*see* Gerrard).
John, Agnes, 19.
„ John ap, 19, 20, 102, 103, 104, 105, 106, 107, 108, 109, 110; lviii, lxxiii, lxxiv, lxxv.
„ Roger ap, 104.
„ Thomas ap, 107, 110.

Johnson, George, 57, 58, 59, 196; xliv, lxxvii.
„ Mr., 151.
„ Peter, 123, 124.
„ Robert, 208.
Joseph, Virgin Mary's husband, lxxx, *n.* 1.
Josiah, King, xxvii.
Joy, Widow (Wedow), 173.

Kay (Key), Cecilea (Cicilie, Cicily), 58.
„ Edmund, 6.
„ Ellen, 101; lxxxiii.
„ George, 58.
„ John, 7, 129, 130.
„ (Sir) Oswald, 3.
Kelly's, 50 *n*; lxxiii *n.*, lxxvi *n.*
Kelsall, Katherine, 135.
„ Richard, 135.
Kendale, Margaret, xlvii *n.*
Kendricke, Master, 141; lxii.
Kenworth, Elena, 113.
Key (*see* Kay).
Killymer, David, 155.
Kilshaw (Kilshae), Thomas, 44.
Kinge, William, 154, 161.
Kirforte, Katarina, 50.
Kirks, Robert, 146, 149.
„ William, 172.
Kitchin, Edward, 167.
„ William, lxxix, *n.* 2.
Knee, Richard, 159, 160.
Knight, Geo. Hy., lxix.
„ William, 146, 167.

Langdale, John, 177.
Langton, Sir Thomas, lxxv, lxxxii, lf. 90 bk.
Large (Larg), Robert, 38, 38 *n.*, 41.
Laton, Robert, 147, 148.
Lawton, Robert, 148.
Leche (Lech, Leeche), Robert, 2, 3, 4, 7, 9, 12, 15, 16, 19, 22, 23, 25, 30, 31, 35, 37, 41, 47, 49, 51, 52, 55, 57, 60, 63, 67, 68, 69, 73, 75, 76, 79, 80, 81, 83, 86, 89, 91, 94, 95, 97, 100, 102, 105, 108, 115, 117, 124, 132, 133, 135, 136, 157, 183, 184, 185, 187, 191, 194, 196, 202.
Lee (*see* Leigh).
Leene, Robert, 146.
Leigh (Lee, Leghe, Leighe), Edward, 139, 140; lxxxiv.
„ John, 105, 106, 107, 107 *n.*, 108, 110, 139; lvi.

Leigh, Mr. (of the Ridge), 5.
„ Mr. (of Shorleye), 180.
„ Oliver, 89, 90, 91; lxxiii, lxxv.
„ Richard; lxxxii.
„ Robert, 124.
Leighton (*see* Laton).
Lenoster, Mr. Robert, 179.
Leycester (Leycestour), B , 179.
„ (Sir) Rafe, 125; lx.
Leyland, Joan (married Rafe Whittall), 12; xx, lxxiv.
„ Rafe, 12.
Leyver, Edmund, 65, 66.
Lightons Wife, lviii.
Lincoln, The Bishop of, lxvi *n.*
„ Bishop's Secretary (Mr. Smith), lxvi *n.*
Lineye (Liney), Alexander, 124, 125, 126; lx.
Lingley (Lyngley), John, 157, 158; lxiii.
„ Richard, 157.
Lister, (Sir) Richard, xl.
„ Richard, xl.
Lithgo, Matthew (Mathue), 122.
Litlour, Cecilia, 209.
„ Elizabeth, 209.
„ Thomas, 209.
Littlehales, Mr. Hy., lxix.
Littleton, xxxvi *n.*
Liverpool, The Mayor of, xlvi.
Livesay, Richard and Ellen, lxxii.
Lloyd (Lloide), David (Dauid, Davyd), 152, 159, 160, 161, 165, 174.
„ Elena (Ellin), 104, 108.
„ Richard, 109.
Lomas, Thomas, 130.
Longstaff, Mr., xxxiii.
Looker, Nicholas, 160, 161.
Loundes, Robert, 121.
Lovetot, Maud, xl.
Low (Lough, Lowe), Agnes, 99.
„ Christopher, 155.
„ Edward, 196.
„ (Sir) Edward, 131.
„ Richard, 45 *n.*, 49, 56, 57, 196; xlv, lxxi.
„ Roderick, lxxx, *n.* 2.
Lowther, Agnes, 113, 115.
„ Sir Richard, xxxii.
„ Oliver, 105, 109, 110.
Loye, Wm., lviii *n.*
Lycurgus, xliii.
Lynaker, Thomas, 165, 178.
Lyngley (*see* Lingley).
Lynyall, Thomas (Mayor of Chester), 155, 156, 157, 158, 160, 161.
Lyons, Mr. Ponsonby, xxiii.
Lythgo (*see* Lithgo).
Lyttleton, Sir John and his Son William, xxxii.

Maddock (Madock), William, 150.
Maddocke, Ellen, lxxii.
Mainwaringe (Manwaring, Maynwaryng),
„ Alicie, 60.
„ (Sir) Arthur, 180.
„ Ellen or Eleanor, 67, 68; xlvi, lxxxv.
„ Humphrey, 134.
„ Laurence, 117, 118, 119.
„ Phillipe, 140.
„ Randulph, 59, 193.
Maisterson, John, 118, 119.
Maker, Mr. , 180.
Makin, Richard, 167.
Malabari, Mr., xxxiv.
Man, Katherine, 63, 64, 65; xlix, lxxxiii.
„ Peter, 65.
„ Seath, 82, 84.
Manley, Henry, 175.
Manwaring (*see* Mainwaring).
Manwell, Thomas, xlix *n.*
Mary, Virgin, and her snow-baby, lxxx *n.*
Maskell, xlvii *n.*
Mason (Maison), John, 30, 31.
„ Margaret (born Dugdale), 30, 31; xviii, lxxxiii.
„ Robert, 30, 30 *n.*, 31; xviii, lxxxiii.
Massey (Massie, Massy), Alice (Alis), 166.
„ Jane (born Sumner), 25.
„ Richard, 166; lii.
„ Robert, 25.
„ Roger, 25; lxxxi.
„ William, 146, 147, 148, 149, 150, 166.
Masterson, Thomas, lxxix.
Matham, Thomas, xxiv.
Mathewe, Andrew, a grocer of London, 185.
Mathue (*see* Alice Ellis, *alias* Mathue, married to Peter Hope), lxxviii.
Melton, Dorothy, xxiv *n.*
„ Sir John, xxiv *n.*
Mercer, Ellin, 187, 188, 190, 191.

Mercer, Robert, 23.
„ Thomas, 145.
Meverill, Mr. , 180.
Michell, John, 33.
Middlehurst, Richard, 201.
„ Thomas, 200, 201; lxxxv, lxxxvi.
Middleton, lv *n.*
Milbourne, Mrs. Agnes, xliii *n.*
Milner, John, 150, 159.
Minshull (Mynshull), Ellen (Elena), 113, 114, 115, 116.
„ Mr. , 116.
Mitchell, Margery, lxxxi, and *n.*
Mitton, Henry, 28.
Moels, Elizabeth, lxxx *n.*
Molinex, Sir Richard, 205, 207.
Monelay (Monelaes, Moneley), Henry, 96, 97.
„ Margaret, 91, 92, 93, 94, 95, 96, 97; lv, lxxiv, lxxv, lxxvi, lxxvii, lxxviii.
Moore, Master, his 'hoore,' 205.
Mordaynte, Mr., 180.
More (Mores), Margery (*alias* Vernon), 16, 17, 18; lxxvii.
„ Master, 17, 18, 205.
„ Randle, 16, 17, 18, 117; lxxvii.
Morgan, Margery (Marggerie), 120, 121; lxxiii, lxxiv.
„ Richard, of Beaumaris, 188, 190.
Morris, Canon, xiii.
„ John, 172.
„ Mr. Wm., lxv.
Moss, James, lxxxvi.
Moston, esquire, 189.
Mountioie (Mountioy), Lord Deputy of Ireland, 175, 176, 179, 180.
Mowbray, Jn., Duke of Norfolk, and Ann his daughter, lxxxvii *n.*
Mullinex, , 168.
„ *See also* Molinex.
Mutchell, Margery, lxxxi.
Mutton, William, 149.
Mynshull (*see* Minshull).

Neadame, Mr. (of Shentone [Shevington]), 180.
Nemor, John, 169.
Newall, Joan, lxxxi *n.*
„ Katarin, 133.
Newparte, Thomas, 162.
Newson, Edward, Vicar of Prestbury, lxxvi.
Newton, John, 70, 71.
„ ( ), 178.
Nicholas, xxxii.
Nicolson, , 169.
„ Henry, lxxx, lxxxi *n.*
„ Isabella, lxxx, lxxxi *n.*
Norfolk, Duke of, lxxxvii *n.*
Northumberland, The Duke of, xl.
Nuttall, Jone, 129, 130; lxxxv.
„ Thomas, 129, 130.

Offley (Offlee), Robert, 172.
Okell, Ellin, 97.
Okes (Okis), Katarina, 87, 88.
Olton, Isabel, 136.
„ John, 135, 136; lxxxv, lxxxvi.
„ Robert, 135, 136, 137.
Ormisdich, Mrs., of Chester, 189.
Orrell, Isabell, xxi.
Orrel, John, lxxii.
Orton, Richard, 208.
Osbaldeston (Osboston), Alexander, 34, 35, 183, 184; lxxxiv, lxxxv.
„ Lady, 35, 183, 184.
„ Margaret (born Hothersall), 34, 35, 85, 183, 184; lxxxiv, lxxxv.
„ Richard, 34.
Otye, Owen, 93.
Oulton (*see* Olton).
Overbury, Sir Thomas, xxx.
Owlthwayt, John, xlvii *n.*

Page, Elizabeth (married to Thomas Dampart), 22; xx, lxxii, lxxvii, lxxix.
„ Rafe: his goods and widow, lxxix.
Parker, Alexander, 28.
„ Barnard, 46.
„ Henry, 28.
„ Janet (Jenet), 28; lxxxii.
„ Laurence, 28; lxxxii.
Parkinson, Elizabeth, 27.
„ John, 27.
Parre, Richard, 197; xxii.
„ Robert, of Backford, xxii, lxxvii.
Partington, Elizabeth, 83 *n.*, 84.
Pattele, Isabell, 128, 129; lix, lxxxiv.
Paul, Mr., 149 (? Mr. Paul Chauntrell).
Pawton, Thomas, 75; liv.
Payne, John, xl.
Peacock, E. B., xlviii *n.*

Pembroke, The Earl of, xli, xlii.
Pendleton, Emme, 131.
„ Richard, 131, 132; lxi, lxxiv.
Penk, Richard, 122.
Percevall (Persivall), (Sir) Richard, 37.
„ Robert, 169.
„ Peter, 127, 128.
Perdita, lv.
Pery, Alis, 194.
Petre, (Sir) William, 181 *n.*
Pharaoh, xxix.
Philippe, Rondal, li.
Phillips, Elizabeth, 157, 158.
Phineus, John, 121.
Phrary, John, 172.
Piccope, Rev., xiv; 1 *n.*, 2 *n.*, 4 *n.*, 6 *n.*, 7 *n.*, 9 *n.*, 10 *n.*, 11 *n.*, 12 *n.*, 15 *n.*, 16 *n.*, 19 *n.*, 21 *n.*, 25 *n.*, 27 *n.*, 29 *n.*, 30 *n.*, 31 *n.*, 32 *n.*, 33 *n.*, 34 *n.*, 35 *n.*, 37 *n.*, 38 *n.*, 41 *n.*, 43 *n.*, 45 *n.*, 47 *n.*, 49 *n.*, 51 *n.*, 52 *n.*, 55 *n.*, 56 *n.*, 57 *n.*, 59 *n.*, 61 *n.*, 63 *n.*, 65 *n.*, 67 *n.*, 68 *n.*, 73 *n.*, 76 *n.*, 78 *n.*, 79 *n.*, 81 *n.*, 131 *n.*, 132 *n.*, 133 *n.*, 134 *n.*, 135 *n.*, 136 *n.*, &c. *See* lxxi, *n.* 1.
Pickforth, Richard, 63, 64; xlvi, xlix, lxv, lxxxiii.
Piers, Margery, 135; lxi.
Pierson, Margaret (Alatt or Pierson), 73, 74, 75.
„ Richard, 73, 74, 75; liv, lxxiii.
„ William, 63.
Pincok, Thomas, 12.
Plant, Sir Robert, lxxxi *n.*
Plato, xliii.
Plumpton, William, 117, 204, 205, 206, 207.
Pole (*see* Poole).
„ Robert, 193, 194, 195, 196.
Pollet, Elizabeth (*alias* Eccles), 62, 63.
„ Hugh, 62, 63; xlix, lxxii and *n.*, lxxxi.
„ Janet, 85.
Poole (Pole, Polle), Elenora, 133.
„ Elizabeth (born Tilston), 1.
„ John, 152.
„ Richard, 1, 17.
„ (Sir) Robert, xxxii.
„ Roger, 47.
„ Thomas, 17, 133, 134, 172.
„ William, 1, 2; lxxi.
Pope, Thomas, 16.
Port, Thomas, 67.
Porter, Richard, 149.
Pott, Sibill, 81, 202, 203.
Powel, Charles, xxxiii.
„ Sir Thomas, xxxiii.
Power, John, xxxi, xxxii.
Preston, John, his daughter Agnes, xxiii *n.*
„ William, 36.
Price, Ellen, 127.
„ Henry, 76, 77, 78, 79; li *n.*, liii, lxxiii.
„ Matilda or Maude (*alias* Gregory), 76, 77, 78, 79; liii.
„ W. H., 50, 61 *n.*; 183, &c.; xi, xv, xxii.
Prieste, Hugh, xlii.
„ Joan, xlii.
Prince, Elena, 93.
„ Philip, 94.
Pringle, Andrew, xxxii.
„ Jonet, xxxii.
Prinros, Henry, 171.
Puleston, Thomas, 105, 106, 109, 110.
Pulford, William, 155.
Pulford's house, lxxix.
Pulle, William, A.D. 1436, lxxxvii *n.*
Puners, Henry, 173.

Rabon, John, 152 (*see also* Rathburne).
Radcliffe, Margaret, 138.
„ Master, 99, 139 (*see also* Ratclif).
Raine, Canon, 44 *n.*, 57 *n.*, 67, 68; xxvii.
Raines, Rev. F. R., xxxii.
Ramsbotham, Elizabeth (married John Bridge), 6, 7, 8, 9; lxxi, lxxii.
„ *See also* Romisbotham.
Ramshae, Randle, 69, 70, 71, 210; xlviii, lxxxvi.
Rand, William, lviii.
Ratclif (Ratcliffe), (Sir) John, 180.
„ Mawde, 149.
„ *See also* Radcliffe.
Rathburne, John, 151.
„ Richard (Mayor of Chester), 174.
„ *See also* Rabon.
Rawlinson, lv. *n.*
Reames, John, 172.
Rehoboam, King, xxvii, xxix.
Res (Rice), John ap, 127, 128.

Res, a beadman, 190/6.
Resadder, 188.
Revington, Thomas, 178.
Reynolds, Mr., xlii *n.*, xlv *n.*
Rice (Res), John ap, 127, 128.
Richard Cœur de Lion, xl.
Richardson, David, 146, 147.
„ Isabell, xlvi *n.*
„ John, 146, 147.
„ Robert, 169.
„ Thomas, 169.
„ Widow (Wedow), 169.
Richmond, Charles, Duke of, xxxiii.
Ricketts, Mr., xliii.
Ricroft (Ricrofte), Ellen (Eleine, Elleine), 46, 59, 60, 61, 196; xlv, xlvi, lxxviii, lxxix, lxxx.
Ridgway, Richard, lxxxi.
Ridley, , 171.
„ John, 158.
Rigmarden, John, xxii.
Rile, Alice (Alis), 111, 112, 113, 114, 115; lxxiii.
„ Robert, 111, 112, 113, 114, 116; lviii, lix, lxxii.
Riley (Rily), Robert, 136.
„ Thomas, 29.
Roales, William, 172.
Roberts, Chas., xl *n.*
Robin, Edward ap, 88.
Rochester, Vicount, xxix, xxx.
Rodon, Peter, lxxix, lxxx *n.*
Rodorye, John, 145.
Rogers, Elizabeth, xxxiii.
Rogerson, Elizabeth, xxii, lxxxvii.
Rokeby, John, xli.
Roland, Randle, 122.
Romisbotham, Roger, 72 (*see also* Ramsbotham).
Rondull, John, 102, 103.
Rope, Alice (Alis), 134.
„ Laurence, 133, 134; lxxxiii.
„ Randle (Rondull), 133, 134.
Round, Mr. P. Z., xlvii *n.*, lxvii.
Roycroft (*see* Ricroft).
Royle (*see* Rile).
Rues, Wedow, 173.
Russell, Lord, 180 *n.*
„ Robert, 88.
Rye, Mr. Walter, xxxi.
Ryles, Robert, 111 (*see also* Rile).

Saiger, William, 33.
Sale, John, 147 (*see* Sele).
Salisbury, William, Earl of, xxix.
Sampson, Willliam, xlv *n.*
Sangermano, Father, xlii *n.*
Santley, Rondull, 119.
Sare, Williams, 178.
Savage, Lady, 172.
Savory, Dr., xxix.
Scattabout, Mawde, 121, 122.
Scons, John, 165.
Scott, Walter, xxxii.
Seaton, Elizabeth, 126; lix.
„ John, 128; lix.
Seddon, Cecilea, 99.
Sedgwick, Mistris, 173.
Sefton, William, 21.
Sele, John, 149 (*see* Sale).
Serjant, Jane, 140.
Seyman, Richard, xli.
Seymor, Sir Robert, xxxiii, xxxiv.
„ Henry (Son of Sir Robert), xxxiii.
Shackilton, James, 28.
Shakspere, 113 *n.*, 142 *n.*; xiv *n.*, xlii, xlviii *n.*, xlix *n.*, l, lv, lv *n.*, lx, lxv, lxxxviii.
Sharington, Mr., xli.
Sharman, Anna, 136.
„ George, 100, 101.
Sharpe, Elizabeth, lxxix and *n.*
„ John, 172.
„ Katharine, lxxix and *n.*
Sharplus, James, 9.
„ Thomas, 56.
Sherington, George, 30.
Shillito, John, Proctor at York, xxvi.
Short, Robert, 18.
Shotilworth (Shuttleworth), Elizabeth, 80; liii, lxxiv.
„ Lawrence, 80.
Sidall, William, 184, 185; xviii *n.*
Sidebotham, Jane, 75; liv.
Sidney, Philip, xlii.
Sill, Norman, lxxxi *n.*
Simon, Thomas, 167.
Simpson, Jn., xlix.
Skelicorne, William, lxxiv *n.*
Slater, Thomas, 169.
Sleves, Robert, 173.
Smalley, Roger, 65.
Smith, Anna, lxxii *n.*
„ James, 13, 14.
„ Jane, 26.
„ Jane (Blackston *alias* Smith), 153.
„ Joan, xlv *n.*

Smith, John, 46, 57, 100 ; lxxiv.
„ John, of Nibley: his 'Lives of the Berkeleys,' xxi, xxvii, xli *n.*
„ Lawrence, 50, 145.
„ Margaret (Wadesworth *alias* Smith), 85.
„ Mr., 168, 178.
„ (Mr.) Challenor, lxvi *n.*
„ Margaret, xxxii, xlix *n.*
„ Rafe, lxxvi, lxxvii.
„ Richard, xxxii.
„ Thomas, 150.
„ *See also* Smythe.
Smithe, Thomas, 184.
Smithyman, William, 169.
Smythe, Augustine, xli.
„ (Sir), Laurence, 50.
„ *See also* Smith.
Snelson, Thomas, 59, 60, 61, 196; xlv, lxxvii, lxxviii, lxxix, lxxx.
Solomon, King, xxviii, xxix.
Somerford (Somerforde, Somerforth), Jane (born Brereton), 25, 26, 27, 28; lxxxii.
„ John, 25, 26, 27, 28; lxxxii.
„ Marie, 181.
„ William, 27, 28.
Somersbee, Parnell, 138.
Somerset, Earl of, xxx.
„ Lady, xxxviii *n.*
Sommer, Jane (married to Roger Massey), 25; lxxxi.
Sonkey, Ellen, 198, 199; l, lxxxii.
Sonkie, William, 199.
Sothworth, Ann (married to Wm. Westby), 35, 36, 37, 38; xx, lxxxv.
„ (Sir) John, 3, 36, 37, 38, 53, 54; xx.
„ Margaret (*alias* Ward), 65, 66, 67; xvii *n.*, xliv, lxii, lxxv, lxxvi.
„ (Lady) Mary, 37.
„ Thomas, 65, 66, 67; xvii *n.*, xliv, lxii, lxxxiv.
„ William, 37.
Soundes, Robert, 121, 122; lxxv.
Southworth, Henry, xxiii *n.*
„ *See also* Sothworth.
Spakeman (Spakman), lxxxv.
„ Leticia (Letice, born Unsworth), 43, 44, 45; lxxxv.
„ William, 43, 44, 45; lxxxv.
Spark, Thomas, 76, 77.
Spencer, Hugh, Lord, xxviii.
Sprack, Wm., xlv *n.*
Spurstowe (Spurstoo), Brigitte (born Dutton), 38, 39, 40, 41; lxxxv.
„ George, 38, 38 *n.*, 39, 40, 41; lxxxv.
„ Randulph, 38, 38 *n.*
„ Richard, 39.
Squire, William, 172.
Stafford, (Capt.) Francis, 168, 172.
„ Sir Humphrey, xl *n.*
Standish, Doctour, his school, 48; xviii.
Stanley, Anne (born Dutton), 47, 48, 49; lxxxv.
„ Bridget, xxiii *n.*
„ Edward, xxiii *n.*
„ Margaret (married to Roland Dutton), 41, 42, 43; xx, lxxxv.
„ Margaret (wife of Thomas), 52, 53, 54, 55; xxi, lxxv, lxxvi.
„ Margaret (lame), 169.
„ Peter, 55; xxiii *n.*
„ Piers, 53, 54.
„ (Sir) Rowland, 48; lxxii.
„ Thomas, 52, 53, 54, 55; xxi, lxxv, lxxvi; (Sir) Thomas, 180.
„ William, 47, 48, 49; lxxxv.
Stanleys of Hooton, xvii, xviii, lxxxviii.
Stansfield, William, 140, 141.
Starkeye (Starkie), [ ] of Wrenburye, 181.
„ Alice (born Dutton), 49, 50, 51; lxxii.
„ Edmund, 29.
„ James, 49, 50.
„ John, 49, 50, 51; lxxii.
Steel, Mrs., xxxiv *n.*
Steele (Stele), Homfri (Homfrey), 128, 129.
„ Margaret, 123, 124; lxxxiii, lxxxiv.
„ Thomas, 98.
„ William, 123, 124.
St. Jerome, xxviii.
St. Vincent, Lord, xliii *n.*
Stockley, Richard, 141.
Stockton, Hugh, 172.
Stone, Coth, 170.

Stones (Stonis), Ellin (Helen), 56, 57; xlv.
Storthes, Gervays, xl.
Strete, Alice (wife of Aynesworthe and Jepson), 185.
„ Cecilea, 122.
„ Katherine, 184, 185, 186, 187; xviii *n.*, xlvi, lxxi.
Stubbes, xv, xxi.
„ Humfre, 175.
„ Philip, xxxiv.
Sudlowe, Ellen, lxxvii.
Suffolk, Earl of, xxix, xxx.
„ (Lady) Frances, xxix, xxx.
„ Katherine (younger sister to Lady Frances), xxix.
Sutton, Agnes, lxxx.
Swan, John, lxviii.
„ (Sir) Robert, 75.
Swetnam, Laurence, lxxxi.
„ Margaret, lxxxi.
„ Thomas, lxxxi *n.*
Swinburne, Judge Henry, d. 1624, xix, xx, xxi, xxviii, xxxv, xxxvi, xxxvii, xxxvii *n.*, xxxviii, xxxviii *n.*, xliii, xlv *n.*, xlvii *n.*, xlviii, li.
Sworton, Rose, 89, 90; lxxiii, lxxv.

Tailiour, Hamlet, Curate of Northwich, lxxvii, lxxvii, *n.* 1.
„ *See* Taylor, lxxix.
Talbot, Emma (married to G. Gerrard), xxii.
„ Grace (born Boyes), 16.
„ John, 16.
„ Mr. , 180.
„ Mistris, 16.
„ Robert, 16; lxxiv.
„ Sir Thomas, lxxv.
Talboys, Sir George, xxiv *n.*
Tarleton, Oliver, 49.
Tatton, Robert, 139.
Taylor (Tailiour, Tauliour), Ann, lxxviii.
„ Geoffrey, 12, 13; lxxxi.
„ Elizabeth, lxxxi *n.*
„ John, lxxviii *n.*
„ Margaret, 117, 118, 119, 120; lix, lxxiii.
Tempest, Sir Richard, xxiv *n.*
Tench, Robert, lxxix.
Thelwall, Galther, 68, 69.
Thirlewinde, John, 99, 100; lxxxi.
Thomas, Jane ap, 106, 110.
„ William, xli.

Thompson, Henry, 162.
Thornton, Randolph, 201.
„ Thomas, 151.
Throgmorton, Frances, 168.
Throp, John, 149.
„ Thomas, 162.
Tilston, Agnes, 1.
„ Elizabeth (married to William Pole or Poole), 1; lxxi.
„ Elizabeth, 121, 122; lxxv, lxxvi.
„ Thomas, 162.
Title, George, 156; lxiii.
„ John, 156.
Tomlynson, Thomas, 175
Tomson, Edward, 200, 201, 202.
Tomstall, Thomas, 140.
Toppinge, Katharine, 206, 207.
Topping's Wife, 117, 204; lviii.
Torbock, Thomas, 1, lxxix.
Totty (Tottie), Oliver, 48.
„ Robert (? Oliver), 49.
„ Margeria, 112.
Trafford, (Sir) Edmonde, 80.
„ Mr., 63.
Turner, Agnes, 203.
Tyrone, Earl of, xxxii.

Underwood, Thomas, 101, 102; lxxxiii.
Unsworth, Leticia (Letice, married to Wm. Spakeman), 43, 44, 45; lxxxv.
„ Thomas, 44.
Urmeston (Urmiston), John, 82.
„ Michael, 149.
„ Mr., lxxvi, *n.* 2.
„ William, 126, 162.

Vaudrey, Oliver, 100, 101; lxxxiii.
„ Robert, 139.
Venables, Anne, 209, 210; l, lxxxiii.
„ Raffe, dead, 209; lx.
Venkatesh, Mr. T. R., xxxv.
Vernon, Margery (married to Randle More), 16, 17, 18; lxxvii.
„ Master, 17.
„ Robert, 17, 18.
Villiers, Edward, xxxii.

Wade, Custance, 111, 112, 113, 114, 115, 116; lviii, lxxii, lxxiii.
„ John, 153.
„ Randle (Rondull), 111, 112, 113, 114, 115; lix.

Wadesworth, Agnes (or Anne), 85; lxxii.
„ Margaret (*alias* Smith), 85.
Wadington, George, 55.
Wagge, Margerie, lxxxii *n*.
Waite, Margaret, 198, 199, 200.
Walchwoman, Margaret, lii.
Walkden, Jane, 56, 57; xlv, xlv *n*., xlix, lxxi.
Walker, Thomas, 140, 141.
„ Isabell (*alias* Bamford), 140, 141.
Wallas, Mr. Graham, xxvii *n*.
Walle, William, 161, 171.
Walley, Elizabeth, 127, 128; lix, lxxxiv.
„ Katherine, 205, 206, 207.
„ *See also* Whalley.
Walmesley, Henry, 34.
„ Laurence, 54.
„ Richard, xxiii *n*.
„ Roger, 100.
„ Thomas, 33, 37.
Walshe, John, 34.
Walton, Robert, 100; lxxxii, lxxxiii.
Warborow, lxxxiv.
Warburton, Grant, 165.
„ (Sir) John, 124.
Ward, (Sir) John, 140, 141.
„ Margaret (Sothworth *alias* Ward), 65, 66, 67; lxxxiv.
Wardel, Jn., xlvii *n*.
Warrington, Dean of, lxxii.
Washington, William, 92, 94.
Watkinson, Edmund, 19, 20.
Watson, William, 162.
Welden, Edw., xl.
„ Tho., xl.
Welstead, Mary, xxxiv.
Wentworth, Michael, xl.
Westbee (Westby, Westbye), Anne (born Sothworth), 35, 36, 37, 38; xx, lxxxv.
„ John, 36, 37, 38.
„ William, 35, 36, 37, 38; xx, lxxxv.
Weste, Joane, 141.
Westminster, Duke of, lxiv.
Weswoll (Wiswoll), Thomas, 146.
Wethers, Robert, 61.
Whalley, Thomas, 177 (*see also* Walley).
Whatbe, Henry, lxxix.
Whatton, Elizabeth, lxxviii, lxxxix.
Whitbrid, Robert, 148.
Whitby, Robert, 147, 148.
Whitehead, John, 208.
„ Katheryne, 165.
Whitfield, Anne (married Thomas Fletcher), 22, 23, 24; lxxix.
„ William, 23, 24; xv.
Whitlock, John, 171.
Whitonge, Jas., lxxii.
Whittacres, Henry, 29, 30; lxxxiii.
„ Margaret (born Hawke), 29, 30; lxxxiii.
Whittall, Joan (born Leyland), 12; xx, lxxiv.
„ Rafe, 12; lxxiv.
Whitwham, John, 85; lxxii.
Whorwood, Margaret, xl.
Wicksted (Wyested), Ellen (born Ball), 51, 52; lxxviii.
„ John, 52.
„ Thomas, 51, 52; lxxviii.
Wilbraham (Wilbram), Ellen, 50.
„ Randulph, 101.
„ Richard, 118 *n*.
Wilcok, Widow (Wedowe), 173.
Wilcokson, Alis, lxxx, *n*. 2.
Wild (Weld), Richard, 88.
Wilkinson, James, 152, 159.
„ Margaret, 85, 86, 87, 88; lxxiii.
Willes, Robert, 155.
Williams, Ellis, 178.
„ esquire, 189, 193.
„ Peers, xxxiii.
Williamson (Williamz), Alice (Alis), 150.
„ Elizabeth, 123.
„ John, 132.
„ Rafe, 125, 126.
„ Robert, 13.
„ Thomas, 150.
„ William, 150.
Willoughbie, Mr., 180.
Willy, Joan, 196; xlvi.
„ John, 196.
„ *See also* Wily.
Wilson, Richard, 149.
„ Robert, 76, 77, 78, 170.
Wily (Willy), Joan, 196; lxxvii, lxxviii.
„ *See also* Willy.
Winstanley, Alexander, 198, 199; l, lxxxii.
„ Alice (born Worsley), 2, 3; xvii, lxxi.

Winstanley, Elizabeth, 83, 84, 85, 198, 199.
„ Humfrey, 2, 3, 4; xvii, lxxi.
„ Peter, 84, 85.
Winterbotham, William, 140.
Wirrall, Margaret, 102 *n.*, 117, 204, 205, 206, 207; lxxiii.
Wiswoll, Thomas, 146.
Witter, Rauff, 147, 148.
Wittoun, Alice, lii, liii.
„ William, lii.
Wodfall, Alice, 196, 197; l, lxxix.
Wolfall, Jane, 205.
„ John, 23.
„ Richard, 117, 204, 206, 207.
„ Robert, 205, 206, 207.
„ *See also* Woolfall.
Wood, Janet, lviii *n.*
Woodcocke, Mathew, 134.
„ Richard, 162, 177, 178.
Woode (Wodde), Matthew, 134.
„ Robert, 10 (*see also* Woods).
Woodfall, Elizabeth, xxiii *n.*
„ Thomas, xxiii *n.*
Woodhouse (Wodhouse), John, 37.
Woodnet, Laurence, 134.
Woodridge, Mr. Chas, lxix.
Woods, James, 141.
„ *See also* Wood.
Woodward, Alexander, xxiii.
Woodward, Cicelie, xxiii.
Woofall, Thomas, 141 (*see also* Wolfall).
Wormley, Margarye, xlix.
Worsley, Alice (married to Humfrey Winstanley), 2, 3; xvii, lxxi.
„ Worsley, James, 2.
Worthington, Charles, 13.
Wright, Gilbert, lxxviii, lxxix, lxxx.
„ Jane, 95.
„ Richard, 118, 118 *n.*, 119, 120.
„ Robert, 5, 122.
Wynne, Godfrey, 153, 161.
Wytter (Witter), Rauff, 147, 148.

Yate (Yates), Anne, 57, 58; xliv, lxxvi, lxxvii.
„ Joanna, lxxvi, lxxvi *n.*, lxxvii.
„ Rafe, lxxvi, lxxvi *n.*, lxxvii.
Yenne, Elizabeth, 15 *n.*
„ John, 15 *n.*
Yeves, William, 171.
Yokin, Thomas, 201.
York, Lord Archbishop of, 31, 45; xvii, xli.
„ Richard, Duke of, lxxxvii *n.*

Zechariah, xxix
Zouch, Ewdo, Lord, xxvii.
Zurich, xxxvii *n.*

INDEX OF NAMES OF PLACES, RIVERS, AND CANALS, &c.

WITH SOME EXAMPLES OF SPELLING.

BY MR. W. H. PRICE.

Acton, 32 *n.*, 70, 90 *n.*
Aighton, xxiii *n.*
Airre (Town in Scotland), 155.
Alne, co. York, xxiv.
Altrincham, 64 *n.*, 139 *n.*
Amounderness (Amundernes), 35, 35 *n.*
Ancrum Moor, xxiv *n.*
Anglesey, 190, 192; xxxi, xxxii.
Arley (Arley Hall), 124, 124 *n.*
Ashton-under-Lyne, 140, 141; lxii.
Astbury (Asbury), 25, 27, 100, 101; lxxxii *n.*
Aston (co. York), xxiv *n.*, xxv, xxvii.
Audlem (Aldlem), 71, 71 *n.*
Audley, co. Staffs. (Aldley), lxxiv, lxxvi.
Awre, xli *n.*
Ayre (*see* Airre).

Backford, xxii.
Baguley (Baguley Hall), 139, 139 *n.*; lxxvi.
Balderston, 65.
Bangor, lxix.
Barthomley (Bartumley), 17, 18.
Bath and Wells, lxviii.
Beaumaris (Bewmarres, Bewmaris), 167, 168, 171, 188.
Bentham, 32 *n.*
Berhampur, xvi.
Berlin, xlii *n.*, xliii *n.*
Berwicke (Barwicke), 118, 119; xxiv *n.*
Bickley (Biclaye), 52, 52 *n.*
Bidstone, lxxxvii *n.*
Birkenhead, 95 *n.*; lxxxvii *n.*
Blackburn (Blagburne), 11, 16, 29 *n.*, 30 *n.*, 33, 34 *n.*, 53, 53 *n.*, 54, 55, 56, 64 *n.*, 65, 66; lxxii.
Blackfriars Church, London, xxxi.
Blackfriars Theatre, xlii.
Bollin, The River, 62 *n.*, 64 *n.*
Bolton le Moors (Bolton), 9, 9 *n.*, 10, 44 *n.*, 50 *n.*, 51, 130; lxxii.
Bombay, xxxv.
Border, Scotch, xxxii.
Bowden (Bawden, The Riddings), 139, 139 *n.*; lxxvi, lxxix, lxxx, lxxxiv.
Bramshill, xxxiii; parish, lxxvi, lxxix, lxxx, lxxxiv.
Bransey, co. Lanc., lxxxvii.
Brayton, co. York, xxiv *n.*
Brempston, co. York, xxiv *n.*
Brereton, 25, 26, 27, 28.
Bridgwater Canal, 63 *n.*
Brimley, 32.
Brindley, 32 *n.*
Broadway, xxxiii.
Brunley, 32 *n.*
Brynn, Parish of Winwick (Brinne Chapel, Brynn Hall), 2, 2 *n.*, 3.
Buckingham, 172.
Buckley Hall, lxxxiii.
Bucklow, 139 *n.*
Budworth, Great (Budworth), 52 *n.*, 86, 87, 97, 99, 124 *n.*, 125 *n.*; lii, lxxv, lxxviii, lxxix.
Budworth, Little, 86, 86 *n.*, 88; lxxiii, lxxiii *n.*
Buerton, 71.
Bunbury (Bunbure, Bunburie, Bunburye), 50, 51 *n.*, 76, 77, 78, 79, 111.
Burnley, 30 *n.*, 32 *n.*
Burton-upon-Trent, 202.
Bury (Burie), 6, 6 *n.*, 7, 8, 53, 54, 55, 129, 130; xxi, lxxv.

Calcutta, xxxiv.

Calder, The River, 46 *n.*
Canterbury, xxxi, xxxii, lxix.
Capenhurst, near Chester, lxxxvi.
Capesthorne, 61, 61 *n.*
Carlisle, lxix.
Carmarthen, lxix.
Carrickfergus, 179.
Chauntrell, 149.
Cheadle (Chedill), 12; lxxvi *n.*
Chelford, 60, 61 *n.*, 63; l.
Chery Norton, 171.
Cheshire (Chessheire, Chesshyre), 1 *n.*, 5 *n.*, 32 *n.*, 41 *n.*, 48 *n.*, 49 *n.*, 50 *n.*, 52 *n.*, 62 *n.*, 63 *n.*, 64 *n.*, 70 *n.*, 90 *n.*, 91 *n.*, 95 *n.*, 101 *n.*, 124 *n.*, 125, 125 *n.*, 179, 180, 181; xiii, xiv, xiv *n.*, xxi, xxiii, xxiii *n.*, li, lvi, lviii, lxiv, lxv, lxv *n.*, lxxv, lxxxvii, lxxxviii.
Chester, 1, 21, 27, 28, 41 *n.*, 42 *n.*, 47 *n.*, 48, 51, 52, 60, 62, 63, 64, 65 *n.*, 68, 69, 71 *n.*, 88 *n.*, 92 *n.*, 93 *n.*, 94 *n.*, 96, 104 *n.*, 111, 112, 112 *n.*, 120 *n.*, 121, 122, 123, 126, 127, 128, 134, 139, 139 *n.*, 146, 147, 148, 149, 150, 151, 152, 153, 154, 155, 156, 157, 158, 159, 160, 161, 162, 163, 164, 165, 166, 167, 168, 169, 170, 171, 172, 173, 174, 175, 176, 177, 178, 179, 180, 181, 182, 189, 191, 192, 193, 194, 201, 208; xiii, xiv *n.*, xv, xix, xx, xxi, xxii, xliv *n.*, xlvi, l, li *n.*, lvi, lx, lxiii, lxiv, lxv *n.*, lxviii, lxix, lxxi, lxxiv, lxxxi, lxxxiii *n.*, lxxxvi, lxxxviii.
„ Bishop's Court, or Consistory Court, xiv, xix, xx, xxi *n.*, lxi, lxvi, lxxxviii.
„ Bishop's Palace, xxii.
„ Bishop's Registry, xiv, xv, xxii.
„ Castle, 157.
„ Castle Jail, 209; lxiii.
„ Common Hall, 156.
„ Cross, lxiv.
„ Dee Bridge (Dye Bridge), 92, 181.
„ Dee, The River, xiv, xv, li, lxiv.
„ Diocese of, 39, 42, 51, 62, 66, 111, 112; xix, xxi, lxxxviii.
Chester, Eastgate (Thestgate) Ward, 172, 173.
„ Ecclesiastical Court, 1. *See also* Bishop's Court.
„ Exchequer of, 150, 152.
„ Holy Trinity (Trinity Ward, Trynitie Ward), 172, 173, 178.
„ Market Place (City Market Place), 150.
„ Market or Common Hall, lxiii.
„ Northgate Jail (Gaile), 148.
„ Northgate Street, 147.
„ Northgate Ward (North Ward), 172, 173.
„ Portmote Court, 173, 174, 177.
„ Prentice Court, 157 *n.*, 174.
„ St. Bridget's (St. Bride's Ward, St. Bridgits, St. Brigitte), 92, 127. 172, 173, 208.
„ St. Giles Ward, 172, 173.
„ St. John Baptist's (St. John's Ward), 133, 172, 173, 201.
„ St. Martin's (St. Marten's Ward), 21, 94, 172, 173.
„ St. Mary's on the Hill (St. Marie, St. Maries, St. Maries Ward, St. Mary apon the Hill), 21, 48, 93, 94, 95, 122, 128, 147, 172, 200.
„ St. Michael's (St. Michaelles, St. Michael's Ward), 96, 172, 173, 208.
„ St. Olave's (St. Olas Ward), 172, 173.
„ St. Oswald's (St. Oswaldes Ward), 96, 123, 172, 189, 191, 193.
„ St. Peter's, 126, 127, 201; li.
„ St. Thomas' (St. Thomas' Ward), 172, 173.
„ Town Clerk's Office, xv.
„ Town Hall, lvi.
„ Walls (Chester City Walls), 144.
Chester-le-Street, Durham, xliv *n.*
Chichester, lxix.
Childwall (Childwell), 23, 24.
China, xlii, *n.* 2.
Chorley, 34 *n.*, 51 *n.*
Christleton, 121.
Church, 29, 33.
Church Kirk, 29, 33 *n.*
Church Lawton, lxxiv.
Clare Priory, xxx.

Clitheroe (Castill in Clidroe, Clidroe), 29, 29 *n.*, 30 *n.*, 45, 45 *n.*, 138; lxi, lxxvi, lxxvi *n.*
Cockermouth, xlix *n.*
Codington, 60.
Colne (Holt House, Colne), 28, 45, 46, 47, 80; xvi.
Congleton, 4, 5, 139 *n.*; xviii.
Cornwall, 181 *n.*
Coventrie and Lichfield, Diocese of, 128.
Cowfild, 146.
Craven, xlvii, *n.* 1.
Crewe, 61, 117 *n.*
Cuerdon (Cuerdon Hall), 34.

Darsbury (Deasbury), 25.
Darwen, 33 *n.*, 34.
Davenham, 26, 58, lxxxii, lxxxvi.
Dean (Deane), 82, 83.
Dee, The River, xiv, xv, li, lxiv.
Deeping St. James, Lincolnshire, xxxiii.
Delamere (Dalamere), 180; lxxiii *n.*
Devon, 181 *n.*
Dodleston, 19, 20.
Dorset, 181 *n.*
Dorsetshire, xl *n.*
Douglas, Isle of Man, lxix.
Downham (Donham), 30, 30 *n.*
Dublin (Dublyn), 167, 174, 175; lv *n.*
Duckworth, 72.
Dunham (Dunhame), 180.
Dunton Basset, Leicestershire, xxxii.
Durham, xxi, xxiii, xxiv *n.*, xliv *n.*, xlix, xlix *n.*, lvi, lxvii, lxviii.
Dutton, 159.

Easingwold, xlvii *n.*
Eastham (Estam), 47, 47 *n.*, 49; lxxii.
East Marches, xxiv *n.*
Eaton (Eton), 87, 181.
Eccles, 99, 100.
Eccleston, 51, 51 *n.*; lxxxi.
„ Great, 51 *n.*
„ Little, 51 *n.*
Edinburgh, xliii *n.*
Egham, Surrey, 181.
Ely, lxviii.
England, 140, 151, 152, 156, 164, 168, 173, 178, 182; xiv, xviii *n.*, xxi, xxiv *n.*, xxxiv, liv *n.*
Engleton, 32, 33 (*see also* Ingleton).
Essex, 152, 168, 170.
Exeter, 15 *n.*; xxix, xlv *n.*, lxix.
Eynsham, Oxfordshire, xxiii, xxiv, xxiv *n.*, xxv, xxvi.
Eyton in Pickering Lyth, xxv, xxvi.

Farndon, 155; xiv, xv, lxxi *n.*, lxxxi.
Fenwick, xxiv *n.*
Flintshire, 102 *n.*, 120 *n.*; lviii.
Flodden, xxiv *n.*
Formby, lxxviii.
Frodsham, lii.

Garstang, li *n.*
Gloucester and Bristol, lxviii.
Goostrey (Gostre), 5, 5 *n.*
Grand Trunk Canal, 52 *n.*
Guildford, 179.

Hadham, 152.
Haigh Parish, Wigan, lxxii, lxxxv.
Haleghden, 102.
Halghton, 104.
Halies, 152.
Halifax (Holifaxe), 72; liv.
Hampford *alias* Hanford, xxxiii, xxxiv.
Handbridge, 146, 154, 169; li, li *n.*
Hankelowe, 181.
Hanmer, 102, 103, 104, 105, 106, 106 *n.*, 107, 108, 109, 110.
Hapsford (Happesford), 155.
Hargrave (Holgreve Hall), 50.
Hartford, lxxv.
Haslington (Hasslington), 17.
Hatton (Chapel of the Hall of Hatton, Hall of Hatton, Hatton Hall, House of Hatton), 39, 40, 41, 42, 43, 48, 49, 50.
Hawarden (Hardn), 18, 19, 171, 171 *n.*; lxiv.
Hazelbeach (Haselbishe), 72, 72 *n.*
Hedley, Durham, xliv *n.*
Hereford, xlvii *n.*, lxix.
Hertford (Hartford), 152.
Hocknell, 152.
Holcrofte, 44.
Holdernesse, Yorkshire, xxvi.
Holgreve, The Hall of, 50.
Holme (Hulme), 68, 68 *n.*
Holt, 155; lxxx *n.*
Hong Kong, xlii, xliii *n.*
Hooton, xviii.
Hothersall, 35.
Hull, 72; liv.
Huntunston, 97.
Hurleston, 90.
Huyton (Hyton), 131, 131 *n.*

India, xxxiv, xlii *n.*
Ingleby, co. Lincoln, xxiv *n.*
Ingleton, 32 *n.* (*see also* Engleton).
Ipswich, 168 ; lxiv.
Ireland, 67, 160, 167, 168, 175, 176, 179, 180 ; xxxii, xlvi, lv.
Isle of Man, lxix.

Kent, xl.
Kidden Hills, ? Riddenhilles, 120, 120 *n.*
Kirkbe, 207.
Kirkham, 34, 35 *n.*, 51 *n.* ; lxxiv.
Knutsford (Knotisford, Knottisford), 4, 5, 125, 126 ; xiv.

Lambeth, Surrey, xxxi.
Lamesley, Durham, xliv *n.*
Lancashire (Lancasher), 3, 6 *n.*, 9 *n.*, 12, 29 *n.*, 30 *n.*, 31 *n.*, 33 *n.*, 34 *n.*, 35 *n.*, 37 *n.*, 44 *n.*, 46 *n.*, 48 *n.*, 50 *n.*, 53 *n.*, 63 *n.*, 64 *n.*, 68 *n.*, 91, 131 *n.*, 170 ; xiv, xiv *n.*, xx *n.*, xxi, xxiii *n.*, lxxv, lxxvi *n.*
Lancaster, 35 *n.*, 164, 169, 180 ; lxxiv.
Lancaster Canal, 30 *n.*
Lashawe, lxxvi *n.*
Lathom (Lathum), 48, 48 *n.*, 49 ; xviii.
Lawton, lxxvi.
Leeds Canal, 46 *n.*
Leicester, 144.
Leigh (Leghe), 44 ; xxii, lxxvi *n.*
Leyland, 12, 34 *n.*
Lichfield (Coventrie and Lichfield), 128 ; lxix.
Lincoln, xiii, xxii, xxiv *n.*
Lincolnshire, xxxiii.
Lincolns' Inn Fields, xxxiii.
Lithe, 13.
Liverpool, 23 *n.*, 30 *n.*, 46 *n.*, 67, 117, 131 *n.* ; xiv, xlvi.
Llandaff, lxix.
London, 13, 14, 15, 29 *n.*, 30 *n.*, 44 *n.*, 46 *n.*, 53 *n.*, 72, 83, 119, 160, 169, 170, 185, 193, 199 ; xiii, xiv *n*, xviii, xxxiii, xxxvi *n.*, xlii, liv, lv, lvii *n.*, lxix *n.*
,, Fleet Prison, xlii.
,, Piccadilly, xlii.
,, Regent Street, xlii.
,, Somerset House, lxvi *n.*
,, Strand, xlii.
Lostock, The River, 34 *n.*
Lostocke, xxiii *n.*
Lough foile, 179.
Lowchurch (Lowe Church), 34, 35.
Lowe, 183, 184 ; lxxxii.
Lowe parish, lxxxii.
Lower Peover (Pever inferiori), 125.
Lymm (Limne), 63, 63 *n.*, 65 ; lxxvi.

Macclesfield (Macclesfelde), 139 *n.*, 180.
Malpas, 52, 52 *n.*, 88, 91 *n.* 104 *n.*, 112 *n.*, 120, 120 *n.*, 121, 125 *n.* ; lxxxiii.
Manchester, 29 *n.*, 30 *n.*, 44 *n.*, 46 *n.*, 82, 124, 164, 185 ; xxii, lxxii *n.*
Marbury (Marburie, Merburye), 1, 2, 52, 52 *n.*
Mellinge, 141 ; lxii.
Mellor (Meller, Melloure), 34, 34 *n.*, 53, 53 *n.*
Mersey, The River, 63 *n.*, 64 *n.*
Middle Marshes, xxiv *n.*
Middlesex, 181 ; lxiv.
Middleton, lxxxiii.
Middlewich (Medii Vici, Medio Vico), 15, 113, 113 *n.*, 114 ; lxxiii *n.*
Minshull (Mynshull), 111, 112, 113, 114, 115.
Morpeth, lvii.

Nantwich (Nauntwich, Vici Malbani, Vico Malbano, Witch Malbank), 32 *n.*, 49 *n.*, 50 *n.*, 52 *n.*, 69, 70, 70 *n*, 71 *n.*, 89, 90, 90 *n.*, 111, 112 *n.*, 117 *n.*, 118, 118 *n.*, 119 ; xlviii, lix.
,, The Bell Inn, 118, 119 ; lix.
,, Market, xlviii.
Neston, Great, 47 *n.* ; lxxviii, lxxx.
Newcastle, lvii, lviii *n.*
Newchurch in Pendle, 29.
Newton Chappel, 140.
Newton in Makerfield, 44 *n.*
New Yaite (Gate), Durham ? lvii.
Nibly, xxvii.
Northampton, 72 *n.*
Northamptonshire, 72.
Northenden (Northerdon, Northredon), 139, 139 *n.*, 140 ; lxxvi.
North Rode, 139 *n.*
Northumberland, xxiv *n.*, xliii *n.*
Northwich, 5 *n.*, 52 *n.*, 64 *n.*, 124 *n.* ; lii, lxxvii.
Norwich, xiii, lxix.
Nuneaton, Warwickshire, xxxii.

Old Withington, 139 *n.*
Ormskirk, 48 *n.*; lxxviii, lxxx, *n.* 1.
Oulton (Olton), 88, 88 *n.*
Over, 87, 87 *n.*, 88 *n.*, 112, 136; lxxiii *n.*
Overton, 102 *n.*, 112 *n.*
Oxford, lxviii.
Oxfordshire, xxiii, xxiv *n.*

Padiam, 30, 30 *n.*
Pendle, 29.
Pendle Hill, 29 *n.*
Peover Lower (Pever Inferiori), 125; lxxvii, *n.* 2.
Peterborough, lxviii.
Pewnal (? Pownall), 180.
Pikeringe Lyth, in York, xxv, xxvi.
Pleasington (Pleddington), 53, 53 *n.*
Plemstow, lxxiv.
Plumpton Castle, xxxii.
Poole, 152, 156.
Poolton or Poulton (Poton), 37, 37 *n.*
Portbury, xli *n.*
Pownall (Pewnal), 180.
Prees (Prise), 128.
Prescot, 51 *n.*, 197.
Prestbury (Presbury), 13, 15, 61, 61 *n.*, 139 *n.*; lxxvi, lxxxi *n.*
Preston, 30, 31, 31 *n.*, 34, 34 *n.*, 35, 35 *n.*, 53 *n.*

Ribble, The River, 29 *n.*, 30 *n.*, 35 *n.*, 38 *n.*
Ribchester, 16, 35 *n.*
Riddenhills (Kidden Hills), 120, 120 *n.*
Ridge, The, 5.
Ridlesdale, co. Northumberland, xxiv *n.*
Ripon, xlvii *n.*
Rishton, Staffordshire, 196; xlvi, lxxviii.
Rochester, lxviii.
Rostherne (Restorne, Rosterne, Rostorne), 59, 60, 75, 97, 98, 99, 123, 124, 125, 126; lxxv, lxxvi, lxxvii.
Runcorn (Roncorne), 201.

St. Asaph, 112 *n.*; lxix.
St. Davids, lxviii.
St. Helens, 51 *n.*
St. Michael on Wyre, 51 *n.*
St. Michael's Castle, xxix.
St. Peters, Chester, li.
St. Quintins, 106.
Salisbury, xiii, xxix, xlv *n.*, lxvi, lxix.
Saltney, near Chester, li.
Samlesbury (Sampsbury, Samsbury), 35, 35 *n.*, 36, 37, 184; xx, xx *n.*, xxiii *n.*
Scotland, 16, 155; xxiv *n.*, xxxi, xxxii, xli *n.*, xliii *n.*
Scrivelsby, co. Lincoln, xxiv *n.*
Sefton, 207.
Shevington (Shentone), 180.
Shirford, Warwickshire, xxxii.
Shorleye, 180.
Skipton Castle, xxxii.
Smallwood (Smalewood), 100.
" Spenne Green, 100.
Sodor and Man, lxix.
Somerset, 181, 181 *n.*
Somerset House, lxvi *n.*
Sondell, 32.
Spenne Green, in Smallwood, 100.
Staffordshire, 196; xlvi.
Staines (Stanys), Middlesex, 181; lxiv.
Standish, lxxiv *n.*
Stanlowe Abbey, lxxi, lxxii, lxxxvii.
Stanney, 152, 156.
Stockport (Stockporte), 62 *n.*, 141.
Stofforth (Stoforth), 82, 82 *n.*
Stokesley, co. York, xxiv *n.*
Streatham, xxiv *n.*
Stretton, 125, 125 *n.*
Suffolk, xxix, xxx.
Swinhed in Rostherne, 99.
Swyne in Holdernesse, Yorkshire, xxvi.

Tabley (Tableye), 180.
Tarporley, 41 *n.*, 48 *n.*, 50 *n.*, 87, 111 *n.*; lxxiii *n.*
Tattenhall (Tatnall, Tattenall), 39, 40, 42, 50.
Tatton, in Rostherne, lxxvi.
Tatton Hall, lxxxi, *n.* 1.
Taxall (Tacksall), 203.
Thornton, in Craven, Yorkshire, xlvii *n.*
Tilston, 125 *n.*
Tinstwick, 172.
Tiverton (Terton), 50, 51 *n.*
Towcester (Totcester), 83, 83 *n.*
Turton (Terton), 50, 51 *n.*; xxi, lxxii.
Tyne, The River, lvi.

Wales (Walles), 91 *n.*, 136, 168, 182, 182 *n.*; lxiv.
Walton on the Hill (Walton), 23, 23 *n.*, 24, 67, 141, 204, 205, 206; lxxv.
Warburton, The Town Field, 64, 64 *n.*; xlvi.

Warmingham (Warmengham), 132, 133.
Warrington (Werington), 22, 25, 44 *n.*, 63 *n.*, 68 *n.*, 125 *n.*; lxxiii, lxxiv.
Warwickshire, xxxii.
Washford, 179.
Waterford, Ireland, 160.
Waverton, 38, 39, 40, 41, 41 *n.*, 43, 48 *n.*, 50.
Weaver, River, 49 *n.*; lxxiii *n.*
Weaverham (Weram, Weverham), 73, 74, 75, 101.
Wem (Wems), 109.
Wendover, 172.
West Derby (Darbye), 44 *n.*, 117, 206.
West Kirkby (Westkirkbie), 95, 95 *n.*, 96.
Westminster, 166; xxxiii.
Whalley, 29, 29 *n.*, 30 *n.*, 32 *n.*, 38, 46 *n.*, 72, 138; lxxii, lxxv, lxxvi, *n.* 2.
Whiston, 131, 132.
Whitchurch, 1 *n.*
Whitegate parish, lxxxiv.
Wickham, 172.
Widford, 13, 14, 15; Widford Hall, 15.
Wigan, 2, 83, 84, 198, 199; xxiii, lxxii, lxxvi *n.*, lxxxi, lxxxii, lxxxv.
Wilmslow (Wilmeslowe, Wilmesly, Wilmysloe), 62, 62 *n.*, 134, 135.
Winchester, lxix.
Winsford, 87 *n.*
Winwick (Winweke), 2, 44, 68, 68 *n.*, 140.
Wirrall, 47 *n.*; lxxxvii.
Withenshawe (Wythenshawe Hall), 139, 139 *n.*
Withington Hall, 139.
Withington, Old, 139 *n.*
Witton, 5, 5 *n.*, 64, 101, 209, 210; lxxv, lxxvii *n.*
Wooler (Wicoller, Wwller), 45, 45 *n.*, 47.
Wootton Fitzpaine (Wotton Phippyn), Devon, xlv *n.*
Worcester, lxix.
Worthenbury (Worthinbury) 91.
Wrenbury (Wrenburie, Wrenburye), 49, 49 *n.*, 129, 181.
Wybunbury, 134.

Yarrow, River, 51 *n.*
York (Yorke), 31 *n*, 114, 162; xvii, xxiv, xxiv *n.*, xxvi, xxvii, xxxv, xli, xlvii *n.*, lxix.
Yorkshire, 32 *n.*; xxiii *n.*

GLOSSARY.

BY MR. P. Z. ROUND.

a, *prep.* (1) on, 23/23; (2) of, 119/38.
abode, *sb.* stay, 193/4.
abject, *adj.* cast off, abandond (child), xxviii.
absent, *adj.* separate, apart, 5/2.
accompanie, *vb.* cohabit (*see* company), 33/34.
after, *adv.* afterwards, 184/14, 201/8.
after-Evensonge, *sb.* "afore dailight was done," 69/2.
agreid, *ptc.* reconciled, 105/16.
Alhalontide, *sb.* All Saints' Day season, 198/12; Alhalowtide, 87/14.
Allholloweday, *sb.* All Saints' Day, 51/14.
allowid, *ptc.* approved, 136/29.
and, *conj.* if, 112/37, 197/21, 208/31.
any whether, *see* whether, 205/3.
apointid, *vb.* made an appointment, 188/37.
arrant, *adj.* infamous, 121/31, 127/19.
articulate, *adj.* charged, stated, 19/31.
as, *conj.* (used redundantly); as when, 137/19; as much as sins (since), 3/16, 40/17, 41/2, 43/19, 49/29.
assured, *ptc.* engaged, affianced, 64/19, lii/32; convinced, xxv/13.
at, *prep.* at the hands of, 4/34; together with, xxiii/2.
aundert, *sb.* afternoon, 117/8; aunderth, 131/36.
avoiding, *sb.* vacating, 148/26.

backside, *sb.* rear (of a dwelling), xlvi, lxxix, note 1; 68/5, 187/16.
backside, *adv.* behind, 101/20.
bagge, *vb.* put in bags, 145/10.
bande, *sb.* bond, 147/33.
banes askinge, asking of banns, 193/34.
bargen, *sb.* covenant, contract, 3/13 (15 note); bargaine, 6/35, 205/24; (2) settlement, payment (under bond), 12/20.
barrell drome, *sb.* barrel-drum, lvii/3.
barthelewne tide, St. Bartholomew's-Day season, 193/30.
beadman, *sb.* bedesman, 190/6.
bear, *vb.*; did bear her in hand = led her to believe, 190/24.
bearbruer, *sb.* beerbrewer, 178/14.
beat the bush, lxxix, note 2; beat the bough, lxxx, note.
bed rotton, *adj.* bedridden (?), 169/2.
beggerly harlot and cutthrote, lvii/23.
behinde-doore worke, *sb.* lv, 97.
beste, *sb.* beestings, lix, note.
betold, *ptc.* betrayed (?), 114/28.
bie, *prep.* concerning, 103/24, 204/21.
bound, *ptc.* engaged, bound over, 200/5, 203/24; bounden, 203/35.
bourd, *sb.* jest, 124/2.
bowed, *ptc.* bent, xlix, note.
bridal, *sb.* wedding feast ("the dinner," 53/14), 31/7, 54/13.
broade, *sb.* breadth, 14/25.
browll, *sb.* lviii/14, but?
brutid, *ptc.* talked of, 111/36.
burnid, *ptc.* poxt, 33/6, 100/17.
burthen, *vb.* accuse, charge, 80/27; burthenid, 91/7.
but, *prep.* except, 187/31.
but, *conj.* unless, 203/25.

carcanet, *sb.* 30.
carder, *sb.* player at cards, gambler, lxii.
cast, *sb.* (1) throw, a stone's cast, 207/1; (2) castes, tricks, 104/1.
cast, *vb.* bestow; cast favour to hym, 4/26; to cast hir favour unto, xxv/17.
cattels, *sb.* chattels, 177/8.
cellered, *ptc.* brought into cellar, 155/21.
certen, *sb.* number, a certen of wyves, 87/8.
chafe, *sb.* anger, heat, 206/35.

chales, *sb.* chalice, 134/11.
charge, *sb.* responsibility; toke apon her charge = solemnly declared, 85/26; did take it apon her charge, 96/5. charges, expense, 202/24.
cheffe, *sb.* napkin, lvii/5.
circumstances, *sb.* ceremonies, formalities, 201/10.
clarted, *adj.* lvii/15, ?
cleane, *adv.* quite, 204/15.
clene, *adj.* pure, 192/3.
clem, *vb.* famish, starve, xxi, 54/28.
close, *sb.* enclosed ground, 104/15.
close, *adj.* fast, 131/6; concealed, 185/38.
cognicion, *sb.* knowledge, 61/24.
cohabit, *vb.* dwell together, 25/11, 36/9.
cohabitacion, xxxvii, note, 29/30.
colourably, *adv.* plausibly, 195/15.
commen, *vb.* converse, 58/2, 70/29, 130/11, 188/27; commune, 57/13; commoned, 125/18.
commorant, *adj.* resident, 139/9.
communicacion, *sb.* conversation, debate, 58/7, 61/14, 187/17, 197/6, 199/8, 200/32, lxxix, note.
company, *vb.* cohabit, 203/9.
conscience, *sb.* solemn or secret opinion, judgment, 19/30, 26/13, 36/17, 59/23, 95/36; inward feelings, sense of right, 80/18.
content, *adj.* pleased; be content = agree, 185/31.
contract, *vb.* affiance, engage, lii/27, 61/8; contractid, 199/14.
convaide, *vb.* carried off, 65/30.
conversacion, *sb.* doings, immorality, lxxvi, note.
conveyance, *sb.* stealthy removal, 39/16, 125/31.
corse, *sb.* corse and recorse = passage in and out, 148/18.
countenance, *sb.* reputation, 173/21.
croft, *sb.* close, 131/30.
crowket-handyd wytch, lvii/14.
cuckold, cuckoldy knaves, lvii/20, 104, 108.
customablie, *adv.* usually, 200/1.
cut a purse, lvi.

daie-holdinges, *sb.* appointments, meetings for reconciliation, 44/30.
daiesman, *sb.* arbitrator, referee, lx, 197/14, 209/34; daiseman, 197/8.
dame, *sb.* mistress, 107/28, 111/13, 19.
daunger, *sb.* power (?), 121/29; offence (or penalty ?), 196/27.
day, *sb.* time, 153/14.
deflour, *vb.* ravish, copulate with, xxix.
delit vpon, xlvi, note 2, love for, desire for. (Cp. "have his pleasure apon her," 79/1.)
delt, *vb.* had intercourse, 53/28.
denaide, *vb.* refused, 126/24.
departe, *vb.* part, separate, xlvii, note 2, 165/36, 198/28; departid, went away, 198/32.
dependinge, *adj.* pending, 192/35.
destetes, *sb.* , 148/3, ?
device, *sb.* bequest, 172 foot.
disagreed, *vb.* (*cp.* dissentid), 31/31.
disburse, *vb.* pay, xli.
discomfort, *vb.*, liv.
dishonesty, *sb.* lewdness, evil doing, 104/32, 115/26, 125/16.
dislove, *sb.* ill-will, 11/32, 55/6.
dissentid, *vb.* refused ratification, 31/31.
divorcement, *sb.*, xxvii, at foot.
doer, *sb.* agent, xxv/34; mover, 84/35.
dole, *sb.* dealing, ado, 4/35, 18/7, 23/27.
draw, *vb.* (1) part, unclasp; drewe handes (*cp.* losid), 68/11, 186/10; (2) betake oneself; drewe into her company, 80/16, 85/20; (3) make, drewe acquaintaunce, 72/17.
dycke, *sb.* hedge, lvii/5.

eame, *sb.* uncle, 132/2.
Egiptians, *sb.* gipsies, 106/7.
entreatid, *ptc.* treated, 206/22.
entrid, *ptc.* sued, 204/22.
escape, *sb.* fault, act of negligence, 152/21.
examied, *ptc.* examined, 167/4.
examinate, *sb.*, xliv, note 3.
extremes, *sb.* uttermost pains (of childbirth), 95/29, 99/30.
extremity, *sb.* severity, hardship, 128/8.

face, *sb.* In the face of the church = in open church, 184/20, 202/12.
fallen, *ptc.* come; Landes fallen vnto her = property inherited, 203/12.
fame, *sb.* repute, 113/2.
fane, *vb.* produce, 150/7.
fansie, *vb.* like, 4/26, 183/20.
favor, *vb.* care for, 7/6; favored, 2/10.
favour, *sb.* liking, affection; cast favour to, 4/26.

feare meanes or foule, lii, fair means or foul.
fele, *vb.* find out, 185/35.
fellowe, *sb.* one fellowe wold tell an other, 196/2; good fellowe, lxxvi, note 1; companion, 88/28.
fells, *sb.* hides, 155/1.
fermour, *sb.* patron, 139/21.
fett, *ptc.* fetched, liv, 74/30.
flight, *sb.* arrow; a flight shot (= bow-shot), 207/26.
flitted, *ptc.* changed his abode, 125/35. So still in South Staffordshire.
for, *prep.* as for, regarding, 193/4, 206/6.
for-bie-cause = forasmuch as, 5/33, 79/18, 115/24, 191/5.
forthe, *adv.* apart, 186/2; furth, forward, 208/31; forth of, away from, li/34.
forther, *adj.* first, previous, 73/8, 190/20.
fortune, *vb.* happen, 204/35.
founde, *ptc.* provided for, 147/10.
frame hoode, *sb.* branks or head-dress for punishing scolds, lvii/8.
fro, *adv.* against; of nor fro, 204/13.
fugitive, *sb.* lx, 124.
furiouse, *adj.* mad, 135/18.
fyne, *vb.* last, feed, lviii/10.

g = z. refuge (*vb.*) = refuse, 191/17.
gestninges, *sb.* hospitalities, entertainments of friends, 18/24.
gestwise, *adv.* guest-fashion; a gestwise, 23/23; as gesteweyes, 41/31; on gestwise, 43/7.
geve ouer = cease from, 129/1, 2.
go, *vb.* walk, xxv/30.
good, *sb.* property, a pece of good, 56/17.
a goode woman, xlv; an honest woman, or wife, after being a concubine, xlv, note 1.
goose and hen thief, lvii/26.
gostly father, godfather, 79/32.
grace, *sb.* (1) disposition (*lit.* share of divine favour); her grace was no better, 180/12. So *II Henry IV.*, V. v. 56, "Make less thy body hence, and more thy grace!" (2) good manners (?), 103/17.
graunt, *vb.* confess, 195/14; grauntith, 116/12; grauntid, 120/5; (= assented), 140/2.
grinning thief, 117, 207.

had, *ptc.* obtained, 2/1; performed, celebrated, 21/20, 28/16, 197/4, xxiv/12; done, 43/17.
haltid, *vb.* limped, lxi, 138/21.
hand, *sb.* in hand = in treaty, 165/8; bear (one) in hand, *see* bear; handes trouthe, contract by joined hands, 188/13; hand in hand, 58/13.
handfast, *adj.* hand in hand (by way of contract), lxxv, note 1, lxxx, note 1.
hang-lipped witches, lvii/15.
hay, *sb.* field, 131/30.
heady, *adj.* wilful, headstrong, 54/27.
hindred, *ptc.* impaired, 104/5.
hold-eyed lymber thief, lviii/9.
holidame, *sb.* halidom, holiness, sacred honour (not Our Lady), 69/15. *Cp.* Alholoweday.
homelye, *adj.* familiar, intimate, 111/26.
honest, *adj.* respectable, 70/20.
honestly, *adv.* decently, 147/20; fairly, 206/22.
hoore, *sb.* whore, 102/25, 117/6, 127/14.
hooremaster, horemonger preiste, lvii/18.
hopping, *sb.* dance, xliv, note 3.
horsekeeper, lxii.
house, *sb.* household (?); in house with = under the same roof with, 195/1, xxvi/1, 39/11.
huggle, *vb.* cuddle, xxxiv.

inconvenient, *adj.* improper, unsuitable, 108/10, 185/3.
instantly, *adv.* urgently, 195/10.
intreaties, *sb.* negotiations, 200/37.
iterate, *vb.* xxviii.

jawde, *sb.* jade, 123/11.
John, Sir John, *n.* parson, priest, lxii.

knowledged, *ptc.* acknowledged, 160/20.

laid bye, were bedded, 78, at foot.
lapp, *vb.* wrap, 128/36.
lather, *adj.* loather, fouler, worse, xlvii, note 2.
leafull, *adj.* lawful, 148/15, 151/19.
leman, *sb.* concubine, lvii/18, 203/8.
light, *adj.* lewd, 32/33, 98 at foot; untrustworthy, lx, 125.

longe of, through, because of, 109/28.
losid, *vb.* unclasped, 184/26. *Cp.* draw.
lowable, *adj.* credible, 107/11.
lucre, *sb.* profit, benefit, xlii, note 2.
lye, *vb.* be; what shuld lye in him, as much as might be in his power, 205/19; lyenge, lodging, 185/23.
lyenge, *sb.* lyenge downe, time of childbed, 90/28.
lymer, lvi, at foot.
lyvinge, *sb.* livelihood, income; 4/23, 5/17, 106/1, 192/11.

made, *ptc.* manufactured, 163/3; assigned, made over, 192/20; shut, lxxxi, note.
malche, *sb.* milch (cow), 141/16.
manesyng, *sb.* menacing, threatening, lii/17.
mangerell, mongrel, lviii/13.
marchandrie ware, *sb.* trading goods, 72/30.
mariage-good, *sb.* dowry, 81/9, 98/27.
marie, *vb.* (intrans.) be married; to marie with him = *nubere ei*, lii/17.
matter, *sb.* case (at law), 122/14, 195/37; matters, affairs, 192/12.
ment, *vb.* thought (?), 197/34.
mercy, call to God's, die, xli.
meryly, *adv.* jestingly, 193/10.
meynie, *sb.* folk, company, 186/5.
milne, *sb.* mill, 97/5.
misdemenour, *sb.* misbehaviour, 80/25.
misliked, *vb.* cared not for, 126/31.
mislyvinge, *sb.* evil living, 80/27.
morowe, *sb.* morning, 111/23.
mother, *sb.* *hysterica passio*, 83/22. See note, p. lv.
muggewede, *sb.* a plant of the genus *Valantia* (Webster), xxiii/3; lv, 83/25.
mynde, *vb.* intend, 206/22; mynded, cared, 126/33; (*ptc.*) disposed, xxiii/3, 185/20.
mynde, *sb.* intent, 185/4, 191/28.

name, *sb.* repute, opinion, 113/31, 121/9; name and fame, lxxix, note 2.
naughtie, *see* noughtie.
neckurcheffe, *sb.* neckerchief, lvii/5.
nominate, *vb.* specify, 197/19.
notice, *sb.* cognizance, 33/9.
notoriouslye, *adv.* well, universally, xxvi/30.

nought, *adj.* valueless, null, 57/3, 194/33; wanton, 92/5, 127/1, 128/23, 205/37, 209/15.
nought, *sb.* fornicator, 129/33.
noughtie, *adj.* naughtie, 75 at foot; lewd, 80/25, 118/19, 203/15, disreputable, worthless, 129/15.
noughtiness, *sb.* wantonness, 92/12.

obligacion, *sb.* undertaking (under penalty), 5/12.
occasion, *sb.* cause, 117/19, 129/9, 206/21, 209/14.
occupie, *vb.* carry on, perform, 163/15; occupide, *ptc.* commissioned (?) 72/30.
on, *prep.* in; on lyve = alive, 191/7, 203/30.
or, *adv.* ere, 204/35.
ordenarie, *sb.* an ecclesiastic having jurisdiction, 42/1; Ordinary, 59/33.
order, *sb.* rule, 193/23.
ordred, *ptc.* treated, 12/9, 117/18.
ouerseer, *sb.* executor, 70/4.
ought, *vb.* owned, 82/15.
owid, *vb.* bore; any hate that (he) owid his wife, 202/14.
ownid, *vb.* attributed, 86/9.
owninge, *sb.* attribution, affiliation, 86/7.

pack, *sb.* load; a pack-a-pack, a-top of, lxxix, note 2. Webster cites *pick-a-pack* (in manner of a pack) from L'Estrange.
paine, *sb.* penalty, 157/12; paines, trouble, 190/20.
pale, *sb.* paling, 117/12.
partie, *sb.* part, side, 201/38; parties, litigants, 209/23.
pass, *vb.* take account, reck; she passid not for his gooddes, 59/29.
pece of good, *sb.* some property, xlix, 56.
peltinge, *adj.* paltry, lv, 98/38.
perfittlie, *adv.* perfectly, 184/22.
play, *vb.* act, perform, behave as; plaid many light points, 32/33; play the hoore, 80/10; plaid the nought, 94/11, 129/33, 209/15.
play, *sb.* in a play, in fun, lxxiv, at foot.
pointed, *vb.* fixed, 188/36.
pointes, *sb.* parts, actions, 32/33.
pokye (pocky) thief, lviii/7.

pollicy, *sb.* artifice, 131/8.
pox, pockes, *sb.* lviii/6, 92/10; *see* burnid.
practisioner, *sb.* practitioner (of surgery), 100/16.
praysed, *ptc.* appraised, valued, 134/4.
pretensid, *ptc.* intended, affianced, 1/12, 2/35, 4/5, 78/30.
procurement, *sb.* management, 196/26.
proxy, *sb.* xxvi, at foot.
purposid, *ptc.* minded; were fullie purposid, had made up their minds, 185/25.
purse, *vb.* take, pocket, xxxix, note 3.
pussie, *sb.* girl, sweetheart, xxxiv.

queane, *sb.* wench, 123/3.
quest, *sb.* inquest, inquiry, 34/28.

rather, *adv.* earlier, sooner, 192/19.
reade, *vb.* guess, 124/8.
reasid, *ptc.* raised, 208/13.
reasoninge, *sb.* dispute, 206/31, 209/16.
recett, *vb.* receive, hide, lviii/9.
reclaime, *vb.* cry out, complain, 45/10.
recorders, *sb.* flutes, 150/25.
recurid, *ptc.* recovered, 146/11.
refuge, *vb.* refuse, 191/17.
rehersall, *sb.* recital, 119/30.
reherse, *vb.* recite, relate, lxxx, note 1.
release, *vb.* ease, 116/28.
remembrid, *ptc.* (reflexive), he is well remembrid that, he well remembers, 7/23; she is not remembrid of, 199/30. But we have "she . . . remembres," 199/3.
repair, *vb.* go, 67/24.
require, *vb.* beseech, 198/15; required, 67/23, 97/35, 196/10; summoned, 135/9.
reteyninge, *ptc.* attendant, 39/20.
rid in a cart, lvii, lix, 128.
right, *sb.* one's due, 204/26.
rise, *vb.* (pt. t.), rose, 107/30.
road, *sb.* rod in length, lxxvi, note 1.
rose noble, *sb.* xlix, note.
rowe, *sb.* alley, 208/6.

se, *vb.* (pt. t.) saw, 194/13; (subj. mood) 205/6; sawe togither, beheld one another, xxv/11.
season, *sb.* time; in the meane season, 188/38.
seducid, *ptc.* led away, 192/13.
send, *vb.* (pt. t.) sent, 109/11, 138/23, 187/37; (ptc.) 189/19.
serve, *vb.* suit, 184/20.
sessed, *ptc.* assessed, 178/23.
set, *ptc.* settled, 190/13.
seve, *sb.* sieve; turn one on a pair of shears, as an exorcism, lvii.
sewid, *vb.* went on, 16/2.
shake-buckler, *vb.* bully, lxii.
sheriffwick, *sb.* sheriffship, shrievalty, 152/21.
sherman, *vb.* shearer (of cloth), 153/3.
shrewdlie, *adv.* harshly, 9/17.
simplicity, *sb.* ignorance, lxxvii, note.
smart, *adj.* lv, note 3.
snigge, *sb.* eel? 116, note.
so, *adv.* provided, 185/38.
sonder, *sb.* in sonder, asunder, 49/13.
sooke, *vb.* seek (?), 141/16.
soole, *adj.* alone, li/14.
soucke, *sb.* nurse's milk, 40/3; suck, 147/11.
spanyell hoore, fawning whore, lvii/9.
stale, *vb.* (pt. t.) stole, 193/33.
stand, *vb.* stick, stand to, abide by, 129/16, 208/10. See note, p. 142.
steg-steiler, *sb.* gander-stealer, lvii/12.
stele, *sb.* stile, 101/20.
stertes, *sb.* by stertes, by fits and starts, 30/4.
stick to that, xlv, 60.
stinged, *ptc.* stung, prickt, incited, xliii.
straite, *adj.* strict, harsh, 53/35.
sure, *adj.* fast, 186/23, 197/15; settled, 200/10.
suspectid, *ptc.* suspectid with, under suspicion (of intercourse), 203/28.
suspicious, *adj.* out of the way, concealed, 101/18, 105/26.
suspiciously, *adv.* clandestinely, surreptitiously, 22/31, 59/2, 106/35.
suter, *sb.* (said of a woman), 194/23.
sutes, *sb.* lawsuits, 192/12.
swelling, *sb.* lxxxi, note.
syde- (long) tayled knave, lvii/22 ('syde' was first 'wide').
sythence, *adv.* since, 36/9.

tables, *sb.* backgammon, lxiii, 180?
tablid, *vb.* (neuter), boarded, 189/15; (*ptc.*) 29/25, 125/9.
tacke, *sb.* lease, 131/29.
take, *vb.* taken her downe, scolded her,

112/13; take to, accept, 158/10; take up, pay off, 164/5; take an othe, exact an oath, swear a person, 186/25.

tar-barrell, lvii/2.

tene, *sb.* passion, vexation, lviii, at foot, 117/16.

thereanendes, *adv.* therefor, for that end, 26/16.

therefore, *adv.* therefor, on that account, 164/18, 19.

thone, the one, 129/32.

thoughts, *sb.* cares, taking thoughts, anxiety, l, 63/9.

title, *sb.* claim, 193/12.

tote, *adj.* peep (hole), spy, lix/5, 113/23. See Skeat, *s. v. tout.*

tralid, *vb.* traild, lxi, 138.

travaylid, *ptc.* busied, lxi, 139/15.

trouthe, *sb.* troth; *see* handes trouthe.

trouthplightid, *ptc.* affianced, 128/20; trouthplight, 128/9.

trouthplightinge, *sb.* betrothal, 128/16.

Twelfth even "in the Christmas," 45/24.

tyme, *sb.* opportunity, 184/20.

tyne, *vb.* shut, 114/34.

uncle in lawe, 3/27.

vnconvenientlie, *adv.* in unseemly wise, 112/12.

vndertake, *vb.* bail, be surety, 149/22, 24.

vnhonest, *adj.* disreputable, 127/34.

vnhonestlie, *adv.* immodestly, 115/21.

vnkindnes, *sb.* ill-will, 203/14.

vnruliness, *sb.* ungovernableness, 109/14.

vnthrift, *sb.* spendthrift, 119/8.

untimeous, too early, xxxi.

upon, *prep.* xlvi, note 2.

vttered, *ptc.* exposed for sale, 153/26.

wagwallet, braggart?, or thief, lvii/22.

waide, *vb.* urged, 61/9.

walkyng staff, *sb.* lii.

ward, *sb.* custody, 195/3.

warned, *vb.* repelled, opposed, 113/24.

wastes, *adj.* impoverished, 4/36.

waytsmen, *sb.* musicians, 150/22 (waytes = hautboys).

whele bed, truckle bed, 88/28.

where, *adv.* whereas, 79/28.

whether, *adv.* whither, 205/3, 69/21.

whitsonmonday, Whitmonday, 50/14.

willed, *vb.* besought, 99/21, 124/31; willid, 133/24, 185/32.

windowes, *sb.* shutters, lvi, 113/24.

wordinge, *sb.* wrangling, 129/9, 206/28.

worke-house, *sb.* outhouse, 185/2.

wright, *sb.* artificer, 129/25.

wyne, *vb.* get, 13/13, 14/10 (Scotch *win*).

worship, *sb.* honour, municipal office, 208/10.

yerlie, yerly, *adv.* early, 7/31, 99/2.

yexcept, *adv.* except, 193/21.

yhoue, *pron.* you, xlvii, note 1.

INDEX OF SUBJECTS.

(IT DOESN'T PRETEND TO COMPLETENESS.)

Absentee Cheshire Landlords in 1578, 180.
Abuse, terms of, in Durham Depositions, lvi—lviii; in Chester ones, *see* Libels, 102—130, 204—210.
Accidentally, 141.
Accompanie together as man and wief, 33.
Acres, 4 to be laid to every Cottage in 1589, xxxiv.
Administration of Testator's goods, lxxviii, note; *see* Inventory.
Adulterers, Chester Sheriff's search for, 194, at foot.
Adulteries, liii—lv, 72—85.
Adultery and folly, 203.
Affiliations, lv—lvi, 85—102.
Age of Consent for girls (12), boys (14), xvii, xix.
Age of marriage in India, 6 to 8, xxxv.
Ages, 2 of men, 6 of women, lxx.
Ale, a cup of, after Trothplight, 68.
Alehouse, a little pelting, 98 at foot, 99.
Alehouse-keeper pulls a woman indoors, lvi, 99.
Allusions to public affairs, liv, note.
Ambitious parents, xxxiv.
Anger, words spoken in, not to be heeded, lix, 127.
Angry words, 204.
Answer at a trial: man refuses to incriminate himself, 81, 101.
Antiquaries, Cheshire, reproacht, lxiv, lxv, lxvii, Dedication; defended, lxx.
Apples; a girl gives a boy two, to marry her, xvi, 45; an Uncle gives his Nephew one, to marry a child, xxii.
Apprentice to a shoemaker, xviii, 5; to a peruke-maker, xxxiii.
Archbishop of York, suit before, 31; punishes a Curate, xvii, 45.
As arrant a hoor as ever went abrode, 121.
As well as any man in England, 202.
Attending, *n.* A.D. 1591 (1611 in *E. E. Dict.*), 147.
Axe, man with one, chivies a woman who cald him names, 117.

Backside, the Mayor of Liverpool's back premises, 68.
Bakers, Chester, Oath of, lxiii, 154.
Banns of Marriage, no, lxxvii; 1, at foot, 19, 194; askt, 59, 61; forbidden, 196.
Barber, not to let unlawful Games be playd, 145.
Bare skin, he never touchid hir, 8.
Bargain or sale of a boy in marriage, xv, 6.
Bargain of Marriage, 6 at foot; 12, 23.
Bark and Crew for Q. Elizabeth's service, 178.
Barley-corn, a woman chews it, 112, 115.
Barley, field of, to be spent in a libel-action, 122.
Bashful woman, 189.
Bastard, father of, declared in church, lvi, 86.
Bastards (generally kept by their Fathers), *see* Affiliations, lv, 32, 69, 70, 85—102; lxiii, 146, 149, 156, 157, 202, 203, 210.
Bastard's mother provided for, at her lying in, 90.
Bawd to her own Daughter, Hy. Glyn's wife was, lvii, note 1.
Beaumont and Fletcher on rape, lxx, note 3.
Bed, man and girl in, together, lv, lxxxi, note 1, 87, 88, 91, 106.
Bedding of married children, xvii, 7, 8, 15.

Bedfellows, uncle-in-law and nephew, 3; friends, 92.
Bedroom, priest's, marriage in, 65-6.
Beerbrewer, a Chester, 178.
Beggars, bastards given to, 97.
Bent or bowd groat, &c., as tokens, xlix, note 1, 73.
Bettering, *n.*, 148.
Bigamy, Indian children's, xvi, *n.*
„ Rafe Holden's, liii, 72.
Bigg and gret in the belly, lxxxi, note.
Births of babies, xv, 40: *see* Affiliations.
Bishop of Chester blamed, lxvi.
Bishop's Court, the remedy for social wrongs, 210.
„ daughter married at 9, xxii.
Blessing, boy asks his Father's, 13, 14.
Blockhouses and a Bulwark for the defence of Hull, 72.
Blue Turquoise, 190.
Bond given to secure a Child Marriage, xix, 5, 9; for other purposes, 154-8, 162, 174, 175.
Book of Common Prayer, 201.
Book, swear upon a, lxxx, note 1; 198.
„ kiss it, 69.
Boy borne in a man's arms to his Wedding, 25; bargaind in marriage, for Father's debt, 23.
Boys of age at 14, xxxv, &c., lxx.
„ at school, xvii, 48. See 'School.'
„ live with father-in-law, xviii, xxiii.
Boys, young, married, xiv—xxxv, 1—55, 203; one cries to go home with his father, 6, and before he's married, 7.
Branks, a Scold's head-dress, lvii, note 2.
Brass to be brought for sale in the Common Hall, 167.
Bread, good and wholesome, 154.
Bread (? poultice) of Mugweed, 83.
Breakfast, 208 at foot.
Breaking into a Cheshire widow's house, and carrying her off, lxxxvi.
Breaking into a Chester citizen's house, and taking him to prison, 159.
Breath went out of his mouth, 131, he died.
Bribe, 2*s.*, to bear false witness, 128.
Bribes for silence: shoes, lv.; shirt, lxxvi, note 2; petticoat, 92;
Bride-ales, xvii, 31; or dinner 53, and supper xxxi; 66.
Bride and Bridegroom held in Nurses or Relatives' arms, when married, xv, xxii, xxiv.
Bride nearly starvd by her heady Mother- and Father-in-law, xxi, 53.
Bridge, Staines, to be broken down, to stop Rebels, 181.
Broade, a fieldes (breadth), 14.
Brutal Stanley mother- and father-in-law, starve their son's Wife, 54-5.
Burials, gifts for, 168, 169.
Burned, she, men, 33, poxt.
Butchers, Chester, Oath of, 153.
Butter and cheese stolen, lx, 124.
Butts of Sack, lxiii, 153.

Candle-light, Child-Marriage by, 2; Adult-, 66.
Candles to be only 4*d.* a pound, 154.
Carnal dole, copulation, 4, 6, 7, 9, &c.
Carrying-off of Women, xlii, note 1; lxxxvi, note 4.
Cart, fornicators ridden in a, lvii, lix, 128.
Cast his love to her, he, 56.
Caused his Daughter to be married, Father, 44 at foot.
Cellered sixe Buttes of Sack, 155.
Chalice worth 30*s.*, 134.
Chandler's Bond to sell Candles at 4*d.* a pound, 154.
Chaplain singing at Aston, 3.
„ doctor, looks at a woman's water, 82, 83.
Charge, take it upon her, 85, 96, oath, conscience?
Charter-coffer, 161.
Check of my Lord Bishop, lxxvii, note 1.
Cheese and butter stolen, lx, 124.
Cheshire Antiquaries blamed, lxv, lxvii; defended, lxx.
Cheshire, its length and breadth, 180.
Chester, *see* Index of Names of Places; Contents, xi, xii; and p. lxiii-iv, &c.; its River and Port, 155; a Row in, 208.
Chief Clerk of the Chester Diocesan Registry, Mr. W. H. Price, thankt for his help in this edition, xv, lxvi.
Childbed, 93, at foot; 95.
Childing of Mothers, lvi, 95, 98.
Child-married couple living together 10 years, 28, lxvi. See 140, 183, &c. &c.

Christening, xv, 8, 9, 50.
Christmas Merriments, xix, 17, 18, 43, 48.
Church dore, wordes of Wedlock spoken at the, 190; meet at, 197.
Church, face of the, 184.
Citation before the Bishop, 59.
Clandestine Marriages, lxii, 140-1, 56, 57, 196.
Cleane striplinge, a, 53.
Clergy, bad state of, lxii; some act as Doctors, 75, 82, 83; some make Wills, 131, 134; one in Chester illustrates a joke of Shakspere's, l-li.
Clergyman, a good, lxi, 139.
Clippinge and kissinge, 53.
Cloth, packs of, carried from Halifax to Hull, 72.
Cock-crowing, Child-Marriage at, xvi, 2.
Cod and Ling, 165.
Cohabiting, or dwelling together; the effect of, xxxvi.
Colourably declare, did, 195.
Colmeis, 172, blackend (? his Colouree = discoloured).
Comaundment, purchasid a, 114, procured a Citation.
Coming and going, 206, 207.
Coming-on disposition, instance of a woman of, 57.
Common Hall of Chester, goods to be brought there for sale, 156, 167.
Common Prayer, book of, 140, 141.
Communion book, 67.
Communion receivd, lxxvii, note 2; 133, 135, 140.
Competentlie preferd, 137, duly provided for.
Compulsion of friends, marriage by, 11, &c. *See* Persuasion.
Concubine, man to marry his, 156.
Conditional Contract of Marriage, xlviii, 71.
Conditions in Marriage-Contracts, renounced by Copulation, xlviii.
Conduit, Chester, the Keeper of, 177.
Conduit-keeper in Chester Market, lxiv, 177.
Conjugal rights, Suit for restitution of, xxi, 52-5.
Conjurors, Dr. Forman and Dr. Savory, xxix.
Conscience, case of, liii, 80, 131, 134; appeal to, 28, 37, 38, 42, 54, 59, 85.
Conscience shuld prick hym, 60.
Consent or Discretion, years of, xvii, xix.
Content and paie, 158.
Contracts, free from all, 194, 210.
Contrary to the locke, 131, on the opposite side to it.
Convaieng away of butter and cheese, 125.
Conversation, 33, goings-on, bad behaviour.
Corn and grain not to leave Chester without the Mayor's consent, lxiii, 145, 163.
Cornets of the Chester Waits, 150.
Corn-field, man and woman in, lxxii, *n.* 1.
Cosin germaine, 84, 200.
Cottage of elder poles, xxxiv.
Council, the Chester, 208, 209.
Counsel's letters about Ratification, 26.
Country, the voice of the, 60.
County-Exchequer bailiff, sent to jail for arresting a man in Chester city, lxiii, 148.
Court, the Bishop's, 210.
„ Civil, suit for debt, 204.
„ of Wards and Liveries, xxiii; xxxix, note 3.
Cousin-germans, 84, 200.
Coventry Plays, the Snow-father in, lxxx, note.
Cow and a panne, 135.
Cow-house of Stanlowe Abbey, lxxi, lxxii.
Cross, a silver-gilt, lent for a Wedding or Wake, 115, 116.
Crosse of gold (silver-gilt), 114, 115, 116.
Cuckold, man cald, 104, 105, 108, 110.
Curate makes a deaf old woman's Will, lx, 134; marries a couple, 52, 53, &c., 140.
Curate punisht by the Archbp. of York for marrying a couple at uncanonical hours, xvii, 45.
Curate takes a companion to hear his remonstrance with a libeller, lix, 129.
Customs-book of Chester, 155.

Daie-holdinges, to get married children together, xx, 44.
Daiesmen or Referees in Libel, 209;

in Trothplight, 197; (friends interfere in other cases).
Damaske sleves, a paire of, 119.
Dampnacion, state of, for oath-breaking, 22.
Damsell, a bigge and mariageable, 47.
Dancing, xxxi.
Daughter, whackt by a Father with his walking-staff to force her into Trothplight, lii.
Dawning of the day, Marriage at the, 196.
Deaf old testatrix, lx, 134.
Debts, acknowledgments of, and arrangements as to, 151, 152, 153, 159.
Delay in suits for Divorce, xx, 11, 12, 16, 198.
Deliberation: best to take it before Trothplight, 67.
Deliverance, 59, childbirth; 95; delivery, 99 foot.
Delt quietly and lovingly together, 53.
Depose upon the holie Evangelist of God, 160.
Depositions in other Dioceses, lxviii.
de presenti aut de futuro, Marriage-contracts, xlv, note 2.
Desperate fellow, a, 92.
Devil to have a man, rather than he a girl, lii.
Diamond carcanet given to girl-bride, xxx.
Diaper table-cloths, 134.
Dicers and carders given Church-livings, lxii.
Dine together, lxxx, note 1; 17, 92.
Discretion, years of, xix.
Divorce before a parson, not lawful, 54 at foot, xxi.
Divorces of Child-Marriages, i—xxxv; of adult ones, 76, 81.
Doctor, l, liv; parson as, 75, 82.
Doctor Canon's wife and children to go back to Ipswich, 168.
Drawinge cover, box with a, 131.
Drink, refused by boy-husband, from his girl-wife, 21.
Drinking together, lxxxi, note 1; xlix, note; 84; at the Bell Inn, Nantwich, 118; 198, 199, 201, 208.
Drowned herself rather than married, she would have, 78.
Drunkard, not a, 109.
Dublin Merchant not to leave Chester without the Mayor's leave, 174; and then to appear before the Lord Deputy in Ireland, 175.
Duke of Westminster to be put in a mine, lxvi.
Durham Depositions, terms of Abuse in, lvi—lviii.

Early marriages in Scotland, xxxi.
Early marriages, main object of, to avoid Wardship, xxxiv, xxxix; but see Notes, lxxxvi.
Early marriages, the benefit of, xlii, xliii.
Earwaker, J. P., his defence of the Cheshire Antiquaries, lxx.
Eases and pleasures, 139, conveniences.
Eel, salt, for a sick woman, 116.
Egyptians, Gypsies, mare bought of, 106.
Entry in the Mayor's book, 161.
Error, Writs of, entries, 175.
Exhortacion to trothplighted couple, 186.
Extremes (in childbirth), 95, 99.
Extremitie, cartid bie, 128.

Face of the church, marry in the, 184, 202,
Falconers and Horse-keepers given benefices, lxii.
Familiarity, 9.
Famished her for want of meate (food), almost, 55.
Famylierlie as man and wief, 112, 113.
Fancy, boys can't, their girl-wives, xx, xxviii, 37, 183, &c.
Fancy, girls can't, their boy-husbands, xviii, xx, 5, 18, 37, &c.
Farmer's wife and her lame goose, lxi, 138.
Father a child on a man, 87, 92, 95, 98, 99,
Father and Mother, before either is 14, have a baby, xxvii.
Father, his, sold hym as his heire, 81.
Father-in-law, boy-husband living with, 12, 29; not stopping the night with, 17; only goes to play at, 24.
Father, old and decayd, Son has to help him, lxiv, 173, 182.
Father thrashes his Daughter with his walking-staff, li, lii.
Fele his mynd, to, 185 (cp. Paston Letters).
Felonousely and fleshly knewe and

ravysshed the said Isabell, lxxxvi, note 4. [This 1436 use of 'felonously' is, at present, the earliest one known.]
Felony to rape a girl under 10, xxxvi, note; not so between 10 and 16, *ib.*
Fermour, 138, lessee.
Fetherbedd and the coveringes, 134.
Feudal dues, early marriage to avoid, xxxiv, xxxix; but see lxxxvi.
Field of wheate and rye, crop on, 134.
Filiation, 86. See 'Affiliations.'
Fireside at evening, 58, 69.
First night, on; boy refuses, xvii, 7-8; woman refuses, 79.
Fishmongers' Company, Stewards of, sent to jail, 165.
Fish to be bought by the Mayor for Chester use, lxiii, 163.
Flemynge knyves, a pair of, 72.
Flesh-meat stopt on Thursday nights, 206.
Flight-shot, a, 207.
Flitted twise within this half yere, 125.
Folly, a husband's, with other women, 203; lust, 60.
Forestallers punisht, lxiii, 155, 165.
Forfeiture of Lease, 147.
Forgiveness, a Libeller to ask, but doesn't, lx, 209-10.
Forgiveness, woman won't ask, 210.
Forther (earlier) promise, 190.
Fortie nightes: woman accused of lying with a man for, 120.
Fortification of our coasts, at Hull, liii.
Foster-mother, 27, -father, 20.
Foule word, one, askis an other, 122.
Four children gotten in lawfull marriage, good evidence of consent, 51.
Four fathers and mothers all under 16, in one house, xxxiii.
Frame and table, Mayor's Award as to a, 165.
Frank and free, 155.
Free country, xxi.
Friends make up a Marriage between two folk, 75.
Fro, 204, against: 'of nor fro,' for or against (his honesty).
Fugitive, a, and a light person, lx, 124.
Furious or lunatic, testatrix was not, 135.

Games, unlawful ones not to be playd, 144, 145.
Gascony wines, 166.
Gauged, Butts of Sack not, 155.
Gentlewoman, an old auncient, 73.
Geve her meate and drinke of the best (when you want to get rid of her), and so lete her departe, 126.
Gifts of Money by the Mayor and Council of Chester, 168—171.
Gifts of Money, Lady Savage's and Robert Offlee's, 172.
Gilt silver cross, 115.
Girdle, silver, 116.
Girl beaten by the Wife of the man who got her with child, 90.
Girl lies in bed to avoid Marriage, liii.
„ too tender and young to speak the words of Matrimony, 26, 39.
Girl married from a boarding-school, xxxiii.
Girl of 9 bears a child, xxix; one under 14 does, xxvii.
Girl rides behind a man, lv, 101.
Girl treats her boy-husband badly, and loves other boys, xviii, 11.
Girl would rather drown than marry, liii, 78.
Girls young, married, xiv—xxxv, 1—55, 203.
Girthing a horse, 83.
Glass windows, 116.
Going to London, xviii, 185, &c.
Going with child, 87, pregnancy.
Gold: she wold not release hym for no gold, 60.
Goldsmith's Bond to provide for his Bastard, 157.
Good, a pese of, 56, property.
Good cheer after a Trothplight, 197.
Good gentleman, a, 119.
Good will betwene you and this maide, 70.
Good will of the Lease, 137.
Goose, one that limpt, and traild its wing, offerd for tithe, 138.
Gown to be given by a Son to his poor Father, 173.
Grace, her, was no better; so she playd the whore, 80; he lackid grace, and cald her 'whore,' 103;
Grain to be brought into Chester for sale, 143.
Grandfather, 37, 38, 40; God, man and wife before, 201, &c.
Grandfather cuts off naughty granddaughter, 32.

Grandfather's wedding-feast for his child-grandson in 1673, xxxi.
Grandmother, 34, 35.
Grants, charters, and priviledges of Chester, 150.
Green, trothplight on a, xlvi, 69; Thos. Ireland of the, 67.
Gret talk rise on hit, 107.
Groat, bent, as a gift or token, xlix, note 1; 73.
Groats, debt of seven, 117, 204-7.
Grocer, of London, a, 185.
Guardians' right to infant Wards' estates and Marriages, xxxix—xli.
Guestways, -wise, girl at Hatton Hall, 41, 43; 48,
Gypsies, mare bought of, 106.

Habilitie, 70, ability, possession of property.
Half-brother, 16.
Handkerchiefs as Marriage-tokens, xlix, 210.
Handkerchiefs not as tokens, 57.
Hands joind and loost at Trothplights, 69, 76, 77, 184, 186, 187, 188, 191, 198.
Handsome man; a girl says he's her child's father, 89.
Harness, red and white, 156, 157.
Harvest, woman with child, to earn money in, lv, 93.
Hatmaker's shop, tools and goods to be seizd if he fails to pay £12, 163.
Hautboys of the Chester Waits, 150.
Hawkers and Hunters made clergymen, lxii.
Hawks, horse and dogs taken to a Chester inn, xliv, 58.
Heady folk, the brutal Mrs. and Mr. Piers Stanley, 54.
Heart of gold as a Token, 188, 192.
He could not do any more than afore, to his Wife, 74.
Hedge, man and girl behind one, lvi, 101.
Her: aunte Emme her children, 132/9.
Herrings, red, bought at Hull, 72.
High way, 141 (marriage in), 207.
„ rate, 9*s.* 8*d.* for, 178.
Hinge-nails of a Will-chest drawn, lx, 131.
Hired servant for all the yere, 205, 207.
Hold thie peace! 99.
Honest name and fame, 96, 103.
Honest porcion of goodes to marry withall, 70.
Honest woman, 97, 208; h. wench and a good laborer, 97.
Hopping, dancing, xliv, *n.*
Horseback, girl carried on, to be married, 36.
House broken into in Chester, lxiii, 157; in Wirral, lxxxvi, *n.*
Housekeeper without suspicion, 68.
Hurt her soule, she wold not, 191.
Husband and Wife, children calling one another, xxxv.
Husband, boy, turns his back on his Wife all night, 6.
Husband runs away when accused of Incompetency, liv, 74.

Illegitimate children, 81; *see* Affiliations, 85—101, Trothplights, 56—69, 184—210, Adulteries, 72—84, and Mayor's Books, 146-9, 157.
Impediment in Wife's body, lxi, 137-8; in husband's, 74.
Incompetence of Husbands: Earl of Essex, xxix; Richard Pearson, 74 (disproved, 75).
Inconstancy of a man, 200.
Inconvenient times for Marriage, xvii, 45, 46,
Indexes to old Cheshire Wills, lxx.
Indian Child-Marriages, xxxiv, *n.*; xxxv;
Indian children's bigamy, xvi, *n.*
Infants, children under 7, xxxv.
Inn, the Bell, at Nantwich: wife invites folk drink at, while her husband's away, lix, 118 at foot.
Innholder's house in Chester, forcibly enterd, and he arrested, 159.
Innuendo, 121, 123, 127.
Inquisitiones post Mortem, xxiii, lxx.
Inventory, a false, lxxii.
Irish Expedition: Earl of Essex's soldiers wreckt in Wales, 168.

Jawde no-bodie . . hoore Jawde, 123, jade.
Jewish Kings, early marriages of, xxvii.
Jointure for a bride, 187.
Journeyman shoemaker, 5, at foot;
Justices of Peace compel a man to take his Wife again, lxi, 137; order a Son to help his poor old Father, 173; at Sessions, 158, 182.

Keeping women: husbands doing so, 202, 203.
Keys of the Chester Treasure-House, 161.
Kin, a man's, abused as well as himself, 204, 205, 206, 207.
Kin, folk too near of, to marry, iii.
Kinswoman taken in for her childing, out of pity, 97.
Kiss, not meant for Marriage, 57; none given, 92, &c.; 184,
Kiss the book, 69.
Kiss, the Parson's right to, at a Marriage, xxxvi, note i.
Kissing after adult Marriage, xxxvi, note 1; 68, 201.
Kissing after Child-Marriages, xix, xxxvi; refused by a girl, xxvi.
Kissing after Trothplights, xlvi, 68; xlvii, note 1; 68, 76, 186, 188, 190, 191, 199.
Knife in bed, husband hadn't a, 22.
Knighthood: prevented Wardship, xli, note 2; ? did not, lxxxvi.
Knocking at the door, 66.
Kye, cows, kept by the Stanlowe monks, lxxii.

Laborer: an honest wenche and a good laborer, 97.
Lame folk, gifts to, 169, 170.
Lame man, says he's not a fit witness to a Trothplight, 68.
Land sold to keep a whore, 122.
Landladie to this Deponentes husband, 209.
Landlord's goodwill of a tenement, 10.
Landlords on their Tenants' side, 201.
Law on Child-Marriages, from Judge Swinburne, xxxv-viii.
Lay in, for childbirth, 69.
Lease of a house in Northgate St., Chester; dispute as to, 147.
Lease worth £100, 134; l. of a dwelling house, 136.
Leather-Searcher's Bond, 162.
Leman and Wife, a man's, both in childbed at once, 203.
Letter by a School-boy saying he will *not* have his Child-wife, xix, 38; written in a high loft at the Bell Inn, Nantwich, lix, 118.
Letters by Lord Darcye, xxvi; Lord Burleigh, 166; Sir Simonds D'Ewes, xxx
Letters to be sent on by Posts, 167, 178.
Libels, lvi-lx, 102—130, 204—210: *see* Contents, lxxii-lxxxv.
Liberties of Chester, 159.
License, none for a Wedding, 140.
License to be a suitor to a girl, 60.
Light person, both of her tonge and of her dede, 96; 98 at foot; man is, 125.
Linendraper, 157.
Ling and Cod, 165.
Little of his wordes, 109.
Liue, in, 137, in lieu, instead; in lue, 156.
Living, girl married for a; but divorst on its failing, 4-6.
Living got by sore working, 126.
Loft, letter written in, 118; man on girl in, 122.
London, going to; *see* Index of Places.
Longe of her tonge, 109, because of it.
Lord Deputie of the realme of Ireland, 176.
Lord Mayor of London, suggestion for his next Children's party, xix.
Love-letter, with a Diamond Carcanet, by Sir Simonds D'Ewes in 1626, xxx.
Lunatic, testatrix not, 135.
Lusty, physic makes a man, 75.

Made her a countenance, 112, pretended, affected.
Maid: she is a good maide, for hym, is a virgin, 11. *See* Servant-maids.
Make nor medle with her, I will, 123.
Malche, 141, milch cow.
Male child, longd for by Indian mothers, xxxiv, *n.*
Marches of Wales, 136.
Mare bought of the Gypsies, 106; turnd out of a close, 104.
Marke, wold have gevin hym a, with a sword, 107/3-4.
Market, Saturday's, walk home from, 70.
Market-place of Chester, man wrongly arrested in, 150.
Marriage a failure, xix. *See* Adulteries.
„ to join a divided house, 14.
„ by moonlight, lxii, 141; by torchlight and candlelight, xvi, 2.

Marriage, clandestine, 56, 57, 140-1, 196.
Marriage of a girl under 12, not conclusive against the King, lxxxvi.
Married children dwelling together 10 years without carnal dole, 11.
Mason of Chester Walls surrenders his Patent, 146.
Mayors' Books, Chester, 1558—1600, English Entries from them, lxiii-iv, 143—180.
Meat-sellers to sell the skins and Tallow too, 154.
Men at service, 76 foot, 78, 79; *see* Service.
Mendinge of the high waies in Chester, 178.
Merchant, rich, fallen into decay, 72.
Merchantry wares like stockfish and herrings, 72.
Merriments at Christmas, 17, 18.
Midlent Sondaie, 123.
Midsummer-Day, merrymaking, on, li.
Midwives fetcht to a woman in childbed, 50; 95, 96, 99, 100.
Milking, women, lix, 111, 112, 115.
Mill, boy wants to go to, rather than be married, 7.
Mill-door, couple behind, lv, 97.
Mind: James mynd and his doinges, 46; she had lefte her mynd with the said Maior, 67.
Ministry (clergy), state of the, lxii.
Misliking between child-husband and wife, 29, &c.
Money, Adult marriages for, xlix, &c.
Money, Child-Marriages for, xv, 4, 6-9, 10, 12, 14, 32, &c.
Money matter, a, 205 at foot, 207.
Monthly sickness or puberty of Indian girls, about 10, xxxv.
Moonlight, marriage by, lxii, 141.
Mortuary due to Rector of Davenham, lxxxvii.
Most notorious hoore, a, 121.
Mother- and father-in-law starve their son's wife, 53-5.
Mother-in-law, a brutal, Mrs. P. Stanley, 53-5.
Mother, the disease of, lv, 83.
Mothers at 9, xxix; under $11\frac{1}{2}$, xxxi; under 14, xxvii.
Mother's mind to marry her boy, xviii, 20.
Mother's right to choose a Father for her Bastard, lvi.
Mugweed, a posset and bread (? poultice) of, 83.

Nag worth 6*s.* 8*d.*, 134.
Nail-drawer, an honest, lx, 131.
Nails drawn out of the hinges of a Will-chest, 131.
Naked, except hir Kirtyll and hir Smokke, lxxxvi, note 4.
Naked sword, one man with, runs after another, 105.
Name and fame, 104. *See* Honest.
Name, 113, report, opinion among the neighbours.
Napkin as a Trothplight-Token, xlix, note 1; 15, note 2;
Naughty life and misdemeanour, 80.
Neighbours bringing food, &c. to one another when sick, lix, 116.
Newland fishe, Linge and Cod, 165.
Night, flitting, with master's goods, 96; marriage by, 140.
Night-visits of men to girls, 87, 88, 91, 199—200.
Nine, a girl of, entitled to Dower, xxxvi, note 2; lxx.
Nobles, half a score of, to get a Divorce, 13; twenty to be rid of a Trothplight, 59; nineteen as a marriage-portion, 64.
Non-resident Landlords in Cheshire, in 1578, 180.
Nought, plaie the, with the said Jone, 129, 130; with another woman's husband, 209.
Nought together, 92, 94, &c.
Noughtie women, kepinge of, 203.
Nuncupative Wills, 131-3; Contents, lxxx, &c.
Nurse got with child by a Boy of nine or ten, xxviii, xxix.
Nurse helps a Girl to say the words of Matrimony, xxiv, xxv, xxvi.
Nurse to a baby-boy, 27; girl, 50, 51.
Nursing of Bastard babies, 65, 146, 149, 156, 157: *see* Affiliations, 85—101.

Oath, deponent will not break his or her, 22.
Offend with man, 96.
Offendid, 138, committed adultery.
Opinion, prejudice, a foolish, 54.
Order of Lawe, bie, 136, 137.

Ordinary, 137, bishop.
Othir boies, she lovid, as well as hym, 12.
Out-house, a work-house, place for work, 185.
Overcame her, and gate her with child, 61.
Overseer and a father to his children, 130.
Overworkt old Londoner, lxv.
Ox, torfled, dislocated a joint, xlix.
Oxen worth 20 marks, 134.

Pack-a-pack, ride, on Kate, lxxix.
Packman, from Halifax to Hull, liv.
Paie his fees, 209.
Painted cloth and a broken wall, only, between man and woman, 58.
Paling, man working at, with an axe, lviii, 117.
Paramour: boy's Mother kept as, before her marriage, xviii, 30.
Parish, all the, knows it, 107; knew her to be Mr. Mores provid hoore, 117.
Parson, 132, rector.
Parson, a bad Chester one illustrates a joke of Shakspere's, l-li.
Parsons, Doctors, 75, 82.
„ illiterate and unfit, lxii.
„ a good one at Northenden, 139.
Part of his bed, wife has not had, this 3 years, 105.
Part of the child, a small, 94 at foot.
Parte, as ever it (the fœtus) & she shuld, 99.
Partlie borne in armes, and partlie led to church, 34, at foot.
Paste and bread, 154.
Patching-up rotten MS., xiv (also done to a Town-Hall MS.).
Patrons plundering the Clergy, lxii.
Peice of mony, a, 24, 57; piece of a lease of a house, 116; of good, property, 56.
Pelting alehouse, a little, 98 at foot.
Penance to be done for adultery, 80.
Penny, drink a, 208.
Persuasion of friends to make children marry, 1, 4, 10, 21.
Persuasion of priest to make boy go to bed with his girl-wife, 6.
Petticoat as a bribe for silence, rejected, 92. *See* Shirt, shoes.
Physic for incompetence, 74.
Physician, 137.
Pig, Referees eat one, l, 197.
Pigs, Tithing of, in Whalley, Lanc., 138.
Pin, a silver, 116.
Places and Times of Child-Marriages, xvi.
Plaid many light points, she, 32, was wanton.
Plaint at law, 174.
Plaintiff not ready for his trial, 174.
Play the nought, 209.
Pleasure, have one's, of a woman, li; lxxvi, note 2.
Pocky knaves bed, that, 92.
Pointed a day to marry, 188.
Poison, wife need not fear, 203.
Politeness to visitors, girl married from, liii.
Pollicy, done for a, 131, rascality, trick.
Poor, gifts to, 168—172.
Poor parents to be helpt by children, 182.
Pore maid Jane (had) grett wronge, 57.
Porte & crekes of Chester, 143.
Portmote, 177.
Posset of Mugweed, lv, 83.
Post haste, 167, 178.
Posts, Letters to be forwarded by, 167, 178.
Poverty prevents child-married folk suing for a Divorce, 16. *See* Delay.
Pox, lvi, lviii, 33, 92, 100.
Precontract, 189, &c.
Precontracts, free from, 189 foot; not free, 79, 185.
Pretie Pussie to huggle, xxxiv.
Priest that served at Waverton, 39.
Priest persuades an unwilling Child-Bridegroom to go to bed with his big-Girl-Wife, 6.
Priest's whore, a, 193.
Priesthood, iniquities covering it, lxii at foot.
Private chapel, 38-9, 40, 41, 49.
Proverb: lix, note; lxxix, note; lviii, note 2; lxxx, note.
Provide a place for her (with child), 124.
Provid hoore, 207.
Psalter-book, Trothplight on, xlvi, 69.
Public affairs, allusions to, liv, note.

Public events alluded to, liv *n.*; Lord Pembroke's command (?), 13; Battle of St. Quintin's, 106; Essex's expedition to Ireland, 168; Queen's service, 178; Letters from Ireland, &c., 178—180.
Pull Roberte Wright out of thie doughter, 122.
Pullid her to bed to hym, he, 99.
Pursuivant, 159.
Put-to the dore, 113, 114.

Queen Elizabeth's Wards in Cheshire in 1578, 180.
Queen's, the, Council, 136.

Rape and conception: odd doctrine as to, xxxvi at foot.
Rape, child can't be begotten in a, xxxvi, note 2; lxx.
Ratifications of Child-Marriages, xx, 49—52.
Recorders of the Chester Waits, 150.
Red and white harness in a Saddler's shop, 156.
Red-herrings and stockfish carried by a packman from Hull to Halifax, 72.
Referees or Daiesmen, about Marriages, 1; in Trothplight, 197; in Libel, 209.
Registrar of the Chester Diocesan Registry, Mr. Jn. Gamon, thankt, lxvi.
Registry-book at Bunbury, 50.
Remembrid he is well, 7, he remembers well.
Rentcharge out of a House, agreement as to, 149.
Rents, some, sent to old wife, 72.
Repentid the said Mariage, he, 46.
Reportinge of these wordes, 114/7.
Reysed this tale hymself, Roger, 108.
Ribbon, gift of some, 72.
Riding on a horse behind a man, girl, 36, lv, 101; servant with his mistress, 82; she bears a child, 83.
Ring as a Trothplight-Token, xlix, 15, note 2; 63, 187, 189, 190, 191, 194; in Marriage, 67, 140, 141, 197.
Rites (Communion) given to a dying man, 133.
River Dee, 145.
Rose-noble, bent, as a Trothplight Token, xlix, note 1.
Rotting leaves of Chester MSS., xiv, lxiii; of Bath and Wells ones, lxviii.
Rowe in the Bridge Strete, Chester, 208.
Rows in Chester, 208.
Ruffians and Shake-bucklers made Ministers, lxii.
Runne his way: incompetent Husband would have, but is fetcht back, 74.
Ruynous house, 99, much out of repair.
Rye field, man and woman in, 106-7.
Rye not to be sold without the Mayor's leave, 162.
Rysed this tale hymself, Roger, 108.

Sack, 6 Butts of, cellard, lxiii, 155.
Saddler to pay a fine, 156.
Satan's Black Book for Cheshire Antiquaries, lxv.
Saturday's market, walk home from, 70.
School-boy, letter from one, xix, 38; at home for the holidays, 3.
School, boys', Dr. Standish's at Lathom, xviii, 48, 49; 19, 24, 29, 30, 36, 39, 139.
Scoldinge wordes, 209.
Scourge for her nowe, in her old daies, 191.
Sculling to Farndon, xv.
Se, *vb.* see to, look after, 1321,
Sealers and Regesters of all Tanned lether, 163.
Searcher of Tand Leather, his Bond, 162.
Seat in church, dispute as to, lxxxiii.
Sea-voyage, Trothplight before, 67.
Secound, 131, sickend.
Seeking beasts, 204; a mare, 104;
Separation of man and wife, 53, xxi.
Servant enticed away from his Master, 205, 206.
Servant-girls and men in the same bed-room, lv, lxxii, note; lxxxii, note; 87, 88, 90.
Service, boys and men at, xvii, xviii, 11, 35 (with therle of Derby), 48; 76, 78, 79, 82.
Service-book, 65; gold and silver laid on it, 66.
Service, girls and women at, xvii, 11, 12, 13, 97.
Settinge & lettinge of the Stalls at Chester Conduit, 177, 178.

Seven, Infants become Children at, xxxv.
Shakspere, his young friend, of his 'Sonnets,' Wm. Herbert, and his Dark Lady, xlii.
Shakspere, illustration of his 'Wench married as she went to the Garden for Parsley to stuffe a Rabit.'—*Shrew*, IV. i. 95-6, l-li.
Shakspere, illustration of his 'behinde-doore worke,' *Winters Tale*, III. iii. 72, lv; 'peltinge,' lv; 'stand-to,' 120, 129; 'convey,' lx, 124.
Shakspere, was one of Robert Cleaver's 'bruite beastes,' xlviii, *n.*
She is non of my wief, 20, no wife of mine.
She is very sory for her offencis, 33.
Sheets, a girl-wife takes them to her boy-husband's bed, xviii, 201.
Sheets, cloth to make s. of, 20, 128, 129.
Sheriffs to pay 28*s.* 10*d.* for a debt, 159; action before, 192, 193.
Shirt, as a bribe to say nothing, lxxvi, note 2.
Shoemaker, apprentice to a, 5.
Shoes, as a bribe to say nothing, lv, 92.
Shop, man got from, to witness a Trothplight, 58.
Sick woman, chickens, spice, &c., for, 116.
Sickly old Priest marries a couple in his bedroom, 66.
Sickly young man, 18.
Sickness, the new, 139, plague.
Silver girdle, pin & Cross, 116.
Silver salt and spoons, 134.
Sisters, two put between boy and girl bride and bridegroom on the wedding-night, xvii, 15.
Skins, fells, heds, and Tallow of beasts, 155.
Skipping on the pavement, a Bride, xxxiii.
Slain, wife need not fear to be, 203.
Slander, she raised such a, 75.
Slater, restricted in buying slates, lxiii, 149.
Small, a woman is, after childbirth, 90; lxxxi, note .
Small while, a, 41 at foot.
Smart: change of meaning in the word, lv, note 3.
Smart houses, naughty doings at, lv, 87.
Smockes and sheetes to lap her hoore ars in, 128.
Snowy morning, lix, 112, 113.
Social side of forefathers' life, xv, lxiv, and all the Volume.
Soldiers, gifts to, 168, 169, 171.
„ at Lithe (for Lord Pembroke's command ?), 13; at St. Quentins, A.D 1557, p. 106.
Soldiers, the Earl of Essex's, cast away in Wales (wreckt in returning from Ireland), gifts to, 168.
Solempnizate, marriage was, 36 at foot.
Son forst to support his poor old Father, lxiv.
Sore workinge, gettith his Livinge bie his, 126.
Sorry, heartily, for his deceit, 56; for her offences, 33.
Soul's health, man has had Bastards against his, 202.
South-Western Rebellion, 181.
Sovereign's Guardianship of Infants, xxxix, lxxxvi.
Spanish-sixpence as a Token, 58.
Spice, ginger, and old ale, as a drink, l, 63.
Spinster spinning at a Customer's, lxxxii, note; 199; at home, xlix, note 1.
Spiritual Law, 138.
Stalls in Chester market, 177.
Standing, can a man get a child, 97, lv.
Stand-to, 120, maintain, hold to, 129, 142, 200.
Statute Merchant, debt secured by, 160.
Statute Merchant, 150, 152, 160.
Stepfather and -mother, 12.
Stepmother, 113.
Sticke to hit, 131.
Stockes, he and his wief were ponished in the, 125.
Stockfish carried inland from Hull, 72.
Stone's cast, a, 206, at foot.
Stout against hym, he was, 94.
Stubbornness, a wife's rightful, 81.
Suck, gave a baby her first, 40, 50.
Sundays on the Dee, xv; a Sonday in the somer season, 99.
Supper, woodcocks for, 58.

Surgeon, 100. *See* Doctors.
Suspiciously married, 59; s. together, 101;
Suspicious place, 101, 105.
Swear trothplighted folk, hesitation to, 186.
Swelling, a woman's with child, lxxxi, note; 90.
Swinburne, Judge (died 1624), xxxv-xxxviii.
Sword, pledgd for 3*s.*, and 3*d.* interest, 146.

Table and frame, Mayor's award as to, 165.
Tablid, boarded, 29, 30, 91, 125 at foot, 139, 189.
Tacke of land, 131.
Tailor working at a customer's house, 198.
Take or refuse her before a Judge, 4.
Take R. Wright in thie doughter in the lofte, 122.
Take unkindness with him, 6.
Taken her downe (blamed her) for adultery, 112.
Tallow of a beast to be 3*s.* 4*d.*, 154.
Tallow, sufficient, to be provided in Chester, 154.
Tand-Leather, Searcher's Bond, 162.
Tenant would favour his Landlord, 84.
Tender and younge, she was then in yeares, 39.
Thames Bridge at Staines, Middx, not to be broken down, 181.
Thatcher, a, who lives on his neighbours, 125.
Thief, and 'grinning thief,' man cald, 117, 204-7.
Thinges done eighty yeres ago, 131.
Thought a truth in it, he, 197.
Threshing in an old house, 204, 206.
Throwne out of window, thinges, 127.
Times of Child-Marriages, xvi,
Tithe-goose demanded: a lame one offerd, lxi, 138.
Tithes: *see* Contents of MS., p. lxxii-lxxxv.
Tithing pig and goose, 138.
Title to a woman, a man's, 193.
Toke away her victualles, 54.
Toke them both sworne, 67/I.
Tokens at and after Trothplights, xlviii-l, &c., 58 (a Spanish 6*d.*); 12*d.*, 59, 60.
Tokens not as Trothplight-gifts, 57, 61, 210. *See* Groat, Handkerchief, Napkin, Ring, Rose Noble.
Tote-hole, Alis lokid in at a, 113.
Town-field, a Trothplight in a, 64.
Travailer bie the Seas, 67.
Treasure-House of Chester, its Key-holders, 161.
Trothplights, xliii—liii; lxxix, note 1; lxxx, note; 56—71, 184—202.
Trothplights, forms of, xlvii, &c.
Truckle- or wheel-bed, lv, 88.
Turquoise ring, 190.
Turves, gathering of, 99, 207.
" going for, 99.
Twelvepence as a token, 59, 60.
Two at a birth, 203.
Two—man and woman—'those 2 will one day make 3,' lviii, note 2.
Two men in bed, with one's Wife between them, 105.
Two shillings a week, for bastard and its Mother, 158.

Uncle-in-law, 3.
Unconveniently together, man and another's wife, 112.
Undertakings, guarantees, for other folk, 149.
Unhonestlie, improperly, shamelessly, 115.
Unkindness grows up, from husband's adultery, 203.
Unlawfull Companie (of a man), 100.
Unruliness of Wife, 109.
Unsemelie for his age: an old man to want a chamber to talk with a woman in, 126.
Unsent for, 133.
Unthift, man cald an, 119.
Utter and sell at reasonable price, 155.

Varying in one's talk, 204.
Vehemently suspected in the matter, 105.
Venereal disease, lvi, 33, 92, 100.
Vicar, 74; his advice about a wife refusing her husband, 79; affiliates a child on a man, 86.
Vicarage of Bowden, 139.
Victualing-house in Chester, 38.
Violins of the Chester Waits, 150.
Virgin Mary bore Christ at 15, xxviii.
Visitation reports a child-married couple not divorst, 16.

Waits, Chester, dispute as to their Hautboys, &c., lxiv, 168.
Wake: a silver-gilt Cross lent to a girl to go to a wedding or wake, lix, 116.
Walking the horses at an inn-door, man, 82.
Walls of Chester: their old Mender resigns, lxiv, 146.
Wards, the Queen's, in Cheshire, in 1578, 180-1.
Wardship, abuses of, xxxix—xli.
Warnid hym, Custance nevir, 113, tried to stop him.
Wars, youth goes to the, 15.
Water, a woman's, sent to a doctor to tell her disease, l, liv-lv, 63, 82, 83.
Welsh witness doesn't know English, lviii, note 3, p. 108.
Wench, 56, girl baby.
Wheel or truckle bed, 88.
Whore, women cald, lvii, lviii, lix, lxxx, 102, 117, 121, 122, 126, 128, 193, 204: *see* Libels.
Whorish casts (tricks) with her, she had, 104.
Widow, a Chester merchant's, has her dead husband's rights, lxiii, 166.
Widow carried off and ravisht, lxxx. *See* xliii, note 2.
Widow not to be hookt, xlix, 63.
Widow, widower, 56.
Wife gets a divorce from an adulterous husband, 81; beats the girl he's got with child, 90.
Wife runs away from her husband, lii; did what she could to have children by him, 73.
Wills, made by Parsons, 131, 134 (*see* 132).
Wills, 130-7. *See* Contents of MS., lxxii—lxxxvi.
Windows, wind-dores, shutters, lvi, 99.
Wine merchants, order as to, 153.
Woman child, a, 84.
Woman, gets between her husband and another man in bed, lviii, 105, 110.
Woman, stops at her Mother's instead of going to her Husband's, 81, 202.
Woman, waits 8 weeks for her incompetent Husband to recover, liv, 74.
Women drinking with men, 84.
Women, their quarrels: *see* Libels, lvi, lx, 102—129, 204—209.
Women, two, mean a rage, lix, note 2.
Women, unmarried, liable to be carried off, xlii, note.
Woodcocks for supper, 58.
Wording, *n.* 206, arguing, quarrelling.
Work-day, marriage on a, 54.
Worke-house, which is an outhouse, 185.
Worship, have borne, in Chester, 208.
Wright, a, bie his occupacion, 129.

Yellow band and green breeches, 171.
Yorkshire heiress given to Gerald de Furnivall, xl.
Youngest mariage that euer he was at, 26.

CORRECTIONS FOR *CHILD-MARRIAGES*, &c.

p. 27, 44, &c, 'morã' is wrongly expanded as 'mora*ns*': it should be 'mora*m*': cp. *Aeneid* x. 888, 'traxisse moram,' and the Chichester Depositions 'moram traxit', 'moram egit'.

There are doubtless other mistakes in the Latin passages, owing to my rustiness. If any are the scribe's, let them be put down to him.

FROM Dr. SHEPPARD, LL.D.,

HIGH SENESCHAL, *CANTERBURY* CATHEDRAL.

Dear Sir,

In reply.

The Archbishop's Consistory Court had cognizance of matrimonial and defamation causes in addition to the jurisdiction in matters of Church discipline.

The Archiepiscopal records are at Lambeth; but I should expect to find those relating to the Acta Curiæ in the office of Sir J. Hassard, or of Dr. Deane.

We—that is, the Prior and Chapter of Canterbury, as temporary *Custodes Spiritualitatis* during vacancies of the See—had jurisdiction in the same cases whilst the various vacancies lasted. No special registers were kept for the law proceedings during these intervals, but *thousands of detached documents*—the original "records" in these suits—have lately come into my hands. Two folio vols. (in the style of scrap-books) have already been filled from this mass, and the contents have been alphabetically indexed. The remainder of this recently discovered collection will be cleaned as soon as possible, and be made available for students.

The "scrap-books" and *Sede Vacante* registers (chiefly on the domestic discipline of our monastery) are all indexed, and can be consulted freely on Tuesdays and Fridays from 11 to 1, by simply walking into the Library and applying to the Sub-Librarian (or to *me*, if I am present; but *adversa valetudine detentus*, I am usually shut up at home).

1. There are *many* volumes of Depositions taken in the Archdeacon's Court in the 15th and 16th centuries. The Archdeacon was more mixed up with shady matters than the Archbishop, and these notes taken down from the lips of the witnesses—all examined on commission—are very *spicy*. See your Chaucer, "The Fox and the Widow's Cock."

2. No registers of Visitations, &c., but a few imperfect notes of visitations of the Nunneries of S. Sepulchre's (Canterbury) and Davington (Kent) are scattered among the loose parchments. There is one *Sede Vac.* Register—Cranmer being dead, and Pole just stepping into his place—with any amount of *abjurations* of all sorts, and disclaiming of wives by *sacerdotes conjugati*. Look on the first page of the June No. of the *Canterbury Diocesan Gazette* (Gibbs, Palace St., Canterbury, price 2*d.*), where is a sketch of the latest found records.

J. B. Sheppard.

Chichester.—The 11 vols. I have examind out of the 21 of the Consistory Court, from A.D. 1556 to 1694, show no Child-Marriages, tho in one case a boy of 12 makes love to a girl—older, I believe—and contracts himself to her. Most of the cases are about Wills and Tithes; several are Libel ones; a few are Trothplights, and a few relate to the execution of Deeds, &c.

There are 40 vols. of 'Books of Instance,' 1519 to 1798; and 64 'Books of Office,' containing Faculties issued to repair Churches, alter Pews, &c., from 1506 to the present time.

The Attestation or Depositions relating to Trials in the "Dean's Peculiars"—Parishes in the City of Chichester (except All Saints), Newfishbourne and Rumboldswhyke—are in 3 vols., from 1606 to 1677; and the Books of Office are in 15 vols., from 1484 to 1853.

For the "Archbishop's Peculiars"—the parishes of Slindon (given to the see by Hen. I. in 1108), East Lavant, Heene, Pagham, Tarring, South Bersted, Patching, Tangmere, &c.—the Attestations or Depositions in Trials are in 2 vols., A.D. 1611 to 1661; while the Books of Office are in 29 vols., A.D. 1537 to 1853.—F., 22 May, 1894.

Carlisle.—Mr. A. N. Bowman, the Registrar, will allow the Registers to be inspected without fee. But he says that 'Mrs. Ware (daughter of the late Bp. Goodwin, and wife of the Bp. Suffragan of Barrow-in-Furness, had an exhaustive search made in the Carlisle Diocesan Register Books for entries relating to Child-Marriages.' She came across only one instance in 1608: see her Paper in vol. xi, p. 220-5 (1889-90) of the 'Transactions of the Cumberland and Westmoreland Antiquarian and Archæological Society.' The entry is,

'*Kirkby Stephen.* [1608].

'Eisdem die et loco comparuit procter Mergera Dowthwait, et allegavit quod fuit contracta in ejus impubertate cum quodam Thomas Fawcett, cum conditione sequenti, Viz^t^. that if she should refuse to marrie with him when she came to lawfull yeares of consent, it should be lawful for the said Fawcett to take the forfeiture mentioned in the condic*i*ons or articles of the same; and if Fawcett should refuse her, then she to take *the* like forfeite.[1] et petiit indicat*rix* (?) ut solemnizetur cum dicto

[1] Mrs. Ware cites from Bp. Nicolson's *Miscellany Accounts of the Diocese of Carlisle*, p. 108, referring to the Register at Threlkeld: 'Formal Contracts of Marriage are herein recorded, and Sureties enter'd for the payment of five Shillings to the poor, by the party that draws back.' But the present Incumbent says 'there is nothing whatever to be found of this nature in the registers at Threlkeld, the entries of which date from 1572.'

Fawcett, alledging that she was willing to have him to her husband according to *the* said articles. Et quia dictus vir non comparuit, dominus (*i. e.* the Chancellor) decrevit diem citandi fore in proximo hoc in loco in causa matrimoniali.'

Mrs. Ware cites from the *Chronicle of Lanercost*, a case which confirms the bedding of the married children (above, p. xvii).

A.D. 1313.

'Eodem anno dominus Thomas de Multuna, dominus Gilleslandiæ, sexto kalendas Decembris obiit. unicam filiam heredem, nomine Margaretam, post se reliquit, quam Robertus de Clifford, filius Roberti de eadem, *septimo suæ ætatis anno*, apud Hoffe, *ipso lecto decubante*, desponsavit. Et vivente dicto Roberto, Ranulphus, Ranulphus de Daker, filius domini Willelmi de Daker, eandem Margaretam nupsit, quia jus habuit ad illam propter pactionem factam ante priores nuptias, inter Thomam de Multuna, patrem dictæ Margaretæ, et Willelmum de Daker.' (She was 17 at her marriage.)

Hereford.—The Registrar, Mr. H. C. Beddoe, writes, "I do not recollect to have seen any papers in this Registry relating to Child-Marriages; but I shall be happy to give you every facility for making search among the papers in the Registry, of course without charge."

Lichfield.—Mr. Hubert C. Hodson, the Registrar, writes, "The original Libels and Allegations in suits before the Consistory Court are deposited here in bundles. Those prior to 1590 are mostly in Latin; and I have not come across any reference to Child-Marriages. The entries in the Court Books are in Latin, and are excessively meagre, mostly consisting of a few lines, to the effect that the Cause was adjourned, or that some one was excommunicated for non-attendance. You can of course see the documents, and copy from their contents, provided that you let me know beforehand when you are coming."

Norwich.—Dr. W. T. Bensly, the Registrar, writes: "You (or any friend deputed by you) are welcome to make searches respecting child-marriages, &c. in the old Deposition-Books in this Registry relating to Consistory Court proceedings, without fee. Office hours, 10 to 4 on week-days, except on Thursdays, when the hours are 10 to 1. The Deposition-Books here begin about the year 1490."

R. CLAY & SONS, LIMITED, LONDON & BUNGAY.